Theories of the Theatre

ALSO BY MARVIN CARLSON

André Antoine's Memories of the Théatre-Libre
The Theatre of the French Revolution
The French Stage in the Nineteenth Century
The German Stage in the Nineteenth Century
Goethe and the Weimar Theatre
The Italian Stage from Goldoni to D'Annunzio

Theories of the Theatre

*A Historical and Critical Survey,
from the Greeks to the Present*

MARVIN CARLSON

CORNELL UNIVERSITY PRESS

ITHACA AND LONDON

First published 1984 by Cornell University Press.
Published in the United Kingdom by
Cornell University Press Ltd., London.

International Standard Book Number 0-8014-1678-7
Library of Congress Catalog Card Number 84-7658
Printed in the United States of America
Librarians: Library of Congress cataloging information
appears on the last page of the book.

The paper in this book is acid-free and meets the guidelines
for permanence and durability of the Committee on Production
Guidelines for Book Longevity of the Council on Library Resources.

*To the many colleagues, past and present,
at Cornell and Indiana, who have provided
inspiration, guidance, and encouragement*

Contents

Preface

ALTHOUGH THEATRE HAS BEEN the subject of speculative inquiry ever since the Greeks, there is by no means a general consensus (perhaps less today than ever) as to just what constitutes or ought to constitute the body of critical theory devoted to this art. The first and in many ways greatest difficulty in pursuing the present investigation was in laying out and attempting to maintain certain boundaries that would allow both flexibility and coherence in the material considered. Neither "theory" nor "theatre" is a term of unambiguous application, so the reader deserves some idea of what has been included and what excluded from a historical survey of Western theatrical theory.

The term "theory," then, I have taken to mean statements of general principles regarding the methods, aims, functions, and characteristics of this particular art form. It is thus separated on the one hand from aesthetics, dealing with art in general, and on the other from the criticism of particular works and reviews of particular productions. Obviously, a certain amount of overlap in these categories is unavoidable. Theatre theory rarely if ever exists in a "pure" form. Observations on theatre will be embedded in or related to observations on other arts or on all art, and so theory is involved with aesthetics. And general principles will most commonly be derived from or illustrated by examples of specific plays or productions, and so theory becomes involved with criticism and reviewing. What I have sought, then, is less a matter of pure cases than of writings in which the theoretical element is paramount, or at least is sufficiently independent from the analysis of an individual work to warrant separate discussion. It would be difficult if not impossible, for example, to discuss the history of Western theatrical theory without devoting a significant amount of space to remarks on Greek tragedy and Shakespeare, but the aim of this book is to trace

9

the development not of interpretations of these dramatists but of the idea—which these interpretations illustrate—of what theatre is, has been, or should be.

Another problem in defining a body of material arises from the variety of modes in which theatre theory has been developed. Professional "theatre theorists" constitute a very modest proportion indeed of those who have considered this subject, and even if we add the theoretical writings of the practitioners of the art, we still have not accounted for the greater part of the available material. Surely no other art has stimulated theoretical speculation from persons in so wide a variety of other fields of endeavor as has theatre; it comes from philosophers and theologians, rhetoricians and grammarians, musicians, painters, poets, and—more recently—sociologists and political scientists, anthropologists and cultural historians, psychologists, linguists, and mathematicians. Behind each theorist lies a whole intellectual world, and often a whole nontheatrical discipline, with concepts, vocabulary, and a substantial tradition frequently quite remote from theatre, but within which a specific theoretical statement about theatre is developed. My aim throughout has been to provide only as much nontheatrical background as I felt was absolutely essential for understanding each writer's contribution to the evolution of theatrical theory. Any less rigid program threatened to lead into the fascinating but infinite regresses of Western cultural and intellectual history.

The word "theatre" presents lesser but by no means negligible difficulties. In English, a distinction is frequently made between "drama" and "theatre," drama being the written text and theatre the process of performance. No general term covers both, as this study does, and I have opted for "theatre" partly for the pleasure of the alliteration and partly because the use of "drama" would be more likely to suggest that I was following the selective model of the two major English-language anthologies of theoretical statements on the art, both of which give only the slightest attention to production or performance theory. In recent years, "theatre" has run into problems from another direction, as a term opposed to "performance" or "spectacle," a development I deal with later in the book. In considering performance theory, I have attempted to limit my observations to those areas in which such theory overlaps with or comments significantly upon theatre. To trace performance in detail—even in the closely related fields of dance and opera, not to speak of happenings, circus, ritual, festival, and ultimately the performance elements of everyday life—would expand this book as radically as the attempt to include generally related social and cultural material. Again, my intent has been not to avoid all reference to these related areas of interest, but rather to touch upon them only as necessary to the understanding of the evolution of theatre theory itself.

All translations, unless otherwise noted, are my own.

MARVIN CARLSON

Bloomington, Indiana

Theories of the Theatre

1

Aristotle and the Greeks

THE PRIMACY OF ARISTOTLE'S *Poetics* in theatrical theory as well as in literary theory is unchallenged. Not only is the *Poetics* the first significant work in the tradition, but its major concepts and lines of argument have continually influenced the development of theory throughout the centuries. Western theatrical theory essentially begins with Aristotle. Still, a few previous writings at least touched on the subject, although aside from some scattered remarks in Isocrates (436–338 B.C.), the only extant significant comments on the drama before Aristotle are found in Aristophanes (c. 448–380 B.C.) and Plato (c. 427–347 B.C.).

The very paucity of Greek critical pronouncements has doubtless encouraged historians of criticism to give more attention to the satirical comments of Aristophanes, in particular in *The Frogs* (405 B.C.), than they have given to literary parodies in later periods. Though *The Frogs* is a rather suspect source for such information, its particular concern, an attempt to judge between Aeschylean and Euripidean styles of tragedy, does give the play a somewhat direct relation to theory. Aristophanes' attacks on Euripides in *The Acharnians* and in *Peace*, like the more famous ones on Socrates in *The Clouds*, are exaggerated and often unfair, but the debate between Aeschylus and Euripides in *The Frogs* seems to attempt a balanced assessment. Aeschylus takes the traditional Greek position that the poet is a moral teacher and that his work must fulfill a moral purpose. Euripides takes the more modern position that art's function is the revelation of reality, aside from moral and ethical questions.

Unquestionably, Aristophanes is on the side of Aeschylus, but Euripides is allowed to make a strong case for his practice. W. K. Wimsatt, Jr., has suggested that literary theory is fundamentally concerned with a "double difficulty": how poetry relates to the world and how it relates to value. *The Frogs* offers the first extended consideration of the second of these basic questions, establishing positions that have been frequently upheld in succeeding centuries.

Plato's famous attack on art in the *Republic* may be seen in part as a development of the types of concerns expressed in *The Frogs*. The first of Plato's complaints, that poets tell corrupting lies about both men and gods (books 2 and 3), closely parallels Aristophanes' criticism of Euripides. Book 10 makes broader charges. Here Plato accuses poetry of feeding and watering the passions instead of discouraging them, and explains the particular deficiency of poetry that his system of philosophy implies. The objects of our sense perceptions are themselves only copies of the ideal forms that compose reality. The artist in turn copies the secondary forms created by nature or by human craftsmen, removing his work one step further from truth. Real artists, says Plato, would be interested in realities, not imitations, and thus would renounce mimetic creation entirely. This is the first full development of another major theme of criticism, the relationship of art to life, and Plato's is the first extant use of the key word *mimesis* (imitation) to describe it. Of course, for Plato this was a pejorative term, and one of Aristotle's successes was to provide a positive function for *mimesis*.

Although Aristotle's *Poetics* is universally acknowledged in Western critical tradition, almost every detail about this seminal work has aroused divergent opinions. Since the original Greek text is not extant, modern versions are based primarily on an eleventh-century manuscript, supplemented by material from an inferior thirteenth- or fourteenth-century version and a tenth-century Arabic translation. Passages are unclear in all three versions, and the style in general is so elliptical that scholars have come to assume that the original manuscript was a series of lecture notes or a work meant to be circulated privately among students already familiar with Aristotle's teachings. In recent years there has been speculation that some of the *Poetics* may come not from Aristotle at all but from subsequent commentators. The date of the composition is also cloudy; though most scholars place it early in Aristotle's career, when he was still under the influence of Plato, some place it much later, when its significance as a rebuttal would be much reduced.

Despite all these problems, the main body of the text is accessible, and its general line of argument and structure are clear. The greatest hurdle for the student of the *Poetics* lies in the interpretation of several key concepts. There is no controversy concerning the significance of these concepts, but major disagreement as to their precise definition. The problems begin with *mimesis* itself, the subject of the first three chapters. Clearly, Aristotle sometimes uses the word to mean simple copying—at the beginning of chapter 4, he says that man learns his earliest lessons through imitation—but equally clearly, Aristotle soon moves on to add something more: for example, in chapter 15 good portrait painters are said to reproduce the distinctive features of a man but at the same time, make him more handsome than he is. What is added is not simply embellishment but fulfillment. What is being imitated is an ideal toward which the example is moving but which it has not yet achieved. Gerald Else calls the transition from Plato to Aristotle a transition from copying to creating,[1] though this does not imply creation from nothing. The term can perhaps be best understood by its relation to the Platonic and Aristotelian views of reality.

The basis of reality, according to Plato, is the realm of pure "Ideas," dimly reflected in the material world and in turn copied by art. Aristotle sees reality as a process, a becoming, with the material world composed of partially realized forms, moving—through natural processes—toward their ideal realizations. The artist who gives form to raw material thus works in a manner parallel to that of nature itself and, by observing the partially realized forms in nature, may anticipate their completion. In this way he shows things not as they are but as they "ought to be." The artist by no means has total freedom in creation. He should represent the process of becoming as he finds it in nature; hence Aristotle's insistence that poetry work by "probability or necessity." In this way the artist frees himself from accidental or individual elements. As Aristotle points out in the famous distinction between poetry and history in chapter 9, "Poetry therefore is more philosophical and more significant than history, for poetry is more concerned with the universal, and history more with the individual."[2]

Chapters 4 and 5 give a brief history of the development of the major poetic genres, with strong emphasis on tragedy; chapter 6, perhaps the best known, sums up previous material in the central definition of tragedy as "an imitation of a noble and complete action, having the proper magnitude; it employs language that has been artistically enhanced by each of the kinds of linguistic adornment, applied separately in the various parts of the play; it is presented in dramatic, not narrative form, and achieves, through the representation of pitiable and fearful incidents, the catharsis of such pitiable and fearful incidents."[3] Aside from the term "imitation," already discussed, the word *katharsis* (purgation) has proved most troublesome in this definition. Aristotle glosses the other words and phrases with reasonable clarity in the following

---

[1]Gerald Else, *Aristotle's Poetics: The Argument* (Cambridge, Mass., 1957), 322.
[2]Aristotle, *Poetics*, trans. Leon Golden, commentary by O. B. Hardison (Englewood Cliffs, N.J., 1968), 17.
[3]Ibid., 11.

chapters, but *katharsis* appears only once again in the *Poetics*, and then in a technical sense to describe Orestes' recovery from madness.

A common interpretation of this term observes that *katharsis* is a Greek medical term and suggests that, in response to Plato, Aristotle avers that tragedy does not encourage the passions but in fact rids the spectator of them. Tragedy would thus function in the manner of homeopathic medicine, treating a disorder by the administration of milder doses of similar agents; in this case, the emotions pity and fear. A passage in book 7 of the *Politics* supports this view, describing how souls with a superabundance of such emotions may be "lightened and delighted" by the cathartic quality of music. (In this same passage Aristotle promises a fuller treatment of *katharsis* in the *Poetics*—a promise which, unhappily, no extant version fulfills.) Among the later critics who subscribed to this interpretation were Minturno in the Renaissance, Milton in the seventeenth century, Thomas Twining in the eighteenth, Jakob Bernays in the nineteenth, and F. L. Lucas in the twentieth (though Lucas disagrees with Aristotle).

The most popular alternative view has read *katharsis* as a moral rather than a medical term, as purification rather than elimination or purgation. In the second book of the *Nicomachean Ethics*, Aristotle condemns both excess and deficiency in the passions; he says that both art and moral virtue must aim at the intermediate. This interpretation was generally favored during the neoclassic period, when a moral tone in tragedy was often sought, and among the critics who advanced variations of this reading were Corneille, Racine, and most notably Lessing.

As concerns in modern times have shifted, for many critics, away from the moral and psychological dimensions of art, it is hardly surprising to find *katharsis* being interpreted as a purely artistic or structural term. A noted exponent of this view is Gerald Else (1908–1982), who has suggested that *katharsis* occurs not in the spectator but in the plot, as it harmonizes disruptive elements within itself. The spectator's ultimate response is to this harmony rather than to the experience of arousal and purgation of emotion.[4] Building upon Else's discussion, Leon Golden, (b. 1930) has suggested that what takes place in the spectators of tragedy is a sort of intellectual enlightenment, whereby they see how disturbing emotions fit into a unified, harmonious world. He proposes "clarification" as a translation of *katharsis*.[5]

Clearly, each of these interpretations grows from a different view of tragedy as a whole, but all agree upon *katharsis* as a beneficial, uplifting

---

[4]Else, *Argument*, 439.
[5]Leon Golden, "Catharsis," *Transactions and Proceedings of the American Philological Association* 93 (1962): 57.

experience, whether psychological, moral, intellectual, or some combination of these. In any case, Aristotle's view of the result of tragedy may be seen, whether calculatedly or not, as a refutation of Plato's charge that art is morally harmful.

The remainder of chapter 6 of the *Poetics* introduces and briefly defines the six elements of tragedy—plot, character, thought, diction, spectacle, and song—which are then developed individually (in descending order of importance) in chapters 7 through 22. Aristotle's emphasis on form and probability led him to place plot (*mythos*) first in importance, indeed calling it the "soul" of tragedy. It must have a proper magnitude, with neither too few nor too many incidents. It must be unified in its action (the only "unity" insisted upon by Aristotle). It may be simple or complex, the latter involving reversal (a change of fortune to its opposite), recognition (a change from ignorance to knowledge), or both.

In chapter 13, as Aristotle begins his discussion of character (*ethos*), there appears another passage that has given rise to much debate: the description of the preferred hero of tragedy. After briefly discussing two possible changes of fortune—the good man falling into adversity and the evil man into prosperity—neither of which inspires the emotions proper to tragedy, Aristotle continues: "What is left, after our considerations, is someone in between these extremes. This would be a person who is neither perfect in virtue and justice nor one who falls into misfortune through vice and depravity: but rather, one who succumbs through some miscalculation."[6] This "miscalculation," called by some the "tragic flaw," is another controversial term, *hamartia*.

The various interpretations of *hamartia* may be generally divided into two groups, those that emphasize the moral aspect of the flaw and those (including Golden) that emphasize the intellectual, making *hamartia* an error of judgment or a mistaken assumption. The former is the traditional interpretation, and for some critics the "flaw" is almost cognate with the Christian idea of sin (indeed *hamartia* is used in this sense in the Gospel of John). Aristotle's own inclusion of such terms as "virtue" and "vice" in this passage seems to point in this direction. Elsewhere, he uses the term more ambiguously, and his central example of tragedy, *Oedipus Rex*, has a hero whose actions seem at least as much uninformed as immoral. In either case, it appears essential that the *hamartia* be unconscious in order for recognition and discovery to occur.

The next chapters move back and forth between considerations of plot and character. Chapter 14 deals with plots that arouse pity and terror, 15 with the goals of character development, 16 with types of

---

[6]Aristotle, *Poetics*, 22.

recognition, 17 with the process of constructing the play. Chapter 18 consists of scattered comments on structure, classification, and the chorus. Probably the most important of these is chapter 15, with its further elaboration of character and especially of the much misunderstood tragic characters "above the common level." In chapter 2, Aristotle makes the famous distinction between comedy and tragedy, that the former represents men as worse, the latter as better than in actual life. Many critics, especially those in the neoclassic tradition, translated Aristotle's "good" (*spoudaios*) character as "noble," and tragedy was made to deal exclusively with kings and princes. Besides converting Aristotle into a prescriptive rule-maker, a position he studiously avoided, this interpretation errs further in not realizing that for him, character (*ethos*) is determined not by birth but by moral choice. "If a speech or action has some choice connected with it, it will manifest character," he notes in chapter 15. "The character will be good if the choice is good."[7] Thus the "nobility" possessed by the tragic character is distinctly more moral than social or political. O. B. Hardison notes further that *ethos* for Aristotle is always directly related to *mythos*; the emphasis is not upon particularizing the character, as in much modern theatre, but upon developing an agent appropriate to the action.[8]

In chapter 19, Aristotle returns to his review of qualitative elements, dismissing thought (*dianoia*) quickly with a reference to the discussion in the *Rhetoric*, then taking up diction (*lexis*), which is treated in chapters 19 through 23. The final elements of tragedy, melody (*melos*) and spectacle (*opsis*), receive no further discussion, leaving for later critics the consideration of the produced work.

The final four chapters compare tragedy with the closely related genre of epic poetry. The important statement, glossed over in periods when verisimilitude became a major artistic concern, that a poet should prefer "impossible probabilities" to "unpersuasive possibilities" occurs in chapter 24. The next chapter defends this assertion against external criticism, the major defense being, as always, inner necessity: objects and events are to be shown not as they are but "as they ought to be."[9] In conclusion, Aristotle pronounces the best tragedy superior as an art form to epic poetry because of its greater concentration and unity and the accessories of music and spectacle. Such are the major features of this central work of Greek criticism, each of them destined to be endlessly explicated and debated during the following centuries.

Aristotle's favorite pupil and his successor as head of the Peripatetic

---

[7]Ibid., 25.
[8]Ibid., 200, Hardison's commentary.
[9]Ibid., 47.

school was Theophrastus (372–287 B.C.), also the author of a poetics, which has unfortunately not survived. Theophrastus was credited by the fourth-century grammarian Diomedes with the definition "tragedy is an action involving a reversal in the fortunes of a heroic character." On the basis of this attribution, Theophrastus has sometimes been credited also with a definition of comedy that Diomedes himself ascribes simply to "the Greeks": "Comedy is an episode of everyday life involving no serious dangers."[10] However, corroborative evidence of this claim is lacking, and scholars now generally argue that both of these subsequently influential definitions are more probably Hellenistic modifications of Aristotle than the work of his pupil. Other authors of this generation are known to have written on the theatre—Heraclides of Pontus, a pupil both of Plato and Aristotle, produced yet another poetics; Aristoxenus of Tarentium wrote on tragic poets and tragic dancing, and Chamelen on satiric drama and ancient comedy—but all of these works are now lost.

After 300 B.C. intellectual life declined in Athens, and Alexandria and later Pergamum emerged as the new centers of learning. Philosophical considerations of art declined, too, as more practical studies and, in literature, textual criticism began to be favored. Extended studies on the drama by the Alexandrian scholars were rare, although fragments remain of a general essay by Aristophanes of Byzantium on theatrical masks and another on the tradition of tragic subjects. More typical of the work of these scholars are the editions of the earlier Greek dramas prepared by Aristophanes of Byzantium and by Aristarchus, often with line-by-line commentary on content and interpretation.

[10]J. H. W. Atkins, *Literary Criticism in Antiquity* (Cambridge, 1934), 1:159.

2

Roman and Late Classic Theory

BY THE MIDDLE of the second century B.C., Latin literature had been established—heavily influenced, of course, by the Greeks—and occasional critical comment may be found in this literature. Plautus (c. 254–184 B.C.), an almost exact contemporary of the Hellenistic scholar Aristophanes of Byzantium, provided a few critical observations in his plays, most notably in the prologue to *Amphitruo*, which show that a definition of genre based on characters was already established. Mercury, who delivers the prologue, calls the play a "tragic-comedy" on the grounds that it contains not only kings and gods but also a servant. The prologues of Terence (c. 185–159 B.C.), which are often replies to his critics, also contain scattered comments on comedy. The prologue to *Heautontimorumenos*, for example, condemns boisterous, action-filled farces and argues that the best form of comedy is that which Terence himself offers, a quiet play with a good, clean style.

Comedy is further defined and analyzed in the puzzling fragment known as the *Tractatus coislinianus*. The only known version of it dates from the tenth century, but scholars are agreed that the work is of classical origin. Some have considered it a distillation or corruption of whatever lost writings Aristotle may have provided on comedy; others have judged it the work of a student of Aristotle or a later imitator. Whatever its source, it is surely in the Peripatetic tradition and provides an important insight into later Greek or early Roman comic theory.

The *Tractatus* classifies poetry as mimetic and nonmimetic; mimetic poetry as narrative and dramatic; and dramatic poetry as comedy, tragedy, mime, and satyr-drama. Its definition of comedy is clearly influenced by Aristotle's definition of tragedy: "Comedy is an imitation of an action that is ludicrous and imperfect, of sufficient length, the several kinds [of embellishment] separately [found] in the parts [of the play]; [presented] by persons acting, and not through narrative; through pleasure and laughter effecting the purgation of the like emotions."[1] The sources of laughter are then listed; some derived from the language (homonyms, garrulity, etc.), others from the content of the piece (deception, the unexpected, debasement, etc.). The *Tractatus* repeats Aristotle's divisions of plot, character, thought, language, melody, and spectacle, giving a sentence of elaboration to each. The characters of comedy comprise buffoons, *eirons* (ironical characters) and imposters, and the language is characterized as common and popular. The quantitative parts of comedy are stated to be prologue, choric song, episode, and exode. The genre itself is divided into Old Comedy, "with a superabundance of the laughable"; New Comedy, "which disregards laughter, and tends toward the serious"; and Middle Comedy, a mixture of the two.

In Roman criticism, rhetorical concerns dominated all others, and the poet and historian, as well as the orator, were analyzed by rhetorical standards. Questions of style and diction became paramount. Cicero (106–43 B.C.), for example, spoke of comedy at some length, not as a dramatic genre, but as a general source for oratorical effect. Even when his examples were drawn from the drama, his interest was in the source of humor and the methods of stimulating laughter in hearers by means of language. With a specificity not at all typical of Aristotle but anticipating the lists of late medieval and early Renaissance critics, Cicero also speaks of the characters suitable for ridicule: the morose, the superstitious, the suspicious, the boastful, and the foolish.[2] And Donatus credited Cicero with a definition of the genre of comedy (doubtless derived from the Greeks) that would be often repeated by later critics: "an imitation of life, a mirror of custom, an image of truth."[3]

Taken as a whole, the writings of Cicero provide for dramatic theory only scattered, if influential, comments. Saintsbury has compared the writings of Cicero to the *Rhetoric* of Aristotle, the Roman equivalent of the *Poetics* being instead the *Ars poetica* of Horace (68–5 B.C.). Certainly the latter is the sole work of the classic period to rival the *Poetics* in its influence on subsequent criticism. Although the *Ars poetica* does not suffer, as does its Greek predecessor, from the basic problem of establishing the text itself, it has not escaped a similar tradition of critical controversy. Its date, its sources, and even its purpose have been endlessly debated; attempts to read the text as a statement of literary theory, which in part it certainly is, have been beclouded by the fact that it is

---

[1]Quoted in Lane Cooper, *An Aristotelian Theory of Comedy* (New York, 1922), 224.
[2]Cicero, *Oratory and Orators* 2.62, trans. J. S. Watson (London, 1855), 295.
[3]J. W. H. Atkins, *Literary Criticism in Antiquity* (Cambridge, 1934), 2:38.

at the same time a work of poetry, with a structure and references determined more often by esthetic than by discursive considerations.

Scholars are now generally agreed that despite its calculatedly fluid form, the *Ars poetica* has a traditional organization based on the common tripartite division of Hellenistic criticism: *Poesis* or general questions concerning poetry; *poema*, or types of poetry; and *poeta*, or the character and education of the poet (the second receives the most thorough treatment). Indeed, there is evidence to suggest that Horace was reworking the writing of one Neoptolemus, a Hellenistic critic who was in turn working under the influence of the Aristotelian tradition. It should be noted, however, that there is no evidence of any firsthand knowledge of Aristotle in Horace or in any Roman author of this period.

One mark of possible, if indirect, Aristotelian influence on the *Ars poetica* is that despite Horace's personal commitment to lyric poetry, he follows Aristotle's practice of considering primarily the drama and secondarily the epic as the most significant poetic genres. Drama occupies most of the major center section of his poem. Decorum and appropriateness, central concerns of Roman criticism, are stressed throughout. Generally, Horace would have poets follow the established paths in such matters as choice of subject, vocabulary, verse forms, and character types. The language and action of individual characters should be in keeping with tradition and the commonly held ideas of how persons of particular ages, social positions, and emotional states should behave. When originality seems required, it must be of a nature that the artist can manage with success and appropriate to the subject being developed.

Unlike Aristotle, Horace, in one brief but striking passage, applies this rule to the actor as well as to the dramatist: if an actor is to make the audience weep, he must first feel grief himself, then seek among the expressions provided by nature those appropriate to the mood and station of the character.

In the most-quoted section of his poem, Horace lays down specific rules. The marvelous and the offensive should be kept offstage and handled by narrative. The play must contain five acts. Gods should appear only when absolutely required to resolve the action. No more than three speaking characters should normally be on stage together. The chorus should maintain a high moral tone and contribute always to the major design of the play.

This last observation leads to a more lengthy consideration of music on the stage and of the satiric drama, both of less specific concern to later critics than the briefer "rules" just given but nevertheless important in their implications. In both passages Horace again champions decorum and appropriateness. Even in the satiric drama, which may include both comic and serious elements, he argues for a kind of purity of genre to be attained by preventing these elements from mixing within the work. The Greek models are to be studied "day and night," with subject, style, and meter to follow conventional, standardized usage. Horace says that he prefers lively work with an occasional flaw (not too many of them, though!) to dull mediocrity, but his emphasis on specific rules and tradition often seems in fact to encourage the latter.

At the end of this central section on the drama, he provides perhaps the most familiar idea among all these much-quoted passages: that the aims of the poet are "to delight" and "to profit." This double emphasis, on pleasure and instruction, was the Romans' great contribution to the central question of art's relation to value and would become—along with the Horatian insistence on appropriateness, decorum, purity of genre, and respect for the Greek "rules"—central to neoclassic dramatic theory.

No other major Roman critic gives drama the central position accorded it by Horace in the *Ars poetica*. Much more commonly the emphasis is on rhetorical theory (as in Quintilian) or style (as in the famous essay on the sublime sometimes attributed to Longinus). When drama is mentioned at all by such writers, it is usually for the purpose of example or illustration only. Quintilian (c. 40–118), in his *De institutione oratoria* (c. 93), praises Menander among comic authors and Euripides among tragedians, but rhetorical rather than poetic criteria determine his choices; he is interested in these dramatists merely as possible models for the orator.[4]

The same observations may be made of Plutarch (c. 50–125), who deals somewhat more extensively with the drama in the surviving synopsis of his *Comparison between Aristophanes and Menander*. Philosophically, Plutarch is much indebted to the tradition of Plato and Aristotle, but his *Comparison* shows a far closer affinity with Horace and Roman rhetorical theory. Menander is praised for his balance, his temperance, his decorum, his ability to suit his style to the "sex, condition, and age" of each individual character. Aristophanes, conversely, is condemned for mixing the tragic and comic, offending good taste and decorum, and not suiting style to speaker. His poetry is written not for the "temperate person" but for the "debauched and lewd," and he gives out his lines "as it were by lot," making no distinction between "son, father, peasant, God, old man or hero." A more careful writer would seek the proper quality for each, such as "state to a prince, force to an orator,

---

[4]Quintilian, *Institutes of Oratory*, 10.1.68-69, trans. J. S. Watson (London, 1871), 2:261.

innocence to a woman, meanness of language to a poor man, and sauciness to a tradesman."[5]

Throughout the late classical period, the attitude toward criticism of such writers as Horace, Quintilian, and Cicero remained dominant. Poetry was studied not for esthetic but for practical reasons, as an aid to more effective speaking and writing. As the medieval trivium of grammar, rhetoric, and logic developed, poetry was normally considered a part of the first, following Quintilian's definition of grammar as "the art of speaking correctly and the illustration of the poets."[6] It is thus in the late classic grammarians that the most substantial theoretical writings on drama from this period are to be found. Foremost among these are the *De fabula* of Evanthius and the *De comedia* of Aelius Donatus, both written during the fourth century and widely distributed and quoted during the Middle Ages and early Renaissance.

The two essays incorporate a wide variety of material clearly drawn from many classic sources and not always self-consistent or entirely coherent. Roughly the first half of each essay deals with the historical development of comedy and tragedy (Evanthius discusses the satyr play as well). Next, the features of the genres are discussed. Evanthius's distinction between tragedy and comedy has a moral tone and a focus on structure that is quite Roman and quite unlike Aristotle:

> In comedy the fortunes of men are middle-class, the dangers are slight, and the ends of the action are happy; but in tragedy everything is the opposite—the characters are great men, the fears are intense, and the ends disastrous. In comedy the beginning is troubled, the end tranquil; in tragedy the events follow the reverse order. And in tragedy the kind of life is shown that is to be shunned; while in comedy the kind is shown that is to be sought after. Finally, in comedy the story is always fictitious; while tragedy is often based on historical truth.[7]

Essentially, this view of the genres dominated medieval and early Renaissance criticism.

Both Evanthius and Donatus identify four structural parts in comedy: the *prologue*, given before the plot begins; the *protasis*, which introduces the action; the *epitasis*, or complication; and the *catastrophe*, or resolution. Donatus adds remarks on the staging of classical drama, the symbolic values of the costumes, the delivery of lines, and the musical accompaniment. Evanthius follows the general Roman practice of sin-

---

[5]Plutarch, *Morals*, ed. W. W. Goodwin (Boston, 1878), 3:11-14.

[6]Quintilian, *Institutes*, 1.4.2, trans. Watson, 1:29.

[7]Evanthius, *De fabula*, trans. O. B. Hardison, Jr., in *Classical and Medieval Literary Criticism* (New York, 1974), 305.

gling out Terence for particular commendation. The virtues attributed to this author are almost a catalogue of those most prized by Latin critics: appropriateness (suiting of character to "moral habits, age, station in life and type"); verisimilitude (which includes defying traditional types: for example, showing prostitutes who are not evil); purity of genre (tempering the emotional element that might give the work too serious a tone); decorum (avoiding topics that might give offense); clarity (rejecting obscure material that would require glossing by antiquaries); and unity (everything composed "from the same material" and forming "a single body").

There is also in the scholiast writings of the late classic period a concern with the emotional effects of the drama, which seems to hark back to Plato's arousal of the passions and Aristotle's *katharsis*. Thus a comment from either Melampus of the third century or Diomedes of the fourth says that the aim of tragedy is to move the hearers to tears; that of comedy, to move them to laughter: "Wherefore, they say, tragedy dissolves life and comedy consolidates it."[8] The author of the third- or fourth-century *De mysteriis* (possibly Iamblichus) says that when we witness the emotions of others in either comedy or tragedy, we qualify our own: we "work them off more moderately, and are purged of them."[9]

A more extended discussion of this subject may be found in the commentaries on Plato by Proclus Diadochus (c. 410–485), the last great figure in the Neoplatonic school of the late classic period. Plotinus (205–70), the leader of this school, opened a way to justify art on Platonic grounds by a redefinition of mimesis. In a famous passage in book 10 of the *Republic*, Plato had attacked art as an imitation of an imitation: a craftsman may create a bed imitative of the abstract and eternal idea, but a painter, considering only external appearance, merely imitates what the craftsman has created. Plotinus, though accepting Plato's concept of eternal ideas, defended art by arguing that the artist imitates not material but spiritual things; that he is a visionary, not a mere observer.[10] While Plotinus himself applied this theory primarily to sculpture, his follower Proclus applied it to poetry, and especially to Homer, though he dealt briefly with the drama as well as the epic.

Yet despite his claim for a visionary element in poetry, Proclus supports Plato's conviction that comedy and tragedy should be banned from an ideal state. In his Neoplatonic view, there are a number of reasons for this prohibition. The soul has three states of being, to any

[8]Quoted in Cooper, *Aristotelian Theory*, 86.
[9]Ibid., 83.
[10]Plotinus, *Enneads* 1.6, "Beauty," trans. Stephen MacKenna (London, 1969), 63.

of which poetry could make its appeal: the divine, offering direct insight into the ultimate good; the rational, dealing with balance and harmony, and instructing men in proper actions and thoughts; and the irrational, seeking to arouse the passions and delight the senses. This third and lowest mode, says Proclus, was where Plato saw the appeal of drama, and for this reason he condemned it. In fact, Proclus believes that comedy and tragedy can present dangers to each division of the soul. He agrees with Plato that on the level of the passions they offer an indulgence in "indecent laughter" and "ignoble tears," nourishing the emotions instead of regulating them. On the rational level, again taking an example from Plato, he asserts that they offer false and misleading information about the gods and heroes, thus confusing men's moral concerns. Most serious, on the highest level, by imitation of a great variety of characters, they tempt the soul into diversity and away from the simplicity and unity that characterize both virtue and God.[11]

Evidently, the late classic writers established two rather distinct traditions in dramatic theory: grammarians such as Donatus and Evanthius, drawing upon the Roman rhetoricians, emphasized structural concerns and the characteristics of the opposed genres of comedy and tragedy; the Neoplatonists focused less on the structure and more on the effect of drama, with the ultimate aim of justifying Plato's banishment of dramatists from the ideal state.

The attacks of the church fathers on the theatre had much in common with this latter approach, in both the condemnatory tone and the emphasis on the effect of the drama. The most extended and bitter early attack came from Tertullian (c. 160–250), whose *De spectaculis* (c. 198) served as a mine of material for antitheatrical tracts for centuries after. Tertullian uses three basic arguments against spectacles, only one of which involves what we might call a theory of the theatre. First, he cites scriptural evidence against spectacles. Second, he seeks to prove their idolatrous nature by their origin, their locale, their equipment, and their concerns. Third, in considering their effects, he expounds a theory similar to that of the Neoplatonists: although God enjoins the Christian to live in tranquility, gentleness, peace, and quiet, the theatre stimulates frenzy and the passions, encouraging a loss of self-control. "There is no spectacle without violent agitation of the soul."[12]

Subsequent Christian commentaries directed against the theatre relied heavily on Tertullian, though his doctrines doubtless received additional support from the general Roman critical enthusiasm for

---

[11]Proclus, *Commentaire sur la République*, trans. A. J. Festugière, 3 vols. (Paris, 1970), 1:68–69.

[12]Tertullian, "Spectacles," trans. Rudolph Arbesmann, in *Disciplinary, Moral, and Ascetical Works* (New York, 1959), 83.

discipline and moderation as well as a revival of interest in Plato. Thus the famous Easter sermon of St. John Chrysostom (c. 347–407) against circuses and spectacles, delivered in 399, condemns theatregoers for abandoning themselves to "transports, to profane cries," and for caring so little for the soul as to "deliver it captive to the mercy of your passions."[13]

From almost the same period (c. 397), the *Confessions* of Augustine (354–430) similarly condemns the theatre's arousal of passions. Typically, however, Augustine goes beyond a mere repetition of conventional conclusions to explore his personal reactions, raising significant questions about the effect of the drama that cannot be found elsewhere in late classic writing. He sees the love of theatre as a "miserable madness" that ensnares man in the passions he should avoid, and speculates further on what makes the tragic emotions attractive: "Why is it that man desires to be made sad, beholding doleful and tragical things, which yet himself would by no means suffer?" Augustine locates this enjoyment in a perverse fascination with grief. Grief is an honorable emotion if coupled with pity or compassion, when it may serve as a spur to relieve the cause of suffering, he says, but if the one commiserating so enjoys the commiseration that he desires someone else to be miserable so that he may have an object of this emotion, a potential good becomes corrupt. This "feigned and personated" misery "which the auditor is not called upon to relieve" is what the theatre offers.[14]

More extensive but, from a theoretical view, less interesting observations on classic theatre may be found in the first two books of *The City of God* (413). Augustine began this monumental apologia in the wake of Alaric's sack of Rome in 410, to answer the charges that this calamity was Jove's judgment on a city weakened by the growth of Christianity. The major comments on pagan theatre come in the second book, which seeks to demonstrate the decay of Roman manners and the moral inadequacies of the pagan gods themselves. Augustine quotes the pagan moralists against the licentiousness of the theatre as a way of challenging the authority of the gods, who reportedly established and enjoyed these spectacles. Plato's banishment of poets is noted with approval, as are Roman legal sanctions against actors. Augustine considers traditional comedy and tragedy the least objectionable theatrical forms, since they at least remain chaste in language, though they sometimes deal with questionable subjects. He notes, though without ap-

[13]St. John Chrysostom, *Oeuvres*, trans. l'abbé J. Bareille, 21 vols. (Paris, 1864–76), 10:488.
[14]Augustine, *Confessions*, trans. E. B. Pusey (New York, 1950), 3.2–4.

proval, that because of the beauty of their language, such works are still read as a part of a liberal education.

Augustine was the last major figure in the early church to apply anything like a critical approach to the theatre. When later church fathers (such as Silvian in the fifth century) spoke of drama at all, it was only to fulminate against its obscenity. Little distinction is made by such writers between different types of spectacles—conventional drama, pantomimes, circuses, and others. Occasional references to comedy and tragedy may still be found after Augustine, but with less and less evidence that these terms have any necessary connection with drama. Already by the time of Boethius (c. 480–524) tragedy was being used to describe a narrative rather than a dramatic genre: "What other thing doth the outcry of tragedies lament, but that fortune, having no respect, overturneth happy states."[15] This understanding of the term predominated during the Middle Ages.

[15]Boethius, *The Consolation of Philosophy*, trans. H. F. Stewart (London, 1918), 181.

3

The Medieval Period

THE CRITICAL AND THEORETICAL WRITINGS of the early Middle Ages devote much attention to scriptural allegory and interpretation, and apply the strategies of these studies to the classic poets, and particularly to Virgil. Remarks on the drama are few, and generally restricted to rephrasing the comments of late classical writers. During these centuries the Eastern Empire, with its capital at Constantinople, became significant in the continuation of classical culture. After the sixth century, when the Latin provinces were lost to invaders, the East became more Greek in character, and Greek became generally accepted as the official language. As a result, the tradition of Greek criticism survived through the next several centuries among the scholars of Constantinople, while writers in the West worked more within the Latin tradition.

Thus, in the Byzantine scholar John Tzetzes (c. 1110–1180) we find an author whose observations on tragedy and comedy show clearly an inheritance from classic Greek sources. He calls comedy "an imitation of an action ... purgative of emotions, constructive of life, moulded by laughter and pleasure." Tragedy concerns deeds "that are past, although it represents them as taking place in the present," while comedy "embraces fictions of the affairs of everyday life." The distinction between the "report" of tragedy and the "fiction" of comedy does not come directly from Aristotle, but seems to derive from an Alexandrian or Attic source. The aim of tragedy, says Tzetzes, is to move the hearers to lamentation; that of comedy is to move them to laughter. The goal of comedy is a sort of social equilibrium. Comedy ridicules the "plunderer and evil-doer and pestilent fellow" and "for the rest settles all into decorum. Thus tragedy dissolves life, while comedy founds it firmly, and renders it solid."[1]

---

[1]Quoted in Lane Cooper, Introduction, in *An Aristotelian Theory of Comedy* (New York, 1922), 86.

In the West, the Carolingian period (eighth to tenth centuries) produced a flowering of poetry and of critical commentary on classical and Christian literature. Little of this concerned the drama, but the continuing importance of Donatus and Horace guaranteed that this genre would receive at least occasional critical attention. The Carolingian *Scholia Vindobonensia* on Horace's *Ars poetica* is the outstanding example; since the *Scholia* comments on Horace line by line, a major part of it necessarily involves the drama. The author clearly has little concept of performance; his model seems to be that of literary recitation. The chorus is seen as a group of well-wishers who play no part in the action but merely listen to the recitation, and the five-act convention is thus curiously explained: "The first act is for the old men, the second for youths, the third for matrons, the fourth for the servant and maid, and the fifth is for the pimp and the prostitute."[2]

During the twelfth century interest in poetic theory grew steadily in the West, but despite promising Horatian titles—the *Ars versificatoria* of Matthew of Vendôme (c. 1175), the *Poetria nova* of Geoffrey of Vinsauf (c. 1200), the *Ars poetica* of Gervase of Melcheley (c. 1215)—such studies invariably considered rhetorical ornament and style, saying little or nothing about the drama. The subject was, however, reintroduced in thirteenth-century criticism when the Neoplatonists and grammarians of the high Middle Ages began to be challenged by the more logically oriented scholastic approach. The great impetus for the shift was the translation of Aristotle from Arabic texts and commentaries, and in poetic theory the central document was the commentary on the *Poetics* of the great Arabic scholar Averroës (1126–1198), translated into Latin in 1256 by Hermannus Alemannus. In his preface to the work, Hermannus made a distinction between two traditional attitudes toward poetry: one, derived from Cicero, considering poetry a branch of rhetoric and therefore concerned with practical or moral philosophy; the other, derived from Horace, calling poetry a branch of grammar and dealing with it in terms of stylistic technique. Aristotle, Hermannus felt, provided a third alternative by making poetry a branch of logic, in which certain effects are achieved by the proper employment of poetic devices. In fact, for both Hermannus and Averroës, these effects were essentially didactic, so the purported new approach became in an important sense a new way of justifying Ciceronian ethical instruction.

Although Averroës used several terms roughly equivalent to "mimesis" (translated by Hermannus as *assimilatio, representatio,* and *imitatio*), the actual Aristotelian concept was too alien for him to assimilate.

---

[2]*Scholia*, l. 190, quoted by O. B. Hardison, in *Classical and Medieval Literary Criticism,* ed. A. Preminger et al. (New York, 1974), 288.

He found instead in chapter 4 of the *Poetics* the suggestion that poetry originated in poems of "beautiful actions" and in "vituperative verses." Thus Averroës begins, "Every poem and all poetry are either praise or blame"—tragedy being an example of the former, comedy of the latter. In this way he placed moral instruction at the foundation of his interpretation and so contributed to the critical inclination—which we find throughout the next several centuries—to assume, incorrectly, a moral base in Aristotle.

In a subsequent passage Averroës explains the relationship between imitation and moral instruction. "Since imitators and makers of likenesses wished through their art to impel people toward certain choices and discourage them from others, they had to treat subjects that, being represented, would suggest either virtues or vices." Thus virtue and vice become the basis of both action and character, with the aim of the representation being "nothing but the encouragement of what is proper and the rejection of what is base."[3]

Such an interpretation would seem to lead inevitably to the idea of poetic justice, with good rewarded and evil punished, but Averroës takes the more difficult path of attempting to reconcile this moral function with the Aristotelian hero who suffers misery and misfortune "without cause," as Averroës put it, since he gave no attention to *hamartia*. Instead, tragedy stimulates the "animal passions, like pity and fear and sorrow" because the mere depiction of virtue will not arouse a perturbation of the soul, and such perturbation alone will stimulate the soul to actually be receptive to virtue.[4]

Averroës calls the arousing of passion one of the three "parts" of tragic action, the other two being indirection and directness, which correspond to reversal and discovery. These also are defined in moral terms. Direct imitation "treats the thing itself"; that is, it shows actions worthy of praise. Indirect imitation shows "the opposite of what is to be praised," causing the soul to "reject and despise" it. These three "parts" make up Averroës' equivalent of Aristotle's plot, or action. The other parts of tragedy are character, meter, belief, melody, and deliberation. The replacement of spectacle by deliberation (*consideratio*) shows clearly how far Averroës was from a theatrical concept of tragedy. Presentation to him meant at most a kind of public reading, and for this he had little respect. The skilled poet "does not need to enhance his reputation through extrinsic aids like dramatic gestures and facial expressions. Only those who parade as poets (although they are really

---

[3]"The Middle Commentary of Averroës of Cordova on the *Poetics* of Aristotle," trans. O. B. Hardison, in ibid., 351.
[4]Ibid., 361–62.

not poets) use these devices."[5] Unity, coherence, and proportion are all praised, not as commendable in themselves but only as they make the work more effective in its moral aim. Similarly, probability and necessity are to be sought because actions like those of real life are those most likely to provide proper stimulation to the soul.

In this odd form Aristotle's *Poetics* entered medieval critical thought, but we should not place on the Arabic scholar or on his faithful Latin translator the whole burden of the misreadings that characterize much subsequent criticism. On the contrary, Averroës' work gained quick acceptance precisely because it harmonized so well with already prevailing critical attitudes. According to his own preface, Hermannus considered translating Aristotle directly, but "because of the difficulty of the vocabulary and for many other reasons" turned to the more comprehensible and more compatible Averroës. Twenty-two years later, in 1278, William of Moerbeke, Bishop of Corinth, did produce a reasonably accurate translation from the Greek, but this was not the Aristotle the late thirteenth century wanted to hear. The translation of Hermannus was widely read and quoted and was printed in 1481, while that of William of Moerbeke created no stir whatever and was not printed until the twentieth century.

The first significant effort to apply the doctrines of Aristotle as interpreted by Averroës seems to have been in the extensive commentaries (1375) on Dante by Benvenuto da Imola. These attempted to demonstrate that the *Divine Comedy* was a work fully in accord with Aristotle's rules, moving from blame in the *Inferno* to praise in the *Paradiso* and even containing the sort of "indirections" Averroës described. For example, the despair of the *Inferno* could be seen as an indirect reflection of the hopefulness of the following *Purgatorio*.

There is no evidence that Dante himself thought of his work in these terms. The faint echoes of Aristotle that may be present in the *Epistle to Can Grande della Scala* (c. 1315) show him much more in harmony with the traditional ideas of comedy and tragedy as they had been handed down through the Middle Ages from Donatus and the grammarians. According to this tradition—formal rather than ethical—comedy dealt with private citizens, was written in humble style, began unhappily and ended happily. Tragedy dealt with kings and princes, was written in elevated style, began happily and ended unhappily. The *Catholican* (1286) of Johannes Januensis de Balbis, a contemporary of Dante, lists precisely these three points of distinction.[6]

---

[5] Ibid., 360.
[6] See Wilhelm Cloëtta, *Beiträge zur Litteraturgeschichte des Mittelalters und der Renaissance*, 2 vols. (Halle, 1890–92), 1:28.

Dante's letter passes over the characters of comedy and tragedy to focus on the language and organization of the genres. Tragedy "begins admirably and tranquilly, whereas its end or exit is foul and terrible" (he explains the Greek "goat-song" as a reference to this end—"fetid, like a goat"). Comedy "introduces some harsh complication, but brings its matter to a prosperous end." In language, tragedy is "exalted and sublime," comedy "lax and humble."[7] Thus Dante's great work, beginning in the horrible and fetid confines of Hell and ending in Paradise, and moreover written in the vernacular, he designates as a comedy. The focus is quite different from that of Averroës, though one central assumption is shared: that comedy and tragedy are terms applied only to varying poetic forms. In both authors, the theatrical connotations of these terms have almost totally disappeared.

The spreading influence of Dante during the following century provided further reinforcement for these already well-entrenched medieval interpretations of comedy and tragedy. Chaucer clearly subscribed to them; in his translation of Boethius (c. 1378), he glosses the famous passage on the wheel of fortune to bring it more closely into line with this critical tradition: "Tragedie is to seyn, a ditee of a prosperitee for a tyme, that endeth in wrecchednesse."[8] A letter of Don Inigo Lopez de Mendoza, Marquis de Santillana (May 4, 1444) observes that the traditional poetic modes are tragedy, comedy, and satire. Tragedy "contains the fall of great kings and princes ... who are born in happy states and live thus for a long time, and then are lamentably brought to destruction." Satire is a work "which strongly ridicules the vices and praises the virtues." Comedy "begins in distress, is resolved in the middle, and ends in joy, happiness, and satisfaction."[9]

The appearance of a powerful dramatic tradition in the late medieval church seems paradoxical in light of the suspicion of the art among the early church fathers, but the new view and the old shared a common theory—that of drama as instruction. Tertullian and Augustine had stressed the pagan origins, subjects, and concerns of classic drama. But could not the attractiveness of drama, dangerous when it preached these values, be turned to good by devoting it to Christian concerns and subjects? Such had precisely been the aim of the Saxon nun Hrotsvitha (c. 935–973). The preface to her collection of Christian comedies expressed concern about those seduced to "criminal actions" by the reading of Terence, and proposed to counter this evil effect by celebrating "the praiseworthy chastity of Christian virgins, while employing

---

[7]*A Translation of the Latin Works of Dante Alighieri*, trans. anon. (New York, 1904), 349.
[8]Gloss to bk. 2.2, line 50, Geoffrey Chaucer, *Works*, ed. Walter Skeat, 6 vols. (Oxford, 1894), 2:28.
[9]Don Inigo Lopez de Mendoza, *Obras* (Madrid, 1852), 94.

the same form of composition which the ancients used to portray the shameful actions of immoral women."[10]

More significant for the development of subsequent religious theatre were those who saw, and began to stress, dramatic elements in the Mass itself. This concept, argued by Amalarius, Bishop of Metz (c. 780–850), was applied with specific reference to the performance of classic drama by a disciple of Amalarius, Honorius of Autun, in his *Gemma Animae* (c. 1100). Again the emphasis was, of course, on the didactic: "It is known that those who recited tragedies in the theatres represented to the people, by their gestures, the actions of conflicting forces. Even so our tragedian represents to the Christian people in the theatre of the church, by his gestures, the struggle of Christ, and impresses upon them the victory of his redemption."[11]

Such concerns were clearly reflected in the development of the cycle dramas, whose authors were well aware that such presentation made the Bible stories not only more vivid and impressive but also more entertaining. Thus medieval drama essentially came into harmony with the Horatian goal "to delight and to instruct," as we may see clearly in the Doctor's description of his function as a character in the *Ludus Coventriae:*

> To [the] pepyl not lernyd—I stonde as A techer
> Of [this] processyon—to [give] informacion
> And to them [that] be lernyd—As a gostly precher
> That in my rehersayl—they may haue delectacion.[12]

---

[10]Hrotsvitha, *Opera* (Leipzig, 1906), 113.

[11]*Patrologiae cursus completus: Patrologia latina* (Paris, 1844–64), 172, 570, trans. David Bevington, in *Medieval Drama* (Boston, 1975), 9.

[12]*Ludus Coventriae*, ed. K. S. Block, Early English Text Society, e.s. 120 (1922), 269.

4

The Italian Renaissance

THE STORY OF DRAMATIC CRITICISM during the Italian Renaissance is essentially the story of the rediscovery of Aristotle, of the establishment of his *Poetics* as a central reference point in dramatic theory, and of attempts to relate this work to the already established critical tradition. Aristotle was known and his works referred to throughout the Middle Ages, but his reputation did not compare with that of Horace, Cicero, Quintilian, Plato, or even Donatus, and the *Poetics* itself was essentially lost to the West until Hermannus's translation of Averroës brought at least this distorted version to the attention of some scholars.

At the end of the fifteenth century, the Latin translation of Giorgio Valla (1498) and a Greek text published in Venice (1508) at last put moderately accurate versions of the *Poetics* at the disposal of Renaissance scholars. They were not at all seized upon with avidity. The late medieval conceptions of the nature and function of tragedy and comedy had evolved as we have seen, from a harmonizing of elements in the Latin rhetoricians and late classic grammarians. These did not in turn harmonize readily with the newly discovered text; for at least a generation there remained a clear preference for the more compatible Averroës. Pietro Pomponazzi, for example, in his *De incantationibus* (1520), cites Averroës in justifying the fables of poets: "They tell untruths so that we may arrive at the truth and so that we may instruct the vulgar crowd, which must be led toward good action and away from wicked action."[1]

The universal opinion of early-sixteenth-century Italian critics was that the classical tradition was essentially a monolithic one, and that

---

[1]Bernard Weinberg, *A History of Literary Criticism in the Italian Renaissance*, 2 vols. (Chicago, 1961), 1:368.

apparent contradictions or inconsistencies were the result of misreadings, mistranslations, or corruptions in the extant texts. Thus the mid-sixteenth-century critics undertook the formidable task of decoding Aristotle, using, naturally enough, the concepts of the already established Latin tradition with its emphasis on moral instruction. The observation in Parrasio's commentary on Horace's *Ars poetica* (1531) that Horace had drawn his precepts from Neoptolemus and Aristotle was echoed in many works of this same decade, and there are Aristotelian touches in parts I–IV of Trissino's *Poetica* (1529) and in the *Poetica* of Daniello (1536). Still, these works seem to draw more on Donatus and the Latin tradition than on the Greek, and moral instruction reigns supreme. Francesco Filippi Pedemonte, in 1546, seems to have been the first critic to quote Aristotle extensively, though as a commentary on Horace. The concepts of mimesis and artistic unity, the definition of tragedy and comedy, probability and necessity, all appear in this commentary, though all are accommodated to Horatian ideas.

The first major commentary to be published on Aristotle himself was that of Francesco Robortello (1516–1568), who occupied the chair of rhetoric at several of the leading Italian universities. In 1548, the same year that his commentary was published, he assumed his first major professorship, at the University of Venice. The commentary drew together scattered observations on the *Poetics* from writers of the previous 20 years and marked the general directions to be followed by subsequent critics.

Perhaps the most urgent problem in harmonizing Aristotle with Horace arose in connection with mimesis. From Aristotle came the idea of mimesis as an end in itself, though Robortello focuses less on mimesis itself than on the audience's pleasure in it: "What other end, therefore, can we say that the poetic faculty has than to delight through the representation, description, and imitation of every human action, every emotion, every thing animate as well as inanimate."[2]

By emphasizing the pleasurable effect of mimesis, Robortello is able to bring Aristotle into line with the Horatian goal of delight, and the Italian critic is quick to add that profit is also involved. The method by which the latter is achieved is the traditional one: the imitation and praise of virtuous men incites men to virtue; the representation and condemnation of vice serve as deterrents. Rhetorical ends are thus substituted for Aristotle's aesthetic ones; the audience is primarily to gain not pleasure from the unity and formal qualities of the work but moral instruction from the various didactic elements. Plot and character

---

[2]Francesco Robortello, *Librum Aristotelis de arte poetica explicationes*, 2, quoted and trans. in ibid., 389.

signify chiefly the actions or personal traits that lead to virtue or vice and thus to happiness or unhappiness.

It should be noted that Robortello restores the idea of performance to dramatic theory. Imitation in tragedy may be considered in two ways, he observes: "either insofar as it is scenic and is acted by the actors or insofar as it is made by the poet as he writes."[3] The former, he suggests, emphasizes action; the latter, character. In either case the audience will be persuaded to moral improvement only if what they experience seems relevant to life as they know it. Thus Horatian utility serves as a justification for Aristotelian probability: "in general, to the extent that the verisimilar partakes of truth it has the power to move and to persuade."[4] Aristotle's "things as they ought to be" is interpreted not philosophically or aesthetically but rhetorically and morally. This linking of the verisimilar with moral instruction was to become, as we shall see, one of the foundation stones of French neoclassic theory.

Appended to Robortello's commentary are several supplementary theses, including one on comedy. Essentially, it simply reworks Aristotle's *Poetics*, substituting comedy for tragedy and repeating anything Robortello considered common to both. The genres are basically distinguished by subject, comedy treating the lowly common people and tragedy involving superior folk. In the parts of comedy and types of plot, on discovery, character, thought, and diction, Robortello generally follows Aristotle closely, though he lays rather more emphasis on appropriateness and verisimilitude. The end of the essay turns to Donatus and Horace as authorities for the parts of comedy, the five-act rule, and an observation that a character in comedy should not be permitted more than five entrances (even fewer in tragedy).

In sum, the effort to accommodate Aristotle to prevailing literary theory is achieved only by radical adjustment of the original text, less by rewriting in the manner of Averroës than by reinterpretation of key concepts. Aristotle's emphasis on the artistic whole disappears, since an artistic effect is not the goal. Instead, the various parts of the work are analyzed for their individual effectiveness in persuading or pleasing an audience. The Horatian ideals of decorum and appropriateness are applied to all aspects of the drama, under the assumption that members of the audience will be most easily persuaded and moved by actions, character, and language that seem in harmony with their already existing conceptions. The concern with verisimilitude explains Robortello's comments on Aristotle's observation that tragedy tries to keep "within a single circuit of the sun, or something near that"; Robortello asserts

[3]Ibid., 393.
[4]Ibid., 392.

that this must mean sunrise to sunset rather than a 24-hour day, since people normally do not "move about or converse" at night. On this point again this first major Renaissance commentary on Aristotle established the general direction for those that followed.

The next year (1549) saw the first translation of Aristotle into the vernacular, by Bernardo Segni, and in 1550 Bartolomeo Lombardi and Vincenzo Maggi published a new commentary, following the example of Robortello. Its methodology and general assumptions are not strikingly different, but certain significant elaboration and qualification may be found. Purgation is dealt with in rather greater detail, and the theory is advanced that pity and terror are not themselves the emotions purged but serve as devices to purge the soul of other disorders of a more social nature, such as avarice or lust. Various parts of tragedy may be designed to give pleasure, but the ultimate aim remains instruction, and the new commentary—far more than that of Robortello—sees this instruction directed not at a selected, receptive public, but at the multitude. This results in even greater stress upon "probability" and "verisimilitude," both now interpreted as what will be accepted by the common crowd. Since the poet's aim is "to teach proper conduct, whether this be introduced into men's souls by false narratives or by true narratives, his desire is fulfilled. But since a poet cannot accomplish this purpose unless he obtains the belief of his audience, he follows common opinion in this respect."[5] Thus plots must be either generally known or readily acceptable, as must characters and style of language.

This leads to the concept of decorum, and to several concepts defining character that are central to neoclassic theory—morality, suitability, and generality. Morality is the aim, the others the means. Poets should imitate "the best people; when they represent their behavior they must make exemplars of it, that is, they must express the highest probity of character in those persons whom they undertake to imitate." But for these exemplars to be effective, they must be general and predictable. The poet "deals with the universal. For if he introduces a king as saying or doing a given thing, what he says or does must belong to those things which are usually or necessarily attributed to kings."

The emphasis on credibility suggests a close adherence to real time. Since both tragedy and comedy "attempt to approach as close to truth as is possible," an audience can hardly accept things done in a month but presented in two or three hours. If a messenger sent to Egypt returns within an hour, what spectator "will not whistle and hiss the

---

[5]Bartolomeo Lombardi and Vincenzo Maggi, *Aristotelis librum de poetica communes explanationes*, 267-68, quoted and trans. in Weinberg, *History*, 1:412.

actor off the stage and judge that an action lacking in all reason was contrived by the poet."[6]

The *Discorso intorno al comporre delle comedie e delle tragedie* by Giambattista Giraldi, or Cinthio (1504–1573), is the first important Renaissance statement on the drama by a practicing playwright, and as is often the case, it takes a much less rigorous stand than the pronouncements of those critics who were not practitioners of the art. The *Discorso* was published in 1554, but the date of its writing is uncertain. Giraldi claimed it as the first exposition of Aristotle's *Poetics* in the vernacular and signed it 1543, but internal evidence places it later; it is likely that he selected the date to establish a claim to precedence and to avoid charges of plagiarism from Maggi.

For almost half a century before Giraldi wrote his *Discorso*, the court and intellectual community at Ferrara, largely under the influence of Ariosto, had been interesed in the revival of the production of classic plays. Giraldi's major contribution to the new repertoire was his tragedy *Orbecche*, strongly influenced by Seneca and first performed in 1541. By 1543, when *Orbecche* was published, Giraldi had written three other plays, and his *Discorso* is at least as much a defense of these works as a commentary on Aristotle. Indeed, a comment in the dedication to *Orbecche* might almost lead us to suspect that Giraldi is headed toward the sort of relativistic criticism that appeared in the nineteenth century: "Aristotle is too obscure to be taken as a guide; it would be better to listen to reason, while taking into consideration the time, the place, and the progress achieved."[7] The final phrase seems almost a prefiguration of Hippolyte Taine's famous *race, moment,* and *milieu* in the nineteenth century, but of course Giraldi has no such radical aim. He is merely allowing himself room for a generous interpretation of the classic sources. In fact, his commentary follows Aristotle with moderate fidelity, though there are a few striking differences, most obviously Giraldi's defense of a happy ending for tragedy and of double plots. Aristotle acknowledges both as possibilities but calls them inferior, saying they are generally employed by authors subservient to audience whim. Still, one by-product of the moralistic bias of Renaissance criticism was a strong concern with audience appeal, and Giraldi is quite willing to challenge Aristotle on this point. His plays, he admits freely, were written

> solely to serve the spectators, and to be pleasing on the stage, and to conform better to the practice of the time. For even if Aristotle says that this caters to the ignorance of the audience, the opposing position has also

[6]Ibid, 415.
[7]G. B. Giraldi Cinthio, *Orbecche tragedia* (Vinegria, 1543), 2.

its defenders. I thought it better to please the one who must listen, despite some loss of excellence (assuming that Aristotle's opinion is the superior one) than to add a bit of grandeur which would displease those for whose pleasure the action is placed upon the stage.[8]

It is essential to remember that this goal of pleasing is never represented as an end in itself. Pleasure remains a means to the end of moral instruction, and Giraldi considers both the idea of purgation and the subject matter of comedy and tragedy in that light: "Tragedy, through pity and terror, shows what we should avoid; it purges those disturbances in which the tragic characters have become involved. But comedy, by setting before us that which is to be imitated, with passions, with temperate feelings mixed with play, with laughter and derisive jests, summons us to the proper way of life."[9]

Giraldi calls for a clear distinction of the two genres in character (royal versus plebian), action (noble versus commonplace), and language (poetry versus prose). Aristotle's concern about the proper "magnitude" of a plot is converted, despite his warning, into the practical matter of the time of presentation. Giraldi considers this to be about three hours for comedy and four for tragedy, though the five acts of the latter may include the events of "a single day." Throughout this commentary we may see working a dynamic by which a concession or exception in Aristotle is seized upon as a general rule, usually in the name of either moral instruction or effectiveness in moving an audience: that is, in keeping with the Horatian aims to delight and to instruct. Thus, for example, where Aristotle admits unfamiliar stories as *possible* bases for drama, Giraldi asserts that invented stories are *as a rule* superior to familiar ones because they provide more interest and are thus more efficacious in their teaching.[10]

The process of reexamination and adjustment of the critical tradition begun by the necessity of accommodating the *Poetics* was broadened after midcentury by the development of a Renaissance dramatic tradition. New plays were appearing regularly, and their relation to classic theory and practice was a matter of continuing concern both to their authors and to contemporary scholars. Giraldi is the outstanding but by no means the only example of a dramatist defending his work by reference to Aristotle when possible, but if necessary by the citation of Roman practice against Greek, Euripides against Sophocles, and audience credibility or satisfaction against all. In the years between 1543 and 1558, Giraldi participated in a controversy over the work of another dramatist, Sperone Speroni (c. 1500–1588). Speroni's *Canace* (1541)

[8]Giraldi, *Scritti critici* (Milan, 1973), 184.
[9]Ibid., 183.
[10]Ibid., 178.

drew attack from Bartolomeo Cavalcanti and others for a variety of reasons, but principally because its protagonists were wicked people, who had been called unsuitable for tragic heroes by Aristotle himself. Speroni admitted his departure from tradition but insisted that the wicked could inspire pity and terror also and that the average person, midway between good and evil, could sympathize with both. Giraldi, asked by Speroni to give his opinion, doubtless disappointed his suitor by taking in this case a firm Aristotelian line and agreeing with Cavalcanti that the leading figure of *Canace* could not inspire a proper purgation and therefore could not improve an audience. There for a time the matter rested, but the questions raised by *Canace* and by the plays of Giraldi remained, and variations of this same debate arose again whenever subsequent dramatists similarly tested the bounds of orthodox theory.

The Florentine comic dramatist Antonfrancesco Grazzini, called Il Lasca (1503–1583), was not particularly revolutionary in his dramaturgy, but his prefaces boldly challenge classic authority. The first prologue to *La gelosia* (1550) complains of the slavish devotion of contemporary authors to classic practice, especially to the improbable device of the discovery of lost relatives. In seeking to follow the ancients, they merely create awkward mixtures of the ancient and the modern. More surprisingly, Grazzini dismisses the widely accepted view of comedy as a didactic instrument: "Whoever wants to learn about the civil and Christian life, does not attend comedies to do so." Those seeking such instruction should rather devote their attention to the "thousands of good and holy books" available and attend sermons "not only during Lent, but all through the year."[11] The prologue to *La strega* (1566) issues an even more direct challenge: "Aristotle and Horace knew their own time, but ours is different. We have other customs, another religion, another way of life, and therefore need to create our comedies in another manner."[12]

Such occasional declarations of independence from practicing dramatists were totally ignored by the continuing tradition of scholarly commentary. The third of the "great commentaries" on the *Poetics*, by Pietro Vettori (1499–1585), appeared in 1560. Vettori was more interested in specific philological questions, less in substantiating any previously held theory of poetry, than Robortello and Maggi had been; this often brought him closer to the conceptions of the original. He correctly, for example, considered purgation as the "end" of tragedy, though he admitted other emotions than pity and terror to bring it about. His

---

[11]Antonfrancesco Grazzini, *Commedie* (Florence, 1859), 5.
[12]Ibid., 173.

tone is less didactic than that of his predecessors, but his emphasis on the feelings and the belief of the audience places him still clearly in the rhetorical tradition.

Besides specific commentaries on Aristotle, general studies of poetry published at this time invariably gave at least some attention to the *Poetics*, and several discussed it extensively. The most comprehensive and best known of these was the huge *De poeta* (1559) of Antonio Sebastiano Minturno, bishop of Ugento (d. 1574). Four years later Minturno published a supplementary work in Italian, the *Arte poetica*, which gave less attention to general theory and more to the analysis of specific types of contemporary poetry. Books 3 and 4 of *De poeta* are devoted to tragedy and comedy, as is Book 2 of the *Arte poetica*.

Minturno—prelate, poet, and critic—was a participant in the Council of Trent, and he produced these two major poetic statements during the same period. One concern of the council, to determine what was to be preserved and supported from the humanist period and the early Renaissance, characterized the bishop's poetic theory as well; it is distinctly more conservative and moralistic than, for example, that of Giraldi. Minturno declares that the end of all poetry is "to instruct, delight, and move," with the further end in tragedy of "purifying of the passions the souls of those who listen."[13]

On the basis of this passage, Minturno is usually credited with adding "to move" to the traditional Horatian "to instruct and to delight." The concept is by no means original with him, however. Robortello spoke of using the verisimilar to move and to persuade; and the idea of arousing pity and terror, whether this was seen as an end in itself (by those critics who emphasized the emotional pleasure of tragedy) or a means to an end (by those who sought moral utility) always implied moving the audience. Drama's arousal of laughter or tears was noted by Horace, and often by subsequent critics. But Minturno seems to have elevated this emotional emphasis sufficiently to expand the traditional dual aim of poetry to a tripartite one. His actual inspiration probably came not from poetic criticism at all, but from the "to teach, delight, and move" of Ciceronian rhetoric, an important source for a number of his ideas.

In the *Arte poetica* Minturno develops these three concerns in an interesting mixture of medieval and Renaissance ideas. Tragedy teaches in the medieval fashion by exhibiting examples of changes of fortune "so we may understand that in prosperity we are not to put our trust

---

[13]Antonio Minturno, *De poeta*, 179, quoted and trans. in Weinberg, "The Poetic Theories of Minturno," in *Studies in Honor of Dean Shipley*, Washington University Studies, N.S. 14 (St. Louis, 1942), 105.

in worldly things, and that there is no one down here so long lived or so stable that he is not frail and mortal, no one so happy that he cannot become miserable, no one so great that he cannot become humble and low."[14] Purgation is understood as related to the insight thus gained, "for no one is so overcome by unrestrained appetites that if he is moved by fear and pity for the unhappiness of another, his soul is not purged of the passions which have been the cause of that unhappy state."[15]

Like other theorists concerned with the moral instruction of the audience, Minturno laid great stress upon verisimilitude. The poet must show only what is true and must imitate it so that his audience accepts it as true; thus a central role is given to appropriateness and decorum. The dramatic genres are distinguished by types of ending (though Minturno would allow tragedies to end happily) and by types of character (great men in tragedy; merchants and common folk in comedy; humble, mean, and ludicrous folk in satiric drama). Citing the practice of the ancients, Minturno advises keeping dramatic action within a day and never prolonging it beyond two, with an actual performance time of not less than three or more than four hours. He echoes Aristotle in calling for unity and completeness in a work, but this unity seems one less of form than of tone, for the various parts of the drama are analyzed for rhetorical effect more than for aesthetic interrelationship.

In the four years between the Latin and the Italian poetics of Minturno, two other widely influential works of the same type appeared: the *Poetice* (1561) of Julius Caesar Scaliger (c. 1484–1558) and Books 5 and 6 of Trissino's *La poetica* (1563). Scaliger's work was even larger and more comprehensive than Minturno's massive *De poeta*, a huge and erudite compendium that demonstrates why at his death Scaliger was widely regarded as the most learned man in Europe. Even more impressive than the size and learning of this study was its organization, for Scaliger was not satisfied, as Minturno had been, with collecting a body of critical ideas not always harmonious with each other; he worked constantly to discover interrelationships and to develop an orderly and consistent system. He was well aware that the system thus created was in contradiction with Aristotle in a number of significant ways, but he unhesitatingly chose consistency over authority. The power of his reputation was such that even when Aristotle's authority was a regular point of reference, critics who did not agree with Aristotle could refer to Scaliger for a possible alternative. Modern dramatic poets like Giraldi

[14]Minturno, *De poeta*, 76, trans. Allan Gilbert, in *Literary Criticism: Plato to Dryden* (Detroit, 1962), 289.
[15]Ibid., 290.

Cinthio and Speroni had already challenged the authority of the ancients; Scaliger was the first major critic to show a similar independence.

Scaliger's definitions of tragedy and comedy depart not only from Aristotle (whom he specifically disavows) but also from the traditional distinctions of the grammarians. Tragedy is "an imitation through actions of some distinguished life, unhappy in outcome, in serious metrical discourse." In a later passage, even the unhappy outcome is discarded, Scaliger suggesting that it is sufficient for tragedy to contain horrible events. Comedy is "a dramatic poem which is filled with intrigue, full of action, happy in its outcome and written in a popular style."[16] Harmony and song are excluded from the definition of tragedy on the grounds that they are involved only when tragedy is staged, not when it is read. "Having a certain magnitude" is discarded as self-evident, and purgation as being not universally applicable. Similarly, in the parts of a tragedy, Scaliger finds some of Aristotle's divisions insignificant, some extraneous, the whole a hodgepodge of unlikely things. Plot he calls complete in itself, character a quality of it, diction an ornamentation of plot, and thought (translated as *sententiae* or aphorisms) a part of diction. Melody and setting are considered entirely external, not essential to tragedy at all.

This arrangement might suggest that Scaliger agreed with Aristotle at least on the primacy of plot. Actually, however, as his definition of tragedy suggests, he considered character more central because, like most of his contemporaries, he saw moral improvement as the true end of drama. At the same time, unlike most of his contemporaries, Scaliger did not attempt to read this attitude into Aristotle but frankly admitted a different focus. "Aristotle asserted that his whole end was imitation," he remarks, only to disagree: "The end of poetry is not imitation, but rather delightful instruction by which the habits of men's minds are brought to right reason, so that through them man may achieve perfect action, which is called Beatitude."[17]

In fact, it is scarcely an exaggeration to say that Scaliger denied mimesis entirely. While earlier critics interpreted Aristotle's terms "appropriate" and "like reality" to mean that dramatic characters should conform to audience expectation or the norms of nature, Scaliger makes no distinction between the things of nature and those of poetry. The creations of Vergil partake of a reality like that of the creations of nature.[18] The concept of verisimilitude is thus given a new and more radical interpretation, which has some similarity to that of the nine-

---

[16]Julius Caesar Scaliger, *Poetice*, 1.5.12, trans. Weinberg in "Scaliger versus Aristotle," *Modern Philology* 39 (1942):338, 345.

[17]Appendix, bk. 7, in ibid., 339–40.

[18]3.25.113, in ibid., 349.

teenth century realists. For Scaliger, drama created a reality in which ideally the audience is unconscious of any artifice. Although Scaliger did not in fact derive from this a narrow interpretation of the unities of time and place, his insistence that theatrical events approximate actuality as closely as possible provided the theoretical foundation for this interpretation, justifying in some measure the French expression the *unités scaligériennes*.

Giangiorgio Trissino died in 1550, long before the publication in 1563 of the final two books of his *Poetica*, and the actual date of their composition is unknown. Trissino achieved his first renown not as a critic but as a playwright; his *Sofonisba* (1515) was one of the first and, many felt, the best of the Renaissance tragedies. He achieved high honors in the church and in diplomatic service as well as in literature and criticism. Although the preface to *Sofonisba* (published in 1524) shows a knowledge of Aristotle unusual for the period, only a few traces of this knowledge appear in the first four books of the *Poetica*, which appeared in 1529. At that time Trissino announced that the remaining two books were in preparation and would shortly appear. Had that promise been kept and had the books been anything like their eventually published versions, Trissino could have gained the credit for introducing Aristotelian criticism to the Italian Renaissance. By 1563, however, when the promised books finally appeared, they were much less revolutionary; indeed, it is probable that their author largely reworked them during the intervening 20 years as Maggi, Robortello, and others brought Aristotle to a position of prominence.

Though part of a general discussion on poetry like that of Scaliger, the final Trissino books are essentially a running translation and commentary on Aristotle, closer in form to the work of Robortello. They attempt no coherent system like Scaliger's but are rather a set of observations upon specific passages, colored predictably by the prevailing rhetorical view of criticism in general. The emphasis on instruction recalls Averroës: poetry imitates "to praise and admire good men" or "to blame and censure bad ones," and Aristotelian suggestions are generally converted into rules. For example, the tragic plot "must" concern "illustrious persons of middling virtue joined by love or by consanguinity."[19]

The appearance in 1570 of the *Poetica d'Aristotele vulgarizzata e sposta*, by Lodovico Castelvetro (1505–1571), was an event of major importance in Renaissance poetics. This was the first of the "great commentaries" on Aristotle to be published in Italian (or indeed in any modern European language) and hence a critical step in making ideas on poetics

---

[19]Trissino, *La quinta e la sesta divisione* (Venice, 1563), 5v.

available to a broad public. Moreover, it was less a commentary than an attempt, even more radical than Scaliger's, to establish a poetic system rivaling that of the Greek philosopher. Castelvetro, like Scaliger, was never reluctant to show how his ideas differed from those he ascribed to his classic predecessor. His text is peppered with variations of the words "according to Aristotle . . . which I esteem to be false." The major disagreements almost all arise from a single cause—a basic shift of critical focus. For Aristotle the focus was the drama itself, its structure and internal relationships. Castelvetro sees the proper concern of dramatic criticism as an analysis of drama in light of the needs and demands of the audience. The stage and the drama, he repeats several times, were invented for the "pleasure of the ignorant multitude" and must be thus considered. Both parts of this phrase had far-ranging implications in Castelvetro's work and separated him sharply not only from Aristotle but from most of his Renaissance predecessors.

The most radical shift, of course, is the promulgation of pleasure alone as the end of poetry. To delight and to instruct (and, occasionally, to move) had been from the outset of Renaissance criticism the rarely challenged bases of poetics; any primary emphasis would surely have been placed on the didactic, with delight regarded as a means of making instruction more effective. Castelvetro, on the contrary, states over and over that "poetry was invented solely to delight and to recreate,"[20] and specifically condemns the teaching function as a false goal.

Equally radical, not only for his own time but in the whole tradition of dramatic criticism, is Castelvetro's unswerving demand that drama be created not for the learned or the aesthetically sensitive but for the uncultured masses, and for these not as readers but as "spectators and hearers." This emphasizes drama as a performed art, and Castelvetro rejects attempts to consider drama apart from performance: "Aristotle is of the opinion that the delight to be obtained from reading a tragedy is as great as that to be obtained from a performance of it; this I aver to be false."[21]

There is a sense in which critics from the late classic period onward focused upon audience effect to a greater extent than Aristotle had. Certainly Tertullian and the fathers of the church were primarily, even obsessively, concerned with that aspect of drama, and the tradition of criticism that drew its inspiration from rhetorical theory shared with that theory a central concern with effect. Castelvetro, however, was as far from these traditions as from Aristotle; he not only focused upon

---

[20]Lodovico Castelvetro, *Poetica d'Aristotele vulgarizzata e sposta* (Basel, 1576), 29.
[21]Ibid., 297

pleasing the audience but advocated, without apology or embarrassment, creating for the lowest common denominator of that audience.

Castelvetro's famous pronouncements on the unities can best be understood in the light of these concerns. The audience he postulates "does not understand the reasons or the distinctions of the arguments—subtle and far from the usage of the unlearned—which philosophers utilize in investigating the truth of things and artists in regulating the arts."[22] They rely instead on common sense and the evidence of their eyes and ears. Thus "it is not possible to make them believe that several days and nights have passed when their senses tell them that only a few hours have passed," and the presentation "should spend the same number of hours in showing an action as would be actually spent." Similarly, the setting must not vary, but be restricted "to that vista alone which would appear to the eye of a single person."[23]

Here in their most rigid form appear the two famous unities of time and place. Castelvetro is quite consistent about them—he accepts no telescoping of either for dramatic purposes. Sometimes his statement that an action may extend up to 12 hours is considered evidence that he is simply following other commentators by taking literally Aristotle's famous "one revolution of the sun," but this is not so. Castelvetro's 12 hours of action would literally occupy that time, and he considers this an outside limit not because of Aristotle but because an audience could not rationally be expected to remain longer than that in the theatre without attending to "the necessities of the body, such as eating, drinking, excreting the superfluous burdens of the belly and bladder, sleeping and other necessities."[24]

Concerning unity of action, Castelvetro is actually more flexible than Aristotle, who made it the major unity. Castelvetro thought the restricted scope˜of the drama, compared with the epic, worked against multiple actions, but the goal of pleasing the audience encouraged them: "There is no doubt that it is more pleasurable to listen to a plot containing many and diverse actions than one which contains but a single one."[25] Thus if the dramatist can achieve this delight within his narrow compass, he gives his audience even greater pleasure because of the difficulty he has overcome. The recognition of difficulty overcome, a part of artistic pleasure noted also by Robortello, seems the single artistic judgment that Castelvetro will allow his untutored audience.

Castelvetro accepts Aristotle's pity and fear in tragedy, but rejects

[22]Ibid., 57, 209.
[23]Ibid., 535.
[24]Ibid., 109.
[25]Ibid., 504.

purgation, which he felt Aristotle invented to answer Plato and make tragedy utilitarian. Instead, he suggests, despite its almost invariably unhappy themes, tragedy gives us "oblique" pleasure. This is achieved in two ways. First, when we feel sadness at the sufferings of another, "we recognize that we ourselves are good, since unjust things displease us," and this recognition is pleasurable. Second, in witnessing distress, "we learn in a quiet and subtle way how subject we are to a multitude of misfortunes," which pleases us more than if we were told this "openly and in words."[26] The latter means to pleasure differs little from the traditional didactic justification of tragedy; clearly Castelvetro, like most critics positing pleasure as the end of art, had difficulty in explaining tragedy's appeal.

Although Castelvetro generally preferred action to narration on stage, he suggested that deeds of "cruelty and horror" be narrated, not on grounds of decorum but because they could not be expected to be done with verisimilitude. This shift from classical tradition to audience psychology was soon echoed in other critics. Giorgio Bartoli, secretary to a nobleman who was to appear in a 1573 revival of *Orbecche*, expressed to his master misgivings about the on-stage deaths in that play: "Certain things are by their nature such that they arouse greater marvel and compassion when we imagine them through somebody's narrative than when we see them, especially certain acts which last a very short time, such as wounding and killing."[27]

A similar focus upon the audience and its concerns characterizes the *Annotationi nel libro della Poetica d'Aristotele* (1575) by Alessandro Piccolomini (1508–1578), a pioneer in the writing of philosophical treatises in the vernacular and the author of two popular comedies. He avoids Castelvetro's scrupulous verisimilitude by arguing that playgoers, however unlettered, know full well that they are not viewing reality. Imitation is not truth itself or it would not be imitation, and the spectators "grant and concede to the imitations all that which is far from the truth and which the art of imitation of necessity requires and brings."[28] Thus Piccolomini, while accepting the unity of time, for example, does not press for minute-by-minute correspondence, even though he accepts Castelvetro's basing of this unity in audience comfort. Piccolomini is convinced that the audience can easily accept the convention of stage time, and the artificial day of a tragedy can be represented in two or three hours, thus freeing the spectators "from the tedium, and from

---

[26]Ibid., 299.
[27]Quoted in Weinberg, *History*, 2:930.
[28]Alessandro Piccolomini, *Annotationi nel libro della Poetica d'Aristotele* (Venice, 1575), 24.

the boredom, and also from the discomfort which they would suffer were the performance to last all day."[29]

It is important to realize, in view of the enormous impact of Castelvetro's rigidly defined concept of verisimilitude upon subsequent critics, particularly in France, that this concept was by no means universally accepted by his Italian contemporaries. Orazio Ariosto (1555–1593), best known for his commentaries on Tasso, took a more liberal view even than Piccolomini in defending a new tragedy, *Sidonia*, which he submitted to the Accademici Innominati of Parma in 1583. Piccolomini agreed with Castelvetro that tragedy must be based upon known stories, since these—accepted as true—would produce a deeper effect. Ariosto, maintaining his right to create a new fable, challenges the belief that audiences need the support of history, calling this merely another aspect of the false assumption that audiences cannot or will not distinguish between the theatre and reality. He attacks this assumption by a *reductio ad absurdum* that anticipates one of Hugo's arguments against the verisimilar basis of French neoclassicism:

> If we wish to concern ourselves with persuading the spectators that the thing represented is really true, it will no longer suffice to make the stage-settings of boards or in any other simulated way, but entire cities will have to be founded; nor will it be sufficient to dress in regal mantles the actors, but we shall have to go about resuscitating from their sepulchres the ashes of those Clytemnestras, of those Oedipuses . . . and place them once again, I do not say upon the stage, but in their royal palaces.[30]

The Latin commentary on Aristotle published in 1585 by Antonio Riccoboni (1541–1599) was the shortest of the "great commentaries," with none of the linguistic and little of the historical material that abounded in Scaliger and Castelvetro. One of the most striking features of this work is its shift in the purpose proposed for poetry. Riccoboni dismisses several suggested by his predecessors: utility as a philosophic concern, only by accident the end of poetry; pleasure as subject to abuse; the Horatian combination of utility and pleasure as internally contradictory; and imitation itself as inadequate to account for all poetry. Thus Riccoboni comes, like Aristotle, to regard plot as the central concern of tragedy; he is the only one of the major commentators to do so.

This disagreement concerning the object of poetic invention should serve as a warning that Italian Renaissance criticism can never be considered a single, unified critical tradition. The late classic view of moral

[29]Ibid., 97.
[30]Dedicatory letter to *Sidonia*, Dec. 25, 1583, quoted in Weinberg, *History*, 2:936.

utility as the end of poetry was perhaps the most widely held critical position, because of both the rhetorical tradition and the need—still strongly felt—to answer the objections of Plato. Yet some of the outstanding critics of the period rejected even this, with Castelvetro emphasizing pleasure, Scaliger imitation, and Riccoboni plot over any moral concern.

Moreover, there were direct challenges to classic authority, anticipating certain key arguments of the romantics. Grazzini, as we have seen, suggested that changing times required changing rules; Giordano Bruno (1548–1600), in a dialogue in *De gli eroici furori* (1585) (written in London and dedicated to Sir Philip Sidney), argued that "poetry is not born of the rules, excerpt by the merest chance"; rather, the rules derive from poetry. "For that reason there are as many genres and species of true rules as there are of true poets." True poets are to be recognized by their fame, and by the delight and instruction they give, not by their observance of rules. Aristotle is of use only to "those who cannot, as Homer, Hesiod, Orpheus and others could, be a poet without the aid of Aristotle."[31]

New works that departed from classic practice, such as Speroni's *Canace* or Ariosto's *Sidonia*, added another dimension to this discussion, and the appearance of wholly new genres placed even greater strain on the classic tradition. Giovanmaria Cecchi (1518–1587) generally followed tradition in his comedies, but he considered his *farsas*, a new form, not obligated to observe the usual rules. The prologue to the *Romanesca* (1585) explains:

> The *farsa* is a third new thing
> Between tragedy and comedy: enjoying
> The liberty of both of them
> And avoiding their restrictions.
> It welcomes great lords and princes
> Which comedy does not; and welcomes
> As do hospitals and inns
> The vile plebian common folk
> Which Dame Tragedy has never wished to do.
> It is not limited to certain themes; it accepts all—
> Light and heavy, sacred and profane,
> Rustic and urban, amusing and sad.
> It cares not for place; its setting may be
> A church, a piazza, or anywhere.

[31]Giordano Bruno, *De gli eroici furori*, trans. Paul Eugene Memmo, University of North Carolina Studies in the Romance Languages and Literatures, 50 (Chapel Hill, 1964), 83.

As for time, if it cannot take place
In a day, it may use two or three.[32]

Much more influential than the *farsa* was the tragicomic pastoral, which stimulated a major literary debate. The opposing sides were led by Battista Guarini (1538–1612), whose *Il pastor fido* (1590) gained an enormous international success despite the protests of traditional critics, and Giasone Denores (c. 1530–1590), professor of moral philosophy at the University of Padua and a staunch defender of classic theory. In 1587 Denores published a *Discorso* attacking the very idea of "pastoral tragicomedy" on formal, stylistic, structural, and—above all—moral grounds. The moral argument was essentially directed toward the subject matter. Denores argued that the activities of shepherds could have little moral relevance to sophisticated urban spectators. Neither the vices leading to tragedy nor the ludicrous vanities leading to comedy suited pastoral situations, and any attempt to introduce them would cause the shepherds to speak or act in unnatural ways, offending both decorum and verisimilitude. Against tragicomedy Denores quoted Cicero on the folly of mixing contrary qualities, Plato on the unlikelihood of a writer's achieving success in both tragedy and comedy, and Aristotle on the purity of genres—all supported by the tradition of regarding the two genres as inalterably opposed in style, in characters, and in emotional tone.[33]

Guarini responded in *Il verrato* (1588), an essay published under the name of a popular contemporary actor, and answered a fresh attack by Denores with a second article in 1593. In 1599 these two articles were combined and published as the *Compendio della poesia tragicomica*, the major document of this controversy. Guarini admits the common Renaissance (though not Aristotelian) distinction between the genres: tragedy containing "important people, a serious action, terror and compassion" and comedy "private characters and affairs, laughter and jests." Still, with the exception of terror, which he considers unique to tragedy, Guarini argues that all these elements do in fact combine in nature. "Can not amusing things intervene between serious matters?" he asks. "Do princes always act majestically? Do they not sometimes deal in private matters?"[34] Thus verisimilitude is pressed into service against the traditional claims of decorum and propriety to justify the mixing of genres, a strategy that the romantics would also employ.

Guarini calls his plot "mixed" rather than "double," meaning that

---

[32]Giovanmaria Cecchi, *Romanesca* (Florence, 1874), 2.
[33]Giasone Denores, *Discorso intorno a que principii, cause, et accrescimenti* (Padua, 1587), 40v.
[34]Battista Guarini, *Il pastor fido*, in *Scrittori d'Italia*, 61 (Bari, 1914), 225–26.

certain homogeneous elements from comedy and tragedy were combined to form a new whole rather than simply placed side by side as separate actions. The blend thus achieved he champions as superior to the earlier genres, since it rejects the bad qualities and extremes of both tragedy and comedy. It does not inflict upon us "atrocious events, blood and death, horrible and inhumane sights," nor does it cause us "to dissolve into laughter, thus sinning against the modesty and decorum of men of breeding." To Denores's charge that pastoral drama is unsuited for moral lessons, Guarini replies that this is not in any case the purpose of drama. He draws the distinction, popular with this generation of critics, between the *instrumental end*, "by means of which the maker introduces into the material which he has at hand the form which is the end of the work," and the *architectonic end*, "for the good and use of which he labors at the work."[35] Thus the instrumental end of tragedy is the imitation of some horrible action, worthy of compassion; the architectonic end is the purgation of terror and pity. Precedence is given to the instrumental end, which seeks through imitation the delight of the audience. Indeed, in modern drama Guarini finds the architectonic end of classical tragedy no longer operable: the correction of harmful excesses of the passions formerly achieved by purgation is achieved in modern times by the teachings of the gospel.

For tragicomedy itself, Guarini provides a definition modeled on Aristotle. It is a play that seeks "to imitate with scenic apparatus an action which is feigned and which contains all those elements of comedy and tragedy which can be united according to verisimilitude and decorum, correctly presented in a single dramatic form with the end of purging with delight the melancholy of the audience."[36] In dealing with both pastoral and tragicomedy, Guarini employs what he considers to be the methodology of Aristotle but not the specific rules. Aristotle, he says, was simply describing the drama as it then existed, not attempting to set standards for all time.

This last major critical controversy of the Cinquecento states or implies almost all the enduring questions of theatrical theory. Perhaps most evident in the argument over *Il pastor fido* is that the so-called Quarrel of the Ancients and Moderns is already under way. The new genre, tragicomedy, is championed as not merely equal but superior to earlier genres, a claim naturally bitterly contested by traditionalists. Behind this debate was a more basic one, concerning what in this period came to be known as the instrumental end of the work. The general supposition in the early Renaissance was that the ancients had discov-

[35]Ibid., 233–35.
[36]Ibid., 524.

ered the basic features of the various possible poetic genres and that these should inform all poetry for all time. Certain poetic universals, similar to Platonic ideas, were assumed. The emphasis of Castelvetro and others on audience effect brought with it an opposing relativistic view: since audiences changed through time, must not poetic genres change also? This seemed especially relevant in the case of drama, directed to a general, popular audience.

Interestingly enough, Aristotle was generally accepted as an authority by both sides. Traditionalists found in him a fixed and limited system, unhappily vague in places and in need of interpretation, but nevertheless prescriptive. Modernists considered his work only descriptive of the theatre known to him and his principles capable of extension to experiments of which Aristotle himself was quite unaware. The former view dominated Italian theory as it was exported to other parts of Europe, but in Italy itself both positions had strong support.

Another controversial issue explored at length was the purpose of drama. As we have seen, the Cinquecento produced a whole series (five, according to Riccoboni) of possible purposes, but the major conflict then and since has been between those who followed the medieval and rhetorical tradition of seeking a moral, didactic end in drama and those who considered its end to be artistic pleasure, derived from the form itself, the mimesis, or admiration of the artist's achievement. Again, the former view had the greater impact outside Italy during the Renaissance period. Aristotle's purgation was considered a process of moral improvement, and his listing of "goodness" among character attributes was taken as an indication that drama should provide moral examples. Poetry, as Plato had suggested, was to serve the ends of the state by useful civic instruction.

The concept of verisimilitude, like the authority of Aristotle, was claimed as an argument by opposing camps; the relationship of art to life was an important question in Cinquecento debate. Critics of this period generally interpreted the classic concept of mimesis as resemblance to nature, leading in its most extreme form to such literalizing of dramatic time and space as may be seen in Castelvetro. A related concept was that of decorum, dear to the Horatians and reinforced by Aristotle's "probability and necessity." Beginning with the idea that a character, to give the best illusion of reality, should follow accepted ideas of how persons of certain ages, ranks, and professions behave, it naturally evolved into a doctrine of fixed types, consistent throughout each work and also from work to work. By the end of the century, writers like Guarini had begun to challenge this idea by citing verisimilitude against it: whatever the generally accepted idea of a type might be, individual men in nature do not always act according to type, and contrasting styles and tones might better represent reality and thus better serve the dramatic illusion. The same argument could be and was used against other rigid elements of classic doctrine, most notably the traditional sharp separation of comedy and tragedy.

In each of these controversies, there were almost as many shades and varieties of opinion as there were critics participating, but the arguments tended to cluster around what might be called a conservative position (championship of the ancients, codification of rules, insistence upon decorum and the purity of traditional genres, subordination of art to moral or social concerns) and a liberal one (championship of the moderns, pragmatic and flexible treatment of classic precepts, art seen as an end in itself). As Renaissance criticism developed elsewhere in Europe, the conservative view predominated; but from the very beginning the counterclaims of liberal critics, among whom practicing dramatists were invariably well represented, provided a significant if less immediately visible part of the developing theory.

5

The Spanish Renaissance

DURING THE SEVENTEENTH CENTURY, when French critics and play-wrights were much preoccupied with the "classical rules" of the drama, they looked frequently to Italian critics for arguments and illustrations. Spain, however, they considered generally free of speculation about or even knowledge of such matters. An oft quoted comment by a French diplomat visiting Spain in 1659 strikingly demonstrates this attitude:

> In the afternoon he and Monsieur de Barrière came to take me to an old play which had been revived, and which was worthless though it was by Don Pedro Calderon. I also went to see this author who is the greatest poet and best wit they have at present. He is a Knight of the Order of St. Jacques and Chapelain of the Chapel *de los Reyes* at Toledo, but by his conversation I saw clearly that he did not know much, for all his white hairs. We argued a bit about the rules of the drama, which they do not know at all in that country and which they ridicule.[1]

Despite this assumption, taken up from the French of this period by later writers, Italy and Spain were closely linked politically and cultur-ally during the Renaissance; in fact, concerns parallel to those of literary critics in Italy were to be found in Spain earlier, and for a time were more widely developed than in France. The early fifteenth century saw there many books on the art of lyric poetry and, in the works of Juan

---

[1]François Bertaut, *Journal du Voyage d'Espagne* (Paris, 1669), 171.

del Encina, the first steps toward a secular drama, though almost nothing appeared at this time in the way of dramatic theory.[2]

The single important statement from this generation may be found in the preface to the *Propaladia* (1517) of Bartolomé de Torres Naharro (d. 1531); it is, in fact, the first treatise on dramaturgy printed in Europe. Naharro, like Encina, visited Rome and was inspired by the literary revival there to write eight plays, published in this collection. He defines comedy, after the ancients, as "the fortunes of common and private citizens, without involving mortal dangers," and tragedy as "the fortunes of heroic figures in adversity." He then cites the traditional late classic types of comedy and its parts, and notes that Horace required "five acts, was much concerned with decorum, etc." But, he continues, "all this appears to me too long to relate and not necessary to hear," and he offers his own simplified definition: "Comedy is no other than an ingenious composition of significant and ultimately light-hearted events, enacted by people."[3]

This is a statement of striking originality, anticipating the independence from classical tradition of the great Spanish dramatists. Naharro allows a broad range for the subject matter of comedy, including "significant" actions, hitherto usually reserved for tragedy. These actions may be drawn from either actual events or imaginary ones. The number of characters allowable in comedy he would place between 6 and 12, though he cites a comedy legitimately requiring 20; the only real test is whether the number causes confusion in the audience. (This comment on presentation is striking, since at the beginning of the sixteenth century many critics in Spain and elsewhere still followed the idea of medieval criticism, reflected by Dante, that comedy and tragedy were essentially poetic terms with no implication of performance.) In short, Naharro speaks always as a pragmatic dramatist, aware of the precepts of Horace and Donatus, but following them only as they harmonize with his practical sense of the theatre.

Pazzi's Latin translation of Aristotle was available after 1536 and Castelvetro's Italian version after 1570, as well as the various Latin and Italian commentaries of the period, but it was not until the end of the century that these seem to have had much effect on the Spanish critical

---

[2]In his introductory material to Spanish Renaissance theory, Barrett Clark (*European Theories of the Drama* [New York, 1965], 58) mentions several essays of this period "touching on the drama," but in fact, except for the most general observations on poetic style, none of them contains any such material. Encino's *Arte de la poesía Castellana*, despite the author's achievement as a dramatist, never mentions the theatre, and the fact that Clark calls Villena's *Arte cisoria* (a cookbook) simply a later title for the totally different *Arte de trobar* (a poetry manual) indicates that his observations on the theory of this period should be read with caution.

[3]Quoted in H. J. Chaytor, *Dramatic Theory in Spain* (Cambridge, 1925), 3.

scene. Spanish translations of Horace's *Ars poetica* appeared in 1591 in Madrid and in 1592 in Lisbon, and the first major Spanish poetics, Alonso López Pinciano's (fl. 1596–1627) *Philosophía antigua poética*, appeared in Madrid in 1596. In its range of discussion on theatrical matters, this ambitious work equals or surpasses most of the more famous Italian works of the century. Its structure takes the form of discussion between Pinciano himself and two neighbors —Ugo and Fadrique—and is often couched in a thesis-antithesis-synthesis arrangement. The lengthy work comprises 13 *epístolas*, the fourth of which deals with distinctions among the poetic genres, the fifth with *fábula* or plot, the eighth with tragedy, the ninth with comedy, and the thirteenth with the art of acting.

Pinciano defines Tragedy as "a sorrowful represented action of illustrious persons,"[4] and "an imitation of a serious action, the hero of which is presented to us as significant but neither wholly good or evil in his characteristics."[5] Comedy is "an imitation of inferior folk, not showing all types of vice but those vices which provoke laughter and ridicule."[6] Much space is devoted to the emotions aroused by tragedy— pity, fear, and admiration—and Pinciano attempts to unite the Aristotelian idea of *katharsis* with the Horatian principles of delight and edification. Of *katharsis* in particular he observes: "Tragedy was created to cleanse the spirit of the passions of the soul by means of compassion and fear. Thus the same plot which perturbs the spirit for a brief time quiets and appeases it for long."[7] The Horatian spirit shows clearly in Pinciano's discussion of character. Characters must be consistent and true to type; those in tragedy should "instruct by their honest and serious speech and by their honest and upright actions"; and all must come to a proper end: "the honest, virtuous, and laudable character . . . must be given a suitable reward and the evil one punished."[8]

Also Horatian are the general rules that appear at the end of the ninth *epístola*: the play must contain five acts; no character should appear more than five times—once in each act—"so as not to annoy with his frequency"; no scene should have more than three speaking characters; no more than one musician should appear; and the action should be restricted to three days. When Ugo reminds Fadrique that Aristotle allowed only one day, Fadrique replies, to the approval of his friends: "The men of earlier times followed the paths of virtue more rapidly and briskly; and thus the time sufficient for them is no t enough today.

---

[4]López Pinciano, *Philosophía antigua poética*, 3 vols. (Madrid, 1953), 1:240.
[5]Ibid., 2:327.
[6]Ibid., 1:241.
[7]Ibid., 176.
[8]Ibid., 2:360.

That is why I agree with those who have written that tragedy may involve five days and comedy three, always admitting that a lesser time is more desirable as it gives less contradiction to verisimilitude, which is essential to all poetic imitation, and more so to comedy than to the rest."[9]

The passage is typical of Pinciano, showing his desire to make the major concepts of classic poetics accessible to his countrymen, while keeping the privilege of filling in omissions in his sources or adjusting them to suit the needs and expectations of his own time. Because the Spanish version of the Quarrel of the Ancients and the Moderns was carried out during the next generation, it is not surprising that both sides mined Pinciano's rich work for support.

Unlike most Renaissance treatises on poetry, Pinciano's discussion contains a substantial section on drama as performance. The final *epístola* is set in the Teatro de la Cruz, where the three friends attend and comment upon a production of *Iphigenia*. They agree that actors should not be condemned because of their profession: "If poetry is, as we have said, an honest work, useful in the world, how can those who execute it be thought vile and infamous?"[10] Fadrique introduces a consideration of acting technique by observing that "gestures and movements are more intrinsic and essential when they reveal more fully the inner workings of the poem. It thus follows that the life of the poem is in the hands of the actor, so much so that many bad actions for a good actor are good and many good ones bad for a bad actor." The best actor "must transform himself into the character he is imitating so that it appears to everyone else no imitation." Pinciano, anticipating the famous discussion of the eighteenth century, responds that it seems more likely that the best artist would concentrate on technique and "move to tears without weeping himself."[11] The conversation goes on to analyze the gestures, bodily postures, and eye movements that naturally accompany certain emotions. Less extended but nevertheless substantial remarks are made upon music in the theatre, stage machinery, settings and costumes—the last especially considered as an extension of verisimilitude, thus anticipating the nineteenth-century fascination with "local color."

Pinciano's emphasis on the moral usefulness of poetry and his defense of the profession of acting suggest, correctly, that the stage was at this time locked in one of its recurrent struggles with the more conservative elements within the church. The heritage of Tertullian

---

[9]Ibid., 3:82–83.
[10]Ibid., 264.
[11]Ibid., 281, 283.

was well known, of course; and as the theatre became more popular in Spain during the 1580s, attacks increased, both in Latin (as in Diego de Tapias's *De eucharistia*, 1587) and Spanish (as in Pedro de Rivadeneira's *Tratado de la tribulación*, 1589). Such works, being largely hortatory, contributed little to actual criticism.[12] The traditional observations of the church fathers were regularly repeated, though with a new emphasis on the generally loose morals and scandalous behavior of contemporary actors.

The dramatists of Spain's golden age often found themselves beset on two sides; the moralists viewed them as a corrupting influence in society, and the classicists complained of their disregard of the precepts of ancient drama. To a certain extent, these two conflicts overlapped, as we can see in Pinciano, where the moral purpose of poetry is emphasized as a part of the classical heritage. Surely the most famous attack on the theatre of this period appears in chapter 48, part 1 of *Don Quixote* (1605) by Miguel de Cervantes (1547–1616), in a section that owes much to Pinciano. Cervantes' curate observes that while the drama "should be the mirror of human life, the model of manners, and the image of the truth, those which are presented now-a-days are mirrors of nonsense, models of folly, and images of lewdness." Neither verisimilitude nor decorum is honored, as Cervantes shows in a series of striking examples very similar to those cited by Sidney a few years earlier in England. Instead of unity of time, we have an infant appearing "in swaddling clothes in the first scene of the first act, and in the second a grown-up, bearded man." Instead of unity of place, we have "a play where the first act began in Europe, the second in Asia, the third finished in Africa, and no doubt had it been in four acts, the fourth would have ended in America." Instead of truthfulness to type, we have "an old man as a swashbuckler, a young man as a poltroon, a lackey using fine language, a page giving sage advice, a king plying as a porter, a princess who is a kitchenmaid." No attention is paid to historical accuracy or even the semblance of probability. Vice is not condemned or virtue rewarded, and plays are so ill written that they do not even satisfactorily fulfill the weakest requirements of social merit: providing the public with harmless amusement to keep it "from those evil humors which idleness is apt to engender." The fault, concludes the curate, is not with the ability of the authors but with their willingness to pander to the low taste of actors and audience, and the best solution would be for some "intelligent and sensible person at the capital to examine all plays before they were acted."[13]

[12]For a detailed listing, see Emilio Cotarelo y Mori, *Bibliografía de las controversias sobre la licitud del teatro en España* (Madrid, 1904), a collection of 213 texts from 1468 to 1868.

[13]Miguel de Cervantes, *Don Quixote*, trans. John Ormsby (New York, 1926), 438–40.

Lope de Vega (1562–1635), while not mentioned by name, is clearly a major object of Cervantes' complaints, and Lope himself admitted the charges. In the *prólogo* to *El peregrino en su patria* (1604), he listed 219 of his plays, following the list with the observation that "foreigners should be advised that Spanish plays do not follow the rules, and that I continued writing them as I found them, without presuming to observe the precepts, because with that strictness they would never have been accepted by the Spanish."[14]

This observation was expanded into a full essay five years later, the famous *Arte nuevo de hacer comedias en este tiempo* (1609), a lighthearted address in rhyme delivered to a Madrid literary society. The tone and major message of the piece are established early:

> Now when I have a comedy to write
> Six keys I use the laws to lock away;
> Plautus and Terence banish from my sight
> For fear of what these injured souls might say....
> Since after all, it is the crowd who pays,
> Why not content them when you write your plays?[15]

Although Lope displays considerable classical erudition, scholars have traced most of his learned references to Robortello, whom he calls "that weighty doctor." The traditional position must be qualified by the demands of the audience; he thus allows kings in comedy, also reminding his hearers that even Plautus showed Jupiter in *Amphitryon*. Tragedy and comedy may be mixed:

> Nature in this must our example be,
> Since she gains beauty by variety.[16]

The same argument is used against a rigid unity of time, though Lope would restrict each act to a day. Kings, lovers, and lackeys should speak in language appropriate to each, and ladies should remain in character even when assuming male disguise. The essay concludes in the same light tone as it began, with the author claiming pleasure as his primary goal and confessing that "all but six" of his 483 plays have offended the rules of "art."

The controversy represented by the opposed positions of Cervantes and Lope de Vega, the two greatest literary figures of the period, inspired a large number of critical statements during the following

---

[14]Lope de Vega, *El peregrino en su patria* (Chapel Hill, 1971), 119.
[15]Lope de Vega, *Arte nuevo de hacer comedias en este tiempo* (Madrid, 1609), 17.
[16]Ibid., 20–21.

decade and has certain features in common with the more famous *Cid* controversy that immediately followed it in France.[17] Significantly, Cervantes himself soon retreated; in the *prólogo* to his *Ocho comedias y ocho entremeses* (1615) and in the *Jornada segunda* of *El rufián dichoso*, one of the eight *comedias*, he takes a much more conciliatory view. A dialogue in the latter between Curiosidad and Comedia deals with elements in this very play that do not suit the classic rules, among them a change from five to three acts and a lack of unity of place. Says Comedia: "The times make all things change / and thus improve the arts." Seneca, Terence, and Plautus were admirable for their own time, but "I have rejected them / In part, and some I've kept / With custom as my rule / Which doesn't bow to art."[18]

Custom (*uso*) and the classic rules (*arte*) were the conflicting concepts championed by the participants in this debate, and the defection of Cervantes apparently caused no lessening of spirit among the defenders of *arte*. Some of these, most notably Cristóbal Suárez de Figueroa in *El pasajero* (1617) and Pedro de Torres Rámila in *Spongia* (1617), combined condemnation of the *comedia* with scurrilous personal attacks on Lope de Vega.

Others took a higher tone, notably Francisco Cascales (c.1564–1642) in his *Tablas poéticas* (1617). This second great Spanish poetics follows the first, Pinciano's, in being cast in dialogue; but it is much simpler, since there are only two speakers, one of whom essentially interrogates the other. Five chapters are devoted to separate poetic genres, one of them to comedy and one to tragedy. Tragedy is defined as "an imitation of a noble action, complete and of suitable grandeur, in smooth dramatic language, which purifies the passions of the soul by means of compassion and fear."[19] Its action is illustrious, magnificent, real, and grand; its characters are compounded of good and evil, since this will arouse the proper emotions. Comedy is "a dramatic imitation of complete and suitable action, humble and smooth, which by means of laughter and distraction cleanses the soul of vices."[20] The tragicomedy is rejected because it was not used by the ancients and because tragedy itself may end either happily or unhappily, requiring no alternate term. Works that mix comic and tragic elements are dismissed as "poetic monsters."

Cascales has no objection to three-act structures, so long as they contain the elements of statement, complication, and resolution. And

---

[17]See J. de Entrambasagus, "Una guerra literaria del Siglo de Oro. Lope de Vega y los preceptistas aristotélicos," in *Estudios sobre Lope de Vega*, vols. 1, 2 (Madrid, 1946–47).

[18]Miguel de Cervantes, *Obras completas*, 6 vols. (Madrid, 1917), 5:97.

[19]Francisco Cascales, *Tablas poéticas* (Madrid, 1975), 185.

[20]Ibid., 201-202.

although he cites Aristotle as arguing for an action of one or two days, he would extend the allowable number by a peculiar scholastic argument: the "truth of imitation" naturally leads an author to keep his action compact, yet a poet may wish, for "ornamentation" or for "the delight of the audience" to skip across time or to leave blanks in his story. Cascales would therefore permit an action of up to ten days "because, according to certain authorities in poetic art, an epic may contain the material for twenty tragedies and comedies, and the epic, containing (at least) a year of events, divided into twenty parts, makes it easy enough for us to allow ten days for a tragedy or comedy."[21]

Lope de Vega and a number of his supporters were the leading defenders of *uso*. Most of them were playwrights, but there were important exceptions, such as Alfonso Sánchez de Moratalla, professor of Greek and Hebrew at Alcalá, and Francisco de Barreda, a prominent priest. In *El meior príncipe Traiano Augusto* (1622), Barreda argued that Plautus and Terence would seem dull and uninspired today in comparison with modern works and that modern writers were quite justified in ignoring traditional rules, which had been on occasion ignored by the classic writers themselves.

Aside from Lope, the major dramatist involved in this controversy was Tirso de Molina (c. 1571–1648), whose *Cigarrales de Toledo* (1621) responds to Cascales in terms similar to those of Sánchez and Barreda but strongly colored by his own experience as a practicing playwright. The *Cigarrales* is organized, like the *Decameron*, as a group of stories and conversations among ladies and gentlemen who have left Toledo to avoid the summer heat. One of the gentlemen, Don Alejo, undertakes the defense of modern Spanish writing that breaks the rules. He attacks unity of time on the grounds of verisimilitude: "Because the ancients decided that a play should present action which had to be completed in twenty-four hours, what greater discomfort could there be than to have in such a brief time a gallant fall in love with a prudent lady, woo and win her and, without a day going by, lead her to accept his love so that having undertaken her suit in the morning he has conquered her by evening?"[22]

The same privilege is claimed for the playwright as that enjoyed by writers of stories, an ability to present as many times or locations as a unified action may require. By the same argument, Tirso would allow mixing of genres and of serious and comic persons in the same play. This is the path to verisimilitude, but need not involve slavish following of history. Tirso defends Lope and himself against the charge by Cer-

---

[21]Ibid., 202.
[22]Tirso de Molina, *Cigarrales de Toledo*, ed. V. S. Armesto (Madrid, n.d.), 125.

vantes that dramatists were distorting historical fact; it is the duty of the poet, says Tirso, to transform both history and nature by imagination, so long as the impression remains true. Like Barreda, Tirso insists that the classic rules cannot be arbitrarily applied to different peoples in different surroundings. Modern works are better suited for modern audiences; indeed, they are better in general, since the art has developed since classic times.

This great dramatic dispute was essentially over by 1626, when Alonso Ordóñez das Seijas y Tovar produced the first vernacular translation of Aristotle's *Poetics* in Spain. Only one more major critical work on the theatre appeared during this period, the outstanding Spanish commentary on Aristotle, Jusepe Antonio González de Salas's *Nueva idea de la tragedia antigua* (1633). By the time of Salas's work, the achievement of Lope de Vega and his contemporaries was so widely and firmly accepted that the use of classic rules to condemn it, in the manner of Cascales, was little to be expected. Salas instead takes the path suggested by Tirso and others: he treats the *Poetics* academically as a historical document on ancient literary theory which modern writers, according to their inspiration or genius, may legitimately reject. The ancient writings should be considered a body of models, rules, and discipline, still of some use if not converted to rigid formulas. This generally pragmatic approach characterizes the work. Salas stresses the importance of the drama as realized on stage and sees the acceptance by an audience not as a bar to following the rules but as a means of better following nature, of which the common folk have an excellent sense.

Salas, like Pinciano and Cascales, observes that the end of poetry is both to delight and to instruct. Although a doctrine of delight alone seems at times implied in Lope de Vega and others, this question was not debated as much in Spain as in Italy. A continual ecclesiastic opposition to the drama, which diminished a bit at the turn of the century but revived in the 1620s, probably encouraged all theorists—whatever their private thoughts—to give at least lip service to a moral end for drama. Tragedy, Salas finds, is more oriented toward purgation than pleasure, and "if it delights in any way, it is with sorrow and tears, as St. Augustine teaches."[23] It instructs by "habituating the soul to such passions as pity and fear," so as "to make them less offensive. And then when those occasions common to mortals arrive in which such passions are aroused by misfortunes, they will certainly be less felt."[24]

Salas traces in much more detail than Aristotle the role of music, dance, spectacle, and acting, considering the history of musical nota-

[23]González de Salas, *Nueva idea de la tragedia antigua* (Madrid, 1633), 210.
[24]Ibid., 17.

tion, machinery, and dancing style. The actor deserves particular attention as the "means and conduit through which the poet communicates his passions and affection to the audience." To achieve this, the actor must remove any personal barriers to transmission and truly experience the passions of the play as "interior feeling" rather than "guileful appearance."

Clearly, in the leading critics of the Spanish Renaissance, we may see already suggested the concerns of subsequent debates on the actor's art, with Pinciano as a champion of technique and Salas of emotional truth.

6

The French Renaissance

THE EARLIEST CRITICAL WRITING in France on the drama is included in Regnaud Le Queux's (d. 1525) *Instructif de la seconde rhétorique* (1501). Its tenth chapter contains detailed advice on the writing of moralities, comedies, and mysteries (the last combined with chronicles, histories, and romances). The morality play is said to deal with "praise and blame" in an "honorable language" with no "foolish jests." Comedy should treat "joyous matter" in a light and melodious fashion and contain nothing to give offense to "all honest folk, especially the ladies." The mystery or chronicle should consider a significant subject and be faithful to the doctrine of decorum; that is, it should hold to the accepted characteristics of different ages, ranks, trades, and sexes.[1]

A much more extensive essay, focusing on comedy, appeared in 1502 in the *Prenotamenta* to Jodocus Badius's (1462–1535) edition of Terence. Badius refers frequently to Donatus and shows a knowledge of other classic authors, among them Diomedes, Horace, Suetonius, and Vitruvius. His long essay considers the differences between comedy and tragedy (following Horace and Diomedes), the origins, types, and parts of comedy (following Donatus), the theatre and its construction, Roman games, comic characters and costumes, the proper language for comedy, decorum, propriety, and verisimilitude; it also includes a life of Terence and a plot summary of the *Andria*. It is, in short, a moderately complete compilation of the theoretical material available to early Renaissance scholars of the drama. Later French editions of Terence, such as that of Robert Estienne in 1529, often included the remarks of Donatus or Diomedes on comedy, following the example of Badius.

---

[1]Regnaud Le Queux, *Instructif de la seconde rhétorique*, quoted (in French) in W. F. Patterson, *Three Centuries of French Poetic Theory*, 2 vols. (Ann Arbor, 1935), 1:153–57.

As for tragedy, early French views of that genre may also be found in prefatory comments to translations of classic works. Thus Lazare de Baïf (d. 1547) prefaced his 1537 translation of Sophocles' *Electra* with a definition beginning, "Tragedy is a morality composed of great calamities, murders and adversities suffered by noble and excellent characters."[2] The dedication *Au roy mon souverain seigneur* to the translation of Euripides' *Hecuba* (1544) (formerly attributed to Baïf but in recent times to Guillaume Bouchetel) shows the influence of both Horatian morality and the medieval wheel of fortune. Poetry seeks to mix pleasure with the good and profitable, and the poet to "laud virtue and condemn vice." Tragedy is the highest form of poetry because of its gravity of style, its grandeur of argument, and the fact that it is addressed to lords and princes. It was "primarily invented to demonstrate to kings and great lords the uncertainty and sorrowful instability of temporal things so that they would not trust in virtue alone."[3]

The 1540s are the watershed years of the French Renaissance, the years in which the first major theoretical works in French poetics were created and the arguments for a modern French literature strongly marshalled. A significant indication of this new direction is Charles Estienne's (1504–1564) "Epistre du translateur au lecteur," which precedes his translation of Terence's *Andria* (1542). It is a lengthy essay, comparable to Badius's *Prenotamenta* but written in the vernacular. Estienne himself summarizes its contents thus: "the origins of plays and different types of them; then how they were performed and in what public places in Rome and elsewhere, the ornamentation of the theatres and the scenes of the comic plays, then the costume of the actors, their method of playing and of speaking."[4] Estienne attempts brief histories and definitions of fable, tragedy, satire, old comedy, and new comedy. Tragedy he distinguishes primarily by its high style and mood: "a grave and exalted argument, the beginning gentle, peaceful, and joyful, the end sad and unhappy."[5]

The following year Estienne translated the Italian play *Gl'ingannati*. No copies of this edition have been preserved, but a second, called *Les abusez* (1548), contains a prefatory "Epistre du traducteur à Monseigner le Dauphin de France." This condenses much material from the *Andria* preface and introduces the question, critical for this period, of composition in the vernacular. French, Estienne asserts, could rival Greek or Latin if its authors would only follow the lead of the Italians in employing classic technique. So far, French comedy has retained only one

---

[2]*Tragédie de Sophocles intitulée Electra*, trans. Lazare de Baïf (Paris, 1537), i.
[3]*La tragédie d'Euripide nommée Hecuba*, trans. Guillaume Bouchetel (Paris, 1544), ij.
[4]*Première comédie de Terence intitulée Andrie*, trans. Charles Estienne (Paris, 1542), iii.
[5]Ibid., iiii.

act of classic comedy; this act ordinarily lacks sense, rhythm, and reason, and it consists of "only ridiculous words, and a little repartee without any other invention or conclusion."[6] Instead, comedies should contain five or six acts, with diverting interludes between them and each act having five or six scenes. Attention must be given to careful construction and to motivation. No one, for example, should remain on the stage "who is not necessary either to speak or to listen to others."[7]

Such stipulations suggest a study of Horace, and indeed a strong Horatian influence can be traced in French criticism from this period on, beginning with Jacques Peletier's (1517–1582) translation, *L'art poétique d'Horace* (1545). In the famous preface to this work, Peletier admits updating it, his purpose—like that of Estienne—being to encourage French authors to develop a significant literature.

Soon after Peletier's translation, and conceived in the same spirit, came the *Art poétique* of Thomas Sébillet (1512–1589). The first major treatise on poetry in the French language, it was published in 1548, the same year as Robortello's edition of Aristotle. Sébillet's comments on the drama are not extensive, but they are more detailed than anything attempted before in France. Under the general heading of dialogue, he considers three forms: the eclogue, the morality, and the farce. The eclogue shows "shepherds and keepers of animals" who discuss "in pastoral terms the death of princes, calamities of the times, changes in Republics, happy outcomes and events of fortune, poetic praises and so forth in very clear allegory." Moralities are likened to classic tragedy in that they treat "grave and serious matters" and indeed would be tragedies but that they lack "a sad and dolorous conclusion." Also like tragedies, moralities "show illustrious deeds, acts of magnificence and virtue, true or at least seemingly true events." He considers the morality containing abstract, idealized characters as only one type, though currently the most popular. Sébillet separates French from Latin comedy; disagreeing with Peletier, he feels that modern Frenchmen would find the latter of "tiresome prolixity." The French comedy, the farce or *sottie* is a simple, short, broad piece designed solely to provoke laughter and with none of the moral aim of classic comedy; in fact, Sébillet considers it more closely related to the Roman mime.[8] (The omission of religious drama from the discussion may seem strange until we recall that the year of this essay is also that in which such drama was banned by the French parliament.)

Despite his confusion of morality and tragedy, Sébillet's ideas are

---

[6]Estienne, *Les abusez* (Paris, 1548), ij.
[7]Ibid., iiij.
[8]Thomas Sébillet, *L'art poétique françoys*, 1555 edition (Geneva, 1972), 60–64.

generally in harmony with those of Baïf's prefaces regarding the subject matter, tone, and unhappy conclusion of tragedy. We should note particularly the inclusion of "seemingly true events" (the *vraisemblable*) in serious drama. This, already a key concept in Italian criticism, was to become even more central in France.

Unfortunately, the great critical work of this highly productive decade, Joachim Du Bellay's (c. 1525-1560) *La deffence et illustration de la langue françoise* (1549), says almost nothing about the drama, but it would probably not have differed radically from Sébillet. Though *La deffence* was conceived in part as a reaction to Sébillet's work, the quarrel was one not of direction but of degree. The Pléiade poets, with Du Bellay at their head, agreed with Sébillet both that French must be established as a major literary language and that the best works of Greece, Rome, and Italy should be the immediate models; however, Sébillet saw this as a gradual evolutionary process, while the Pléiade called for a sharp break with the medieval past and with Latin, and urged a calculated fresh beginning. A certain pride on both sides maintained debate for several years, but ultimately Du Bellay and Sébillet found more to agree upon than to debate, and they ended by accepting and even praising each other's works.

Another more conservative critic contributed to the controversy. In 1550, Guillaume des Autelz (c. 1529–1581) launched a determined attack on *La deffence* in his *Réplique aux furieuses défenses de Louis Meigret*. The work defends, on didactic grounds, the medieval French morality which the Pléiade wished to reject in favor of classic models. The morality is "more profitable" than comedy or tragedy "because these both tend more to corruption than to good information of manners, one giving every example of lasciviousness, the other of cruelty and tyranny."[9] His argument appears to be drawn from the *De institutione reipublicae* (1494) of Francesco Patrizi, bishop of Gaeta, who stated that Plato was mistaken in wishing to banish poets from his ideal city, since the enticements of fiction were an excellent aid to teaching. Still, Patrizi contended, tragedy and comedy should be banned, the first because "it has within it a certain excessive violence mixed with despair which readily changes stupid men into madmen and drives the unstable to frenzy," the second because it "corrupts the mores of men, makes them effeminate, and drives them to lust and dissipation."[10] Des Autelz admits the artistic inferiority of the morality to classic drama but argues that rather than discard it, modern poets should revivify it through

[9]Guillaume des Autelz, *Réplique aux furieuses défenses de Louis Meigret*, quoted (in French) in Patterson, *Three Centuries*, 1:362.
[10]Francesco Patrizi, *De institutione reipublicae* (Paris, 1534), 27.

what can be learned in formal matters from the classics. Thus, in France, the emphasis on the moral end of drama drew its early arguments not primarily from Horace—as in Italy—but from a desire to keep the positive elements in the late morality plays.

The most extensive response to opponents of the Pléiade was provided by Jacques Peletier, the translator of Horace, in *L'Art poétique* (1555). Chapter 7 of his second book is devoted to comedy and tragedy, which he champions over such medieval genres as the morality. Drawing upon Horace, Donatus, and Diomedes, he calls the five-act structure the only important similarity between comedy and tragedy. Comedy shows men "of base condition"; tragedy portrays "kings, princes, and great lords." Comedy has "a joyous issue"; tragedy, "an end always lamentable and sorrowful or horrible to see." Comedy has an easy and popular style; tragedy, like the epic, deals in a sublime manner with great events. Peletier says little of the ends of drama but clearly sees a moral purpose involved at least in tragedy, whose function is to teach the audience "to fear the gods, renounce vice, turn aside from evil, and respect virtue."[11] He calls comedy "a mirror of life"—an expression he attributes to Livius Andronicus—and since it reflects life, it must remain true to accepted "types": old men must be avaricious or prudent, young men ardent and loving, nurses diligent, mothers indulgent, and so on. This truth to type, decorum to the Italians, Peletier calls *"bienséance"*—a critical term that would gain enormous popularity in France during the next century.

If Aristotle was known at all to Sébillet or Peletier, his influence was slight, but the next decade established him as a major authority in France, as he had already become in Italy. The two most important works in effecting this were Guillaume Morel's edition of the *Poetics*, which appeared in Paris in 1555, and the *Poetices* of Scaliger in 1561. Scaliger is generally considered part of the tradition of Italian Renaissance criticism, and we have already considered him in that context. Nevertheless, he bore a special relationship to France as well: he became a French subject in 1528, and his major work (written in Latin) was published at Lyons, an important French intellectual center which also saw the publication of Peletier's *Art poétique*. Scaliger is thought by some scholars to have been acquainted with members of the Pléiade; whether he was or not, he clearly served as a major link between the French and Italian criticism of the mid-sixteenth century, and he may be called the first critic in France to look primarily to Aristotle for poetic authority.

There are also some hints of Aristotle in the essentially medieval "Brief discours pour l'intelligence de ce théâtre" with which Jacques

---

[11]Jacques Peletier, *L'art poétique* (Lyons, 1555), 70.

Grévin (1538–1570) prefaced his tragedy, *La mort de César* (1561). Aristotle is cited as the authority for Grévin's definition of tragedy: "an imitation or representation of some fact illustrious and grand in itself, as for example the death of Julius Caesar."[12] The concept of verisimilitude appears in Grévin's justification for his departure from the tradition of a singing chorus: "Since tragedy is nothing other than a representation of truth or that which has the appearance of it, it seems to me that when the troubles (as they have been described) come to republics, the common folk would have little occasion to sing."[13] On these grounds Grévin takes the significant further step of declaring a certain independence from classic models, arguing that various nations do things in different ways.

The influence of both Aristotle and contemporary Italian theory is much more distinct in "L'art de la tragédie," a preface to *Saül le furieux* (1572) by Jean de la Taille (1540–1611). This brief (five-page) essay is of particular importance, since it brings into French criticism the then current Italian attitude of seeking primarily in Aristotle and secondarily in Horace the "laws" of the theatre. Castelvetro's *Poetica*, published two years earlier, is the most likely source for several of Jean de la Taille's ideas. Tragedy, he says, treats of unusual events and great catastrophes—such as "banishments, wars, plagues, famines, captivities, the execrable cruelties of tyrants"—since these are more moving than common misfortunes, and "the true and only end of tragedy is to move and to arouse in a marvelous manner the emotions of each of us."[14] This clear shift from moral to artistic ends indicates the new influence of Aristotle, and the emphasis on the extraordinary and the emotional opens a line of interpretation of tragedy that would influence the French neoclassical concept of admiration (see Chapter 8). Later, about the beginning of the eighteenth century, a growing interest in psychology and new attention to Longinus would bring critics back to a very similar view of tragedy's purpose.

De la Taille echoes the Aristotelian notion that the ideal tragic hero should be neither wholly good nor wholly evil and specifically rejects poetic justice as essential for tragedy. He also rejects abstract characters such as Death, Truth, or Avarice. He champions the unities and offstage action in the name of verisimilitude: "The story and the play must be always represented in the same day, the same time and in the same place; and one must also avoid doing anything on the stage that cannot be easily and honestly done there; that is, one should not perform

---

[12]Jacques Grévin, *Le théâtre de Jacques Grévin* (Paris, 1562), iij.
[13]Ibid., iiij.
[14]Jean de la Taille, *De l'art de la tragédie* (Paris, 1574), ij.

murders and other deaths, pretended or otherwise, for everyone will always see that it is nothing but a feint."[15] The emphasis throughout, as in Aristotle, is on the unified and well-constructed plot. Matters must be carefully arranged to arouse the proper emotions in the spectators and to lead directly and inevitably to the resolution. Nothing should be present which is "useless, superfluous, or out of place."

De la Taille has less to say on the subject of comedy, but the prologue to his *Les corrivaux* (1573) calls for the writing of classic comedies instead of "low and foolish" farces and moralities, and claims that true comedy "presents as in a mirror the natural, and the manner of action of all members of the populace, such as old men, youths, servants, well-born young ladies, and so on."[16]

Although Jean de la Taille and others were advocating the famous neoclassic unities, these were by no means rapidly or universally accepted; for almost half a century there was continuing discussion over their necessity. Jean de Beaubreuil in the preface "Au lecteur" to his tragedy *Regulus* (1582) admits to "long intervals of time" in his drama but insists that these are necessary for understanding the story, and he scoffs at those "too superstitious" authors, "who think that nothing can be presented in a tragedy except what could happen during one day."[17] Pierre de Ronsard (1525–1585), on the other hand, in his scattered comments on the drama, clearly subscribes to tradition and rule-centered criticism. The goal of both comedy and tragedy is didactic, he argues, and best achieved through verisimilitude, leading in turn to the unities. Best of all is a "minute to minute" correspondence with real life.[18]

Two works composed at the end of the century may be taken as suitable summations of French critical theory during this period: *L'art poétique françois* (1598) by Pierre de Laudun d'Aygaliers (1575–1629) and *L'art poétique* (1605) by Jean Vauquelin de la Fresnaye (1536–1606) both contain substantial commentary on the drama. Laudun generally takes a flexible view of classic models and rules, especially in his remarks on tragedy; he covers comedy quickly, citing its traditional themes and characters. His distinctions between the genres are drawn largely from Scaliger and contain the usual observations on character, language, style, and tone. His flexibility appears in his emphasis on the historical accuracy of tragedy and his attention (in the tradition of Castelvetro) to audience effect. He denies, for example, the assertion that tragedy

---

[15]Ibid., iij.
[16]De la Taille, *Les corrivaux* (Paris, 1574), iij.
[17]Jean de Beaubreuil, *Regulus* (Limoges, 1582), i.
[18]Pierre de Ronsard, "Préface sur la *Franciade*," *Oeuvres*, texte de 1587, 8 vols. (Chicago, 1966–69), 4:14.

should as a rule have fewer characters than comedy: this number should be determined by the truthful telling of a story, not by arbitrary rule. Modern writers must not be bound by classic practice, "since no person today would have the patience to listen to a tragedy in the form of an Eclogue having only two characters, and yet tragedy is created only to please the audience."[19] An extended attack on the unity of time is based on the same arguments: we are not bound to such a rule even if the ancients were, any more than we are bound "to the measures of feet and syllables with which they made their verses." Moreover, tragedy deals with matters such as the fortunes and glories of kings and princes, and "the greatest absurdities" would attend an attempt to cover such matters in a single day. Corneille's *Le Cid*, in the following generation, would encounter precisely this problem.

Vauquelin's *L'art poétique* clearly represents the opposing, conservative, viewpoint on such matters. He defines tragedy as an imitation not of life but of a "grave and true action,"[20] which allows him to reject Laudun's argument against the unity of time on the basis of fidelity to history. "The theatre," he says, "should never be occupied by an argument which requires more than a day to be achieved."[21] Vauquelin would adhere strictly not only to the unities but to the five-act structure and to a maximum of three speaking persons on stage. The aim of poetry is to teach, to profit, or both, but in tragedy and comedy the emphasis is on instruction. "Tragedy shows only virtuous actions, magnificent and grand, royal and sumptuous; comedy only actions worthy of blame."[22] The original purpose of tragedy, Vauquelin declares, was the teaching of princes, showing them the catastrophes arising from wickedness and pride. He observes, however, that some classic tragedies ended happily; he commends this arrangement, which could show virtue rewarded—an early statement of the doctrine that would come to be called poetic justice. Vauquelin considers verisimilitude more important to pleasure than to instruction, but this aim, while secondary, is still of consequence. Therefore, he would ban violent action from the stage and keep character true to history and to type. A long section is devoted to *bienséance*, or making each character appropriate to age and station in life.

We can see outlined in these almost contemporary poetic studies, at the opening of the great classic period in French letters, the same general contrasted positions on the perennial questions of theatrical theory as we found at this same time in Italy. The traditional, classics-

---

[19]Pierre de Laudun d'Aygaliers, *L'art poétique français* (Geneva, 1969), 159–61.
[20]Jean Vauquelin de la Fresnaye, *L'art poétique* (Paris, 1885), 134.
[21]Ibid., 78.
[22]Ibid., 135.

oriented, and rule-dominated attitude of Vauquelin is the critical stance we most associate with the period that follows, but the counterposition represented by Laudun persists as well, continually challenging and modifying the other.

7

The Renaissance in England and the Netherlands

DURING THE EARLY TUDOR PERIOD, English criticism focused upon the rhetorical study of literature. Although certain aspects of this study, particularly the development of the concept of decorum, had significant impact on subsequent dramatic theory, no systematic discussion of the drama was produced in England at this time. The concerns and the methods of these authors correspond closely to those of the Italian humanists of the later fifteenth century; drama was of interest to them primarily for its style, its educational function, and its important part in the beloved classical inheritance. Still, scattered through the writings of the humanists and accompanying the academic dramas attempted by some early Tudor authors are comments that give us some insight into their ideas about the drama.

Sir Thomas More (1478–1535), for example, in his *Utopia* (1516) cites the impropriety of mixing serious and comic material, "for by bringing in other stuff that appertains not at all to the present matter, you must needs mar and pervert the play that is at hand, even though the stuff you bring in be much better."[1] Sir Thomas Elyot (c. 1490–1546) in *The Governor* (1531) took up tragedy and comedy as part of his general defense of poetry. He reproves those who call all poetry nothing but bawdry and unprofitable lies, and defends the dramatic genres on traditional neoclassic moral grounds. Comedy is "a picture or as it were a mirror of a man's life" wherein men are warned against evil and schooled to resist it by beholding "the promptness of youth into vice, the snares of harlots and bawds laid for young minds, the

---

[1]Thomas More, *Utopia*, trans. Ralph Robinson, text modernized by Mildred Campbell (New York, 1947), 61.

deceit of servants, the chances of fortune being contrary to men's expectation."[2] Tragedy should preferably be read by men in mature years, whose reason has been "confirmed with serious learning and long experience." Then in such works they shall "execrate and abhor the intolerable life of tyrants and shall contemn the folly and dotage expressed by poets lascivious."[3]

At Oxford and Cambridge, Aristotle (at least in fragmentary form) and Horace were studied, and classic plays were read and occasionally performed during the first part of the sixteenth century. At both universities the 1540s saw the publication of original Latin works on classic models, often with prefaces showing a clear awareness of classical doctrine. The preface to the earliest of these, *Christus Redivivus* (1541) by Nicholas Grimald (c. 1520–1562), indicates the interests of a school dramatist of this generation. The matter given the most attention is "appropriate diction"—Grimald makes inescapably clear the rhetorical basis of this concern in a quotation from his master Johannes Aerius: "Who, experienced in the art of oratory, does not give a meagre, terse, and colloquial diction to characters who report an occurrence, and who speak in rapid dialogue, to those bringing consolation, or good news; to those who applaud, a fluent, pleasant, graceful style; and to the vainglorious, the boasting, the indignant, a keen, ardent, grandiloquent speech."[4] Grimald touches also on the unities, remarking that his variety of scenes can be easily reduced to a single setting, and citing the *Captivi* of Plautus as a precedent for his mixture of sad and happy elements and the extension of action to several days.

The defense of the theatre as a moral instrument in a well-ordered state, touched upon by Elyot, was given its fullest development to date in William Bavande's *The Good Ordering of a Common Weal* (1559), translated from a Latin work by the Italian Johannes Ferrarius (Montanus). Bavande was a member of the Inns of Court, in the circle that included Thomas Sackville and Thomas Norton (authors of the early tragedy *Gorboduc*, 1561) and translators of Seneca such as Jasper Heywood. Politics and literature were of major interest to these young scholars, and Bavande's political and moral defense of theatre may be taken as representative of their opinions. Plays by dissolute actors exhibiting corruption and vice are to be condemned, he asserts, but plays teaching moral lessons are a boon to society, serving "partlie to delight, partlie

---

[2]Thomas Elyot, *The Book Named the Governor*, ed. and modernized by S. E. Lehmberg (New York, 1962), 47–48.

[3]Ibid., 33.

[4]Nicholas Grimald, *Epistola nuncupatoria* to *Christus Redivivus*, trans. L. R. Merrill in *The Life and Poems of Nicholas Grimald*, Yale Studies in English, 69 (New Haven, 1925), 109.

to move to embrace ensamples on vertue and goodnesse, and to eschue vice and filthie liuying."[5] Classic stories involving wickedness and vice are acceptable, provided they illustrate some moral lesson. The story of Agamemnon and Clytemnestra, for example, can be used "for an argumente, that the loue of an aduoutresse is so unpacient and madde, that she will not spare, nether her owne housebande or frendes to ease her stomacke."[6]

Moral lessons of this type may be found in many justificatory essays of the 1560s, such as Alexander Nevyle's preface to *Oedipus* (1560), which called this play "a dredfull Example of Gods horrible vengeaunce for sinne,"[7] or Arthur Brooke's to *Romeus and Juliet* (1562), which claimed that this story taught virtue by the miserable example of "a couple of unfortunate lovers, thralling themselves to unhonest desire; neglecting the authority and advice of parents and friends; confering their principal counsels with drunken gossips and superstitious friers, etc."[8]

The first complete translation of Horace's *Ars poetica* into English was completed by Thomas Drant in 1567. The translation, a rather free one, tended to adjust Horace to suit prevailing critical opinion. Nevertheless, it provided an important stimulus by codifying a body of critical theory in the vernacular and thus making it more generally accessible.

As usual, Horace proved more readily assimilated into modern theory than Aristotle. The Aristotelian idea of imitation was suggested in the 1570 translation by Thomas Browne of the *Nobilitas literata* by the Strasburg humanist Johann Sturm; and the same year, the posthumous *Schoolmaster* of Sturm's friend and correspondent Roger Ascham (1515–1568) discussed the same concept: "The whole doctrine of comedies and tragedies is a perfect Imitation, or fair lively painted picture of the life of every degree of man."[9] More clearly Aristotelian is Ascham's according of the highest honors to tragedy, though he does so on predictably moral grounds, calling this genre "the goodliest argument of all, and for the use either of the learned preacher, or a civil gentleman, more profitable than Homer, Pindar, Virgil, and Horace."[10] There is little pure Aristotle in Ascham, however, despite his repeated advice to follow the precepts of the Greek scholar.

The sole reference to *katharsis* during this period seems to be that in a 1576 translation by Robert Peterson of Giovanni della Casa's *Galateo*,

[5]William Bavande, *A woork of Ioannes Ferrarius Montanus touchynge the good-orderynge of a commonweele* . . . (London, 1559), 81.
[6]Ibid., 103.
[7]Alexander Nevyle, *The Tenne Tragedies of Seneca* (Manchester, 1887), 162.
[8]Arthur Brooke, "To the Reader," in *Romeus and Juliet* (London, 1908), lxv.
[9]Roger Ascham, *The Whole Works*, 2 vols. (London, 1864), 2:213.
[10]Ibid., 228.

which reported and disagreed with a theory that men needed to weep more than to laugh; for this reason tragedy was invented, that "they might draw teares out of their eyes that had neede to spend them. And so they were by their weeping heeled of their infirmitie."[11] The same end, observes the writer scornfully, could be achieved by strong mustard or a smoke-filled house.

The decade of the mid-1570s to mid-1580s was notable in English criticism for its large number of attacks on the theatre—often, though by no means exclusively, the work of Puritan writers. The defenses of Elyot, Bavande, and others imply a certain moral opposition to the drama at the time they were written, but the occasional complaint became a flood of opposition after 1576. Burbage's opening of the first public theatre in that year served to mobilize the forces of a growing religious conservatism in England, and a series of sermons at Paul's Cross by Thomas Wilcox and others opened the campaign with all the fervor of a new crusade.

The first systematic attack appeared in 1577, John Northbrooke's *Treatise wherein Dicing, Daūcing, Vaine plaies or Enterludes . . . are reprooued by the authoritie of the worde of God and auncient Writers*. This dialogue between Youth and Age rehearses traditional charges against the theatre, drawing—as the title suggests—equally upon classic authors and church fathers. Somewhat surprisingly, however, after condemning the obscenity and baseness of drama in general, Age approves academic plays in Latin and English as useful scholarly exercises. The conclusion contains a traditional distinction of genres: "A tragedie, properly, is that kinde of playe in which calamaties and miserable ends of kings, princes, and great rulers, are described and set forth, and it hath for the most part a sadde and heavy beginning and ending. A comedie hath in it humble and private persons; it beginneth with turbulent and troublesome matters but hath a merie end."[12]

George Whetstone (c. 1544–1587), in his preface to *Promos and Cassandra* (1578), the source play for *Measure for Measure*, answered such attacks by recalling the high esteem of drama in classic times and by the usual moral defense: "By the rewarde of the good the good are encouraged in wel doinge; and with the scowrge of the lewde the lewde are feared from euill attempts." The preface, though brief, contains the most complete summary that had yet appeared of English neoclassic ideas on the drama. After a brief survey of French, Spanish, Italian, and German drama, it condemns the English dramatists for gross indecorum (using "one order of speach for all persons"); for corrupting

[11]Giovanni della Casa, *Galateo*, trans. Robert Peterson (London, 1576), 31.
[12]John Northbrooke, *Treatise . . .* (London, 1577), 104.

their plays "to make mirthe" ("manye tymes they make a Clowne com-panion with a Kinge"); for basing their work on impossibilities; and for generally ignoring the unities and verisimilitude ("in three howers ronnes he throwe the worlde, marryes, gets Children, makes Children men, men to conquer kingdomes, murder Monsters, and bringeth Gods from Heauen and fetcheth Diuels from Hel").[13]

Pamphlets and counterpamphlets multiplied after 1579 in a series launched by Stephen Gosson (1554–1623), a former actor, with his vitriolic *The Schoole of Abuse*. In combativeness if not in concerns, this conflict anticipated the more famous critical quarrels of the next century in France. The moral tone of Gosson's attack has led later commentators to conflate him with the Puritans, but his arguments and examples are in fact drawn primarily from classical humanism, and his uneasiness with poetry closely echoes that of Plato. He admits that good art may instruct by virtuous example—"the notable exploytes of woorthy Cap-taines, the holesome councels of good fathers, and vertuous liues of predecessors"[14]—but notes that the power of art may as easily be turned to evil as to good. Poetic works "slip downe into the hart, and with gunshotte of affection gaule the minde, where reason and vertue should rule the roste,"[15] and by subjugating reason, they hamper man's special power to make moral choices. Thus, until all poetry is placed in the service of virtue, it should be avoided. This work was dedicated to Sir Philip Sidney (1554–1586), a wealthy courtier with a reputation as a generous patron. Sidney, far from being pleased, seems to have been inspired—in part, at least—to begin his famous *Defense of Poesy* as a refutation of the Platonic doctrine advanced by Gosson. Sidney's work was probably written between 1580 and 1583 but not published until 1593.

In the meantime a number of speedier rebuttals appeared, most notably a defense (the title page has been lost) by Thomas Lodge (c. 1558–1625), a young student at the Inns of Court who launched his literary career with this pamphlet. Lodge admits that poetry has been abused but defends it as an art inspired, according to both Biblical and pagan sources, by the deity. It would be a disservice to man and to morals to reject so effective an instrument for moral instruction: "You say unlesse the thinge be taken away the vice will continuue, nay I say if the style were changed the practise would profit."[16]

Gosson replied in a hastily written *Apologie of the Schoole of Abuse* (1579)

---

[13]George Whetstone, Dedication to *Promos and Cassandra*, in G. G. Smith, ed., *Elizabethan Critical Essays*, 2 vols. (London, 1904), 1:59.
[14]Stephen Gosson, *The Dramatic Criticism*, ed. A. F. Kinney (Salzburg, 1974), 82.
[15]Ibid., 89.
[16]Thomas Lodge, *A Reply to Stephen Gosson's Schoole of Abuse* (London, 1879), 41.

and in the more considered *Players Confuted in Fiue Actions* (1582), the fullest and best developed of this series of arguments. Its five "actions," analogous perhaps to the five acts of a play, are based upon Aristotle's four causes—efficient, material, formal, and final—with a concluding section drawing together all four to the single end of arousing emotion. The efficient cause of plays, Gosson argues, is their origin in pagan religion, and being originally celebrations of heathen gods, they are "the doctrines and inuentions of the deuill."[17] Their material cause is "such thinges as neuer were," the devil being the father of lies and deceptions: distorted and exaggerated emotions, fantastic events, and "many a terible monster made of broune paper." Even when treating true events, the poet makes them "seeme longer, or shorter, or greater or lesse than they were."[18] The formal cause is the manner of representation itself: to act is to lie, and to lie is to sin—a favorite argument with later Elizabethan critics. The fourth action describes the purpose of plays: "to make our affections overflow" and elevate them above reason and temperance, "which is manifest treason to our soules, and deliuereth them captiue to the deuill."[19] Therefore, concludes the fifth action, plays work to lead men to vanity, apostacy, iniquity, riot, and adultery.

The general lines of argument traced by Gosson were followed by other writers such as Philip Stubbes in his *Anatomie of Abuses* (1583). Lodge withdrew from the controversy in 1584, but others continued the debate, and in that same year Oxford University found the matter of sufficient interest to propose as a subject for disputations for the M.A. degree "whether dramatic presentations should be prohibited in a well organized state."[20]

After 1585 the number of significant attacks on the theatre apparently diminished, though William Rankins's *A Mirrour of Monsters* (1587) and John Rainold's *Th'Overthrow of Stage-Playes* (1599) show that the question remained of interest. In the closing years of the century, however, defenses and theoretical works constitute the more significant documents. William Webbe's *Discourse of English Poetrie* (1586), the most extensive treatment of the subject to that point, discusses tragedy and comedy but adds little to the standard postclassical and medieval distinctions. Scarcely more elaboration is found in George Puttenham's *Arte of English Poesie* (1589), but while not considering directly the attacks of Gosson and others, Puttenham does provide counterarguments that anticipate those of Sidney. He defends fiction as being both more

---

[17]Gosson, *Criticism*, 151.
[18]Ibid., 161, 169.
[19]Ibid., 181.
[20]Andrew Clark, *Register of the University of Oxford* (Oxford, 1887), vol. 2, pt. 1, p. 171.

pleasing and more effective than historical truth, which can fulfill and historically has fulfilled an important social function; thus it may be defended on moral grounds, even though its great end is emotional and its chief purpose man's recreation and delight.

The central critical work of this period, Sir Philip Sidney's *Defense of Poesy* (1595), is a milestone of Renaissance thought not only for England but for Europe in general. It is in part a reflection of the English situation—a culmination of English critical thought to that time and a response to English attacks on imaginative literature—but it is also a synthesis of Renaissance critical thought in general, drawing heavily upon Aristotle but not neglecting Plato and Horace or the great Italian commentators, especially Scaliger and Minturno.

Sidney's essay consists of three major parts: the first a description of poetry, its heritage, its nature, its relationship to history and philosophy, and its forms; the second a response to arguments against poetry; and the third a commentary on contemporary poetry in England. His definition of poetry draws upon both Horace and Aristotle: it is an "art of imitation . . . that is to say, a representing, counterfeiting, or figuring forth; to speak metaphorically, a speaking picture, with this end—to teach and delight."[21] Sidney's idea of imitation transcends the phenomena of nature; the poet makes manifest the ideal forms in the mind of the Creator, which are distorted in natural phenomena. His concept of imitation is thus closer to Neoplatonist than to Aristotelian thought. Sidney also stresses a moral purpose: virtuous action is the end of all earthly learning, and poetry—more specific, more focused, more moving than its closest rivals philosophy and history—is best suited to this. Comedy and tragedy are defined in terms of their moral utility, the first imitating "common errors" in "ridiculous and scornful sort," and the latter "making kings fear to be tyrants" and teaching to all "the uncertainty of the world."[22]

Poetry has been abused, he says, as any good thing may be, but that should not prevent us from using it properly. As for the charge that poetry lies, Sidney points out that its departure from reality does not mislead, since all recognize that it works in allegory and figure. "What child is there that, coming to a play, and seeing Thebes written in great letters upon an old door," he asks, "doth believe that it is Thebes?"[23]

In his concluding section, doubtless influenced by the Italian commentators on Aristotle, Sidney gives a primacy to tragedy that is new to English scholarship. His observations on this genre unhappily run

[21]Sir Philip Sidney, *The Defense of Poesy*, ed. A. S. Cook (Boston, 1890), 9.
[22]Ibid., 28.
[23]Ibid., 36.

counter to the practice of the great Elizabethan dramatists who shortly followed, but Sidney can hardly be faulted for not anticipating this. His arguments and illustrations are based upon the best previous authorities and a sound knowledge of contemporary practice. Following Castelvetro, he denounces the common abuse in England of the unities of time and place: "Asia of the one side, and Afric of the other," and the adventures of a man's entire life and more in two hours' space.[24] Following Scaliger, he seeks "stately speeches and well-sounding phrases climbing to the height of Seneca's style, and as full of notable morality."[25] Following Minturno, he links commiseration with admiration, rather than terror, as the primary emotions of tragedy.[26] He would allow the mixing of comic and tragic elements when the play requires it, but condemns the indiscriminate use of this mixture by English playwrights.

Turning more briefly to comedy, he distinguishes between delight, which has "a permanent or present joy," and laughter, which "hath only a scornful tickling." The two can and in comedy should be combined, but the true end must be pleasurable instruction. The proper material for comedy is harmless human foibles: "a busy loving courtier, a heartless threatening Thraso, a self-wise-seeming schoolmaster, a wry-transformed traveller."[27]

This concern with refining comedy and removing it from the domain of farce may be found also in the prefaces of John Lyly (1553–1606), the most interesting critical statements by a practicing dramatist of the period. Comedy's intent, said he, is "to moue inward delight, not outward lightness, and to breede (if it might bee) soft smiling, not loude laughing."[28] On the question of the moral purpose of drama or that of the distinction of genres, however, Lyly's romantic imagination separates him sharply from Sidney. The prologue to *Endimion* (1591), for example, makes no apology for a work without moral function, which is "neither Comedie, nor Tragedie, nor storie, nor anie thing" but a mere pastime or fancy.[29]

Traditional genres are also briefly discussed in the anonymous *A Warning for Fair Women* (1599), which features Tragedy as a choric commentator and opens with a bantering debate between History, Comedy, and Tragedy. Though Comedy sneeringly defines tragedy as "How

[24]Ibid., 48.
[25]Ibid., 47.
[26]Ibid., 50.
[27]Ibid., 51–52.
[28]John Lyly, Prologue to *Sapho and Phao* (1584), in *Complete Works*, 3 vols. (Oxford, 1902), 2:371.
[29]Lyly, Prologue to *Endimion*, in ibid., 3:20.

some damnd tyrant, to obtaine a crowne, / Stabs, hangs, impoysons, smothers, cutteth throats," Tragedy defines herself by effect rather than subject: "I must have passions that must move the soule, / Make the heart heave, and throbe within the bosome, / Extorting tears out of the strictest eyes."[30] The subject of this particular play is in fact domestic rather than royal, drawn from a well-known contemporary crime. At the conclusion Tragedy admits the difficulty of building "a matter of importance" on a popular subject, but argues that truth to history is to be given preference over artistic embellishment.

Few of the great English Renaissance dramatists gave specific attention to the theory of the drama. Only scattered and fragmentary observations may be gleaned from Marlowe, Kyd, and Shakespeare, though Shakespeare's practice unquestionably provided a source of incalculable influence on later theorists. The first English dramatist to produce a significant body of critical commentary was Ben Jonson (1573–1637), who was clearly more concerned than his predecessors with the literary dimensions of his work. The influence of Sidney can be clearly seen in Jonson's Prologue (written about 1612) to his first play, *Every Man in His Humour* (1598), which repeats in much abridged form Sidney's arguments for the unities and echoes his aim of comedy: "to sport with humane follies, not with crimes."[31]

In the Induction to *Every Man out of His Humour* (1600), Jonson gave detailed consideration to the sort of "humane follies" that should be the province of comedy and, in so doing, departed distinctly from the ideas of Sidney. Drawing upon medieval physiology, he observed that a normal personality resulted from the balance of four bodily fluids, or humours, corresponding to the four primary elements of earth, air, fire, and water. This idea Jonson extended metaphorically, ascribing to a "humour" any case "when some one peculiar quality / Doth so possesse a man, that it doth draw / All his affects, his spirits, and his powers, / In their confluctions, all to runne one way."[32] The subject of comedy should thus be a dominant, distorting personality trait, not a simple caprice or affectation. The purpose of comedy remains moral, to "scourge" such distortions by holding them up to ridicule. Poetry, says the Dedicatory Epistle to *Volpone* (1607), should serve "to informe men, in the best reason of liuing."[33]

The Prologue to *Volpone* boasts that the play is "refined / As best criticks haue designed," that its author has observed the unities of time,

---

[30]*A Warning for Fair Women*, ed. Charles Cannon (The Hague, 1975), 98.
[31]*Ben Jonson*, ed. C. H. Herford and Percy Simpson, 11 vols. (Oxford, 1925-52), 3:303.
[32]Ibid., 432.
[33]Ibid., 5:20.

place, and person and has departed from "no needful rule."[34] This last comment should serve as warning that Jonson was willing to depart, when he felt it necessary, from the demands of neoclassic theory. The Induction to *Every Man out of His Humour* lists certain "lawes of Comedie"—equal division into acts and scenes, proper number of actors, use of the chorus, and unity of time—but argues that a poet need not hold too closely to these and that in fact classic authors themselves did not always do so.[35] Similarly, the Dedicatory Epistle to *Volpone* cites classic practice in defense of the play's dark conclusion, which "may, in the strict rigour of comick law, meet with censure," despite its strict morality.[36]

The same flexibility may be seen in Jonson's much briefer remarks on tragedy in the preface to *Sejanus* (1605). Those features of tragedy which Jonson claims for the play—dignity of persons, lofty style, sententious observations, and verisimilitude—clearly reflect Senecan practice and late classic theory rather than Aristotle. Jonson admits that his work lacks a chorus and offends unity of time, but he argues that it is neither necessary nor possible in modern times to observe "the ould state, and splendour of *Drammatick Poemes*" while preserving "popular delight."[37] Thus, like most of his fellow dramatists in England and elsewhere during this period, Jonson confesses that the taste of the public must be given preference over classic rules.

Other critical comments of the time, mostly brief notes serving as prefaces to plays, are generally in harmony with Jonson, acknowledging the classical (Roman) rules but finding them often incompatible with contemporary taste. John Webster (c. 1580–1625), in his preface to *The White Devil* (1612), readily admits that his work is "no true Drammatiche poem," arguing like Lope de Vega that he is well aware of the rules, but that the most perfect tragedy—observing all the laws, such as elevated style, grave persons, and a sententious chorus—would be poisoned by "the breath that comes from the uncapable multitude."[38] In a less apologetic dedication to *The Revenge of Bussy d'Ambois* (1613), George Chapman (c. 1559–1634) echoes Jonson and Sidney in the requirements of tragedy: "things like truth ... material instruction, elegant and sententious excitation to virtue, and deflection from her contrary."[39]

[34]Ibid., 24.
[35]Ibid., 2:436–37.
[36]Ibid., 5:20.
[37]Ibid., 4:350.
[38]John Webster, *Complete Works*, ed. F. L. Lucas, 4 vols. (New York, 1966), 1:107.
[39]George Chapman, *The Plays and Poems*, ed. T. M. Parrott, 2 vols. (New York, 1961), 1:77.

John Fletcher's (1579–1625) brief address "To the Reader," which introduces *The Faithful Shepherdess* (1609), is unusual in claiming without apology new concerns for the drama. Fletcher, clearly inspired by Guarini, calls his work a pastoral tragicomedy, and considering both terms susceptible to misinterpretation, provides his own definition of them. He defines "pastoral" according to the classical concept of decorum: "a representation of shepherds and shepherdesses with their actions and passions, which must be such as may agree with their natures; at least not exceeding former fictions and vulgar traditions." His definition of the mixed genre of tragicomedy contains indirect definitions of the two traditional genres. It is "not so called in respect of mirth and killing, but in respect it wants death, which is enough to make it no tragedy, yet it brings some near it, which is enough to make it no comedy, which must be a representation of familiar people, with such kind of trouble as no life be questioned; so that a god is as lawful in this as in a tragedy, and mean people as in a comedy."[40]

The few remarks on the drama by Francis Bacon (1561–1626) in *De augmentis scientiarum* (1623) reflect the still-prevalent humanist concern for seeking moral instruction as well as Bacon's own strong preference for philosophy over poetry. The latter he sees as essentially a pleasant but unprofitable stimulation of the senses. Drama "would be of excellent use if it were sound," but it is generally much corrupted and subject to little discipline and thus rarely achieves the stimulation to virtue that it had for the ancients, who used it more carefully. A significant original note is struck by Bacon when he considers the sources of the theatre's power, one of the earliest recognitions of group psychology: "Certain it is, though a great secret in nature, that the minds of men in company are more open to affections and impressions than when alone."[41]

The last major work of English Renaissance criticism was the *Timber or Discoveries* of Ben Jonson, published posthumously in 1640. This commonplace book, apparently never intended for publication, draws together observations from a large variety of sources, recast to reflect Jonson's own concerns. Current scholarship is strongly reflected, though Jonson avoids, as always, the slavish following of authority, observing, "It is true they open'd the gates, and made the way, that went before us; but as Guides, not commanders. . . . Truth lyes open to all; it is no mans *severall*."[42] The final section of the book is devoted to drama and is heavily indebted to the work of the Dutch critic Daniel Heinsius (1580–1655), at times translating him word for word. Criticism from

---

[40]John Fletcher, *The Faithful Shepherdess*, in *The Dramatic Works in the Beaumont and Fletcher Canon*, ed. Fredson Bowers, 5 vols. (Cambridge, 1966–76), 3:497.
[41]Francis Bacon, *The Advancement of Learning*, ed. Joseph Devey (New York, 1905), 116.
[42]*Jonson*, 8:567.

the Netherlands, especially that of Heinsius, exerted a great influence in European letters at the opening of the seventeenth century; not only Jonson but the next generation of French critics, as well as Racine and Corneille, drew as heavily upon Heinsius as upon any Italian source for the fundamentals of neoclassic dramatic theory.

The great years of Dutch Renaissance scholarship began with the founding of the University of Leyden in 1575. In 1590 Julius Caesar Scaliger's son Joseph, having inherited his father's position as one of Europe's leading scholars, joined the faculty, remaining until his death in 1609. His favorite pupil was Heinsius, who carried on the Scaliger tradition in his highly influential *De tragoediae constitutione* (1611). Heinsius, like Jonson but unlike many of his Italian predecessors, saw in Aristotle not a lawgiver but a philosophic observer, who simply noted the features of phenomena and—whenever possible—drew general conclusions. This may be why Heinsius, despite his admiration for the Scaligers, did not attempt to stake out a critical position and indicate just where it departed from that of the Greek critic. His definition of tragedy follows Aristotle closely: "an imitation of a serious and complete action, which is of a proper magnitude; composed of harmonious, rhythmic and pleasing language, so that the various kinds are found in different parts, not narrated but effecting through pity and terror the expiation of these. Thus tragedy is an imitation of the serious and grave while comedy is joyous and pleasant."[43] Heinsius translates *katharsis* as *expiatio* rather than the more literal and traditional *purgatio*, arguing that Aristotle, unlike Plato, did not see the passions themselves as evil, only their deficiency or excess. Thus the proper function of tragedy is to expose the public to pity and horror so that those deficient in them may learn to feel these passions, and those with an excess may become habituated or sated and thus achieve a more moderate emotional state.

There is some echo here of Minturno's idea, based in turn on medieval notions of tragedy, that man prepares himself for the blows of fate by observing the catastrophes experienced by others. Heinsius, however, would school the passions for enduring not only great calamities but also the stresses of everyday life. In this way a didactic purpose for tragedy is achieved. This concern brings Heinsius closer than many of the Italians to an understanding of Aristotle's interest in creating empathy with the tragic hero, who like ourselves should be a mixture of good and evil, though Heinsius is more restrictive than Aristotle in defining the tragic flaw. Evil, Heinsius feels, cannot be knowingly com-

[43]Daniel Heinsius, *De tragoediae constitutione* (Amsterdam, 1643), 18.

mitted by other than an evil man; to be effective, then, tragedy can be based only upon unpremeditated wrongdoing.[44]

The Horatian interest in the didactic may also be seen in Heinsius's discussion of comedy. A misreading of Aristotle's comment on laughter as a species of the ugly or bad, consisting of some defect or ugliness that is neither painful nor harmful, leads the Dutch critic to express serious misgivings about the arousal of laughter. These are repeated by Jonson, who now calls this arousal "a fault in Comedie, a kind of turpitude, that depraves some part of a mans nature without a disease,"[45] a curious idea faithfully mirrored by later English neoclassic critics.

Considering the emphasis placed on the three unities in subsequent years, especially in France, it might be well to note that Heinsius, like Aristotle, has comparatively little to say on this question. The unity of action is of primary concern to him; it is the subject of his fourth chapter and is repeatedly mentioned elsewhere. The unity of time is suggested in several passages, but Heinsius, again like Aristotle, sees verisimilitude as faithfulness to the essence of a species, not to individuals (which is what separates the poet from the historian). He is therefore little concerned with the sort of illusion in the theatre championed by Castelvetro. Of unity of place he says nothing.

The first summation of the body of rules developed by the neoclassic critics of the late sixteenth and early seventeenth century was provided by the period's second major Dutch critic, Gerardus Joannes Vossius (1577–1649) in his *Poeticarum institutionum libri tres* (1647). This Latin compendium contained no direct references to the vernacular critics of Italy, France, Spain, or England, or to the specific literary debates that had constituted an important part of the vernacular criticism in most of these countries. Instead, Vossius attempts to sum up the contributions of Horace, Aristotle, Scaliger, Donatus, Minturno, and his own countryman Heinsius. He follows the general neoclassic idea that poetry should "teach with delight." But he agrees with Scaliger that the mere presentation of good and evil actions on stage will lead men to imitate the first and avoid the latter, rather than with Chapelain and La Mesnardière in France, who insisted upon the specific rewarding of virtue and punishment of vice. Tragedy he defines as a "dramatic poem" including "grave and serious" actions and "illustrious but unhappy" characters, which affects the purgation of general "moods" rather than of the specific emotions of pity and terror.[46] Catharsis, in

[44]Ibid., 76–77.
[45]*Jonson*, 8:643.
[46]Gerardus Vossius, *Poeticarum institutionum*, 2 vols. (Amsterdam, 1701), 2:11.

fact, holds little interest for him; he explains the murders, incests, and similar "shameful and atrocious acts" in tragedy as stimulants not to terror but to the "*admirabile*," which he uses in the sense of the amazing or surprising, similar to the *merveilleux* of the period's French critics.[47] Both derive from Aristotle's comment that terror and pity are best produced where events come on us by surprise.

Like Heinsius, Vossius ignored the question of unity of place entirely and had little to say concerning unity of time. Unity of action was of major interest to him, however, and his discussion of it, running to several chapters, is one of the most thorough of the period. A drama must contain only one action and one hero, he contends, though the action will have subordinate parts, so joined by probability and necessity that none can be omitted or changed without damage to the whole. Secondary actions may be used for ornamentation, provided they are tied to the main action and never rival it in interest.

All of these concerns would be further developed by D'Aubignac and others in his generation, who regularly looked to Vossius for guidance as their predecessors had looked to Heinsius.

[47] Ibid., 2:13.

8

Seventeenth-Century France

AFTER THE WRITINGS of Vauquelin and Laudun at the turn of the century, almost 20 years passed before any major critical statements on the drama (with the arguable exception of Heinsius's work) appeared in France. The dominant drama as the century began was that provided by Alexandre Hardy and others who, like Lope de Vega, sought popular success in defiance of classical rules. Ironically, the only sort of theatre that was both moderately faithful to these precepts and still popular was the pastoral, a type unknown to antiquity and regarded with suspicion by the more conservative Italian neoclassicists. Still, the wide success of such plays as Guarini's *Pastor fido* provided encouragement to critics and occasionally to playwrights interested in establishing in France the tradition of Italian neoclassic criticism. The most famous of the Italian rules, that of the "three unities," seems to have disappeared from the French consciousness after being promulgated by such writers as Ronsard and Jean de la Taille; it did not reappear until about 1630. Then, almost simultaneously, several writers reopened a discussion of the unities, causing much subsequent debate as to who actually discovered or rediscovered them.[1]

It would be more accurate to say that only unity of place reentered critical discussions at about this time, since unity of action and unity of time were generally espoused, at least by conservative critics, in a fairly unbroken line from Jean de la Taille to Jean Chapelain (1595–1674). They were advocated, as we have seen, by Vauquelin in 1605 and again by Chapelain in one of his first critical essays, the *Préface de l'Adone du Marin* (1623). The most famous French statement on the drama of the

---

[1]For a summary of various claims, see H. C. Lancaster, "The Unities and French Drama," *Modern Language Notes* 44 (Apr. 1929): 209–17.

1620s, the 1628 preface to Schélandre's *Tyr et Sidon* by François Ogier (d. 1670), seemingly mounts a general attack on the rigid strictures of neoclassic criticism, but in fact devotes its attention almost entirely to the unity of time. Although Ogier was hailed in the late nineteenth century (when his long-forgotten preface was rediscovered) as a significant precursor of the romantics in their desire to free the artist from classic bonds, it is important to remember that in his own time Ogier was taking a conservative position. The drama he was defending was already well established by the work of Alexandre Hardy and others. What he was resisting was (for the French) the more modern Italian style of drama, which did in fact ultimately triumph.

Ogier knew well enough that, despite Hardy's popularity, students of dramatic theory would demand arguments drawn from tradition and from classic rather than modern practice. He thus attacked the unity of time by two strategies that were used also by Italian critics. First, he pointed out exceptions to this unity in the works of the classic authors themselves–Sophocles, Menander, and Terence. Further, he praised them for this liberty, noting that some classic dramas were marred by too rigid an observance of the rule. Some caused "a number of incidents and encounters to take place in one and the same day, which probably cannot have happened in such a short period of time," and others avoided this difficulty only by "lengthy enumeration of tiresome intrigues" offstage, which served in the end only to irritate and bore the spectator.[2]

His second strategy was to emphasize differences between Greek and modern society. Whether the rules were suitable for the Greeks or not, Ogier felt they should not be imposed upon dramatists working in a different culture. "The Greeks worked for Greece, and were successful in the judgment of the cultured people of their day, and we shall imitate them much better if we grant something to the genius of our own country and to the preferences of our own language than if we compel ourselves to follow step by step their plan and their style."[3]

The freedom championed by Ogier continued to have spokesmen in following years, but the dominant critical tradition opposed it. Not only were the unities of action and time continually reaffirmed as essential to the drama, but soon after Ogier wrote, the unity of place began to be regularly added to them. In 1630 the dramatist André Mareschal observed, in the preface to his *Généreuse Allemande*, that he had not confined himself "to those narrow bonds of place, time, and

[2]Jean de Schélandre, *Tyr et Sidon* (Paris, 1624), a, vi.
[3]Ibid., e, iii.

action which are the principal concern of the rules of the ancients."[4] But in the same month, Chapelain defended these three unities in a letter that contained most of the standard arguments of the proponents of regularity.

Though Chapelain lauds the ancients, his arguments are based not upon authority but upon a theory of how drama works. He denies the idea that drama was created only to give pleasure (though he noted that even if it were, adherence to the rules would give more pleasure than rejection of them); rather, the principal end of scenic representation is "to move the soul of the spectator by the power and truth with which the various passions are expressed on the stage and in this way to purge it from the unfortunate effects which these passions can create in himself."[5] To do this most effectively, the drama must echo the conditions of real life, and so the performance must be "accompanied and supported" by verisimilitude (*vraisemblance*), the key concept in Chapelain's writing. The great discovery of the ancients was the value of "removing from the spectators any occasion to reflect on what they are seeing and to doubt its reality." For the support of this illusion, the unities are required, as is the concept of decorum, which—by presenting traditional and expected features of various ages and social conditions—offers nothing to strain the spectator's credulity.

Chapelain does not argue for a minute-to-minute correspondence of stage and real time; he allows the action to be extended by assuming that extra time passes during entr'actes and interludes but thinks the depiction of a total period of more than 24 hours would strain belief too far. The unities of action and place are closely tied to this view, since extending a story over a long period of time would involve several actions, thus blurring the focus of the drama, and several locales, thus undermining illusion. A spectator should not be asked to imagine "that the same stage, which had never left his sight, had become another place than the poet had designated it at first."[6] Also in the interest of verisimilitude, Chapelain suggested that French authors follow the example of certain Italian and Spanish dramatists who had begun to write in prose.

These ideas were first successfully employed in the theatre by Jean Mairet (1604–1686), whose preface to *Silvanire* (1631) was a central manifesto of the new approach. The preface is in the form of a small *Ars poetica*, beginning with a section on the poet and poetry, then discussing the various genres, and concluding with a long section on com-

---

[4]André Mareschal, *La généreuse Allemande*, Preface to *Seconde journée* (Paris, 1630), 2.
[5]Jean Chapelain, *Opuscules critiques* (Paris, 1936), 119.
[6]Ibid., 123.

edy. The definitions of tragedy and comedy are solidly traditional. Tragedy is "the mirror of the fragility of human things," dealing with kings and princes, beginning in joy and ending in misery. Comedy shows the private affairs of people of medium condition, beginning in distress but ending happily. Its moral function is "to show fathers and children how to live well together."[7] Mairet cites three "laws" for comedy: that its story be believable, that it consist of a single action, and that it follow the unity of time, "a fundamental law of the theatre." He does not mention unity of place, but it is clearly involved in that of time, since he speaks of the absurdity of an actor appearing in Rome in the first act and in Athens or Cairo in the second. Like Chapelain, he cites verisimilitude as the basis for this concern, since drama—unlike history—is "an active and emotional presentation of things as if they are truly happening at that time."[8]

The arguments thus expressed in 1630–1631 were repeated in a number of letters, prefaces, and manifestos between 1631 and 1636. Isnard, in a preface to Pichou's *La filis de Scire* (1631), called for an exact correspondence between real and stage time. Chapelain, in a *Discours de la poésie représentative* (1635), repeated his contention that the ancients developed the rules of unity of place and the "natural day" on the "foundation of versimilitude." In this same essay Chapelain speaks of *bienséance*, a key term of French classicism and closely related to verisimilitude. The word had been used by Pelletier in 1555 and by Vauquelin in 1605 as a translation of the Latin "decorum," but like the concept of the unities, it entered the period of its greatest influence after 1630. Chapelain's use of the term is traditional: "to make each character speak according to his condition, his age, his sex." He specifically disclaims any moral tone for the word. *Bienséance*, however, like the English word "propriety," may be taken as a synonym for suitability, as Chapelain illustrates it, or may further imply moral decency, a meaning often associated with the concept by later critics.

While theoreticians like Chapelain and some dramatists supported Italianate regulations, other writers (mostly playwrights connected with the Hôtel de Bourgogne and more sensitive to popular taste) took a more relaxed view. Thus Scudéry, in the preface to his *Ligdamon et Lidias* (1631), asserts, like Lope de Vega, that he has read all the authorities on drama but has consciously chosen to defy them in order to please his public. Similarly, Rayssiguier noted in his adaptation of Tasso's *Aminte* (1632) that "those who wish to gain profit and approval

[7]Jean Mairet, *Silvanire* (Paris, 1631), x–xi.
[8]Ibid., xiii.

for the actors who recite their verses are obliged to write without observing any rules."[9]

These were the general lines of argument for and against the neoclassic rules that were followed by participants in the famous *Cid* controversy, which followed the premiere of Pierre Corneille's (1606–1684) play in 1637. The enormous success of *Le Cid* aroused the jealousy of rival dramatists and inspired several of them to publish attacks on it. The first of these to make charges of interest to students of dramatic theory was Georges de Scudéry (1601–1667), whose *Observations sur le Cid* (published anonymously in 1637) attempted to demonstrate "that the subject is worthless, that it defies the major rules of a Dramatic Poem, that its development is lacking in judgment, that it has many bad verses, that almost all of its beauties are plagiarized."[10] Scudéry collapses Aristotle's remark about the single revolution of the sun with his observations about the proper magnitude of a beautiful object, making the unity of time a criterion for this beauty. Even so, he condemns Corneille, who literally confined his action to 24 hours, for crowding in the historical events of several years, thus offending both history and verisimilitude. The play's greatest flaw, however, in Scudéry's eyes, was its immorality. Since drama was invented "to instruct in a pleasing manner," the stage "must always show virtue rewarded and vice punished," whereas Corneille shows a daughter content to marry the murderer of her father.[11]

Corneille replied to this attack with a scornful *Lettre apologitique*, which did not condescend to answer Scudéry's specific charges, but other anonymous writers attempted point-by-point refutations: *La deffense du Cid* and *La voix publique à M. de Scudéry* (both 1637). The "bourgeois of Paris" credited with *Le jugement du Cid* (1637) boasted, "I have never read Aristotle, and I know nothing of the rules of the theatre, but I judge plays according to the pleasure they give me."[12] On such grounds, of course, Scudéry's concerns about the unities, bad verses, and even morality could be dismissed. In the meantime, other pamphlets appeared on the opposing side. The dramatist Jean de Claveret, rather gratuitously attacked in Corneille's letter to Scudéry, responded with a personal attack of his own, the *Lettre du Sr. Claveret au M. Corneille*, inspiring in turn an anonymous answer, *L'amy du Cid à Claveret*. All of these pamphlets, with at least as many more, appeared in the early months of 1637, and by spring the debate threatened to degenerate

---

[9]Quoted in René Bray, *La formation de la doctrine classique en France* (Lausanne, 1931), 268.

[10]Armand Gasté, *La querelle du Cid* (Paris, 1898), 73.

[11]Ibid., 79–80.

[12]Ibid., 231.

into a battle of personal insults. At this point Scudéry wrote to the newly founded Académie Française, admitting his authorship of the *Observations*, which had initiated the controversy, and requesting the Académie to investigate his charges and assess their validity.

Corneille accepted this proposal, though with some misgivings, when he heard that Cardinal Richelieu himself approved of it. It was long commonly assumed that Richelieu was among the enemies of the play and used the Académie as an indirect means of chastising Corneille, but more recent scholarship has challenged this idea.[13] Richelieu seems to have been interested instead in resolving an artistic debate that had grown increasingly personal and antiproductive and in adding to the authority and luster of his recently formed Académie. While the investigation proceeded (a period of six months), so did the battle of pamphlets, even though Richelieu had letters sent to Scudéry and Corneille in an effort to lower the tensions.

The most interesting of these pamphlets was the *Discours à Cliton*, containing a *Traicté de la disposition du poëme dramatique*, which is a lengthy and impassioned defense of the freedom earlier urged by Ogier. "The object of dramatic poetry," it claims, "is to imitate every action, every place, and every time, so that nothing of any sort which occurs in the world, no interval of time however long, no country of whatever size or remoteness should be excluded from what theatre can treat."[14] Like Ogier, this anonymous author insists that modern writers must be allowed to form their own rules, and that the modern consciousness will not be content with the simple and limited view of reality that classic authors presented. Since the modern knowledge of the world and of history is greater, it requires more complex expressions. The unity of action allows only one kind of story to be told in the theatre, whereas any kind should be accommodated there. "Nature creates nothing that Art cannot imitate: any action, any effect can be imitated by the Art of Poetry. The difficulty is to imitate and to make the measure and proportion of the imitations suitable to those things imitated."[15]

The eagerly awaited *Sentimens de l'Académie française sur la tragi-comédie du Cid*, largely the work of Chapelain, appeared late in 1637. It was a thorough study, containing a point-by-point commentary on Scudéry's complaints and a scene-by-scene analysis of *Le Cid*. In many particulars it took issue with Scudéry, particularly concerning the believability of the actions, the motivation of particular scenes, and the acceptability of certain expressions. Scudéry was also charged with being insuffi-

[13]See, e.g., Louis Batiffol, *Richelieu et Corneille* (Paris, 1936).
[14]Gasté, *Querelle*, 255–56.
[15]Ibid., 360.

ciently Aristotelian in his analysis. The criticism of Corneille, however, was much more severe. Chapelain agreed with Scudéry that Corneille, in attempting to follow the unities, had shown too much action for a single day and thus offended verisimilitude.

The ethics of the play stimulated even stronger condemnation. Chapelain begins his analysis with a discussion of the functions of drama and of criticism. In drama a work cannot be called good, "however pleasing it may be to the common folk," if the precepts of the art are not observed and if "the experts, who are the true judges, do not support with their approbation that of the multitude." The precepts required by the experts are those—such as decorum, verisimilitude, propriety, and poetic justice—which teach virtue "in a manner in conformity with reason." Educated and cultivated men (such as critics) will not suffer from witnessing deviations from these precepts, but it is their responsibility to insist that authors shun such deviations, since these might corrupt the ignorant multitude: "Evil examples are contagious, even in the theatre; all too many real crimes are caused by feigned representations." Corneille's depiction of "a girl introduced as virtuous" consenting to wed her father's slayer (even after due hesitation) is simply not acceptable on moral grounds, and Chapelain will have nothing to do with Corneille's defense that the story was a true one: "There are monstrous truths which must be repressed for the good of society," he concludes. "It is primarily in these cases that the poet should prefer verisimilitude to truth."[16]

With this document, the major part of the *Cid* controversy ended, though other writings of lesser interest continued the debate into the following year, and Corneille, as we shall see, continued throughout the rest of his career to refer back to the questions here raised. Despite its ferocity and fame, the controversy took up the space of scarcely more than a year. It did not, as is sometimes claimed, fix the rules of neoclassism in France; these were already in the ascendant among critics and gaining in popularity among dramatists before *Le Cid*, although there was continuing opposition to them both before and after 1637. The emphasis on the moral function of drama, too, had long been part of traditional critical discussion. The major significance of the controversy was thus not in its content but rather in the interest it aroused in the general public consciousness. The question of the rules of drama became a concern for anyone interested in letters or arts, not merely a few specialists. And with this controversy, France replaced Italy as the European center for critical discussion of the drama; for the next century and a half French critics would largely define its terms.

[16]Ibid., 366.

Despite its occasional disagreements with him, Scudéry took the judgment of the Académie as a complete vindication of his position and sought to seal his victory by writing a rival play to *Le Cid* using a similar subject but avoiding Corneille's faults. The result was *L'Amour tyrannique* (1639), which did in fact achieve considerable success. The second edition of the play appeared with a *Discours de la tragédie* by Jean-François Sarasin (1614–1654), a poet and critic of some repute who had not previously contributed to the Scudéry-Corneille debate.

Sarasin avoids all mention of *Le Cid*, saying that he is writing only in praise of Scudéry's play and will not consider "the vices of others." *L'Amour tyrannique*, he claims, is as great as anything produced by the Greeks and would surely have been taken as a model by Aristotle had it been available to him. Doubtless remembering that the Académie took Scudéry to task for not casting his remarks in Aristotelian order, Sarasin is careful to follow the Greek critic, or, to be more accurate, careful to follow Aristotle as interpreted by Heinsius in *De tragoedia constitutione*. In many passages, he translates the Dutch writer almost literally.

Sarasin begins with the purpose of tragedy and interprets Aristotle's *katharsis* as a process of "molding the passions and guiding them to that perfect philosophical equilibrium" which in turn is the basis for "the acquisition of virtue and the mastery of knowledge."[17] He specifically disclaims the "pleasure of the people" as the final end of drama. Sarasin also eliminates spectacle and music from his discussion, the first because it concerns only the scene designer, the second because it is no longer relevant to drama. Turning then to plot, he praises Scudéry for the inevitability of his climax, his regard for the unities, his arousal of pity and terror, his Aristotelian central character, and the relevance of all his poetic material to the central action. Though the conclusion is happy, there are no comic elements in the play, so the appellation of tragedy is proper to it. (A major contribution of this essay was Sarasin's attempt to claim as tragedies plays like *Le Cid* which, because of their endings, had previously been generally styled tragi-comedies.) The promised observations on character, thought, and language are in fact not included in this essay. The author pleads personal business as his excuse for not completing it; however, he recommends the soon-to-be-published work on poetic theory by Hippolyte-Jules Pilet de la Mesnardière (1610–1663) for a full discussion of these topics.

Sarasin, like Scudéry, submitted his essay to the Académie for its

---

[17]Jean-François Sarasin, *Oeuvres*, 2 vols. (Paris, 1926), 2:3.

opinion, but Richelieu, perhaps to avoid further literary debate, pronounced himself pleased by Scudéry's drama and informed the Académie that further discussion was not required. Richelieu probably considered that the anticipated *Poétique* of La Mesnardière, which he had commissioned, would resolve any outstanding questions, but the death of the Cardinal prevented the completion of this huge work; only a first section appeared, in 1639, but the loss does not seem to be great. La Mesnardière, primarily a physician and secondarily a minor poet and member of the Académie, was not a distinguished choice to provide the major book on poetic theory with which France would challenge Italy. The completed section is little more than a prolix and rambling commentary on Aristotle, Scaliger, and Heinsius. La Mesnardière is even stronger than Sarasin in his contempt for the "vile multitude" and their taste, but despite frequent references in Latin and Greek, his own "informed" critical standards are not particularly clear. He is surprisingly flexible on the unities, allowing more than 24 hours if the events require it, and approving the representation of various places, provided they could all be reached in a short period of time.

The most distinctive feature of La Mesnardière's work was its emphasis on moral instruction and poetic justice, clearly an inheritance from the *Cid* controversy. Heroes were to be models of virtue, guilty— if at all—only "of some fragility which deserves to be forgiven."[18] Evil characters should be avoided if at all possible. La Mesnardière devotes several chapters to character delineation, placing much emphasis on faithfulness to type and to expectation: "Age, passions, present fortune, condition of life, nationality, and sex" should determine personality and action, and the poet should avoid such contradictory creations as "a valiant maiden, a wise woman, or a judicious servant."[19] The aim was verisimilitude, since the play was to present specific models of virtue, and these, to be effective, should be as accessible as possible to the audience.

Another and more significant work interrupted by the death of the Cardinal was that of François Hédelin, Abbé d'Aubignac (1604–1676), another of Richelieu's protégés, and one to whom the Cardinal had turned for ideas for the general reform of the French stage. D'Aubignac, who hoped to become the first director of a national theatre, drew up recommendations on architecture, scenery, stage morality, seating, and control of audiences. He defended the moral, religious, and social utility of a national theatre so ably in his *Dissertation sur la condemnation des spectacles* (1640) that Richelieu urged him to create a guidebook for

[18]Hippolyte-Jules Pilet de La Mesnardière, *Poétique* (Paris, 1639), 314.
[19]Ibid., 120-21.

would-be dramatists. This was the *Pratique du théâtre*, put aside at the Cardinal's death, and not completed and published until 1657.

Had d'Aubignac finished his essay in the early 1640s, according to plan, it would have been the first major European summary of a century of neoclassic literary criticism. Instead, that summation was first provided by Vossius, upon whose work d'Aubignac then drew heavily for his theoretical background. The two works are in many ways parallel, but there are significant differences. Both are in a sense textbooks, attempts to summarize the existing state of criticism and to present it in a clear and memorable way, not merely for fellow specialists but for students and would-be poets. D'Aubignac confined himself to the drama, while Vossius considered all poetic genres. Moreover, as d'Aubignac himself observed, previous writings on theatre, including the work of Vossius, had tended to be commentaries on Aristotle, containing general maxims on such matters as the origin of dramatic poetry, its development, its definition, its types, the unity of action, the measure of time, the beauty of events, emotions, manners, language, and similar concerns. He, however, was attempting something new, an application of these matters to the specific problems of writing a play: "how to prepare the incidents, to unite the times and places, the continuity of the acts, the connection of scenes, and so forth."[20] D'Aubignac's goal was to create the first practical manual of playwriting, and his work indeed became a standard reference for practicing dramatists in France and elsewhere for the rest of the century.

Inevitably, the *Pratique* contains a certain amount of theory, upon which d'Aubignac's practical observations are based. He also seeks to defend the theatre, as in his previous writing, against those who found it an idle or immoral pastime. Theatre, he argues, adds to the joy of life and the glory of a nation, provides distraction for idle minds, inspires a people with examples of heroism, and—most important— shows, by the reward of virtue and punishment of vice, the proper way to live.

D'Aubignac followed La Mesnardière in emphasizing the importance of verisimilitude in making such examples effective. Actors must speak as if they were truly their characters, behave as if they were truly in the place represented, and pretend that no audience is present. All must be done "as if it truly is happening. The thoughts must suit the characters, the time and the place; results must follow from causes."[21] This seemingly reasonable approach leads d'Aubignac at times to rather

---

[20]François Hédelin, Abbé d'Aubignac, *La pratique du théâtre* (Amsterdam, 1715), 16–17.
[21]Ibid., 32.

bizarre conclusions, perhaps most strikingly when he discusses the unity of place. The stage floor, which cannot be changed, must always represent the same area, he says; the wings may change if this is done in keeping with the principle of verisimilitude. For example, they may represent a castle which is burned and so becomes a ruin, revealing a new perspective beyond.

This rigid dedication to verisimilitude causes some tension in dealing with the marvelous (*merveilleux*), a concept sanctioned by both Aristotle and Vossius. D'Aubignac essentially accepts the resolution to this problem advanced by Chapelain, who allowed surprise in the drama only when, once experienced, it would seem a reasonable effect of antecedent causes. Castelvetro had observed that "the unbelievable cannot be marvelous,"[22] which Chapelain restated as "the marvelous can only be produced by verisimilitude."[23] As Vossius became more widely read in France, his *admirabile* further reduced this tension by gradually taking on the shading of something to be admired rather than something surprising or even unnatural, a significant shift that influenced the later critical writings of Corneille.

The overly literal aspect of d'Aubignac's reasoning seems farfetched today, but the great majority of his observations are still valid. He discusses the necessity of introducing characters properly, ways to subordinate episodes, the importance of preparation and foreshadowing and the gradual building of emotion. He considers various styles of speech, asides and soliloquies, proper subjects for the drama and proper development of them. "The best arrangement," he suggests, "is to begin the play as near as possible to the catastrophe, so as to give less time to the developments of the scene and to have more liberty to expand the passions and those speeches which are most pleasing"[24] (advice followed with great effect by Racine, who studied d'Aubignac's manual faithfully). He paid particular attention to continuity of dramatic action, even through interludes and moments of repose on stage. "From the opening of the scene to the catastrophe, from the moment the first actor appears on stage until the last leaves, the major characters must always be in action, and the theatre must be involved continually and without interruption with the depiction of the designs, expectations, troubles, passions, disturbances and other such agitations, so that the spectators believe that the action has never ceased."[25] (This emphasis on unity through continuity hints at what Stanislavski would call the "through line of action.")

[22]Lodovico Castelvetro, *Poetica d'Aristotele vulgarizzata e sposta* 5.2 (Basel, 1576), 612.
[23]Gasté, *Querelle*, 365.
[24]D'Aubignac, *Pratique*, 113.
[25]Ibid., 79.

Although d'Aubignac had many kind words for Corneille and frequently cited his works as examples, Corneille was by no means satisfied with d'Aubignac's system, which was still very close to that of Corneille's antagonists in the *Cid* controversy. Hence, he prefaced each volume of a three-volume edition of his works, published in 1660, with a theoretical essay providing his own ideas on dramatic art. In a letter of August 25, 1660, he explained that in his "very difficult work on a very delicate subject," he had "made several new explications of Aristotle and put forward several propositions and several maxims unknown to the ancients. I have refuted those on which the Academy based the condemnation of *Le Cid* and I do not agree with M. d'Aubignac, even with all the good things he says about me. When this appears, I have no doubt it will arouse antagonism."[26]

Indeed, these three essays, essentially an apologia for Corneille's own work, constitute the century's most fully developed statement of disagreement with the prevailing assumptions of French neoclassic theatrical theory. The first essay accepts Aristotle as the central authority on drama and declares the author's allegiance to dramatic rules, but his interpretation of both the rules and the ideas of the philosopher placed him, as he well knew, in direct opposition to most contemporary theorists on many key questions. This is clear from the opening of the first essay, where he boldly proclaims pleasure to be the sole end of dramatic poetry. Moral purpose arises only because we are pleased by seeing the workings of a moral universe; this is a by-product of the art, not its end.

Having de-emphasized the moral function, Corneille is naturally less concerned with its traditional corollary, verisimilitude. In fact, he upbraids critics for focusing on "the probable" of Aristotle and neglecting "the necessary," resulting in "a very false maxim, that the subject of a tragedy must be based on verisimilitude."[27] On the contrary, the best subjects go beyond the verisimilar and need the authority of history or of common knowledge for their belief. This is why Aristotle said that it was "not art, but happy chance" that led poets to the few family histories providing suitable material for tragedy.

In his distinction between comedy and tragedy, Corneille takes another unorthodox view: neither the endings nor the type of character involved determine genre, but rather the gravity of the concerns. Tragedy requires "an illustrious, extraordinary, and serious action" involving such matters as death, banishment, or loss of states; comedy "restricts

[26]Pierre Corneille, *Oeuvres*, 12 vols. (Paris, 1862), 10:486.
[27]Ibid., 1:14.

itself to common, playful subjects."[28] Even love interests should be avoided in tragedy—a dictum ignored by Racine but generally followed in the early eighteenth century. At best, Corneille would allow the term "heroic comedy" to be applied to plays where a noble character rejects love for glory or duty. Turning to manners or character, Corneille translates the Aristotelian conditions as "good, suitable, similar, and equal." The first causes him the most difficulty, since he refuses to accept the common translation of it as simply "virtuous," an interpretation suggesting a moral purpose. He suggests instead the meaning that characters should be no more evil than is necessary for their actions.

The second essay deals specifically with tragedy, beginning with a consideration of catharsis. Even by considering this subject at some length, Corneille was departing from standard French practice, for such writers as Chapelain, Scudéry, and d'Aubignac referred to it only vaguely or not at all. Noting that Aristotle never defined the concept, Corneille attempts a definition of his own: "Pity for a misfortune into which we see men like ourselves fall leads us to fear a similar misfortune for ourselves. This fear leads us to a desire to avoid it, and this desire leads us to purge, moderate, rectify, and even eradicate in ourselves the passion which, in our eyes, plunged the persons we pitied into misfortune."[29] Little wonder that this convoluted idea did not prove usable even to Corneille himself. He later admits that though he believes this is what Aristotle meant, "I doubt if it is ever achieved, even in those tragedies which have the conditions Aristotle demanded."[30] Therefore, Corneille calls for a more flexible approach to the emotions. Purgation (which he sees in a strong moral light) may be stimulated by secondary characters, and may involve neither pity nor terror. An example is the death of the Count in *Le Cid*, which functions to "purge us of that sort of pride envious of the glory of others."[31] In his remarks on *Nicomède*, Corneille goes even further; he proposes a new emotion, admiration (perhaps suggested by Vossius' *admirabile*), as preferable to pity and terror for the purging of unacceptable passions. Corneille would also broaden Aristotle's idea of the best tragic hero, allowing him to be a completely good man or an utter villain, provided that his deeds, his suffering, or his punishment offer us the emotions proper to tragedy and to purgation.

The third essay deals with the unities, and here again Corneille claims to accept the tradition but in fact interprets it in a quite individual manner. Unity of action in comedy "consists of the unity of intrigue

[28] Ibid., 25.
[29] Ibid., 53.
[30] Ibid., 57.
[31] Ibid., 60.

or of the obstacle to the plans of the leading actors"; in tragedy it involves a single peril—"whether the hero succumbs to it or escapes."[32] Ideally, the drama should be restricted to a time equal to that of the presentation and to a single place, but few events in history provide material for drama so circumscribed; therefore, time may be expanded to a full day and events of several days be included so long as they do not unduly strain credulity. Several locations within a single city are acceptable for the same reason, though Corneille also argues for the "theatrical fiction" of a neutral room belonging to no one character but available to all for private conversations[33]—a device frequently employed by Racine.

As Corneille anticipated, his *Discours* set off a fresh round of critical controversy, which was complicated and before long eclipsed by the emergence of a new figure, who opened a fresh set of critical perspectives—Molière (1622—1673). The young Molière, fresh from the triumph of *L'école des maris* (1661), entertainingly separated himself from the widely discussed *Discours* in his preface to *Les fâcheux* (1662): "It is not my purpose to examine here whether all this might have been better done and if all those who were diverted by it laughed according to the rules. The time will come for me to publish my remarks on the plays I have written, and I do not give up hope that one day I, like a great author, will show that I am able to cite Aristotle and Horace!"[34]

Such a cavalier attitude toward criticism, even from a writer of comedy, was certain to arouse protest; and following the great success of *L'école des femmes* (1662), traditionalist critics, moralists suspicious of the drama, and jealous rival dramatists united in attacking the young author. The second great theatre dispute of the century thus grew out of much the same situation as did that over *Le Cid*; Molière in turn found himself under attack for plagiarism, immorality, and indifference to the rules of dramaturgy.

The attacks began in the salons and were first put into print by the young Jean Donneau de Visé (1638–1710), who sought to establish a literary reputation for himself by criticizing the leading dramatists of the day in his *Nouvelles nouvelles* (1663). By presenting his critique of Molière as a discussion among three informed critics, de Visé gives it an air of objectivity and is able to disguise his most severe criticisms. In fact, specific complaints are few, and Molière's work in general is praised for its naturalness, but his latest play is called "a monster" wherein "no one has ever seen so many good and bad things mixed

---

[32]Ibid., 98.
[33]Ibid., 121.
[34]Molière, *Oeuvres*, 13 vols. (Paris, 1873), 3:29.

together."[35] In the same publication, de Visé called Corneille's *Sophonisbe* (1663) boring throughout, lacking in both pity and terror, mixed
in tone, offensive to good taste, and too filled with incident.

These attacks on leading dramatists were the opening shots in an
exchange that enlivened the French theatrical scene for the next several
years. A month after de Visé made his comments, d'Aubignac, still
smarting from Corneille's thinly disguised attack on him in the three
Discours, published a commentary on *Sophonisbe*, supporting de Visé
and condemning Corneille's indifference to the rules. The "neutral
room" is "based on a false principle," and Corneille's argument that
he must sometimes stretch the rules to be faithful to history is dismissed
as invalid: "One should never insist on the details of history when they
do not suit the beauty of the theatre."[36]

Like the earlier *Cid* controversy, this one began with purely literary
questions, but again, as the argument grew more heated and positions
more rigid, personal attacks began to replace critical discussion. D'Aubignac essentially withdrew all his earlier praise for Corneille, and the
truly significant difference between them—Corneille's attempted fidelity to historical sources and the mores of the characters as he saw
them versus d'Aubignac's desire in the name of beauty, order, delicacy,
and good taste to adjust, soften, and accommodate material to contemporary fashion—was quite lost in overstatement and invective. After
writing a justificatory prologue, *Au lecteur*, to his *Sophonisbe*, Corneille
wisely withdrew from the debate, leaving d'Aubignac to vent his irritation on de Visé, who had decided to support Corneille's position after
all.

In the meantime, the debate launched by de Visé over Molière's *Ecole
des femmes* also continued, but more in the form of new plays than in
prefaces and pamphlets. Molière responded to his detractors in the
Critique de l'Ecole des femmes, presented June 1, 1663. In it, the characters
mention all the charges brought against Molière: his lack of taste (even
obscenity), his pandering to the pit, and most important, his departure
from the rules of art. The poet-critic Lysidas charges that Aristotle and
Horace would condemn Molière's work; Dorante replies that in fact
Molière has followed the rules, and that even had he not, the play has
pleased its audience, and that is the greatest of all rules. To the charges
that the play lacks in action and is inconsistent in characterization,
Dorante insists that dramatic "action" may be involved even in monologues or shifts in emotional states, and that a character who is foolish
in certain matters and sensible in others is not inconsistent.[37]

[35]Pierre Mélèse, *Donneau de Visé* (Paris, 1936), 17.
[36]D'Aubignac, *Remarques sur Sophonisbe* (Paris, 1633), 27.
[37]Molière, *Oeuvres*, 3:364–65.

The *Critique*, which was performed along with *L'école des femmes*, added to its popularity and thus further aroused Molière's opponents. De Visé, who considered himself ridiculed in the character of Lysidas, created a strident and acrimonious countercomedy, *Zélinda*, which attempted to arouse against Molière all the presumed objects of his satire— women, people of quality, rival actors and authors, men of religion, and literary critics. The Hôtel de Bourgogne company, the major rival of Molière's troupe, presented another response, Boursault's *Portrait du peintre*, which parodied Molière's *Critique* by absurdly exaggerating the praise for the playwright. Molière answered with the *Impromptu de Versailles*, in which he and members of his company appeared under their own names to discuss their rivals and these attacks.

From the point of view of dramatic theory, the main contribution of this last play was its consideration of the function of comedy. In the *Critique*, the character of Dorante had argued that comedy was more difficult to write well than tragedy because tragedy can depict a largely imaginary world of fancy, while comedy must depict a reality recognizable to all. Much of the *Impromptu* may be considered as an elaboration of this passage. Molière laughs at the actors of the Bourgogne who, under the influence of their tragic dramatists, depart from nature to indulge in declamation and claptrap. Far better, he insists, to draw upon the examples of nature, though he is careful to deny the charge that his satire is directed against specific individuals. The basis of comedy is "to represent in general all the defects of men, and especially the men of our own time."[38]

After the *Impromptu*, Molière contributed no further to the debate, leaving others to answer subsequent plays directed against him by de Visé and the younger Montfleury. New attacks were mounted in response to his *Tartuffe* (1664), but these came primarily from religious conservatives rather than rival actors and dramatists; their focus was thus on the morality of drama rather than its theory or practice. In his 1669 preface, Molière no longer speaks of comedy as rendering defects agreeably on stage but as aiming to correct men's vices by exposing them to ridicule—a distinctly more utilitarian purpose, probably inspired less by a change in his personal convictions than by a realization that this was a more expedient position.

During these same years Jean Racine (1639–1699) was emerging as a major dramatist and, like Corneille and Molière before him, creating enemies through his success. In the prefaces to his plays, we find him defending himself and justifying his dramatic practice. Of the three great dramatists of the century, he is the most faithful to the neoclassic

[38]Ibid., 414.

tradition, though as a practicing playwright, he recognizes the necessity of a certain flexibility in the interpretation of the rules. He takes great care to show how the plays accord with historical fact, but Racine does not, like Corneille, consider historical accuracy important in itself. Rather, he is concerned with a close adherence to what the general public accepts as history, the more important goal being verisimilitude. In the preface to *Bérénice* (1674) he states flatly, "Only verisimilitude can move us in a tragedy,"[39] and in that to *Mithridate* (1673) he suggests that "the pleasure of the reader may be redoubled" upon learning that almost all historians agree with the offered representation of Mithridate.[40] Racine is at the same time far more willing than Corneille to depart from historical fact. In the second preface to *Andromaque* (1676) he readily admits that he has changed the facts "in order to conform to the idea we have now of that princess."[41]

Racine does not normally link this emphasis on verisimilitude, as do many neoclassic writers, with moral purpose; only in the preface to *Phèdre* (1677) does he defend drama as moral instruction and claim the purpose of tragedy to be the praise of virtue and the exposure of the hideousness of vice. Far more typical is his statement in the preface to *Bérénice* that the chief rule in tragedy is "to please and to move" and all others are subordinate to that.[42] To achieve this pleasure, the action must be great and the actors heroic, the passions must be aroused, and everything in the drama must partake of a majestic sadness. Even the first half of the preface to *Phèdre* reflects Racine's more common position, noting the pains taken by the author to soften the odiousness of his heroine.[43] The latter part of this preface is thus so far out of harmony with Racine's other statements about the purpose of tragedy that it should probably be considered less an artistic credo than a device to reconcile the dramatist with the religious fathers of Port-Royal—a goal which it did in fact achieve.

As for the unities, Racine simply follows them with little critical comment. In the preface—his first—to *Alexandre* (1666) he complains of critics who cite Aristotle against him unfairly and defends his simple and straightforward construction in which all scenes are logically linked and all interest is steadily maintained.[44] Simplicity of plot is required by the unity of time, and the preface to *Britannicus* (1670) condemns

[39]Jean Racine, *Oeuvres*, 8 vols. (Paris, 1885), 2:377.
[40]Ibid., 3:17.
[41]Ibid., 2:41.
[42]Ibid., 307.
[43]Ibid., 3:299–303.
[44]Ibid., 1:157.

the practice of authors like Corneille (clearly meant though not named) who present a month's worth of action in a single day.[45]

During the years in which Racine's prefaces were appearing, three other French writers made major contributions to the theory of the theatre, the essayist Charles de Marguetel de Saint-Evremond (1610–1703), René Rapin (1621–1678), and Nicolas Boileau-Despréaux (1636–1711). The year 1674 saw the appearance of two of the most influential summations of French neoclassic criticism, Rapin's *Réflexions sur la poétique* and Boileau's *Art poétique*. The two form a striking critical diptych, since Boileau's work is a series of critical observations in poetic form, clearly looking to Horace as a model, while Rapin's is the last of the great sixteenth- and seventeenth-century commentaries on Aristotle.

The *Réflexions* begins with general observations on the poet and poetry. Rapin considers serving the public good by the improvement of manners to be the principal end of poetry. Pleasure is an important means to this end, since virtue itself is naturally austere and can be made more attractive by the emotional lure of poetry. But pleasure will result only if the poem is based upon verisimilitude, and this in turn results from following the rules—the unities, in particular. These guarantee that the work will be "proper, well-proportioned, and natural, since they are founded upon good sense and reason rather than on authority and example."[46] Rapin, like Racine, would allow verisimilitude to untrue events, provided that these conform to generally accepted ideas or can be made convincing. A poet should not, however, in an attempt to inspire admiration, go beyond what audiences can accept as reality. Rapin cites Spanish and Italian writers who have erred in this, and he doubtless had Corneille in mind as well.

Near the end of this section, Rapin adds a rule derived, he says, from Horace rather than Aristotle, to which all other rules are subordinate: this is *bienséance*. "Without it all other rules of poetry are false, because it is the most solid base of that verisimilitude which is so essential to this art."[47] He defines the term by a series of negative examples: shifts in tone, inadequate foreshadowing, characters developed inconsistently or contrary to type, offenses against morality or belief—in short, "everything which is opposed to the rules of the time, of manner, of feelings, of expression."[48] In this way he expands the traditional doctrine of decorum so that not only the general poetic assumptions but the moral and social assumptions of the public are made criteria for judging poetic creations.

---

[45]Ibid., 2:280.
[46]René Rapin, *Les réflexions sur la poétique* (Geneva, 1970), 26.
[47]Ibid., 66.
[48]Ibid., 67.

Rapin considers individually each of the three "perfect types" of poetry: epic, tragedy, and comedy. Aristotle favored tragedy, Rapin avers, because of its moral function. It uses the passions to moderate passionate excess, teaches humility by showing the fall of the mighty, teaches men to moderate their pity and bestow it upon suitable objects, and gives them courage to face the difficulties of life. Rapin considers modern French tragedy distinctly inferior to that of the Greeks: the subjects are more frivolous, and the deeper emotions are rejected in favor of love intrigues (this complaint became a staple of later neoclassic criticism). Moreover, the plots are poorly constructed, characters poorly motivated or inconsistent, and natural and impassioned dialogue replaced by surprising and marvelous events inconsistent with verisimilitude.

Comedy fares somewhat better, Rapin believes, though it also suffers at times from vulgarity, inadequate preparation of the incidents, and insufficient attention to *bienséance*. Despite continued reference to Aristotle, this discussion of comedy as well as tragedy is dominated not by Aristotle's concerns but by those of French classicism: verisimilitude, *bienséance*, and the improvement of public manners. The essence of comedy is considered to be ridicule, and its end is "to cure the public of their faults and to correct people by the fear of being mocked."[49]

Boileau's *Art poétique*, following Horace, is much more laconic than Rapin's essay, devoting only 159 verses to tragedy and 93 to comedy. The moral emphasis so clear in Rapin is almost totally absent in Boileau, who stresses pleasurable emotion: "The Secret is, Attention first to gain; / To move our minds, and then to entertain." On the traditional rules, however, the two critics are in close accord. Boileau rejects the Spanish plays which may portray an entire lifetime and observes: "That unity of Action, Time, and Place / Keep the Stage full, and all our Labors grace."[50] Like Rapin, he rejects historical truth when it does not harmonize with verisimilitude. His discussion of character generally follows Horace, stressing consistency and appropriateness to type, with a suggestion of Aristotle's tragic flaw: "Yet to great hearts some Human frailties joyn."[51] Character also dominates Boileau's briefer discussion of comedy, which is described as the portrayal of folly in natural colors. The comic poet, he says, should seek truth to nature and avoid buffoonery and coarse jesting.

Saint-Evremond, exiled from France, lived the last 40 years of his life in London, where he wrote most of the essays for which he is

---

[49]Ibid., 114.
[50]Nicolas Boileau-Despréaux, *L'art poétique*, trans. John Dryden, *Works*, 19 vols. (Berkeley, 1956–79), 2:138.
[51]Ibid., 140.

remembered. His exile gave him a more cosmopolitan view than most of his contemporaries; he agreed with the main assumptions of neo-classic French criticism, but he was unusually open to the achievements of the English, Spanish, and Italian theatre as well. He attempts to deal with each national tradition on its own terms and to discover the strengths and weaknesses of each in an objective manner. In "Sur nos comédies" (1677) he contrasts French and Spanish drama, pointing out that the Spanish, following the tradition of Moorish and chivalric tales, will produce comedies no more regular than these models and quite unlike the rulebound plays of the French. "De la comédie anglaise" (1677) notes that the English have little regard for unity of action, but that they achieve an agreeable variety of incident instead. The English feel that "liberties taken in order to please the better are to be preferred to exact rules," and those who enjoy lifelike characters and effective ridicule of man's follies will find some English comedies "as much or more to their taste as any they have ever seen."[52] Saint-Evremond acknowledges the genius of Aristotle, but insists that no theorist or system was "so perfect that it can regulate all nations and all centuries."[53]

There is a certain ambiguity about the purpose of drama in Saint-Evremond's writings. In theory he supports moral utility, but his descriptions of the drama and his own reactions to it focus more on the stimulation of emotion. He renounces the attempts, dating from the early Renaissance, to accommodate Aristotle and Greek tragedy to Horace's profit and pleasure. Whatever Aristotle meant by *katharsis* (and Saint-Evremond suspects that Aristotle himself did not know what he meant), it had no moral function. Greek tragedy, if it taught anything, taught only fear and apprehension, and Plato had ample justification for condemning it. Modern tragedies are a hundred times more useful for both individuals and for society, since they make villainy detestable and heroism admirable: "Few crimes go unpunished, few virtues unrewarded."[54]

Saint-Evremond's definition of tragedy, which he calls "new and daring," does not stress the utilitarian, however; rather, it is "a greatness of soul well expressed which excites in us a tender admiration, the sort of admiration which ravishes the mind, elevates the courage, and touches the soul."[55] His emphasis on admiration instead of pity and terror recalls Corneille, as does his relegation of love interests in tragedy to a distinctly minor position: the "tenderness of love" should never be

[52]Charles de Saint-Denis, sieur de Saint-Evremond, "De la comédie anglaise," in *Oeuvres*, 5 vols. (Paris, 1740), 3:234.
[53]Saint-Evremond, "De la tragédie ancienne et moderne," in ibid., 3:148.
[54]Ibid., 182.
[55]Ibid., 183.

the central concern of tragedy, though it should not be rejected either, especially not in favor of pity and fear. The dramatist must seek a proper emotional balance; Saint-Evremond deplores a tendency in some of his contemporaries to substitute for action "tears and long discourses," as he remarked in the amusing little essay "To an author who asked my opinion of a play where the heroine does nothing but lament herself" (1672).

Before taking leave of Saint-Evremond, we should look briefly at a famous controversy in which he played a significant role; though this debate added little of substance to dramatic theory, or indeed to literary theory in general, it did signal an interesting change in intellectual perspective during this period, which had its effect upon the strategies of criticism. As we have seen, the relative merits of classic and modern authors had been debated from the outset of the Renaissance—in the arguments over the pastoral and tragicomedy in Italy, in the conflict between Lope de Vega and Cervantes in Spain, in the *Cid* controversy in France—but the so-called Quarrel of the Ancients and the Moderns is traditionally considered to have begun in 1687, when Charles Perrault shocked many members of the French Academy with the *Siècle de Louis le Grand*, a poem that elevated a number of modern writers above the Romans and Greeks. Most of the leading writers and critics of the period were drawn into the resulting dispute, with Boileau and Racine defending the ancients, Saint-Evremond and Perrault the moderns.

Generally speaking, the champions of the ancients insisted upon faithful adherence to classical models, classical subjects, and Aristotle's rules—or rather to these rules as they were traditionally understood. The modern attention to *bienséance* pressed most of them to adjust classical practice for contemporary appreciation, but this was seen as a way of fulfilling, not replacing, that practice. The moderns, arguing on the bases of progress, changing taste, and—occasionally—the replacement of paganism by Christianity, sought new and more flexible subjects and structures, often emphasizing the emotional and psychological in reaction to the ancients' emphasis on reason and good sense. Saint-Evremond took this argument to England, where it became known as the Battle of the Books, after the major work in the quarrel, written in 1697 by Jonathan Swift.

Saint-Evremond was the last major contributor to dramatic theory in France in the closing years of the century. Critical prefaces by the dramatists Noël Le Breton, sieur de Hauteroche and Boursault essentially recapitulated the established critical tradition as represented by Rapin and Boileau. Edmé Boursault (1638–1701) also produced a lengthy and learned compilation of and response to attacks on the theatre from Tertullian on, the *Lettre sur les spectacles* (1694), which aroused a good deal of interest but added nothing original to this perennial debate. The most interesting remarks on the drama at the century's close were in André Dacier's (1651–1722) edition of the *Poetics* (1692) (accepted as standard for most of the following century in both France and England) and scattered through the writings of Pierre Bayle (1647–1746), best known for his voluminous *Dictionnaire historique et critique* (1697).

Dacier's reading of Aristotle is in close accord with the neoclassic tradition; he sees Aristotle not as an arbitrary lawgiver but as the enunciator of doctrines harmonious with reason and recognizable as correct by all mankind. Dacier accepts nothing of Saint-Evremond's cultural relativism: "Good sense and proper reason are the same in all lands and all centuries."[56] Similarly, a tragedy is the imitation of "an allegorical and universal action" which is "applicable to everyone"[57] in moderating and correcting the passions by pity and terror. If tragedy does not fulfill a moral aim, it should be condemned even if it pleases. This is the major failing of modern plays, which deal with the particular rather than the universal and which stir up the passions without improving their audiences. Comedy also has a moral function, correcting vice by ridicule.

Both Dacier's respect for the rules and his emphasis on moral purpose were challenged by Bayle, who focused upon the theatre as pure entertainment. Comedy, he observed, "must be thought of as a feast given for the people, and therefore what is important is that the food appears good to the guests, and not that it was prepared according to the rules of the art of Cuisine."[58] Vice indeed might be ridiculed, since this could amuse the public, but the major vices such as avarice, envy, or illicit love were beyond the reach of theatrical effect. It is perhaps not surprising that along with moral instruction Bayle rejected verisimilitude, allowing dramatists freedom to distort and exaggerate for the entertainment of their audience.[59]

The challenges to neoclassicism mounted by such critics as Bayle and Saint-Evremond were significant, anticipating more numerous and detailed challenges in the next century, but remained for some time a clear minority. For most of the following century, the tradition of Boileau, Racine, and Dacier remained dominant, even in the comments of such critics as Voltaire, who claimed to be expanding the boundaries of this tradition.

[56]André Dacier, *La poétique d'Aristote* (Amsterdam, 1733), viii.
[57]Ibid., x.
[58]Pierre Bayle, "Continuation des pensées diverses (1704)," in *Oeuvres diverses*, 3 vols. (The Hague, 1737), 3:202, x.
[59]Bayle, "Nouvelles de la République des lettres" (April 1684, June 1686), in ibid., 1:40, 570.

9

The Restoration and Eighteenth Century in England

THE CIVIL AND RELIGIOUS STRIFE that engulfed England in the mid-seventeenth century brought an end for a time to critical concerns; with the closing of the theatres, writings on the drama, except for religious denunciations, could hardly be expected. When the tradition was reestablished by John Dryden (1631–1700) and others in the 1660s, the whole landscape of European criticism had altered. The preeminence once Italy's had been assumed by France, where the positions developed by the generation of Corneille provided the general framework for discussions of dramatic theory for the remainder of that century and much of the next. England was particularly open to French influence because many leading members of the royalist party spent the middle years of the century in exile in Paris, absorbing the cultural views of that capital. It is highly significant that the major documents of English literary criticism between Jonson's *Discoveries* in 1640 and Dryden's *Essay of Dramatic Poesy* in 1668 were both written in Paris: the preface to *Gondibert* (1650) by William D'Avenant (1606–1668) and a letter of response (also 1650) by Thomas Hobbes (1588–1679).

Minor but interesting comments on the drama are found in both works. D'Avenant attempts to isolate the features that are most praiseworthy in English as distinct from French drama. In addition to the coherence of acts and the dynamic of the main plot, he finds English drama "pleasant and instructive," filled with "shadowings, happy strokes, secret graces" and "drapery." This "second beauty" lies in the "underwalks, interweaving, or correspondence of lesser design in Scenes."[1] His is an early defense of the more complex actions of English drama.

---

[1] William D'Avenant, *Gondibert: An Heroick Poem* (London, 1651), 22–23.

Hobbes divides poetry into heroic, scommatic (satirical), and pastoral types, each of which may be either narrative or dramatic. A moral purpose is assumed in all to be achieved by the depiction of vice's punishment in tragedy (the heroic dramatic form) or by ridicule in comedy (scommatic dramatic). Ridicule works by mirth and laughter, which Hobbes, defying Heinsius, finds perfectly suitable to comedy.[2]

The reopening of the theatres in 1660, after a hiatus of nearly 20 years, naturally inspired a number of pronouncements on the drama. The wide acquaintance with French models caused a new concern for harmonizing French and English practice, or, when that appeared impossible, deciding which was to be preferred. Should dramatists follow the loose plot arrangements of Shakespeare or the tighter structure of Corneille, employ blank verse like the former or rhyme like the latter?

Such concerns mark the first piece of dramatic theory to appear in the new era: Richard Flecknoe's (c. 1600–1678) *Short Discourse of the English Stage* (1664), which prefaced his play *Love's Kingdom*. Flecknoe's clear preference is for the sparer French style of drama; English plots suffer from "huddling too much matter together" so that author and auditors alike become lost and confused. He praises the recent introduction of scenery but warns that this may tempt authors to stress spectacle over content and thus betray "the chiefest end" of the stage, which is "to render Folly ridiculous, Vice odious, and Vertue and Noblenesse so aimiable and lovely, as, every one should be delighted and enamoured with it."[3]

A similar deference to French practice may be found in Dryden's first significant statement on the drama, his preface to *The Rival Ladies* (1664). His major concern is a defense of rhyme, used, he says, by the English before Shakespeare and in modern times by all "the most polish'd and civiliz'd nations of Europe"[4] as a check to the wild and lawless imagination of the poet. This contention was challenged almost at once by Dryden's brother-in-law, Robert Howard (1626–1698), in the preface to his *Four Plays* (1665), which announces its intention of defending English practice against that of other nations. He condemns the classic and French custom of replacing much action by narration, noting that anything makes a greater impression presented than related and that those who insist upon the latter do so "more upon the Account that what the *French* do, ought to be a Fashion, than upon the Reason of the thing."[5] Howard does feel compelled to disapprove of the English practice of mixing comic and tragic elements as putting too great a

[2]Thomas Hobbes, *An Answer to Davenant's Preface* (London, 1651), 84.
[3]Richard Flecknoe, *Love's Kingdom* (London, 1664), 67v.
[4]John Dryden, *Works*, 19 vols. (Berkeley, 1956–79), 8:99.
[5]Robert Howard, "To the Reader," in *Dramatic Works* (London, 1722), A4v.

strain on audience emotion, but he takes sharp issue with Dryden on the use of verse. His essential argument is based on verisimilitude: rhyme may be proper to a poem, which is a premeditated form of expression, but the stage should give the illusion of naturally occurring speech. If the poet's exuberant fancy needs to be checked, says Howard, the poet should learn to discipline himself by less artificial means.

This debate is continued, on a much more elaborate scale, in the outstanding work of dramatic theory of this period: Dryden's *Essay of Dramatic Poesy* (1668). Here, rather than dogmatize, Dryden follows the Socratic model used by a number of Renaissance theorists, casting his discussion in the form of a conversation between Crites, Eugenius, Lisideius, and Neander. The discussants first agree upon a definition of a play: "a just and lively Image of Humane Nature, representing its Passions and Humours, and the Changes of Fortune to which it is subject; for the Delight and Instruction of Mankind."[6]

Then they embark upon the first major debate, whether the ancients or moderns were superior artists. Crites holds that poetry was held in higher esteem among the ancients, that they were spurred by emulation rather than malice, and that their achievement was such that the best drama still follows their rules—that of the unities, for example. Eugenius responds that the ancients neither invented the unities nor observed them; that the Greeks had so little idea of structure that acts were unknown to them; that classic plots were threadbare and obvious; that classic characters, far from capturing the richness of nature, were developed within the narrow bonds of traditional types. Their teaching was no more successful than their dramaturgy, for instead of punishing vice and rewarding virtue, they often showed prosperous wickedness (as with Medea) or unhappy piety (as with Cassandra). Moderns, he contends, have learned from both the virtues and the faults of the ancients to create a superior drama.

The discussion next shifts to a comparison of English and French drama, with Lisideius defending the French and Neander—Dryden's mouthpiece—defending the English. Lisideius commends the strict regard for the unities in France, the refusal there to mix comic and serious elements, the economic plotting, the expert narration that permits the avoidance of duels and battle on stage, the well-motivated characters, and the skill in verse.

Neander's reply is the most lengthy in the essay and the most fully developed—hardly surprising, since the preface to the work announces unequivocally that its goal is "chiefly to vindicate the honour of our *English* Writers, from the censure of those who unjustly prefer the

[6]Dryden, *Works*, 17:15.

French before them."[7] Neander, recalling the definition of a play as a "lively imitation of Nature," charges that the French in fact follow not nature but artistic rules, achieving only an artificial beauty. French plots are bare, passions cold, variety stifled by the strict separation of genres, believability sacrificed to a rigid adherence to the unities. Neander admits that English drama is at times excessively violent, but "if we are to be blam'd for showing too much of the action, the *French* are as faulty for discovering too little of it."[8] These general observations are followed by extended and thoughtful analyses of Shakespeare, Beaumont and Fletcher, and Jonson.

The final section of the essay returns to the question of rhyme and blank verse. Crites essentially repeats the arguments already advanced by Howard, emphasizing the artificial quality of rhyme in a form devoted to imitating nature. Neander responds that no one in fact speaks either blank verse or rhyme, so only the skill of the poet can give either the illusion of natural speech. The distinction between them is that blank verse is closer to common speech and thus more suitable for comedy; rhyme, a more noble speech, should be used for tragedy, which shows "Nature wrought up to an higher pitch."[9]

This debate continued in two more documents of 1668, Howard's preface to *The Duke of Lerma* and Dryden's *Defense of An Essay of Dramatic Poesy*. Howard's brief essay is neither very clear nor very convincing, shortcomings that Dryden pointed out at considerable length. Neither essay added much to the argument over rhyme, but Howard's disagreement with Dryden on the unities of time and place led to more original observations. Howard scoffs at Dryden's assertion that two rooms in the same house or two locations in the same town are more acceptable than widely separated locations, arguing that there are no degrees of impossibility. Dryden insists that such degrees do exist, that "in the belief of fiction, reason is not destroyed, but misled, or blinded," and that it "suffers itself to be so hoodwink'd, that it may better enjoy the pleasures of the fiction: But it is never so wholly made a captive, as to be drawn head-long into a persuasion of those things which are most remote from probability."[10] This early and striking statement of the phenomenon Coleridge would call the "willing suspension of disbelief" allows Dryden to handle with unusual clarity the long-confused problem of verisimilitude and the unities. Place and time in the theatre must be considered as both real and imaginary: "The real place is that Theatre, or piece of ground on which the Play is acted. The imaginary,

---

[7] Ibid., 17:7.
[8] Ibid., 51.
[9] Ibid., 74.
[10] Ibid., 9:18.

that House, Town, or County where the action of the *Drama* is supposed to be ... the imagination of the Audience, aided by the words of the Poet, and painted Scenes, may suppose the Stage to be sometimes one place, sometimes another, now a Garden, or Wood, and immediately a Camp."[11]

In defending rhyme, Dryden went so far as to assert that "delight is the chief, if not the only end of Poesie,"[12] but few contemporary critics so lightly dismissed the moral function. Thomas Shadwell (1642–1692), in his preface to *The Humourists* (1671), took "leave to dissent from those, who seem to insinuate that the ultimate end of a Poet is to delight," which would make the poet "of as little use to Mankind as a Fidler, or Dancing-Master, who delights the fancy only, without improving the Judgement."[13] Indeed, so important was the moral function in Shadwell's eyes that he elevated comedy above tragedy—because the former, in rendering vices and fopperies ridiculous, "is a much greater punishment than Tragedy can inflict upon 'em."[14] His preface to *The Royal Shepherdesse* (1669) claims that the work follows the rules of morality and good manners by exalting virtue and condemning vice. Others may seek popular success by avoiding moral lessons, but "he that debases himself to think of nothing but pleasing the Rabble, loses the dignity of a Poet."[15] Shadwell displays no interest in the debate over verse, and little in language in general. He follows Jonson's view that the essence of comedy is in character, in holding "humours" from everyday life up to ridicule and correction.

Dryden, in his preface to *The Mock Astrologer* (1669), condemned this view of comedy as too narrow, qualifying somewhat his earlier praise of Jonson. The ideal comic poet should portray the humours, which are amusing in themselves, but add to them his own verbal wit, in the manner of Fletcher or Shakespeare. He quotes Quintilian: "It is easy to make fun of folly, for it is laughable in itself. ... What gives rise to refined laughter is what we add of our own."[16]

Few theorists of this generation gave much detailed attention to traditional tragedy, and few dramatists attempted it. John Milton's (1608–1674) preface to *Samson Agonistes* (1671) is thus a rather isolated document, the more so because of its highly conservative conclusions. Milton defends the chorus (long since given up even by many Italian critics), the rule of 24 hours, simplicity of plot, verisimilitude and de-

---

[11]Ibid., 171.
[12]Ibid., 5.
[13]Thomas Shadwell, *Complete Works*, 5 vols. (London, 1927), 1:183–84.
[14]Ibid., 184.
[15]Ibid., 100.
[16]Dryden, *Works*, 3:244.

corum, and purity of genre. He holds tragedy to be "the gravest, moralest, and most profitable" of poems, though he seeks its instruction not primarily in the events portrayed, but rather in the moral thoughts expressed in the text. Indeed, his citation of Aristotle on the end of drama—"raising pity and fear, or terror, to purge the mind of those and such like passions, that is to temper and reduce them to just measure with a kind of delight, stirr'd up by reading or seeing those passions well imitated"[17]—comes close to rejecting the traditional idea of moral instruction altogether.

The genre which at this time quite eclipsed tragedy in England was the heroic drama, an extremely popular and highly mannered form, the artificiality and bombast of which was amusingly parodied in George Villiers, Duke of Buckingham's *The Rehearsal* (1672). Although the parody was far-ranging, the primary object of attack was Dryden, the leading exponent of the genre, who both explained and defended it in the preface to his *Conquest of Granada* (1672). William D'Avenant, says Dryden, laid the foundations for this form by drawing upon elements of Italian opera and the dramas of Corneille, but his experiments still lacked significant elevation of characters and events. These Dryden found in the heroic poems of the period and concluded "that an Heroick Play ought to be an imitation, in little, of an Heroick Poem: and consequently, that Love and Valour ought to be the Subject of it."[18] The arguments against heroic drama can all be reduced to the single complaint that it is artificial, but the heroic poet "is not ty'd to a bare representation of what is true, or exceeding probable."[19] His realm is that of the imagination, his subject the majestic and noble, his emotions admiration and wonder. Naturally, such a form required the heightening of all the elements, including language. Once again Dryden dismisses those who would remove verse from the stage; they are followers of the false idea of drama as a reflection of commonplace reality.

In the Epilogue to the second part of *Conquest*, Dryden offers historical support for heightened language. Drama, to succeed, must adapt to the age. Jonson could rely upon "Mechanique humour" because he wrote "when men were dull, and conversation low."[20] But in the present, more refined age, love and honor are exalted, wit more developed, and language refined; all this must be reflected by the drama. Dryden credits the influence of the court with this improvement of manners and hence of the stage.

The year 1674 marks the beginning of a new phase in English dra-

[17]John Milton, *Works*, 18 vols. (New York, 1931–38), 1:331.
[18]Dryden, *Works*, 11:10.
[19]Ibid., 12.
[20]Ibid., 201.

matic criticism: the methods and assumptions of French neoclassic criticism received their first widespread and thoughtful attention in England with the appearance of Boileau's *Art poétique* and Thomas Rymer's (c. 1643–1713) translation of Rapin (misleadingly entitled *Reflections on Aristotle's Treatise of Poesie*). In 1680 there were translations of Horace by the Earl of Roscommon and John Oldham, Sir William Soame's *Art of Poetry*, and a translation of Boileau revised and adapted by Dryden—who ingeniously substituted English names and examples for those of the original French. D'Aubignac's *Pratique* appeared in English in 1684 as *The Whole Art of the Stage*, and the *Mixed Essays of Saint-Evremond* became available to English readers in 1686. Thus within a decade the major works summarizing contemporary French critical thought appeared in England, exerting a powerful influence on the critics of that nation.

In his preface to the translation of Rapin, Rymer calls attention to Rapin's praise of English poets but notes that they are in general defective in the rules of their art, a defect that the study of such writers as Rapin and Aristotle could correct. It is characteristic of all Rymer's criticism that he regards the neoclassic rules not as a learned and esoteric body of specialized knowledge but as the naturally developed dictates of common sense: Aristotle's observations are not "the dry deductions of his metaphysics" but observations of the actual practice of successful poets, reduced to general principles. They are thus "convincing and clear as any demonstration in *Mathematicks*. 'Tis only needful that we understand them, for our consent to the truth of them."[21]

Rymer's views are more fully developed in his *Tragedies of the Last Age* (1678), which considers three plays by Beaumont and Fletcher in some detail as examples of the inferiority of Elizabethan to classical drama. He does not stress such "outward regularities" as the unities, which he calls the mechanical parts of tragedy, but focuses on the more essential matters of fable and character. Again, common sense is advanced as the ultimate judge of value, unaffected by changes in culture or custom. He seems to depart from his French models by asserting that the primary end of poetry is pleasure and that some poems can please without profit, but he goes on at once to assert that whoever writes a tragedy "cannot please but must also profit." This leads him to the dynamic of tragedy: "beside the *purging* of the *passions*; something must stick by observing that constant order, that harmony and beauty of providence, that necessary relation and chain, whereby the causes and the effects, the virtues and rewards, the vices and their punish-

---

[21]Thomas Rymer, *Critical Works* (New Haven, 1956), 2–3.

ments are proportion'd and link'd together."[22] This linking together
of vice and punishment, virtue and reward was what in Rymer's eyes
made drama more universal than and superior to history. The Greeks
realized that it was the poet's duty to "see justice exactly administered,
if he intended to please."[23] Thus the highly influential idea of poetic
justice made its appearance in English criticism.

Rymer's demands on the subject of characterization follow naturally
from this concern. He subscribes to the neoclassic idea of decorum,
not only because it accords with probability and thus with common
sense, but because it supports the universalized morality of poetic justice. Historical kings might have been corrupt and cruel, but poetic
kings must be just, noble, and heroic. If virtue is always rewarded, "it
is not necessary that all Heroes should be Kings, yet undoubtedly all
crown'd heads by *Poetical Right* are Heroes."[24] By the end of the century
this rigid interpretation of suitable character types, poetic justice, and
stage morality, even in the name of reason and common sense, came
under increasing attack, especially after Rymer's notorious rationalistic
condemnation of *Othello* in 1692. The nineteenth-century critics came
to regard him, largely on the basis of this essay, as the prototype of
the inflexible critic, blinded by limited critical standards; Macaulay went
so far as to call him the worst critic that ever lived.

In the 1670s and 1680s, however, few voices were raised in protest
to Rymer's pronouncements, though Samuel Butler (1612–1680) argued in a lively though not very substantial poetic essay *Upon Criticism*
(c. 1678) that "An *English* poet should be try'd b'his Peers / And not
by *Pedants* and *Philosophers*."[25] Rymer was at this time sufficiently in
harmony with the critical taste of the period to be generally accepted
as equal in stature to Dryden himself, and the observations of the two
were often similar. Dryden too considered contemporary drama more
refined and polished than that of the Elizabethans, and deferred to
classic authority as codified by the French. In the "Apology for Her-
oique Poetry" that prefaced his *State of Innocence* (1677) he went so far
as to call Rapin "alone sufficient, were all other Critiques lost, to teach
anew the rules of writing."[26]

Dryden, as a practicing poet and a critic with greater sensitivity than
Rymer to the beauties of Elizabethan drama, clearly chafed far more
under the restraints of neoclassic regulations. Though he quoted with
approval Rymer's criticism of Fletcher and Shakespeare, he could not

[22] Ibid., 75.
[23] Ibid., 22.
[24] Ibid., 42.
[25] Samuel Butler, *The Genuine Remains in Verse and Prose* (London, 1759), 165.
[26] Dryden, *Dramatic Works*, 6 vols. (New York, 1968), 3:418.

escape the latter's power. In the prologue to *Aureng-Zebe* (1676) he confessed, "In spite of all his pride a secret shame / Invades his breast at Shakespear's sacred name"; under Shakespeare's influence he had even "grown weary of his long lov'd mistress, Rhyme."[27] The full effect of this was seen in his subsequent *All for Love* (1678), a reworking of *Antony and Cleopatra* along fairly strict neoclassic lines, with careful attention to decorum, morality, and the unities but without Dryden's "long lov'd mistress, Rhyme."

The tension between classic principles and traditional English practice is again reflected in Dryden's *Troilus and Cressida* (1679), whose preface "The Grounds of Criticism in Tragedy" is one of the first detailed discussions in English of Aristotle's principles. Introducing this essay is the definition of tragedy as "an imitation of one entire, great, and probable action, not told but represented, which by moving in us fear and pity, is conducive to the purging of those two passions in our minds."[28] The final phrase Dryden interprets, following Rapin and general neoclassic theory, in a moralistic, indeed Horatian manner. "To instruct delightfully is the end of all poetry,"[29] he avers, and pity and fear serve this end by ridding man of pride and lack of commiseration. The tragic hero must serve as the focus for these emotions and so must be sympathetic, more virtuous than evil, consistent, and faithful to type.

The parts of the definition that caused Dryden the most difficulty were those hardest to reconcile with the practice of Shakespeare. The "one entire action" seemed to rule out subplots, and the restriction of emotions aroused to pity and fear seemed to rule out tragicomedy, both highly attractive to Dryden. In the preface to his next play, *The Spanish Friar* (1681), he admitted mixing serious and comic elements "for the pleasure of variety," since audiences "are grown weary of continu'd melancholy scenes." He does not shelter himself entirely behind audience taste, however, but argues that tragicomedy should be respected as a distinct form, as difficult to create as tragedy, "for 'tis more difficult to save than 'tis to kill," and much art and judgment are required "to bring the action to the last extremity, and then by probable means recover all."[30]

Despite such arguments, Dryden was never able to harmonize his work as a dramatist completely with his understanding of the rules of drama. Eventually, faithfulness to neoclassic principles won out over pragmatism and personal taste. In 1693 he still defended tragicomedy,

[27]Ibid., 4:87.
[28]Ibid., 5:14.
[29]Ibid., 16.
[30]Ibid., 122.

but only if it had one main action and the "underplot or second walk of comical characters and adventures" was kept clearly subordinate.[31] Two years later, he renounced even this compromise and pronounced English tragicomedy to be "wholly Gothic, notwithstanding the success which it has found upon our theatre." Such works as Guarini's *Pastor fido* and his own *Spanish Friar* he now calls unnatural minglings, in which the conflicting claims of mirth and gravity create an effect as unpleasant as "a gay widow laughing in a mourning habit."[32]

The 1680 translations of Horace and Boileau clearly influenced the *Essay on Poetry* (1682) written by the Earl of Mulgrave (1648–1721), which advanced similar doctrines in poetic form. Mulgrave drew upon the same critical tradition as Dryden and Rymer but disagreed sharply with them on the superiority of the contemporary English theatre. Its indifference to such technical matters as the unities is, he observes, "too well known to be taught here"; he gives his attention instead to its "less obvious errors," among them unjustified verbal embellishment, unnaturally witty and simile-laden conversation, and extended and frequent soliloquies. Shakespeare and Fletcher he holds up as models of a spare and honest drama now almost forgotten. In a minor but significant part of the essay considering the morality of art, Mulgrave condemns the ribaldry and obscenity of the "nauseous songs" of a certain "late author"—presumably the Earl of Rochester.

A spirited rebuttal to this last point was offered by Robert Wolseley (1649–1697) in the preface to *Valentinian* (1685). A poet, argues Wolseley, should be free to depict anything in nature, concrete or abstract, beautiful or ugly, good or evil; he is not to be judged by the worth of his subject but by his skill in the treatment of it. In fact, he says, the author attacked by Mulgrave did use art for moral ends—the exposure of vice and the lashing of folly—yet the ultimate test of art's worth is not moral but aesthetic. Indeed, "the baser, the emptier, the obscurer, the fouler, and the less susceptible of Ornament the Subject appears to be, the more is the Poet's Praise, who can infuse dignity and breathe beauty upon it."[33] This bold claim found few supporters, for public and critical opinion during the Restoration generally followed the French concern for the morality of art so clear in the contemporary reactions to Corneille and Molière. In this matter, Mulgrave more accurately reflected the temper of the time, and within a decade condemnations of the immorality of the theatre would dominate critical writing in England.

An attempt to mediate between the rival claims of profit and pleasure

---

[31]Dryden, *Essays*, 2 vols. (Oxford, 1900), 2:102.
[32]Ibid., 147.
[33]J. E. Spingarn, ed., *Critical Essays of the Seventeenth Century*, 3 vols. (Bloomington, 1957), 3:16.

was made by Sir William Temple (1628–1699) in his essay *On Poetry* (1690). He calls the question of which is primary "rather an Exercise of Wit than an Enquiry after Truth," since poetry generally mixes the two.[34] It was Temple, much influenced by Saint-Evremond, who wrote the first major English contribution to the Quarrel of the Ancients and the Moderns, *Upon Ancient and Modern Learning* (1690). In general, he judged poetry to have declined since classic times but made an exception for the drama. He joined Rapin and Saint-Evremond in the praise of English comedy, which he considered richer and livelier than that of the ancients or of other modern nations. The cause, Temple thought, was the English climate, ease of life, and freedom of expression, which allowed the development of a much greater variety of eccentricities—the English "humours"—here than elsewhere.

This idea that the strength of English drama lay in the English concept of humour gained wide currency among Temple's contemporaries. William Congreve (1670–1729), in *Concerning Humour in Comedy* (1695), precisely repeats (without attribution) Temple's assessment of the superiority of English comedy and its source in the physical and political environment of the country. Congreve distinguishes humour from affectation and external habit, defining it as "a singular and unavoidable manner of doing or saying any thing, Peculiar and Natural to one Man only, by which his Speech and Actions are distinguish'd from those of other men."[35]

Critical concern was, however, shifting away from the matter of comedy to its morals. James Wright's "Of Modern Comedies" in *Country Conversations* (1694) and the anonymous *Reflection on our Modern Poesie* (1695) both complained that modern comedy seemed often to neglect its moral purpose in seeking mere pleasure, and to ridicule religious matter as readily as vice; still, neither of these works could be styled a call for reform. More distinctly polemic was the preface to *Prince Arthur* (1694) by Sir Richard Blackmore (1650–1729), which charged modern poets with conspiring "to ruin the End of their own Art, to expose *Religion* and *Virtue*, and bring *Vice* and *Corruption of Manners* into Esteem and Reputation."[36] Greek drama, asserts Blackmore, was established by the state for moral instruction. Its heroes suffered punishment for impiety and gained praise for virtuous action, and the chorus "was wholly employ'd in rectifying their [the Athenians'] mistakes about the *Gods* and their Government of the World, in moderating their Passions, and purging their Minds from Vice and Corruption."[37]

---

[34] William Temple, *Essays* (Oxford, 1909), 43.
[35] Spingarn, *Critical Essays*, 3:248.
[36] Ibid., 3:229.
[37] Ibid., 3:228.

Blackmore clearly struck a responsive note. *Prince Arthur* was re-printed twice, while in the theatre Cibber's highly moral *Love's Last Shift* (1696) enjoyed a huge success, and complaints were often heard about the immorality of other plays. The appearance of Bossuet's *Maximes et réflexions sur la comédie* (1694) in France probably added fuel to the fire, for the *Gentleman's Journal* of November 1694 remarked that "the controversy is now as hot for and against the lawfulness of the French stage, as it was of late about the ancients and moderns." Petitions addressed to King and Parliament protesting the immorality of contemporary life and literature were given sympathetic hearing.

Against this background appeared the period's most famous attack on the theatre, Jeremy Collier's (1650–1726) *Short View of the Immorality and Profaneness of the English Stage* (1698). In a sense the work may be seen as a particularly striking contribution to the tradition of antitheatre tracts, the tradition that included William Prynne in the Jacobean period and Stephen Gosson in the Elizabethan. But while Collier's fulminations have a similar feel, his approach ties him more directly into the mainstream of theatre criticism than his predecessors had been. Wishing not simply to discharge his wrath against the stage but to force reforms, Collier drew the greater part of his critical support from authorities and arguments generally accepted by the leading literary theorists of the day. The church fathers are not neglected, of course, but their comments are briefly summarized in the final chapter, while the authorities cited in the previous five chapters are the classic dramatists, Aristotle, Horace, Quintilian, Heinsius, and Rapin.

Collier's central argument is for the moral end of drama, as his opening statement makes clear: "The business of *Plays* is to recommend Virtue, and discountenance Vice; To shew the Uncertainty of Humane Greatness, the suddain Turns of Fate, and the Unhappy Conclusions of Violence and Injustice. 'Tis to expose the Singularities of Pride and Fancy, to make Folly and Falsehood contemptible, and to bring every Thing that is Ill under Infamy, and Neglect."[38]

Each chapter considers a way in which the present theatre works against this end. The first discusses its immodest and obscene language; the second, profanity and blasphemy. Modern authors employ more of both than did the classics, asserts Collier, despite the latitude of paganism and the blemishes of its gods. The third and fourth chapters draw most heavily on generally accepted critical dicta. Against the argument sometimes made by Dryden and others that evil characters might be presented in a favorable light for the pleasure of the audience,

---

[38]Jeremy Collier, *A Short View of the Immorality and Profaneness of the English Stage* (London, 1698), 1.

Collier quotes Rapin and Jonson in support of poetic justice. Evil must be punished, he insists. The search for amusement at any cost leads to a disregard for the proprieties of age, sex, and condition, thus flying in the face of decorum, and tempts authors to indulge in mere ribaldry, which was condemned by both Aristotle and Quintilian as a source of laughter. In dealing with four specific plays by Dryden, D'Urfey, and Vanbrugh, Collier finds offenses not only to morality but to the accepted standards of the drama: improbable plots; inconsistent characters, untrue to type, who speak inappropriately; even disregard of the unities. The concluding chapter is essentially a compilation of antitheatrical comments from pagan and Christian authors.

Although, as we have seen, Collier by no means initiated debate over the morality of the stage, even in his own generation, the effect of his essay so far outweighed that of its immediate predecessors that it is not inaccurate to credit him with launching the battle of pamphlets on this question that continued for the next quarter-century in England. Of the more than 80 known contributions to this dispute,[39] fortunately only a few need engage our attention as contributions to dramatic theory.

Most of the dramatists attacked in the *Short View* produced responses, though none of major significance. Dryden, who in previous controversies had shown himself a powerful adversary, now—much to the chagrin of Collier's opponents—made no official reply. However, in his *Poetical Epistle to Motteux* (1698) and his preface to *The Fables* (1700), his position on the debate and his reason for not engaging in it are clear. He charges Collier with a want of good manners and civility, and even with finding blasphemy and bawdry in places where none was intended. Nevertheless, "in many things he has taxed me justly," Dryden admits, "and I have pleaded guilty to all thoughts and expressions of mine, which can be truly argued of obscenity, and profaneness, or immorality, and retract them."[40]

Probably the most effective response to Collier was written by John Dennis (1657–1734), a protégé of Dryden who, after the master's death in 1700, was for a time generally considered England's leading literary critic. Dennis's early critical writings were all defenses of Dryden. The *Impartial Critick* (1693) scoffed at Rymer for attempting to introduce Athenian drama into England, where climate, politics, and social customs were all different. In 1698 his "Remarks on a Book entitled *Prince Arthur*" responded in part to criticisms of Dryden made in Blackmore's

---

[39]See Rose Anthony, *The Jeremy Collier Stage Controversy 1698–1726* (Milwaukee, 1937), for a complete listing.
[40]Dryden, *Essays*, 2:272.

preface. Collier's essay not surprisingly inspired a more extended defense, the *Usefulness of the Stage to the Happiness of Mankind* (1698).

Unlike most disputants in this quarrel, Dennis does not undertake a series of specific rebuttals to Collier; indeed, he begins by admitting that the stage is now prey to great abuses which demand reform. "My business," he says, "is a Vindication of the Stage, and not of the Corruptions or the Abuses of it."[41] Properly employed, the stage is useful to the happiness of mankind, the welfare of the state, and the advancement of religion. Treating happiness first, Dennis suggests that drama works in such a way as to stimulate the passions while not denying the reason. This makes it enjoyable and useful for all men but particularly for the English, a splenetic race who tend to stifle their passions with too much reflection. Government is especially well served by tragedy, which discourages rebellion by showing the ill effects of ambition and desire for power. Moreover, it diverts men from their grievances by showing others in greater distress than themselves and banishes seditious thoughts by filling the mind with images of compassion, duty, and patriotism. Both church and state profit from the purging of the passions and the teaching of humility, patience, and duty, the traditional business of tragedy. Specifically religious subjects have no place on the stage, but drama teaches religion indirectly; for without a belief in God and particular Providence, the working out of tragic fate (particularly of poetic justice, which Dennis considers essential) would be impossible. Like Collier, Dennis buttresses his logical arguments with citations from ancient and modern authorities.

The emphasis upon the raising of passions as a stimulus to happiness in the early part of this essay and upon moral purpose in the latter part may suggest a duality in Dennis's thought on the purpose of drama, but in fact he fuses the two ideas, following a generally Horatian pattern. In the *Grounds of Criticism in Poetry* (1704), he makes pleasure a subordinate end and "reforming the Minds of Men" the chief end of poetry. Both, however, are achieved by exciting passion. Lesser poetry does so by depicting objects in natural life; this is the method of comedy and of the less elevated passages in tragedy. Greater poetry does so by arousing Enthusiasm, a concept for which Dennis draws upon Longinus and religious thought. Tragedy at its finest arouses deeper feelings, not directly but by stimulating its audience to the subsequent arousal of ideas in meditation (a concept something akin to Wordsworth's famous "emotion recollected in tranquillity").

This interest in emotion, especially in its deeper and more evocative aspects, might have led Dennis, like later critics, to a doctrine of in-

[41]John Dennis, *Critical Works*, 2 vols. (Baltimore, 1939–45), 2:147.

dividual genius had he not been so firmly schooled in the teachings of Dryden and the French neoclassicists. Thus he argued that the greatest geniuses were always scrupulous in their observance of the rules of art. If the purpose of poetry was "to instruct and reform the World, that is to bring Mankind from Irregularity, Extravagance, and Confusion, to Rule and Order,"[42] then it naturally followed that rule and order must characterize poetry itself. Indifferent observance of the rules, Dennis concluded, was the cause of the low state of poetry in his own day.

The new generation of writers and critics that appeared after 1705 agreed with Dennis on a few matters—such as the folly of Italian Opera, which he judged "a mere sensual Delight, utterly incapable of informing the Understanding, or reforming the Will; and for that very reason utterly unfit to be made a publick Diversion."[43] In general, however, they found his dedication to neoclassic regulations and his tone of high religious seriousness increasingly pompous, pedantic, and old-fashioned. And it is true that after 1705 a certain petulance and rigidity marked his attempts to defend his opinions against a new, more flexible literary orthodoxy. In his early career, Dennis had sounded a positive, even exuberant note in defending the mainstream of English literature against the moralism of Collier or the rationalism of Rymer, and as the eighteenth century opened, he was moving toward the same flexible position as the new generation; his interest in Longinus, in the psychology of the author and the spectator, in the effect of climate and environment on literature all show this. But the dynamics of the ensuing debates caused him to abandon these interests in his determined defense of neoclassic rules.

Signs that the authority of these rules was weakening began to appear in England immediately after Dryden's death. One of the first was the informal "Discourse upon Comedy" (1702) by the dramatist George Farquhar (1678–1707). This essay in the form of a letter to a friend considers the apparent paradox that plays written according to the widely accepted rules of art are nevertheless dull and ineffective. The problem, suggests Farquhar, lies in looking to authorities like Aristotle, "who was no Poet, and consequently not capable of giving Instructions in the Art of Poetry,"[44] rather than to the basic purpose of the art. If the end is known, the means can be discovered by reason rather than by reliance upon possibly false authority. Comedy, then, is a "well-fram'd Tale handsomly told, as an agreeable Vehicle for Counsel or

[42]Ibid., 1:335.
[43]Ibid., 385.
[44]George Farquhar, *Works*, 2 vols. (New York, 1967), 2:335.

Reproof."[45] Since our follies and pleasures are different from those of the ancients, our comedies must seek new means to achieve these ends. Modern authors should not be condemned if they ignore the unity of time or place, which the mind may easily do, but only if they "have left Vice unpunish'd, Vertue unrewarded, Folly unexpos'd or Prudence unsuccessful."[46]

The theatre comments of Sir Richard Steele (1672–1729) in *The Tatler* (1709–1710) with their striking observations on contemporary actors and productions, may be said to have begun the modern review. They contain little formal theory, but the delight in Shakespeare and the emphasis on the pragmatic test of what is effective in the theatre clearly show Steele to be an observer with little interest in traditional rules. The most conventional part of his observations is his interest in moral concerns. "It is not the business of a good play to make every man a hero," he observes, "but it certainly gives him a livelier sense of virtue and merit than he had when he entered the theatre."[47]

Steele apparently stimulated an interest in the theatre in his co-worker on *The Tatler*, Joseph Addison (1672–1719), who produced a more substantial body of theoretical writing. Tragedy, which received his principal attention, is dealt with in Nos. 39, 40, 42, and 44 (April 1711) of *The Spectator*. These essays essentially echo neoclassic ideals. Though Addison ignores most of the specific rules on structure and the unities, he condemns tragicomedy and would allow subplots only where these "bear such a near Relation to the principal Design, as to contribute towards the Completion of it, and be concluded by the same Catastrophe."[48] The didactic aim of tragedy is essential to Addison, and he considers the neglect of it the major fault in modern drama. However, the means of moral instruction in his view were sharply different from those advocated by Dennis and his tradition. The doctrine of poetic justice Addison considered a ridiculous idea with "no foundation in Nature, in Reason, or in the Practice of the Ancients."[49] Good and evil happen to all, and if we deny the clear workings of the world and solve all problems by the end of the play, we undermine the arousal of pity and fear stipulated by Aristotle. Addison is frequently credited with making the first formal attack on this doctrine in England, but in fact Steele anticipated him in *The Tatler* No. 82 (Oct. 18, 1709),

---

[45]Ibid., 336.

[46]Ibid., 343.

[47]Richard Steele, No. 99 (Nov. 26, 1709), *The Tatler*, ed. G. A. Aitken, 4 vols. (New York, 1970), 2:334.

[48]Joseph Addison, No. 40, *The Spectator*, ed. Donald F. Bond, 5 vols. (Oxford, 1965), 1:171.

[49]Ibid., 169.

calling poetic justice a "chimerical method" of disposing of dramatic fortunes, where "an intelligent spectator, if he is concerned, knows he ought not to be so; and can learn nothing from such a tenderness, but that he is a weak creature, whose passions cannot follow the dictates of his understanding."[50]

Dennis, long a champion of poetic justice, denied Addison's assertions in a letter "To the *Spectator*" (1712), pointing out that Aristotle himself demanded this doctrine when he insisted that a completely good man should not be plunged into adversity. Reason and Nature, too, support poetic justice as the unalterable foundation of tragedy, "for what Tragedy can there be without a Fable? or what Fable without a Moral? or what Moral without poetical Justice?"[51] As for Addison's claim that good and evil happen to all, Dennis replies that we cannot know what pleasures or pain men feel inwardly; moreover, even if this life does not make all things right, God will reward and punish hereafter. The dramatist, whose world ends with the fall of the curtain, must settle his reckonings within the drama. The arguments of the *Spectator* are the sort used by inferior artists to justify their work: "Men first write foolish ridiculous Tragedies, which shock all the Rules of Reason and Philosophy, and then they make foolish extravagant Rules to fit those foolish Plays."[52]

The focus upon reason in Dennis and emotion in Addison suggests why these two critics, who could agree on a moral end for tragedy, could so disagree on the question of poetic justice. Each saw differently what could be learned from tragedy. Dennis felt that we learn virtue by seeing its rewards; Addison (and Steele) believed that the spectacle of tragedy teaches, more obliquely, such things as humility, forbearance, and distrust of worldly success.

On tragedy's secondary aim, to delight, the divergence was even more striking. The question of why tragedy, with its painful subject matter, should cause pleasure in the spectator and indeed be more deeply satisfying than cheerful comedy became a question of greater importance as critics in the eighteenth century turned their focus from form to effect. The Renaissance critics had given some thought to this matter and provided two basic responses to the question. The more common of the two looked to the ethical content of tragedy and found the explanation for tragedy's attractiveness in the cultivation of the moral sense, the discharge of socially unacceptable emotions, the pleasure of seeing error punished. Less common, and often subordinated to the

---

[50]Steele, *Tatler*, 2:233.
[51]Dennis, *Critical Works*, 2:19.
[52]Ibid., 18.

first idea was the second, that we take pleasure in the skill of the artist, in the difficulties overcome and the ability to present convincingly the admirable and the marvelous. Subjects that would cause distress in nature present the greatest challenge to the artist, and thus give the greatest pleasure if he succeeds in making them pleasant by artistic skill.

In the seventeenth century the new psychological theories of such writers as René Descartes and Thomas Hobbes provided another way of dealing with this question by looking more closely at emotions themselves. Descartes considered all emotions as various stimulations of the animal spirits and, as such, pleasurable so long as they were held somewhat in check by the brain. Thus pleasure may come even from sadness and hatred "when these passions are only caused by the stage adventures which we see represented in a theatre, or by other similar means which, not being able to harm us in any way, seem pleasurably to excite our soul in affecting it."[53] This concept clearly influenced such French critics as Rapin and, through them, Dennis. In theory the knowledge that we are in a theatre should suffice to render painful feelings safe and thus pleasurable, and Dennis makes this very point in *The Advancement and Reformation of Poetry*.[54] Nevertheless, the controlling element remains the reason or will, and the depiction of unwarranted suffering or unmerited reward could overcome the distancing effect of artifice and let free the passions to cause us displeasure. Thus poetic justice for Dennis related necessarily to Cartesian pleasure.

Hobbes's attitude toward the relation between the passions and pleasure differed sharply from that of Descartes. Some emotions, said Hobbes, are pleasant. These, men pursue. Others are painful; these, men avoid. Why then are men attracted to the spectacle of tragedy? Although Hobbes does not speak directly of theatrical representation, a key passage in the chapter he devotes to a study of various passions in *De corpore politico* (1650) provides a clear parallel to it. He considers the pleasure men gain from seeing their fellowmen in danger at sea or at war when they themselves are safe: "As there is novelty and remembrance of own security present, which is delight; so is there also pity, which is grief. But the delight is so far predominant, that men usually are content in such a case to be spectators of the misery of their friends."[55] The specific examples Hobbes gives are the same used by Lucretius: "It is sweet, when on the great sea the winds trouble its waters, to behold from land another's deep distress; not that it is a pleasure and

[53]René Descartes, *Philosophical Works*, trans. E. S. Haldane and G. R. T. Ross, 2 vols. (Cambridge, 1911), 1:373.
[54]Dennis, *Critical Works*, 1:264.
[55]Thomas Hobbes, *The Elements of Law*, ed. F. Tönnies (Cambridge, 1928), 35.

delight that any should be afflicted, but because it is sweet to see from what evils you are yourself exempt."[56] This for Addison and Steele was the basis of tragedy's pleasure, though it should be noted that in the mechanistic and self-oriented doctrine of Hobbes there is no suggestion of learning or moral improvement. Addison and Steele, in favoring the Hobbesian view, had to introduce this element.

In the same chapter of Hobbes's work occurs his famous statement on laughter, based upon the same idea of pleasure resulting from a sense of relative security, this time intellectual rather than physical. The passage is quoted with approval by Addison in *The Spectator*, No. 47 (1711): "The passion of laughter is nothing else but a sudden glory arising from sudden conception of some eminency in ourselves, by comparison with the infirmities of others or with our own formerly."[57] Again it should be noted that Addison adds a moral concern to Hobbes's concept; for example, in *The Spectator*, No. 446 (1712), Addison condemns the modern stage for seeking comedy in subjects "improper for ridicule," chief among them marital infidelity, which should arouse "Horror and Commiseration rather than Laughter."[58] These natural feelings are not aroused, however, because modern dramatists attempt to engage our sympathy, even our admiration, for such vicious characters as the elegant debaucher and the clever cheating wife.

Actually, on this point Dennis was more in harmony with Hobbes. It was his belief that the "chief Force of Comedy must consist in exciting Laughter," and that the source of laughter was invariably "lively Ridicule."[59] Addison was clearly uneasy with the potential cruelty and abuse of this flat assertion, and Steele challenged its validity. While traditional neoclassicists like Dennis and D'Aubignac had judged Terence inferior to Plautus precisely because the former was deficient in laughter, the essence of comedy, Steele praised Terence for what had previously been thought a defect. The Romans, he felt, should be honored for producing a work like the *Heautontimorumenos*, which contained "in the Whole not one Passage that could raise a Laugh." "How well disposed must that People be," he continued, "who could be entertained with Satisfaction by so sober and polite Mirth."[60]

"Sober and polite mirth" became for Steele the aim of comedy, more suited than ridicule and laughter to achieving the moral aim he sought. Colley Cibber and others had responded to the critical and public demand at the close of the seventeenth century for a more moral theatre

---

[56] Hobbes, *De rerum natura*, trans. H. A. J. Munro (London, 1914), 41.
[57] Addison, *Spectator*, 1:32.
[58] Ibid., 4:68.
[59] Dennis, "On the *Vis Comica*," (1717), in *Critical Works*, 2:160.
[60] Steele, *Spectator*, 4:280.

by placing the amoral rake of Restoration comedy in a plot leading to his remorse and reform. Steele's *Lying Lover* (1704) followed this pattern, and the preface called it "a Comedy, which might be no improper Entertainment in a Christian Community." Though the hero "makes false Love, gets drunk, and kills his Man," in the final act he "awakes from his Debauch" with "Compunction and Remorse." The emotions aroused by this action, Steele admits, may be "an Injury to the Rules of Comedy; but I am sure they are a Justice to those of Morality."[61] Such plays still were disposed to work by negative example, but an empathy with the major character who was brought to conversion replaced traditional ridicule for the unconverted characters of Jonson or of Molière.

By 1720 Steele had developed another approach; he hoped to demonstrate virtue positively rather than negatively, and to make his leading character exemplary throughout. In *The Theatre* No. 19 (1720) he mentioned a play in progress whose major character "bears unprovok'd Wrongs, denies a Duel, and still appears a Man of Honor and Courage." Such an example should be of great use, he suggests, since young men are already tempted to imitate the fopperies of the stage. "How warmly would they pursue true Gallantries, when accompanied with the Beauties with which a Poet represents them, when he has a Mind to make them amiable?"[62]

This "play in progrese," which became *The Conscious Lovers*, was frequently mentioned during the next two years by Steele and his friends as one that would tower above its competitors and open a completely new direction for English comedy. The new direction was no secret, and Dennis was sufficiently offended by it to argue the counterposition even before the play opened. In No. 65 of *The Spectator*, Steele had singled out George Etherege's comedy for attack as "corrupt and degenerate," a "perfect Contradiction to good Manners, good Sense, and Common Honesty,"[63] the ruling concerns of his reformed comedy. Dennis, in "A Defense of Sir Fopling Flutter" (1722), denied the validity of Steele's experiment. Horace, Aristotle, and Rapin had all called ridicule and laughter the basis of comedy, he pointed out, and what "but corrupt and degenerate Nature" can be the proper subject of ridicule? Comedy should never attempt to provide us with positive examples for imitation, "for all such Patterns are serious Things, and Laughter is the Life and the very Soul of Comedy. 'Tis its proper Business to expose Persons to our View, whose Views we may shun,

---

[61]Steele, *Plays* (Oxford, 1971), 115.
[62]Steele, No. 19, *The Theatre* (Oxford, 1962).
[63]Addison, *Spectator*, 1:280.

and whose Follies we may despise; and by shewing us what is done upon the Comick Stage, to shew us what ought never to be done upon the Stage of the World."[64]

Steele's famous preface to *The Conscious Lovers* (1723) did not argue this point further but simply affirmed his contention that comedy could best achieve its aim by touching its viewers' hearts rather than by stimulating their laughter, by dealing in sympathy and admiration rather than in ridicule. "Anything that has its Foundation in Happiness and Success, must be allow'd to be the Object of Comedy," he argued, "and sure it must be an Improvement of it, to introduce a Joy too exquisite for Laughter, that can have no spring but in Delight."[65] Such a joy, appealing to "Reason and Good Sense," may well produce, instead of laughter, sympathetic tears.

A lively exchange of pamphlets and letters continued this argument for the next several years but added little of substance to the positions already expressed by Dennis and Steele. Probably the only one worth noting is Dennis's own *Remarks on a Play, Call'd, The Conscious Lovers, A Comedy* (1723), in which Dennis attacks in detail both play and preface. In response to Steele's oft-quoted "joy too exquisite for laughter," Dennis replies that joy, like other emotions, may appear in many types of poetry, but only "that kind of Joy which is attended with Laughter, is the Characteristick of Comedy."[66]

In tragedy as in comedy, Steele's critical observations were much in tune with the sentiments of the period though in conflict with tradition. Besides attacking the doctrine of poetic justice, he advanced as early as 1710 the even more unorthodox idea (in No. 172 of *The Tatler*) that the misfortunes of princes and great men affect us only slightly, being remote from our own concerns. "Instead of such high passages, I was thinking it would be of great use (if anybody could hit it) to lay before the world such adventures as befall persons not exalted above the common level."[67] A play with characters of everyday life, all laudable, their misfortunes arising from unguarded virtue rather than calculated vice—clearly these are the elements of the sentimental drama, and a number of tales written by Steele for *The Tatler* needed only to be cast in dramatic form to create that genre. The first moderately successful attempt at doing so was Aaron Hill's *Fatal Extravagance* (1721), the prologue to which takes precisely the position suggested by Steele:

[64]Dennis, *Critical Works*, 2:215.
[65]Steele, *Plays*, 298.
[66]Dennis, *Critical Works*, 2:260.
[67]Steele, *Tatler*, 3:306.

None can their pity for those woes conceal
Which most who hear perhaps too deeply feel.
The ranks of ruined kings of mighty name,
For pompous misery, small compassion claim.
Empires o'erturned, and heroes held in chains,
Alarm the mind but give the heart no pains.
To ills remote from our domestic fears,
We lend our wonder, but withhold our tears.[68]

The great success of *The London Merchant* (1731) by George Lillo (c. 1693–1739) eclipsed all previous attempts at domestic tragedy and established it as the prototype of such drama. It was not widely imitated in England but served as a powerful stimulus to continental writers, led by Denis Diderot and Gotthold Lessing (see Chapters 10 and 11). Lillo's dedication develops more fully the critical position sketched by Steele and Hill. He claims to quote Dryden in calling tragic poetry "the most excellent and most useful kind of writing," then derives the rather surprising corollary that "the more extensively useful the moral of any tragedy is, the more excellent that piece must be of its kind."[69] The end of tragedy becomes solely moral: "the exciting of the passions in order to the correcting such of them as are criminal, either in their nature or through their excess." This being the case, there is no need to confine tragedy to characters of high rank; indeed "moral tales of private life," dealing with situations familiar to their audiences, are more likely to achieve the desired moral instruction.[70]

The next generation of major English writers on tragedy returned from ethical to psychological concerns, asking not how tragedy could best move its audiences to virtue but why painful events that would cause us discomfort in life are pleasurable in the theatre. In considering this question, David Hume (1711–1776) looked back to Descartes, and Edmund Burke (1729–1797) to Hobbes, but each added important modifications to these theories.

In "Of Tragedy" (1757) Hume approvingly cites Jean Dubos, whose *Réflexions critiques sur la poésie et sur la peinture* (1719) had followed Descartes in looking upon any emotional stimulation as potentially pleasurable. Were this our only concern, however, unpleasant events in life could also give us pleasure, says Hume. He adds the important proviso, suggested by Fontenelle, that since stimulation which is too extreme is irritating, we need a controlling element, provided in the theatre by the knowledge that after all we are witnessing a fiction. This knowledge

---

[68]Aaron Hill, *Works*, 4 vols. (London, 1753–54), 1:291.
[69]George Lillo, *The London Merchant* (Lincoln, 1965), 3.
[70]Ibid., 4.

allows the spectator to convert the passions aroused by sorrowful events into equally strong or even stronger feelings of enjoyment on the success of the work of art. Hume condemns the triumph of vice not, like Dennis, for moral reasons, but for aesthetic ones; such a spectacle is likely to arouse emotions too strong for the distancing power of art to manage. Properly constituted, tragedy moves the spectators into a realm of its own, separate from the real world. In so doing, it does not diminish or weaken the painful emotions that would be aroused were the depicted events real but transforms them "by the infusion of a new feeling."[71] Thus Hume arrives at a view almost diametrically opposed to the dedication to verisimilitude preached by Lillo. Instead, he anticipates Kant and the romantics in the concept that art offers its own realm of experience, attained by a disengagement of worldly interest, in which the emotions of everyday life are significantly transformed.

Edmund Burke, addressing this same problem in his *Philosophical Enquiry into the Origin of Our Ideas of the Sublime and Beautiful* (1756), admits that some pleasure can arise from the awareness that tragedy is a fiction but denies that this is a significant part of our emotional reaction. If men enjoy only fictional tragedy, why do they flock to public executions, even in preference to the most perfect dramas? Why do they delight in observing the ruins of earthquakes and conflagrations? Apparently it is because they are fascinated by great destruction, provided they are not themselves threatened. Clearly, this view is close to that of Hobbes, but Burke does not place the source of pleasure in immunity itself; rather he makes the immunity a precondition to taking "delight in the sufferings of others, real or imaginary."[72]

Henry Home, Lord Kames (1696–1782), in his *Elements of Criticism* (1762), follows Hume and Burke in analyzing literature through psychology and the emotions and specifically condemns the French, who base their work instead on the practice of Homer or the authority of Aristotle. In interpreting tragedy, however, he comes to a conclusion strikingly different from that of either Hume or Burke. Despite their differences, both earlier writers saw emotional distancing as essential to the tragic effect, while Kames stresses emotional involvement: tragedy arouses persons "of any degree of sensibility" to sympathy, an emotion that "attracts us to an object in distress, the opposition of self-love notwithstanding."[73] Since this is a manifestation of the better, more altruistic side of our nature, it not only brings us satisfaction, even at

---

[71]David Hume, *Four Dissertations* (London, 1757), 193, 199.
[72]Edmund Burke, *Philosophical Enquiry* (London, 1756), 78.
[73]Henry Home, Lord Kames, *Elements of Criticism*, 2 vols. (London, 1762), 1:448.

the cost of some pain, but makes better persons of us. Thus, by way of the emotions, Kames returns to the moral function of poetry.

Since the beginning of the century, as may be seen in the Dennis-Steele controversy, the authority of neoclassic rules had been challenged by appeals to reason and—as the years passed—to psychology. On these bases Kames attacked the rigidity of French neoclassicists, and so did his contemporary Samuel Johnson (1709–1784), the leading critic of the age. The most concise statement of Johnson's attitude, along with a number of specific observations on the drama, may be found in *The Rambler*, No. 156 (1751). Not all rules handed down to us, says Johnson, have equal claim to our regard: "Some are to be considered as fundamental and indispensable, others only as useful and convenient; some as dictated by reason and necessity, others as enacted by despotick antiquity; some as invincibly supported by their conformity to the order of nature and operations of the intellect; others as formed by accident, or instituted by example, and therefore always liable to dispute and alteration."[74] It is the duty of every writer to distinguish the rules of nature from those of custom, and to hold fast only to the former. Among the rules of custom, Johnson places the unity of time, the five-act structure, the limitation of only three speaking characters on stage. Reason and nature support the unity of action and the single outstanding hero, and would seem to allow the mixing of comic and tragic elements—though Johnson expresses some uneasiness about this latter practice and wonders whether Shakespeare himself might not have achieved greater effects had he not "counter-acted himself" by placing buffoons in his tragedies.[75]

By 1765, however, when Johnson wrote the preface to his edition of Shakespeare's works, this hesitation about mixed genres had been overcome. The only sort of poetry that can "please many and please long," he says, involves "just representations of general nature," at which Shakespeare is unsurpassed.[76] In mixing comic and serious elements, Shakespeare exhibits "the real state of sublunary nature, which partakes of good and evil, joy and sorrow, mingled with endless variety of proportion and innumerable modes of combination." Admittedly, this is contrary to traditional rules, "but there is always an appeal open from criticism to nature." Johnson, who takes a clear Horatian view of the end of poetry—"to instruct by pleasing"—here argues that mixed drama instructs best because it most truly represents the manner in which the world operates.[77] This argument led Johnson to agree with Addison

[74]Samuel Johnson, *Works*, 14 vols. (New Haven, 1958–78), 5:67.
[75]Ibid., 69.
[76]Ibid., 7:61–62.
[77]Ibid., 66–67.

on the concept of poetic justice. In *Lives of the English Poets* (1780), he wrote, "Since wickedness often prospers in real life, the poet is certainly at liberty to give it prosperity on the stage. For if poetry is an imitation of reality, how are its laws broken by exhibiting the world in its true form?"[78]

Nevertheless, there were occasions, at least earlier in his career, when Johnson expressed concern that too severe a flouting of the spectator's natural wish to see evil punished and good rewarded could diminish a play's effectiveness. He could not go so far as Addison, who wrote that Tate's adaptation of *King Lear*—which allowed Cordelia to live on in happiness—destroyed "half the beauty" of the play.[79] Johnson confessed himself so shocked by Cordelia's death that he could not endure reading the ending of the play over again until he undertook to edit it in 1765. Though "a play in which the wicked prosper, and the virtuous miscarry, may doubtless be good, because it is a just representation of the common events of life," the love of all reasonable beings for justice will still surely create a greater pleasure for them if the ends of justice are observed, "other excellencies" being equal.[80]

Johnson generally approved of the trend toward developing tragedies from middle-class situations, again on the basis that they are true to reality: "What is nearest us touches us most," he says in a letter of 1770. "The passions rise higher at domestic than at imperial tragedies."[81] The sentimental comedy, however, found no support in Johnson's writings. He constantly held up mirth as essential to comedy and praised Goldsmith's *She Stoops to Conquer* as a work which answered "the great end of comedy—making an audience merry."[82]

In fact, in the years just after 1750, sentimental drama for a time almost disappeared. Authors such as Samuel Foote, Arthur Murphy, and George Coleman returned to the traditional aim of comedy, to expose the "follies and absurdities of men," as Foote remarked in his preface to *Taste* (1751).[83] But a new generation of sentimental dramatists, dominated by Richard Cumberland (1732–1811), appeared in the 1760s, and Cumberland's view of comedy, as stated in his *Memoirs* (1806), is clearly much closer to Steele than to Johnson or Foote. He castigates William Congreve and George Farquhar for making vice amusing and for overlooking any wickedness if committed with wit. Instead, said Cumberland, it was the duty of the dramatist "to reserve

[78]Johnson, *Lives of the English Poets*, 2 vols. (London, 1905), 2:135.
[79]Addison, No. 40, *Spectator*, 1:170.
[80]Johnson, *Works*, 7:704.
[81]Johnson, *Letters*, 2 vols. (New York, 1892), 1:162.
[82]James Boswell, *Life of Johnson*, 6 vols. (Oxford, 1934–50), 2:233.
[83]Samuel Foote, *Works*, 2 vols. (London, 1799), 1:iii.

his brightest coloring for the best characters, to give no false attractions to vice and immorality, but to endeavor, as far as is consistent with that contrast, which is the very essence of his art, to turn the fairer side of human nature to the public."[84] Accordingly, he frequently sought heroes for his dramas among those who had in the past been traditional subjects of ridicule—the Scotsman, the Irishman, the Colonial, and the Jew.

Unquestionably, the best known document in the debate over the primacy of sentiment or mirth in comedy, which continued throughout the eighteenth century, is the *Essay on the Theatre* (1773) by Oliver Goldsmith (1728–1774). Indeed, the fame of this short essay, reinforced by the appearance soon after of Goldsmith's own *She Stoops to Conquer* and the plays of Richard Brinsley Sheridan, the most durable English plays of the century, has considerably distorted our view of what was actually happening in the dramatic theory and practice of this period. The rhetoric of Goldsmith's essay, which—as its subtitle explained—compared "laughing and sentimental comedy," and the achievement of the subsequent plays have created an impression that sentimentalism reigned virtually unchallenged before Goldsmith, and that it was dealt a mortal blow by Goldsmith and Sheridan. Neither of these common assumptions is correct. The tradition of mirthful comedy continued through the century and quite dominated the stage in the generation of Foote and Murphy. Johnson's scattered comments on comedy do not give sentimental comedy even passing mention. Neither Goldsmith's own plays nor those of Sheridan are free of sentimental elements, despite the attention to laughter. And finally, the popularity of sentimental comedy, despite the success of these dramatists, continued unabated through the closing years of the century.

Goldsmith's essay should therefore properly be regarded not as a watershed in English dramatic taste but rather as a statement, like those of Steele before *The Conscious Lovers*, preparing the public for a striking new play by suggesting it would open a new era. Goldsmith returns to the traditional view that "Comedy should excite our laughter by ridiculously exhibiting the Follies of the Lower Part of Mankind,"[85] and condemns as a defect that tendency toward sentimentality in Terence which was praised by Steele. Sentiment is not only less amusing but less instructive than laughter, since it causes us to sympathize with the possessors of foibles and faults. Its apparent popularity comes only from the ease with which sentimental comedy can be written, says

---

[84]Richard Cumberland, *Memoirs* (London, 1806), 141.
[85]Oliver Goldsmith, *Collected Works*, 5 vols. (Oxford, 1966), 3:210.

Goldsmith, and if audiences demand something better, it will soon disappear.

The eighteenth-century critics from Dennis to Goldsmith who appealed to Aristotle as authority almost invariably read him in the light of French interpretation. This was hardly surprising, since the standard English translation from 1705 until 1775 was in fact done not from the original but from the French version of Dacier. An anonymous translation of 1775 gave a more faithful rendition of some passages, but not until 1788, with the translation by Henry James Pye (1745–1813), did England have an Aristotle largely free of the French. The translation by Thomas Twining (1735–1804) the following year soon replaced Pye's; it was even more accurate and long remained the standard English version. The commentaries of Pye and Twining are most significant, therefore, in their independence of French influence, but Twining goes further, rejecting the Horatian coloring that had so long modified Aristotle's statement of the purpose of poetry. Nowhere, he says, does Aristotle support "an idea which rational criticism has now pretty well exploded—that utility and instruction are the end of poetry."[86]

Pye, despite his faithfulness to Aristotle, risks several significant disagreements with him, most notably on the low position accorded by the Greek philosopher to spectacle. Though Pye admits that theatre is inferior to painting in general visual effect, he argues that the power of acting raises drama above every other art. He is especially struck by the actors in comedy and domestic tragedy, where representation appears to merge with reality. "I rise from seeing such tragedies as George Barnwell, The Fatal Curiosity, and The Gamester, with nearly the same sensation as if I had been actually present at scenes of the same kind in real life."[87] Even tragedy, somewhat more removed from everyday life, benefits from the modern achievements of acting and scenery, which together make it seem more real than anything witnessed by the Greeks. Pye goes so far as to speculate that had Aristotle seen Garrick in Lear or Siddons in Isabella, he might well have placed much more importance on the presentation of the drama.

This apotheosis of the actor in the midst of a commentary on Aristotle is a striking illustration of how the art of acting had risen in critical acclaim during the eighteenth century. As Pye suggests, the brilliance of David Garrick (1717–1779) and his contemporaries surely had much to do with this, and it is not entirely coincidental that the first writings on the general theory and practice of this art (instead of the descriptive

---

[86]Thomas Twining, *Aristotle's Treatise on Poetry* (London, 1789), 561.

[87]Henry James Pye, *A Commentary Illustrating the Poetics of Aristotle* (London, 1792), 116–17.

anecdotes that had always been popular) appeared during Garrick's career. Garrick himself penned one of the first, *A Short Treatise on Acting*, in 1744. He defines acting as "an entertainment of the stage, which by calling in the aid and assistance of articulation, corporeal motion, and ocular expression, imitates, assumes or puts on the various mental and bodily emotions arising from the various humours, virtues, and vices, incident to human nature."[88] Human nature, the raw material of the actor, must be closely observed but never simply imitated, since every character will express the passions in a different manner. His observations must be "digested" in the actor's mind, "cherished by the genial warmth of his conception," translated by his judgment, raised to perfection, and made his own.

The actor's manner of expressing the passions occupied the subsequent *Essay on the Art of Acting* (1746) by Aaron Hill and *Treatise on the Passions* (1747) by Samuel Foote. Hill attempts to reduce acting to a programmatic, almost mechanistic craft. He considers all dramatic passion essentially reducible to ten emotions: joy, grief, fear, anger, pity, scorn, hatred, jealousy, wonder, and love. He defines each of these, illustrates it by examples from the drama, and analyzes it in terms of physical manifestations. Nevertheless, he specifically warns actors against attempting to imitate passions mechanically; first and always, the imagination must create the passion in the mind as strongly as it would in nature. This in turn will naturally impress the form of the passion first upon the muscles of the face, then upon the muscles of the body, and thereby upon the sound of the voice and disposition of the gestures. His delineation of the end results of this process apparently is designed only as a check so that the actor can be sure he has felt the emotion deeply and properly.

The announced aim of Foote's essay—"to trace the Rise and Progress of the Passions, together with the Effects on the Organs of our Bodies"—seems similar, but audiences rather than actors are the potential readers; the essay would presumably provide examples whereby they might judge the accuracy of stage imitations.[89] In fact, Foote avoids the rigidity of Hill's approach. After general observations on the passions, he echoes Garrick's comment that their effects are quite different in different men, and generally mixed and complicated.

A much more extensive treatise on the art of acting by Pierre Rémond de Sainte-Albine was translated into English, with English examples by John Hill, as *The Actor* in 1750. Its emphasis on the emotionality of the actor—particularly upon the necessity of an actor's being naturally en-

---

[88]David Garrick, *An Essay on Acting* (London, 1744), 2.
[89]Foote, *A Treatise on the Passions* (London, 1747), 3, 8.

dowed with the proper emotional cast for the character he plays—
stimulated reactions from theorists who felt that the technical and rational side of the actor's art was being forgotten in the stress upon the
utilization of the passions. The most famous of these was the *Paradoxe
sur le comédien* of Diderot, which is discussed in a later chapter, but in
England too there was some resistance to the emotional emphasis of
these early essays and some attempts, as the century progressed, to
discover a middle ground. Thus James Boswell (1740–1795), in an essay
"On the Profession of a Player" (1770), speaks of a "double feeling" in
the actor as the source of the "mysterious power by which a player
really is the character he represents." The feelings and passions of the
character being portrayed, Boswell suggests, "must take full possession
as it were of the antechamber of his mind, while his own character
remains in the innermost recess."[90]

[90]Boswell, "On the Profession of a Player," *London Magazine*, Sept. 1770, 469–70.

10

Eighteenth-Century France

THE EARLY EIGHTEENTH-CENTURY French theatre in large part echoed the concerns and approaches of the late seventeenth century, but with markedly reduced power. The occasional observations on dramatic theory during the century's first decade, primarily from practicing dramatists, show these authors as unwilling to depart significantly in their thinking from previous theorists as from the models of Molière and Racine. Tragedy is generally considered, despite the veneration of Molière, as innately superior to comedy, although Alain-René Le Sage (1667–1748) in his *Le diable boiteux* (1707) concludes a comic quarrel between tragic and comic dramatists with the observation that creating the two sorts of drama requires a different genius but equal skill.[1] In a critique on his own best play, *Turcaret* (1709), Le Sage revives the characters of the devil and Don Cléofas from *Le diable boiteux* to comment on the play before and after its presentation. The devil complains that the characters are not sympathetic enough, though he admits that the comedy does serve the required end of "making vice hateful." Then a Spanish cavalier complains that the play has insufficient plot, but Don Cléofas explains that the French, unlike the Spanish, elevate the study of character over complex action.[2]

Prosper Jolyot de Crébillon (1674–1762), the leading tragic author as the century began, held closely to the neoclassic creed in both plays and prefaces. In the preface to *Atrée et Thyeste* (1707), he boasts of what care he took to soften the cruel details of the original drama, so as to offend neither the "delicacy" of his audiences nor the *bienséances*. In

[1]Alain-René Le Sage, *Oeuvres*, 12 vols. (Paris, 1828), 1:220.
[2]Ibid., 2:508–10.

the preface to *Electre* (1708), he admits creating an intrigue somewhat more complex than in the original but pleaded that this fault be excused, since it made the play more interesting for a modern public. Even so, in the preface to his collected works (1750), he apologizes for the offenses to the rules occasionally found in his plays, however much these pleased the public. It is a dangerous error, he says, "to pretend that a flaw which produces great beauties should not be considered a flaw."[3]

The first major poetics of the new century was provided by the philosopher François de Fénelon (1651–1715) in his *Lettre écrite à l'Académie française sur l'éloquence, la poésie, l'histoire, etc.* (1714), written as a guide to the work of the Académie and at the request of its president. One section is devoted to tragedy and another to comedy, both excellent summaries of neoclassical critical opinion of this period, colored by a strong moral concern. Tragedy should show "great events" and arouse "strong passions," but never in such a way as to corrupt its audience. Thus it should not portray corrupted passions, even to cure them, nor should it depict profane love—a subject shunned by the ancients though not, unfortunately, by Racine. The language of tragedy should be suited to character and situation; it may, when the nature of things demands it, be simple and unadorned. Comedy, dealing with private life, has a generally lower tone, though circumstances may occasionally elevate it. Fénelon praises Molière even above Terence, though the French author is taken to task for occasional unpolished language, exaggerated characters, and ridicule of virtue, which Fénelon attributes to the unfortunate influence of the older Italian comedy.[4]

A much more wide-ranging discussion of theatrical matters may be found in the *Réflexions critiques sur la poésie et sur la peinture* (1719) by Jean Dubos (1670–1742). Dubos, following the reasoning of Descartes, views the function of art as a stimulus to the emotions, and tragedy as superior to comedy because it moves more deeply and involves the grand emotions, pity and terror, rather than the lesser emotions of amusement and scorn. To feel these emotions, the spectator must identify to some extent with the hero, who must therefore never be an evil man but rather someone estimable who is excessively punished for his errors. A certain distance is also critical to prevent these powerful emotions from arousing pain. Thus tragedies should be set in remote times and places and involve characters somewhat apart from us. This not only allows the spectator to experience tragic emotions in a safe manner but contributes to another emotion central to the genre—

---

[3]Prosper Jolyot de Crébillon, *Oeuvres*, 2 vols., (Paris, 1818), 1:45.
[4]François de Fénelon, *Oeuvres*, 10 vols. (Paris, 1822), 1:178–91.

admiration. "No man can be admirable," says Dubos, "if he is not seen from a certain distance."[5] The usual quotation from Lucretius is cited to support emotional distancing, and Dubos expands upon it to explain the delight of the Romans in gladiatorial contests.

From a purely didactic point of view, he goes on to say, this distancing makes tragedy less effective than comedy. Comedy still requires some distance, for spectators will be hurt rather than reformed if the ridicule of social errors cuts them too deeply. As a rule, however, comedy can be effective only when it is close to the situations it seeks to improve, while the necessary remoteness of the characters and events of tragedy make the lessons of that genre vague and imperfect.[6]

Dubos is also a significant pioneer in the first extended considerations of the art of acting, devoting eight chapters to declamation, movement, and gesture. With extensive quotations from classic authors, he reconstructs a classic theatre—the actors highly trained in voice and movement, their performance controlled by musical notation. In striking anticipation of Wagner, Dubos argues for a similar subordination of the actor to music in the modern theatre, to guarantee that even mediocre actors will perform passably and to unify the work of art: "The declamation of a play which has been composed from beginning to end by a single person must be better conducted and better organized than a declamation where each actor delivers his role according to his own fancy."[7] Dubos recognizes that this would place some restraint on superior actors but thinks the balance of the whole is more important. Emotional truth need not be compromised, since the composer must always leave a certain freedom in interpretation of accents, sighs, inflections, and so on to the individual performer, as opera demonstrates. Moreover, Quintilian reports that Roman actors, despite the control of their declamation by the poet, often left the stage in tears after touching scenes.

The traditional rules of tragedy, given little attention by Dubos, were of great concern to Antoine Houdar de La Motte (1672–1731), who penned faithful imitations of Racine accompanied by bold prefaces announcing a challenge to the rules—which the works never mounted. Each of his tragedies—*Les Machabées* (1721), *Romulus* (1722), *Inès de Castro* (1723), and *Oedipe* (1726)—was printed with a *Discours sur la tragédie*. In these La Motte advances pleasure, to be achieved by the arousal of emotion, as the dominant end of drama. He disclaims any attempt to "enlighten the soul about vice or virtue by painting them in

[5]Jean Dubos, *Réflexions critiques*, 3 vols., (Paris, 1733), 1:148.
[6]Ibid., 13–17.
[7]Ibid., 3:311.

the true colors," but seeks only "to stir the passions by mixing them together."[8] The rules, invented only to insure pleasure, should never be invoked against a work which pleases without them, and the unities of time and place should never be made barriers to pleasure. Rigidly observed, they do not aid verisimilitude, as has been traditionally claimed, but in fact hinder it: "It is not natural for all parts of an action to occur in the same apartment or the same place," he observes, and "a length of time suitable and proportionate to the nature of the subjects" is surely to be preferred to "a precipitation of events which has no air of truth."[9]

La Motte is more tolerant of unity of action, but he would broaden its scope to create a new unity, the unity of interest, which is his most original—though not his clearest—contribution to French dramatic theory. While unity of action focuses our attention upon a single problem or question, it does not guarantee that we will keep the various major characters of the play constantly in mind as our attention shifts from one aspect of the problem to another. Unity of interest keeps all the major characters at least emotionally present. For example, though *Le Cid* is weak in unity of action, it possesses unity of interest, our sympathy being equally aroused by Rodrigue and Chimène as they undergo parallel suffering. In the name of unity of interest, La Motte could and did justify departures even from the traditional idea of unity of action.

La Motte's prefaces stimulated a rebuttal from Voltaire (1694–1778), the first of his lifelong literary debates. In the preface to the 1730 edition of his first play, *Oedipe*, Voltaire observed that since the principles of all arts are drawn from nature and reason, it seemed as futile for the playwright to speak of rules in a preface to a tragedy as for a painter to prepare the public by dissertations on his canvases or for a musician to attempt to demonstrate that his music ought to please. Nevertheless, the attempts by La Motte to overthrow the "good and necessary" rules of the great masters required a response. Unity of interest, when effective, is the same as unity of action, and this unity demands the others, since changes of location or extended periods of time necessarily will involve several actions. La Motte had cited opera as a genre that successfully ignores these restrictions; Voltaire called that argument an attempt "to reform a regular government by the example of anarchy," opera being "a bizarre and magnificent spectacle which satisfies the ears and eyes rather than the mind."[10]

Further, Voltaire was offended by La Motte's observations on lan-

---

[8]Antoine Houdar de La Motte, *Oeuvres*, 10 vols. (Paris, 1753–54), 4:182.
[9]Ibid., 38, 40.
[10]Voltaire, *Oeuvres*, 52 vols. (Paris, 1877–85), 2:52.

guage. In the preface to *Oedipe*, La Motte, had argued for the use of prose in tragedy, on the grounds of greater verisimilitude and greater freedom for the poet (but cited the public's conservatism and the actors' lack of training in prose delivery as his reasons for not making this attempt himself).[11] But the experience of all peoples of the earth, Voltaire argued, had demonstrated that prose could not attain the power of poetry. True, some Italian and English poets rejected rhyme in certain tragedies, but only because they could employ patterns of vowel sounds and repeating syllabic stress that the French language, for all its clarity and elegance, did not possess.

La Motte's reply, the *Suite des réflexions sur la tragédie* (1730) expressed only token resistance to Voltaire. He observed that though a single action could in theory occupy several locations and more than one day, this had never happened in his own plays, and indeed he considered their strict observance of the unities a strength. He admitted the necessity of unity of action, though he still argued that interest could be separated from it. Prose he now defended primarily on the grounds of "tolerance for those who have great talent for tragedy but not for versification," and he suggested that if experiments with prose tragedy proved unsuccessful, the idea be abandoned.[12]

Once having vanquished La Motte, Voltaire took a distinctly less rigid position in regard to traditional French dramatic practice. Both the play *Brutus* (1731) and its preface, the *Discours sur la tragédie*, implicitly and explicitly challenged certain assumptions of the French theatre. The influence of Voltaire's two years in England (1726–1728) was clear from his opening praise of the freedom enjoyed by English poetry. The French author is "a slave to rhyme," sometimes forced to consume four lines to express what an Englishman can say in one: "The Englishman says whatever he wishes; the Frenchman whatever he can." Still, Voltaire maintains that rhyme is necessary in France, repeating his argument that the less flexible language demands it and interestingly picking up one of La Motte's arguments, that French ears are accustomed to it.

Voltaire also attempts to balance the relative strengths and weaknesses of French and English drama. Of all English tragedies, only Addison's *Cato* is "well written from beginning to end"; the rest lack "the purity, the regular conduct, the proprieties of art and style, the elegance, all the subtleties of art" of the French.[13] Yet the delicacy of French poets and audiences can lead to a certain dryness and lack of

---

[11] La Motte, *Oeuvres*, 4:390–91.
[12] Ibid., 439–40.
[13] Voltaire, *Oeuvres*, 2:312, 314.

action. English plays, though often monstrous, have vigor and admirable scenes. They demonstrate that artists of genius may break effectively with certain traditional practices—such as limiting the number of speaking actors to three or banning all brutal action—provided that the "fundamental laws of the theatre," such as the three unities, are observed.

Finally, Voltaire defends the introduction of a love element in *Brutus*, a practice frowned upon by strict neoclassicists. Since all theatre, tragic or comic, is "the living picture of human passions," love may be shown in tragedy if it is essential to the central action, is a truly tragic passion, and conforms to the moral demands of the genre by "either leading to sufferings and crimes, to demonstrate how dangerous it is, or giving way to virtue, to show that it is not invincible."[14]

There are many distinct echoes of *Othello* in Voltaire's *Zaïre* (1732), but the play remains quite faithful to traditional French practice, as do the two *Epîtres dédicatoires* (1733 and 1736), even though these contain warm praise for the English and are addressed, in defiance of tradition, to an English merchant. The only important literary debt to the English that Voltaire acknowledges in the *Epîtres* is the "bold step" of placing on stage historical figures—"kings and ancient families of the realm"[15]— a step he realized more fully in *Adelaïde du Guesclin* (1734). Otherwise Voltaire's attitude seems best expressed by his parallel between English science, especially the work of Newton, and French dramaturgy: "You should submit to the rules of our theatre, as we should embrace your philosophy. We have made experiments on the human heart as valid as yours in physics."[16]

Two essays in the *Lettres philosophiques* (1734), one on tragedy (XVIII) and one on comedy (XIX), provide a fuller development of these ideas. In the former Voltaire again praises Addison for writing the first "reasonable" English tragedy but finds this work nevertheless cold and lifeless; English writers have learned to respect French rules, but not how to bring them alive. Thus the "brilliant monsters" of Shakespeare are still "a thousand times more pleasing than the informed work of the moderns."[17] Shakespeare is both the glory and the curse of the English theatre. "A genius full of force and fecundity, nature and the sublime, without the slightest trace of good taste or the least knowledge of the rules," he created works so powerful that even his faults have been respected and imitated. Thus later English dramatists used material as grotesque as the strangling of Desdemona, the jesting grave-

[14]Ibid., 324.
[15]Ibid., 542.
[16]Ibid., 554.
[17]Ibid., 22:456.

diggers in *Hamlet*, or the puns of the aristocrats in *Julius Caesar*,[18] but these authors achieved at best brilliant isolated passages amid a barbarous disregard of propriety, order, and verisimilitude.

Voltaire's opinion of English comedy, especially that of Congreve, is much more favorable. He finds it rigorously true to the rules, full of subtle characters and wit, and commendably natural, though he sees an unfortunate tendency in authors other than Congreve to allow natural speech to slip from frankness into obscenity. The end of comedy, as of tragedy, is for Voltaire always moral and didactic.

The moral lessons to be taught were, of course, those of the Enlightenment—civilization, benevolent royalism, and enlightened religion. Man's natural desire for the good led to a desire for what the English called poetic justice, described (though not with that term) in the *Dissertation sur la tragédie* that prefaced *Sémiramis* (1748): "All men have a deeply seated sense of justice" and thus "naturally expect that heaven will avenge the innocent and in all times and all countries witness with pleasure a supreme being punishing the crimes of those beyond the reach of mortal judgment."[19] In setting forth the moral purpose of theatre, Voltaire essentially followed the doctrines of Dacier and Rapin: "True tragedy is the school of virtue, and the only difference between purified theatre and books of morality is that instruction in the theatre is through action which engages the interest and is embellished by the charms of an art originally invented only to instruct the earth and bless heaven."[20]

Taken as a whole, Voltaire's dramatic theory, despite his frequent claims of innovation, remains strongly conservative. A somewhat greater interest in visual spectacle (especially the exotic), though not to the extent of challenging unity of place; a somewhat greater freedom in expression, though not enough to erode traditional French poetic form; a somewhat greater freedom in subject matter, allowing figures from French history to join Greeks and Romans as possible subjects; and a new emphasis on the emotional, especially the sentimental—these essentially exhaust his innovations.

Voltaire did move in the major direction of the period's innovation, which led through the *comédie larmoyante* (tearful comedy) to the *drame bourgeois* (middle-class drama), but other writers preceded him along this path, in both theory and practice. The first major theoretical justification of the *comédie larmoyante* was the preface to *Le glorieux* (1732) by Nericault Destouches (1680–1754). However amusing and enter-

[18]Ibid., 745–50.
[19]Ibid., 4:504.
[20]Ibid., 505.

taining a comedy might be, Destouches judged it "an imperfect and even dangerous work" if it did not seek "to correct manners, to expose the ridiculous, to condemn vice, and to put virtue into such a favorable light as to attract the esteem and veneration of the public."[21] Thus comedy was charged with essentially the same moral obligation as Voltaire and others applied to tragedy. In emotional tone, if not yet in language or subject matter, the two genres began to converge. Destouches, disturbed by this, argued in his preface to *L'amour usé* (1742) against the introduction of the "tears of Melpomene" into the domain of laughter.[22] But the sentimental and moralistic taste of the time found virtuous tears congenial, and other dramatists were far less hesitant than he to turn comedy away from laughter and make it a showcase for virtuous action.

Chief among these was Pierre Nivelle de La Chaussée (1691–1754), whose first play, *La fausse antipathie* (1733), contained distinct though cautiously developed sentimental elements. The prologue shows the Genius of the Comédie paralyzed by the conflicting demands of a diverse public. Thalia comes to her rescue with La Chaussée's new play, though the goddess expresses some misgivings about it: she would have preferred "a better made fable, a little more of the comic, a clearer plot."[23] The author carried this self-deprecation further in his *Critique de la fausse antipathie* (1734), written, like the *Critique* of Molière, in response to his detractors, but unlike that of Molière, freely admitting the charges. The characters Imagination and Denouement denounce the work, Melpomene and Thalia each insist it belongs to the other, and Momus—asked to arbitrate—is forced to give it a new name, *épi-tragi-comique*.

La Chaussée could afford such self-deprecation. A few conservative critics continued to complain of his loose plots and substitution of emotionality for laughter, but when *La fausse antipathie* was followed by the even more successful *Préjugé à la mode* (1735), La Chaussée's fame was assured. The following year he was admitted to the Académie, and the reception speech by the Archbishop of Sens warmly praised the dramatist's new approach: "Continue, Monsieur, to furnish our youth with what I will not call spectacles, but useful lessons, which, while pleasing their curiosity will recall them to virtue, to justice, to the sentiments of honor and right that Nature has engraved on the hearts of all men."[24]

The success of La Chaussée apparently inspired Voltaire to try his hand at this new style of comedy, and in the preface to *L'enfant prodigue* (1736) he expressed a tolerance for experimentation in comedy much

[21]Nericault Destouches, *Oeuvres*, 6 vols. (Paris, 1811), 2:308.
[22]Ibid., 5:284.
[23]Pierre Nivelle de La Chaussée, *Oeuvres*, 5 vols. (Paris, 1762), 1:26.
[24]Ibid., 5:191.

greater than he showed in the case of tragedy: "There are many fine pieces in which gaiety reigns, others totally serious, others mixed, others with such sadness as to provoke tears. No type should be excluded, and if I am asked which is the best, I should answer 'The one which is done the best.' "[25] A comedy should not be condemned for failing to produce laughter but only for failing to interest its audience, and no play should be condemned for being of a new type, but only for not representing well the values of that type. This argument would be widely employed, of course, by the romantics.

There is also a hint of romantic theory in the preface to *Nanine* (1749), where Voltaire argues for a mixture of sentimental and comic elements in a single play, since they are so mixed in real life. At this point, Voltaire apparently feels that traditional comic responses must remain dominant; he insists that comedy should move the passions only if it subsequently "moves honest men to laughter," and that if it arouses only tears, it becomes "a most vicious and disagreeable genre."[26] Even so, the preface to *L'Ecossaise* (1760) comes close to echoing Steele's sentimental "joy too exquisite for laughter" in claiming that the honest man will smile at this play "with the smile of the soul," which is "preferable to the laughter of the mouth." Voltaire seems more concerned with avoiding "characters who study to be pathetic" than with pathos itself, but in any case the emotional questions are, as always, subordinated to ethical ones: "What is much more important, is that this comedy possesses an excellent morality ... while losing nothing of what can please honest men of the world."[27]

The great intellectual summation of the age, Diderot's *Encyclopédie*, began to appear in 1751. Its editor and chief architect, Denis Diderot (1713–1784), was also the major author of this great work, but despite his interest in the theatre, he entrusted the major articles on drama primarily to Jean François Marmontel (1723–1799), a protégé of Voltaire whose liberal ideas and great success at the Comédie Française with *Denys le Tyran* (1748) and *Aristomène* (1749), just as the *Encyclopédie* was being launched, made him a logical choice for the task.

The third volume of the *Encyclopédie*, appearing in 1753, contained Marmontel's observations on comedy. Like Voltaire, Marmontel stresses the morality of the drama: the function of comedy is to encourage us to laugh at the flaws of others like ourselves and thus to learn to avoid these flaws. "It has been found easier and more certain to employ human malice to correct the other vices of humanity, rather as one uses dia-

[25]Voltaire, *Oeuvres*, 3:443.
[26]Ibid., 5:10.
[27]Ibid., 411.

mond points to polish the diamond itself."[28] Comedy may be of three types, depending on its object. If it seeks to render vice odious, it becomes comedy of character; if it shows men as the playthings of events, it is comedy of situation; if it seeks to make virtue loved, it is comedy of sentiment. Marmontel considers the first the best, but all three are valuable, and the sentimental comedy—calling forth tears instead of laughter—should not be scorned as a modern innovation, since Terence used it.

The subsequent entry on *"Comédien"* was written by the Abbé Mallet, who had contributed the entry on *"Acteur"* in the first volume. Both mentioned the contrast between the official English honor of actors and French scorn for them, but without calling the English attitude superior, as Voltaire memorably did. It was Diderot who supplied this conclusion in observations of his own appended to the *"Comédien"* entry. Since the goal of the theatre is "to stimulate virtue, inspire a horror of vice and expose folly," the actors charged with this task, he argued, are performing a vital role in society and deserve the greatest respect and encouragement.

Marmontel's *"Décoration"* in the next volume (1754) condemned contemporary practice in both scenery and costume for its indifference to verisimilitude. Instead of relying upon traditional elegant tragic dress and ornate wigs, he advised, actors should try to suit costume to character and situation. In this concern Marmontel echoed Voltaire but drew a conclusion unacceptable to Voltaire, that unity of place should be disregarded. Marmontel condemns the neutral stage that this unity had encouraged in France as an artistic hindrance: "The lack of decoration leads to the impossibility of scene changes, and this confines authors to the most rigorous unity of place; an irritating rule which forbids to them many beautiful subjects."[29]

In the seventh volume of the *Encyclopédie* (1757) appeared an article on the city of Geneva, written by d'Alembert (1717–1783), which proved to be one of the most controversial entries in this highly controversial work. In addition to observations on the city's religious beliefs by no means in harmony with those held by most of the city fathers, there was a passage (probably suggested by Voltaire) arguing that Geneva was mistaken in outlawing theatre to protect its youth. If actors were often immoral, said d'Alembert, it was society's fault for ostracizing them in the first place. Let Geneva accept actors and plays, and regulate them wisely, and it could establish a school of virtue for all of Europe.

Jean-Jacques Rousseau (1712–1778), then living in Geneva and dis-

---

[28]Denis Diderot et al., *Encyclopédie*, 36 vols. (Lausanne, 1779–82), 8:552.
[29]Ibid., 10:449.

turbed by the growing influence of Voltaire and of worldly Parisian ideas in this (in Rousseau's opinion) still unspoiled community, was spurred to reply to this proposal. His first major published work, the *Lettre à M. d'Alembert* (1758), cast Rousseau in the role of a modern-day Plato defending a Calvinist republic from corruption. Indeed, in an appended essay, *De l'imitation théâtrale*, Rousseau appeals to Plato directly, expanding upon comments drawn from the second book of the *Laws* and the tenth of the *Republic*.

The *Lettre* is itself a lengthy essay, exploring so wide a range of Rousseau's concerns that it has been called his own encyclopedia. Nevertheless, the theatre serves as a unifying theme, especially in respect to its effect upon audiences. One cannot speak of public amusements as good or bad in themselves, says Rousseau, since man is so modified by religion, government, laws, customs, predispositions, and climate that one cannot ask what is good for men in general but only "what is good in any particular time and country."[30] For his Geneva, at least, Rousseau sees no profit in theatre, and much potential harm. He denies instruction as its major aim; rather, its exists primarily to amuse and must thus conform to and flatter public opinion. It "reinforces the national character, augments natural inclinations, and gives new energy to all the passions." At best then, theatre might encourage those already virtuous, but it would similarly encourage those inclined to vice. The doctrine of catharsis Rousseau denies entirely, insisting that the arousal of emotions can in no way remove emotions. "The only instrument which can purge them is reason, and I have already said that reason has no effect in the theatre."[31] Indeed, if we wish to learn to love virtue and to hate vice, the best teachers are reason and nature. Theatre is not needed to teach this, even were it effective in doing so.

It may be that theatre, by appealing to man's natural benevolence, calls up a shadow of goodness, but it remains a shadow, since the conventions of drama inevitably remove the experience there from application to everyday life. Even Molière, whom Rousseau praises as the best of comic writers, seeks primarily "to ridicule goodness and simplicity and to engage our interest on behalf of characters who employ ruses and lies."[32] (A major example of a virtuous character so ridiculed is Alceste in *Le misanthrope*, with whom Rousseau clearly feels deep sympathy.) And both tragedy and comedy have become steadily more decadent since Molière, chiefly by the development of love interests, which Rousseau, echoing Pascal,[33] considers to have the most bale-

[30]Jean-Jacques Rousseau, *Oeuvres*, 25 vols. (Paris, 1823–26), 2:21.
[31]Ibid., 24–26.
[32]Ibid., 45.
[33]Blaise Pascal, ch. 24,40, *Pensées, édition variorum* (Paris, n.d.), 383.

ful influence on morality. If love is presented effectively, the play seduces us from the higher passions of virtue and duty; if ineffectively, the play is a bad one. Moreover, placing an emphasis on love forces the drama to favor youth over age and sentiment (the concern of women) over virtue (the concern of men)—both inversions of natural order.

Turning from the plays themselves to the stage and the players, Rousseau develops in his own manner many of the traditional arguments of Christian moralists, beginning with examples from the early church fathers. The actor, by practicing the art of lying and of putting on false appearances, is inevitably corrupted, and women, by denying their natural modesty as well, are particularly so. If there is no danger of corruption, asks Rousseau, why does d'Alembert suggest that wise regulation be used? Geneva already has the only safe regulation: a total ban on players. Were the ban relaxed, lesser regulation would be difficult to pass or enforce. The social life of the city, now consisting of simple, innocent, virtuous pleasures among close friends and family, would be disrupted by so attractive an entertainment.

If any theatre is to be introduced into Geneva, it should be theatre suited to a small republic still close to nature and natural virtue—open-air spectacles with dancing, gymnastics, and innocent celebration by the entire population. In these final suggestions, the leaders of the French Revolution found the inspiration for their great festivals. A century later, Rolland and others revived again in France this Rousseauean ideal of a populist communal theatre totally opposed to the major tradition, and it flourished anew in the Russian Proletcult and in populist theatre theories of the mid-twentieth century.

Rousseau's attack could hardly have come at a more unfavorable time for Diderot. The enemies of the free thought expressed in the *Encyclopédie* were gaining in power and had already used the ill-starred Geneva article to raise questions about censorship. The defection of Rousseau, a former contributor to Diderot's project, was a new and serious blow. D'Alembert withdrew soon after, and early in 1759 the *Encyclopédie* was suppressed by royal decree.

During this turbulent period Diderot began to develop a new interest: playwriting. He produced two works of striking originality with highly significant accompanying essays, *Le fils naturel* (1757), and *Le père de famille* (1758), which suggest reforms in theatre vastly more revolutionary than any of those trumpeted by Voltaire. Diderot considered his reforms, once articulated, to be so self-evident as to win immediate acceptance, but the antagonism aroused by the *Encyclopédie* controversy and Rousseau's essay, made this an idle dream. The ultimate impact of his ideas was enormous, but the immediate effect on the theatre and drama of his own time proved slight.

The germ of Diderot's subsequent dramatic theories may be found in his early, rather salacious novel, *Les bijoux indiscrets* (1748), which devoted two chapters (34 and 35) to observations on the theatre. Here pleasure is given preference over rules, and the source of pleasure is said to lie in the illusion of reality. Despite one's awareness of always being in a theatre, the representation closest to nature will please the most. Modern theatre constantly diminishes this pleasure, however, by the "exaggerations of the actors, their bizarre dress, the extravagance of their gestures, their peculiar rhymed and rhythmic speech and a thousand other dissonances."[34]

Diderot's interest in greater realism pervades the *Entretiens* (1757), three dialogues between "Dorval" and "Moi" that accompanied *Le fils naturel*. These attacked almost every aspect of the contemporary French stage as an offence to verisimilitude. The stage space, already too small, is further encumbered by spectators (eventually removed upon the insistence of Voltaire). The settings are traditional and used for play after play; instead, Diderot insists, one should "bring into the theatre Clairville's salon [the setting for *Le fils naturel*] just as it is."[35] Diderot supports the unities, at least insofar as they support verisimilitude, and he would allow shifts of scene or lapses in time only if they take place between acts, a practice modern realism has faithfully followed. Instead of traditional dialogue, rhythmic, rhymed, and highly self-conscious, Diderot calls for (and uses in his own play) broken and irregular phrases copied from everyday speech. Pantomime, he says, should often be developed instead of declamation. In scenes of great emotion, the poet should allow actors the freedom composers give to great musicians, to develop a passage according to their own inspiration. The poet must recognize that in life a man in the grip of passion "begins many ideas but finishes none," and instead of polished phrases will blurt out words accompanied by "a series of weak and confused noises, expiring sounds, stifled accents which the actor knows better than the poet."[36]

Traditional stage movement, he points out, is as far removed from reality as is speech. Actors remain equidistant in artificial semicircles, never daring "to look each other in the face, turn their backs to the spectator, move close to one another, part, or rejoin." Diderot suggests instead fluid, natural movement and casual arrangements suggesting the groupings in painting. The *coup de théâtre* should be replaced by the

---

[34]Diderot, *Oeuvres complètes*, 13 vols. (Paris, 1969–), 1:637.
[35]Ibid., 3:150.
[36]Ibid., 140.

tableau, "an arrangement of those characters on stage so natural and true that if it were faithfully rendered by a painter it would please on canvas."[37] Thus, both visually and aurally, in this major essay Diderot lays the groundwork for the standard compositional practices of the modern stage.

He also emphasizes moral instruction over pleasure as the end of drama, thus bringing his argument more in harmony with general Enlightenment views. He therefore stresses not so much the pleasure given by verisimilitude as its effectiveness in such instruction: "Can you not conceive of the effect produced upon you by a real setting, realistic costumes, dialogue appropriate to the situation, dangers which would cause you yourself to tremble for your parents, your friends, yourself? Domestic catastrophes of common life will affect us more than the fabulous death of tyrants or the sacrifice of children to pagan gods."[38]

The argument that a play will serve as a better example of virtue if it is founded on verisimilitude was not new to French criticism, of course. As we have seen, La Mesnardière and others were centrally interested in this point. Traditionally, however, this line of argument had been used by both French and Italian critics to justify traditional and expected character types and situations. Diderot's shift from popular opinion to observed reality as the basis of verisimilitude was a significant change in the strategy of this argument, and surely is indebted at least in part to English writers, particularly Lillo.

Lillo's *London Merchant* is one of the two earlier models Diderot cites for his own experiments, the other being Terence's work (he does not acknowledge the sentimental comedy of La Chaussée, another possible precursor). Morality and verisimilitude would be best served, suggests Diderot, by a new genre midway between comedy and tragedy, the *genre sérieux*, which would depict the passions and circumstances of everyday domestic life. The new genre would also require new subjects: its plays would be based not upon the peculiarities of an individual character but upon social and familial roles—the concerns of the new middle class. The businessman, the politician, the citizen, the public administrator, the husband, the brother or sister, the family father could now serve as the center of a drama.[39]

And indeed Diderot employed the last suggested subject in his next drama, *Le père de famille* (1758), which appeared with a *Discours sur la poésie dramatique.* In this, a more formal system of genres is proposed, making up a sort of spectrum: at one end traditional or gay comedy,

---

[37]Ibid., 127–28.
[38]Ibid., 186.
[39]Ibid., 191.

"the object of which is ridicule and vice"; next the *comédie sérieuse*, of which *Le père de famille* is an example and "the object of which is virtue and the duties of man"; then the *genre sérieux*, now called the *drame*, "the object of which is our domestic misfortunes"; and finally traditional tragedy, "the object of which is public catastrophes and the misfortunes of the great."[40]

Succeeding chapters make up a sort of manual of playwriting (the first major attempt at this since D'Aubignac): how to draw up a plan, arrange incidents, handle exposition, develop characters, structure acts and scenes. The would-be author is urged to pay particular attention to the much neglected matter of pantomime, without which "he will be unable to begin, conduct, or end his scene truthfully."[41] Costume and scenery should both be simple, natural, carefully done, and suited to the specific demands of the play.

A key section of this essay, devoted to "manners," repeats Diderot's conviction of the moral utility of drama, with particular attention to refuting Rousseau. All conditions of men and all public instruction can be attacked for their abuses in the same way that Rousseau attacks actors and the drama, insists Diderot. Instead of such focusing on the errors of the past, one should look to the possibilities of the future. Any people "which has prejudices to destroy, vice to root out, follies to expose" has need of the drama, and any government will find it an effective means for "preparing for a change in the law or the extinction of a custom."[42] Diderot accepts Rousseau's assumption of the basic goodness of man but for that very reason argues that the theatre, by portraying virtuous actions, can recall the rogue from his erring path. "The auditorium of the theatre is the only place where the tears of the virtuous man and the rogue are mingled. There the rogue feels discomfort over the injustice he has committed, feels sorry for the evils he has brought about, and is indignant toward a man of his own sort."[43] He thus leaves the theatre more disposed to do good than if a harsh and severe orator had condemned him. For this reason, philosophers should not oppose imitative artists but encourage them to use heaven's gifts for expressing the love of virtue and hatred of vice.

This appeal to reason and natural goodness was in harmony with much of the intellectual writing of the period, but it clearly did not alleviate the suspicions of religious conservatives, who were almost as leery of humanist ethics as they were of the drama. A major spokesman

[40]Ibid., 413.
[41]Ibid., 490.
[42]Ibid., 480.
[43]Ibid., 417.

for this position was Jean Gresset (1709–1777), a one-time poet and playwright whose early work, in philosophy if not in technique, was close to that of Diderot. In 1749, however, Gresset published a letter announcing his renunciation of theatre on religious grounds, and in 1759, in response to the gibes of Voltaire and others, produced *Lettre sur la comédie*, a widely read essay that dismissed the so-called "moral utility" of drama as a sophistic argument. "I now see clearly," he stated, "that the sacred laws of religion and the maxims of profane morality, the sanctuary and the theatre, are absolutely unreconcilable; and all the arguments of opinion, *bienséance*, and purely human virtue gathered in favor of dramatic art have never, nor should they ever win the approbation of the church."[44]

Attacks from former supporters like Rousseau and Gresset were particularly damaging to Diderot and his cause, but he persevered in the face of continual opposition. Work on the *Encyclopédie*, though the project was banned, continued clandestinely; his plays, though not produced, were published and widely read; and after 1760 his fortunes took a turn for the better. *Le père de famille* was performed in 1761 (though *Le fils naturel* had to wait another decade), and the long-delayed final volumes of the *Encyclopédie* appeared as a group in 1765–1766, with comparatively little opposition.

These final volumes contain further discussion of the drama, still primarily by Marmontel. The entry on tragedy is the most extensive, including both a history and an analysis of the genre. Aristotle and Corneille are cited as the "two famous guides," but Corneille's observations are quoted with a warning that they were written in part as justification of his own practice. Tragedy is defined as the representation of a heroic action calculated to arouse pity and terror (admiration, says Marmontel, is more the concern of the epic). It should inspire "the hatred of vice and the love of virtue" and should "purge those passions which are vicious and harmful to society."[45] The ancients tended to show their heroes suffering from external causes, or fate, while the moderns tend to show the suffering resulting from internal causes, the passions. The intimacy of the modern theatre reinforces the latter trend, but poets should nevertheless resist carrying intimacy too far, creating heroes too close to us, or allowing romantic interests to dominate in tragedy. Such practices, of which even Racine was guilty, reduce the veneration for tragic heroes that is essential to the power of the genre. Rather surprisingly, nothing is said of Diderot's own new genre, the *drame*; only a brief notice under "*Tragique bourgeois*" recognizes the

[44]Jean Gresset, *Oeuvres*, 2 vols. (London, 1765), 1:330.
[45]Diderot, *Encyclopédie*, 33:837.

emotional power of depicting the sufferings of persons like ourselves, but it denies to such representations the title of tragedy, since they lack the dignity and grandeur proper to inspire the pity and terror demanded in true tragedy.

Such downgrading of the *drame* by comparison with traditional tragedy, although common among conservative critics of the 1760s, was warmly and wittily attacked by Beaumarchais (1732–1799). In the *Essai sur le genre sérieux* that prefaced his drama *Eugénie* (1767), citing Diderot as his inspiration, Beaumarchais defines a play as "a faithful picture of human actions" that seeks to stir men's emotions and improve their morals, both of which are purposes better achieved by this new drama than by traditional forms. "It is the essential aim of the serious drama, other things being equal, to offer a more powerful interest and a morality which is more relevant than that of heroic tragedy and more profound than that of gay comedy."[46] Classic tragedy, showing the working of destiny, teaches us only fatalism and resignation. If it affects us, it does so not because of its remoteness and grandeur, but on the contrary because—despite these aspects—we recognize a bond between its heroes and ourselves. In other words, tragedy affects us "only insofar as it approaches the serious drama, by showing us men and not kings."[47] The traditional rules do not acknowledge the serious drama, but rules have never produced great art; they are themselves derived from original works of genius produced not by rule but by inspiration. The greatest poets have always ignored the rules, sought the new, and pushed out the frontiers of art.

Clearly there is more than a hint of romanticism in this striking little essay, though Beaumarchais is careful to qualify his more radical assertions and to refrain from direct attacks on the pillars of French neoclassicism. No such restraint is shown in the subsequent writings of Louis-Sébastien Mercier (1740–1814), a clear precursor of Hugo and Stendhal who paid for this prescience by being virtually ignored by his contemporaries. Scattered through his numerous prefaces and articles, and developed in more detail in *Du théâtre* (1773) and *De la littérature et des littératures* (1778), is a poetic based upon the ideas of Diderot but far more radical. Mercier sees the entire development of French theatre since the end of the sixteenth century as misguided, corrupted by deference to arbitrary and foolish regulation. He singles out Boileau and Racine for particular attack, as the leaders of a literature totally estranged from reality. Mercier's vision of theatre, like that of Diderot

---

[46]Pierre Augustin Caron de Beaumarchais, *Théâtre complet*, 4 vols. (Paris, 1869–71), 1:25–26.
[47]Ibid., 29.

and Beaumarchais, is one of social and moral improvement, and like them he insists that this can best be achieved by a drama closely following observed reality. Shakespeare, not Racine, provides the best example; in *Tableau de Paris* (1788), Mercier advises: "Read Shakespeare, not to copy him, but to immerse yourself in his grand and relaxed manner, simple, natural, strong, eloquent; study him as the faithful interpreter of nature, and you will soon realize that all these uniform constipated little tragedies, devoid of action or real design, offer you only a hideous thinness and dryness."[48]

It is significant that Mercier cautions against merely substituting Shakespeare for Racine as a model. Like the romantics, he condemns all imitation, and one of the lessons to be learned from Shakespeare is precisely that every artist must develop "his own unique and sharply defined style;"[49] indeed, "it is essential that every work have its own particular and individual organization."[50] Of the traditional unities, Mercier would retain only unity of action, interpreted in a manner close to the organic unity of the German romantics. The traditional genres, too, are incompatible with Mercier's view of each work as unique. In a passage suggesting Hugo, not only in its content but in its bombast, he cries, "Fall, fall, you walls separating the genres! Let the poet's view range freely across the open countryside and never let him again feel his genius locked into cells where art is circumscribed and diminished."[51]

Mercier's interest in the drama as a reflection of everyday life led him much further than Diderot toward the democratization of the theatre: he extended to the proletariat the serious attention that Diderot had accorded to the bourgeoisie. In the preface to *La brouette du vinaigrier* (1775), he called the dramatist a "universal painter. Every detail of human life is equally his object. The royal mantle and the worker's frock are equally subjects for his brush."[52] Such statements anticipate the concern of the naturalists a century later to expand the subject matter of serious drama. Mercier's democratic interest is evident also in his attempt to stimulate republican virtues and to unite all classes in patriotic fervor by means of historical drama. True tragedy, he says, should return to the practice of Greek drama, which appealed to all classes, showed the people their true interests, and aroused an enlightened patriotism and love of country.[53]

Mercier's own attempts at such theatre, his *"pièces nationales,"* were

---

[48]Louis-Sébastien Mercier, *Tableau de Paris*, 12 vols. (Paris, 1782–89), 4:103.
[49]Mercier, *Du théâtre* (Amsterdam, 1773), 330.
[50]Mercier, *De la littérature et des littératures* (Yverdon, 1778), 127.
[51]Ibid., 105.
[52]Mercier, *Théâtre complet*, 3 vols. (Amsterdam, 1778), 3:116
[53]Mercier, *Du théâtre*, 39–40.

not particularly successful, but both in theory and practice he provided a crucial link between the patriotic manifestations that Rousseau considered perhaps the only form of spectacle suitable for his republic, and the pageants and dramas of the Revolution. In the *Discours préliminaire* to *Charles IX* (1789), by Marie-Joseph Chénier (1764–1811), the major historical play of the Revolution, there is an interesting blend of Mercier and traditional eighteenth-century ideas. The "end of tragedy," says the author, is "to move men's hearts, to cause tears of pity or admiration to flow, and by all this to inculcate in men the important truths, to inspire in them a hatred of tyranny and superstition, a horror of crime, a love of virtue and liberty, a respect for laws and morality, the universal religion."[54]

The development of acting theory, in France as in England, became an established critical concern during the eighteenth century. A pioneer work is Luigi Riccoboni's (1676–1753) "Pensées sur la declamation" (1738), which condemns contemporary French acting style (including both gesture and speech) as studied and artificial. Before considering matters of projection and style, he says, actors should seek to capture the "tones of the soul," too varied and complex to be learned mechanically. Only by "feeling what one says" can an actor achieve these tones and thus achieve the major goal of the stage, which is "to give illusion to the spectators."[55] Luigi's own son, Antonio Francesco Riccoboni (1707–1772), takes issue with this theory in his short *L'art du théâtre à Madame xxx* (1750). According to the younger Riccoboni, an actor who actually felt the emotions of his part would be unable to act. His goal should be rather to understand fully the natural reactions of others and to imitate them on stage through complete control of his expression.[56] In brief form, this is the idea that would be most fully developed by Diderot in the subsequent famous *Paradoxe*.

A more extended treatise on acting, generally supporting the view of the elder Riccoboni, appeared in 1749: *Le comédien* by Pierre Rémond de Sainte-Albine (1699–1778). Like the almost contemporary English essay of Foote, it seeks to bring order to an art previously scarcely considered, but Sainte-Albine's essay treats the subject at much greater length and depth. It begins with a consideration of the actor's emotional gifts—wit, feeling, and enthusiasm. The best actors will be well endowed with these, and those who argue that an actor can be too emotional have confused true emotion with the flamboyant imitation of deep feeling. Not all actors will possess these gifts in equal measure, but it is

[54]Marie-Joseph Chénier, *Oeuvres*, 5 vols. (Paris, 1824–26), 1:152.
[55]Luigi Riccoboni, *Réflexions historiques et critiques sur les différents théâtres de l'Europe* (Paris, 1738), 31, 34.
[56]Antonio Francesco Riccoboni, *L'art du théâtre à Madame xxx* (Paris, 1750), 73–75.

essential for actors in each type of role to possess them in the proper degree for that type: those who would make us laugh must have the gift of gaiety and wit; those who play heroes must have elevated souls; those who seek to stimulate tears must feel sentiment keenly themselves; and those who play lovers must be persons born to love. Physical as well as emotional expectations must be satisfied. Though many physical types are acceptable on stage, heroes must have imposing bodies and lovers attractive ones; actors must look the proper age for their roles and have the natural vocal qualities suitable to their characters.

What Sainte-Albine proposes, in short, is the general application of the Horatian rule of decorum in character types to the actors' portrayal of these types. The goal, as always, is verisimilitude, and the first 11 chapters of the second part of the essay deal with specific means of obtaining truth in presentation through gesture, movement, and vocal delivery.

So far, the relationship between this treatise and traditional neo-classicism is clear, but beginning with chapter 12, Sainte-Albine turns his attention to a more modern question. He distinguishes between the average spectator and those of "taste and discernment," saying that all he has written so far is necessary to satisfy the first, but that the second requires more: "In their judgment, there is between acting which is natural and true and that which is ingenious and delicate the same difference as between the book of a man who has only knowledge and good sense and the book of a man of genius. They require the actor not only to be a faithful copier, but that he be a creator as well."[57] For this, the "fine points" of the art must be added to truth. Fidelity to nature is still essential, but the best actors will embellish the text or correct its deficiencies with individual touches uniquely their own in order to add richness, variety, grace, and depth to the truth.

Sainte-Albine's essay was adapted for English readers by John Hill as *The Actor* (1750, revised 1755), which closely followed the French original but gave English examples. In 1769 the work in much reduced form was translated back into French by Antonio Fabio Sticotti as *Garrick ou les acteurs anglais*. This version, about half the length of its predecessors, focuses more upon the qualities of the actor than on his technique. Most of Hill's first section—how the actor should suit the role physically and emotionally—is included, but only one brief chapter remains of the material on truthfulness to nature and the fine points of the art. Probably this is due to the stronger moral tone of Sticotti's work. It stresses the instruction of the spectator, which is best achieved

---

[57]Pierre Rémond de Sainte-Albine, *Le comédien* (Paris, 1749), 228–29.

when the actor "adds to superior talents the virtues of the honest man and the qualities of the useful citizen."[58]

Diderot, asked to review Sticotti's essay for the *Correspondance littéraire* in 1770, sharply disagreed with it, and went on to elaborate his observations into the most famous treatise on acting of the eighteenth century, the *Paradoxe sur le comédien*, written about 1773, though not published until 1830. In Diderot's earlier writings, the occasional comments on acting had been generally compatible with Sticotti and Sainte-Albine, stressing the emotional suitability of the artist to the role: thus Dorval in the *Entretiens* remarks "Poets, actors, musicians, painters, the best singers, the great dancers, tender lovers, the truly devout, all this enthusiastic and impassioned company feel deeply and reflect little."[59] During the next decade, however, Diderot's opinions underwent a major change. His association with sculptors and painters, especially Chardin, led him to give increasing attention to technical mastery in art, and the visit of Garrick to Paris in 1764 clearly added to his growing conviction that training and discipline were at least as critical to the great actor as feeling.

In fact, Diderot has come to view sympathetic feelings (*sensibilité*) as the source of mediocre acting and its absence necessary for the greatest performance. Great actors, he contends, do not abandon themselves to feeling but "imitate so perfectly the exterior signs of feeling that you are thereby deceived. Their dolorous cries are noted in their memory, their despairing gestures are carefully rehearsed, they know the precise moment when their tears will begin to flow."[60] The actor who relies upon sympathetic imagination plays erratically and at best produces the effect of life but not of art, since the images of passion in the theatre are not true images but are heightened and idealized according to the rules and conventions of the art. Truth for stage purposes is the conforming of action, diction, expression, and gesture not to life but "to an ideal type invented by the poet and frequently enhanced by the player."[61] However realistic this may appear on the stage, it would immediately strike us as false or grotesque on the street. Art is a product of careful study and preparation, not spontaneity; indeed, the greatest poet will so clearly delineate his characters that the actors have simply to present them without being tempted to add anything of their own for clarity or emotional effect.

Clearly, by the final third of the eighteenth century, not only had a certain body of acting theory appeared but two fairly distinct critical

[58]Antonio Sticotti, *Garrick ou les acteurs anglais* (Paris, 1769), 3.
[59]Diderot, *Oeuvres*, 3:143.
[60]Ibid., 8:640.
[61]Ibid., 10:435.

positions on the art had been established. One held that acting was essentially a rationalistic process, a study of the technical means for obtaining a graceful depiction of idealized reality. The other stressed emotional insight and sympathetic imagination, demanding that the actor go beyond reason to tap the inner springs of feeling. Obviously these positions reflected in a general way the contemporary conflict in criticism between those who looked backward to the classical tradition stressing reason, rules, and *bienséance* and those who anticipated romanticism by championing inspiration, genius, and particularized reality. It should be remarked, nevertheless, that Diderot's position also anticipated certain romantic concerns. Though he would have agreed with Horace and Quintilian on the validity of rules and technique, he rejected totally their requirement of empathy, bringing him much closer to the detached "romantic irony" of the artist, which appeared in German romanticism.

The opposition on the question of involvement in acting was by no means confined to critics and theorists. France's leading actors added to the debate with strong advocacy of one side or the other. Hyppolite Clairon (1723–1803), whose ability Diderot warmly praised, was in complete accord with his ideas on the art of acting. In her *Mémoires* (1798) she dismissed as foolish the idea of applying her own sentiments and feelings to the diverse characters demanded of her. Art, not sympathy, was the key to her roles: "If ever I have seemed to impersonate them in a purely natural manner, it is because my studies, supported by some fortunate gifts I may have received from nature, have led me to the perfection of art."[62] Clairon's leading rival, Marie-Françoise Dumesnil (1713–1803), answered in her own *Mémoires* (1800) that Clairon was describing an art of the drama but not of the theatre, of reciting but not of creation. Rebutting Clairon section by section, Dumesnil argued that while her rival might gain admiration through sheer technique, she would never move an audience to tears; she lacked what Dumesnil considered the basic requirement for a tragic actor—"a sense of pathos."[63]

[62]Hyppolite Clairon, *Mémoires* (Paris, 1798), 30.
[63]Marie-Françoise Dumesnil, *Mémoires* (Paris, 1800), 59.

11

Germany to Hegel

IT WAS NOT UNTIL THE PERIOD of Gotthold Lessing (1729–1781) that Germany emerged from more than a century of political and religious strife and cultural subservience to other nations, to create its own modern tradition of literature and criticism. Lessing contributed to both, producing the first truly significant German plays and the first major German pronouncements on dramatic theory. He was not without predecessors in either, however.

The leader in German Renaissance poetics had been Martin Opitz (1597–1639), a faithful follower of Aristotle, Horace, and Scaliger, who attempted in his *Buch von der deutschen Poeterey* (1624) to apply the precepts of these critics, as he understood them, to German literature. Opitz's *Buch* is brief, scarcely 50 pages, but it was reprinted and read as the basic German poetics up to the time of Lessing. The fifth chapter considers comedy and tragedy, essentially defining them as did the neoclassicists in France. Tragedy should avoid persons of low station or commonplace events, use elevated language, and deal with such topics as murder (especially of children and parents) and war. Comedy should depict lower people in everyday situations, use humble language, and deal with such topics as greed, deception, youthful frivolity, and the avarice of old men.[1]

In the preface to his translation of Seneca's *Trojan Women* (1625), Opitz discusses the function of tragedy, which he calls "nothing other than a mirror held up to those who base their activity or inactivity on luck alone." The demonstrated misfortunes of such persons arouse in us compassionate tears and teach us both to develop caution and wis-

---

[1]Martin Opitz, *Gesammelte Werke*, 4 vols. (Stuttgart, 1968–79), 2, pt. 1, 364–65.

dom in our own lives, and to bear suffering with greater strength and less fear.[2]

The theories of Opitz were further developed in the plays and prefaces of Andreas Gryphius (1616–1664), the major serious German dramatist of the seventeenth century. Gryphius, like Opitz, saw as the function of tragedy a teaching of stoic resignation to the workings of fate. "In this tragedy and those which follow," he stated in the preface to *Leo Armenius* (1646), "I attempted to represent the fragility of all human things."[3] He also points out that the work is strictly faithful to the rules, its time, for example, lasting from noon until before sunrise the following day.

This strongly neoclassic approach, looking to Scaliger and Heinsius, was challenged after the death of Opitz by Georg Philipp Harsdoerfer (1607–1658), who produced a far more detailed poetics than Opitz in his *Poetischer Trichter* (1648), a curious blend of neoclassic ideas and the freedom seen in the dramas of the English and Spanish Renaissance. Harsdoerfer rejected Opitz's stoic interpretation of tragedy in favor of a moral didacticism more in harmony with contemporary neoclassic thought in France and England. Tragedy he defined as "the noble and serious presentation of a sorrowful story of weighty matters, leading the spectators to astonishment and pity, not only by words but by realistic portrayals of misfortune."[4] "Astonishment" suggests the "admiration" of Corneille or the Dutch critics, but Harsdoerfer defines it in such a way as to make it in fact an elaboration of fear. It is of two sorts, that which "chills the spectator" by showing such things as "frightful tortures and atrocious cruelties" and that which "arouses fear by the spectacle of a great person in peril." Tragic emotions are not aroused, as Opitz and Gryphius suggested, to teach endurance but to be purged, and the means by which this is accomplished is poetic justice. The tragic hero is "a model of all virtues" who suffers greatly during the play but is rewarded at the end. Since it is highly pleasurable "to see a character at the end of a play in a quite different situation from at the beginning," tragedy should depict "innocence oppressed and vice triumphant, all changed into pleasure at the resolution."[5] The end of tragedy is not resignation but the reestablishment of justice in the world of the play, and harmony in the soul of the spectator. Any device that will aid this end is permissible, according to Harsdoerfer, including the mixing of the comic with the serious and total rejection of the unities.

The historical tragedies of Daniel Casper von Lohenstein (1635–

[2]Ibid., 2, pt. 2, 430.
[3]Andreas Gryphius, *Werke*, 4 vols. (Hildesheim, 1961), 2:14.
[4]Georg Philipp Harsdoerfer, *Poetischer Trichter*, 3 vols. (Nuremberg, 1648–53), 2:80.
[5]Ibid., 83–84.

1683) reflect many of the ideas of Harsdoerfer, but the sort of freedom from classical restraints that he approved was more radically demonstrated in the popular *Haupt- und Staatsaktionen* (Chief and state plays) of the same period. These largely improvised performances combined events in high places with the antics of Hanswurst, the traditional fool; they carried the mixing of styles and freedom of form to an extreme beyond the tolerance of most theorists.

In fact, the first influential critic of the eighteenth century reacted to such liberties by developing a system of stifling rigidity. This was Johann Christoph Gottsched (1700–1766), professor of poetry at Leipzig University and the leader of eighteenth-century rationalism in German dramatic theory. Two concerns dominated Gottsched's critical writings: an insistence on the moral function of drama, and a demand for the virtual identity of dramatic and empirical reality. The mechanical approach of his aesthetics is well illustrated in what is probably the best-known passage in his voluminous works, a virtual recipe for playwriting in the fourth chapter of his *Versuch einer critische Dichtkunst* (1730):

First of all, select an instructive moral lesson which will form a basis for the entire plot in accordance with the goals which you wish to achieve. Next, lay out the general circumstances of an action which very clearly illustrates this chosen instruction.... Next, you must determine what effect you wish to achieve in this creation; do you desire to make a fable, a comedy, a tragedy, or an epic of it? Everything will influence the names given to the characters who will appear in it. A fable will use animal names.... If you want to make a comedy ... the characters must be citizens, for heroes and princes belong in a tragedy. The one who does wrong must by the end of the play be the object of scorn and laughter.[6]

Gottsched is as rigid as Castelvetro or Dacier on the unities of time and place, and for the same reason—their contribution to verisimilitude. The best plots are those in which stage time and real time coincide exactly, and eight or ten hours is the absolute maximum allowable for a believable plot. Moreover, these hours must be during the day, not at night, since the characters need to sleep. Thus a plot "must begin about noon and last into the evening or begin early in the morning and end by afternoon."[7] Similarly, "the spectator remains seated in one place; thus it follows of necessity that the persons performing must all remain in one place."[8] Further, this should not be the sort of neutral

[6]Johann Gottsched, *Schriften zur Literatur* (Stuttgart, 1972), 97–98.
[7]Ibid., 164–65.
[8]Ibid., 174.

space favored by Racine; the setting should be as true to historical reality as possible.

Speech and action must also follow observed reality, and on these grounds Gottsched opposes monologues, asides, and similar rhetorical flourishes. So concerned did he become with the question of verisimilitude that by 1851, in an essay entitled *Ob man in theatralischen Gedichten allezeit die Tugend als belohnt und das Laster als bestraft vorstellen muss* (whether one in dramatic works must always show virtue triumphant and vice punished), he proposed that even poetic justice should be set aside if it could not be made compatible with the illusion of reality. At this point Gottsched seemed to be moving in the direction of the late nineteenth-century naturalists, but in several significant ways he remained committed to traditional artifice. Despite his rejection of asides and monologues, he felt tragedy should retain the Alexandrine verse form and the formal, stylized language associated with it. He also remained firmly neoclassic on the matter of dramatic character, insisting that characters remain true to general traditional types and that their speech contain nothing vulgar or idiosyncratic.

A distinct alternative to the theories of Gottsched was provided by his pupil Johann Elias Schlegel (1719–1749), whose extensive writings on the theatre include the first appreciation of Shakespeare to appear in German, the *Vergleichung Shakespeare und Andreas Gryphius* (1741). Frederick V's project to establish a new theatre in Copenhagen inspired Schlegel's two major writings on the drama, both highly influential for subsequent theorists and practitioners: the *Schreiben von Errichtung eines Theaters in Kobenhagen* (1746), dealing with practical theatre management, and the *Gedanken zur Aufnahme des dänischen Theaters* (1746), dealing with dramatic theory and the repertoire. Schlegel's disagreements with Gottsched appear early in the latter work. No eighteenth-century critic would be likely to reject moral purpose in poetry entirely, but Schlegel, unlike Gottsched, always places it in a distinctly subordinate position. "A play upon which much art has been lavished but which lacks the art of pleasing belongs in the study and not on the stage," he observes. "On the other hand, a play which fulfills only this chief end has the right to be enjoyed on this ground alone, even by people of taste and learning."[9]

This emphasis on pleasure rather than moral instruction led Schlegel away from the concern for verisimilitude that marks Gottsched's writings, toward an emphasis on imagination and on the aspects of drama that make it *unlike* nature. Every art has its own conventions, Schlegel says, by means of which the artist concentrates and makes more effec-

[9]Johann Schlegel, *Werke*, 5 vols. (Leipzig, 1764–73), 3:270.

tive his raw material. Unity of place, for example, is of value not because "the spectator remains seated on his bench and so the play must remain in one place" (as Gottsched argued) but for concentration of focus: "When the unities of time and place are observed, the spectator can give his undivided attention to the plot, the characters, and the emotions."[10] For Schlegel, probability in drama depends not upon the resemblance of the world of the theatre to external experience but on the internal consistency and believability of the plot, an idea much closer to Aristotle and to subsequent romantic theory than to Gottsched and neoclassicism: "Given events have verisimilitude if the causes from which they spring are made clear."[11] Once again there is an emphasis on art over nature, since it is one of the concerns of the artist to clarify cause and effect.

Schlegel is also far more willing than Gottsched to depart from traditional generic types. Looking pragmatically to contemporary theatre practice, he proposes a spectrum of dramatic types similar to that evolved by Diderot, based upon the effect sought and the type of character portrayed. First came traditional tragedies, with plots involving elevated characters that seek to arouse the passions, then four types of drama all classed as comedic: plots involving elevated characters that seek to arouse laughter; plots involving low characters that seek to arouse laughter (traditional comedy); plots involving low characters that seek to arouse the passions (Diderot's *drame*); and plots involving both high and low characters, or with "mixed" personages, that seek to arouse some laughter and some passions.[12]

The dramatist Christian Fürchtegott Gellert (1715–1769), who occupied the chair of poetry at Leipzig after Gottsched, modified Gottsched's rationalist approach in another way. While accepting Gottsched's didacticism and interest in French models, Gellert looked for inspiration not to neoclassic tragedy but to the *comédie larmoyante*, and argued in *Pro commoedia commovente* (1751), his inaugural lecture at Leipzig, that comedy instructed best when it aroused compassion rather than satirical laughter.

The writings of Gellert and Schlegel helped to prepare the way for the first great theorist of drama in Germany, Gotthold Ephraim Lessing (1729–1781), who set himself firmly in opposition to Gottsched and to the veneration of French neoclassicism. His major work in dramatic theory was the *Hamburgische Dramaturgie* (1769), a collection of 100 essays that he was commissioned to write as a means of informing the

[10]Ibid., 293–94.
[11]Ibid., 282.
[12]J. Schlegel, *Werke*, 3:276.

public about the plays offered at the newly formed National Theatre in Hamburg. In addition to reviewing individual productions, these essays ranged widely over questions of dramatic theory and technique; they provided, in their totality, the critical foundation for the establishment of a modern German theatre.

In the final essay of the *Dramaturgie*, Lessing acknowledges Aristotle's *Poetics* as his major critical touchstone, a work "as infallible as the Elements of Euclid." The works of the classic French stage, he says, presumably based on Aristotle, are in fact often founded on misapprehensions and distortions of Aristotle's ideas, severely restricting the artists' potential. The English, unaffected in general by the pedantic French misreadings, have produced works both more vital and truer to the real spirit of the Greek theorist.

Thus, although Lessing's work is not, as has sometimes been claimed, essentially a commentary on Aristotle,[13] it nevertheless frequently returns to the *Poetics*, not only because Lessing found a number of concepts in Aristotle useful to his own critical system, but also because he recognized that it would be difficult if not impossible to remove the strictures of French neoclassicism from German letters except by challenging the original authority for those strictures.

Tragedy is, not surprisingly, the central concern of the *Dramaturgie*, and it is upon the emotional effect of this genre that Lessing places the greatest emphasis. In essay 77 he states that Aristotle never gave an exact logical definition of this genre, but when the accidental qualities are removed from his general observations, a fairly precise definition emerges, "namely, that tragedy, in a word, is a poem which excites pity." Fear, Lessing feels, works with pity in the process of catharsis, but is not a direct goal of tragedy. The pity aroused by the sufferings of persons like ourselves ends when the play ends, and fear of similar misfortunes for ourselves then replaces it. "This fear we carry away with us, and just as it helps, as an ingredient of pity, to purify pity, it now also helps to purify itself as a passion of independent existence."[14] Other emotions may also be purified by tragedy, but these are subsidiary. What is sought is an emotional balance: tragedy should work to diminish pity and fear in those who have an excess of these emotions and to increase them in those who are deficient. Lessing specifically rejects Corneille's attempt to include admiration among the tragic emotions; he considers it more appropriate to the epic.

Eighteenth-century humanitarianism, even sentimentality, doubtless contributed strongly to Lessing's preference for pity. Goodness and

---

[13]See, e.g., E. Gotschlich, *Lessings Aristotelische Studien* (Berlin, 1876).
[14]Gotthold Lessing, *Gesammelte Werke*, 10 vols. (Berlin, 1968), 6:391.

sympathy were closely related in his mind, and the process of arousing the latter was therefore automatically a moral one. On these grounds he was forced to call Christian Felix Weisse's *Richard der Dritte* (1759), which served as a basis for much of his discussion of tragedy, a failure: Richard, a thorough villain, could not arouse the pity necessary for moral improvement. Still, Lessing admitted that the audience derived pleasure from the play, and in attempting to explain this, he moved significantly from moral to formal considerations. The play, he suggested, had passages of poetic beauty; even more important, it created a powerful drive, which he described in terms suggestive of Stanislavski's later "through line of action," which bound audience interest to the play. "We so love anything that has an aim that this gives us pleasure quite independent of the morality of the aim."[15]

Although the *Dramaturgie* has little to say directly about the new middle-class tragedy that Lessing himself was instrumental in establishing, the emphasis on sympathetic identification with tragic characters and actions clearly points in this direction. Essay 59, for example, scoffs at those who consider "pompous and tragic" to be synonymous. In ancient tragedies a certain reserve of speech was justified because the conventions of the drama forced the characters to speak in public before a curious chorus, but no such conventions hamper the moderns, who should therefore show men speaking as they truly speak. "Feeling can have nothing to do with stilted, selected, pompous speech. This neither arises from feeling nor gives rise to it. Feeling deals in the simplest, commonest, plainest words and expressions."[16]

This interest in simplicity and the natural was reinforced by Lessing's reading of Diderot, whose two plays and prefaces Lessing translated in 1759 and who is extensively cited in the *Dramaturgie*. Lessing's own brief preface to *Das Theater des Herrn Diderot* compared the French author favorably with Aristotle and recommended Diderot's writings as an excellent corrective for Gottsched's.

On such questions as the unities or separation of the genres by tone and character type, Lessing takes a generally flexible position. He calls the unities conventions required by the use of the chorus (following Castelvetro and d'Aubignac) and not essential to drama. Essay 7 advances an interesting distinction between comedy and tragedy: both deal with subjects outside the normal workings of society's laws, but comedy considers those moral flaws too insignificant for society to regulate; tragedy, those events too great for rational comprehension or control. Nevertheless, Lessing refuses to restrict comedy and tragedy

[15]Ibid., 403.
[16]Ibid., 304.

to such manifestations, remarking that "genius laughs at the boundary lines criticism draws."[17] In a later passage (essay 70) he contributes to the theoretical groundwork for a modern concept of tragicomedy, rejecting the sort of crude mixing together of kings and clowns found in the *Haupt- und Staatsaktionen* in favor of an interpenetration of emotional reactions where tragedy and comedy are both present, yet "one does not merely follow upon the other, but necessarily arises from it, when seriousness stimulates laughter, sadness pleasure, or vice versa so directly that we cannot abstract one or the other."[18]

Such observations suggest a flexibility of theoretical approach and an exultation of individual expression typical of the romantics, but Lessing's idea of genius and individuality is much more conservative. Geniuses are great not because of their defiance of the rules but because they are endowed by nature with an innate understanding of them. The genius, says essay 96, "has the proof of all rules within himself." The critics who cry that "genius rises above all rules" do not understand what genius is. It is not oppressed by the rules; it is the fullest expression of them.[19] It is true that the regulations of French classicism are oppressive, but that is because many of them are derived not from the rules nature gives to each art but from custom and convention.

In the preface to the *Dramaturgie*, Lessing promises to consider the art of the actor as well as that of the poet. It is essential for the dramatic critic "to know how to distinguish infallibly, in every case of satisfaction or dissatisfaction, what and how much of this is to be placed to the account of the poet or of the actor. To blame one for what is the fault of the other is to injure both." Particular care must be taken in the criticism of acting, since the art is transitory. This prevents it from being reexamined, as the work of a poet can be, and makes it more vulnerable to the passing mood of the spectator.[20]

Despite this promising beginning, Lessing was prevented by the protests of the Hamburg actors from providing any significant criticism of their work, and after restricting himself to guarded remarks in the first 25 essays, he gave up the attempt. His more general remarks on the art add little to the standard French works of the period. He translated Francesco Riccoboni's *Art du théâtre* as *Die Schauspielkunst* in the fourth and final issue of a periodical he established to consider theatre matters, the *Beyträge zur Historie und Aufnahme des Theaters* (1750). Later he translated a part of Sainte-Albine's essay and, as has been noted, Diderot's *Entretiens* (though he was not acquainted with the as yet unpublished

[17] Ibid., 41.
[18] Ibid., 353.
[19] Ibid., 482.
[20] Ibid., 9–10.

Paradoxe). From these sources he evolved a position attempting to balance technique and emotion but rather favoring the former: emotional identification, though important, is never sufficient alone; although an actor should be able to provide a suitable emotional base for his expression, it will not properly affect the audience unless he is proficient in the basic techniques of the art which, like those of poetry, should be founded upon general, universal, and unalterable rules.[21]

Lessing's championship of Shakespeare and his willingness to give free rein to the occasional genius did not seriously qualify his basic commitment to the tradition and the ideals of the enlightenment. The clear break with this tradition comes in the next few years; it is first strikingly seen in the writings of Johann Gottfried Herder (1744–1803) and Johann Georg Hamann (1730–1788). During this generation the long-protracted Quarrel between the Ancients and the Moderns seemed at last decided in favor of the Moderns, and the *Sturm und Drang* movement launched by Herder, a great outpouring in the 1870s and 1880s of literary works stressing inspiration and individualism, provided major critical concepts for the subsequent romantic movement and thus for the development of modern theatrical theory.

Hamann was more a religious mystic than a critic, but he prepared the way for the far more influential Herder with his rejection of the neoclassic love of order, decorum, probability, and the idea of *la belle nature*. He considered poetry a sacred, primal expression, parallel to religion and myth, snatched by the genius directly from God. His comments on the theatre are few and oracular but highly suggestive. Not surprisingly, in view of his religious fervor, he conjured up ecstatic visions of the medieval theatre, but his love of Shakespeare proved more stimulating to his contemporaries. "What is it in Homer which makes up for his ignorance of the rules which Aristotle thought up after him, and what is it in Shakespeare which makes up for his ignorance or his overstepping of these critical laws?" he asked, and responded, "Genius is the universal answer."[22]

Since it was Hamann who introduced Herder to Shakespeare, studying *Hamlet* with him in the original, it is hardly surprising that the spirit of Hamann infuses Herder's major essay, *Shakesper* (1773). There is the same mystic exultation, the same ecstatic view of the poet as quasi-divine creator of infinitely suggestive patterns. Herder compares the dynamics of a Shakespearian play to the interplay of waves upon the surface of the ocean: "Scenes of nature ebb and flow; affect one another

[21]Ibid., 508–9. See also Otto G. Graf, "Lessing and the Art of Acting," *Papers of the Michigan Academy of Science, Arts, and Letters*, 40 (1955), 293–301.

[22]Johann Hamann, *Sämtliche Werke*, 6 vols., (Vienna, 1949–57), 2:75.

however disparate they appear; work together to create and to destroy, so that the vision of the creator, who at first appeared to have thrown them together in a drunken, disorderly manner, may be fulfilled."[23] The classic unities are of course condemned, but rather than emphasize the freedom of genius, as Hamann had done, Herder develops a more reasoned argument, reminiscent of Lessing, that Shakespeare—writing in a different culture and different time—could hardly be expected to create plays in the same way as the Greeks. Their "rules" may have been natural for them but become artificial when transplanted to alien surroundings, as had happened in France. "Sophocles remained true to Nature when he created an action in a single place and at one time; Shakespeare could remain true to her only if he developed his world-historical events and human fates through all the times and places where they occurred."[24]

Naturally, Herder also finds the traditional interest in genre irrelevant to Shakespeare, recalling Polonius's foolish listing of dramatic types and concluding that none of Shakespeare's plays were "Greek Tragedy, History, or Pastoral, nor should they be." Every play, in the broadest sense, belongs to a single genre, which is History. Beyond that, each play has its unique unifying mood, which Herder calls its soul;[25] it may be derived from the images, the incidents, the references, and the evocation of the physical setting.

All of Herder's concerns—the new idea of nature, the emphasis on the sensual and metaphorical, the historical relativism, and the search for an individual unifying principle within each individual work—are clearly laying the foundations of romantic aesthetic theory. Johann Wolfgang von Goethe (1749–1832) in his early years held views extremely similar to those of Herder. In a brief, ecstatic speech for Shakespeare's birthday, *Zum Schäkespears Tag* (1771), Goethe compared his experience of reading his first Shakespeare play to that of a man blind from birth miraculously given sight, to a prisoner leaping into the open air and casting his former fetters away: "I did not hesitate for a second to renounce the theatre of rules. The unity of place seemed to me oppressive as a prison, the unities of action and time burdensome chains on the imagination." The French he dismissed as pitiful dwarfs attempting to wear the massive armor of the Greeks, as unconscious self-parodists. Shakespeare's creations, on the other hand, were "embodiments of nature," Shakespeare the "historian of mankind." Like Herder, Goethe avoided the exaltation of formlessness itself but claimed

---

[23]Johann Herder, *Sämmtliche Werke*, 60 vols. (Stuttgart, 1827–30), 5:220.
[24]Ibid., 220.
[25]Ibid., 226.

for Shakespeare's works a mysterious inner unity: "His plots are, to speak in the conventional manner, not plots at all, but his plays all turn around a secret point (which as yet no philosopher has seen and defined) in which the essential characteristic of his own ego, the alleged freedom of the will, clashes with the necessary movement of the whole."[26] This conflict of ego and universe, mentioned by both Herder and Goethe, would also become a staple of romantic critics seeking a model to replace the discarded neoclassic structure.

The hero of Goethe's *Wilhelm Meisters theatralische Sendung* (written between 1777 and 1785) undergoes a conversion to Shakespeare similar to Goethe's own. When he heaps praise upon Corneille and especially upon Racine, his colleague Jarno urges him to read the English dramatist. Wilhelm, intrigued by reports of an author specializing in "mad and bizarre monstrosities, which outrage all *bienséance* and all *vraisemblance*," agrees. Having read a few plays, he is transported with enthusiasm. "These are not fictions; one seems to have opened before him the grand books of Fate while the tempest of the most passionate life roars and thrashes back and forth the pages." The characters "seemed natural men and yet not so"; they were "mysterious and complex creations of nature" whose inner workings could only be glimpsed "like watches embedded in crystal."[27]

Wilhelm's first encounter with Corneille, in Goethe's book, prefigures that with Shakespeare and leads to a strong defense of French neoclassicism: "Hardly had I read a few plays than my spirit was in tumult and I was carried away with the irresistible desire to write in the same style." Enthusiasm aside, young Wilhelm gives a balanced and thoughtful view of such vexing questions as that of the unities. Any rule "drawn from the observation of nature and suitable to an object" should be accepted, and the three unities appear not only "necessary to the drama but an ornament of it." The unities have been misused, encouraging critics to view drama in a fragmentary way, "like dividing a man into soul, body, hair, and clothing," but are essential if viewed as parts of an organic whole. Indeed, one should not stop with three but consider a dozen or more—including unity of manners, of tone, of language, of character, of costume, of setting, of lighting. "For if the word unity means anything, what could this be but an interior wholeness, a harmony of parts among themselves, suitability, and verisimilitude." Under these conditions, unity of action—the most important of the three—may mean either simplicity of action or "adroit and intimate fusion of

---

[26]Johann Goethe, *Sämtliche Werke*, 41 vols. (Munich, 1909–20), 1:174.
[27]Goethe, *Wilhelm Meisters theatralische Sendung* (Stuttgart, 1911), 311, 321–22.

several actions."[28] The later Goethe, who argued for a rational and flexible classicism, seems clearly prefigured in this early passage.

In the early writings of Friedrich Schiller (1759–1805), the tenets of neoclassicism, especially as developed by Lessing, are much more dominant than in Goethe. Under the influence of Shakespeare and Goethe's youthful *Götz von Berlichingen*, Schiller created *Die Räuber* (1781), perhaps the best known example of *Sturm und Drang* theatre. Nevertheless, when the work was published, Schiller accompanied it with a preface which in apparent sincerity apologized for its deficiencies by neoclassic standards. One of the major differences between classicism and romanticism was a shift in general focus from plot to character, and Schiller admits that in order "to illuminate the souls" of the leading characters, the unities have been sacrificed and more incident included than Aristotle would permit. More serious still, in order to portray his characters honestly and richly, Schiller included "good qualities with their bad," a practice which he asserts may be excused if the play is only read, but runs the risk of being considered a defense of vice on the stage, where audiences are less thoughtful and less select.[29]

The moral obligation of theatre is much more fully developed in *Die Schaubühne als eine moralische Anstalt betrachtet* (The Stage viewed as a Moral Institution, 1784), which marshalls the traditional pragmatic defenses of the theatre: its championship of virtue and condemnation of vice, its guide to practical wisdom and civic life, its value for steeling man to bear the reversals of fortune, its preaching of tolerance, its harmonizing of national interests. The essay concludes by describing a kind of apotheosis of theatrical enlightenment, when "men of all ranks, zones, and conditions, set free from the bonds of convention and fashion, merge back into a single race, forgetting themselves and the world as they approach their heavenly source."[30]

In *Über die tragische Kunst*, another early essay, Schiller again echoes Aristotle and Lessing, defining tragedy as a "poetic imitation of a coherent series of particular events, an imitation which shows us men in a state of suffering and which aims at arousing our pity."[31] He goes on to comment on imitation, action, coherence, and completeness in essentially Aristotelian terms, and echoes Aristotle further in characterizing the hero and in distinguishing history, which must be faithful to recorded facts and whose end is to teach, from poetry, which follows "natural truth" and seeks to move.

The choice of pity as the central emotion of tragedy comes, of course,

[28]Ibid., 74–77.
[29]Friedrich Schiller, *Sämtliche Werke*, 16 vols. (Stuttgart, 1893–1904), 2:3.
[30]Ibid., 12:59.
[31]Ibid., 13:236.

not from Aristotle but from Lessing, who also gave Schiller the idea of emotional balance. Pity must be neither too weak (for then we remain unmoved) nor too strong (for then we feel pain as well). Most effective are situations wherein both the oppressor and the oppressed gain our sympathy, which can occur when the oppressor acts against his own inclination. There is always a danger that sympathy will become so strong as to cause pain, but Schiller proposes a counterbalance in "supersensuous ideas, moral ideas," to which the reason "clings as to a kind of spiritual support, to right and raise itself above the fogs of the sensuous to a serener atmosphere." He cites the moral *sententiae* of classic drama as a kind of distancing device to accomplish precisely this effect. The goal is a lifting of the spirit beyond pity or compassion to an intuition or consciousness of "a teleological coherence of all things, a sublime order of a benevolent will."[32] Thus tragedy leads at last to the eighteenth-century ordered universe and justifies God's ways to man.

The years of Schiller's early theoretical studies also saw the publication of the major philosophical works of Immanuel Kant, and although these had little to say directly about literary theory, they provided an intellectual background, concepts, and terminology of enormous importance for subsequent theorists, first in Germany and then throughout Europe. This influence is at work in Schiller, whose study of Kant led him away from the eighteenth-century theodicy of Lessing and set him on the path that would lead to the romantic theories of the theatre.

If, as Kant argued, the universe is incomprehensible to man, then the purpose of tragedy can hardly be to provide a rationalist's apologia for it, and Schiller had to seek elsewhere for the key to tragedy's power. His fullest attempt to do so appears in *Über das Pathetische* (1793), which opens with a clear shift in position from his previous writings. "The depiction of suffering, as suffering alone, is never the end of art, though it is of the utmost importance as a means of attaining this end. The highest aim of art is to represent the supersensuous, and this is achieved in particular by tragedy."[33] Schiller now describes the supersensuous in terms drawn directly from Kant. The world is divided into two realms, that of the senses and that of reason; the former is the sphere of appearance and of necessity, the latter of moral freedom. Art theoretically could provide a bridge between freedom and necessity, between the individual and the world, and even if an ultimate harmonization of these spheres proved impossible, art could at least make us aware of the tension between them and thus give us an inti-

[32]Ibid., 227, 229.
[33]Ibid., 14:66.

mation of the "supersensuous" that lies beyond both understanding and reason.

This same insight, says Schiller, is sometimes found in nature, in what he calls the sublime—an apprehension quite different from beauty, which is based on harmony and balance. The sublime arises instead from disjuncture; in the face of overwhelming and irresistible natural phenomena, the mind nevertheless insists upon its individual freedom of action, and from this conflict arises an apprehension of the supersensuous. Though Kant does not develop this idea in relation to art, Schiller does so in his essay *Über das Erhabene* (On the Sublime, 1801) as well as in *Über das Pathetische*. The pathetic, he asserts, arises from two conditions: first suffering, by which the natural sensuous side of man is engaged; then moral freedom, by which man declares his independence from suffering. As in Kant, this disjuncture between the effect of suffering on the sensuous man and lack of effect on the moral man gives rise to the sublime, and "only in so far as it is sublime does the pathetic have aesthetic value."[34] In tragedy this sublimity is achieved in action—either mediately, when a character chooses suffering out of a sense of duty, or immediately, when he accepts it as expiation for a violation of duty.

At this point in its development, Schiller's argument seems headed for a conflict with Kant, since the emphasis on moral choice suggests a moral or didactic aim, while Kant explicitly insisted on the autonomy of art and its freedom from all utilitarian ends. Therefore, in the latter part of his essay, Schiller attempts to reconcile the moral choices of the reason with the free, disinterested play of the imagination; he emphasizes that though the reason acts in accordance with moral law, it does so as a free choice, and this possibility of freedom is what engages our aesthetic feeling. "The degree of aesthetical energy with which sublime feelings and acts take possession of our souls does not at all depend upon the interest of the reason, which requires every action to conform *absolutely* to the idea of the good. It depends instead on the interests of the imagination, which requires only that conformity with good should be possible, or in other words, that no feeling, however strong, should repress the freedom of the soul."[35] This allows Schiller also to justify evil characters, if they show a great force of will and thus a greater aptitude for real moral liberty than is seen in weak or in untested virtue.

If man gains anything from tragedy, in Schiller's system, other than aesthetic pleasure or an apprehension of the supersensuous, it seems

[34]Ibid., 72.
[35]Ibid., 93–94.

to be a kind of stoicism from the observance of the hero's opposition of free will to suffering: in *Über das Erhabene*, Schiller calls tragedy an "inoculation against unavoidable fate." This stoicism, related to the apprehension of the supersensuous, led Schiller increasingly to a view of art as a means of transcending reality. In the preface to *Die Braut von Messina*, entitled *Über den Gebrauch des Chors in der Tragödie* (On the Use of the Chorus in Tragedy, 1803), he stated that the object of art was not to give man a transient dream of liberty but to make him "absolutely free," which it achieves "by awakening, exercising, and perfecting in him a power to remove the world of the senses to an objective distance," thus to acquire "a dominion over the material by means of ideas."[36] Schiller sees the chorus as an admirable instrument for achieving this distancing, for expressing general ideas in corporeal form, and for preventing too great a realism in the drama from submerging our freedom in the tempest of the emotions.

Schiller's best known critical treatise, *Über naive und sentimentalische Dichtung* (1795–1796) has little to say directly about the drama but provides some significant critical strategies and orientation for subsequent theorists of the genre. Here Schiller recasts ancient and modern as naive and sentimental poetry. Naive poetry, the general mode of antiquity, was in unquestioned harmony with the natural world. Sentimental poetry, the usual modern mode, is conscious of a gulf between the real and the ideal. It is this self-divided and self-conscious intellectual concern with problems of expression that marks the modern author. He cannot easily return directly to nature and to the spontaneous and impersonal expression of the ancients, but he can hope at last to return indirectly, by way of reason and freedom, so that the sentimental may achieve in its own way the same ideal as the naive.

Schiller divides sentimental poetry into types based not on traditional genres, but on modes of feeling, all derived from a consciousness of the gap between ideal and real. Elegiac writing mourned the lost ideal, idyllic writing treated the ideal as real in the past or future, and satiric writing focused upon the real in light of the ideal. The concept of naive and sentimental as developed by Schiller proved extremely useful to subsequent German writers as they sought to classify modern poetic modes and to work with the differences between classicism and romanticism.

Crucial in the codification and dissemination throughout Europe of the critical insights and methods of Herder, Kant, and Schiller were two brothers, Friedrich (1772–1829) and August Wilhelm Schlegel (1767–1845), nephews of Johann Elias Schlegel. During the late 1790s

[36]Ibid., 6:177.

they were part of the same intellectual circles in Jena and Weimar that included Goethe and Schiller. For the drama, the more important of the two was August, who dealt with this genre in considerable detail and in 1808 devoted to it one major series of lectures in Vienna, which was translated into all major European languages and became one of the most widely read works of German romantic theory.

In defining the dramatic, Schlegel first stresses that its dialogue must imply life and action, must be designed to be exhibited on stage, and thus must contain a theatrical as well as a poetic element. To be poetic, a drama must be "a coherent whole, complete and satisfactory within itself" and must "mirror and bring bodily before us ideas, that is to say necessary and eternally true thoughts and feelings which soar above this earthly existence."[37] To be dramatic, it must work to "produce an impression on an assembled multitude, to fix their attention and to arouse their interest."[38] The spectators are to be brought out of themselves by a kind of magic spell, which, Schlegel notes, makes the drama a powerful instrument for good or evil and thus justifies the concern it has always caused legislators.

In his earlier (1789) lectures in Jena, Schlegel defined tragedy as "the direct representation of an action in which the struggle between man and fate is resolved" and comedy as "the direct sportive representation of human characters in an action."[39] The two genres are explored in more detail in the Vienna lectures with emphasis on their disparate moods—seriousness or earnestness in tragedy, sportiveness or playfulness in comedy. The earnest tone of tragedy Schlegel explains, not surprisingly, by the romantic yearning for the unattainable. Reason impels man always to seek some aim in existence, but reason keeps lifting that aim higher and higher until it comes to the end of existence itself, "and here that longing for the infinite which is inherent in our being is baffled by our finite limitations."[40] The melancholy that results and the prostration or stoic defiance with which this melancholy is accepted are the basis of tragic poetry. Clearly, this formulation draws upon the same sources as the disjuncture between the real and the ideal that concerned Schiller.

Schlegel also reflects Schiller in seeking different emotional moods as the bases for various genres. Comedy, which Schlegel finds in its purest form in Greek Old Comedy, contrasts completely with the mood of tragedy. If earnestness derives more from our moral side, sport derives more from the sensuous, though it differs from simple animalistic

---

[37]August Schlegel, *Sämmtliche Werke*, 12 vols. (Leipzig, 1846–47), 5:30.
[38]Ibid., 31.
[39]A. Schlegel, *Vorlesungen über philosophische Kunstlehre* (Leipzig, 1911), 161, 179.
[40]A. Schlegel, *Werke*, 5:41.

pleasure because human consciousness recognizes sportiveness for what it is. Reason and understanding voluntarily put aside the pain of disjuncture in the human condition to assume "a forgetfulness of all gloomy considerations in the pleasant feeling of present happiness."[41] Everything must be taken in the "spirit of play" for the delight of the fancy—an idea clearly related to Schiller's "play-urge" (*Spieltrieb*), the term he gave in his *Über die ästhetische Erziehung des Menschen* (1793–1794) to aesthetic activity that transcends the opposed impulses of the sense and the reason to achieve a delight in activity for its own sake, aside from moral or utilitarian ends. Such play "makes man whole and unfolds both sides of his nature simultaneously."[42]

The essence of classic tragedy Schlegel finds in fate or destiny, against which man and at times even the gods must struggle. The result is almost invariably a series of terrible and painful events, and Schlegel considers various theories as to why we find the spectacle of such events pleasurable. He discounts the theories of poetic justice, of purgation, of pleasure in the stimulus of the emotions, and of pleasure in the contrast between our own safety and the danger observed in the theatre; he sides with Schiller in arguing that the moral freedom of man is best displayed when in conflict with the sensuous, and the greater the opposition, the more significant the demonstration. Citing Kant's idea of the sublime as his inspiration, Schlegel defines the aim of tragedy as an attempt "to establish the claims of the mind to an inner divinity." To achieve this, "all earthly existence must be held as worthless; all sufferings must be endured, and all difficulties overcome."[43] In a famous phrase, he characterizes the chorus as "the ideal spectator," using "ideal" in Schiller's sense to suggest the distancing function of the chorus. "It mitigates the impression of a heart-rending or moving story while it conveys to the actual spectator a lyrical and musical expression of his own emotions, and elevates him to the region of contemplation."[44]

A major concept in Schlegel's criticism is that of organic unity, an idea advanced by Herder but much more fully developed by Goethe. The rejection of the organizing principles of neoclassic theory left the late eighteenth-century innovators with the necessity of finding another basis of organization, especially for their beloved Shakespeare, or else to pronounce his work entirely devoid of form—an unthinkable alternative. However, the identification of the genius with nature, suggested by Lessing and others, provided a solution. If a genius like Shakespeare created in the same manner as nature, one could apply organic prin-

[41]Ibid., 42.
[42]Schiller, *Werke*, 6:144.
[43]A. Schlegel, *Werke*, 5:76.
[44]Ibid., 77.

ciples to his creations, and this biological metaphor soon assumed a major role in German poetic theory. In Goethe's *Wilhelm Meisters Lehrjahre*, Wilhelm protests against the slightest adjustment of *Hamlet* on precisely these grounds: "Wilhelm absolutely refused to listen to the talk of separating wheat from chaff. 'It is not a mixture of wheat and chaff,' he said, 'It is a trunk, boughs, twigs, leaves, buds, blossoms, and fruit. Is not each one there with the others and by means of them?' "[45]

Schlegel, whose first enthusiasm for Shakespeare was stimulated by *Wilhelm Meister*, absorbed and then championed this organic concept. In his Vienna lectures he remarked, in speaking of Shakespeare, that genius is never without form but that one must distinguish between mechanical and organic form. The first is externally imposed, as in French classicism; the second, as in Shakespeare, is innate: "It unfolds itself from within, and becomes defined simultaneously with the full development of the germ." This form creates a "significant exterior" that gives a faithful testimony to a "hidden essence."[46] The traditional unities of time and place, of course, are a part of mechanical form and thus of little consequence. Schlegel calls unity of action essential, but for this he suggests "a deeper, more intrinsic, more mysterious unity than that which satisfies most critics." This is not discovered by empirical evidence, or by any sort of experience, but by the mind's apprehension of a unity in the higher sphere of ideas. The "unity of interest" that La Motte would substitute for the traditional unities seems to Schlegel a possible term for this concept, provided that it does not refer to the interest in the destiny of a single character but "is taken to mean in general the direction which the mind takes at the sight of an event."[47]

Schlegel thinks it characteristic of Greek art that it continuously sought homogeneity by excluding all heterogeneous elements and by combining and adjusting the rest into a harmonious whole; thus each genre, like an organic species, became clearly defined. But with the passage of time, the spirit of poetry has manifested itself in other ways. Again the metaphor is organic: the spirit "creates a body of a different composition from the nutrimental substances of an altered age."[48] It is thus both incorrect and misleading to impose old names on new kinds of poetry. The terms comedy and tragedy are not applicable to most modern drama; it should simply be called romantic. The classic poet rigorously separated dissimilar elements, while the romantic delights in mixtures and contrarieties. The classic poet sought eternal order; the romantic seeks the secret chaos at the heart of the universe from

[45]Goethe, *Werke*, 5:247.
[46]A. Schlegel, *Werke*, 5:157.
[47]Ibid., 19, 21.
[48]Ibid., 6:158.

which new forms arise. Schlegel compares classic tragedy to a group in sculpture, romantic drama to a vast canvas where larger, richer groups appear with all the surrounding background and the emotional qualities of light and color. One must view such matters as the disregard of the unities and the mixing of comic and tragic elements not as mere indulgences of the poet but as features, even beauties, of the modern concept of poetry.

Goethe, too, continued to explore the differences between ancient and modern poetry, but with much less enthusiasm than Schlegel for the modern. In *Shakespeare und kein Ende!* (1813–1816), he produced this table of antitheses:

Ancient	Modern
Natural (Naive)	Sentimental
Pagan	Christian
Classic	Romantic
Realistic	Idealistic
Necessity	Freedom
Destiny (*Sollen*)	Will (*Wollen*)

Most of these oppositions are standard in the theory of the period, but Goethe develops the final pair in his own manner. In Greek drama, an unalterable destiny foreordained the catastrophe and the defeat of the opposing human will. In modern drama, the focus is on the will and hence upon the free choice of the individual. This distinction was made also by Schiller, who considered the change essentially positive. Modern social theorists would agree, since in this view the classic mode represents society as unalterable, whereas the romantic shows it susceptible to change and reform.

Goethe, however, finds the shift an unfortunate one: "The *Sollen* is despotic, whether it derives from the Reason, as do the laws of society or custom, or from nature, as do the laws of development, growth and departure, life and death. We tremble before all of these without considering that they aim for the good of the whole. The *Wollen* on the contrary is free and appears free and advantageous to the individual. Thus it flatters men and rules over them as soon as they become acquainted with it."[49] Through the *Sollen*, tragedy became great and powerful; through the whimsical *Wollen*, it has become weak and insignificant, its power dissolved in indulgence and caprice.

Shakespeare alone, in Goethe's opinion, avoided this degeneration by combining the virtues of the old and new, allowing destiny the advantage but keeping it in balance with the will. In so doing, he provided a model for subsequent authors, but not—Goethe now be-

[49]Goethe, *Werke*, 26:48–49.

lieves—for the stage: the poetic vision of Shakespeare is too large and too complex for physical embodiment, and is suited only to a theatre of the mind. Earlier writers on Shakespeare deplored the primitive conditions of the Elizabethan stage as checks on his genius, but Goethe argues, to the contrary, that the crude and undeveloped theatre of Shakespeare's time freed him from thinking about the stage and left his poetic fancy free to develop. Like Johnson and Tate before him, and in a strikingly similar metaphor, Goethe calls Shakespeare's actual achievement as a dramatist brilliant but intermittent: his theatrical accomplishments were "only moments, scattered jewels, which are separated by much that is untheatrical." Goethe's idea of what constituted these "jewels," however, is much different from that of the eighteenth-century critics and closer to the modern concept of a "poetry of the theatre." Nothing is theatrical, he says, "except what is immediately symbolic to the eye; a significant action which evokes a still more significant one." As an example, Goethe cites the moment when Prince Hal removes the crown from his sleeping father, places it on his own head, and proudly struts about.[50]

In his later years, Goethe ceased to consider Shakespeare a theatrical writer at all and, indeed, praised him for never allowing his genius to be restricted by the demands of the stage. In 1826 he sharply disagreed with Ludwig Tieck (1773–1853), who was urging that producers recognize the "unity, indivisibility, and inviolability" of Shakespeare's plays and put them "on the stage without revision or modification from beginning to end."[51]

The relationship of the theatre to morality, particularly in regard to the concept of catharsis, occupies Goethe in his *Nachlass zu Aristoteles Poetik* (1827), his last significant essay on the drama. Once again he stresses the goal of the dramatist as the attainment of harmony by the reconciliation of opposing elements; but he remarks that this reconciliation, which he equates with Aristotle's *katharsis*, occurs on the stage, not within the spectators. It is a mistake, he insists, to claim for the theatre a beneficial effect on the audience of either a moral or an emotional nature. That is the domain of philosophy and religion, not theatre. "If the poet has fulfilled his obligation on his side, tying together his knots meaningfully and untying them properly, this same process will be experienced by the spectator—the complications will perplex him, and the solution enlighten him; but he will not go home any the better for it."[52]

---

[50]Ibid., 52.
[51]Ludwig Tieck, *Werke*, 30 vols. (Vienna, 1817–24), 30:63.
[52]Goethe, *Werke*, 19:62.

German romanticism as a literary movement was inseparable from the philosophy of the period. Kant, as we have seen, had a profound influence upon Schiller and indeed upon all of Schiller's generation; two of Kant's followers, Johann Gottlieb Fichte (1765–1814) and F. W. J. Schelling (1775–1854)—both professors at Jena—lived, worked, and debated with the Schlegels and their circle and were greatly influential in establishing the framework of romantic theory.

Fichte wrote little on literary matters, but his treatise *Grundlage der gesammten Wissenschaftslehre* (1794) exercised great influence on the Jena romantics, especially the Schlegels. Schiller, following Kant, had divided feeling and reason, perception and understanding, and had seen an essential aspect of art, the sublime, precisely in the inevitable disjuncture between man's perception of the physical facts of the universe and his inability to grasp intellectually their essence—the transcendental *Ding an sich*. Fichte extends the range of man's mind to bridge even this final gulf. The human ego, he argues, is in fact one with the metaphysical essence of the universe, and thus the transcendental "other," which Kant postulated, is an illusion. The external world can be treated as a mental concept, and created or destroyed by man's will.[53] The struggle between the world of natural phenomena and that of moral freedom is thus internalized and given an ethical dimension, since the disjuncture that concerned Kant and Schiller can, according to Fichte, be not only experienced and described but overcome by the will, in elevating the individual ego into the absolute. To do this, the individual must transcend individuality and the illusory world of the senses.

The aesthetics of the Schlegels closely reflected this philosophic system, both descriptively and morally. They saw in the ego's creation of the non-ego (the external world) a parallel to the poet's creation of his fictive universe, and felt that by emphasizing the poet's distance from and superiority over his universe, they could provide a model for the ego in its striving after the absolute. To describe this poetic strategy, Friedrich Schlegel introduced a major new term to the critical vocabulary—irony. The ironic poet simultaneously revels in the pleasure of creation and recognizes its unreality in relation to the infinite, celebrates the achievement of a work eternally becoming, and simultaneously recognizes its failure. In his *Kritische Fragmente* (1797), Schlegel says that ironic works deal in "transcendental buffoonery. Inwardly, their spirit surveys everything and rises above all that is limited, even above

[53]Johann Gottlieb Fichte, *Sämmtliche Werke*, 8 vols. (Berlin, 1845–46), 1:227.

one's own art, virtue, or genius; outwardly, in execution, they follow the approach of a good Italian buffo."[54]

The concept of irony was more fully developed by the philosopher Karl Wilhelm Ferdinand Solger (1780–1819), whose final work was an extensive review of August Schlegel's *Vorlesungen über dramatische Kunst und Literatur* (1819). Solger disagrees sharply with Schlegel's emphasis on the distinction between comedy and tragedy, which stressed the prevailing mood of each. There is, Solger argues, a more fundamental mood found in both genres, and that is irony, the basis of all drama and indeed of all art. The temporary union of the absolute and the accidental, of the world of essence and that of phenomena, can be achieved in art, in a work that simultaneously gives an insight into eternal reality and acknowledges its own inadequacy to embody that reality. Comedy and tragedy have "an inner similarity. The whole conflict between the incomplete in man and his higher calling involves making us appear as something worthless, only in opposition to which something truly valuable can appear."[55]

Actually, this is not far from the idea of irony proposed by Friedrich Schlegel, but Solger established himself as the first "serious" and "philosophic" developer of this concept by pointing out (correctly) that August Schlegel paid little attention to irony at all and (less correctly) that Friedrich Schlegel saw it merely as a way of giving free reign to subjective playfulness. Hegel's subsequent acceptance of Solger's claim solidified the impression of a greater division between Solger and Schlegel than in fact existed. Solger certainly deserves credit for a fuller development of this concept than Schlegel gave it, but he did not depart radically from Schlegel's basic premise, nor did Solger himself deny the subjective—even frivolous—side of romantic irony, as we may see in his unqualified admiration for the free-wheeling, self-destructive comedies of his close friend Ludwig Tieck.

Solger's interpretation of comedy and tragedy does show a clear break with the Schlegels, as well as with Schiller. Since both genres are based upon irony, both must provide in some way at least a momentary glimpse of eternal order. The tragic hero for Solger represents not freedom in Schiller's sense but mere individuality, even caprice, and the absolute is affirmed by his destruction. In tragedy the species is affirmed over the individual, and the individual death is a kind of martyrdom in the name of the absolute. Subsequent theories of tragedy in nineteenth-century Germany, most notably those of Hegel and Heb-

[54]Friedrich Schlegel, *Kritische Ausgabe, Lyceum der schönen Künste*, Fragment 42 (Munich, 1967), 182.
[55]Karl Wilhelm Solger, *Nachgelassene Schriften und Briefwechsel*, 2 vols. (Leipzig, 1826), 2:513.

bel, moved in this same direction. Moreover, Solger does not agree that comedy, as Schlegel suggested, is a celebration of the sensuous and of chance and caprice, since chance and caprice can never in themselves create the beauty necessary to artistic production. "A higher order must be recognizable through them, and this can be achieved only through irony."[56] This, says Solger, is as true of Shakespeare as it is of Aristophanes.

A somewhat different approach to tragedy was offered by F.W.J. Schelling, Fichte's successor in Jena and one of the those who influenced Solger. Almost all of Schelling's specific comments on drama are clustered at the end of his *Philosophie der Kunst* (written in 1802–1803 and published in 1809). In his theory of genres, Schelling sets up a distinctly dialectical system with echoes of both Schiller and the Schlegels. He considers the epic the first poetic form to evolve, calling it a somewhat naive form based upon necessity but one in which necessity is accepted as a fact of nature and life, with no implication of conflict with freedom. As the individual becomes conscious internally of this freedom, a reaction to the epic appears as lyric poetry, which, being entirely subjective, also avoids open conflict with necessity. From these opposed genres comes the synthesis of drama, which explores the conflict between freedom and necessity but creates an equilibrium between their demands. Drama is thus "the hypothetical form which shall become the final synthesis of all poetry."[57]

Schelling goes on to base the subdivisions of comedy and tragedy upon this equilibrium. In tragedy, necessity is the objective element and freedom the subjective; freedom in the person of the hero struggles on its own ground to achieve the required equilibrium that is both defeat and victory—necessity is recognized without the destruction of freedom itself. In comedy, freedom is objective and necessity subjective. Here, as in the works of Aristophanes, the ground of the confrontation is that of freedom, in a universe seemingly devoid of destiny, where subjective necessity must establish a claim for itself. The end of both tragedy and comedy is a condition of stasis.

Like Solger, Schelling stresses the subjection of the hero to an absolute order in tragedy, but while Solger focuses upon the order, Schelling's emphasis is upon the hero. He quotes Aristotle approvingly on the ideal hero for tragedy, the basically good man who errs and must atone, citing Oedipus as the central example. What is beautiful in such a spectacle? It is the hero's realization that his error is less a crime than a partial perspective, and his subsequent sacrifice of himself to the

---

[56]Ibid., 536.
[57]Friedrich Schelling, *Sämmtliche Werke*, 6 vols. (Stuttgart, 1839), 5:692.

absolute. The voluntary assumption of guilt and suffering to restore the moral order is the highest expression of free will: "It is the loftiest thought and the greatest victory of freedom, to take on punishment for an unavoidable misdeed, in order thus in the loss of freedom itself to make manifest this freedom, and to go down to defeat with a declaration of the freedom of the will."[58] It is in this free assumption of "necessity" or "guiltless guilt" that tragedy lies, not in the unhappiness of the conclusion. The gods cannot, as in the epic, participate actively as independent agents, for this would compromise the freedom of the hero. They must either represent necessity or be themselves in conflict with it, as in the *Orestia*.

As for the unities, Schelling, like Schlegel, approves only of the unity of action, which he calls an external reflection of the inner unity of the work. He also sees the chorus as an instrument for "elevating the spectator directly to the higher sphere of true art and symbolic representation."[59]

Schelling sees character as even more important in modern drama, which resembles the epic in its mixture of comic and tragic elements and, more significantly, in its inability to embody the conflict between freedom and necessity. Catholicism, he suggests, offers a possible modern parallel in its doctrine of original sin, an inevitable error which is part of the dynamic of grace. For this reason he considers Calderón, as a Catholic tragic dramatist, the only modern whose works equal those of Sophocles in power. Shakespeare, a Protestant, was forced to find another and somewhat lesser tragic vision, which he based on character, laying upon it "so significant a charge of fate that it can no longer be regarded as representative of freedom, but as irresistible necessity."[60] This concept of character as destiny, suggested also by Schlegel, became a standard romantic explanation for the particular power of modern tragedy. Schelling is careful, however, to distinguish this new idea of fate or destiny, which he calls "nemesis," from classic necessity. The latter, he says, is found in reality, the former in the historical process. Tragedy based on character ultimately confronts not freedom with necessity but freedom with freedom, in a continuing succession that echoes the process of history itself. It is this historical focus that made Shakespeare the greatest poet of the individual, the "characteristic," but also deprived him of the concentrated universality, the assumption of the many into a unity, that characterized the classic authors. His world is always the world of reality, never of convention or idealism.

[58]Ibid., 697.
[59]Ibid., 705.
[60]Ibid., 720.

The *Philosophie der Kunst* ends with a passage calling for a rediscovery of this lost universality, which Schelling, in anticipation of Wagner, thinks may be achieved by a true union of the arts in the Greek manner, of which modern opera is only a caricature. When the presently separated arts of music, poetry, dance, and painting are reunited, the present "realistic external drama," in which the people take part only politically and socially, will be replaced by an "internal, ideal drama" which will unify them essentially as a people.[61]

The lyric poet Friedrich Hölderlin (1770–1843) derived from Fichte, Kant, and Schiller a concern with the modern concept of opposition between the self and the world, which he most often expresses as a conflict between man's creations—art or culture—and nature. The unity once enjoyed by man is now lost: "We are at variance with nature, and where there was once unity, so we may believe, there is now opposition."[62] Hölderlin argues that nevertheless man could strive, through culture, to obtain a new unity superior to the old. In *Über den Unterschied der Dichtarten* (1799), he takes issue with Fichte's theory of the all-embracing consciousness, arguing that consciousness is impossible in a subject without an object. Only when the whole becomes divided into opposing parts is consciousness possible, but once this division takes place, art can seek a reunification which will encompass the consciousness thus gained. Schiller's vision of sentimental poetry reachieving the unity of the naive would be thus superior to the naive in its original state. Hölderlin saw tragedy as a means of approaching this unity, based on an "intellecutal perception" that recognizes both the parts and the more fundamental unity, which "can be apprehended by the spirit and which arises from the impossibility of a separation and a unification both of which are absolute."[63]

Hölderlin began his tragedy *Empedokles* in 1798, and it became the focus of his thoughts on this genre. The fragmentary essay *Grund zum Empedokles* (1799) is the fullest statement of these thoughts, beginning with a philosophical consideration of the opposition and eventual union of nature and art. Art is the "flower, the perfection of nature," but in itself it is incomplete, just as nature is. Though divided, the two are harmonious; each completes the other and supplies its lack. "Divinity is between the two."[64] The poet's task is to reconcile these opposed realms, for the poet's senses arrange the undifferentiated material of life (*die aorgischere Natur*) into forms apprehensible by man's intellect and aesthetic taste (*der organischere künstlichere Mensch*). The tragic hero

---

[61] Ibid., 736.
[62] Friedrich Hölderlin, *Sämtliche Werke*, 6 vols. (Stuttgart, 1944–62), 6:203.
[63] Ibid., 4:267.
[64] Ibid., 152.

like Empedokles is a representative individual who has discovered or sensed the potential unity, but who arises among a people whose self-confidence and trust in reason has blinded them to the power and significance of nature. The resulting opposition of nature and culture, recognized only by the hero-poet, Hölderlin calls the "fate" of the era.[65] In order to achieve for his people the unity he intuits, the tragic hero pushes their self-assertion to its furthest limit, "seeking to overcome conquering nature itself and to gain a total understanding of it."[66] By pushing the opposition to an intolerable extreme, he achieves the longed-for unity, but only at the cost of his own destruction by the forces he has challenged. His death, his reduction to nothingness, demonstrates negatively the power of nature, and he becomes a "sacrifice of his era," ending the alienation of his society through his own destruction.[67]

The romantic critic Adam Müller (1779–1829) looked for inspiration to the Schlegels rather than to Kant or Schiller and attempted, through the Schlegels' historical relativism, to avoid the classic-modern dualism so much in evidence in the writings of his contemporaries. He suggested that although all poetry belongs to one great organism, each work contributing to and affecting the whole, each work is at the same time part of another organic whole, the total social system of its own era: "Scientific, economic, and religious concerns condition poetic ones."[68] This approach gave Müller a tolerance for a wide variety of works that was unusual in critics of his generation.

In *Über die dramatische Kunst* (1806) he even defends the artificiality of the French classic stage, calling his contemporaries' arguments from nature beside the point. French and Roman drama he terms "representative," while Greek and romantic drama (headed by Shakespeare) is "individual," and different standards should be applied to them. Romantic drama can properly be held up to nature, but representative drama must be judged according to the ideals, however artificial, of its own time. Racine's stage, for example, was "a rostrum set up for that particular place, for that particular time, for that court, for that genuine popular gathering of talents which assembled during the century of Louis XIV," and any attempt to stage it according to "nature" would destroy its effectiveness. Its very essence is formal and oratorical.[69]

For modern Germany, Müller proposed a theatre that would stand "between the marketplace and the church," serving as a link between

---

[65]Ibid., 154.
[66]Ibid., 158.
[67]Ibid., 153.
[68]Adam Müller, *Kritische, aesthetische, und philosophische Schriften*, 2 vols. (Berlin, 1907), 1:110.
[69]"Apologie der französischen dramatischen Literatur," in ibid., 269.

the concerns of everyday life and those of eternity. Tragedy, of course, tends toward religion, comedy toward trade. "Tragedy lifts man above his everyday existence, his individual and isolated commerce with his neighbors, to convey him to the heights and depths of humanity," while comedy "gives amusement to the spirit elevated by the all-powerful emotions of religion and carries back on light, gaily colored wings to the home, the market, and the activities of the day."[70] Both genres are affirmative, comedy stressing joy and life, and tragedy the conquering of death by a vision of a higher life to come.

Although this strong traditional religious element in Müller (a convert to Catholicism) found few echoes in the critics of the next generation, another aspect of his vision was much more in harmony with subsequent writers. In seeing the theatre as a mirror not of nature but of the political, economic, and religious concerns of a specific community, Müller anticipated much theory of the later nineteenth and the twentieth century, and he was particularly prescient in the ideal he saw for the working of theatre. He condemned his contemporary theatre as one "divided in half by the proscenium, on one side of which are those on the stage who are only seen and on the other those in the audience who only see." The fool in Shakespeare and the Greek chorus suggest another and better arrangement, where the drama becomes truly integrated with the life of the community. It will then "return at last to its original form, when it was a communal celebration, not a one-sided spectacle, a cold representation, or a petty mirror of manners."[71]

The German romantic dramatists contributed little to dramatic theory. Ludwig Tieck, whose comedies were held up as examples by the Schlegels, Solger, and Müller, was interested more in history, especially of the Elizabethan drama, than in theory. His monumental book on Shakespeare was never completed, and the parts of it that did appear essentially echoed the observations of the critics and philosophers with whom Tieck was in contact. Much more original were his studies on Elizabethan staging and costuming, pioneering efforts in the reconstruction of the actual production methods of Shakespeare's time.

Heinrich von Kleist (1777–1811) produced one striking and evocative essay, *Über das Marionettentheater* (1810), which anticipated the fascination the puppet exerted on drama theorists a century later. In this brief work the narrator is informed by a leading dancer at the opera that a marionette can achieve a grace impossible for a human because

---

[70]"Vorlesungen über die deutsche Wissenschaft und Literatur" (1806), in ibid., 129–30.

[71]Ibid., 198.

it lacks consciousness and cannot, like a human actor, falsify the dance "by locating the soul (*vis motrix*) at any other point than that of the center of gravity of the movement."[72] The human can occasionally slip into moments of unconscious grace, spontaneous reflections of the infinite, but these are rare and unreproducible by conscious activity. Only perhaps at the end of time can such grace return, "when knowledge has, at it were, gone through the infinite."[73]

More substantial were the observations of the Austrian dramatist Franz Grillparzer (1791–1872), whose poetic dramas of historical and mythological subjects carried on the tradition of Goethe and Schiller, but did so in the darker, more resigned, and fatalistic tone typical of the Restoration period. Like Kleist, Grillparzer saw man as victim to forces beyond his rational understanding or control. His essay *Über das Wesen des Drama* (1820) begins with the observation that the essence of drama lies in strong causality, since that is what makes the fiction command our belief. Causality makes necessity a major concern of the drama, at the expense of freedom. Nature and similar forces independent of man's will work so strongly upon his actions that they seem to crush any desire for freedom in men of unhappy temperament, passion, or upbringing, and "even the best among us know how often they have taken the worst course through such influence, which can reach so great a degree of intensive and extensive power that it becomes a wonder it can be resisted at all."[74]

Tragedy, says Grillparzer, deals always with freedom and necessity, and one must always triumph. Recent authors, headed by Schiller, have shown freedom the victor, though Grillparzer pronounces himself "quite of the opposite opinion." The elevation of the spirit that comes with such a victory has nothing to do with tragedy, which, as Aristotle noted, arouses feelings not of joy and triumph but of pity and fear. It should lead men "to recognize the nullity of the earthly and the dangers that the best must face and suffer."[75] The theatre does not and should not seek to offer its audience pleasant entertainment or trite morals, though it should provide a kind of exhilaration, which Grillparzer describes in a note written about 1820 as "an elevation of the spirit, an exaltation of the whole existence, a stimulation of the emotions, such as often does not occur in the whole course of one's everyday life." The source of this exaltation is "an overview over the totality of life; insight into oneself; the meshing together of one's own sufferings and those of

[72] Heinrich von Kleist, *Sämtliche Werke* (Munich, 1912), 884.
[73] Ibid., 888.
[74] Franz Grillparzer, *Sämtliche Werke*, 37 vols. (Vienna, 1909–48), 14, pt. 1, p. 31.
[75] Ibid.

others."[76] This vision of the end of tragedy is remarkably similar to that of Grillparzer's contemporary, Schopenhauer.

The theologian Friedrich Schleiermacher (1768–1834) considered the art of acting in his lectures on aesthetics in 1832–1833 and argued for the human actor an ability to draw upon natural grace which Kleist had called almost impossible. For Schleiermacher, art is essentially the expression of emotion, but he finds art not in the sort of spontaneous, totally free expression pictured by Kleist, but in expression modified and transfigured by *Besonnenheit* (deliberation or illumination). This is the internal process that imposes upon spontaneous emotions order and harmony, the marks of the absolute, of Platonic form. In this process the unique emotional experience of the individual is made one with the infinite—self-expression apotheosized. It should be noted that for Schleiermacher the expression of this is enough, even if communication does not occur. The value of the work lies in itself, and the effect on an audience "cannot indeed be an object of the artist's consideration."[77]

German metaphysical writing after Kant was forced to define itself in terms of Kant's pervading dualism. The philosophers Fichte and Schelling and the literary critic Friedrich Schlegel, as we have seen, attempted to overcome this dualism by placing the absolute within the realm of artistic apprehension. Other philosophers such as Solger and Schleiermacher, and poets such as Kleist, felt that the gap between human perception and the higher world could not be bridged except perhaps in momentary and unplanned flashes of transcendence. The last major German philosophers of the early nineteenth century, Arthur Schopenhauer (1788–1860) and Georg Wilhelm Friedrich Hegel (1770–1831), considered the question of tragedy in a striking manner from these two opposed positions—Schopenhauer from that of dualism, Hegel of monism.

Schopenhauer defined Kant's *Ding-an-sich*, the unknowable essence, as Will, which manifests itself in the actual processes and objects of the sensuous world by ceaseless striving and conflict, devoid of aim or reason. Only by a recognition and rejection of all these manifestations—that is, of the world itself—can man escape the power of Will. Eastern mysticism, which had fascinated Schlegel as well, provided Schopenhauer with a model philosophy for this rejection. In his central work, *Die Welt als Wille und Vorstellung* (1819), Schopenhauer suggests that art under certain circumstances can provide temporary relief from the ceaseless striving of the Will, and thus a taste of the joy of total negation.

[76]Ibid., 7, 2, 332.
[77]Friedrich Schleiermacher, *Aesthetik* (Berlin, 1931), 4.

He considers tragedy the highest of the poetic arts because it is best suited to achieve this effect. He denounces as ridiculous the common romantic interpretation of tragedy as a struggle of man's free will against fate or destiny, since fate is all-powerful and all-pervasive. All life is struggle, and the so-called struggle against fate is actually only a meaningless conflict between different manifestations of the Will. Tragedy should rather lead us to look beyond this conflict to a "disinterested contemplation of the process." We should follow the example of the tragic hero, who, purified by suffering, sees through the "veil of Maya." His egoism and striving disappear, to be replaced by a "complete knowledge of the essence of the world, which brings to the Will a *quietus*, produces resignation, the surrender not only of life, but of the very will to live."[78] Because he finds this spirit of resignation more common in modern than in classic tragedy (since the Greeks tended to stress Stoic acceptance of the blows of fate), Schopenhauer considers modern tragedy superior.

In general, he favors tragedies of everyday life, since these remind us most strikingly of our own situation, and he praises the relationships between Hamlet, Laertes, and Ophelia and between Faust, Gretchen, and her brother for their domestic quality. Characters should be drawn from life, combining good and evil traits, wisdom and folly, as men do in nature. Still, Schopenhauer does not reject the traditional princely hero, whose more significant fall seems to point to the basic workings of the universe. His ideal dramatist seems to be one who, like Shakespeare, could provide both a sense of commonplace life and characters of more elevated stature.

Since tragedy leads to a denial of the will to live, comedy, its opposite, must assert that will; therefore Schopenhauer views it with some scorn. Comedy cannot avoid depicting adversity and suffering, since these are essential to the human condition, but it shows them as "transient, dissolving into joy, and mingled with success, victory, and hope, which triumph in the end." The curtain then must be quickly lowered "so that we may not see what comes after," the inevitable return of suffering and strife. Comedy can thus offer little of interest to the "reflective spectator," who recognizes that the view of life it offers is accidental and transient, and therefore fallacious.[79]

The *Parerga* and *Paralipomena* also give brief attention to the art of acting. In his earlier writings Schopenhauer, stressing the necessary verisimilitude of dramatic characters, said that the best dramatists spoke "like ventriloquists," giving equal truth and naturalness to every char-

---

[78]Arthur Schopenhauer, *Sämmtliche Werke*, 6 vols. (Leipzig, 1888), 2:299.
[79]Ibid., 3:500.

acter. The actor can never be as protean as this, since his own individuality can never be entirely effaced. Still, he must be a "capable and complete specimen" with sufficient intelligence and experience to understand his character, enough imagination to stir his own inner nature by fictitious events, and enough ability to display this inner nature to others. If he possesses these, he can create "a thousand extremely different characters all on the common basis of his individuality."[80]

Hegel's writings serve, in many respects, as a summation of the entire German philosophic and aesthetic tradition. He dealt with drama in general and tragedy in particular in a more profound and detailed manner than any writer since Lessing; indeed, modern critics have tended to echo the observation first made by A.C. Bradley in 1909 that Hegel was the only philosopher after Aristotle to treat tragedy "in a manner both searching and original."[81] Bradley goes on, in this highly influential lecture, to outline Hegel's theory as he understands it; his concise summary, less than 30 pages in length, has not surprisingly served for many subsequent English and American scholars as the essence of Hegel's thought on this subject. One effect of this is the general assumption, despite Bradley's own qualification of these points, that Hegel favored Greek over modern tragedy and that he saw the essence of tragedy in a conflict of two incompatible goods, best illustrated in Sophocles' *Antigone*. In fact, Hegel describes other sources of the tragic, and he lauds the moderns and Shakespeare in particular to such an extent that his translator, Bernard Bosanquet, argued that in the Hegelian system the romantic arts represent not a decline from but a culmination of the classic.[82]

Most of Hegel's observations on art may be found in the *Vorlesungen über die Aesthetik*, notes from a series of lectures in the 1820s, published in 1835. Here he adds to the traditional classic and romantic categories a third type of art, the symbolic. In symbolic art, the earliest form, man is aware of vague powers in the natural world and the course of human events, but is able to suggest them only by approximate and often distorted images. In classic art man discovers an outward form congruent with spiritual understanding. The best example is classic sculpture, which most nearly unites form and idea. Classic art is the most harmonious and beautiful, but since it remains bound to the visible and the finite, it is not the fullest realization of the spirit. Romantic art seeks this higher fulfillment by transcending the harmonious balance of form and idea, and accepting the conflict and disjuncture of a higher

[80]Ibid., 6:469–70.
[81]A. C. Bradley, *Oxford Lectures on Poetry* (London, 1950), 69.
[82]Bernard Bosanquet, *A History of Aesthetic* (London, 1949), 352.

level of experience. Painting, music, and poetry are the major romantic arts, and poetry, which unites the subjectivity of music with the objectivity of the visual arts, is potentially the richest of these.

The final section of Hegel's *Aesthetik*, where he deals most fully with tragedy, begins by calling dramatic poetry not only the "highest phase of the art of poetry" but "indeed of every kind of art." This is so because drama uses the only appropriate medium for presentation of the spiritual life, the human voice, and combines the objectivity of the epic mode with the subjectivity of the lyric. In order for this combination to be fully manifested, Hegel agrees with Schlegel that a "complete scenic presentation" is essential.[83]

Hegel's discussion of dramatic poetry is divided into three parts. The first deals with dramatic composition as a form of poetry, especially as it contrasts with the epic and lyric modes. Among other matters, Hegel here considers the parts of the drama, its diction and dialogue, and the three unities. He calls action the only essential unity, and for this action to be dramatic, it must involve the quest for a remote goal. Resistance to this quest is also essential, since genuine unity "can only find its rationale in the entire movement which consists in the assertion of this collision relative to the definition of the particular circumstances, characters, and ends proposed, not merely under a mode consonant to such ends and characters, but in such a way as to resolve the opposition implied."[84]

The brief second section deals with aspects of the drama as a performed work of art. Music and scenery are touched upon, but the most attention is given to the actor and his contrasting responsibilities in the ancient and modern theatre. The ancient formal theatre of masks and declaimed speech required great mechanical technique, but the actor's major responsibility was to enter with all his faculties into the part "without thereto adding anything peculiar to himself." The modern theatre, emphasizing the individual personality, demands more of the actor, not only "to assimilate profoundly the spirit of the poet and the part he accepts," but then "to supplement the part with his own creative insight, to fill in gaps, to discover modes of transition and generally, by his performance, to interpret the poet."[85]

The final section, on the types of dramatic poetry, with the focus on tragedy, is the most famous and most extensive of the three. Having already discussed the central importance of conflict in drama, Hegel analyzes the particular forms that such conflict took in Greek tragedy.

[83]G. W. F. Hegel, *The Philosophy of Fine Art*, 4 vols., trans. F. P. B. Osmaston (London, 1920), 4:248.
[84]Ibid., 259–60.
[85]Ibid., 287, 289.

The major form, developed by Aeschylus and brought to its peak by Sophocles, was the opposition "between ethical life in its social universality and the family as the natural ground of moral relations."[86] This is the conflict, most brilliantly illustrated in *Antigone*, between opposing goods, whose only flaw is that each demands the unqualified subjection of the other, and it is, of course, the view of tragedy most commonly associated with Hegel.

A second form of Greek tragedy is represented by *Oedipus*, in which a man carries out a volition unaware of its criminal nature. The Greeks, says Hegel, did not distinguish between deeds done in ignorance and in knowledge and thus portrayed here a tension that to modern consciousness is irrelevant; guilt or innocence in the modern sense is not involved. The heroes of classic tragedy do not choose "but are entirely and absolutely just that which they will and achieve."[87] The positions held by these heroes are not shown to be fallacious, but their one-sidedness is canceled by a final reconciliation that centers not on punishment or reward but on the establishment of harmony. This condition of stasis and resolution is represented by the chorus, "which attributes without reserve equal honor to all the gods."[88]

In modern tragedy, the hero embodying a single ethical position is replaced by characters "placed within a wide expanse of contingent relations and conditions, within which every sort of action is possible." The conflict thus becomes internal, and character, as earlier romantic theorists had observed, becomes the center of tragedy. Modern tragic heroes act not "in the interest of the ethical vindication of the truly substantive claims, but for the simple reason that they are the kind of men they are."[89] Hegel sees the conflict in *Hamlet* arising not from the opposing demands of vengeance and Christian morality, but from Hamlet's unwillingness to pursue any energetic course. Such indecision is typical of modern characters but rare in Greek drama, though it can be found in Euripides, the most modern of the Greeks. The reconciliation offered in Greek drama by the establishment of social and ethical harmony cannot easily be achieved in modern tragedy; it offers a colder and more abstract reconciliation, gained from the fulfillment of our realization that a character like Hamlet is doomed from the outset.

The conservative foundations of Hegel's aesthetic are more apparent in his views on comedy than in those on tragedy, but in both cases we see that he is at pains to preserve an essentially Platonic idea as the base of reality, an unchanging foundation of truth, nobility, and good-

---

[86]Ibid., 318.
[87]Ibid., 320.
[88]Ibid., 321.
[89]Ibid., 335.

ness. What he seeks and seems to find in classic drama is a dynamic which by a dialectic process pointed toward this idea, and what disturbs him most in modern drama is the development of oppositions and conflicts which do not appear to suggest the same revelation. In Aristophanes and in certain of the romantics, he seems to find a comic view that assumes a basically harmonious universe accepting all conflict and contradiction as transient and not serious. True comedy must possess "an infinite geniality and confidence capable of rising superior to its own contradictions, and experiencing therein no taint of bitterness or sense of misfortune whatever."[90] Plautus, Terence, and Molière are all pronounced lacking in such a spirit.

Hegel's commentators agree that he holds Greek drama in high esteem, but debate whether he finds modern drama as potentially successful even though in different terms. Clearly, Hegel was somewhat ambivalent on this matter. He recognized the power and richness of the modern approach and the impossibility in any case of returning to a classic world view. Nevertheless, he obviously felt some nostalgia for what he saw as the clear-cut relation to the absolute in Greek drama. The more ambiguous modern expressions gave him some uneasiness, at times even with Shakespeare, whom he warmly admired. In romantic irony he saw some possible reflection of the Aristophanic spirit, but at the same time recognized that drama might easily move beyond the use of irony to expose the contradictions of partial perspectives to a position of total subjectivity which would challange the absolute itself. The characters of Shakespeare were still based on "firm and decisive delineation," but other modern poets carried the ironic stance so far as to create characters "so essentially diverse that they are incapable of all homogeneous relation."[91] The resulting drama reflected not the absolute, but a universe of mere chance, caprice, and subjective experience.

Hegel's dismissal of this alternative did not mask the tension, and theorists after him increasingly accepted the aspects of romantic thought that he attempted to deny, at last even basing aesthetic systems directly upon them. The subjectivity and chance he so deplored came for many to be an essential part of the theory of art.

[90]Ibid., 302.
[91]Ibid., 324–25.

12

Italy and France in the Early Nineteenth Century

FRANCE, WHICH HAD REPLACED ITALY as the leading nation in literary theory in the seventeenth century, made the tradition of neoclassicism almost a national possession. The rise of a rival approach to literature in Germany (and to a lesser extent in England) at the beginning of the nineteenth century could hardly have avoided resistance from the French, especially since the new movement tended to define itself in large part by opposition to the French tradition. To make matters worse, French critical hegemony was challenged by the country's political enemies, so that support for neoclassicism became a patriotic act, strongly encouraged by Napoleon himself. Even after Napoleon's fall, though Schlegel's lectures on the drama and Madame de Staël's *De l'Allemagne* were published (both in 1814), resistance to the new movement remained strong. Not until the 1820s did romanticism gain spokesmen and native works powerful enough to establish it in France.

The dynamics of these years in Italy formed an interesting contrast to those in France. Here too the literary tradition, heavily influenced by the French, was strongly neoclassical. Goldoni had broken with the tradition of commedia dell'arte to establish modern Italian comedy, with strong inspiration from Molière, and he had spent his final years in Paris. Italy's first major tragic writer, Alfieri, wrote his early tragedies in French, drew heavily upon the model of Racine, and planned like Goldoni to settle in Paris—only to be driven out by the Revolution. The Italian eighteenth-century critical tradition, too, from Giovan Crescimbeni's (1663–1728) *La belleza della volgar poesia* (1700) and Gian Gravina's (1664–1718) *Della tragedia* (1712) through Antonio Conti's (1677–1749) *Lettera* in *Le quattro tragedie* (1751) and Alfonso Varano's (1705–1788) *Discorso sul teatro italiano* (1771), followed the general directions of French neoclassicism, supporting the unities, strict separation of genres, elevated language for tragedy, decorum, and moral uplift.

As the nineteenth century opened, however, this literary and critical tradition was no longer supported in Italy, as it was in France, by political convictions. On the contrary, northern Italy, first under French and then—after 1812—under Austrian occupation, began to seek a new national literature as a part of the growing desire for a free Italian state. Romanticism in Italy came gradually to be associated with this political dream, and neoclassicism with the forces of occupation and suppression.

Ironically, it was the forces of occupation themselves that introduced the new movement to Italy. When the Austrians replaced the French in Milan, they brought with them the ideas of German romanticism, and when the *Bibliotheca italiana* was founded in Milan to acquaint the Italians (so the authorities hoped) with German culture, it was at first an outlet for such expression. In the first issue Madame de Staël (1766–1817) published an article, *Sulla maniera e l'utilità delle traduzioni* (1816), that called upon Italian writers to break with traditional forms and mythological subjects and to seek more modern models in Shakespeare and the Germans. The ensuing flurry of essays supporting and attacking this advice is considered the beginning of the romantic movement in Italy.

Among these first manifestos, the most significant was the *Lettera semiseria di Grisostomo a suo figiuolo* (1816) by Giovanni Berchet (1783–1851), a translator of German and English literature and strong supporter of Madame de Staël. The most famous phrase in this essay is Berchet's distinction between classicism and romanticism as "the poetry of the dead" and "the poetry of the living."[1] This distinction refers not to history but to the choice of subject and methodology: the romantic writer deals with his own culture, speaks to the common man, and imitates nature; the classic author deals with the cultures of the past, writes for scholars, and creates "an imitation of imitations."[2] Thus Homer, Pindar, Sophocles, and Euripides were "in their own time romantics of a sort, since they wrote not of the Egyptians or Chaldeans, but of the Greeks."[3]

Berchet does not deal at length with the drama, but he does challenge some basic tenets of neoclassic dramatic theory as examples of arbitrary and unnatural rules. He divides poetry into four elementary forms—lyric, didactic, epic, and dramatic—and considers further genre divi-

---

[1]Giovanni Berchet, *Opere* (Naples, 1972), 463.
[2]Ibid., 464.
[3]Ibid., 463.

sions foolish and pedantic. "If poetry is the expression of living nature, she should be as much alive as the thing she represents, as free as the thought that springs from it."[4] The division of drama into tragedy and comedy and the unities of time and place Berchet considers unnatural restrictions of this necessary freedom. He points out that even rigorous purists have allowed the traditional 24-hour rule to be stretched another half-day, although only three hours of actual playing time have elapsed. "But an additional minute will overburden the poor human mind. The precision of calculation cannot be in doubt, since Good Taste itself, armed with a piece of chalk, writes on the board the motto 36 = 3."[5] Similarly, Berchet scoffs at the idea of a spectator so deluded in the theatre that he accepts a stage setting for reality and therefore cannot accept its change.

Silvio Pellico (1789–1854), whose tragedy *Francesca da Rimini* (1815) anticipated certain practices of the romantics, was the compiler of *Il conciliatore*, a journal founded in 1818 that opposed the pro-Austrian leanings of the *Bibliotheca italiana* and became the leading voice of the new movement in Italy. Pellico contributed a number of articles on theatrical subjects to this influential journal before its suppression in 1820. Soon thereafter, he was imprisoned for his association with the outlawed patriot organization, the *Carbonari*.

In two articles on the tragedies of Alfieri (1818), Pellico argues against restrictive definitions of dramatic genres. He admits the definition that tragedy is the representation of a heroic action exciting in us compassion and terror, but likens it to a definition of clothing as any garment protecting men from the cold or from immodesty: Greek robes, Turkish gowns, or modern Parisian fashions suit the definition equally well. Similarly, Shakespeare's *Othello* "with its multitude of characters and no unity whatever of time or place still excites compassion and terror, and is every whit as true a tragedy as the one which produces these same effects with three characters and all the most revered unities."[6]

As theatrical conditions change, Pellico argues, dramatic form must change as well. What was proper for a Greek outdoor theatre, seating an entire population before a permanent scenic structure, with a great distance between spectator and performer, will not be suitable for modern audiences: a few hundred persons in a smaller, more intimate space where scenery can be rapidly and easily changed. The subject matter of drama should change, too, and Pellico's essay ends with the rhetorical

[4]Ibid., 468.
[5]Ibid., 489.
[6]Silvio Pellico, "Due articoli sulla 'Vera idea della tragedia di V. Alfieri,' " *Conciliatore*, Sept. 6, 1818, in Egidio Bellorini, ed., *Discussioni e polemiche sul romanticismo*, 2 vols. (Bari, 1943), 1:408.

question, easily answered by his readers: "What are the heroic actions most important for Italy to celebrate? Those of the fatherland or of foreign nations? Mythologic or historic? The most ancient or the less remote of our own century?"[7]

The other leading *Conciliatore* writer on the drama was Ermes Visconti (1784–1841), who produced one of the best brief summaries of the aims of the new movement in *Idee elementari sulla poesia romantica* (1818) and a sprightly *Dialogo sulla unità drammatiche di luogo e di tempo* (1819). Though four persons participate in the *Dialogo*, essentially the discussion is between the romantic Romagnosi and the classicist Lamberti. The unity of time is the central matter discussed, and Romagnosi follows the standard practice of focusing on illusion. If a spectator can accept 24 hours in three, why arbitrarily stop his imagination at that point? He concludes that in the theatre two sorts of time are operating: the time actually required for the development of the events portrayed, and the time a spectator's attention may be engaged without fatigue. Trouble arises when the two are confused. The dramatist's goal should be "to distribute the scenes within real time and do it in such a way that all which is not described but presented occupies a time approximately equal to that which the same matter would occupy in reality."[8]

Alessandro Manzoni (1785–1873), the most famous author of this generation, did not write for the *Conciliatore*, but shared many of its ideals. His tragedy *Il conte di Carmagnola* (1820) was the first major Italian drama to fulfill the conditions laid down by Pellico, Berchet, and their circle. The play dealt with a subject drawn from Italian history, defied the traditional unities, and crowded the stage with characters speaking in a language strikingly less rhetorical than that of traditional tragedy. In the play's *Prefazione* he argued for an openminded criticism, a passage later quoted by Goethe, who found much to admire in this play: "Every composition presents to whoever wishes to examine it the necessary elements upon which a judgment may be based; and to my mind they are these: what is the author's intention, is this intention reasonable, and has the author achieved it? To set aside such an examination and insist upon judging all works according to rules whose universality and certainty are questionable is to open oneself to a distorted judgment of the work."[9] In a later letter (1827) Manzoni remarks that it was from Schlegel that he learned to regard literary works as "organic and not mechanical in form," based upon internal relationships rather than external standards. Thus every

[7]Ibid., 1:415.
[8]Ermes Visconti, "Dialogò sulla unità drammatiche di luogo e di tempo," in ibid., 2:44.
[9]Alessandro Manzoni, *Tutte le opere*, 6 vols. (Milan, 1957–74), 1:105.

composition possessed "its own special nature and reason for existence and thus must be judged by its own rules."[10]

The major concern of the *Prefazione* to *Il conte di Carmagnola* is with the unities of time and place, which Manzoni—quoting Schlegel—calls non-Aristotelian and unsuited to modern drama: even classic critics like Batteux and Marmontel have had to accept a stretching of the unity of time to 24 hours, clearly in defiance of a strict argument for verisimilitude. Ultimately, Manzoni's argument is a moral one: that the theatre should improve mankind, and any arbitrary and restrictive regulations tend to hinder its effectiveness. Bossuet and Rousseau were correct in condemning the immorality of the theatre, but they did not realize that what offended them resulted not from the nature of drama but from the French rules, a point Manzoni promises to explain in future writings. Again following Schlegel, he points to the chorus as a significant instrument in tragedy, a "personification of the moral thoughts inspired by the action."[11]

Il conte di Carmagnola and its preface gave Manzoni the position of leader of the Italian romantics and thereby made him the inevitable focus of neoclassic attack, not only in his own country but even in England and of course in France. Stung by these attacks, Manzoni singled out for rebuttal the one by the minor French critic Victor Chauvet, and published in 1823 an extended essay, *Lettre à M. C—— sur l'unité de temps et de lieu dans la tragédie.*

Chauvet had argued that the unities of time and place were originally derived not from the demands of verisimilitude but from the necessity of unity of action and consistency of character. Manzoni responded that unity of action implies not a single event (the catastrophe) but a series of events closely related, requiring no particular duration or locale. Characters must be well-drawn and clearly motivated whatever the length of action, but their goals may change during a play, which is quite proper whether unity of time is followed or not. Indeed, action and character may be clarified when the author does not strictly follow unity of time but skips over nonessential material (during the intervals). This "historic" approach, opposed to the classic, mixes "the serious and the burlesque, the touching and the low," as can be seen in Shakespeare, who "observed this mixture in reality and wished to portray the strong impression it made upon him."[12] The poet should be true to history, exposing its actual dynamic, which the unities often prevent. He must be as faithful as the historian to the facts of history but express them

[10]Manzoni, *Carteggio*, 2 vols. (Milan, 1921), 2:359.
[11]Manzoni, *Opere*, 1:108.
[12]Ibid., 2:1676, 1694.

poetically, tell not only what happened but why and with what emotional effects.

In the latter part of this essay Manzoni turns again to the moral concern of drama, noting that French authors have been frequently condemned for overemphasizing love intrigues. This results, he suggests, from the domination of the unities: these prohibit the authors from dealing with the great actions of history, which have complex and lengthy developments, and force them to write about love, "this passion being of all the richest in rapid incidents, and thus best suited for being confined within these rules."[13] Moreover, most French dramatists compounded this error by seeking to excite the passions of the spectator and draw him emotionally into the action instead of seeking the proper emotions of tragedy, which come only when the spectator is lifted "into the pure regions of disinterested contemplation" where "the useless sufferings and vain pleasures of men" arouse the proper feelings of pity and terror. Yet the end of tragedy remains for Manzoni not emotional but moral, and the distance he seeks does not remove men from the world as Schopenhauer wished, but provides them with a perspective for clearer understanding of an action, in the manner of Brecht. Emotions serve to attract and please us, but only so that they may in turn arouse "the moral force by means of which we control and judge them." The tragic poet, "in bringing before us events that do not interest us as actors, where we are only witnesses, can help us learn the habit of fixing our thoughts on those calm and great ideas which overpower and dissolve everyday realities and which, when more carefully developed and accessible, will unquestionably improve our wisdom and dignity."[14]

During the years between 1816 and 1820, as romanticism was developing in Milan, one interested observer was the young Frenchman Henri Beyle, later known as Stendhal (1783–1842), a devotee of Shakespeare and Byron and a subscriber during these years to the major British journal of literary criticism, the *Edinburgh Review*. Stendhal wrote two unpublished essays for *Il conciliatore*, dealing with the implications of romanticism for the drama; these essays served as the basis for his later *Racine et Shakespeare*. When Stendhal returned to Paris in 1821, romanticism (the actual term was not yet in use; Stendhal was one of the first to employ it, in 1823) was still widely regarded as a suspicious foreign movement. Translations of Schiller and Shakespeare appeared that year, however, and François Guizot (1787–1874), in the preface to the latter, was bold enough to urge abandoning the classic system,

[13]Ibid., 1700.
[14]Ibid., 1710.

the Alexandrine verse form, and even the unities. "The classic system was born from the life of the time, a time which has passed," he said. "It seems to me that only the system of Shakespeare can furnish a model for genius to follow now."[15]

A major test of Shakespeare in France occurred in the summer of 1822 with the arrival of a troupe of English actors to perform his works. They were shouted from the stage by patriotic Frenchmen, who called Shakespeare an aide-de-camp of Wellington, and this scandal spurred Stendhal to submit an article to the *Paris Monthly Review of British and Continental Literature*—the first chapter of *Racine et Shakespeare* (1823). A second chapter appeared in the same journal, and a third was added to complete a separately published brochure before the end of the year. Italian ideas are strong in the work, especially in the opening chapter, a significant part of which is a direct translation of sections of Visconti's *Dialogo* from the *Conciliatore*. It is clear that Stendhal kept closely in touch with developments in Milan; since he associated in Paris with Manzoni's friend and translator Fauriel, he was probably acquainted as well with the *Lettre à M. C———*, which Fauriel published, along with the French translation of Manzoni's play, the week after the appearance of *Racine et Shakespeare*.

Stendhal's opening chapter poses the question, "In order to create tragedies capable of interesting the public of 1823, must one follow the practice of Racine or that of Shakespeare?" The major part of this essay is a dialogue between an academician and a romantic, drawn largely from Visconti. Perhaps the most interesting observation in this dialogue on the much-discussed problem of dramatic illusion is the admission by the romantic that in fact there are moments of "perfect illusion" in the theatre (though they last for only fractions of seconds), and these are indeed the essence of the pleasure one finds in tragedy—but they come at moments of reflection, not of action nor of admiration, and they are more common in Shakespeare than in Racine.

Stendhal's emphasis on pleasure as the purpose of tragedy is one idea that markedly separates him from the Italians, especially from Manzoni. This famous distinction opens the third chapter of his essay: "Romanticism is the art of offering the public literary works which, given their present habits and beliefs, are capable of giving them the greatest possible pleasure. Classicism, on the other hand, offers them the literature which gave the greatest possible pleasure to their grandparents."[16] Applying this distinction, Stendhal finds not only Shake-

---

[15]François Guizot, "Notice biographique et littéraire," *Oeuvres complètes de Shakespeare*, trans. Le Tourneur, 13 vols. (Paris, 1821), 1:151.

[16]Henri Beyle, *Oeuvres complètes*, 79 vols. (Paris, 1927–37), 13:43.

speare but Sophocles, Euripides, and Racine all romantics, since they wrote according to the prejudices and fashions of their day. The nineteenth-century authors who bore their audiences by imitating Racine or Sophocles are examples of classicism. It is even possible to be a classicist by imitating Shakespeare instead of seeking to reflect the concerns of one's own time—Stendhal cites Schiller as an example. We are closer to Shakespeare than to the Greeks because he also lived in a period of political upheaval and uncertainty, but our public is more refined and educated than his, so a new sort of drama must be created for them.

In his second chapter, *Le rire*, Stendhal took up the matter of comedy, here following Schlegel and the Germans more closely than the English or Italians. Like the Germans, he found Aristophanes the great comic master and comedy strongly conditioned by the social circumstances of its creation. Aristophanes had the good fortune to live in a society of lighthearted people who sought happiness everywhere and encouraged him as part of their universal amusement. Molière, though a man of genius, was far inferior as a comic author because of the rigidity of his society: under Louis XIV all sought to follow a single social model, and laughter could be directed only against those who imitated this model poorly. The result is that as social conditions have changed, Molière is no longer funny. In 1822, Stendhal reported, *Tartuffe* aroused only two laughs in the audience.[17]

Stendhal's essay aroused a greater literary debate over the new movement than Paris had yet seen. Articles and pamphlets appeared on both sides, and at the Académie Française romanticism was officially condemned. In a speech on April 24, 1824, the academician Louis Auger (1772–1829) denounced German romanticism as a purely theoretical movement, with no relation to reality, which had not yet produced a single play of significance. French romanticism was worse still, a bastard offspring "lacking the energy, the boldness, and the excesses of German romanticism."[18] In August the Comte de Frayssinons, Grand Master of the University of Paris, called romanticism an attack on the monarchy and organized religion.[19]

Stendhal completely revised his essay to respond to these attacks; it reappeared in 1825 in the form of a series of letters between a classicist and a romantic, as *Racine et Shakespeare II*. Challenged to provide a brief definition of romantic tragedy, he offered, "a tragedy in prose which lasts several months and is set in various locales."[20] Many of the

[17]Ibid., 38.
[18]Léon Séché, *Le cénacle de la muse française* (Paris, 1908), 79.
[19]Ibid., 237.
[20]Beyle, *Oeuvres*, 13:89.

great events of French history, he notes, would be best treated in this manner (as, for example, a drama based on Napoleon's 100 days after Elba), events that Voltaire and Racine were prevented from considering. Dismissing the Alexandrine as a device to hide foolishness (*un cache-sottise*), he calls for an end to "epic and official language" and for the replacement of tirades by simple speeches "lively with natural brilliance." Men of genius like Molière and Racine created great works despite the rules, not because of them. Indeed, repeating Berchet's argument, Stendhal now claims Molière for romanticism, since "all great writers were romantic in their own times."[21] The classicists are those who copy these masters instead of imitating nature. As for the charges from classic critics that romanticists have created theory but no major works, it is the censorship of church and state which gives classicism artificial support by preventing new experimental works from appearing.

The major period of romantic theory in France was launched by Victor Hugo (1802–1885) in his famous preface to his play *Cromwell* (1827). Few of its ideas were totally original, even in France, but Hugo presented them with a color and force that made him at once the critical spokesman for the new movement. The preface begins with a survey of literary history in the manner of the German romantics, showing how each period evolved its own distinctive type of poetry—the primitive lyric ode, the epic of the classical period, and the drama of modern times (which Hugo, doubtless influenced by Chateaubriand, dates from the arrival of Christianity). These three periods are the poetic equivalent of childhood, youth, and maturity and represent a constantly repeated natural process. Thus the major periods in Western literature that culminated respectively in the Bible, Homer, and Shakespeare can be seen repeated on a smaller scale in each historical period. The movement is always from lyric to epic to dramatic, from the ideal to the grandiose to the human. So in the Bible the sequence runs Genesis, Kings, Job; in Greek literature, Orpheus, Homer, Aeschylus; and in French literature, Malherbe, Chapelain, Corneille.

The central concept in this essay, and indeed in much of Hugo's writing, is that of the grotesque as the organizing principle of the third phase of this recurring sequence. Classic art recognized only the harmonious and beautiful as its province, but Christianity forces the poet to deal with the full truth of reality: "that the ugly exists there beside the beautiful, the deformed next to the graceful, the grotesque on the reverse of the sublime, evil with good, darkness with light."[22] The artist now accepts this world as God created it, with its diversity and its

---

[21]Ibid., 106, 109.
[22]Victor Hugo, *Oeuvres complètes*, 18 vols. (Paris, 1967–70), 3:50.

contradictions. The poetry born of Christianity, the poetry of our time, is the drama, since drama is the only poetic form that seeks the real, doing so in imitation of nature by "combining the sublime and the grotesque" and seeking "the harmony of contraries."[23] The grotesque is moreover not simply an appropriate element of the drama but one of its greatest beauties, as we see in Shakespeare, whose genius combined Macbeth and the witches, Hamlet and the gravediggers, Lear and the Fool.

The same application of common sense that demolishes the traditional but artificial distinction of genres, says Hugo, may be used to demolish the unities of time and place (unity of action having been long since universally accepted as valid). Verisimilitude, traditionally offered in defense of these rules, is precisely what destroys them. Modern writers recognize that nothing could be more false and artificial than the neutral meeting place of a Racinian tragedy; they know that "an exact and unique location is one of the first elements of reality."[24] Similarly, every action dictates its own necessary duration. The only rules to which an artist should submit are the general laws of nature and the special rules, unique to each individual creation, which unify that creation. No treatise on poetry can ever codify these rules; they are infinitely variable, and unique to each work. The artist must look neither to rules nor to other artists, even the greatest, but must "take council only of nature, truth, and inspiration."[25]

This is not to say that art should seek merely to duplicate nature, a goal Hugo calls ridiculous. He accepts heightening and concentration, even (unlike Stendhal) the use of verse. Poetic speech discourages laziness and self-indulgence in the dramatist, forcing him to cast his thoughts in a more memorable and striking form for his public. If the drama is a mirror, it should not be an ordinary one, giving back a faithful but dull image of reality. It should be rather a "concentrating mirror which, far from weakening the colored beams, gathers and concentrates them, to make a gleam a light and a light a flame."[26] The poet must still select and refine, but his goal is not the beautiful (as in classicism) or the commonplace (as some misguided romantics seem to wish) but the characteristic, concentrating upon the essential elements of historical reality.

A rather more extreme version of this same concept was expressed by Alfred de Vigny (1797–1863) in the preface to his novel *Cinq-Mars* (1827), *Réflexions sur la vérité dans l'art*. Vigny distinguishes between the

[23]Ibid., 60.
[24]Ibid., 63.
[25]Ibid., 69.
[26]Ibid., 70.

True (*le Vrai*), which is the totality of objective facts and events and is the province of historians, and Truth (*la Vérité*), which is an attempt to explain and understand these facts in terms of human imagination, the province of the poet. Truth is "better than the True, an ideal ensemble of its principal forms ... the sum total of all its values." It is this truth which is the goal of dramatic art. Of course, the dramatist must start by mastering the True of the age he is depicting, but this is merely a task of "attention, patience, and memory." Then the real work of "choosing and grouping around an invented center" begins; the work of "imagination and the great Common Sense which is genius itself."[27]

Hugo's manifesto in *Cromwell* was seconded within a year by two other significant defenses of romanticism, Charles Augustin Sainte-Beuve's (1804–1869) *Tableau de la poésie française au XVIe siècle* (1828) and Emile Deschamps's (1797–1871) preface to *Etudes françaises et étrangères* (1828). Sainte-Beuve urges the French to look back to the Renaissance for inspiration rather than to the rule-laden seventeenth century. It is true that no great dramatic genius, no French Shakespeare or Lope de Vega had appeared then; but the freedom enjoyed by the generation of Hardy, and the resistance expressed then to the unities and the Alexandrine, provided a significant precedent for the present romantics.[28]

Deschamps, like Hugo and Sainte-Beuve, bases his discussion upon the idea of literary evolution, since "the men of true talent in every age are always endowed with an instinct which pushes them toward the *new*."[29] Dramatic art has always been one of the glories of France. Molière stands unchallenged as the comic master of Europe, and though Shakespeare holds a similar stature in tragedy, he stands alone in England, while France has a long and unbroken tradition of masters in this genre. The vein is now exhausted, however, and modern French drama is composed almost entirely of lifeless imitation of the great French masters. To break this cycle of imitation, French authors must either create or translate, and the genius of invention now being dulled, Deschamps councils translation—particularly of Shakespeare, "with his magnificent development, the variety of his characters, the freedom of his conceptions, his effective mixtures of comic and tragic, in short, with all his new and original beauties and even with those flaws inseparable from them, which at least are not the flaws of our own poets."[30]

[27]Alfred de Vigny, *Oeuvres complètes*, 6 vols. (Paris, 1914–35), 5:viii.
[28]Charles Augustin Sainte-Beuve, *Tableau de la poésie française au XVIe siècle*, 2 vols. (Paris, 1876), 1:427.
[29]Emile Deschamps, *Oeuvres complètes*, 6 vols. (Paris, 1872–74), 2:260.
[30]Ibid., 284.

Deschamps hastens to explain that he is not advocating translations of total fidelity. The good translator will carefully remove that material forced upon Shakespeare by the "bad taste of his times" but will retain everything else and add nothing to the original. Such a translation will show the French that true romantic drama is to be found not in the disregard of the unities or breaking tragic declamation with farce interludes, but "in the individualized painting of characters, in the continual replacement of recitation by action, in the simplicity of the poetic language or the coloring, in short, in a totally modern style."[31]

Deschamps himself attempted to provide such a translation, collaborating with Alfred de Vigny on a *Roméo et Juliette*, the performance of which was blocked by conservative forces. Vigny, undaunted, proceeded on his own to translate *Othello* as *Le more de Venise* (1829), which was produced successfully at the Comédie a few months before Hugo's more famous *Hernani*. In an introductory *Lettre*—which Vigny, following the example of Voltaire, addressed to an English lord—the dramatist describes his goal as threefold: to create a modern tragedy which in conception would offer "a sweeping picture of life instead of the restricted portrayal of the denouement of an intrigue"; in composition would offer "characters, not roles, and peaceful undramatic scenes mixed with scenes of comedy and tragedy"; and in execution would offer "a familiar style, comic, tragic, and sometimes epic."[32] Vigny suggests that the best way of testing the merit of these goals is translation of an already proven foreign work, rather than an original piece that might suffer from weaknesses of its own. Shakespeare, accepted by generations of Englishmen, seems an ideal choice, especially since Shakespeare seized the reality of his own times, with little regard for tradition or rules. The old classic system, he says, provided security for dramatists of the second rank and produced works of harmony and coherence. Still, like the theocratic and feudal systems, it became at last outmoded and needed to be replaced.

Vigny's idea of relating a work to its historical setting is of course commonplace among the romantics, but he carries it further than most. "To present a tragedy is nothing else than to prepare an evening, and the most accurate title ought to be the date of the performance."[33] Thus the event of October 24, 1829, a unique combination of the dramatist's goals, the actors' interpretation, and the public's response, was to Vigny the true *More de Venise*. (Here he strikingly anticipates many twentieth-century theorists who regard drama as occasion.)

[31] Ibid., 285–86.
[32] Vigny, *Oeuvres*, 3:xiv.
[33] Ibid., xii–xiii.

The growing respectability of romantic ideas at this time is clearly illustrated in the work of another translator, Benjamin Constant (1767–1830). In 1809 Constant had translated Schiller's *Wallenstein* and added a preface, *Quelques réflexions sur la tragédie de Wallenstein et sur le théâtre allemand*. In 1829 he reworked this preface, with significant alterations, as *De la Guerre de Trente Ans*. In 1809 Constant had stressed the difficulties of adjusting the German play to French practice: the use of Alexandrines, the elimination of secondary characters and scenes of local color, the general narrowing of focus both in action and character to suit the unities of time and place. He had viewed these as justifiable changes, however, since what was appropriate for Germany could prove pernicious in France. The Germans, Constant suggested, had a native passion for truth, historical accuracy, and moral verisimilitude that served as a natural check on their imagination and their desire to please the public. French authors, obsessed with popularity, needed external restraints to keep them from seeking easy success to the detriment of art. Thus the unities, for example, served the French well "despite the problems they impose and the faults they may occasion."[34]

In 1829 Constant expressed a very different opinion. He still thought the French spirit required more guidance than the German, but not so much as to imply "a puerile respect for superannuated rules." He now found the unities of time and place "particularly absurd," forcing the poet to neglect in character and events "the truth of gradation, the delicacy of nuance." Instead of condemning all shifts in time and place, as he had in 1809, he rejected only those that were "too frequent or too abrupt." Instead of devotion to arbitrary rules, he called for flexibility and a regulatory system in both theatre and society that would unite "order and liberty."[35]

Constant expresses rather bolder and more original ideas in his *Réflexions sur la tragédie*, also published in 1829. Here he suggests that there are three possible bases for tragedy. The first is passion, usual in French classic tragedy: Phèdre, Andromaque, Oreste exist only for their passions; they have little individualized character otherwise. Shakespeare and the Germans, however, and following their example, the romantic theatre, base tragedy on character. A third possibility, so far unexplored, is the individual in conflict with society, and Constant recommends this as a basis for the tragedy of the future. Passion, he says, which the French narrowed to love, has been conventionalized and exhausted. Character offers more variety, but it also restricts an author

[34]Benjamin Constant, *Quelques réflexions sur la tragédie de Wallenstein et sur le théâtre allemand* (Paris, 1809), xxiii.
[35]Constant, *Oeuvres* (Paris, 1957), 918.

by limiting him to traits that serve the action. The struggle of man's moral force against the world, its "circumstances, laws, institutions, public and private relations" is, however, "the most important feature of human life" and an inexhaustible source of tragic situations. Moreover, the "network of institutions and conventions which envelops us from birth to death" has for us the same power that fate had for the Greeks, and its portrayal will arouse in modern man the recognition and terror central to classic tragedy.[36]

Victor Hugo and Alexandre Dumas (1802–1870) had little interest in the possible reform of the French stage through translations, in the manner of Deschamps, Vigny or Constant; they preferred to experiment with original works based on episodes in French history. Hugo's *Marion de Lorme* (1829) attempted to carry out those ideas expressed in the preface to *Cromwell*, though the work was blocked by the censor, forcing Hugo to turn instead to his *Hernani*. In the meantime Dumas's *Henri III et sa cour* (1829) was performed with success at the Comédie. Essentially as romantic as the work of Hugo, *Henri III* did not arouse similar protest, doubtless because Dumas made no attempt to set himself up as the leader in theory or practice of a new movement. On the contrary, his brief preface to *Henri III* credits Hugo and others with inventing the method he followed and indeed surpassing him in it. Dumas claims no interest in founding a genre, but he does betray a distinct romantic bias: "I establish no system because I have written, not according to a system, but following my conscience."[37] In the subsequent preface to *Napoléon Bonaparte*, he again disclaims any system, any school, any banner. "To amuse and to interest, those are the only rules which I will not say that I follow, but which I admit."[38]

The success of Hugo's *Hernani* (1830), considered by both classicists and romantics as the key test of romantic ideas in the theatre, established, by its success at the Comédie, the new drama in France. Its preface is much shorter and less detailed than that of *Cromwell* but is interesting for its much more political focus. Here Hugo echoes Stendhal and the Italians in seeing romanticism in literature as a manifestation closely allied to liberalism in politics. "*Ultras* of all sorts, classicists or monarchists," he says, seek in vain to hold back the revolutionary tide and to preserve the *ancien régime* "both in society and in literature."[39] The general public now insists upon liberty, though not license; in letters as in society, it calls out not for anarchy but for new and more flexible laws.

[36]Ibid., 951–52.
[37]Alexandre Dumas, *Théâtre complet*, 15 vols. (Paris, 1863–74), 1:115.
[38]Ibid., 314.
[39]Hugo, *Oeuvres*, 3:922.

The revolution of 1830 removed at least for a time the threat of censorship and opened the theatres to works such as Hugo's *Marion de Lorme* that had previously been banned. Although Hugo viewed the revolutionary upheavals with some misgivings, he enthusiastically hailed the freedom they brought to artists. He wrote a new preface to *Marion de Lorme* in 1831, blaming the censor for blocking the development of a "true, conscientious, sincere art"; 1830 would eventually be recognized as "no less a literary than a political date." In literature as in politics, men must work to establish a new and more humane order. The poet's responsibility was "to create a theatre in its entirety, a vast yet simple theatre, one varied, national in its historical subjects, popular in its truth, human, natural, and universal in its passions."[40] Classicism and romanticism, like all old factional terms, must be swallowed up in the united consciousness of the masses, upon which the art of the future must be based.

Hugo attempted to follow this program of romantic historical drama for the next several years, from *Le roi s'amuse* (1831) to *Ruy Blas* (1838) but other romantic dramatists were experimenting in different directions. The most influential of these was Dumas, who departed most significantly from Hugo in *Antony* (1831), his tragedy of modern life, which was also freed for presentation by the abolishment of censorship. This popular and influential work contains Dumas's best analysis of his aims in writing it. In act 4, scene 6, the dramatist Eugène speaks of the problems facing a contemporary playwright. Comedy, "the painting of manners," has since the Revolution become difficult if not impossible to create, because all social classes have been confounded. "Nothing indicates a profession, no circle marks off certain manners or customs; all is mixed together, nuances have replaced colors, and the painter requires colors, not nuances." Drama, dealing with the passions, presents another difficulty. The characters, emotions, and actions of history are known and accepted by all, but if one tries to expose the heart of man in a modern setting, one is accused of exaggeration. The spectator is likely to say, "That is false; I don't act that way; when the woman I love deceives me, I suffer, of course—yes, for a while—but I don't stab her or die myself, and the proof of it is that I am still here."[41]

Nevertheless, Dumas attempted in *Antony* to stage not merely a scene of contemporary life but a dramatization of a personal emotional crisis. "Antony," he says in *Mes mémoires* (1852), "is myself, except for the murder." The play is not a drama, not a tragedy—not even a play, but

---

[40]Ibid., 4:465–66.
[41]Dumas, *Théâtre*, 2:52–53.

a "scene of love, jealousy, and wrath in five acts."[42] That the play was attacked for its immorality is a charge that Dumas credits entirely to his having the action in the present. With changing laws and mores, attitudes toward adultery have changed, and what Molière could treat as comedy now demands tears and condemnation. Equally important is the loss of distance. We do not recognize ourselves in Georges Dandin, Harpagon, or Pierrot, who neither speak nor dress as we do, but when an author is bold enough to present in modern dress "manners as they are, passion as it exists, crime as it is hidden," then the public "recognizes itself as in a mirror, frowns instead of laughing, attacks instead of approving, and growls instead of applauding."[43]

With *Antony*, the *drame*, which writers of the previous century had seen as a vehicle for the promulgation of morality, took on a moral ambiguity that made it a pioneer in what would become a favorite type of nineteenth-century theatre, the "shocking" drama of contemporary life.

Despite Dumas's analysis, historical dramas were not exempt from charges of immorality, as Hugo discovered when *Le roi s'amuse* was suppressed. The problem was more political than social—a play showing a king of France as a debaucher of young girls and frequenter of low taverns proved intolerable just a few days after the attempted assassination of Louis-Philippe—but Hugo felt called upon to stress the moral function of the theatre in the prefaces to this play and his next, *Lucrèce Borgia* (1833). The theatre, he said, has "a natural mission, a social mission, a humane mission" never to send its audiences away "without bearing with them some austere and profound morality." The shift from verse to prose, though not commented upon in the preface, presumably helped make the morality more accessible to the masses.

Even so, the precise content of this austere morality is not clear. It seems to involve the demonstration of the workings of fate (or providence, as Hugo calls it in speaking of *Le roi s'amuse*), the interjection of reminders of human mortality ("Remember that thou art dust") into all scenes of gaiety, and an attempt to find in the most hideous characters and actions a touch of humanity and goodness (Triboulet's fatherly or Lucrèce Borgia's motherly compassion, for example). The drama should "touch upon everything without being stained by anything, take a moral and compassionate view of all things deformed and repulsive." The most hideous object can become "holy and pure" if touched with "a religious idea."[44] Clearly, this idea reflects Hugo's continuing interest

[42]Dumas, *Mes mémoires*, 5 vols. (Paris, 1954–67), 4:302.
[43]Ibid., 305–06.
[44]Hugo, *Oeuvres*, 4:656.

in the juxtaposition of the beautiful and the ugly, now given a religious dimension; its effect on characterization became particularly important once the neoclassic types, upheld by the old concept of decorum, began to be undermined by the romantics through the conscious introduction of contradictory elements. (In this respect the writers of melodrama, unlike Hugo, closely followed tradition.)

The preface to *Marie Tudor* (1833) turns from a moral emphasis to a balanced consideration of beauty and didacticism in drama, explained in the sort of opposing terms that always attracted Hugo. There are two means of raising passions in the theatre, he asserts, the grand and the true. The former, the method of Corneille, seizes the masses; the latter, the method of Molière, seizes the individual. The greatest artists, like Shakespeare, combine these opposites. Hamlet is "colossal, but real"; he is man, yet also mankind. The true is the source of morality; the grade, of beauty. The preface to *Angelo* (1835) continues to develop these ideas, claiming that the play is "not entirely royal, for fear that the possibility of application would disappear in the grandeur of its proportions; not entirely bourgeois, for fear that the smallness of the characters would nullify the magnitude of the idea; but princely and domestic—princely because the drama must be grand, domestic because the drama must be true."[45] Not for Hugo the attempt to capture the passions of princes in the domestic setting of an *Antony*; the historical dimension is essential to gain the stature he seeks. When he speaks of the *drame* (for example, in the preface to *Ruy Blas*, 1838) as "the third great form of art, containing, merging, and making fertile the first two [comedy and tragedy],"[46] it is always the historical and never the domestic drama that he had in mind.

Earlier in this preface Hugo suggests another tripartite arrangement, with a third genre that does not combine the best features of comedy and tragedy—the melodrama. Each genre appeals to a different part of the audience, he points out. Women, interested in the passions and emotions, seek the pleasure of the heart in tragedy. The general crowd, interested in an action-filled plot and sensational effects, seeks the pleasure of the eyes in melodrama. Thinkers, interested in human beings and their motives, seek the pleasure of the mind in comedy. Though he suggests that each fills a legitimate need, Hugo calls the melodrama "vulgar and inferior" to the others.[47]

The exact relationship between the melodrama and the romantic drama was debated during this period and has been debated ever since.

[45]Ibid., 5:683.
[46]Ibid., 670–71.
[47]Ibid., 669–70.

Hugo sought, as the preface to *Ruy Blas* clearly shows, to dissociate himself from the popular form. Still, his work, especially when he wrote in prose, had enough in common with that of the popular melodrama authors that his opponents conflated the two—either as a rhetorical strategy or because, from the viewpoint of neoclassicism, the two forms were virtually indistinguishable. The critic Jules Janin, writing of *Angelo*, reported, "Its admirers said 'It's Shakespeare!' and its detractors 'It's Pixérecourt!' "[48]

The most common modern distinction was set forth succinctly by François Ponsard in an 1852 review:

> I would call any play either a drama or a tragedy if it were primarily concerned with the representation of character, the development of passions, or the re-creation of the spirit and manners of a period, and it subordinated the plot to this dominant idea. Any play, on the contrary, which seeks only to astonish and move the spectator by a rapid succession of adventures and unexpected turns would be a melodrama. Each of these works has its own particular laws which must be observed.[49]

Scorned by both classicists and romantics, the melodrama inspired few contemporary theorists to consider what its "particular laws" might be, or even to defend it as worthy of serious consideration. Charles Nodier (1780–1844), in the introduction to Guilbert de Pixérecourt's *Théâtre Choisi* (1841), presented the most extended defense of the genre. He stresses the moral function of the melodrama, its emphasis on justice and humanity, its stimulation of virtue, its arousal of tender and generous sympathy, and above all its embodiment of the "morality of the Revolution," which showed that "even here below, virtue is always rewarded and crime is never without punishment."[50] Melodramatic theatre has thus replaced the departed church as the source of moral instruction, and the uncontested contemporary popularity of the genre explains why crime has never been so rare, especially among the lower classes. The new romantic dramas have shown the artistic potential of melodrama by elevating it with "the artificial pomp of lyricism," but unhappily their authors have not always been faithful to the essence of melodrama—its morality.[51]

Nodier considers only one criticism of the genre at any length, that of style. He admits that the language of the melodrama is often exaggerated and affected but asserts that it serves its purpose well. That

[48]Jules Janin, *Histoire de la littérature dramatique*, 2d ser., 6 vols. (Paris, 1853–58), 4:368.
[49]François Ponsard, *Oeuvres complètes*, 3 vols. (Paris, 1865–76), 3:372–73.
[50]Guilbert de Pixérecourt, *Théâtre choisi*, 4 vols. (Paris, 1841–43), 1:iii.
[51]Ibid., vii.

purpose is to delight and impress the multitude, to strike their imagination and seize their memory; true popular drama has always done this, which is why Aristophanes and Plautus are now so difficult to read.

Nowhere in Nodier is there the interest, so typical of romantic theory, in distancing this new genre from what has gone before. On the contrary, in stressing instruction and delight, and defending poetic justice, he appears to be attempting to stress a certain continuity with the neoclassic tradition. This tendency is equally clear in the theoretical statements of the founding father of melodrama, Guilbert de Pixérecourt (1773–1844). In his *Dernières réflexions de l'auteur sur le mélodrame* (1843), Pixérecourt remarks that with the exception of two plays, "I have represented in my dramas the three unities as much as possible. I have always thought that there should be complete unity in a dramatic work."[52] In Pixérecourt's opinion the concept of unity extended also to unity of vision between writing and production, causing him to demand a single theatre artist involved with the entire process of production, of the sort later championed by Wagner: "A theatre piece can only be well conceived, well constructed, well set into dialogue, well rehearsed, and well played under the auspices and by the efforts of a single man having the same taste, the same judgment, the same mind, the same heart, and the same opinion."[53]

Like Nodier, Pixérecourt condemns the romantic drama, for its disregard of the unities, its multiplication of scenes, and most of all for its lack of morality and its interest in the lowest vices—adultery, rape, incest, parricide, prostitution; he finds the plays "evil, dangerous, immoral, and devoid of interest or truth."[54] What then prevented Pixérecourt from making common cause with the neoclassicists, who shared these same complaints? The language of melodrama was surely a major obstacle, as Nodier suggested, but there were others. The melodrama's interest in spectacle and in mixing tones also clearly offended such neoclassic critics as Jean-Louis Geoffroy; writing of Pixérecourt's *La rose blanche et la rose rouge* (1809), he said, "The determining characteristics of melodrama are the abuse of pantomime and machines, combats, dances, the mixing of tragedy and low comedy, declamation and bombast."[55]

Despite its lack of critical respectability, the melodrama proved a popular and durable form. Nor was it the only competitor the romantic drama faced in its search for audiences after its triumph over neoclassicism. While the melodrama, developed in the popular boulevard

[52] Ibid., 4:496.
[53] Ibid., 497.
[54] Ibid., 497–98.
[55] Ibid., 2:506–07.

theatres, drew from the romantic drama the more proletarian audiences, the "well-made play" of Eugène Scribe (1791–1861) and his followers also challenged romanticism, first at the more bourgeois boulevard houses and then at the stronghold of traditional drama, the Comédie Française itself. The influence of Scribe on subsequent drama can hardly be overestimated. The realistic dramatists of the later nineteenth century—most notably Ibsen—drew upon his technique of careful construction and preparation of effects, and through their example the well-made play became and still remains the traditional model of play construction.

Yet Scribe, unlike Hugo or even Pixérecourt, saw himself not as a reformer or founder of any school, but simply as the successful practitioner of a craft. He wrote no prefaces, issued no manifestos; his works spoke for themselves. His single extended critical comment occurs in his reception speech to the Académie Française (1836), which argues, surely with gentle irony, the superiority of song over drama and denies that comedy reflects the manners of its own society. Quite the contrary, in fact: during the licentious Regency period, comedy was cold, correct, pretentious, and decent; during the bloody Revolution, it was humane, benevolent, and sentimental. The reason, says Scribe, is that spectators go the theatre "not for instruction or improvement but for diversion and distraction, and that which diverts them most is not truth but fiction. To see again what you have before your eyes daily will not please you, but that which is not available to you in everyday life—the extraordinary and the romantic."[56]

Even within the romantic drama, the system advanced by Hugo was by no means universally accepted. Dumas's *Antony*, as we have seen, offered quite another sort of drama, as did Alfred de Vigny's *Chatterton* (1835). Vigny's preface, *Dernière nuit de travail*, disclaims all theoretical purpose: "The most vain of vanities is perhaps that of literary theories, which have their moment of popularity and are soon ridiculed and forgotten."

Nevertheless, the preface advances a distinct theory of the drama, and the remark on vanity probably comes less from general disillusionment than from Vigny's realization that in 1835 he was advancing ideas he had rejected in 1829. The public now merely smiled at the grand effects "to delight the eyes by childish surprises"—a reference that could apply to either Hugo or Pixérecourt—and the time had come for a simpler and more serious drama, which Vigny called "the drama of thought." Its focus would be on internal action—the "wounding of a soul"—which would have "the most complete unity, the most severe

---

[56]Eugène Scribe, *Oeuvres complètes*, 16 vols. (Paris, 1854), 1:6.

simplicity." The action would be all catastrophe and denouement, (the very sort of thing Vigny condemned in 1829): "the story of a man who writes a letter in the morning, who awaits the response until evening; it arrives and kills him—but here the moral action is everything."[57] This format has been described as a return to the principles of Racine, but surely it might be more accurately called an anticipation of those of Ibsen. The structure, the internalization of the action, the modern setting, and even the theme—"the stifling of a spiritual man by a materialist society"—strongly suggest the work of the later dramatist.

Finding suitable interpreters for the new drama was a continual problem for the romantic dramatists. The best trained actors in France were of course rigorously schooled in traditional methods, and those from the melodrama theatres had power but little polish—even Marie Dorval and Frédérick Lemaître, the greatest actors of the time. Hugo remarked on the unevenness of Lemaître's playing, his tendency to rely upon brilliant moments and flashes of genius;[58] Dumas, in his *Mémoires*, commented that no French actress—Dorval included—could do justice to characters like Juliet because they were unable to manage the shifts of emotional tone that Shakespeare required.[59]

Certainly, theoretical writing on acting in the early nineteenth century provided little basis for the development of a romantic approach to the art. François-Joseph Talma (1763—1826), the great actor of the Napoleonic period, died before the triumph of romanticism, though throughout his career he moved toward the flexibility it would offer. His *Quelques réflexions sur Lekain et sur l'art théâtral* (1825) suggests this tension; the comic actor representing everyday persons, he said, draws directly upon his own nature, while the tragic actor must preserve the ideal forms created by the poet in all their majesty, yet do so through "natural accents and true expression." He must seek "grandeur without pomp, nature without triviality—a union of the ideal and the true."[60] Talma takes issue with Diderot on the matter of sensibility, ranking it above intelligence because the latter leads to regular but cold playing, the former to deeply moving performance. In the style of a good romantic, Talma swears he "prefers sublime acting to perfect acting."[61]

The following year Aristippe Bernier de Maligny (d. 1864) published his detailed *Théorie de l'art du comédien* (1826), which distinguished between "actors by imitation," who were neither outstandingly good nor outstandingly bad; "actors by nature," who relied upon genius and

[57]Vigny, *Théâtre*, 2 vols. (Paris, 1926–27), 2:240–41.
[58]Jules Claretie, *Profils de théâtre* (Paris, 1902), 51.
[59]Dumas, *Mes mémoires*, 3:57.
[60]François-Joseph Talma, *Mémoires de Lekain* (Paris, 1825), xliii.
[61]Ibid., xxxvii.

were sometimes brilliant and sometimes detestable; and "sublime actors," who "coldly observed human nature" but subsequently "rendered it with spirit and energy."[62]

While the work of Talma and Sainte-Albine (republished in 1825) remained the best general theoretical statements, the most famous, or notorious, acting work of the period is surely that of François Delsarte (1811–1871), who began his *Cours d'esthétique appliqué* in 1839. The unfinished work, handed down in sometimes contradictory forms by his disciples, gained a reputation quite the opposite of what its originator intended. Delsarte, reacting against the mechanical and formalized actor training of his time, attempted to return to nature by carefully observing and recording those expressions and gestures produced not by art but by instinct and emotion. But when these were codified for his students, the result was yet another mechanical system, the formal details of which were so rigorously taught by Delsarte's disciples for the remainder of the century that even today his system is almost a synonym for mechanical, arbitrary expressions and gestures, the very thing it was created to prevent.

[62]Aristippe Maligny, *Théorie de l'art du comédien* (Paris, 1826), 42.

13

Nineteenth-Century England

THE SIMILARITY OF Samuel Taylor Coleridge's (1772–1834) ideas to those of the German romantics, the Schlegels in particular, is so great that a major element in Coleridge scholarship has been an analysis of borrowings. For our purposes, the question of how much of Coleridge's thought was original is less important than the fact that Coleridge introduced to English criticism the revolutionary romantic idea that a play could possess a sort of unity different from that of neoclassic critical concern, an organic unity supported from within and unique to the work itself. Thus in the famous essay "Shakespeare's Judgment Equal to His Genius,"[1] Coleridge takes issue with the "popular notion" that Shakespeare "was a great dramatist by mere instinct, that he grew immortal in his own despite." The source of this mistaken idea lies "in confounding mechanical regularity with organic form." It is true that Shakespeare did not observe the first, but like nature herself he was always faithful to the second. In this respect his genius required judgment, since genius is never lawless; it acts "creatively under laws of its own origination," which allow organic form to shape and develop a perfect outward form from within.[2]

In Coleridge's notes to *Romeo and Juliet*, he dismisses the unities of time and place as "mere inconveniences attached to the local peculiarities of the Athenian drama" and calls action the only unity that "de-

---

[1]The critical writings of Coleridge are often scattered and fragmentary, and their titles sometimes suggest a nonexistent order. So it is with this "essay"—actually a series of six fragments, all probably written between 1808 and 1819, collected and united by nonoriginal connecting matter and given a title by Coleridge's first major editor, his nephew Henry Nelson Coleridge.

[2]Samuel Taylor Coleridge, *Complete Works*, ed. W. G. T. Shedd, 7 vols. (New York, 1853), 4:51, 54, 55.

served the name of a principle." Then, echoing Schlegel (who was in turn quoting La Motte), Coleridge suggests substituting "interest" for "action":"Instead of unity of action, I should greatly prefer the more appropriate, though scholastic and uncouth, words homogeneity, proportionateness, and totality of interest—expressions which involve the distinction, or rather the essential difference, betwixt the shaping skill of mechanical talent, and the creative, productive, life-power of inspired genius."[3]

This unity meant for Coleridge that each drama grows from an organizing idea as a plant grows from a germ (indeed his criticism uses "germ" and "idea" almost interchangeably). It starts with an imbalance or opposition which the play must resolve. The imbalance may be within a single character (like Hamlet, who possesses "a great, an almost enormous, intellectual activity, and a proportionate aversion to real action,")[4] or in a set of circumstances (as in the blind but determined family feuds that oppose the young lovers in *Romeo and Juliet*). Beyond these imbalances, which provide a guiding force for the action of the drama, there is a concern for harmony, not merely in the ultimate resolution of the imbalance but even within the imbalance itself, so that conflicting forces still remain part of the same imaginary world. This is in part achieved by action (every scene in *Romeo and Juliet*, comic or serious, from the opening quarrels of the servants to the final tableau over the lovers' bodies grows from the same germ) and partly by tone (all the characters in this drama, for example, share in the precipitation characteristic of youthful passion).

There is always a sense of the reconciliation of opposites in Coleridge's concept of organic unity. At times it suggests Hugo's conciliation of the sublime and the grotesque, but Coleridge applied this dialectic much more broadly, looking to the process of reconciliation itself, rather than the reconciliation of any specific opposition, as the dynamic of art. His ultimate model, however, was apparently the Kantian opposition of reason and understanding, reconciled by the imagination. In the essay "On Poesy or Art," strongly influenced by Schelling, Coleridge writes: "In all imitation two elements must coexist, and not only coexist but must be perceived as coexisting. These two constituent elements are likeness and unlikeness, or sameness and difference, and in all genuine creations of art there must be a union of these disparates."[5] "The Drama Generally and Public Taste" speaks of "one great principle" common to all the arts, which was an "ever-varying balance, or

[3]Ibid., 110.
[4]Ibid., 145.
[5]Ibid., 381.

balancing, of images, notions, or feelings, conceived as in opposition to each other."[6]

The simultaneous perception of opposites lies behind Coleridge's most famous concept concerning the theatre: the "willing suspension of disbelief." This particular formulation appears in the *Biographia Literaria* (III, 6), but the concept also appears in various guises, and with more elaboration, in his writings on Shakespeare. Thus in defining the stage in "Progress of the Drama," he speaks of a "combination of several, or of all the fine arts to a harmonious whole having a distinct end of its own," this end being that "of imitating reality (objects, actions or passions) under a semblance of reality." The key word is semblance, and this requires a contribution from the spectator. Plays "are to produce a sort of temporary half-faith, which the spectator encourages in himself and supports by a voluntary contribution on his own part."[7] In his notes on *The Tempest*, Coleridge compares a play to a dream: "In sleep we pass at once by a sudden collapse into this suspension of the will and the comparative power: whereas in an interesting play, read or represented, we are brought up to this point, as far as it is requisite or desirable, gradually, by the art of the poet and the actors; and with the consent and positive aidence [*sic*] of our own will. We *choose* to be deceived."[8]

No other major English critic of his time was so close as Coleridge to the concerns and critical strategies of the contemporary German theorists. The English empiricist tradition that characterized the period's other leading critics had generally little tolerance for such abstract speculation. William Hazlitt (1778–1830), for example, scoffed at the metaphysics of Coleridge or Schlegel: "Truth in their view of it, is never what is, but what, according to their system, *ought* to be."[9] Hazlitt therefore erected no system, developed no philosophy of art, but considered specific works more in the light of the physical than the metaphysical, the physiological rather than the philosophical.

Nevertheless, certain common concerns are to be found throughout his writings. Despite his mistrust of the Germans, he shares with them an interest in character rather than action as the central element of drama: what makes Shakespeare preeminent among poets is his brilliance in realizing individual characters, each "as much itself, and as absolutely independent of the rest, as if they were living persons, not

[6]Ibid., 41.
[7]Ibid., 86–87.
[8]Ibid., 73.
[9]William Hazlitt, "Schlegel on the Drama," in *Collected Works*, ed. P. P. Howe, 21 vols. (London, 1930–34), 16:58.

fictions of the mind."[10] Hazlitt thus holds in common with Schopenhauer the idea that the great dramatist creates characters that are not
reflections of himself but unique individuals such as nature might have
fashioned. Good and evil characters alike are permitted to speak for
themselves without moral commentary by the poet. "In one sense
Shakespeare was no moralist at all," says Hazlitt, writing on *Measure for
Measure*. "In another he was the greatest of moralists. He was a moralist
in the same sense in which nature is one." The genius of Shakespeare
was for sympathetic identification "with human nature in all its shapes,
degrees, depressions, and elevations."[11] This focus on sympathetic
expression, found throughout Hazlitt's criticism, is diametrically opposed to the common romantic idea that the poet expresses feelings
generated within himself by the contemplation of nature. Hazlitt's poet
brings to objective reality only a conscious sensitivity; Shakespeare "was
nothing in himself; but he was all that others were, or that they could
become."[12]

It is not surprising that with this orientation Hazlitt considers superior those arts that most directly express human life. Paintings of
human beings, for example (other things being equal), are superior to
landscapes. Dramatic poetry is superior to lyric poetry because of its
fuller exploration of human character, and tragedy is the highest form
of drama because of the range and intensity of its concerns. Again, its
effect is based on sympathy, the audience being moved by the work
just as the poet was originally moved by nature. The Germans argued
that tragedy offers metaphysical insight; Hazlitt suggests instead an
emotional insight with a distinctly moral tone. Tragedy "substitutes
imaginary sympathy for mere selfishness. It gives us a high and permanent interest, beyond ourselves, in humanity as such." It makes man
"a partaker with his kind. It subdues and softens the stubbornness of
his will. It teaches him that there are and have been others like himself,
by showing him as in a glass what they have felt, thought, and done.
It opens the chambers of the human heart."[13]

The dynamic of comedy is just the opposite; here, not sympathy but
detachment is sought, and for this reason Hazlitt finds it an inferior
form. It appeals "to our indolence, our vanity, our weakness and in-
sensibility" while "serious and impassioned poetry appeals to our
strength, our magnanimity, our virtue, and humanity."[14] He evolves a
rather detailed taxonomy of comedy, dividing it into the merely laugh-

[10]Hazlitt, *Lectures on the English Poets*, in ibid., 5:50.
[11]Hazlitt, *Characters of Shakespeare's Plays*, in ibid., 4:346–47.
[12]Hazlitt, *Lectures*, in ibid., 5:47.
[13]Hazlitt, *Characters*, in ibid., 4:200.
[14]Hazlitt, *Lectures on the English Comic Writers*, in ibid., 6:23.

able, which owes its effect largely to surprise; the ludicrous (the usual realm of comedy), where "some deformity or inconvenience" contrary "to what is customary or desirable" is added to surprise; and the ridiculous, the realm of satire and the highest degree of comedy, "which is contrary not only to custom but to sense and reason."[15] Comedy's major devices are humor and wit; the former involving the simple portrayal of the ludicrous in an accidental situation or character, the latter heightening this artificially by an unexpected comparison or contrast.

Though sympathy makes serious drama preferable to comedy in Hazlitt's opinion, he considers the mixture of sympathy with comedy a blemish and judges Restoration comedy superior to that of Shakespeare on these grounds. The affectations and artificiality of the society being ridiculed are so patent that "we are almost transported to another world, and escape from this dull age to one that was all life, and whim, and mirth, and humour."[16] For Hazlitt, this is not the fairytale world it is for Charles Lamb, however; the vices and follies depicted are real enough to their contemporary audiences, who respond by correcting or at least hiding these faults. Hazlitt sees comedy in its traditional Horatian role as the lash of folly and corrector of manners; moreover, he is so convinced of its effectiveness in this role that he believes it "naturally wears itself out—destroys the very food on which it lives; and by constantly and successfully exposing the follies or weaknesses of mankind to ridicule, it in the end leaves itself nothing worth laughing at."[17]

Tragedy also gradually exhausts its material, because it is so successful a stimulus of interests and passions that men come to prefer it to life. "We learn to exist, not in ourselves, but in books." Men's passions thus become "ideal, remote, sentimental, and abstracted,"[18] and Hazlitt's theatrical public at length encounters a dilemma like that of Schiller's sentimental poet: its literary and critical self-consciousness stands as a barrier between itself and nature. Hazlitt suggests no formula for surmounting this modernist dilemma. The drama, in his theory, seems headed for extinction, a victim of its own success.

Charles Lamb's (1775–1834) critical assumptions closely parallel Hazlitt's. He is probably most notorious among those interested in theatre for his argument that Shakespeare's plays are better read than acted, but his writings in fact show as sympathetic and intimate an acquaintance with the performed work as that of any other major critic of his

---

[15]Ibid., 7–8.
[16]Ibid., 70.
[17]Hazlitt, "On Modern Comedy," in ibid., 4:10.
[18]Ibid., 13.

generation. Like Hazlitt, Lamb contrasts tragedy and comedy on the basis of sympathy and detachment, and in the essay "Stage Illusion" (1825) he suggests how this affects the art of acting as well. Lamb quickly dismisses the idea of perfect illusion on the stage—a certain distancing seems both inevitable and useful—and considers the different degree of illusion in comedy and tragedy. As in Hazlitt, sympathy is the key. The comic actor, portraying defects and infirmities in human nature, must not involve himself too deeply in them, or we as spectators may become too involved. "To see a coward *done to the life* upon a stage would produce anything but mirth," so the comic actor must show by "a perpetual sub-insinuation to us, the spectators, even in the extremity of the shaking fit, that he was not half such a coward as we took him for."[19] By this rather Brechtian distancing, the comic actor avoids engendering the sort of sympathy proper to tragedy. Dramatic delight requires "a judicious understanding, not too openly announced, between the ladies and gentlemen on both sides of the curtain."[20]

It is upon the essential distance in comedy that Lamb bases his famous defense of Restoration comedy, "On the Artificial Comedy of the Last Century" (1822). The emotional distancing in such plays should remove them from any moral considerations, he asserts; they are "a world of themselves almost as much as fairyland," a "passing pageant, where we should sit as unconcerned at the issues, for life and death, as at the battle of the frogs and mice."[21]

Lamb's major commentary on tragedy is the well-known "On the Tragedies of Shakespeare considered with reference to their fitness for stage representation" (1811), which argues that "the plays of Shakespeare are less calculated for performance on a stage than those of almost any other dramatist whatever."[22] There have been attempts to explain this prejudice on the basis of Lamb's dissatisfaction with the theatre of his own time; however, though he does criticize unfavorably the acting of Mr. K (John Philip Kemble) and Mrs. S (Sarah Siddons), his general theory of the drama seems to lead to the same conclusion regardless of the quality of performance in any particular era. Like Hazlitt, Lamb considers tragedy the highest poetic genre, thanks to the emotional identification it inspired, and Shakespeare the supreme tragic poet, thanks to his ability to lose himself entirely in his creations. A similar annihilation of self should ideally occur in the spectator (always allowing for the minimum distancing the mind must impose to prevent actual pain or suffering), but the physical reality of the stage constantly

[19]Charles and Mary Lamb, *Works*, ed. E. V. Lucas, 5 vols. (New York, 1903), 2:163.
[20]Ibid., 165.
[21]Ibid., 144.
[22]Ibid., 1:99.

works against this. "What we see upon the stage is body and bodily action; what we are conscious of in reading is almost exclusively the mind and its movements."[23] In reading we can draw from our imagination only such elements of costume, scenery, and physical action as we need to participate fully in the "thoughts and internal machinery" of the character, while on stage we must have a multitude of detailed and specific externals, many of which are potentially distracting. When these are ill done (as in painted representations of rocks and trees), they disturb the illusion; even when they are well done (as in the choice of an effective gesture), they may still distract from the essence of the drama. Lamb saw Mrs. Siddons's much-admired dismissal of the guests in the banquet scene of *Macbeth* as a case in point: when a striking gesture rivals moments of internal action, he contends, it serves to "level" all aspects of the drama, and to make "tricks, bows, and courtesies of importance."[24]

A similar but somewhat more moderate view is expressed by Sir Walter Scott (1771–1832) in his "Essay on the Drama" (1814), written for the *Encyclopaedia Britannica*. The object of every artist, says Scott, is to bring to his audience "the same sublime sensations that had dictated his own compositions," and the drama, with the physical aid of representation, "has a better chance of attaining its object, especially when addressing the sluggish and inert fancies of the multitude." Still, for persons of more taste and discernment, Scott agrees with Lamb that such crude stimulation is unnecessary, and even harmful. He questions whether "with all these means and appliances, minds of a high poetic temperature may not receive a more lively impression from the solitary perusal, than from the representation, of one of Shakespeare's plays."[25]

The tradition of English romantic criticism represented by Hazlitt and Lamb was carried on to midcentury by the younger writers Thomas De Quincey (1785–1859) and Leigh Hunt (1784–1859). De Quincey's most famous essay, "On the Knocking at the Gate in Macbeth" (1823), analyzes in some detail the source of the "peculiar awfulness and depth of solemnity" aroused in him by this particular moment. For years, he reports, he attempted in vain to comprehend this rationally; at last, like a good romantic, he turned to his feelings and eventually found an explanation in a process suggesting the romantic juxtaposition of opposites. A world of darkness, inhuman and hellish, has taken possession of the play during the murder, and the knocking signals the sudden shift from that world to its opposite: "The reaction has com-

[23]Ibid., 108.
[24]Ibid., 111.
[25]Walter Scott, *Miscellaneous Prose Works*, 6 vols. (Edinburgh, 1827), 6:368–69.

menced; the human has made its reflux upon the fiendish; the pulses of life are beginning to beat again; and the re-establishment of the goings-on of the world in which we live first makes us profoundly sensible of the awful parentheses that had suspended them."[26]

De Quincey's most important attempt at a more general theory of drama may be found in his "Theory of Greek Tragedy" (1840), a work which he himself considered highly original but which in fact has much in common with Schlegel. All comedy, he says, bears a family resemblance, since it springs from the same sources: "the ludicrous of incident, or the ludicrous of situation, or the ludicrous which arises in a mixed way between the character and the situation."[27] Tragedy is a much more varied form, so different in Greece and England as to be almost unrecognizable as the same genre. Everything in Greek tragedy tends to make it abstract and remote from real life: the religious origins, the vast theatres, the masks and cothurni, the chorus. It is a drama not of action or developing passions but of "fixed, unmoving situations," of "tableaux vivants" played before a cosmic canvas. Its mode is suffering, not conflict, "for suffering is enduring and indefinite," not conditioned by the temporal. English drama sought life and action, conflict and movement.

De Quincey summarizes these two approaches in "The *Antigone* of Sophocles as Represented on the Edinburgh Stage" (1846): Greek tragedy offers "the abstraction of a life that aspires, the solemnity of a life that is thrown to an infinite distance," while English tragedy offers "breathing life—life kindling, trembling, palpitating."[28] Both affect us profoundly but in quite different ways, the one by its depth of unmitigated gloom, the other by its tumultous conflicts and its alternating waves of light and darkness, as observed in that central moment in *Macbeth*.

Among the English essayists of the romantic period, Leigh Hunt wrote most prolifically on the drama, publishing hundreds of essays and reviews between 1805 and the 1830s. Like Hazlitt and Lamb (whom he called, in 1831, the best dramatic critics England had yet produced), he avoided the abstract aesthetic concerns of Coleridge and the Germans, but he shared with them a fairly consistent if unstated theory of the drama, distinctly romantic in inclination.

For Hunt, drama is "the most perfect imitation of human life," representing man "in all his varieties of mind, his expressions of manner, and his power of action," and also "the first of moralities because it

---

[26]Thomas De Quincey, *Collected Writings*, 14 vols. (Edinburgh, 1889–90), 10:393.
[27]Ibid., 342.
[28]De Quincey, *Works*, 15 vols. (Edinburgh, 1862–63), 13:217. (This section of the 1890 *Collected Writings* is defective.)

teaches us in the most impressive way the knowledge of ourselves."[29] Hunt admits that little in the contemporary theatre approaches this ideal, but like other romantics he takes refuge in Shakespeare, the universal model and infallible genius of the theatre: "The more this unmatched poet is considered the more he will be found superior to all times and circumstances."[30]

Though Hunt also addresses himself to the question of imitation and the relationships between tragedy, comedy, and observed reality, his discussion of these genres has a somewhat different focus from that of Lamb and Hazlitt. Rather than stressing emotional sympathy or detachment, Hunt follows a more traditional neoclassic line, seeing comedy as a play close to real life in which the players "act naturally," while the characters in tragedy "require an elaboration of language and manner which they never use in real life."[31] Hunt is well aware that such a distinction can lead to an abstract and mechanical presentation of tragedy, and warns authors and actors not to forget that the imitation of passion is the essence of tragedy.

It is precisely upon this point that he criticized the acting of Kemble, who "knew there was a difference between tragedy and common life, but did not know in what it consisted, except in *manner*, which he consequently carried to excess, losing sight of the passion." Edmund Kean, on the other hand, knew that if his acting were based on passion, manner would follow as a matter of course "as the flower issues from the entireness of the plant, or from all that was necessary to produce it." Kemble "began with the flower" and "had no notion of so inelegant a thing as a root, or as the common earth, or of all the precious elements that make a heart and a life in the plant, and crown their success with beauty."[32]

The major romantic poets in England all tried their hand at the drama, but only a few of their efforts, headed by *The Cenci* (1819) of Percy Bysshe Shelley (1792–1822), achieved even a modest reputation in the theatre. Their contributions to dramatic theory are even slighter, though Shelley offers a fairly extended commentary on the drama in his *Defense of Poetry*, written about 1821 but not published until 1840. The essay draws upon Sidney, Plato's idea of poetic inspiration, and recent romantic thought. The first of its three sections defines poetry and discusses how it achieves its effects: poetry is a product of the imagination that synthesizes things known into eternal truths, giving both pleasure and moral improvement.

[29]Leigh Hunt, *Critical Essays on the Performers of the London Theatres* (London, 1807), 1.
[30]Hunt, *Dramatic Criticism* (New York, 1949), 190.
[31]Ibid., 1–2.
[32]Hunt, *Dramatic Essays* (London, 1894), 224.

The second section gives a brief history of European poetry and contains Shelley's specific remarks on the drama. He anticipates Wagner in hailing the Greeks as possessing the only true theatre yet known— a perfect fusion of all the arts: they "employed language, action, music, painting, the dance, and religious institution, to produce a common effect in the representation of the highest idealism of passion and power." Like Wagner, Shelley condemns the modern period for separating and weakening the individual arts. He also regrets the loss of the mask as a means of abstracting expressions and making them complete and eternal, and disapproves of the practice of mixing comedy and tragedy unless comedy can be made "universal, ideal, and sublime" as it is in *King Lear*.[33]

Turning to the moral side of the theatre, Shelley argues that as long as drama is allied with poetry it can touch with majesty and beauty "the brightest rays of human nature," encouraging and even propagating them. But when society decays, drama decays with it, losing its contact with poetry and turning to sterile imitation or gross flatteries of the morals of the age. The darkest example of this in England is the poetry and drama of the Restoration. It is the duty of the poets to rescue the drama from its thrall to social circumstance and restore it to its function as a mirror of the highest and greatest thoughts and feelings of mankind. The final third of the essay explores this duty in the famous panegyric on poetry that concludes, "Poets are the unacknowledged legislators of the world."[34] Dramatists who, like Shakespeare and the Greeks, bring poetry to the theatre share in this glory and this responsibility.

The deaths of De Quincey and Hunt in 1859 essentially ended the tradition of romantic criticism in England and diminished still further the already comparatively minor contributions being made there to dramatic theory. The general Victorian view of literature as either utilitarian and morally uplifting or else frivolous, if not actually degrading, did not encourage speculative thought on the drama, which was generally viewed in the latter light. Early nineteenth-century drama was certainly undistinguished, as the romantic theorists were well aware, but after 1850 complaints about its insubstantiality began to take on the color of moral condemnation as well. For many respectable Victorians, the very experience of going to the theatre was suspect, and though Shakespeare (with the cruder passages removed) was revered, many took Lamb's advice and enjoyed his pleasure in the home rather than in the theatre.

---

[33]Percy Bysshe Shelley, *Works*, 8 vols. (London, 1880), 7:114.
[34]Ibid., 144.

The reactions of Thomas Babington Macaulay (1800–1859) to Hunt's and Lamb's praise of Restoration comedy anticipates this Victorian temper. Macaulay shared the common English distaste for critical abstractions; in his essay "Lord Bacon" (1837) he declares all theory "useless" and argues in good Victorian fashion that utility and progress are the true aims of man, and philosophy mere word-spinning. Plato, Aristotle, and their followers "despised what was practicable; they filled the world with long words and long beards; and they left it as wicked and as ignorant as they found it."[35]

Given utility and progress as the two available justifications for human endeavor, Macaulay can find no defense for the authors he discusses in "Comic Dramatists of the Restoration" (1841). He has enough nineteenth-century liberal tolerance to prevent his calling for the suppression of the works of Wycherly, Congreve, Vanbrugh, and Farquhar, but not enough to discover anything redeeming in them. "This part of our literature is a disgrace to our language and to our national character," he complains; it seeks, as the Elizabethans never did, "to associate vice with those things men value most and desire most, and virtue with everything ridiculous and degrading."[36] Lamb is mistaken in calling it a world of fantasy; the world portrayed is quite recognizable as that of contemporary society, and to that society these dramatists preach a corrupt morality. Such observations bring Macaulay close to the view of Steele, or even Collier, on Restoration comedy, but he tempers his condemnation with historical justification: we should view these plays in context as a reaction to the "extreme and foolish restraints" of the Puritan commonwealth and preserve them as illustrations of the character of "an important epoch in letters, politics, and morals."[37]

The leading drama critic of mid-nineteenth-century England was George Henry Lewes (1817–1896), whom Bernard Shaw characterized as "the most able and brilliant critic between Hazlitt and our own contemporaries."[38] This is not a greatly exaggerated claim, but Lewes did not achieve the position of a major theorist. He was an insightful and thoughtful reviewer, who commented wryly himself on the difficulty of creating substantial and sustained theoretical statement within the context of journalistic criticism: "I should like to send Quintilian to a 'first representation' with the necessity of his proceeding straight from the theatre to the printing office, and there sitting in judgement on the new work, his article to be read by thousands before he is awake

---

[35]Thomas Babington Macaulay, *The Works of Lord Macaulay*, 8 vols. (London, 1866), 6:220.
[36]Ibid., 490–91.
[37]Ibid., 493–94.
[38]George Bernard Shaw, *Our Theatres in the Nineties*, 3 vols. (London, 1931), 3:163.

on the morrow!"[39] He did, however, formulate several ideas that earn him mention among the dramatic theorists from whose ranks he appeared to exclude himself. The most important of these is the concept of realism, which enters English criticism in Lewes's writings first on the novel, then on the drama. "What we most heartily enjoy and applaud," he wrote in 1847, "is truth in the delineation of life and character: incidents however wonderful, adventures however perilous, are almost as naught when compared with the deep and lasting interest excited by any thing like a correct representation of life."[40]

Thus, at almost precisely the same time that the French drama was turning toward realism with the *école de bon sens* (see Chapter 19), Lewes was introducing this mode to England. It is important to realize that Lewes was no more calling for Zolaesque naturalism than were his French contemporaries, however, as we may clearly see from his remarks in *On Actors and the Art of Acting* (1875). He calls this art one "of representation, not of illusion"; it should "represent character with such truthfulness that it shall affect us as real, not to drag down ideal character to the vulgar level."[41] Natural expression must be converted by the actor into art, just as theatrical language is drawn from daily speech but "purified from the hesitances, incoherences, and imperfections." In real life, men and women rarely express their feelings openly, and an honest imitation of this reticence would be totally ineffective on stage. Thus the actor must find "well-known symbols" of what an individual may feel so that the spectators "recognizing these expressions, are thrown into a state of sympathy."[42]

The actor must also consider another of Lewes's concerns, the relativity of "truth." Having inherited from romanticism a view of historical relativism Lewes attempts to view each work so far as possible in the light of the concerns, needs, and expectations of its own time. Similarly, "natural" acting must take into account the demands of any particular play and its audience. "Naturalness being truthfulness, it is obvious that a coat-and-waistcoat realism demands a manner, delivery, and gesture wholly unlike the poetic realism of tragedy and comedy," he observes, and condemns actors who confuse the style of ideal life with that of ordinary life.[43]

Lewes's historicist orientation placed him in conflict with the majority of his contemporaries on two important issues. The first had to do with the imitation of past models. One might suppose that with the passing

[39]George Henry Lewes, "Criticism," *Leader* 2, 71 (Aug. 2, 1851): 735.
[40]Lewes, "Recent Novels: French and English," *Fraser's Magazine* 36 (Dec. 1847):687.
[41]Lewes, *On Actors and the Art of Acting* (London, 1875), 112–13.
[42]Ibid., 119, 124.
[43]Ibid., 115–16.

of classicism, reliance upon the practice of earlier dramatists would no longer be a serious concern; but even in France, as we have seen, theorists felt the need to caution poets that they must avoid merely substituting imitation of Shakespeare for imitation of Racine. In England this note was rarely struck; on the contrary, the lesser dramatists of Shakespeare's era were rediscovered and lavishly praised by the critics of Lamb's generation and imitated—with what success, we know— by most young English playwrights of the period with literary pretensions. In 1850, Lewes termed this veneration for past models "the greatest injury yet sustained by the English drama"; he called for a theatre reflecting his own time: "idealized of course, but issuing out of the atmosphere we breathe." This was true of Elizabethan drama when it was written, he argued, but when it was transported to a later era, nothing was left of it but the poetry, and this misled modern dramatists to think that poetry alone would suffice to create drama—a dreadful error.[44]

The same emphasis on poetry marked contemporary interpretations of Shakespeare, the area of Lewes's second significant disagreement with Lamb and others. These writers, he noted in "Shakespeare's Critics: English and Foreign" (1849), were profoundly mistaken in stressing Shakespeare's poetic skill and forgetting that his major concern was to write and produce successful plays. His poetic gifts were great, but focusing upon them had led to the "extraordinary fallacy" of Lamb's preference for reading these works, whereas in fact, Lewes contended, stage production could create "an infinitely grander effect than could have been reached by any closet reading."[45]

Matthew Arnold (1822–1888) in his inaugural lecture at Oxford in 1857, "On the Modern Element in Literature," praised the drama as a more lasting and enjoyable form than the epic, since it avoids local and transient descriptions of details of life and concentrates on "the actions of man as strictly determined by his thoughts and feelings." This makes it "always accessible, always intelligible, always interesting."[46] At this time, Arnold dreamed of creating his own major tragedy in the Greek style, but only one of a number of attempts was carried to fruition—the dull and sterile *Merope* (1857), which even its author had to admit was "calculated rather to inaugurate my Professorship with dignity than to move deeply."[47]

Little more is heard of the drama in Arnold's writings. His most

[44]Lewes, "The Old and Modern Dramatists," *Leader* 1, 19 (Aug. 3, 1850):451.
[45]Lewes, "Shakespeare's Critics: English and Foreign," *Edinburgh Review* 90 (1849):62–63, 68.
[46]Matthew Arnold, *The Complete Prose Works*, 11 vols. (Ann Arbor, 1960–77), 1:34.
[47]Arnold, *Letters, 1848–1888*, 2 vols. (London, 1895), 1:60.

substantial later comments appear in the essay "The French Play in London" (1879), in which he attacks the English fad for French theatre. The French, more mechanical, more dominated by artificial rules, and subservient to the inflexible Alexandrine, are deficient "in power, in penetrativeness, in criticism of life, in ability to call forth energy and joy."[48] Even Molière, their greatest genius, was so restricted by this tradition that he was unable to create tragedy, a more profound and difficult genre than comedy. The only thing the English can learn from the French, says Arnold, is that the state should become involved in the support and encouragement of the drama.

George Meredith's (1828–1909) "On the Idea of Comedy" (1877) is well known, not only because it has wit and charm, but because it is one of the few English essays of the period to consider a question of abstract literary and dramatic theory. Meredith divides the "powers of laughter" into satire, irony, and humor, according to the degree of sympathy with the object of laughter. Satire, the weapon of open ridicule, is the cruelest; irony leaves the victim discomfited but unsure whether the attack was truly meant; humor mixes pity with exposure and may even allow sympathy to overcome laughter entirely. The comic spirit is the perception that informs them all. Since society is based upon common sense, the comic spirit deals with the ever-recurring and ever-changing follies that depart from this basis. The test of true comedy, says Meredith in a famous phrase, is "that it shall awaken thoughtful laughter."[49] His favored examples, Menander and Molière, are products of societies where the ideal mixture of feeling and intellect was present to produce the comic spirit.

During the 1880s in England, the central concern of theatrical theory turned to the art of acting. The immediate stimulus seems to have been a small book, *L'art et le comédien* (1880), by the French actor Constant Coquelin (1841–1909), best remembered for his creation of Rostand's Cyrano de Bergerac. The book, translated into English in 1881, begins with a defense of the actor as an independent artist who uses the creation of the dramatist as a basis for a new creation of his own. Coquelin strongly supports Diderot's idea of acting and calls the paradox the only reason acting can be considered an art: "One can only be a great actor on condition of complete self-mastery, and ability to express feelings which are not experienced, which may never be experienced, which from the very nature of things never can be experienced."[50] Naturalism is mistaken, says Coquelin, in assuming that

---

[48] Arnold, *Works*, 9:69.
[49] George Meredith, *Works*, 29 vols. (New York, 1909–12), 23:46.
[50] Constant Coquelin, "Art and the Actor," trans. Abby Alger, in *Papers on Acting*, ser. 2, vol. 2 (New York, 1915), 56.

nature pure and simple can be effective on stage. The theatre must heighten and select with wisdom and taste. Too frequent a use of conventions will destroy all truth in the theatre, but too great a fidelity to fact will destroy all illusion and all effect.

Coquelin's essay initiated a series of English observations. In a preface, "On the Stage," to her *Notes upon Some of Shakespeare's Plays* (1882), Frances Kemble (1809–1893) distinguishes between the dramatic, which is the "passionate, emotional, humourous element" in human nature, and the theatrical, which is the conscious, artificial reproduction of this. The greatest actor must have a talent for both, must be able to conceive passion and also to present it. There is a certain analytic quality in the theatrical, but the dramatic has "a power of apprehension quicker than the disintegrating process of critical analysis."[51] The best actors therefore rely most strongly upon their dramatic talent, and use the theatrical only insofar as necessary to adjust to the physical demands of the theatre.

Coquelin's championship of Diderot encouraged an English translation of the *Paradoxe* in 1883, with a preface by Henry Irving (1838–1905). Irving disagrees sharply with Diderot and Coquelin, calling the paradox an ingenious but totally wrong-headed idea. The great actor does not deny his sensibility; he feels emotions perhaps more keenly than others and uses these feelings in his art. Against Diderot, Irving cites Talma, who said that sensibility should take possession of an actor and shake him to his very soul before the intelligence could select and utilize this experience on stage: "If tears be produced at the actor's will and under his control, they are true art; and happy is the actor who numbers them among his gifts."[52] Irving made essentially the same points in an address, "The Art of Acting," at Harvard, and he arranged for an English publication in 1877 of Talma's essay to counteract the influence of Coquelin and Diderot.

Among the various commentaries on these two essays, one of the most perceptive was that written by a student of nineteenth-century acting, Fleeming Jenkin (1833–1885), in the *Saturday Review*. Quoting both Kemble and Talma, Jenkin suggests that the training of the actor is largely a training in emotional memory. All actors must possess the sensibility Talma describes, which manifests itself in flashes of profound and honest emotion. Later, when alone, the actor fixes the spontaneous outpourings of this emotion—his tones, cries, gestures, and actions—so that these may be reproduced at will and, if necessary, adjusted or recombined. This sets up a circle of effect: "If by the aid of memory

[51]Frances Kemble, *Notes upon Some of Shakespeare's Plays* (London, 1882), 3.
[52]Denis Diderot, *The Paradox of Acting*, trans. Walter H. Pollock (London, 1883), 10.

we perfectly reproduce a tone or cry, that tone or cry brings back simultaneously a close reproduction of the feeling by which it was first created."[53]

A further essay by Coquelin, "L'art du comédien" (1886), was published in English by *Harper's* in 1887. Here Coquelin speaks of a necessary dual personality in the actor. The "first self" conceives the character to be created in terms of the "second self," his instrument. Great actors will always keep this second self rigorously under the control of the first. When the second, the ego, becomes dominant, the actor's individuality eclipses the role, and characterization is lost amid picturesque detail. Coquelin cites Irving as an example of this error, of one who chooses effect over analysis. The basis of the actor's art should be a thorough understanding of the character, discovered in the text by the first self. The second should then ideally be "a soft mass of sculptor's clay, capable of assuming at will any form."[54]

Irving felt obliged to respond to this view, and within a month he contributed to *Nineteenth Century* a rebuttal entitled "An Actor's Notes."[55] Once again he insisted upon the efficacy of occasionally losing oneself in passion on the stage, but his focus is on Coquelin's apparent ideal of an actor so denying his own individuality that nothing of it remained in the various characters he played. Irving considers this neither possible nor desirable; all great actors, such as Salvini, Booth, or Kean, put a personal stamp on the great roles they play, making each of these creations in some sense their own.

Dion Boucicault (c. 1820–1890) suggested, in an essay in the *North American Review*, that a carelessness in distinguishing dramatic genre might explain the apparent conflict between these two major artists. In his work as a dramatist, Boucicault felt that an author writing comedy was called upon to be "circumspect and calculating, careful in the selection of thoughts, a fastidious spectator of the details of his work, thoroughly self-conscious and deliberate"; in writing tragedy or scenes of deep pathos, however, he must be impulsive and spontaneous: "passion wields his pen."[56] Similarly, the comic actor would do well to heed Coquelin, and keep a certain calculation in all he does, but the tragic actor should rather hearken to Irving. The inclination of contemporary tragedians such as Bernhardt to follow Coquelin's method resulted, he said, from an analytic consciousness forced upon the French theatre by Zola and does not lead to the greatest tragic expression.

Coquelin's reply appeared in the *Harper's Weekly* in November 1887,

[53]Fleeming Jenkin, "Talma on the Actor's Art," *Saturday Review* 55 (Apr. 28, 1883):542.
[54]Coquelin, "Acting and Actors," *Harper's* 74 (May 1887):894.
[55]Henry Irving, "An Actor's Notes," *Nineteenth Century* 21 (June 1887):800–803.
[56]Dion Boucicault, "Coquelin-Irving," *North American Review* 145 (Aug. 1887):159.

with an introductory statement by Brander Matthews summing up the controversy to date. Coquelin agrees with Boucicault that different attitudes toward drama explain his conflict with Irving, but ascribes this not to a focus upon different genres, but to national traits. The English tend to favor originality and the French, tradition; the English, the specific and the French, the general. Shakespeare creates great individuals, Molière great types. The great French actors have always been able to express themselves within a tradition and so are more conscious of their work than the English, who favor inspiration. He does not deny the power of spontaneous emotion but feels that it cannot be properly utilized, either in rehearsal or in performance, unless the actor is already so well studied in his part, so "penetrated with the essence of his personage," that the emotion can be effectively and theatrically used.[57]

The best-known document from this lively controversy, and the lengthiest treatment of the actor's art to appear in England to that point was William Archer's (1856–1924) *Masks or Faces?* (1888). The evolving debate was moving away from the comparatively minor question of whether actors really feel the emotions they express to the more basic one of how actors design and control their presentation. Archer, however, remained with the first: "To feel, or not to feel?—That is the question."[58] He prepared a lengthy questionnaire about whether and when actors truly wept, blushed, and so forth, on stage, and sent it out to the leading players of the day. The critic Francisque Sarcey, whom he asked to supervise this survey in France, would have nothing to do with it. "I regard this procedure," he replied, "which is American in nature, as inimical both to criticism and to art."[59] Still, Archer did receive replies from a number of leading British and a few French actors (he does not say how many). Out of the welter of often contradictory evidence thus unearthed, he developed a position that guardedly supported Coquelin. "The greatest virtuoso of mechanical mimicry" cannot be expected to attain "the subtle and absolute truth of imitation which is possible to the actor who combines artistically controlled sensibility with perfect physical means of expression." Since nobody had advocated "mechanical mimicry" anyway, the phrasing here suggests Coquelin, though Archer goes on to remark that the production and reproduction of a precise shade of feeling comes not from "the unaided action of the will" but from "the intervention of imaginative sympa-

---

[57]Coquelin, "A Reply to Mr. Henry Irving," trans. Theodore Child, *Harper's Weekly* 31, no. 1612 (Nov. 12, 1887):831.

[58]William Archer, *Masks or Faces?* (London, 1888), 211.

[59]Ibid., 7.

thy."[60] Coquelin would probably still agree, but on these terms Irving's position could probably be accommodated, too, while the more basic question of the relation between the text, one's actual emotions, imaginative sympathy, and the will is, unhappily, never directly faced.

Although England produced no theorist-playwright between 1850 and 1890 to champion the drama of socially engaged realism (as Dumas *fils*, in particular, did in France), the Victorian essayists Lewes, Arnold, and Meredith, prefigured by Macaulay, generally accepted it as the suitable dramatic form for their era. The assumption was sharply challenged by Oscar Wilde (1854–1900) at the end of the 1890s. He argued that form, not content, was the most important consideration in art and that life should serve art, not vice versa. Wilde's fullest discussion of this position appeared in three articles in *Nineteenth Century*, subsequently gathered in the collection entitled *Intentions* (1891). These were "The Decay of Lying" (January 1889), and the two parts of "The Critic as Artist" (July and September 1890). In dialogue form, all three consider the relationship between art and life.

In "The Decay of Lying," Vivian—Wilde's mouthpiece—argues that the current decadence in art results from art's having turned toward nature and truth. The Elizabethans inherited a drama powerful in abstraction and perfection of form, which they took to new heights but then began to betray. Even in Shakespeare a decline may be observed: "It shows itself by the gradual breaking-up of the blank verse in the later plays, by the predominance given to prose, and by the overimportance assigned to characterisation."[61] This trend toward realism has been a failure, since it denies what gives art its power. If art's subjects are not remote, we risk becoming emotionally involved and losing our aesthetic pleasure: "The only beautiful things are the things that do not concern us." Art restored to its proper power will not be a model *of* life but a model *for* it, since life always seeks to find expression, and "art offers it certain beautiful forms through which it may realize that energy."[62]

In "The Critic as Artist," Wilde discusses the ethical and the aesthetic views of art, citing Plato and Aristotle as the great early examples of these two attitudes. Plato, the moralist, was concerned with the importance of art to culture, making it a means to another end. Aristotle properly regarded art as an end in itself and thus came closer to its essence. His *katharsis* was a purifying and spiritualizing process, an initiation into a higher sphere than that of normal reality. Goethe

---

[60]Ibid., 208.
[61]Oscar Wilde, *Works*, 15 vols. (London, 1969), 8:24.
[62]Ibid., 56.

correctly saw this as an aesthetic process rather than a moral one, as Lessing mistakenly supposed. All art is thus detached from morality "except those baser forms of sensual or didactic art that seek to excite to action of evil or good." Action is the sphere not of art but of ethics, and "the aim of art is simply to create a mood."[63] It begins not with an idea but with an artistic form, a form that itself suggests "what is to fill it and make it intellectually and emotionally complete." The artist with something to say, or even with some specific feeling to communicate, cannot abandon himself entirely to the demands of this form: "All bad poetry springs from genuine feeling" and all great poetry from "the worship of form."[64] Although Wilde does not apply this doctrine specifically to the debate about acting, his position on the question is clearly implied: the actor relying upon his own emotions would, like the poet, be necessarily inartistic, since true art comes not from life but from form. "Do you wish to love?" asks Wilde. Then "use Love's Litany, and the words will create the yearning from which the world fancies they have sprung."[65]

Stout opposition to this formalist view of the drama was mounted by the most prolific author/critic of the late nineteenth century in England, George Bernard Shaw (1856–1950), who insisted—beginning with his earliest theatre reviews and his first major critical essay, *The Quintessence of Ibsenism* (1891)—that the primary aim of art should be didactic. It has often been observed, with considerable justice, that *Quintessence* in fact reveals more about Shaw than about Ibsen. It might be more accurate to say that Shaw took one aspect of a very complex dramatist, that of the iconoclast who insists upon telling truths society would rather not hear, and dealt exclusively with this aspect. Shaw asks why Ibsen's plays drove otherwise stable gentlemen, like the dramatic critic Clement Scott, to paroxysms of excoriation; he was doubtless right in ascribing this effect to Ibsen's "messages." Ibsen's greatest technical novelty, says Shaw, was to alter traditional dramatic structure to reflect his didactic aim. "Formerly you had in what was called a well-made play an exposition in the first act, a situation in the second, an unravelling in the third. Now you have exposition, situation, and discussion; and the discussion is the test of the playwright."[66] In such a play there is no clear-cut conclusion, just as there are no clear heroes or villains; there is instead a serious consideration of significant contemporary questions.

The preface to Shaw's first play, *Widowers' Houses* (1893), insisted that it be judged on the proper grounds, as "a propagandist play—a didactic

---

[63]Ibid., 183.
[64]Ibid., 207.
[65]Ibid., 208.
[66]George Bernard Shaw, *Works*, 37 vols. (London, 1930–50), 19:145.

play—a play with a purpose," though at the same time he characterized it as "a technically good practicable stage play" for those who seek only entertainment in the theatre.[67] It was, of course, precisely this blend of didacticism and theatrical skill that characterized much of Shaw's work and assured his continued popularity, while the plodding moralist Eugène Brieux, whose bravado in dealing with forbidden topics on stage and whose scorn for Scribean structure led Shaw, ill-advisedly, to rank him with Molière and Shakespeare,[68] is now almost totally forgotten.

True drama, says Shaw in the preface to *Mrs. Warren's Profession* (1894), is found only in the problem play, "because drama is no mere setting up of the camera to nature; it is the presentation in parable of the conflict between Man's will and his environment: in a word, of problem."[69] The task of the dramatist becomes the isolation of a problem, the clarification of its terms, and— perhaps—the arrangement of argument in such a way as to suggest a solution. By selection and arrangement of material "from the chaos of daily happenings," the dramatist can change us "from bewildered spectators of a monstrous confusion to men intelligently conscious of the world and its destinies."[70] A German theorist employing these same terms would doubtless be thinking in metaphysical fashion, but Shaw remains firmly within the down-to-earth English pragmatic tradition. In "The Problem Play" (1895), he asserts that "the general preference of dramatists for subjects in which the conflict is between man and his apparently inevitable and eternal rather than his political and temporal circumstances, is due in the vast majority of cases to the dramatist's political ignorance (not to mention that of his audience)."[71] Whether the dramatist should simply present a problem in sufficiently clear terms for the audience to think it through on their own or whether he should seek to bring them to a particular conviction is a question never clearly answered in Shaw's writings, though he seems to be tending toward the latter view after 1900. In either case, it is clear that a thoughtful consideration of social questions remains for Shaw the primary requisite for significant drama.

As a champion of didactic theatre, Shaw develops in his own terms a theory of drama with striking correspondences to those of earlier instruction-oriented theorists such as Minturno and d'Aubignac. Like them, Shaw argues that if an audience is to be properly engaged by the moral questions debated on the stage, they must be presented by

---

[67]Shaw, *Prefaces* (London, 1934), 670.
[68]Ibid., 196–218.
[69]Shaw, *Works*, 7:167.
[70]Shaw, *Prefaces*, 205.
[71]Shaw, *Shaw on Theatre*, ed. E. J. West (New York, 1959), 65.

the dramatists and actors with a familiar world, essentially like their own. Thus the verisimilitude so dear to Horatian neoclassicists reappears in Shaw's championship of realism. "The beginning and end of the business from the author's point of view," Shaw wrote in his famous letter to his Irish colleague Matthew McNulty, "is the art of making the audience believe that real things are happening to real people."[72] This naturally placed Shaw in direct opposition to conventional actors and their traditional stage business; he fulminated against them throughout his career. The appendix to *The Quintessence of Ibsenism* describes the problems Ibsen's characters give to the conventional actor who insists upon "reducing his part to one of the stage types with which he is familiar, and which he has learnt to present by rule of thumb."[73]

Like much of his criticism, Shaw's famous negative comments on Shakespeare are based upon moral arguments. The essay "Better than Shakespeare?" prefacing *Caesar and Cleopatra* (1900) argues that Shakespeare suffers an inherent disadvantage in respect to any modern dramatist simply because he cannot deal with questions of our own time in our own terms.[74] But for Shaw, Shakespeare's inadequacy goes much deeper: his real lack is his unfortunate inability to commit himself to questions of real psychological and social importance. In such crucial matters, Shakespeare is "absurdly dwarfed" by a dramatist like Ibsen, and Ibsen's achievement, if less permanent by conventional literary standards, is vastly to be preferred. *A Doll House*, Shaw predicts, will be "as flat as dish water" when *A Midsummer Night's Dream* is still as "fresh as paint." But it will have "done more work" in the world, and that "is enough for the highest genius, which is always intensely utilitarian."[75] What work does it do in the world? That question is the ultimate touchstone in all of Shaw's criticism of both playwriting and performance.

[72]Ibid., 153.
[73]Ibid., 1.
[74]Shaw, *Shaw on Shakespeare*, ed. Edwin Wilson (New York, 1961), 219.
[75]Ibid., 63.

14

Russian Theory to 1900

THE FIRST MAJOR RUSSIAN LITERARY CRITIC was Vissarion Belinsky (1811–1848), who is generally given credit for establishing the emphasis on social and political concerns that has been a major feature of the Russian critical tradition ever since. Actually, this position was developed fully only in the final phase of his work, after 1842. Before 1840, Belinsky wrote largely under the influence of the German romantic theorists, stressing organic unity, the close relationship of artistic expression and national spirit, and the freedom of art from essentially didactic concerns. For a brief period in the early 1840s, his concern with protecting the artist from becoming a caterer to "petty passions and partisan ravings" led him to separate art almost entirely from social questions. His later position sought to retain for art its social function while protecting its aesthetic integrity. As he said in "A Survey of Russian Literature" (1847): "Without a doubt art must be, first and foremost, art—and then only can it be an expression of the spirit and direction of social life during a given period."[1]

Belinsky's most extended comments on drama appear in a major essay, "The Division of Poetry into Kinds and Genres" (1841). In almost every point it follows the Hegelian system, which Belinsky was studying at the time. He classifies poetry as epic, lyric, and dramatic, with drama, a fusion of the other two, being the highest form. Tragedy portrays the conflict of opposing principles, represented by characters of heroic stature. So convinced is Belinsky of this Hegelian view that he blames the lack of any major tragedies in Russian literature on the lack of any significant ideological struggles in Russian history. In "The Russian Theatre in Petersburg" (1841), he observes: "A variety of passions, the

---

[1]Quoted in Viktor Terras, *Belinskij and Russian Literary Criticism* (Madison, 1974), 102.

clash of internal interests, and the differentiation of society—these are the conditions without which there can be no drama; and nothing of the kind ever existed in Russia."[2]

Belinsky's idea of comedy is also Hegelian, opposing to tragedy's world of necessity a world of chance and illusion. In the essay "Woe from Wit" (1840), Belinsky applies this interpretation to the work of Nikolai Gogol and Alexander Griboedov, calling their comic worlds pictures of a negative reality, a world of illusory activity. To the extent that this negative reality is actually operative in the experienced world of Russian society, such plays can by indirection suggest the positive ideal that they subvert. In this sense, rather than in the traditional sense of teaching a specific moral lesson, comedy can be considered didactic.

The two major Russian dramatists of the early nineteenth century, Alexander Pushkin (1799–1837) and Nikolai Gogol (1809–1852), each provided some critical observations on their craft. Pushkin's were primarily inspired by his own *Boris Godunov* (1827) and are clearly strongly influenced by European romanticism. In an unpublished "Letter to the Publisher of the *Moscow Messenger*" (1828), Pushkin acknowledges "Our Father Shakespeare" as his primary inspiration and model. "To his altar" Pushkin "brought him as sacrifices two classical unities, barely preserving the third." Moreover, he discarded a fourth traditional unity, that of style; exchanged Alexandrines for blank verse and occasional prose; and did not follow the traditional division into acts. Instead of respecting these tried and proven rules, he sought to create "a faithful depiction of characters and the true, with the development of historical personages and events" in order to produce "a truly romantic tragedy."[3]

Pushkin finds the traditional idea of verisimilitude ridiculous. "Of all genres, the most unrealistic (*invraisemblable*) is the drama," he wrote in 1825, "and in the drama, the tragedy; because for the most part the spectator must forget time, place, and language."[4] In an 1829 draft for a preface to *Boris Godunov*, he asked, "what kind of verisimilitude is there in a room divided into two parts, one of which is occupied by two thousand people supposedly not visible to those who are on the stage?"[5]

In the essay "On National Drama and on *Marfa Posadnitsa*" (1830), Pushkin seeks in the history of the drama the sort of verisimilitude truly proper to this genre. When the crude thrills and easy farcical

[2] V. G. Belinskij, *Polnoe sobranie sočinenij*, 13 vols. (Moscow, 1953–59), 5:497 (trans. in ibid., 174).

[3] Alexander Pushkin, *The Critical Prose*, trans. Carl R. Proffer (Bloomington, 1969), 66–67.

[4] Ibid., 40.

[5] Ibid., 98.

laughter of early popular entertainments dulled, he says, dramatists came to realize that only the exploration of human passions remains eternally interesting. Thus the only important verisimilitude in drama is "truth of passions, verisimilitude of feelings in the proffered circumstances," and this should be respected in both high comedy and tragedy.[6] The great popular dramatists, like Shakespeare, continued the tradition of appealing to the multitude, though with new interest in emotion and with great poetic insight. But court dramatists, like Racine, felt themselves inferior to their more select audience and restricted their genius by following arbitrary and artificial rules that they thought would please these alien superiors. The problem for Russian tragedy, which began in imitation of this artificial model, is to find an idiom, which it has never possessed, accessible to the common people.

Gogol's major comments on the theatre also cluster about his most famous play, *The Government Inspector* (1836). While it was in rehearsal, Gogol wrote the posthumously published essay "The Petersburg Stage in 1835–36," in which he praises the romantic movement for breaking the fetters of neoclassic drama but argues that the time has come for a more calm and controlled art, utilizing the best of both romanticism and classicism. It should be socially oriented, exposing the ills of contemporary society, and its major weapon should be laughter, which Gogol considers the most effective of social correctives.

The generally unfavorable critical reception given *The Government Inspector* inspired Gogol to write a dramatic commentary, "After the Play," which showed members of the audience discussing the work in the theatre lobby. The two complaints most often brought against Gogol's work were that it contained no central love interest and that it attacked the government. Two art lovers consider the first of these problems, the second arguing that comedy was originally "a social, popular creation," as seen in Aristophanes, and that it later became unnaturally restricted to "the narrow path" of romantic interest. Thus the true social aim of comedy has been lost, and not even the best authors are able to give the genre much significance. Nevertheless, tragedy and comedy should ideally both express "the same lofty idea"— that of "law, justice, and duty."[7]

This assertion leads naturally to the other major attack on the play, and a "very modestly dressed man" argues that Gogol's attack was not on the government itself but on individual corrupt officials. Such exposures of hypocrisy would not harm the government but fortify it, by showing the people "that abuses come not from the government but

---

[6]Ibid., 131.
[7]Nikolai Gogol, *Oeuvres complètes* (Paris, 1966), 1058–59.

from people who do not understand its needs; who do not wish to be accountable to it."[8] At the end of the scene the author, left alone, speculates on the function of laughter, the great poetic force for the elevation and ennoblement of mankind, "without whose penetrating force man would become disheartened by the triviality and vanity of life." Such laughter, he concludes, does not lead to revolt, as some claim, but promotes tolerance and understanding. It touches the rogue who sees his roguery exposed; more important, it provides a deep and luminous experience for the good man. Those who call laughter low have simply never felt its power to liberate and to elevate.[9]

When Gogol in his later writings shifted from social to religious concerns, he still kept his view of laughter as a great liberating agent. In another essay in dramatic form "The Conclusion of *The Government Inspector*" (1846), the "first comic actor" praises laughter as a creation "to mock all which degrades the true beauty of man" and calls on all men to join in laughing both at others and at themselves. Here *The Government Inspector* is interpreted not as social commentary but as religious allegory. It shows no representative Russian town but "the town of our souls," and the true inspector is "our awakened conscience which suddenly and abruptly obliges us to look within us with un-clouded eyes." Those who can laugh at what they find within themselves experience not a political but a spiritual cleansing, and comedy partic-ipates in what Gogol calls the new concern of poetry: "a battle not for temporal liberty (for our rights and privileges) but for our soul."[10]

This view of the noble mission of poetry and drama gave Gogol the basis for a defense of the art against writers such as Count A. P. Tolstoy (1801–1873), who raised many of the old ecclesiastic arguments against the theatre. In the essay "On the Theatre" (1845), Gogol accused Tol-stoy of one-sidedness, of condemning all theatre because some of it was corrupt. Everything in the world, said Gogol, can be an instrument for the service of God. The theatre at its best can fulfill this function by renewing the spectator "through living representations of noble deeds," which would send the audience out of the theatre with new strength "after having seen a heroic exploit well represented."[11]

This religious note was not often struck in the theatre writings of the next generation. The majority of the Russian critics who followed Belinsky tended to continue his emphasis on the social importance of poetry and were thus called the civic or democratic critics, while those who reacted against this emphasis and focused on formal or organic

[8]Ibid., 1061–62.
[9]Ibid., 1088–89.
[10]Ibid., 1718.
[11]Ibid., 1556.

concerns were called the aesthetic or conservative school. Although the two groups were of almost equal importance between 1850 and 1880, the former were so much more congenial to subsequent Soviet thought that the latter have faded into relative obscurity.

Nikolai Chernyshevsky (c. 1828–1889), highly regarded by both Marx and Lenin, is probably the best known of the civic critics. He was the leader of the "men of the sixties," a group of writers who championed scientific materialism, utilitarianism, and social progress. The central premise of Chernyshevsky's dissertation *The Aesthetic Relation of Art to Reality* (1855) is that art is inferior to reality, and that its primary goal is not to imitate but to reproduce reality, "to compensate man in case of absence of opportunity to enjoy the full aesthetic pleasure afforded by reality."[12] Closely allied to this function is a second, to explain and to pronounce judgment on reality. Art "will present, or solve, the problems that arise out of life for the man who thinks."[13]

Chernyshevsky found the metaphysical basis of Hegelian aesthetics totally unacceptable, and in his remarks on tragedy he takes pains to remove all traces of transcendentalism. The idea of a force in the universe called destiny or fate, according to Chernyshevsky, is a remnant of savage man's proclivity to personify forces in nature; scientific man knows that nature is neutral, that guilty and innocent, famous and obscure persons suffer alike. The German idea of necessity must be purged from tragic theory and the concept be reduced to more basic and pragmatic terms. "The tragic is a man's suffering or death—this is quite enough to fill us with horror or sympathy" without reference to any "infinitely mighty and irresistible force." Some have said that purely accidental death is not tragic. "This may be so in tragedies written by authors, but not in real life,"[14] and real life is as always the standard by which artistic success must be measured.

The aesthetic or conservative critic most concerned with the drama was Apollon Grigoriev (1822–1864), whose criticism reflects two major influences. One is German romanticism, particularly Schelling's view of art as organic process; the other is the "native soul" movement (*pochvennichestvo*), which sought to encourage a distinctly Russian culture drawn from the people and the land. Grigoriev found these two concerns united in the plays of his friend Alexander Ostrovsky (1823-1866), which the critic called a "mirror of the national consciousness."[15]

---

[12]N. G. Chernyshevsky, *Selected Philosophical Essays*, trans. anon. (Moscow, 1953), 373.
[13]Ibid., 375.
[14]Ibid., 311.
[15]Apollon Grigoriev, *Russkij teatr*, in *Epocha* 1-2 (1864): 423; quoted (in German) in Jürgen Lehmann, *Der Einfluss der Philosophie des deutschen Idealismus in der russischen Literaturkritik des 19. Jahrhunderts* (Heidelberg, 1975), 185.

Like Pushkin and Wagner, Grigoriev believed that the greatest theatre must arise from the people, the masses, and that it must give expression to something akin to what Wagner called the "collective need." Thus it is misleading to call Grigoriev an aesthetic critic to the extent that the term implies an "art for art's sake" attitude. It is true that he scorned the strict materialism of Chernyshevsky, but he felt that poetry was much involved in life on a deeper, more philosophic level: it should not provide instruction on the social questions of the moment, but it should give insight into the popular consciousness and into the general historical development from which social questions emerge. The dramatist must be "a priest who believes in his god and who for that reason never gives the masses the least hint of insincerity in his worship, who instructs the masses, who puts before them the summit of their own world view."[16]

Both Belinsky and Grigoriev laid great stress on the importance of the actor, whom they saw not as a simple intepreter but as a major creator, scarcely less important than the poet himself. Grigoriev speaks of the great actor as a magician, able to make something powerful and significant even out of unpromising material. Pavel Mochalov (1800–1848), whose reliance upon emotion and inspiration often led him strikingly away from tradition and, some felt, even from the clear intent of the text, was warmly praised by both these critics;[17] they condemned those actors who relied upon "routine and triviality." Since he relegated the great majority of the actors he reviewed into the latter category, Grigoriev was both feared and hated by members of the Moscow stage in the 1850s and by those in Petersburg in the next decade.

Mochalov's search for inner truth clearly contributed to the tradition of great Russian acting, which reached its most famous incarnation in Stanislavski. The main elements of talent, wrote Mochalov, are "spiritual profundity and a flowing imagination." The actor must have "the ability to imagine what he himself is living with the mind and soul of the audience"; he must "force the audience to share his joy and tears" and at last to forget itself in the emotional world he has created.[18] A similar vision was expressed by Mochalov's revered contemporary, Michael Shchepkin (1788–1863). In a letter to an actress in 1848, he contrasted two actors, equally devoted to their art and each working conscientiously: one is intelligent and reasoned, and "has achieved the art of pretense to a high degree"; the other expresses true feelings by

[16]Grigoriev, *Sobranie sočinenij*, 3:57; quoted in ibid., 186.
[17]See Belinskij, "Gamlet, drama Šekspira i Močalov v roli Gamleta," *Polmoe sobranie sočinenij*, 3:329, and Grigoriev, *Vospominanija* (Moscow, 1930), 405.
[18]Quoted in Toby Cole and Helen Chinoy, *Actors on Acting* (New York, 1954), 415.

means of "a flaming-soul, heavenly spark." Shchepkin considered the second far superior in effect.[19]

After the critical writings of the 1860s, little significant theatre theory was written in Russia until the end of the century. The various comments of Anton Chekhov (1860–1904) on the drama, scattered through his letters, are for the most part observations on specific plays or questions of technique. He did, however, address himself to the long-debated question of the artist's relationship to social issues in several of his letters to editor and critic A. S. Suvorin (1834-1912). Suvorin accused Chekhov of too general an objectivity in his writing, of an unwillingness to take sides, but Chekhov insisted that the artist's duty was not to solve problems, but only to state them clearly. "The artist should be, not the judge of his characters and their conversations, but only an unbiased witness";[20] he places the evidence before the jury of readers and spectators and allows them to pronounce judgment.

A quite opposite position was taken by Leo Tolstoy (1828–1910). In *What is Art?* (1897), Tolstoy establishes a definition of art and the criteria by which good art can be separated from bad. He begins by summarizing the traditional theories and finds their emphasis on beauty unacceptable because it makes art simply a means of pleasure, whereas its more important function is the communication (Tolstoy calls it the infection) of feeling. Like Pushkin and Grigoriev, Tolstoy deplores the removal of art from the people and its corruption by small elites for their own pleasure. He considers the symbolist drama of Henrik Ibsen, Maurice Maeterlinck, and Gerhart Hauptmann, along with similar experiments in the other artistic modes, perversely difficult. The business of art is not to make obscure; on the contrary, it is to make "comprehensible and accessible what in the form of reasoning may remain incomprehensible and inaccessible."[21] Whether art is good or bad depends upon the quality of the feelings it expresses. Good art must contribute to the progress of the human soul, and just as "truer and more necessary knowledge crowds out and takes the place of unnecessary knowledge," art can aid its audience in evolving "better feelings"—those of human sympathy and brotherhood.

Tolstoy was inspired to apply these general observations to Shakespeare in particular by an essay, "Shakespeare and the Working Classes," written by Ernest Crosby, an American author and legislator. Crosby, much influenced by Tolstoy's writings, condemned Shakespeare for his indifference to the feelings of the common man. Tolstoy's planned

---

[19]Trans. David Pressman, in ibid., 423.
[20]Anton Chekhov, May 30, 1888, in *Letters*, trans. Constance Garnett (New York, 1920), 88. See also letters of Oct. 27 and Apr. 1, 1890.
[21]Lev Tolstoy, *Complete Works*, trans. Leo Wiener, 12 vols. (London, 1904), 11:232.

preface to this work grew into a major essay in its own right, *Shakespeare and the Drama* (1906). After a ruthless analysis of *King Lear* reminiscent of Rymer's analysis of *Othello*, Tolstoy speaks more generally of Shakespeare's unmotivated characters, his anachronisms, his carelessness in differentiating individual speech. But if Shakespeare lacks a proper command of the technical requirements of his genre, he fails even more seriously in content and sincerity. He is always artificial and obsessed with word play; he despises the masses and has no interest in improving the existing order of society. Any significant drama must have something to say about "man's relation to God, to the universe, to all that is infinite and unending," and the Shakespearian dramas fail in this because their author lacks what a great dramatist must have, "a definite view of life corresponding to the highest religious understanding of a given period."[22]

Tolstoy explains the veneration of Shakespeare as a historical accident. German aesthetic critics of the romantic period, seeking to break free from the restrictions of French classicism, seized upon Shakespeare as a weapon and, lacking any real artistic sense, lauded even his worst faults. So voluminous were the writings of these critics, buttressed by the great authority of Goethe, that a Shakespeare industry was established which now proceeds by its own momentum and which no one dares challenge. Young dramatists stifle their natural aesthetic and ethical feelings to follow the false model of Shakespeare, with the result that the drama, "the most important sphere of art," has become "merely an empty and immoral amusement for the empty and immoral crowd."[23]

[22]Tolstoy, *Recollections and Essays*, trans. Aylmer Maude (Oxford, 1952), 376.
[23]Ibid., 380.

15

The Germanic Tradition in the Late Nineteenth Century

IN EARLY NINETEENTH-CENTURY GERMANY the dominant philosophers, Kant and Hegel, and the dominant dramatists, Goethe and Schiller, all had in one way or another supported a view of art as idealization, the revelation of universal, eternal truth hidden behind mundane, empirical reality. The concept of drama as idealized life or revealed truth remained strong in the theorists and the dramatists who followed them. The refusal of Georg Büchner (1813–1837) to accept this dominant opinion explains in large part why his powerful dramas had to wait for several generations before being recognized as among the period's major contributions to the theatre.

For Büchner, idealized reality was not superior but inferior to nature, since it removed from consideration an important part of reality. The most extended defense of his ideas occurs in a letter to his family, written July 28, 1835, concerning his play *Dantons Tod*. The duty of the dramatist, Büchner avers, is to re-create history in a more direct and living form than that provided by the historian. He must "place us in the life of an era, give us characters instead of characterization and forms instead of descriptions." His major task is "to come as close as possible to history as it actually happened" and to be "neither moral nor immoral, like history itself." To those who ask the poet to show the world "as it should be," Büchner replies that he does not wish to make the world "better than God did, who surely made the world as it ought to be." The idealist playwrights have created only "marionettes with skyblue noses and affected pathos" whose sorrow and happiness have little relevance to us. Instead, drama should offer "people of flesh and blood," whose actions have the power truly to arouse our emotions.[1]

---

[1]Georg Büchner, *Sämtliche Werke und Briefe*, 4 vols. (Hamburg, 1967–71), 2:443–44.

Although there is a hint in Friedrich Hebbel of the sort of anti-idealism Büchner expresses, it was not until the appearance of naturalism half a century later that a view of drama similar to Büchner's gained wide currency. In the meantime, the theories of Hegel and the dramas of Schiller provided the major intellectual orientation of the Germanic theatre. Nowhere is the Hegelian influence clearer than in subsequent speculation on the nature of tragedy. The aesthetician Friedrich Vischer (1807–1887), much read in the late nineteenth century, clearly reflects the Hegelian approach in the 1837 *Über das Erhabene und Komische* and capitulates to the Hegelian system almost completely in his *Ästhetik* of 1847–1858. In both works he describes the evolution of the tragic idea in triadic form. First comes the vague perception of the absolute "as the dim basis of an eternal natural power," which arouses in man a feeling not of guilt but rather of inadequacy as he becomes aware of his "temporal, individual existence."[2] This perception can appear in tragedy but not as its basis; its proper domain is history or epic poetry. The second stage allows true tragic expression. Here fate appears as the force of justice, moving into the ethical realm, and the struggle is often between different claims to right or between individual knowledge and divine knowledge, as in *Oedipus*. The third, and purest tragic form allows the fullest expression both of the absolute and of the total claim of the individual. The opposing claims enter a struggle which, through the purifying "fire of suffering," brings them "to a higher unity in the absolute spirit."[3]

In the theories of tragedy advanced by Kierkegaard, Hebbel, and Nietzsche during the next generation, the influence of Hegel continues, but these authors were not content to organize their observations, as Vischer had, within the capacious framework of the Hegelian system. To a thinker such as Søren Kierkegaard (1813–1855), the great triumph of this system, its internal logic and its organized exploration of spirit and consciousness, was also its greatest flaw. He saw Hegel's emphasis on universals and striving for ultimate harmony by essentially rationalistic means as a mistaken return, after Kant's revolution, to something resembling the intellectual world of Lessing. Kierkegaard may be viewed as a new romantic reaction to this approach, emotional and individualistic, preaching not harmony but paradox, and seeking the ultimate not by logic but by individual religious insight.

Either/Or (1843), Kierkegaard's first major work, contains an essay on tragic theory, "The Ancient Tragical Motif as Reflected in the Modern," but its function within Kierkegaard's writings requires some ex-

---

[2]Friedrich Vischer, *Kritische Gänge*, 6 vols. (Leipzig, 1914–22), 4:65, 70.
[3]Ibid., 89.

planation. Kierkegaard's general approach is Socratic; he speaks in many voices and suggests his argument in a poetic rather than a logical manner. *Either/Or* explores two contrasting modes of existence, the asthetic, based on subjectivity and leading ultimately to despair, and the objective, based on moral duty and leading ultimately to crisis by conflict with the irrational. A third stage of existence, the religious, transcends the limitations of both aesthetic pleasure and ethical self-assurance to choose God by an act of faith. The essay on tragedy should be viewed within this context, since it is purportedly the work of one of Kierkegaard's aesthetic personae, an artist identified only as "A," who reads this paper as a work in progress before a society of fellow aesthetes. It must be thus considered not as Kierkegaard's own "theory of tragedy," but as a theory evolved within the aesthetic dimension of his thought: both comedy and tragedy are manifestations of contradictions arising from partial perspectives, and will disappear when the transcendent religious stage (the real focus of Kierkegaard's concern) is reached.

The essay by "A" rejects equally the tragic reconciliation of Hegel and the tragic resignation of Schopenhauer. The concept of the tragic hero has shifted since classic times. In classic tragedy the hero was still tied to his entire society, pitted against the power of fate. His suffering, shared by others, gave rise to tragic sorrow. In modern tragedy, the hero is more isolated, more reflective, more conscious of guilt and less of fate. We, aware of his isolation, feel greater pain in his suffering but less sorrow. Our age, having lost the "substantial categories of family, state, and race," leaves the individual to himself so that "he becomes his own creator; his guilt is consequently sin, his pain remorse; but this nullifies the tragic."[4] A dialectic between guilt and innocence, individuality and fate, pain and sorrow is necessary for true tragedy, but this seems impossible in the present age. Instead, we have a predominance of comedy and irony, modes that acknowledge and are built upon isolation and disjuncture.

In two essays on the art of acting, "The Crisis and a Crisis in the Life of an Actress" (1848) and "Herr Phisto as Captain Scipio" (1848), the personae adopted by Kierkegaard again work entirely from within the aesthetic consciousness. Art is considered as a transparent medium through which shine ideal forms, and the question is how best the actor may realize this transparency. A distinction is made, suggestive of Diderot, between the "direct, fortuitous youthfulness" of the beginning actress who achieves great success by being naturally attuned to her

---

[4]Søren Kierkegaard, *Either/Or*, trans. David and Lillian Swenson, 2 vols. (Garden City, N.Y., 1959), 1:147.

role, and the rarer but more aesthetic success of the mature actress who, by "full and conscious, well-earned and dedicated command over her essential power," returns to the portrayal of the inner ideal but does so in an ideal way.[5] Her original unreflective inwardness may bring her into such harmony with ideality that her interpretation even reveals to the poet himself "the original he was trying to copy,"[6] but this transient grace departs with age; only the reflective actor can maintain such transparency throughout a career. The ideal actor presents "a totality thoroughly reflected upon in every detail," and the ideal spectator or critic should observe and understand the performance with a reflection no less detailed and circumstantial.[7]

Germany's leading dramatist at midcentury, Friedrich Hebbel (1813–1863), like Kierkegaard, rejected Hegelian reconciliation as an overly rational and overly optimistic approach to reality, but while Kierkegaard found in religious faith another center for existence, Hebbel found at the center of the universe only unresolved and unresolvable conflict. He challenges Hegel's claim that philosophy has replaced art as the highest interpretation of life and asserts that, on the contrary, Hegel's philosophy masks the terrible reality of existence by its process of unifying theses and antitheses into ever higher syntheses. In this way it is doomed to eternally approach the center of life by creating logical circles of ever-decreasing circumference, while art can look symbolically but directly into the turbulent center itself. Art is "realized philosophy just as the world is realized Idea"; it is the drama, not philosophy, that can "mediate between the Idea and the condition of man and the world."[8] To do this, the drama must reflect the historical process, become the mirror of the day—indeed of the hour—and express the spirit of its own age, whatever its actual subject.

In "Ein Wort über das Drama" (1843), Hebbel lays out a general theory of tragedy based upon the common philosophic division of life into Being and Becoming (*Sein* and *Werden*). *Sein* represents the "original nexus" (like Hegel's *Geist*) from which the individual manifestations of *Werden* spring. As the individual seeks to express his own form and focus, he necessarily departs from the mean and thus inevitably releases an opposing force to restore the equilibrium he has disrupted. Dramatic guilt is the inescapable result of this process of individualization. Unlike Christianity's original sin, which is concerned with the direction of the human will, this guilt arises from the mere working of the will, and "it is a matter of total indifference dramatically whether the hero fails at

---

[5]Kierkegaard, *Crisis in the Life of an Actress*, trans. Stephen Crites (London, 1967), 86–89.
[6]Ibid., 77 and note.
[7]Ibid., 111.
[8]Friedrich Hebbel, *Sämtliche Werke*, 24 vols.(Berlin, 1901–7), 11:56–57.

a praiseworthy or a reprehensible ambition."[9] The hero is destroyed not for evil deeds, mistaken judgments, or even hubris, but simply because he is an individual: "All action, when confronted with fate, that is with the world-will, dissolves into suffering."[10] As a simile for life, Hebbel suggests a great river in which individuals are lumps of ice that must inevitably be melted and absorbed into the flow.

Since little of Hegelian reconciliation was left in this theory, it is not surprising that the Hegelians generally attacked Hebbel as pessimistic and even philosophically bankrupt. He held his ground, however, insisting, in a doubtless unconscious echo of Büchner, that "it is foolish to require of the poet what God himself does not provide: reconciliation and the resolution of dissonances." All that can be asked of the poet is to show "that the catastrophe is inevitable, that it, like death, is established by birth itself."[11] The only solace offered is that of the reaffirmation of the unchanging Idea, and Hebbel suggested that tragic heroes should not die "sullen and unreconciled" but gain in death "a clear view of the individual's relation to the whole." Instead of a true Hegelian reconciliation, Hebbel saw this as a kind of Stoic acceptance of the inevitable.

Nevertheless, his rejection of Hegelian optimism did not take Hebbel in the direction of Schopenhauer, to a desire to reject the workings of the will to life altogether. He saw the will as a necessary part of life's process, and the drama a means of providing, if not a reconciliation of life's dualism, at least a temporary resolution of dissonance "as soon as this appears too prominently"; his image is of two circles in water that merge into a single large one. There always remains a more fundamental dissonance that neither drama nor philosophy attempts to resolve, the original one that caused individuation or duality in the first place. Tragic guilt is inevitable because this inner cause remains unrevealed, even when the individual gains a partial insight and dies in peace. "I have never found the answer to this," says Hebbel, "nor will anyone else who seriously considers the problem."[12]

These general observations on the dynamics of tragedy are given a more particular focus in the "Vorwort zur 'Maria Magdalena' " (1844). Here Hebbel repeats his contention that the function of drama, "the summit of all art," is to illustrate "the existing state of the world and man in their relationship to the Idea."[13] He argues that great drama can occur only when some significant change is occurring in this re-

[9] Ibid., 11:4.
[10] Ibid., 11:52.
[11] Hebbel, *Tagebücher*, 4 vols. (Berlin, 1903), 2:269.
[12] Hebbel, *Werke*, 11:31–32.
[13] Ibid., 40.

lationship, a situation which has appeared only three times in the history of the drama. The first was during the period of Greek tragedy, when the old naive conception of the gods was challenged by the new concept of fate. The second was at the time of Shakespeare, when the rising Protestant consciousness shifted attention to the individual, and the conflict between man and fate changed to a tragic dualism within the single individual. In his own age a new source of tragic dualism had appeared—intimated, Hebbel thinks, in certain of Goethe's works—a dualism within the Idea itself, or at least in that part of it that we can comprehend. "The existing institutions of human society, political, religious, and moral" have become problematic, he says, and tragedy can be developed on the basis of perceived contradictions in these manifestations of the Idea. Modern man does not desire to overthrow traditional institutions, but to reestablish them on firmer, less contradictory foundations. Drama of social criticism can be a major aid in this process.

This provocative essay concludes with a spirited defense of bourgeois tragedy, which, it argues, has been cheapened by inferior craftsmen who neglect the essence of all tragedy: that it must portray universal conflict through individual cases. Modern authors, says Hebbel, have substituted external and avoidable conflicts such as lack of money or class conflict for the pathos of tragedy. Further, they have either artifically heightened and falsified the speech of their characters in an attempt to ennoble them or have turned them in the name of realism, into "living blocks of wood, whose very ability to say Yes and No is cause for no little surprise."[14] A rich and interesting language of the people is available to the perceptive artist, but even more important, the bourgeois tragedy will be significant only to the extent that it deals, as great tragedy has always done, with the basic tensions of the human condition.

The tone of resignation and pessimism so often found in Hebbel's writing helps to mark him as one of the last representatives of the generation, beginning with Schopenhauer and Grillparzer, that rejected the moral optimism and even the revolutionary zeal found in Schiller. The next generation, whose coming to maturity was signaled by the revolutionary upheavals of 1848–1849, tended to agree with Hebbel that art should be concerned with contemporary society, but with a reforming enthusiasm much closer to that of Schiller. A central example of this new generation of theatre theorists is Richard Wagner (1813–1883). Wagner was just beginning to gain a reputation when involvement in the 1848 riots in Dresden forced him to exile in Zurich, where he remained for ten years. During this time he wrote most of

[14]Ibid., 63.

his prose works and solidifed the theories that supported his greatest operas and profoundly influenced the course of modern theatre.

The exile came, if such a circumstance can ever be positive, at a most favorable time for Wagner. With *Tannhäuser* (1845) and *Lohengrin* (1848), he had pushed traditional romantic opera to its limits and was ready to launch into something much more experimental. His exile gave him the time and opportunity to chart out a new path and to harmonize it with those growing social concerns that had led to his involvement in Dresden politics to begin with. The title of his first major essay, *Die Kunst und die Revolution* (1849), made this clear, and in his later introduction to this essay in the *Gesammelte Schriften* (1872), he wrote: "I believed in the Revolution, as in its necessity and its irresistibility . . . and felt called upon to indicate the path to its salvation." This did not mean, he explained, that he wished to suggest the form of the necessary new political order; his concern was with the new art, which must be built simultaneously with that political order on the ruins of the discredited past.[15]

Die Kunst begins with a rapturous invocation of ancient Greek drama, a political and spiritual creation at which the whole people (*Volk*) gathered "to understand themselves, to comprehend their own activities, to achieve an inner unity with their being, their fellowship, their god."[16] With the decline of Athens came the decline of this drama, and as the common Greek spirit "split into a thousand egotistic concerns, so the unified art work of tragedy split into separate artistic genres,"[17] and philosophy replaced art as the interpreter of reality. The Romans and the Christians rejected the drama for opposite reasons, the former by a denial of spirituality, the latter by a denial of sensual pleasure. When art revived in the Renaissance, it appeared as an amusement for the rich and powerful. A pleasure meant for all mankind became an indulgence of the affluent. Both artists and audiences were thereby corrupted, art becoming a trade and a tool of capitalism. Greek art was conservative, "the deepest and noblest expression of the people's consciousness," but to regain this function, art must be revolutionary and begin by rejecting what it has become under the influence of modern society.[18]

The essay *Das Kunstwerk der Zukunft* (1850) uses less of the rhetoric of revolution and seeks the source of this new art in the *Volk*. Wagner defines the *Volk* as "the sum total of all those who feel a common

[15]Richard Wagner, *Gesammelte Schriften und Dichtungen*, 10 vols. (Leipzig, 1871–72), 3:2.
[16]Ibid., 11.
[17]Ibid., 12.
[18]Ibid., 21.

need,"[19] as opposed to those who feel no true need but substitute for it the indulgence of luxury, capitalism, and godless science. Each sub-division of art has become corrupted, dance turning to mime, music to abstract form, song to operatic aria, and drama itself to "the dead form of literature."[20] The *Volk* must respond to their felt need, reunify the arts, and rediscover the only real, free, and universally meaningful art work, a total work like that of Greece.

Oper und Drama (1851), Wagner's major theoretical text, continues to explore the unhappy state of art and to suggest how it must be changed. In the first of its three sections, *"Die Oper und das Wesen der Musik,"* Wagner summarizes the history of opera to illustrate what he sees as the basic fallacy of the genre: "that a means of expression (music) has been made the end, and the end of the expression (drama) the means."[21] The second section, *"Das Schauspiel und das Wesen der dra-matischen Dichtkunst,"* undertakes a parallel survey of dramatic poetry which, by allying itself with literature, has degenerated to "shallow realism." It has lost the basic purpose of Greek drama, which was to convey "the content and essence of myth in the most convincing and intelligible form."[22] The final section, *"Dichtkunst und Tonkunst im Drama der Zukunft,"* discusses the reunification of the separated arts of poetry and music, and what each would gain thereby. Poetry, whose medium is words, necessarily addresses itself primarily to the understanding, while music speaks directly to the emotions. If a single artist, both musician and poet, could unite them, he would fulfill the need of the *Volk* for an expression of their total being.

The great sociopolitical document of the period, the *Communist Manifesto* of Karl Marx (1818–1883) and Friedrich Engels (1820–1895), appeared on the eve of the revolutionary upheavals of 1848. A significant body of modern theatre criticism acknowledges Marx as its intellectual father, though the writings of Marx and Engels on literature and art in general and on drama in particular are neither extensive nor easily reducible to a system. Nevertheless, since those that exist are relatively consistent among themselves and within the total context of Marxist philosophy, they have served as a basis for a subsequent variety of more comprehensive theories. Key documents for the drama are the letters of opinion solicited in 1859 from both Marx and Engels by Ferdinand Lassalle (1825–1864) on his historical drama *Franz von Sickingen*. Their responses, though not coordinated, are strikingly similar. Both speak first of the strongly favorable impression the work made

[19]Ibid., 48.
[20]Ibid., 112.
[21]Ibid., 231.
[22]Ibid., 4:34.

upon them subjectively, then turn to matters of form. Marx advises more care with the poetic lines; Engels approves of the general structure but calls the play literary rather than theatrical. To suit it better for the stage, he advises reducing the monologues, even at the expense of intellectual content, and giving greater attention to how characters do what they do.

Both writers feel that Lassalle's play suffers from following Schiller rather than Shakespeare as a model: that is, realism has been sacrificed to abstract ideas and individuals made mouthpieces for particular intellectual positions. The general and occasionally the individual could be found in the play, but rarely if ever the mediation between the two that Georg Lukács later called the "typical."

Both letters also deal briefly but suggestively with the idea of the tragic hero and sources of the tragic. The real tragic element in the fate of Sickingen, the play's hero, says Engels, is that he was born out of his time: the national revolt of which he dreamed could have been successful only if the knights had aligned themselves with the peasantry, an alignment historically impossible during that period. A tragic conflict is implied "between the historically necessary postulate and the practical impossibility of its realization."[23] Marx's analysis is similar, calling Sickingen "a Don Quixote, although historically justified."[24]

Another significant statement on theatre appears in a letter of June 5, 1890, from Engels to Paul Ernst concerning Ernst's interpretation of Ibsen. Engels takes Ernst to task for a simplistic pigeon-holing of Ibsen and for the assumption that class structures in contemporary Germany and Scandinavia are identical. In a key sentence, Engles warns that "the materialist method is converted into its direct opposite if, instead of being used as a guiding thread in historical research, it becomes a ready-made pattern by which one tailors historical facts."[25] In these few pronouncements on the drama, the fathers of Communism—within a system dominated by historical consciousness—seem to advise a flexibility of interpretation, a general avoidance of open tendentiousness or propagandistic writing, a portrayal of significant typical figures in historical situations, a respect for such past models as Shakespeare, and a possibility of modern tragedy's focusing upon the disjuncture of the individual and the historical moment.

The spirit of social revolution likewise informs the small book *Das moderne Drama* (1852) by the literary theorist and historian Hermann Hettner (1821–1882). Like Wagner, Marx, and Engels, Hettner argues

---

[23] Karl Marx and Friedrich Engels, *Werke*, 39 vols. (Berlin, 1956–69), 29:604.
[24] Ibid., 591.
[25] Ibid., 37:411.

that the drama of the future can "only be social and historical,"[26] reflecting both the social and emotional needs of its audience. Kings and significant heroes are no longer the best choice for historical subjects, "because now and in the future we shall be much more occupied with social questions than with political conflicts," and for the exploration of such questions, the bourgeois social drama is much more suitable than historical drama as it has been traditionally conceived.[27]

Hettner identifies three types of tragedy. First is the tragedy of condition, in which a significant character is pitted against the external world, as in the contemporary fate tragedies. Next, tragedies of passion show the hero in conflict with himself, a popular type in Shakespeare and Schiller. Third, the tragedy of idea, highest of the three, should be the goal of serious drama in the future. This drama also involves internal conflict, but it is caused not by weaknesses or deficiencies in the character, as in Wallenstein or Hamlet, but by conflicting obligations and ideals. Sophocles' *Antigone*, Goethe's *Faust*, and the plays of Hebbel point the way to a new middle-class drama of social conflict dealing with the crises arising from social man's own development. Hettner looked to a dramatist friend, Gottfried Keller, to fulfill this vision. It was a disappointed hope, but a quarter-century later another young writer, Henrik Ibsen, was strongly impressed by Hettner's book and carried its ideas to brilliant fruition.

Hettner launched his critical career with *Gegen die spekulative Æsthetik* (1845), a pamphlet criticizing, in the name of realism, the metaphysical approach to art that had dominated German theory for the preceding half-century. In Germany as in France, the fashionable philosophic trend was toward empiricism and the concerns of this world increasingly occupied literary theorists.

Gustav Freytag (1816–1895) carried empiricism even further, considering the drama as an artifact pure and simple, not even a social and political one. His *Technik des Dramas* (1863) seeks to set down the basic rules of drama, resulting in a structure quite similar to the contemporary French well-made play. Freytag's approach is, at least in his own eyes, purely pragmatic. He analyzes the dramatic work of five acknowledged masters—Sophocles, Shakespeare, Lessing, Goethe, and Schiller—to find "the fundamental laws of dramatic construction"[28] common to all. The general basis of his system is Aristotelian. Action is primary (though a controlling idea precedes action and guarantees its unity). Unity, probability, and magnitude are each given a separate

[26] Hermann Hettner, *Das moderne Drama* (Berlin, 1924), 9.
[27] Ibid., 75–76.
[28] Gustav Freytag, *Die Technik des Dramas* (Darmstadt, 1965), 7.

chapter and shown to inform the major works of Freytag's selected dramatists.

In dealing with tragedy itself, Freytag departs from Aristotle. Man's view of himself and his universe has changed through the centuries, and the great poet will reflect the highest concerns of his contemporaries. He should "trouble himself very little" about the purpose or effect of tragedy but "make an upright man of himself, then with a gay heart take on a subject which concerns strong characters in a significant struggle, and leave to others the high-sounding words guilt and redemption, refinement and elevation."[29] We are no longer deeply moved by Greek tragedy because we see the universe as essentially rational and events explicable by human action: "We recognize no fate on the stage but that which arises from the nature of the hero himself."[30] Human reason in the greatest modern drama is equated with divine reason, and the effect sought is "beautiful transparence and joyous elevation." The character of the modern poet, his "free manliness," liberates his hearers and makes them stronger and nobler. Freytag considers this result related to Aristotle's *katharsis*, an effect rarely achieved in the less enlightened world of the Greeks.

Probably the best-known part of Freytag's book is the section that he calls the "pyramidal structure" of the most effective drama. This consists of five parts and three crises. The first part is the *introduction* of characters and situation. The first crisis brings the dramatic forces into play and initiates the *rising movement*, leading to the *climax*, the peak of the pyramid and emotional mid-point of the drama. The second crisis, or tragic moment, ends the climax and introduces the *falling movement*, or return. Between this and the final part, the *catastrophe*, may come a third crisis, the moment of final tension. Freytag applies these general observations to the work of major Greek, English, and German dramatists, then proceeds to more detailed technical advice: how to arrange and place monologues and messenger speeches, how to construct dialogue and ensemble scenes, how to motivate exits, how to reveal character. Finally, he turns to the specific concerns of putting the play on stage—the adjustment of the script to specific actors, the necessity of cuts and alterations, the length of acts according to contemporary taste, the role of the playwright in the rehearsal process. This section most clearly demonstrates Freytag's pragmatic orientation. His suggestions are specific and practical, based not upon any theory of drama but upon the contemporary working conditions of the German theatre.

Freytag's book, translated into English in 1894, served well into the

[29]Ibid., 77.
[30]Ibid., 81.

twentieth century as the standard manual for young playwrights, even though its rather facile optimism, its simplistic view of Greek tragedy, and its mechanistic approach aroused some protest along the way. Wilhelm Dilthey (1833–1911), the philosopher, psychologist, and aesthetician, expressed such criticisms in a lengthy review, published the year of the book's appearance, in the *Berliner Allgemeinen Zeitung*. Dilthey looks back to romantic theory and particularly to Schopenhauer in dismissing Freytag's interpretation of catharsis, essentially the removal of unpleasant emotions, as "worthless for our understanding of tragedy today."[31] Instead, he suggests as the function of tragedy the lifting of man to a higher consciousness, to the free realm of the universal.

He does not deny Freytag's theory of dramatic structure but questions its significance. Even if it is possible to abstract the "typical" form of an artistic mode, this sort of mechanistic and scientific procedure seems to Dilthey to ignore what is the essence of art and, worse, to misdirect future artists by encouraging them to focus on codified rules. "Æsthetics, like ethics, is not concerned with the rules of nature, but with masterpieces."[32] The true organizing principle of the great work, as opposed to the typical work, would be less like Freytag's pyramid than like the "inner form" of the romantics, the secret soul of the drama, which dictates not merely the general course of the action but the placement of every character and every scene.

This organizing principle derives in turn from the artist's psychic reaction to the world, for which the work of art serves as an objective symbol. In "Die Typen der Weltanschauungslehre" (1911), Dilthey postulates three types of world view, suggesting that each era has been dominated by one of these, which placed its stamp upon all the psychic products of that era—philosophy, society, literature, and art. The first view is positivism, which sees nature as a blind, purposeless creative force. Naturalism in art reflects this view. The second, objective idealism, is pantheistic, seeking a unified spirit that can organize man, nature, and society in a coherent whole. It is represented by authors like Goethe and Shakespeare. The third is dualistic idealism, which emerged in philosophy with Kant; it sees the human spirit independent of nature and creating its own order and meaning. Corneille and Schiller reflect this view.[33] Variations of Dilthey's approach, seeking to relate artistic and intellectual manifestations within a particular period on the basis of a presumed common psychic ground, were extremely popular in Germany through the first half of the twentieth century.

[31] Ibid., 331.
[32] Ibid., 340.
[33] Wilhelm Dilthey, *Gesammelte Schriften*, 19 vols. (Leipzig, 1914–82), 8:110–12.

A distinctly less sophisticated reaction to midcentury empiricism was provided by Otto Ludwig (1813–1865), one of the period's most popular dramatists. He rejected equally the socially engaged drama urged by such writers as Hebbel and Hettner and the concern with technique seen in Freytag. In both of these he saw an emphasis on the intellectual side of drama at the expense of the more essential emotional side. Freytag, said Ludwig in 1863, "lacks passion; he does not understand it, and without this no one can be a dramatist"; his book reveals nobility of character and high culture, but it considers "only the externals, and not the essence" of drama.[34]

The clearest development of Ludwig's own theory of drama may be found in his *Dramaturgische Aphorismen*, especially in the group written between 1840 and 1860. As the comments on Freytag suggest, he finds the essence of tragedy in emotional conflict, but within the hero rather than between man and fate or man and society. Tragic conflict must arise "from the deepest core" of the hero's self, "from an absolute contradiction in his own nature, so that the conflict is, so to speak, latent in the beginning and is awakened and laid open to view by the situation."[35] This formulation suggests Hegel's description of modern tragedy, and Ludwig's analysis of the evolution of it is similarly Hegelian. The tragedy Ludwig champions he calls poetic realism, which he sees as a synthesis of the partial perspectives offered by naturalism and idealism. From naturalism, it takes the elements of the real world; from idealism, the artistic unity arising from harmony and contrast. Naturalism gives it material; idealism, form.

There is a kind of moral world order implied in Ludwig's tragedy, since the internal conflict gives rise to guilt and itself arises from the workings of passion. He describes this process in "Shakespeares Kunst," a section of his *Shakespeare-Studien* (1871): "Passion must be the chief motive, not reflection . . . . The tragic is the ever-necessary nexus of guilt out of passion and of suffering out of guilt. External reality is only a symbol of this necessary internal struggle."[36] In his emphasis on unity, both internal and external—which he often describes in organic terms—and in his emphasis on character over plot, Ludwig shows a clear romantic influence, but his central vision of tragedy looks back to the eighteenth century and the hero who creates his own instability by an excess of passion, thus bringing on his own deserved punishment.

A much more radical interpretation of tragedy was advanced in the first major work of Friedrich Nietzsche (1844–1900), *Die Geburt der*

---

[34]Otto Ludwig, *Gesammelte Schriften*, 6 vols. (Leipzig, 1891), 6:320.
[35]Ibid., 5:429.
[36]Ibid., 163.

Tragödie aus dem Geiste der Musik (1872), the most influential theoretical statement on the drama in German in the latter nineteenth century. The book has many flaws, and no one has pointed them out more uncompromisingly than did Nietzsche himself in an 1886 preface to the work: "an impossible book . . . badly written, ponderous, embarrassing, mad and confused in imagery, sentimental, in places saccharine to the point of effeminacy, uneven in tempo, without the will to logical clarity, very convinced and therefore disdainful of proof, even of the propriety of truth . . . an arrogant and rhapsodic book."[37] Still, for all its flaws, this evocative text has inspired a wide range of modern critics.

In fact, despite its rather florid style, Nietzsche's book has a fairly logical structure. It is divided into 25 chapters: the first seven consider the conditions under which tragedy arose in ancient Greece, the next nine discuss its decline and death, and the final nine suggest how tragedy may be reborn in modern times.

The book begins with the duality upon which Nietzsche's theory of tragedy, and indeed his entire metaphysical system, is based: he distinguishes the Apollonian and Dionysian modes as ruling "the separate art worlds of dreams and intoxication." Apollo is the god of dreams, beautiful illusions, and a principle of individuation such as Schopenhauer described. Dionysus is the god of intoxication and loss of the self in primordial unity, in the maelstrom of continual creation and destruction. There is a suggestion of Hegel in this dualism and, beyond Hegel, of the general romantic proclivity to see the world in terms of oppositions: classic-romantic, ancient-modern, naive-sentimental, and so on. Indeed, Schlegel, at one point in his lectures, seems to anticipate the very dualism described by Nietzsche:

> The whole of ancient poetry and art is, as it were, a rhythmical nomos, a harmonious promulgation of a world permanently established, submitting to a higher order, and reflecting in itself eternal images. Romantic poetry, on the other hand, expresses a secret attraction to a chaos which lies concealed in the very bosom of the ordered universe, and is perpetually giving rise to new and awe-inspiring births; the life-giving spirit of primal love moves here anew upon the face of the deep.

Schlegel goes on to point out that the former is individualistic, the latter general, and closer to the "secret of the universe."[38] All that is needed to make this observation totally Nietzschean is to upset the implied balance of the duality, to make the Platonic "eternal images" of classic

---

[37]Friedrich Nietzsche, *Werke*, 3 vols. (Munich, 1954–56), 1:11.
[38]August Wilhelm von Schlegel, *Vorlesungen über dramatische Kunst und Literatur*, 2 vols. (Bonn, 1923), 2:114.

art illusory, and to emphasize the "life-giving" chaos as the basis of the universe. This is essentially what Schopenhauer did, and it is hardly surprising that Nietzsche cites Schopenhauer as his major philosophic inspiration.

There is nothing Schopenhauerian, however, in Nietzsche's final view of the purpose of tragedy. For Schopenhauer, tragedy led man to a negation of the Will by a revelation of the purposelessness of the universe, but Nietzsche saw tragedy as the great life-affirming response to such a vision. The Greek tragedian, "having looked boldly right into the terrible destructiveness of so-called world history as well as the cruelty of nature," might well have succumbed to that which Schopenhauer advocated, "a Buddhistic negation of the Will"; instead he was "saved by art," and through his art, life also is saved.[39] This was the great insight of classic Greece; having looked into the horror of the Dionysian world of existence, it created the Apollonian dream-world of Olympus. Each new emergence of the former strengthened and enriched the latter. In this process of playing off dream against intoxication, the Greeks shared in "the eternal core of the world," which Nietzsche saw as a suffering and self-contradictory being that seeks relief, redemption, even distraction by continual creation and destruction. Human existence is "merely images and artistic projections for the true author"; we are "aesthetic phenomena."[40]

To regard man and the world as aesthetic phenomena suggests Schopenhauer's passing show and seems to make the Apollonian vision itself a sort of escapism. But Nietzsche sees the Apollonian spirit not as a means of avoiding or denying the Dionysian, but as a necessary complement to it. The denial of either involves a denial of both, and it was precisely by abandoning Dionysus, says Nietzsche, that Euripides found himself abandoned by Apollo. At its greatest, tragedy may veil the true Dionysian, but ultimately the Apollonian drama itself is forced "into a sphere when it begins to speak with Dionysian wisdom and even denies itself its Apollonian visibility." Thus a union is accomplished: "Dionysus speaks the language of Apollo; and Apollo, finally, the language of Dionysus; and so the highest goal of all tragedy is achieved."[41]

The middle section of Nietzsche's *Die Geburt* tells how this goal was lost, beginning with Euripides, who—under the influence of Socratic thought—renounced Dionysus in favor of an art presumably based on morality and rationalism. This illusory view has prevailed down to our own day, but contains the seeds of its own destruction. Science, spread-

---

[39]Nietzsche, *Werke*, 1:48.
[40]Ibid., 40.
[41]Ibid., 120.

ing toward infinity in all directions, will inevitably discover that human logic cannot penetrate the deepest mysteries of the universe or correct all contradictions. When this realization is reached, a tragic vision will again be demanded, and a new Socrates, who understands the spirit of music, may appear. The book concludes with Nietzsche's belief that the world stands upon that threshold.

Not surprisingly, so odd and idiosyncratic a work met with considerable resistance. The philosopher's praise of Wagner as one of the pioneers pointing the way to the new tragic art gained him the support of Wagnerians, but the intellectual community in general and classicists in particular generally received *Die Geburt der Tragödie* in silence; the few who acknowledged it at all dismissed it on grounds of faulty scholarship. Only in the twentieth century has it become widely accepted as a work of major poetic insight, despite its blemishes.

The dominant theory of drama in the 1870s followed the more moderate and traditional directions suggested by Hebbel, Freytag, and Ludwig. Well-constructed plays dealing with contemporary social conditions, especially those of marriage and family, were dominant, and the critical theory supporting them was strikingly close to that of Dumas *fils* or Francisque Sarcey in France. The influential Berlin critic and dramatist Paul Lindau (1839–1919) explained that his tragic drama *Marion* (1870) sought to demonstrate "how the prevailing conditions alone suffice to bring about this tragedy" and that the "two decisive factors in human life"—education, and the way marriage is arranged and families established—now "lead inevitably to the weakening of the family and to the moral and physical destruction of the individual."[42]

In Berlin as in Paris, this sort of engaged social drama was bitterly attacked by members of the new naturalist movement that emerged in the 1880s. Some, such as Michael Georg Conrad (1846–1927), founder of the naturalist journal *Die Gesellschaft* in Munich, did it through an unqualified acceptance of Zola's theories (see Chapter 16). More typical of German naturalists was Heinrich Hart (1855–1906) in Berlin, whose essay "Für und gegen Zola" (1885) calls Zola's naturalism an extreme reaction against the pomposity of French romanticism—a corrective fortunately not necessary in Germany. Hart saw in Zola a danger of loss of artistic control and an unfortunate openness to the base and unpleasant in human existence. He called instead for nature controlled and refined by artistry—essentially what Ludwig meant by "poetic realism." "What our stage needs," he wrote in the early 1880s, "is an overcoming of the prosaic and commonplace which now rules there"

---

[42]Paul Lindau, *Dramaturgische Blätter*, 2 vols. (Stuttgart, 1874–75), 1:209.

and a turn toward "deep, internal, emotional poetry, which bears profound thoughts on its wings and joins heaven and earth with its vision."[43]

This conviction appears clearly in Hart's major theatre essay "Das 'deutsche Theater' des Herrn L'Arronge" (1882), which calls the drama "the summit of all art" and asserts that the stage "opens to us the pure world of ideas, free of any restrictions or chance occurrences; it shows us man in his essence, in the full range of his deeds and actions; it is the mirror of mankind, and brings man to consciousness of his feelings and drives."[44] Such a goal might possibly lead to the abstract drama of the symbolists, but Hart was satisfied with depictions of social conflict and scenes of family life, provided these were developed "artistically" and "in harmony with the poetic creations of our nation."[45]

Hart blames the decline in drama partly on dramatists who neglect this poetic dimension, but partly also on directors, actors, and even designers and machinists who attempt to usurp the dramatist's position of superiority. He dismisses as a pernicious doctrine the assertion that "the play in written form is only a half-completed work of art." The actor "adds nothing to the clarity of the character as it is created in the imagination of the reader" except a "greater effect on the senses," which indeed is the purpose of presentation as a whole.[46] Hart therefore urges the dramatist to oversee the process of production in order to protect his original vision.

An idealized naturalism similar to Hart's was championed by the Berlin critic Otto Brahm (1856–1912), founder of the Freie Bühne, which served in Berlin (like Antoine's Théâtre-Libre in Paris) as the pioneer theatre for modern ideas of staging and dramaturgy. In his survey of contemporary Parisian theatre, *Pariser Theatereindrücke* (1880), Brahm seconded Zola in condemning the contemporary French stage for relying upon convention rather than seeking nature; in the article "Der Naturalismus und das Theater" (1891), he stated that the theatre "can recover its great spiritual power over the life of the Germans only by walking the path of naturalism."[47]

Brahm's critical vocabulary clearly owes much to Zola, but its intellectual basis is the German philosophic tradition. Brahm regards as true but unfortunate Zola's statement that reality is always seen "through a temperament"; he argues that the greatest dramatists, such as Goethe and Shakespeare, reduce this subjective element almost to nothing. When temperament is dominant, "we have only a mere thesis play";

[43] Heinrich Hart, *Kritische Waffengänge*, 6 nos. (Leipzig, 1882–84), 2:28.
[44] Ibid., 4:20.
[45] Ibid., 24–25.
[46] Ibid.,18.
[47] Otto Brahm, *Kritiken und Essays* (Zurich, 1964), 418.

when its influence is mastered, we have "the pure work of art," which can be judged "on purely artistic grounds."[48] In this way Brahm's naturalism, partly in reaction to the social drama of Lindau's generation, recalls the metaphysical idealism of the early nineteenth century.

Brahm further sides with those romantic idealists who saw the ideal not as an immutable absolute but as a process, in constant change. Goethe and Shakespeare reflect no permanent classic ideal, but a dynamic of change and constant organic growth. In an 1887 review of Ibsen's *Ghosts*, Brahm condemns those who would criticize Ibsen on the basis of rules drawn from Aristotle and Lessing, since theory itself must change "to accommodate the ever-changing rules of art."[49] The battle cry of the new art, he states in the first issue of *Freie Bühne für modernes Leben* (1890), is "the single word, truth," and this truth is not fixed, not to be discovered by consulting the old authorities, but is revealed in the struggles of actual existence.[50] Naturalism itself, the living art of the time, will invariably be replaced by other approaches as this process continues.

Brahm's theories on acting, discussed in "Von alter und neuer Schauspielkunst" (1892), reflect this same interest in change and development in art. The impetus for these observations was an attack by the Berlin critic Karl Frenzel (1827–1914) on trends in acting related to naturalism: "Young actors now preach the most fantastic theory of a new art of acting, somewhat in the manner of the impressionist painters, which imitates nature at any price, rejecting the beauty of humanity to return grotesquely to a disgusting bestiality."[51] Brahm responds by admitting an affinity between his work and that of certain "impressionist" painters (Millet in particular) but denies the goal of "imitating nature at any price." He condemns the surface realism of the Meininger and such historical painters as Piloty, but feels that Millet offers something more, an "intimate observation of nature" and a capturing of "inner truth." Similarly the actor must be not simply a keen observer of the details of daily life but a human being of rich and pure personality, one who experiences life deeply and attempts to present nature "in her entirety, her fullness of soul."[52]

Brahm's major goal in founding the Freie Bühne was to provide a hearing for new works that would revitalize the German stage, "which is in danger of losing touch with modern German life."[53] Gerhart

---

[48]Ibid., 486.
[49]Ibid., 103.
[50]Ibid., 317.
[51]Ibid., 465.
[52]Ibid., 473.
[53]Heinz Selo, *Die "Freie Volksbühne in Berlin"* (Berlin, 1930), 185.

Hauptmann (1862–1946), Brahm's leading dramatist, provided him with a series of plays in the early 1890s which dealt with significant social questions in a strikingly realistic manner. His work was held up as an example by champions of naturalism such as the Munich critic Hans von Gumppenberg (1866–1928), who, in "Wohin mit dem Drama?" (1892), called for a theatre scrupulously reproducing everyday life. He particularly praised Hauptmann's *Die Weber* (1892) for its realistic characterizations and its use of dialect—"the only true living speech"—instead of conventional theatrical language.[54]

An interesting rejoinder to this article was published in a subsequent issue of the same journal, the *Münchener Kunst*, by the dramatist Julius Brand (1862–1895). Brand objected to the use of dialect, indeed to the whole concept of the "slice of life," which he called suitable for the novel but not for the stage. The drama, he said, by its nature involves "conflict, explosion, struggle, dialogue, dualism, dialectic." It cannot show the "secret inner workings of the spirit" that cause these explosions, "because it is much too deficient in psychological-physiological analysis."[55]

Of course, this assertion would hardly be accepted by any symbolist, whose concern would be precisely to capture those "secret inner workings." Thus the Viennese critic Hermann Bahr (1863–1934), in his highly influential *Die Überwindung des Naturalismus* (1891), argues that naturalism brought about its own destruction, its increasingly precise and detailed examinations leading at last to a multitude of evanescent sense impressions; the art of the future, Bahr felt, must turn to psychology and to the reporting of these impressions.

Bahr did not find such a direction inimical to drama. Indeed, among the members of *Junge Österreich*, as he called the writers in the new style, he included Arthur Schnitzler (1862–1931) and Hugo von Hofmannsthal (1874–1929); these young Viennese dramatists looked to the philosopher Ernst Mach (1838–1916) for inspiration, especially to his *Die Analyse der Empfindungen und das Verhältniss des Physischen zum Psychischen* (1886–1900), which denied the possiblity of ascertaining subjective reality. All experience, says Mach, is totally conditioned by the observer; however, the observer himself is not fixed but is a constantly changing constellation of impressions. Reality is thus not only subjective but in constant flux.

The evanescent impressions and shifting emotions of life became the concern of these dramatists—not without a sense of skating on the edge of a metaphysical abyss. In the poetic *Einleitung* to Schnitzler's play *Anatol* (1892), Hofmannsthal wrote:

---

[54]Hans von Gumppenberg, "Wohin mit dem Drama?" *Münchener Kunst* 2, 39 (1892):360.
[55]Julius Brand, "Das Drama," *Münchener Kunst* 2, 41 (1892): 387.

In this way we play theater,
Thus we play our private plays,
Early-ripened, tender, sad,
The comedy of our own soul,
All our feelings past and present,
Evil things in charming form,
Polished words and lively pictures,
Half-formed personal sensations,
Agonies and episodes . . . .[56]

The new "impressionist" approach, clearly akin to French symbolism, was advocated in Berlin by such journals as the *Blätter für die Kunst*, founded in 1892, and the *Dramaturgische Blätter*, founded in 1898. For the latter, Johannes Schlaf (1862–1941), one of the pioneers of German naturalism, wrote an essay "Von intimen Theater" (1898), announcing that the essence of modern drama involves a shift to internal action. The dramatist must learn to work in indirect ways, to create dialogue and situations that reveal "the inner movement of the soul."[57] Two articles that same year by the poet Rainer Maria Rilke (1875–1926) called for a drama "more concentrated, more searching" than life. Rilke denounced "fourth-wall" realism, observing that to be truly reflective of human existence the stage had not one wall too few, but three too many. "It must find room for all which fills our days and from childhood on moves us and makes us what we are."[58]

Alongside the growing interest in an internal, psychological theatre in Berlin at the close of the century, there developed a quite different concern with the theatre as a social phenomenon. This approach, too, had its roots in naturalism but was brought to prominence by the growing political strength of socialism. Brahm's interest in plays dealing with "modern German life" ensured that the Freie Bühne would offer works dealing with contemporary political questions though Brahm's theory itself had no strong political coloration. In a period of growing socialist consciousness, his program inspired a desire to establish a similar theatre for the proletariat; on March 23, 1890, the *Berlin Volksblatt*, the chief publication of the Social Democrats, published a manifesto by Bruno Wille (1860–1928), "Aufruf zur Gründung einer Freien Volks-Bühne." The taste of the German people, said Wille, had "been corrupted in all levels of society by certain economic conditions," and the theatre, which should serve as a moral guide and a "powerful stimulus to thinking about the great questions of the time," had be-

[56]Arthur Schnitzler, *Gesammelte Werke*, 9 vols. (Vienna, 1922–28), Abt. 2, pt. 1, p. 12.
[57]Johannes Schlaf, "Von intimen Theater," *Dramaturgische Blätter*, 2, 1 (1899):36.
[58]Rainer Maria Rilke, "Theater," *Dramaturgische Blätter* 1, 38 (1898):296; 1, 40:312.

come—under the influence of capitalism—a mindless entertainment. The Freie Bühne had raised hopes of something better, but its audience remained essentially bourgeois, and a theatre was needed to create, significant drama for the working class.[59]

Wille's announced program suggested no tension between cultural improvement of the proletariat and political stimulus, but before long these developed into rival concerns. Wille's opponents, insisting upon closer ties with the Socialist party, wrested control of the Freie Volks-bühne from him, and he departed to found a rival theatre, the Neue Freie Volksbühne. The directorship of the original organization was then offered to Franz Mehring (1846–1919), a leading Berlin journalist and editor and a recent, influential, and highly visible convert to the Social Democratic party. Mehring was the first literary theorist to at-tempt to apply the principles of Marxism to European literature, and his administration of the Freie Volksbühne, during which he continued to write critical articles, coincided with the appearance of his first major essay on Marxist thought, "Über den historischen Materialismus" (1893), and his first substantial work dealing with literature in these terms, *Die Lessing-Legende* (1892).

Die Lessing-Legende considered the inspiration of Lessing's original works and the development of his subsequent reputation as products of social and economic forces. It also referred to the founding of the Volksbühne as another manifestation of these forces; Mehring called it one of the first fruits of the rising proletarian consciousness and of a developing proletarian aesthetic, which would "relate to proletarian politics as the bourgeois aesthetic relates to bourgeois politics."[60] The coming of naturalism was a step in the right direction, but true pro-letarian theatre was yet to be achieved. In the earlier *Kapital und Presse* (1891), Mehring had praised naturalism for breaking with empty for-malism and bourgeois apologetics but deplored the tendency of nat-uralist authors to select subjects "of hopeless and disconsolate pessimism" that eroded man's desire to improve his society; he warned that the movement, still in its infancy, could easily "lose its way or even begin moving backward."[61]

"Der heutige Naturalismus" (1893) develops these observations fur-ther. Naturalism is praised for "the courage and love of truth to portray contemporary conditions as they are," but it has gone only halfway toward the goal of truly depicting a proletarian society. Since this society has not yet come into being, this second half of the path will require

[59]Siegfried Nestriepke, *Geschichte der Volksbühne* (Berlin, 1930), 10.
[60]Franz Mehring, *Die Volksbühne* 9, 2 (1901):10.
[61]Mehring, *Kapital und Presse* (Berlin, 1891), 131.

a "higher courage and a higher love of truth, so as to depict conditions as they must become and as they are daily becoming."[62] A certain paradox is involved, for Mehring simultaneously calls upon art to prepare the way intellectually and emotionally for the new order and argues that art can only reflect the order in which it was created.

During the 1890s, the failure of naturalism to provide the sort of theatre he proposed led him increasingly to feel that indeed this literature must wait for the reorganization of society. In 1895 he wrote, "The time has not yet come, though it is certain to come, for the proletariat to produce a dramatic poet from its own womb."[63] Mehring saw the new symbolist dramas—and particularly the turning of Hauptmann, whose early works he had praised, in that direction—as confirmation of his worst fears. He characterized Hauptmann's *Hannele*, with its excursions into fantasy, as an "infinitely sentimental and emotional presentation of the sort that used to be created in the musical comedies of the Royal Prussian Theatre for the most lachrymose souls of the Stock Exchange."[64] Mehring became convinced that the theatre as it was must disappear completely, along with its society, before a new and higher art could appear. Only when "the declining bourgeoisie can no longer create great art and the ascending proletariat can not yet create great art" will sufficient desire arise among the latter to lead at last to a "greater, higher, more noble art than men's eyes have yet beheld."[65]

[62]Mehring, *Die Volksbühne* 1, 3 (1892):12.
[63]Ibid., 3, 9 (1895):3.
[64]Mehring, "Ein Traumstück," *Die Neue Zeit* 12, 1 (1893):246.
[65]Mehring, *Gesammelte Schriften und Aufsatze* (Berlin, 1929–31), 230.

16

France in the
Late Nineteenth Century

THE TRIUMPH OF ROMANTICISM in the French theatre was neither unqualified nor long-lasting, at least in the form championed and exemplified by Hugo. Within a decade after the preface to *Cromwell*, even sympathetic critics like Théophile Gautier were complaining that the high tide of romanticism had passed without establishing the modern theatre it promised. The vision of a theatre of truth and contemporary relevance remained, but the search for the dramatists to accomplish this turned away from the established romantics. In 1838, Honoré de Balzac (1799–1850), who for a time apparently considered himself a possible candidate for the role, wrote: "It is no longer possible for the theatre to be anything but true, as my novels have attempted to be. But the creation of truth is not given to Hugo, whose talent carries him into lyricism, nor to Dumas, who has gone past it never to return; he cannot be again what he has been. Scribe is finished. New talents must be sought."[1]

That same year, the enormous success of the actress Rachel in revivals of the French classics brought new life to a tradition many had dismissed as gone forever. Alfred de Musset (1810–1857) was inspired to take a fresh look at the tragic genre in "De la tragédie à propos des débuts de Mlle Rachel" (1838). Rachel had proved, he said, that henceforth both the classic and the romantic approach must be accepted as a part of the continuing French tradition. One could not, however, return to the style of Corneille and Racine, so Musset turned to the question of what form modern tragedy should take.

He begins with a brief history of the genre, pointing out that a key

[1]Honoré de Balzac, *Correspondance*, 5 vols. (Paris, 1960–69), 3:475.

change occurred when Christianity and modern philosophy destroyed the classic belief in fate or destiny. This left providence and chance as ruling forces, neither of them tragic: the one leads only to happy conclusions; the other provides no shape or coherence for a drama. Corneille, faced with this dilemma, turned to the depiction of passion as the source of tragedy, thus inaugurating the modern drama: "a passion and an obstacle; that sums up almost all of our plays."[2]

In Racine, the development of the passion became the source of the plot, and action essentially disappeared—a trend encouraged, says Musset, by the encumbrance of spectators on the stage. The drama, restoring this action, achieved great popularity but, in refusing to follow the rules, denied itself the greatest power of theatre. The unities and other rules are not arbitrary but essential components of the art: "An architect uses wheels, pulleys, framework; a poet uses rules, and the more precisely these are observed, the greater will be the effect and the more solid the result."[3] Musset recommends the development of a modern tragic style with subjects drawn from French history, as in Chénier and Hugo, but with respect for the unities and in poetic but simple and straightforward language.

When in 1843 François Ponsard's (1814–1867) *Lucrèce*, widely regarded as a counterromantic work, achieved a marked success almost simultaneously with an indifferent reception of Hugo's new work, *Les Burgraves*, Ponsard was at once widely hailed as the leader of the eagerly sought new school, which came to be known as the *école de bon sens*. Although the writings of Ponsard and others in this group were in some respects simply a revival of neoclassic subjects and methods, these authors were not mere epigones. Their success was due not to nostalgia, but to relevance, for much more accurately than Hugo or Dumas, they reflected the concerns and the ideals of the new bourgeois society of the 1840s. Although they wrote in verse, it was simple and direct, as Musset had advised, purged of the flamboyant ornamentation of romanticism. Reason and moderation replaced emotion and excess, and perhaps most important, duty to family and society was stressed instead of the exaltation of the individual ego.

In an "A propos" to *Agnès de Méranie* (1847), his second play, Ponsard answered the attacks of the romantics on his work by asserting that romanticism was already becoming as inflexible and as removed from life as the late imitators of classicism, that uninspired copies of Shakespeare had replaced uninspired copies of Racine. He called for the rejection of formulas and doctrines, of concern with innovation or

[2]Alfred de Musset, *Oeuvres complètes*, 10 vols. (Paris, 1866), 9:325.
[3]Ibid., 333.

imitation, in favor of a recognition that all art was simply good or bad. For Ponsard, the "only sovereignty to be admitted" was that of "good sense. I hold that all doctrines, ancient or modern, should be continually submitted to this supreme judge."[4] Only "good sense," clearly the mid-nineteeenth-century version of the previous century's "reason," could save drama from doctrinal disputes and pedantry.

The Racine-Shakespeare confrontation was considered more fully in Ponsard's "Discours de réception à l'Académie Française" (1856), which praised Shakespeare as a great dramatic genius but championed Racine as a corrective needed once again, because French writers were embracing all of Shakespeare, even his faults. Had Shakespeare dominated the French stage for 200 years and Racine then been discovered, said Ponsard, unbounded enthusiasm would have been felt "for his language, always pure, harmonious, noble without pomp, natural without banality, and for the severe majesty of his tragedies, where a clear, logical, believable, and united action unrolls in a controlled manner."[5] The French should now recover these virtues of the classic French stage and use them to temper the recent enthusiasm for alien drama, not in the spirit of reaction or blind patriotism, but in the objective desire to move forward, utilizing the best of both traditions. The goal should be simplicity and truth, and Racine "is simple, very simple, simpler and more natural than Goethe; as natural as Shakespeare, when Shakespeare himself is natural."[6]

Emile Augier (1820–1887) championed the cause of Ponsard and the return to the traditional values of French drama while he was dramatic critic of the short-lived *Spectateur républicain* (July to September 1848), but he wrote little subsequent criticism. As a dramatist, on the other hand, he eventually far surpassed Ponsard in popularity and influence. In his plays he began to apply, first in verse and then in prose, the ideas of the *école de bon sens* to contemporary subjects; in this manner he and Dumas *fils* established the post-1850 social drama, the first major postromantic school in France.

La dame aux camélias (1851) by Alexandre Dumas *fils* (1824–1895) was the first great success of this school. It bore some relationship to the elder Dumas's *Antony* but was even more direct in its utilization of personal experience and specific contemporary references. The preface to the play (written in 1867) describes the physical appearance and summarizes the life of the "real" Marguerite Gautier—Marie Duplessis, who died in 1847. Although not all of his subsequent plays were so

[4]François Ponsard, *Oeuvres complètes*, 3 vols. (Paris, 1865–76), 3:352.
[5]Ibid., 1:27.
[6]Ibid., 24.

directly drawn from personal experience, Dumas *fils* sought always to depict, as realistically as possible, the society and the individuals around him. He repeats this idea constantly. The world of *Le demi-monde* (1855), the preface assures us, is "absolutely true." Jeannine in *Les idées de Madame Aubry* (1867), says Dumas, "really lived"; he kept a drawing of her in his desk. In the preface to *Le fils naturel* (1858), he describes himself as "someone who passes by, who regards, who sees, who feels, who reflects, who hopes and who says or writes down whatever strikes him in the form which is the clearest, the quickest, the most suitable for what he wishes to say."[7] The preface to *Un père prodigue* (1859) goes so far as to deny the necessity of imagination in a dramatist. "We have only to observe, to remember, to feel, to coordinate and to restore, in a particular form, what every spectator should at once recall having seen or felt without taking note of it before. Reality as a base, possibility in facts, ingenuity in means, that is all that ought to be asked of us."[8]

Clearly, Dumas saw the poet not as the unique, isolated genius of romanticism but as the representative of mankind in general, different only in that he observed more thoughtfully and recorded his observations more carefully than others so that they could be recognized as part of common experience. There is certainly a suggestion of "slice of life" realism in this, and Dumas *fils* unquestionably contributed to the development of that approach, but it was by no means his aim. He recognized the importance of style and of artistic form, warmly praising those achievements in Scribe despite the vacuity of his characters. The ideal drama must excel in both technique and observation: "The dramatist who knows *man* as Balzac did and the *theatre* as Scribe did will be the greatest dramatist who ever lived."[9]

The other clear distinction between Dumas *fils* and subsequent realists was Dumas's dedication to the moral purpose of drama. "The pure and simple reproduction of facts and men is the job of the photographer," he says in the preface to *Le fils naturel*. "All literature which is not concerned with perfectability, morality, the ideal, the useful, is in a word an unhealthy and rickety literature, dead at birth."[10] Theatre should show man as he is, but only to indicate to him thereby what he can become and how he may achieve this. Dumas finds the expression "art for art's sake" "totally devoid of meaning." His didacticism, which is increasingly obvious in his later dramas, marks the prefaces as well; they often contain extended discussions of such matters as prostitution,

---

[7] Alexandre Dumas *fils*, *Théâtre complet*, 8 vols. (Paris, 1890–98), 3:10. (These prefaces were almost all written in 1868 for a collected edition of the plays.)
[8] Ibid., 211–12.
[9] Ibid., 219.
[10] Ibid., 31.

motherhood, and preservation of the family. Both plays and prefaces become tribunals, as they became later for Shaw, but unhappily those of Dumas *fils* are much less often enlivened by objectivity or wit.

It was precisely this didactic quality that most offended the major new dramatists and theorists of the 1870s. Villiers de l'Isle-Adam (1838–1889), in the preface to his striking little play *La révolte* (1870)—which anticipates the subject of Ibsen's *A Doll House*—rejected the request of those who asked "what he wanted to prove": all he wished was "simply to paint in *La révolte* the sad condition of a commendable man in the toils of an overenthusiastic woman."[11]

Emile Zola (1840–1902) went much further, charging that didacticism actually prevented Dumas *fils* from achieving a significant success in what Zola felt should be the next stage of theatrical evolution, the "naturalist" theatre. In his essay on Dumas in *Nos auteurs dramatiques* (1881), Zola concludes: "In sum, Balzac desires to portray and Dumas to prove. That says it all. Dumas, like Sand, is in the idealist school. The world as he sees it seems badly constructed, and he feels a constant need to rebuild it. In the preface to *Le fils naturel* he declares quite clearly that he desires to play the role of moralist and legislator. I have other ideas." These other ideas, Zola explains, are based on the belief that "in the present era of experimental science," the artist should emulate the scientist, in both method and aim, the method being the careful study of objective phenomena, the aim "an exact analysis of man."[12]

The scientific metaphor—much influenced, as he readily admitted, by the physiologist Claude Bernard's *Introduction à l'étude de la médecine expérimentale* (1865)—is constantly present in Zola's theory. He frequently describes the work of the author as the conducting of an experiment in the manner of the scientist. The novelist, says Zola in *Le roman expérimental* (1880), "collects observed facts, chooses a point of departure, and establishes a solid ground upon which characters can walk and phenomena develop." He then allows the characters to develop "as required by determinism and the phenomena being studied," and observes and records the result. The "experimental novel" is thus "a verbal report of an experiment that the novelist conducts in the presence of the public," its goal being "the scientific knowledge of man, in his individual and social action."[13]

Zola points out that naturalism, "the return to nature and to man, direct observation, exact anatomy, acceptance and portrayal of that

[11]Villiers de l'Isle-Adam, *Oeuvres complètes*, 11 vols. (Paris, 1914–31), 7:xix.
[12]Emile Zola, *Oeuvres complètes*, 50 vols. (Paris, 1927–29), 43:133.
[13]Ibid., 41:16–17.

which exists," has important literary antecedents.[14] Whenever a writer seeks to capture truth, naturalism is to some degree involved. Homer was a naturalist in his way, as was Aristotle, but it was not until the eighteenth century that something akin to modern naturalism began to develop. Rousseau's interest in nature and the Encyclopedists' spirit of inquiry opened the way for modern naturalism, and certain late eighteenth-century French authors like Mercier and especially Diderot (whom Zola says "upheld the same ideas as I")[15] first applied these concerns to the theatre. Romanticism, in its revolutionary frenzy, prevented the orderly development of naturalism, but by clearing away the exhausted classic tradition and freeing artists from outworn conventions, it made an important contribution to naturalism's eventual triumph.

Unfortunately, Zola, like Diderot, proved far more influential as a theorist than as a practicing dramatist, though his works did provide models for the upcoming generation of French naturalists. The preface to his best-known play, *Thérèse Raquin* (1873), served as a kind of manifesto of naturalism, his generation's preface to *Cromwell*. It suggests ideas more fully developed in *Le roman expérimental* and *Le naturalisme au théâtre* (1881), all based on Zola's conviction "that the experimental and scientific spirit of the century will prevail in the theatre, and that there lies the only renewal possible for our stage."[16] The logic of this play was to be not that of facts but of "sensations and sentiments; and the denouement a mathematical result of the problem posed."

The mathematical and scientific imagery so common in Zola's writings can be misleading unless we recognize that Zola never forgot the contribution of the artist's personality. A work of art, he says in *Le roman expérimental*, is always "a bit of nature seen through a temperament."[17] Nor does he regard the effect of the artist's temperament as negative; on the contrary, it intensifies and shapes, ideally without removing the work from nature. Zola never champions "mere photography"; he recognizes that the artist's personal contribution makes nature into art, but he does warn that the artist must never distort or falsify to suit either his own concerns, the conventions of the form, or the tastes of his public.

The setting of *Thérèse Raquin*, according to its preface, was brought completely into accord "with the ordinary occupations of my characters, so that they would not 'play,' but 'live' before the audience."[18] This idea

[14] Ibid., 95.
[15] Ibid., 42:154.
[16] Ibid., 38:iii.
[17] Ibid., 41:92.
[18] Ibid., 38:iii.

is much more fully developed in the sections "Le costume" and "Les décors" of *Le naturalisme au théâtre*, where Zola explores the implications of the more natural style on settings, costumes, and acting. In each area he sees major changes required, since in each area theatrical conventions now reign.

The state of French acting, for example, can be inferred from the major acting text of the period, Joseph Samson's (1793–1871) *L'art théâtral* (1863), in which Samson, the leading teacher of acting at the Comédie Française, put forward his ideas on the art in general as well as on specific major roles in the repertoire. The form immediately betrays the content, for the two-volume work is composed of eight "songs," each a poem composed in the traditional Alexandrines of the classic French stage. Samson takes it for granted that an actor's lines will be in verse; the only question is whether he should "declaim or speak" them—stress the verse or try to convert it into prose. Samson's solution, not surprisingly, is the classic ideal mean:

> Avoid them both; shun all misguided schemes.
> Seek out the truth between the two extremes—
> The heart's desires in cadence to expose
> Or Alexandrines to reduce to prose.
> For such excesses there is no defense—
> A shock alike to ears and to good sense.[19]

Samson does not deny the "divine flame" of inspiration but has the greatest scorn for actors who rely upon it. Instead, he advises:

> Meditate, plan, and test all in advance.
> Such careful work will give you confidence.

Then, secure in every detail, the actor can

> Add to effects learned with deliberation
> The tones and movements drawn from
> inspiration.[20]

To Zola, of course, such advice represented a system of "deplorable tradition" that has "nothing in common with real life." The presumed best actors in France, he noted, spoke artificially, did not relate to each other, played toward the audience, and entered and exited as if by rule. In contrast, he praised the performance of a troupe of Italian actors, led by Tommaso Salvini, then visiting Paris. "The audience did

[19]Joseph Samson, *L'art théâtral* (Paris, 1863), 56.
[20]Ibid., 20.

not seem to exist for them. . . . They turned their backs to the orchestra, entered, said what they wished to say, and left, naturally, without the least effort to attract attention to themselves. This doesn't seem like much, but it is enormous for us in France."[21]

Equally important, if the actors were to give the impression of living the role, was to place them in costumes and settings appropriate to their condition. For Zola this was not simply an extension of the romantic interest in local color. He stressed that people act as they do in real life in part *because* of the clothing they wear and the surroundings in which they live. The old abstract or metaphysical tragic hero required only three neutral walls to enclose him, but "the physiological man of our modern tragedies demands more and more imperiously to be determined by the decor, by the milieu of which he is the product."[22]

Clearly, the physical surroundings were becoming as important to the drama as the characters themselves, and the concerns of dramatic theory, which had expanded to include the art of the actor in the eighteenth century, began in the nineteenth—most significantly with the writings of the naturalists—to include considerations of costume and setting as well. The primary influence on Zola's interest in milieu appears to have been Hippolyte Taine (1828–1893), whose discussion of the effects of environment on literature Zola cited approvingly to open his essay on costume.

Taine's *Histoire de la littérature anglaise* (1863) served as an important link between the critics of the German romantic tradition and those like Zola, who looked to nineteenth-century scientific thought for models of critical and literary procedure. Taine agrees with the Germans that each work of art must be viewed on its own unique terms as an organic whole. "All original art creates its own rules, and no original art can submit to the rules of another; it carries its own counterweight and receives no counterweight from elsewhere; it forms an inviolable whole; it is an animate being which lives on its own blood, and which languishes or dies if one removes some of its own blood to replace it with the blood of another."[23]

Again like the Germans, Taine couples this idea of uniqueness with a historical and national view of literature, seeing a relationship among all the works of a particular period. Following Hegel, he sees such a relationship developing in an evolutionary way, with each age reacting to or assimilating the doctrines of the age before. His major contribution is a much more programmatic view of this process than that of

---

[21]Zola, *Oeuvres*, 42:120.
[22]Ibid., 105.
[23]Hippolyte Taine, *Histoire de la littérature anglaise*, 5 vols. (Paris, 1866–71), 3:177.

most of his predecessors, possibly reflecting the English empirical interest in facts and data. In attempting to isolate the "primordial forces" that work upon literature to create its features in each period, he proposes his famous triad: *race, moment,* and *milieu. Race* comprises "the innate and hereditary dispositions which man brings with him into the world," often tied to variations in human physiology; *milieu* is made up of the external surroundings of a people—climate and geography, as well as social and cultural assumptions; *moment* is the "acquired momentum" of what *race* and *milieu,* working together, have already produced at the specific point in time when an artist or a work appears.[24]

By the careful analysis of these variables, Taine argues, the productions not only of literature but of all arts, as well as those of philosophy, science, and industry—indeed, all human endeavor—can be explained. Each one has "for its direct cause a moral disposition; the cause given, they appear ... each is bound up with its causes just as a physical phenomenon is with its condition, as the dew with the fall of the temperature, as dilatation with heat."[25] The causes of human action, analyzed with sufficient precision (a process that Taine admits is still in its infancy), can not only explain the past but predict the future. Each of Zola's naturalist works can be viewed as an experiment in such analysis, a demonstration of the causes and effects of human action.

Before Zola began his campaign to revitalize the theatre through naturalism, Edmond (1822–1896) and Jules (1830–1870) de Goncourt had attempted a much more modest turn toward realism in their plays *Henriette Maréchal* (1863) and *La patrie en danger* (1867). The former was produced without success, the latter not produced at all for more than 20 years, and Edmond de Goncourt's later prefaces to them seem to reflect irritation with both the indifference of the public and the usurpation by Zola of the position of major dramatic reformer. In an 1879 introduction to the two plays, Goncourt excludes himself from the realist tradition entirely and calls Zola to task for attempting to impose realism on an art form that is "a box of conventions, a pasteboard creation." Realism is impossible without psychology, and Goncourt does not find "the boards a proper ground for profound and intimate studies of manners";[26] for that sort of creation, the novel is much superior to the stage. Indeed, Goncourt, replying indirectly to Zola's assertion that the theatre must become naturalistic or cease to exist, concludes that in 50 years it will be replaced by the novel.

In 1885, for a second edition of *Henriette Maréchal,* Goncourt takes

[24]Ibid., 1:xxiii–xxx.
[25]Ibid., xlii–xliii.
[26]Edmond and Jules de Goncourt, *Préfaces et manifestes littéraires* (Paris, 1888), 136.

a somewhat more positive position. He still considers the theatre in its terminal illness, but since it is "not yet dead" and might linger for some time in a languishing state "like the present Catholic church," one might seek to prolong its existence by a "transfusion of new elements into its old organism." These will not be the facts, events, or situations of true human life espoused by Zola, for Goncourt still insists that these are inappropriate to this "pasteboard temple of convention." Instead, dramatists should develop first a "literary spoken language," a poetic style without the learned verbal displays of the romantics or the flat banalities of the naturalists. With this they should create portrayals of "sentiments in their characters which are in accord with nature."[27]

The theatre most associated with French naturalism was André Antoine's (1858–1943) Théâtre-Libre, which opened in 1887. Antoine wrote little theory, but in May 1890 he published a brochure that attempted to explain to the public the goals and procedures of his theatre. It essentially follows Zola in calling for a theatre based upon truth, observation, and the direct study of nature, denouncing the traditional training of actors as "perhaps dangerous—and at the very least useless and above all badly organized."[28] Such training emphasizes traditional types, traditional gestures, and especially traditional elocution. Antoine's actors "will come back to natural gestures and will substitute *composition for effects achieved solely by means of the voice*." This new acting, of course, must take place in realistic settings where an actor can develop, "simply and naturally, the simple gestures and natural movements of a modern man living his everyday life."[29]

One of Antoine's dramatists, Jean Jullien (1854–1919), became the leading critical spokesman for Antoine's venture. The preface to his *L'échéance*, dedicated to Antoine and produced at the Théâtre-Libre in 1889, provides a good summary of Jullien's ideas, again strongly influenced by Zola. Zola's definition, a "fragment of nature seen through a temperament," becomes Jullien's more famous dictum: "A play is a slice of life placed on the stage with art."[30] By art, Jullien does not mean traditional construction; indeed, he dismisses preparation, exposition, and denouement as "useless." The spectators need not be taken into the author's confidence or given superfluous details to make them feel they know the characters. What the theatre should offer is neither character analysis nor well-made plots, but action, full of surprises and often unresolved, just as it is in real life. The art of the theatre consists in the dramatist's "living for a long time mentally with

[27]Ibid., 112–13.
[28]Quoted in Toby Cole and Helen K. Chinoy, *Actors on Acting* (New York, 1970), 212.
[29]Ibid., 214.
[30]Jean Jullien, *Le théâtre vivant* (Paris, 1892), 11.

his characters, coming to think like them and thus gaining a language proper to each of them and being able to write a real dialogue without seeking to make effects in an inappropriate style." It involves "structuring the acts and scenes logically on a solid base composed of observed facts instead of being concerned with the clever linking of conversations," and of making certain that such technical matters as "entrances and exits are justified by nature."[31]

The mode of presentation is also of much concern to Jullien. Like Diderot, he places strong emphasis on pantomime; indeed, his concern with action leads him to place movement over language in importance to the dramatist. *L'échéance*, he says, "could as well be performed in pantomime as spoken,"[32] and he urges all dramatists to strive for this degree of visual clarity. No previous critic—not Diderot, who urged that whole scenes be presented in pantomime, and not Goethe, who saw the symbolic visual image as central to theatrical effect—went so far as Jullien, who suggested that the essence of drama may not be found in the words at all. (A significant part of the theatrical theory of the twentieth century would concern itself with this possibility.)

Jullien, like Antoine, urges actors to abandon traditional character types and seek no longer "to enter the skin of a role, but to adapt the role to themselves"[33] and perform "as if at home, ignoring the emotions they arouse in the public." In perhaps his most memorable phrase, Jullien says that the proscenium opening should be considered "a fourth wall, transparent for the public, opaque for the actor."[34] Other production suggestions reinforce this vision of the theatre as an illusion of real life. The auditorium should be darkened, the footlights abandoned, properties real rather than painted on the scenery, costumes appropriate to the character. The spectator "must lose for an instant the feeling of his presence in a theatre" and, sitting in darkness before a lighted box, should "remain attentive and no longer dare to speak."[35] Only in this way, says Jullien, can the theatre be considered a serious art.

Many of these same concerns may be found in what is probably the best-known statement of the ideas and practices of the naturalist theatre, August Strindberg's (1849–1912) preface to *Miss Julie* (1888), which was written under the influence of Zola and his disciples and presented at the Théâtre-Libre. The objective stance advocated by Strindberg suggests Zola's scientific detachment pushed almost to parody. He ad-

[31]Ibid., 14.
[32]Ibid., 15.
[33]Ibid., 18.
[34]Ibid., 11.
[35]Ibid., 10.

mits that his play may now seem tragic, but "a time may come when we have grown so developed and enlightened that we shall view with indifference life's spectacle, now seeming so brutal, cynical, and heartless." The pity spectators may be tempted to feel for Miss Julie is, says Strindberg, a sign of weakness; he urges his audience to seek joy in his play, joy in "the strong and eternal struggles of life" and pleasure in adding to one's knowledge of them.[36] Like Zola, he carefully analyzes the various forces working upon his characters, listing in detail the psychological, physiological, social, and environmental reasons for his heroine's actions. Modern characters indeed should have no "character" in the traditional sense of a predictable set of reactions drawn from type; they should instead reflect the variety of forces playing upon them. They should be "vacillating, disintegrated . . . conglomerations of past and present stages of civilization."[37]

In his own technique, Strindberg shows a strong debt to the naturalists. His dialogue avoids "symmetrical, mathematical construction" and lets "people's minds work irregularly, as they do in real life."[38] He calls for a realistic interior with real objects, instead of pots and pans painted on the walls, and for the abolition of the unnatural illumination of footlights. He sets his entire action within a single interior, and observes unity of time even to the extent of replacing traditional intermissions with a pantomime and a dance that allow the action to flow without interruption. He considers it too utopian to expect the actors to treat the stage as "a real room with the fourth wall missing," but he hopes someday to see actors willing to ignore the audience and play within the scene to each other.[39] He would also like to see makeup abolished, or at least reduced to a minimum.

The Darwinian tone of the struggle between Jean and Miss Julie also suggests naturalism, though Strindberg's analysis of it is strongly colored by concerns of his own: the male-female conflict, the confrontation of classes, the morally superior Aryan (a Nietzschean echo) whose sense of honor hampers him in any struggle with a morally inferior but therefore more ruthless adversary. Strindberg attempts in this essay to interpret internal struggles, psychological and physiological, in essentially naturalistic terms, but the scientific objectivity championed by Zola is ultimately impossible for so subjective an artist, and his subsequent theoretical writings are much more in harmony with symbolist and psychoanalytic criticism.

Zola, following Taine, believed that "any established and lasting gov-

[36]August Strindberg, *Six Plays*, trans. Elizabeth Sprigge (Garden City, 1955), 62–63.
[37]Ibid., 65.
[38]Ibid., 69.
[39]Ibid., 73.

ernment has its own literature," an idea ultimately derived from the historicism introduced by the German romantics. He thus considered naturalism the inevitable literature of the Republic of 1870, a government based on positivist thought and a scientific analysis of the needs of the nation.[40] In fact, naturalism reflected the new Republic in less positive ways, which understandably are not remarked upon by Zola. The stinging defeat of Napoleon III by the Prussians in 1870 was for many an invitation to cynicism rather than scientism, and a distinctly dark and pessimistic note pervaded the naturalist movement, opening Zola to attack from several groups. There were those who admired the technical competence of Scribe and his school and who found naturalist slices of life unattractive, all the more so when they seemed to specialize in the sordid and depressing. There were the writers Zola called idealists, who charged him with denying the spiritual, and more significant, side of man. Finally, there were even those who turned Zola's own arguments against him, saying that by emphasizing man's baseness he was betraying the scientific objectivity he claimed as his goal.

Among the defenders of Scribe was the leading French theatre critic of the later nineteenth century, Francisque Sarcey (1827–1899), who provided an informed, often subtle and perceptive, view of the French stage from 1860 until his death. His clear preference for the classics and for the well-made plays of Scribe, Augier, and Dumas *fils* over the naturalists' slices of life and the subsequent reveries of the symbolists eventually earned him the quite unmerited reputation of being a narrow traditionalist, and his goal of applying common sense and values understandable to the average playgoer have been cited by those who thought him something of a philistine as well. In fact, his observations on even the genres with which he had little sympathy contain striking insights, but for his contribution to dramatic theory in general, we must look primarily to his observations on the well-made play and its practitioners.

Sarcey's *Essai d'esthétique de théâtre* (1876) defines dramatic art as "the ensemble of universal or local, eternal or temporary conventions by the aid of which one represents human life on a stage so as to give to the public the illusion of truth."[41] Each part of this somewhat cumbersome formulation is in fact important to Sarcey, but the heart of his aesthetics and his criticism is found in the words "to the public"; the effect on the public remained always his touchstone. Thus he acknowledges Hugo's argument that in reality tears sometimes mingle with laughter and the sublime is seen juxtaposed with the grotesque,

---

[40]Zola, *Oeuvres*, 41:32.
[41]Francisque Sarcey, *Quarante ans de théâtre*, 8 vols. (Paris, 1900–1902), 1:132.

but this is not necessarily an argument for doing the same thing on stage in imitation of reality. The question for Sarcey is not whether "buffoonery and horror are mixed in life," but whether "twelve hundred persons gathered in a theatre auditorium can easily move from tears to laughter and from laughter to tears."[42] It it this concern, he suggests, that underlies the old ideas of the distinction of genres and the unity of impression. Only if the public can come to accept abrupt changes would Sarcey allow them; he does admit that the dramatists of his own time can introduce a degree of the grotesque that would have been unacceptable in 1817, the ideas and the taste of the public having changed since then.

Sarcey specifically dissociates himself from establishing rules for all time. He is not interested in whether a new work may be a lasting masterpiece but only in whether it will please the contemporary taste. Thus he can give high praise to an admittedly minor drama, such as George Ohnet's *Le maître de forges* (1883), which fulfilled this condition. "While a school of turbulent revolutionaries claim to overthrow from top to bottom the old rules and bring us a new art, here is a man who succeeds ... simply because he knows his craft, because he gives us what we used to call a well-made play." Sarcey then lists the components of such a work: the drama is "founded upon sentiments which everyone understands and which interest everyone because they are the sentiments common to human nature; it is clearly laid out, logically developed, and furnished with a happy denouement."[43]

Clarity and logic of structure are the qualities of drama Sarcey most admires, and the keystone of the structure is the *scène à faire* (the obligatory scene), a term he invented which became a central concept in the analysis of play construction. His analysis of the opening action of Emile Augier's *Les Fourchambault* (1878) illustrates this concept at work. Sarcey praises the play as an excellent example of construction in general: "These two acts are no vain conversation from which emerges a drama which has no relation to it. There is not a word spoken which does not subsequently serve either to elucidate the action or to explain the character of those who will take part in it. As the curtain falls on the phrase 'It is my father,' I see at once two obligatory scenes coming, and I know they will take place—the scene between the son and the father he is going to save and that between Bernard and his brother Leopold." The precise turn these scenes will take is unknown, but Sarcey calls this very uncertainty one of the great charms of the theatre. "I say aside to myself 'Ah! They are going to speak together! What will

[42]Ibid., 140.
[43]Ibid., 7:201.

come of that?' And this is so much the thought of the entire audience that when the two persons confront one another in the obligatory scene a universal shiver is felt throughout the auditorium."[44] This craft, this careful arrangement of anticipation and fulfillment, was what Sarcey and the public he represented admired as the essence of theatrical experience.

The logical approach to dramatic structure represented by Sarcey and the spirit of codification inspired by the physical sciences in the nineteenth century reached a kind of apotheosis in *Les 36 situations dramatiques*. This periodic table of the drama, created by Georges Polti (b. 1868), was published in the *Mercure de France* in 1894 and subsequently as a separate volume. Taking his cue from Goethe's remark to Eckermann that Gozzi had limited the tragic situations to 36, Polti set himself to discover, as Goethe had been unable to do, what precisely these situations were. He attempted to isolate 36 "basic" emotions upon which the situations could be based, and announced that he had succeeded.

In fact, his list is a hodgepodge of elements. Some are infinitives: "to supplicate," "to obtain," "to sacrifice to an ideal," "to kill an unknown victim," "to sacrifice all to passion." Others are modified or unmodified nouns: "revolt," "disaster," "the savior," "madness," "unequal rivals," "adulterous murder," "judicial error." Still others are phrases, such as "vengeance pursuing a crime." Nevertheless, all are carefully worked out through possible variations. A complex plot could combine two of them for (he says, with a regrettably weak grasp of mathematics) a total of 1,332 situations, and by a process of further combination Polti offers to the theatre directors of Paris 10,000 different scenarios—a thousand the first week, if they wish. "The day of imagination is over," he declares. "It must be replaced now by a higher and more modern principle, logic."[45]

Despite the scientific flavor of this approach, it won no praise from Zola, who deplored the calculation and manipulation involved in any approach to drama that sought to establish patterns. He regarded such attention to dramatic structure as a resurgence of the old practice of making actors and actions mere cogs in a dramatic machine with little relation to real life. By the 1880s, however, Zolaesque naturalism itself was under serious attack, and its enemies were by no means restricted to proponents of the well-made play.

Ferdinand Brunetière (1849–1906) sought to discredit Zola in the name of Zola's own deity, scientific realism. In *Le roman naturaliste*

[44]Ibid., 5:94–95.
[45]Georges Polti, "Les 36 situations dramatiques," *Mercure de France* 12 (1894): 244.

(1882), Brunetière charged that Zola's lack of taste and wit, as well as of psychological finesse, led him into "literary pessimism and investigation of the crude and gross," masquerading as objective presentation of material.[46] His characters thus became either puppets, devoid of life, or mere animals with nothing human about them. In his passion to avoid the lyric excesses of the romantics, Zola had distorted reality just as severely in the opposite direction.

The same argument was repeated in a much less reasoned and more personal attack in 1887, the notorious *Manifeste des cinq*, which appeared on the first page of the *Figaro* on August 18. Here five young authors renounced naturalism and charged Zola with debasing literature and making his movement almost synonymous with scatology. They speculated that certain psychological and physical defects in Zola himself had stimulated his interest in the vulgar and obscene, or that he was simply tempted by the profits to be realized from titillating the public. In either case, he had corrupted the famous formula of naturalism to make it "a fragment of nature seen through a morbid sensorium."[47]

The attacks on Zola with his own weapons, accusing him of personal biases and unscientific use of material, doubtless wounded him more than the attacks of a new generation of idealists, but in the critical consciousness of the period, the latter were more effective. The preface to the younger Dumas's *L'etrangère* (1879) pointed the way to this new orientation. Dumas charges that Zola, in his desire to place on the stage the exact replication of life, has lost sight of both the methods and the purpose of art. The novelist can, if he wishes, deal in real blood and bodies or show scenes of the most embarrassing intimacy, but the form and function of theatre do not allow this. Every art has its necessary conventional omissions—sculpture lacks color, paintings lack relief—and the denial of these conventions in the name of more faithful reproduction of nature will only convert the arts into inferior copies of a greater and richer original. Nature is "the base, the proof, the means of art," but not art's end. The artist's task is more difficult than simply to reproduce nature; it is "to discover and reveal to us that which we do not see in what we daily observe," to give "a soul to material things, a form to the things of the soul, and in a word, to idealize the real that is seen and make real the ideal that is felt."[48]

This preface and the early criticism of Brunetière represent what might be called the first stage of the idealist reaction, which sought in part to defeat Zola on his own terms: that is, by repeating the charges

---

[46]Ferdinand Brunetière, *Le roman naturaliste* (Paris, 1882), iii.
[47]Quoted in Matthew Josephson, *Zola and His Time* (New York, 1928), 313–15.
[48]Dumas *fils*, *Théâtre*, 6:178.

that he was exclusively interested in the baser side of man and thus could not claim naturalism as a true picture of the human condition. "The great error of the century," wrote Brunetière in 1890, "has been to mingle and confuse man with nature, never stopping to consider that in art, in science, and in morality, man is man only to the extent that he distinguishes himself from nature and becomes an exception to it."[49] Naturalism, he charged, dealt with the actual rather than the real and contented itself with the mere piling up of factual data, which would never create a picture of the blend of physical and spiritual that makes man truly human. In his *Etudes critiques* of 1880, Brunetière even tried to deny Zola's work the title of naturalism. True naturalism would depict "all of nature, interior as well as exterior, invisible as well as visible," and authors falsely call themselves naturalists "when they do not express one side of human nature with as much vigor and precision as the other." Zola's approach necessarily created something "narrow, incomplete, and mutilated."[50] Thus Brunetière would call idealism to the aid of naturalism, to create a balanced and complete depiction of man in literature.

This essentially rationalistic and moderate attempt to reform naturalism was quite overshadowed by a much more thoroughgoing idealist reaction, which sought to provide not merely a necessary corrective but a superior and quite different alternative. The critics and writers in this movement agreed that Zola had ignored the interior, the invisible, the spiritual in man, and made these elements their exclusive concern. Wagner was for this reaction what Shakespeare had been for the romantics, and the *Revue wagnérienne*, founded early in 1885, became the central organ for their critical pronouncements. The articles, mostly analyses and exaltations of Wagner's works, do not include any well-organized manifestos, but certain themes are regularly repeated. Perhaps most common is the rejection of the "real" world of the naturalists in favor of the ideal world of art. Teodor de Wyzewa (1862–1917), one of the founders of the influential review, describes the task of art according to Wagner as an attempt to re-create the world, "to build the holy world of a better life above the world of everyday profane appearances."[51] The common nineteenth-century idea of art as the expression of a particular society, suggested by Schlegel and championed by Taine, was denied by the Wagnerians, who saw art as a mystic expression of a deeper reality, untouched by changing secular concerns. At least on the question of art as expressive of the particular or the

[49]Brunetière, *Nouvelles questions de critique* (Paris, 1890), 393.
[50]Brunetière, *Etudes critiques sur l'histoire de la littérature française* (Paris, 1880), 335.
[51]Teodor de Wyzewa, "Notes sur la peinture wagnérienne," *Revue wagnérienne* 2 (1886): 102.

general, they renounced the position of romanticism and returned to that of classicism.

The other Wagnerian concept of great interest to these French critics was that of the integration of the various arts, each exposing a part of this deeper reality to create an aesthetic whole more profound and complete than anything attainable by a single art. Wyzewa briefly recapitulates Wagner's explanation of the process: "The soul first receives Sensations, which it organizes into Notions, which mixed with other and more powerful Sensations give way to Emotions. Art has attempted to reflect each of these modes of the soul—plastic art the Sensations, literature the Notions, music the Emotions. Wagner has sought, by creating a total work of art, a unity of these elements to reflect the total life of the soul."[52]

The major movement that developed from the antirealist theorists of the 1880s was symbolism, and the *Revue wagnérienne* was in a real sense the first journal devoted to this movement. Still, the adoption of Wagner as a guiding spirit caused from the outset a tension in symbolist theory, since the movement's leaders in France never fully accepted Wagner's primary emphasis on music, or his belief in the performed work as the ideal total artistic expression. Nowhere is this tension more evident than in the comments of Stéphane Mallarmé (1842–1898), whose "Richard Wagner, rêverie d'un poëte français," published in the *Revue wagnérienne* of August 8, 1885, was probably that journal's most famous article.

As its title suggests, the essay is more a prose-poem meditation than a critical article, but it makes clear both what attracted and what disturbed Mallarmé in Wagner's work. Mallarmé praises the rich, almost holy experience that Wagner's drama seeks and his success in utilizing the power of all the arts, especially music, to spiritualize the stage and give authentic inner life to previously inert matter. At the same time, Mallarmé disagrees with Wagner's choice of music rather than poetry as the essential unifying element of the total work of art. Nor does he accept Wagner's vision of this work as existing in solid, three-dimensional form; ultimately, the world of the spirit could only be re-created, asserts Mallarmé, in its own domain, the imagination. "A spiritual fact, the preparation or blossoming of symbols requires a place to develop other than the fictional foyer of vision under the eye of a crowd. A holy of holies, but mental."[53] The physical presence of actors and scenery could only lessen the potential expressiveness of art.

---

[52]Ibid., 103.
[53]Stéphane Mallarmé, "Richard Wagner, rêverie d'un poëte français," *Revue wagnérienne* 1 (1885): 199.

Wyzewa had demonstrated the same concern, remarking "A drama, read, will appear to sensitive souls more alive than the same drama given on stage by living actors."[54] This distinct antitheatrical bias in the symbolists shows clearly that Wagner was by no means the only influence on their critical thought. Equally important was the tradition of idealist theory in France, scorned by Zola and temporarily overshadowed by naturalism, but still vital and available to help nourish the antirealist reaction of the 1880s.

It is hardly surprising, given the extreme position taken by naturalist theorists in emphasizing concrete physical detail in the theatre, that the idealists reacted with a total rejection of such concerns. The most significant expression of this position during the 1870s was in the theatre essays by Théodore de Banville (1823–1891) that appeared between 1869 and 1881 in the *National*. Writing in 1873, the year of *Thérèse Raquin*, Banville calls poetry "the great evoker, the great magician, the great maker of prodigies and miracles. She knows how to and is quite willing to do all this unaided, but only on the express condition that she is unaided." Against a simple curtain, she can create the Doge's palace, Hamlet's castle, Caesar's Rome, and Cleopatra's Egypt, but if one insists upon "real silk, real cloth of gold, trinkets of the period, a real Spanish madonna (as was used in *Ruy Blas*!), props, furnishings, projected electric lights," then a jealous muse like poetry will say, "Since you wish to join to me inert and stupid matter, let the matter do for itself and make your miracles without me!" No detail of costume or setting should be allowed to distract from "the ideal harmony aroused in the mind of the spectator by the genius of the poet."[55]

It is equally mistaken, Banville continues, to credit to the skill of the actor the power of the theatre. Without a poet, the actor is helpless. "The stage would never have been able to imitate great events except with unreal and lifeless mannequins, while the verse of Victor Hugo, with an evocative word, gives them life."[56] Banville does not renounce physical staging but clearly deemphasizes it, encouraging poetry to paint the scene. The romantics, he charges, discarded the unity of place only to be forced, by their love of lavish settings, to restore it for each act. The stage should, on the contrary, be a neutral playing space, perhaps with only a backdrop and wings, so that plays can follow the example of Shakespeare "where a single action continues without interruption in quite different locales."[57] Banville's own most ambitious

[54]Wyzewa, "Notes," 102.

[55]Théodore de Banville, *National*, Dec. 22, 1873; quoted in Maximilian Fuchs, *Théodore de Banville* (Paris, 1912), 342.

[56]*National*, Apr. 14, 1879; Fuchs, 343.

[57]*National*, Sept. 24, 1877; Fuchs, 354.

play, *Le forgeron* (1887), might be easily staged in such a manner, but recognizing the grip realism still exerted on the stage, he wrote it only for reading. Mallarmé warmly praised this "spectacle in an armchair" as an example of the best theatre, a theatre of the mind.

For some symbolists the theatre of the mind, completely etherealized and uncontaminated by physical presentation, became the only theatre worthy of the name of art. Mallarmé, though clearly tempted by such an alternative, continued to accept theatre as a performed art, in part because he saw drama as an art for the people as well as for the solitary reader and in part because he felt that sounds, colors, even odors, if always subordinated to poetry, could enrich the poetic effect. Both of these attitudes were supported by the ideas of Wagner, though Wagner also provided support for the etherealization of the theatre by his insistence that in his own work external action was subordinated to interior movements of the soul. The process of achieving this subordination, of spiritualizing the art form the naturalists had so physicalized, was the focus of the symbolists in the theatre, both in theory and in practice.

The writings of Mallarmé on the drama are of two general types. There are his comments on contemporary productions in his capacity as dramatic critic for the *Revue indépendante* in 1886–1887, and the theoretical observations scattered throughout his writings, especially in those dealings with *Le livre*, his great, never completed work. Neither provides a very clear expression of his theory. In the former he attempts to find the positive features even in drama that interests him little, in the hope of eventually improving it; his own vision is suggested only indirectly. In the latter his pronouncements are generally poetic and oracular, difficult to reduce to theoretical form.

Much more accessible are the writings of Mallarmé's disciples, several of whom provided what amounted to manifestos of the new movement. The best known of these, *La littérature de tout à l'heure* (1889) by Charles Morice (1861–1919), mentions theatre only in passing. Morice admits that Wagner envisioned the theatre as the temple for the "rites of the aesthetic religion," but today's theatre is so far from such an apotheosis that our civilization may pass away before this vision is fulfilled. In any case, "these things are too remote to be considered" in a book that is "necessarily initial and general."[58]

Other theorists were more willing to attempt a symbolist aesthetic of the theatre, which meant primarily finding some way to reconcile the physical component of stage presentation with the poet's abstract vision. Two basic strategies evolved. One was that of a subgroup of symbolists

[58]Charles Morice, *La littérature de tout à l'heure* (Paris, 1889), 290.

whom Saint-Pol-Roux (1861–1940), their leader, called the *idéoréalistes*. As the term suggests, these writers sought to combine features of realism and idealism. Wagner's great insight, said François Coulon in the *Mercure de France* of October 1892, was that only in the theatre could all the arts be synthesized and the greatest poetic vision brought to the general public. Poetic geniuses like Rimbaud or Mallarmé had no hope of reaching the average reader, who would put their poems aside as too difficult. But in the theatre "if spectators, even hostile, experience a formidable struggle of human passions in an *idéoréaliste* drama, they will perhaps give us their attention even when they do not understand the symbol of the piece, a symbol accessible only to the elite."[59] Thus an artist like Wagner could provide for his superior public a play of ideas in their eternal manifestations, while the public on a lower level could be simultaneously moved by realistic human emotions and conflicts.

A different approach was suggested by Camille Mauclair (1872–1945), who in 1893 aided Aurelian Lugné-Poe (1869–1940) in the founding of the Théâtre de l'Oeuvre, the theatre that was to symbolism what Antoine's Théâtre-Libre had been to naturalism. In "Notes sur un essai de dramaturgie symbolique" in the *Revue indépendante de littérature et d'art* of March 1892, Mauclair attempted a theory of symbolist drama. The contemporary theatre, he suggests, shows three distinct conceptions of drama. First is "the vision of modern life from the psychological point of view"—the positivist theatre of Henry Becque and Jean Jullien. Second is the metaphysical theatre of Maurice Maeterlinck, a sort of theatre of Platonic dialogue, "more philosophical in essence than dramatic." The third conception, the symbolist, differs profoundly from the others; its goal is to create "philosophic and intellectual entities" through "superhuman characters in an emotional and sensual decor."[60]

This goal, says Mauclair, requires unusual attitudes toward both the setting and the leading characters. Both, of course, are to be purged of all traces of specific time and place, of anything individualistic. Only what is eternal and fixed is to be suggested. The setting need not be an empty void, but it must shun all specific detail. "A simple shade of green will perhaps give a better impression of a forest than a cardboard cutout, imitating nature leaf by leaf. An intense purple background will perhaps inspire the joy of a triumphant dawn."[61] The leading actors will "have no value except as incarnations of the Idea they symbolize." They will move little and will "enunciate eternal ideas" in "magnificent

---

[59]François Coulon, "Essai de rénovation théâtrale," *Mercure de France* 6 (Oct. 1892): 158.

[60]Camille Mauclair, "Notes sur un essai de dramaturgie symbolique," *Revue indépendante de littérature et d'art* 22 (Mar. 1892): 309.

[61]Ibid., 311–12.

language, resplendent with poetry." Mauclair agrees with the *idéoréal-istes* that the "unlettered or indifferently meditative multitude" cannot be expected to share the enthusiasm of the "artist-spectator" for the pure Idea, but he goes beyond their suggestion of providing an interesting surface story for this public; he suggests surrounding statuesque abstract central figures with realistic secondary characters, who would carry on everyday activities and by their comments help the audience to understand the central figures. They would serve the role of the classic chorus, "being intermediaries between the ideality of the drama and the intellect of the public."[62] In this way idealism and realism, passion and poetry, psychology and dream could be united on the stage.

Statements such as these from Mallarmé, Coulon, and Mauclair suggest a static, highly abstract, trancelike theatre, and the opponents of symbolism were inclined to regard it in these terms. However, when Lugné-Poe and Mauclair organized the Théâtre de l'Oeuvre, their theory and practice tended toward a more lively and colorful theatre, strongly engaged both in art and in life. The Oeuvre had, they suggested, two distinct aims. The first, as Mauclair described it, was "to struggle, to create out of the currents of ideas, out of controversies, to rebel against the inertia of spirits who tend to be a bit delicate, to make use of our youth no longer to excuse experiments but to live violently and passionately through our works." Mauclair praised the plays of Ibsen as models for such theatre, since these included not only "masterpieces of symbolism" like *Rosmersholm* and *The Master Builder*, but socially engaged drama like *An Enemy of the People*, which "made cry out on stage an anguished crowd of contemporary social questions."[63]

The second aim concerned "not sociology but art itself"; it involved the more familiar side of symbolism, the evocative and dreamlike drama, but presented with all the resources of theatrical spectacle. Mauclair and Lugné-Poe deplored the physical detail of Zola's theatre but did not champion a neutral void as the best alternative. Lighting, color, movement, even scenic display were not to be rejected, so long as they served the end of evocation rather than verisimilitude. The physical presence of the actor remained the most stubborn tie to everyday reality and tempted Mallarmé, like Lamb in England early in the century, toward a theatre for the solitary reader. But Lugné-Poe saw highly theatrical alternatives—"shadow figures, perhaps larger than life, marionettes, the English pantomime, the clown pantomime, macabre or funny . . . or perhaps all of these mixed together in great fairytale spectacles?" Lugné-Poe proposed these as experimental possibilities

[62]Ibid., 314.
[63]Mauclair, "Communications," *Mercure de France* 9 (Oct. 1893): 191.

and promised to try out as many as his budget would permit.[64] In fact, he never actually pursued the symbolist possibilities of nonhuman figures in the theatre, but the concept emerges again, to be explored more fully, in the writings of Edward Gordon Craig in England and William Butler Yeats in Ireland.

The physical resources necessary to stage "fairytale spectacles" were also beyond the reach of Lugné-Poe's theatre, and he became more interested in the possibilities of the essentially unadorned stage, especially after becoming acquainted with contemporary English experiments in performing Shakespeare in this manner. A pair of important articles in the *Mercure de France* in 1896 by Lugné-Poe and Alfred Jarry (1873–1907) addressed themselves to this approach.

Jarry's article, "De l'inutilité du théâtre au théâtre" (On the Uselessness of the "Theatrical" in Theatre), appeared in September. It dismisses from consideration the best way of pleasing the infinite, mediocre multitude and concerns itself with the perhaps "500 persons who have a touch of Shakespeare or Leonardo in them." Among the things these 500 find most "horrifying and incomprehensible" in the contemporary theatre are the decor and the actors "which encumber the stage to no purpose." The settings are hybrids, neither artificial nor natural. If real settings are desired, performances should be given outdoors; if artificial ones, then the 500 are entitled to settings that embody the world "as the playwright has seen it"—that is, with its *inner* meaning exposed. Jarry suggests that the best setting would be an unpainted backdrop or the reverse side of a set. "Each one can then imagine for himself the place he wishes, or better still, if he knows what he wishes, the real decor can appear on the stage by exosmosis."[65]

The actor could also become abstract and evocative by using the universal gestures of the marionette, by wearing a mask that would suggest different expressions by slightly changing its relation to the light, and by speaking in a special voice—the "sort of voice the mouth of the mask would make if the muscles of its lips could move." Indeed, to avoid any possible intrusion of the particular, Jarry advocates the delivery of the entire play in a monotone.[66]

In a sequel to this article, published under the same title the following month, Lugné-Poe cites the experiments of the Elizabethan Stage Society in London as an example of the successful application of Jarry's ideas. He avoids Jarry's elitism, however, pointing out that in fact all ranks of Elizabethan society accepted the bare stage of Shakespeare,

[64]Aurelian Lugné-Poe, "Lettre-programme," *Gil Blas*, Aug. 9, 1893.
[65]Alfred Jarry, *Oeuvres complètes* (Paris, 1972), 406–7.
[66]Ibid., 409.

with scenery painted by the poet's words. Nor does Lugné-Poe go so far as to call for a reinstitution of the mask, but he does urge actors to discard all the trappings of the conventional theatre and the busy details of naturalism. "Standing apart before the crowd, glowingly illuminated, he must quickly understand that the multiplicity of gestures is odious, that if he is to succeed in giving artistic form to the abstraction he incarnates, he must be sparing of effects or abandon them. Otherwise he will be a criminal to this art."[67]

At the premiere of his play *Ubu roi* at the Oeuvre on December 10, 1896, Jarry presented a brief *discours* which repeated in a jocular way several matters from his *Mercure de France* article. Some actors, he announced, have been willing to perform in masks "in order to become precisely the interior man and the soul of the life-sized marionettes you are about to see." The setting is described in a manner that suggests less the neutral background previously advocated by both Jarry and Lugné-Poe than the antilogical visualizations of the later surrealists. Jarry calls it a "perfectly exact" setting, for just as it is "easy to set a play in eternity by, for example, firing revolvers in the year 1000 or thereabouts, so you will see doors opening onto snow-covered plains under a blue sky, fireplaces with clocks on them opening to serve as doorways, and palm trees at the foot of beds being grazed on by little elephants perched on whatnot shelves."[68]

This question of symbolist staging was dealt with in detail in the theories of Adolphe Appia (1862–1928), whose work, though it gained recognition too late to influence Oeuvre productions, sprang from precisely the same roots and became one of the twentieth century's most significant contributions to the theatre. Appia was a lifelong friend of Houston Stewart Chamberlain (1855–1927), a leading French Wagnerian, but the productions at Wagner's festival theatre in Beyreuth, so lavishly praised in the *Revue wagnérienne* by Chamberlain and others, seemed to Appia totally unworthy of Wagner's genius. With a penetration and profundity of thought never before accorded this aspect of the theatre, he began to consider the proper visual setting for the Wagnerian works. His first brief essay on this subject, *Notes de mise en scène pour L'Anneau de Nibelung* (written in 1891 but not published until 1954), advances a theory of staging completely unlike anything in the European theatre of that time. Instead of the cluttered, detailed, illusionistic settings employed even at Beyreuth, Appia calls for a stage that anticipates the interests of the symbolists—a simple arrangement

---

[67]Lugné-Poe, "De l'inutilité du théâtre au théâtre," *Mercure de France* 20 (Oct. 1896): 97.
[68]Jarry, *Oeuvres*, 400.

of spatial forms, evocative rather than specific, which would give major emphasis to light and the movement in space of the actor; the intent is to capture the organic unity of the stage work, so that the visual elements would be as well integrated into the Wagnerian total work of art as the musical and poetic ones.

These ideas are developed further in the small book *La mise en scène du drame Wagnérien* (1895), published in Paris with the aid of Chamberlain. Here Appia argues that Wagner demands a new approach to staging unlike that of either conventional opera or spoken theatre. Music, unlike spoken theatre, controls time as well as expressing emotional changes, and thus the operatic composer has always more control over stage movement and even the proportions of the setting than does the regular dramatist. In the new theatre as conceived by Wagner, the poet-musician should control all aspects of production, including setting, and these should form a whole unique to each work. The setting should no longer rely "upon conventions, as the opera normally does, nor upon an imitation of life, as does the spoken theatre." Instead, "each drama will determine its own staging" unique to itself.[69] The sole inspiration of the design must thus arise from the work itself, not from convention or external reality. The present system of staging prevents the actor, when animated by music, from relating in any unified way to the inanimate setting around him. The solution is to allow this setting also to be conditioned by music. Scene painting must be replaced by lighting, which shares the animation of the living actor and can serve as the unifying element between him and the neutral stage space required by the movements of the music.

A further elaboration of these ideas appears in *La musique et la mise en scène*, which Appia, in hopes of making a greater impact in Wagner's homeland, arranged to have published first in a German translation, *Die Musik und die Inscenierung* (1899). Despite its difficult style, this book at last began to gain attention for Appia's ideas. The brilliant accompanying sketches for settings proved at least as influential as the text, and countless young designers in Europe and America during the next generation were influenced by Appia's revolutionary abstract style.

Die Musik begins with the problem that most occupied Wagner: the dramatist's lack of control over the ultimate presentation of his work on the stage. Music, which both creates and controls time and emotion in Wagner's theatre, provides a solution, but if it is to unify everything, its domain must extend to the physical setting. This it can do only by renouncing those elements necessary to the traditional theatre, where the dramatist's incomplete work is filled out by the additions of the

---

[69]Adolphe Appia, *La mise en scène du drame wagnérien* (Paris, 1895), 12.

actor and scene painter. Actor and scenery should not add new information but simply express the life already in the work. The new problem becomes that of integrating the living actor into inanimate settings, and this can best be done by the mediating presence of light. The actor, relieved of "filling out" the role with his own experience, becomes another medium (though the most important one) for the dramatist's expression. Thus the symbolist vision of the ideal actor, what Craig called the Über-marionette, is clearly required in Appia's theatre. By means of music "the living human body throws off the accident of personality and becomes purely an instrument for human expression."[70] Appia in fact urges the would-be actor of the new theatre to shun traditional plays; they are now "poison" to him, since the tendency to bring his own emotional life and spiritual values to the interpretation is so persistent, so difficult to overcome, that a single wish to go back to them can be enough to make him unequal to the struggle.[71]

Clearly, the actor as an original artist is demoted in this system, subordinated to the artistic ensemble expressed in the master score (the *partitur*) and controlled by music. He nevertheless remains the central element of the production, the bearer of the word-tone text and the animate entity whose movement, though defined by light and controlled by the *partitur*, conditions the physical surroundings of the stage space. "What music is to the *partitur*, light is to the presentation," says Appia, "an element of pure expression as contrasted with those elements bearing a rational meaning."[72] Still, it is the actor who gives to these two great expressive elements tangible form for the audience, which is the basis of theatre. The ideal theatre should be totally flexible (even its floor, ceiling, and walls) behind the proscenium arch, so that every drama can be developed in its own unique performance space— another idea of Appia's that became highly important in the twentieth century. The two mottos for his book Appia drew from Schopenhauer: "Music in and through itself never expresses the phenomenon but only the inner essence of the phenomenon"; and from Schiller: "When music reaches its noblest power, it becomes form"—both strongly suggestive of symbolist thought.

The leading dramatist of the symbolist movement, Maurice Maeterlinck (1862–1949), frequently wrote of the relationship between internal life and its external figuration on the stage. Like Appia and the symbolists in general, he saw the theatre's previous interest in the accidental and the realistic as a major barrier to deeper expression, but

---

[70] Appia, *Die Musik und die Inscenierung* (Munich, 1899), 36.
[71] Ibid., 43.
[72] Ibid., 81.

unlike Appia, Maeterlinck never found what he considered a satisfactory way of resolving the tension between the spiritual vision of the poet and the physical world of the theatre and the actor. Some of his earliest writings suggest that Lear, Hamlet, Othello, and Macbeth "can not be presented, and it is dangerous to see them on the stage." The "shadow of an actor" stands between us and the "real" Hamlet, who is a figure of our dreams: "Every masterpiece is a symbol and the symbol can never support the active presence of a man." To diminish this problem, Maeterlinck suggests the use of masks, or even of sculpted or wax figures, marionettes, or shadows instead of living actors.[73] Indeed, his first dramas were written for marionettes.

Something of this conviction remains throughout Maeterlinck's work, but he continued to seek some satisfactory way to bend the physical theatre to suit his dreams. His essay "Le tragique quotidien" in *Le trésor des humbles* (1896) champions a new sort of drama, a static drama of internal action and reflexion, of revelation by the simplest of means. In the most famous passage of this essay, he proposes an ideal that seems to deny the significance of action itself, accepted as the heart of drama ever since Aristotle: "I have come to believe," he said, "that an old man sitting in his armchair, simply waiting by his lamp, listening unconsciously to all the eternal laws which reign around his house ... I have come to believe that this unmoving old man is living in reality a deeper, more human and more universal life than the lover who strangles his mistress, the captain who wins a victory, or the 'husband who avenges his honor.' "[74]

Maeterlinck does not advance the idea of static drama as totally new; he cites *Prometheus, The Suppliants*, and *Oedipus at Colonus* as Greek examples. In such plays the inner life is revealed not by actions but by words. They contain two dialogues, one which is necessary to the action and another "which seems superfluous. But examine it carefully and you will see that it is the only dialogue to which the soul listens deeply, because only here does one speak to the soul."[75] Ibsen is a master of this dialogue of the "second degree," and the strangeness of the conversations in a play like *The Master Builder* comes from an attempt to blend both dialogues in a single conversation.

Maeterlinck eventually drew back from the ideal of static drama, admitting in the preface to his collected plays (1903) that the abstraction easily available to the lyric poet was not really possible for the dramatist. "He is obliged to bring the idea that he has created of the unknown

---

[73]Maurice Maeterlinck, "Le théâtre," *La jeune belgique* 9 (1890): 331.
[74]Maeterlinck, *Le trésor des humbles* (Paris, 1898), 187–88.
[75]Ibid., 193.

down into real life, into the life of every day. He must show us how, in what form, in what conditions, according to what laws, to what end, those superior powers, those infinite principles, those unknown influences which as a poet he senses pervade the universe, work upon our lives."[76] In *Le drame moderne* (1904) he went so far as to state that "the sovereign law, the essential exigency of theatre will always be *action*,"[77] though of course in the modern drama, dealing with psychology and the moral life, this action is normally that of internal conflict, such as that between duty and desire. The philosophy of Maeterlinck's later years, based on a search for inner harmony that would fortify man against the forces of destiny and death, was ultimately incompatible with his earlier view of theatre: when harmony is at last achieved, all conflict will disappear, and with it the drama, which is the expression of conflict.

This conclusion contrasts sharply with that of Ferdinand Brunetière, who evolved at this time a somewhat similar and much better-known theory of drama as the conflict of opposing duties and desires. Brunetière, as we have seen, first achieved critical prominence in the 1880s as a leader of the reaction against Zola and the naturalists. Nevertheless, Brunetière was far from denying the scientism that Zola claimed as his authority; indeed his own critical method was openly and proudly derived from Darwin, and he attempted to apply the doctrine of evolution to literary history.

Brunetière accepted the forces of race and environment suggested by Taine, but placed more stress than Taine on a Hegelian series of reactions, on the influence of works upon subsequent works. Changes of taste, he says, can be best explained by a kind of dialectic process: Racine wished to do "something different" from Corneille; Diderot wished to do "something different" from Molière; the romantics wished to do "something different" from the classicists. And the writer who successfully achieves "something different" can be explained in terms of Darwinian natural selection. The great original dramatist, a Shakespeare or a Molière, is the better endowed specimen who suddenly appears amid the undifferentiated crowd like the bull with better horns or the horse of exceptional swiftness. "Forthwith not only is the variety modified, but new species have come into being: psychological drama, the comedy of character, the novel of manners. The superior adaptability and power of survival of the new species are at once recognized and proved, indeed, in practice. It is in vain that the older species

---

[76]Maeterlinck, *Théâtre*, 3 vols. (Brussels, 1908–10), 1:xii.
[77]Maeterlinck, *Le double jardin* (Paris, 1904), 119.

attempt to struggle; their fate is sealed."[78] Once the new literary species is established, it is carried on by lesser successors with declining distinction and originality until it becomes weakened, impoverished, and unable to survive the challenge of new rivals. "A genre is born, grows, attains its perfection, declines, and finally dies."[79]

Brunetière applied this evolutionary criticism in detail to the French theatre in a series of lectures given at the Odéon and published as *Les époques du théâtre français* (1892). In the opening lecture he proposed to consider not only the development of French drama and the relation of major works to one another but to seek the general "laws" of the theatre, "supple, plastic, and organic" principles that provide a foundation for all drama in all times, as opposed to the more rigid rules of a particular period, which must be rejected as the genre evolves.[80] In his summation, Brunetière proposes three such laws. The first connects the theatre with other genres and with life itself; it requires that the action turn upon "some question of general interest"—upon a case of conscience or a social question. The third law, common to all genres, is that as an art evolves, it always retains something from previous forms; it "employs the debris of what it has overthrown." The first law ties the work to the present, the third to the past.

The second law is the only one specifically tied to the drama, and in "La loi du théâtre," his introduction to the 1893 *Annales du théâtre et de la musique*, Brunetière advances this as the theatre's *only* law. In the lectures Brunetière states it thus: "A theatrical action must be conducted by wills, which, whether they are free or not, are at least always conscious of themselves."[81] "La loi du théâtre" elaborates the concept, demonstrating that the formula of a will seeking some goal and conscious of the means it employs can be seen operating in all dramatic genres, in tragedy as well as in farce, in Shakespeare as in Racine. It does not, however, so operate in the lyric or the novel, and only those novels that happen to involve the working of such a will can be successfully adapted for the stage.

This law also provides a means of differentiating between various dramatic "species"—"much as one does with the species in nature."[82] This is done by considering the obstacles against which the will is directed. In tragedy these are or seem to be insurmountable—the decrees of fate for the Greeks, providence for the Christians, the laws of nature or of an internal fatality in modern times. Here the defeat of the hero

[78]Brunetière, *Etudes critiques*, 23.
[79]Brunetière, *L'évolution des genres dans l'histoire de la littérature* (Paris, 1890), 23.
[80]Brunetière, *Les époques du théâtre français* (Paris, 1892), 8–9.
[81]Ibid., 367.
[82]Brunetière, "La loi du théâtre," *Annales du théâtre et de la musique* (1893), xi.

is preordained. If he has a chance of conquering his obstacle—an internal passion that may be overcome, or something external such as prejudice or social convention that may give way to determined effort—then we have drama. In comedy, of course, the will of the hero triumphs.

Finally, Brunetière suggests that the greatest drama will be produced when an entire people is engaged in a project of the will. Greek tragedy flourished at the time of the Peloponnesian Wars, Spanish and English as these nations were reaching for global power, French as the nation was achieving unity and influence. When national will is weak or absent, the drama will decline and its rival form, the novel, will flourish.

The influence of Schopenhauer, to whom Brunetière confessed a great intellectual debt, can be clearly seen in this formulation, but Brunetière uses Schopenhauer's terminology to arrive at very different and, in the drama, almost opposite conclusions. In his intellectual battle with such impressionist critics as Anatole France (1844–1924), Brunetière used Schopenhauer as a means of establishing a fixed point for critical reaction. If will is common to all men, then upon it understanding and communication can be postulated. It provides between ourselves and the dramatic hero a base for the emotional sympathy sought by the English critics and in danger of being lost both by the objectivity of the naturalists and the subjectivity of the impressionists. Thus, for Brunetière, the idea of the will led to a deeper involvement in the drama, not at all to the distancing that Schopenhauer sought. Further, far from accepting Schopenhauer's goal of withdrawal from life, a conclusion much closer to Maeterlinck's later (and vaguer) overcoming of conflicts of the will through enlightenment, Brunetière felt that a recognition of will as the basis of existence led to a commitment to action as self-definition, both of individuals and of nations, in an almost existentialist manner.

The philosopher Henri Bergson (1859–1941) also reacted against the scienticism of Zola and his generation, giving his attention, as did the symbolists, not to the utilitarian world of the senses and of reason, but to the inner world of the emotions and of intuition. The most famous concept in Bergson's system is the *élan vital*, the "vital impulse"—a current of inner life, which we can perceive by instinct or intuition but which is utterly inaccessible to rigid intellectual systems or to the scientific accumulation of data that so fascinated the naturalists. Bergson's famous essay *Le rire* first appeared as two articles in the *Revue de Paris* in 1900. Although it is indeed primarily a study of the sources of laughter, it includes a general theory of art and drama that demonstrates how these relate to Bergson's overall philosophic system. In this system the artist plays a special role since he, like the philosopher, possesses the special gift of touching the inner world of the *élan vital*. Were this gift possessed by all men, there would no longer be any need for art, "or rather we should all be artists, for then our soul would continually vibrate in perfect accord with nature."[83]

There is, however, in most men a veil between themselves and such consciousness: "Not only external objects but even our own mental states are screened from us in their inner, their personal aspect, in the original life they possess."[84] Instead of this highly variable and individual inner essence, we see the generalities and respond to the labels that make everyday life easier to live. It is the artist who from time to time brushes conventional generalities aside and brings us face to face with reality itself. What has been called artistic idealism is in fact realism of the highest order.

Drama is no exception to this. It provides glimpses into the secret, hidden part of our nature which the necessity of living in society and of submitting to the rules of reason and propriety has obscured. Beneath this veneer, the "cooling crust" of civilization, lies the dark and turbulent world of nature, the elemental passions of individual man. These have only been repressed, not obliterated, and in tragedy they rise temporarily to the surface. Art must always express the individual, because that is the nature of the hidden world. The great tragic heroes like Hamlet must be unique, as must the vision that creates them. We can therefore never see the precise individual vision Shakespeare saw in the creation of his work, but we can recognize the sincerity of his attempt to penetrate the veil of the general, and this serves as a stimulus to us to seek our own individual insight.

Genuine art is always disinterested; that is, it turns away from the external world and society to seek and express individual intuition. Comedy "lies midway between art and life"; that is, it does not, like tragedy, turn its back on life to seek pure nature. Instead, it turns its back on art and "accepts social life as a natural element."[85] It thus deals not with the individual but with types and generalities. Its purpose is not a deeper understanding of the self and experience of the *élan vital*, but an affirmation of the social order. "The comic expresses, above all else, a special lack of adaptability to society." The subject of comedy is the social misfit, and our laughter has always the unavowed intention "to humiliate and thus to correct our neighbor, if not in his will, at least in his deed."[86] This social utilitarianism removes comedy from the sphere of art.

Bergson finds rigidity or inelasticity involved in all aspects of the

[83]Henri Bergson, *Le rire* (Paris, 1900), 158.
[84]Ibid., 159.
[85]Ibid., 170.
[86]Ibid., 146, 148.

comic. Whenever the human body, its actions, its gestures, or its language become mechanical, the comic appears. The *élan vital* forces society itself to shift constantly, always evolving new systems or generalities to which social man must adapt; failure to do so exposes one to the chastening power of laughter. Throughout the essay this is presented as a positive process, but in closing, Bergson recalls that laughter is after all a weapon of intimidation by society and cannot be considered either kindhearted or just. It is like a gay and sparkling froth on the surface of social life, but to the philosopher, aware of the richer rewards offered by tragedy, the substance of comedy is scanty and its aftertaste bitter.

17

The Early Twentieth Century, 1900–1914

BY 1900 THE GREAT YEARS OF SYMBOLISM were past in France, but
the influence of symbolist ideas continued to spread into other countries.
In England significant contributions were made early in the new century to the symbolist theory of theatre by the critic Arthur Symons
(1865–1945), the designer Edward Gordon Craig (1872–1966), and the
poet-playwright William Butler Yeats (1865–1939). Symons was a key
figure in importing and promoting symbolist ideas in England, and
despite his reputation as a mystic, vague, and impressionistic critic, he
has in fact left some of the clearest and most concise statements of
symbolist aesthetic from this period. "The Ideas of Wagner" (1905)
lays out the theoretical bases of Wagner's work more clearly than Wagner ever did; "A New Art of the Stage" (1902, 1906) is a perceptive
introduction to the work of Craig, and "A Symbolist Farce" (1888) to
the importance of Jarry's *Ubu roi*. In his more general theory, too,
Symons may more properly be regarded as a guide to the thinking of
the period than as an originator of ideas, but he is one of the most
informed and engaging guides the period offers, and most of the central concepts of symbolist theatre are explored among his essays.

Symons himself considered his various collections of essays as together
presenting a system of aesthetics; the collection *Plays, Acting, and Music*
(1909) covers the theatrical arts. It begins with "An Apology for Puppets,"
agreeing with Maeterlinck (to whom the book is dedicated) and Craig that
human beings are distracting in a play because they are always subject to
"personal caprice." The puppet must portray the more general and universal,
and hence the more emotional and poetic, idea. Such ideas are finer and
deeper than the "merely rationalistic" concerns of modern drama.[1]

---

[1]Arthur Symons, *Plays, Acting, and Music* (New York, 1909), 8.

In the essays on individual actors and actresses—Bernhardt, Coquelin, Réjane, Irving, Duse—Symons extends the metaphor of the puppet to living artists. He suggests that there are three kinds of actors: those like Réjane, who seek reality and seem to portray real people in real situations; those like Bernhardt and Irving, who depart from nature with superb artistry and technique; and those like Duse, who do not "act" at all but simply reflect the essential mood or soul of the drama. These last, of course, function for the script like ideal puppets and are for Symons the greatest artists. Duse "thinks on the stage"; she "creates out of life itself an art which no one before her had ever imagined: not realism, not a copy, but the thing itself, the evocation of thoughtful life."[2] Bernhardt, who is a far greater actress in the conventional sense of the word, can make an inferior play a moving experience, which Duse cannot, but when a play touches the depths of the human condition, then Duse's art is far more profound than anything the brilliant surface technique of Bernhardt can achieve.

English actors, says Symons in "On Crossing Stage to Right," are addicted to physical action, which often distracts from the soul of the drama. "Two people should be able to sit quietly in a room, without ever leaving their chairs, and to hold our attention breathless for as long as the playwright likes."[3] Great drama must be a mixture of life and beauty, he says in "A Theory of the Stage," of both action and poetry and inner harmonies. Action alone is "a violent thing which has been scornfully called melodrama," but it is life and action that dominate the modern prose theatre. Thus we have actors who understand only action, playwrights like Shaw, "a whimsical intelligence without a soul,"[4] and stage settings that are costly and inartistic attempts at reality. The drama should turn from Shaw and Pinero to Yeats and Maeterlinck, with staging by artists like Craig, who gives "suggestion instead of reality, a symbol instead of an imitation."[5]

Craig began his career as an actor with Henry Irving, then turned to design and to the development of a new symbolist-oriented aesthetic for the theatre. His first major critical statement, *On the Art of the Theatre*, appeared in 1905. It is in the form of a dialogue between a stage director and a playgoer, and advances several ideas that permeate Craig's later writings and indeed much twentieth-century theatrical theory. The stage director begins by stressing the holistic nature of theatre. It is "neither acting nor the play, it is not scene or dance" but consists of a compound of the more basic elements of action, words, line, color, and

[2]Ibid., 65.
[3]Ibid., 171.
[4]Ibid., 200, 207.
[5]Ibid., 165.

rhythm.[6] A distinction must be made between the written text and the performed work. When a text is complete in itself—as are the plays of Shakespeare, for example—stage performance can add nothing, and the theatre of the future should turn away from such literature to find texts that are complete only when presented. The new theatre will thus be based not on the art of the dramatist but on that of the stage director, who will control, even if he does not specifically create, every element of the production. The actor too must be subordinate to the total design; he must concentrate upon the rhythm of the total production, not his own thoughts or emotions. Though Craig lays little stress on the *partitur* of Appia or Wagner, he seeks the same goal: the subordination of all elements to a single artistic vision.

These ideas are further elaborated in various essays published in *The Mask*, an international journal on the history and theory of dramatic art which Craig produced in Florence between 1908 and 1929. Among the first articles appearing in this journal was Craig's most controversial, "The Actor and the Über-Marionette" (1908). Here Craig condemns the art of acting, indeed argues that it cannot properly be called an art at all, since the actor, being flesh and blood, is always prey to emotion, and emotion introduces the accidental, which is inimical to art. Craig urges actors to reduce this element in their work by renouncing impersonation and representation, and to seek a new form based on "symbolical gesture."[7] He agrees with Lamb that a physical imitation of Lear on the stage will always be ridiculous. Therefore, the stage should never attempt to reproduce nature, but to create its own forms and visions never yet seen in nature. The actor, as we know him, bound to nature, must disappear; in his place must come "the inanimate figure— the Über-marionette,"[8] a figure of symbolist vision that "will not compete with life" but "go beyond it" to trance and vision.

In later writings Craig suggests that his ideal need not be a literal marionette; a human actor, if purged of the accidental, might fulfill this goal. Henry Irving indicated the way by moving away from the traditional "spasmodic and ridiculous expression of the human face" and toward the mask, which will be the medium of the future. Only the mask, contends Craig in "The Artists of the Theatre of the Future" (1911), can truly portray "the emotions of the soul," the essential moods of humanity.[9]

Strikingly similar conclusions were reached by William Butler Yeats, though he devoted more attention than Craig to the contents and

[6]Edward Gordon Craig, *On the Art of the Theatre* (Chicago, 1911), 138.
[7]Craig, "The Actor and the Über-Marionette," *Mask* 1, 2 (April 1908): 5.
[8]Ibid., 11.
[9]Craig, "The Artists of the Theatre of the Future," *Mask* 1, 3 (May 1908): 58.

dynamics of those mysterious depths to be revealed by the mask. Throughout his work he struggled with a central question: how to make the drama spiritually significant. The theatre of his own time, indeed of his own tradition, had, he felt, sacrificed vision to the intricacies of character study and surface reality. Rejection of this trend became an important part of his search for what he called "the theatre's anti-self."[10] Documentation of this search is scattered throughout Yeats's theoretical writings and reviews, but the most complete expression can be found in three key essays: "The Tragic Theatre" (1910), "Certain Noble Plays of Japan" (1916), and "A People's Theatre" (1923).

The first of these deals more with a statement of Yeats's goals than with a means of achieving them. He challenges the "dogma of printed criticism" that character is essential to drama, looking instead to lyric expression as the essence of great and serious theatre. Character, he says, is the essence of comedy; it defines the individual and separates him from ourselves, whereas tragedy "must always be a drowning and breaking of the dykes that separate man from man."[11] In tragic art the real world is but slightly touched upon, "and into the places we have left empty we summon rhythm, balance, pattern, images that remind us of vast passion, the vagueness of past times, all the chimeras that haunt the edge of trance." Contemporary reference and personal emotion must be purified by "ideal form, a symbolism handled by the generations, a mask from whose eyes the disembodied looks."[12]

The mask, a central image for Yeats, provides a technical means of achieving the expression of the ideal, the superhuman, the other-worldly. It is one of the conventions of Japanese Noh drama that he praises most strongly: "The face seems the nobler for lacking curiosity, alert attention, all that we sum up under the famous word of the realists, 'vitality'."[13] Verse, ritual, music and dance, the mask, stylized gesture, and nonrealistic decor must all unite to hold the door against a "pushing world." The "unimaginative arts" of the West, concerned only with putting a frame around a piece of the observed world, should be replaced by arts that "enable us to pass for a few moments into a deep of the mind that had hitherto been too subtle for our habitation."[14]

In *Per Amica Silentia Lunae* (1918), Yeats distinguishes between human and superhuman reality, the *anima hominis* and *anima mundi*, suggestive of the physical and spiritual worlds often posited by the German romantics. The former is the realm of tangible but transient

---

[10]William Butler Yeats, *Plays and Controversies* (New York, 1924), 215.
[11]Yeats, *Essays and Introductions* (New York, 1961), 241.
[12]Ibid., 243.
[13]Ibid., 226.
[14]Ibid., 224.

partial phenomena, of conflicting forces and of evil, which is the expression of conflict. For those who transcend this world of division and incomplete forms, there is the realm of homogeneous, eternal, complete being, which is "all music and all rest."[15] Any man or group operating in the lower realm will engender conflict because all perspectives there are partial, and whatever they reject develops as a force to oppose them. This force, suggesting Schopenhauer's opposing Will, Yeats calls the "Daemon." It forces the tragic hero to the ultimate confrontation with self and reality that leads both to tragic defeat and unification in the higher sphere. It "brings man again and again to the place of choice, heightening temptation that the choice may be as final as possible, imposing his own lucidity upon events, leading his victim to whatever among works not impossible is most difficult."[16] In good symbolist fashion, Yeats placed this force within the protagonist: hence the continued search for an internalized theatre.

Societies, like men, suffer from conflict, according to the same dynamic. Thus subjective reality, repressed in literature since the Renaissance, now appears as an opposing Daemon, to which Yeats sees himself as contributing. "I seek not a theatre, but the theatre's anti-self," he writes in "A People's Theatre."[17] While the popular theatre continues its objective course, ever more concerned with seeing and understanding, the anti-theatre will develop the rejected experiences of feeling and imagination to emerge eventually in a moment of revelation when the objective has completed its cycle and can no longer avoid confrontation with its Daemon. In the meantime, the work of the spiritual dramatist must be clandestine, almost subversive. "I want to create for myself an unpopular theatre and an audience like a secret society where admission is by favor and never to many," suggests Yeats; there a a few sympathetic initiates will experience "a mysterious art, always reminding and half-reminding those who understand it of dearly loved things, doing its work by suggestion, not by direct statement, a complexity of rhythm, color, gesture, not space-pervading like the intellect but a memory and a prophecy."[18]

Not surprisingly, when Gordon Craig established an international committee for his visionary new school on the art of the theatre in 1913, Yeats was one of the two representatives from Britain. The other was Edward Lord Dunsany (1878–1957), who similarly championed the cause of symbolist drama, both as essayist and playwright. In "Romance and the Modern Stage" (1911), he calls for a return of poetic

---

[15]Yeats, *Per Amica Silentia Lunae* (London, 1918), 71.
[16]Ibid., 79.
[17]Yeats, *Explorations* (New York, 1912), 215.
[18]Ibid., 213.

vision to the theatre. The concerns of business and of the utilitarian, the sham truths of politics and advertising, have driven romance from our lives; and the only force pitted against these in the drama, that of realism, seeks to expose the shams but offers nothing positive in their place. We need a drama to "build new worlds for the fancy, for the spirit as much as the body needs sometimes a change of scene."[19] We need poets to "see through the dust of ephemeral things to the cool eternal spaces that lie all around," to see once again "the lost idyllic things and give them back to the people, who are wearier with waiting for them than they have said or known."[20] Only in this way will simplicity and beauty return to our world, and we shall then find ourselves better prepared to deal with the problems of our time. Moreover, we shall pass on to our children the only lasting inheritance man has ever discovered: romance and song.

John Galsworthy (1867–1933), in "Some Platitudes concerning Drama" (1909), suggests that there are two main channels open for future English drama: the poetic prose drama of the symbolists, which sought "to disclose the elemental soul and the forces of nature," and the drama of naturalism "faithful to the seething and multiple life around us."[21] His own preference is clearly for the latter, the character of which he discusses in some detail. Like Zola, Galsworthy considers the artist and the scientist "the only two impartial persons" in society. The artist should set before the public "the phenomena of life and character, selected and combined, *but not distorted*, by the dramatist's outlook," and this should be done "without fear, favor, or prejudice, leaving the public to draw such poor moral as nature may afford."[22] In such a drama the interplay of character is naturally elevated over plot, indeed "a human being is the best plot there is,"[23] and the dramatist's task is essentially to assemble interesting characters, set them in motion with a dominant idea, and record their actions and dialogue.

A very similar philosophy is expressed by St. John Hankin (1869–1909) in the preface to his *Three Plays with Happy Endings* (1907). Responding to critics who complained that these plays in fact end unhappily or do not "end" at all, he replies that he selects an episode in the life of his characters when something of importance has to be decided, "and I ring up my curtain. Having shown how it was decided and why it was so decided, I ring it down again." There is no attempt

[19]Edward Lord Dunsany, "Romance and the Modern Stage," *National Review* 57 (July 1911): 834.
[20]Ibid., 829.
[21]John Galsworthy, *The Inn of Tranquillity* (New York, 1912), 200–201.
[22]Ibid., 190.
[23]Ibid., 193.

to "prove" anything, for "it is the dramatist's business to represent life, not to argue about it."[24]

In the original version of his essay, Galsworthy insisted that the poetic and naturalistic approaches must remain separate, that effective blending of such disparate styles was impossible. Some of his contemporaries disagreed, however, chief among them John Millington Synge (1871–1909) and John Masefield (1878–1967), who both attempted precisely this "ill-mating of forms." Synge found in rural Ireland an imagination and a language that allowed him to achieve the combination he expressed in the preface to *The Playboy of the Western World* (1907): "One must have reality and one must have joy."[25] Places where language and imagination are still rich and living allow a writer "to be rich and copious in his words, and at the same time to give the reality, which is the root of all poetry, in a comprehensive and natural form."[26] Masefield, in a 1911 preface to his *Tragedy of Nan* (1908), called tragedy "a vision into the heart of life," leading the multitude "to a passionate knowledge of things exulting and eternal." Contemporary playwrights, in his view, lacked the essential power to achieve the "power of exultation which comes from a delighted brooding on excessive, terrible things," and until that power returned, authors would have to strive humbly toward recapturing it with whatever materials life might present.[27] So Synge by choice and Masefield by default tempered poetic vision with reality and did so with sufficient success that in revising his essay, Galsworthy gave grudging acknowledgment to their work as a "seeming blend of lyricism and naturalism." He hastened to add, however, that their reality was so remote from our own that "we really cannot tell, and therefore do not care, whether an absolute illusion is maintained."[28]

Other significant approaches to the drama in England at this time, which did not really fit either of Galsworthy's alternatives or even a blend of them, can be seen in the writings of two of the best-known critics of the drama, Bernard Shaw and William Archer. Shaw continued (see Chapter 13) to champion didactic drama, and his program of instruction was incompatible with either lyricism or naturalism. His preface to *The Shewing-Up of Blanco Posnet* (1907) announced flatly, "I write plays with the deliberate object of converting the nation to my opinions in these matters."[29] In a lecture entitled "Literature and Art" (1908) Shaw insisted that "all art at the fountainhead is didactic," and

[24]St. John Hankin, *Dramatic Works*, 3 vols. (New York, 1912), 3:120–21.
[25]John Millington Synge, *The Complete Works* (New York, 1935), 4.
[26]Ibid., 3–4.
[27]John Masefield, *The Tragedy of Nan* (New York, 1921), vii.
[28]Galsworthy, *The Inn*, 202.
[29]George Bernard Shaw, *Works*, 33 vols. (London, 1930–38), 13:380.

that "nothing can produce art except the necessity of being didactic," denouncing in scriptural terms (he was speaking from a pulpit) "the man who believes in art for art's sake" as "a fool; that is to say, a man in a state of damnation."[30]

Shaw felt that the modern drama had evolved a new genre, based on realism and social comment, to fulfill the didactic aim, and he condemned authors who attempted to revert to traditional genres such as comedy and tragedy, just as he condemned actors who continued to approach their roles according to the stock expectations of hero or villain, melodrama or farce. In "Tolstoy: Tragedian or Comedian?" (1921), Shaw argues that traditional tragedy, a simple and sublime form unable to vary its approach, ended with Wagner; comedy, more open to change, gradually evolved into a "higher form"—the modern mixture of elements that he calls tragicomedy. Once again Ibsen is hailed as the great pioneer, "the dramatic poet who firmly established tragicomedy as a much deeper and grimmer entertainment than tragedy." His heroes, for all their sufferings, are still comic heroes, and their trials are no longer "soul-purifying convulsions of pity and horror, but reproaches, challenges, criticisms addressed to society and to the spectators as a voting constituent of society."[31] The suffering of such heroes is not hopeless, because it results from "false intellectual positions, which, being intellectual, are remediable by better thinking."[32]

Archer was inclined to share Shaw's views on the social function of drama, but as a critic he directed his attention more to form than to content. His *Play-making* (1912), essentially a manual of instruction for the well-made play, seeks to discover the "essence of drama" and finds it not in Brunetière's conflict but in crisis. "A play is a more or less rapidly-developing crisis in destiny or circumstance, and a dramatic scene is a crisis within a crisis, clearly furthering the ultimate event." Indeed drama "may be called the art of crises," while fiction in general is "the art of gradual developments."[33] The basis of this observation, as we would expect in Archer, is empirical and pragmatic. He calls it "an induction from the overwhelming majority of existing dramas, and a deduction from the nature and inherent conditions of theatrical presentation."[34] There is always room for experimentation; indeed, some recent dramas have successfully avoided the marked crisis in broad pictures of social phenomena. But generally speaking, the dramatist is

---

[30]Shaw, *Platform and Pulpit*, ed. Dan Laurence (London, 1962), 44.
[31]Ibid., 45.
[32]Shaw, *Works*, 29:277.
[33]William Archer, *Play-making* (Boston, 1912), 36.
[34]Ibid., 50.

safest in remaining with proven formulae: "The forms and methods which have been found to please ... will probably please again."[35]

The dramatist Henry Arthur Jones (1851–1929), in his introduction to an English translation of Brunetière's *Law of the Drama* in 1914, tries to reconcile Archer and the French critic. He praises both for insisting upon plot and form in a period when many dramatists ignore these critical matters with the justification that they are interested only in psychological or social "ideas." True drama, he says, whatever its use of "idea," must always involve opposition; the characters must be "consciously or unconsciously 'up against' some antagonistic person, or circumstance, or fortune." The course of the dramatic action is determined by the reactions, "physical, mental, or spiritual," to this opposition, and the drama ends when the reaction is complete. The most arresting and intense drama arises "when the obstacle takes the form of another human will in almost balanced collision."[36] The view of life Jones presents, a continual warfare of opposing forces, recalls Schopenhauer, but Jones does not suggest that viewing this conflict in dramatic form will distance us from it; rather he believes that our recognition of such warfare as the basis of life will assure our interest in the spectacle.

The approach to drama represented by critics like Archer was a common one in England and America in the years just after 1900. Drawing upon such sources as Sarcey, Freytag, and Brunetière, its supporters viewed the drama as a genre created to achieve particular effects within the theatre and regarded the form of drama—the structure of incident, the portrayal of conflict or crisis—as the basis of such effects. A major spokesman for this position in America was Brander Matthews (1852–1929), named by Columbia in 1899 the first professor of dramatic literature in an English-speaking university. The appointment was highly appropriate, since it was Matthews's constant aim to justify the study of drama as an art separate from literature, comprehensible not in the study but only in the theatre.

In *The Development of the Drama* (1903), Matthews insists that there is no masterpiece of drama, however remarkable its poetic power, that is "not sustained by a solid structure of dramaturgic technic";[37] in *A Study of the Drama* (1910), he asserts that it is "impossible to consider the drama profitably apart from the theatre in which it was born and in which it reveals itself in its completest perfection."[38] Dramatic technique and historical realization in the theatre are Matthews's invariable concerns. Literary quality may be added, or studied for its own sake,

---

[35]Ibid., 48.
[36]Quoted in Barrett H. Clark, *European Theories of the Drama* (New York, 1947), 469.
[37]Brander Matthews, *The Development of the Drama* (New York, 1903), 16.
[38]Matthews, *A Study of the Drama* (New York, 1910), 3.

but it is not essential. Matthews defines drama as "a story in dialogue shown in action before an audience"[39] and argues that such basic concepts as Brunetière's law of conflict and Sarcey's obligatory scene grow naturally from the needs of the theatre audience, which reacts as a crowd and not as isolated individuals. The appeal of drama is always "to the mass and to the communal desires of the main body."[40] Thus the only true test of drama is whether it pleases the mass audience—the test always advocated by Sarcey—and it is significant that in the essay "Three Theorists of the Theatre" (1916), Matthews ranks Lessing and Aristotle as the foremost writers on this art; "at an interval after them and far in advance of any fourth claimant," he put Sarcey.[41]

The critic Clayton Hamilton (1881–1946), a student of Matthews, dedicated to him his book *The Theory of the Theatre* (1910), which opened with a Matthews-inspired definition that Hamilton said summed up "within itself the entire theory of the theatre": "A play is a story devised to be presented by actors on a stage before an audience."[42] According to Hamilton, the major implication of this view is that the dramatist, aware that his work will be interpreted by actors, necessarily develops a dynamic clash of wills, and knowing that it must appeal to a heterogeneous audience, necessarily gives it a strongly emotional orientation.

The Matthews-Hamilton position was sharply challenged by another professor at Columbia, Joel Elias Spingarn (1875–1939), the chief American exponent of Benedetto Croce (1866–1952). In his key essay, "New Criticism" (1910), Spingarn calls for a rejection of all traditional rules, concepts of genre, moral judgments of art, history of themes— indeed of historical concerns of any kind—and for a criticism that recognizes every work as a fresh attempt at expression, an individual creation "governed by its own law."[43]

The "new critics" of the 1940s did not acknowledge Spingarn as one of their number, but this concern with the unity and form of the individual work is nevertheless echoed in their approach. Neither the old nor the new "new criticism" gave much attention to the script in the theatre, in which both followed Croce. Croce's *Estetica* (1902), in the section entitled "The Activity of Externalization," warned that the technical means of the arts, like genres and traditional rules, should be rejected as critical tools because they tend to define or limit artistic expression. Drama *in some cases* does require actors and scenery, but one should avoid making such "externals" absolute: "We can obtain

---

[39]Ibid., 92.
[40]Ibid., 93.
[41]Matthews, *The Principles of Playmaking* (New York, 1919), 81.
[42]Clayton Hamilton, *The Theory of the Theatre* (New York, 1910), 3.
[43]Joel Elias Spingarn, *Creative Criticism* (New York, 1931), 22.

the effect of certain plays simply by reading them; others need declamation and scenic display."[44] Spingarn rightly saw the position taken
by Matthews and Hamilton as a challenge to Croce on this point, and
following Croce, he called their emphasis on performance a confusion
of aesthetics with cultural and social history. Theatre conditions and
theatre audiences, he observed, have no more relation to drama as an
art than a history of publishing has to poetry.[45]

Spingarn's opponents could have turned for support to Croce's major
contemporary rival in aesthetic theory, George Santayana (1863–1952),
though if any of them did so, the evidence is slight. Santayana's specific
comments on the drama in his major work on aesthetics, *The Sense of
Beauty* (1896), are brief. He agrees with Aristotle that plot is the essential
element of drama, since it is the formal principle, and calls character
only "a symbol and mental abbreviation for a set of acts."[46] Further,
he specifically rejects what in 1903 he called "the barren and futile
transcendentalism" of Croce[47] by insisting upon the importance of the
physical medium of art. "There is no effect of form which an effect of
material could not enhance," he observes, "and this effect of material,
underlying that of form, raises the latter to a higher power and gives
the beauty of the object a certain poignancy, thoroughness, and infinity
which it otherwise would have lacked."[48] The marble of the Parthenon
and the gold of a king's crown are not for Santayana mere accidental
features but are essential to the aesthetic experience, and his argument
could clearly be applied with equal force to the material presentation
of the drama.

The English critic A. B. Walkley (1855–1926) advanced a rather apologetic refutation of Spingarn in the London *Times* of March 20, 1911,
taking the position that the dramatist is more restricted than any other
artist because he must work under particular performance conditions.
A painter can use any color suggested by his imagination, but a dramatist works for a particular stage and with actors who, "as no two things
in the universe are identical," can never possibly "coincide exactly with
the dramatist's preconceived personage." He is further limited by "the
peculiar psychology of the crowd he addresses," which may put him
in the position of a painter, for example, whose public cannot distinguish the color red.[49]

Spingarn's response, "Dramatic Criticism and the Theatre" (1913),

[44]Benedetto Croce, *Aesthetic*, trans. Douglas Ainslie (London, 1929), 116.
[45]Spingarn, *Criticism*, 31.
[46]George Santayana, *The Sense of Beauty* (London, 1896), 175.
[47]Santayana, "Croce's Aesthetics," *Journal of Comparative Literature* 1 (Apr. 1903): 191.
[48]Santayana, *Sense of Beauty*, 78.
[49]A. B. Walkley, "Criticism and Croce," *London Times* (Mar. 20, 1911), 12.

focused upon the argument of audience psychology, an argument he traced from Castelvetro through Diderot and Sarcey to Archer, Walkley, and "their noisy but negligible echoes in our own country."[50] The true poet, says Spingarn, will write to express his inner vision, whether his result suits the external conventions of his period or not. Performance, like financial reward, may serve as a stimulus but not as a creative impulse, and the circumstances of performance are "only one, and a very insignificant one, of all the influences that have gone to make up dramatic literature."[51]

The positions thus established by Spingarn and Matthews each included such disdain for the other that accommodation was impossible, and the subsequent writings of these two influential professors, and of their many disciples, nourished opposing critical camps in American dramatic theory for many years thereafter.

Symbolism, a minor concern in English and American dramatic theory during this period, played a far more significant role in Russia, both directly and as a stimulus to subsequent antirealist theatre theory. Translations and studies of such writers as Baudelaire, Mallarmé, Wilde, and Nietzsche during the 1890s prepared the way. In the pages of the *World of Art*, a journal published in St. Petersburg from 1898 to 1904, Serge Diaghilev (1872–1929) and Alexander Benois (1870–1960) challenged the general critical assumption that art should have a utilitarian aim; they called for "pure expression" in line, mass, and color; for the total work of art in the manner of Wagner; and for the evocative, nonreferential example of music as a model for all art in the manner of Mallarmé.

In Russia as elsewhere, the symbolists, even those who praised drama as the highest of the arts, almost without exception turned most of their creative and critical attention to lyric poetry. Nevertheless, they produced a number of striking plays and a body of theory that exercised great influence on the brilliant generation of theatre directors who emerged at the opening of the new century. The poet and theorist Valery Bryusov (1873–1924) was credited with inaugurating the movement against naturalism in the Russian theatre; his article "Unnecessary Truth," which appeared in the *World of Art* in 1902, was that journal's first major statement on the theatre and a kind of manifesto of the new movement. Bryusov was already a leading figure in the movement, having published symbolist poems of his own and translations of the French and, in 1900, founded in Moscow the Scorpion Press, which published such innovative authors as Ibsen, D'Annunzio, and Schnit-

[50]Spingarn, *Criticism*, 76.
[51]Ibid., 90.

zler. In "Unnecessary Truth" he urged the theatre to turn away from the sort of reproduction of reality offered by Stanislavski (see Chapter 19), toward conscious stylization. Instead of being cluttered with the details of everyday life, the stage must supply only "that which is needed to help the spectator to picture as easily as possible in his imagination the scene demanded by the plot of the play."[52] Though the dramatist furnishes the primary form, the central creative artist in the theatre is the actor, and both script and setting exist only to give the actor the fullest creative freedom. The end of all art is the communication of the impulses and sensations of the soul, and "the theatre's sole obligation is to assist the actor to reveal his soul to the audience."[53]

Bryusov's ideas first bore fruit in the theatre when Vsevolod Meyerhold (1874–1940), dissatisfied with Stanislavski's emphasis on psychological realism at the Moscow Art Theatre, left to establish his own company in the Ukraine. Here in 1903 he founded the Fellowship of the New Drama, whose literary manager, Aleksei Remizov (1877–1957), enthusiastically followed the new vision of Bryusov. In one of the first articles to appear in the *Scales*, a literary journal started by Bryusov in 1904, Remizov set down the goals of the "New Drama"—to create a theatre which "seized with unquenchable thirst would go in search of new forms for the expression of eternal mysteries," which would no longer be a game, an entertainment, or a copy of human infirmity, but "a cult, a mass, in the mysteries of which perhaps the Redemption is concealed."[54]

In fact, the aesthetic of Remizov has a somewhat different focus from that of Bryusov. Bryusov is the outstanding example of the first phase of Russian symbolism, sometimes called the "decadent" phase and strongly influenced by Mallarmé and the French. His theatre, like theirs, was abstract, evocative of inner states. Remizov and others, drawing more heavily on the German philosophic tradition, particularly Wagner and Nietzsche, began to champion a theatre of spiritual ecstasy and mass participation. The leaders of this approach were Vyacheslav Ivanov (1866–1949) and Fyodor Sologub (1863–1927). Ivanov cites both Nietzsche and Wagner in an essay on the mask in 1904 and calls for a new theatre to restore the ancient relation between the poet and the masses. Both need this relationship, he says, for the people provide the poet with symbols, the spontaneous expressions of their Wagnerian collective need, and the poet works these symbols into the myth that

---

[52]*Mir iskusstva* 4 (Petersburg, 1902), quoted in Vsevolod Meyerhold, "The New Theatre Foreshadowed in Literature," in *Meyerhold on Theatre*, trans. Edward Braun (New York, 1969), 39.
[53]Ibid., 38.
[54]Quoted in Harold Segel, *Twentieth Century Russian Drama* (New York, 1979), 65.

answers that need.[55] Through the example of the hero, the myth restores to the people its sense of the "total unity of suffering." This is best achieved by use of the mask, since the characters of the greatest tragedies are "masks of the one all-human I."[56] This transfiguration links Greek and modern religious insight: Dionysus, the sacrificial hero, becomes an avatar for Christ, and the suffering and death he undergoes becomes a crucifixion to purify mankind of its sins.

Sologub, in "The Theatre of One Will" (1908), similarly called for a theatre of "enchantment and ecstasy," the product of a Wagnerian single creative vision reflecting a Nietzschean reality: "the eternal contradictoriness of the world, the eternal identity of good and evil and other polarities."[57] To express this, the actor must abandon all his training and tricks, indeed give up the art of acting itself and become merely a marionette, a transparent expression of the poet's vision. When this vision is revealed to the spectator, he may be inspired to share it, as a choric participant. The action of the tragedy of the future will be accompanied by the liberating power of dance, and the crowd which has come to look on will be drawn into "the rhythmic frenzy of body and soul, plunging into the tragic element of music."[58]

In practice, such theorists discovered—as did others later in the twentieth century—that the calculated revival of ritual religious experience is a difficult if not impossible undertaking. In Schiller's terms, they were sentimental poets vainly attempting to create a naive consciousness. This tension is particularly clear in the symbolists who followed Wagner in seeking a poetry of the people, since their creations were without exception highly refined and abstract, and far from the interests or even the comprehension of the common man. It is hardly surprising that other symbolists not only admitted but championed a much more aristocratic view. Thus the Belgian symbolist poet and playwright Georges Rodenbach (1855–1898), in the *Figaro* of September 17, 1896, dismissed the goal of art for the masses: "Art is not created for the people. It is essentially complex, composed of nuances, while the people love only the most direct, clear, and simple presentations of life." Drama for the people must "lower itself to the people's level" and thus become "only a means of propaganda in the service of ideas called philanthropic or the interests of politicians"—in short, "only a parody of art."[59]

[55]Vyacheslav Ivanov, "Poèt i Čern," *Vesy* 3 (1904): 41, trans. (into German) in Armin Hetzer, *Vjačeslav Ivanovs Tragödie "Tantal"* (Munich, 1972), 99.
[56]Ivanov, "Novye maski," *Vesy* 3 (1904): 57, in ibid., 101.
[57]Fyodor Sologub, "The Theatre of One Will," trans. Daniel Gerould, *Drama Review* 21, 4 (Dec. 1977): 94.
[58]Ibid., 98.
[59]Quoted in Maurice Pottecher, "Le théâtre populaire," *Revue de Paris* 4, 4 (July-Aug. 1897): 211.

Edouard Schuré (1841–1929), an early French champion of Wagner and explorer of the occult, took a broader but ultimately equally aristocratic view of the drama in *Le théâtre de l'âme* (1900). The theatre of the future, he suggests, will take three principal forms, corresponding to "the three levels of life, consciousness, and beauty."[60] First would come the "rural and provincial Popular Theatre" of life, envisioned by Rousseau and being developed in France by Maurice Pottecher. Next would be the "City Theatre" or "Theatre of Conflict," an intellectual drama exposing contemporary social reality in the manner of Ibsen or Hauptmann. Then, for the elite disciples of beauty, a "Theatre of Dreams" or "Theatre of the Soul," following the example of Maeterlinck, would "tie the human to the divine," reflecting eternal truths in the mirror of history, legend, and symbol.[61]

Nonsymbolists could accept Schuré's general divisions of the serious drama of the period but not his analysis of the functions of drama or the conclusions he drew from it. Those involved with establishing theatres for the people were generally inspired by quite different concerns, sociological rather than philosophical. They wanted to improve life rather than art and drew upon Rousseau in preference to Wagner. This was true both of the German *Volksbühne* theorists and subsequently of the two major French spokesmen for a *théâtre du peuple*: Maurice Pottecher (1867–1960) and Romain Rolland (1866–1944). Pottecher, whose people's theatre—founded in rural Bussang in 1895—served as a model and inspiration for this movement, was willing to concede a crudeness in the taste of his public; he insisted, however, that one should not pander to them with "gross melodramas" and "circus farces" but seek to elevate them to purer feelings and higher thoughts through a theatre "not propagandistic but truly educative, by means of a language the spectator can understand and representation of heroic acts."[62]

Rolland applauded Pottecher's work but was disturbed by its limitation to small, geographically restricted audiences. Looking back to Rousseau's *Lettre à d'Alembert* and to the festivals of the French Revolution, Rolland denounced both the traditional classics and contemporary bourgeois drama as irrelevant and incomprehensible to the proletariat; he called for a new repertoire open to their needs and interests. The *Revue d'art dramatique*, which Rolland edited from 1900 to 1903, became a rallying point for populist theatre in France, publishing manifestos, encouraging the writing of populist drama, and urging the government (in vain) to become involved in this cause.

---

[60]Edouard Schuré, *Le théâtre de l'âme*, 2 vols. (Paris, 1900), 1:xiii.
[61]Ibid., xv.
[62]Pottecher, *Le théâtre du peuple* (Paris, 1899), 16.

Rolland himself contributed a series of dramas dealing with the events of the French Revolution, and a variety of articles analyzing the inadequacies of the theatre of the past and outlining the needs of the future that were collected in his book, *Le théâtre du peuple* (1903). Like Pottecher, he envisioned a theatre accessible to the workers without being condescending, and educative without being pompous or exclusive. He proposed for it three basic concerns: to provide relaxation for its patrons after a day of labor, to give them energy for the day to come, and to stimulate their minds. "Pleasure, strength, intelligence—there are the major conditions for a people's theatre." Such a theatre would not teach moral lessons but gradually raise the taste of its audience, create in them a fraternal bond, and "let more light, air, and order into the chaos of the soul."[63] Rolland's vision was not achieved, but his concerns have continued to be represented in French theory, most recently by such figures as Gatti, Benedetto, and Mnouchkine.

Jules Romains (1885–1972) came to support populist drama as much for philosophic as for social reasons. Accepting Bergson's concept of life as a continuous psychic stream, Romains felt that the collective expresses the flow of this stream more clearly and richly than do the casual and more random activities of individuals; he coined the term *"unanimisme"* for works that focus upon the group. In the preface to his first play, *L'armée dans la ville* (1911), he calls the group the basis of all drama: "What is a scene but the life of a precarious, emotional group? An act is a filiation of groups." The drama has developed only one group extensively, the couple, but the time has come to explore larger groups in "superior syntheses" that will restore to the drama the depth and spirituality it has lost. The focus on the individual is an outdated convention and prose drama a degenerate error. The drama of the future, he urged, must not only depict the crowd but be addressed to it, treating subjects of mass appeal on a proper stage and in language suited to raise the spirits of a whole people.[64]

After the Russian Revolution, the populist visions of writers like Rolland had a significant impact in that nation, but in the early years of the century the more mystic Dionysian view of Ivanov and Sologub seemed more attractive. A number of the symbolists wrote modern mystery plays, and Meyerhold considered Ivanov—along with Bryusov—a major source of inspiration for the new theatre. Meyerhold himself spoke of a universal, festive theatre that would "intoxicate the spectator with the Dionysian cup of eternal sacrifice" and make the spectator a "fourth *creator*, in addition to the author, the director, and

---

[63]Romain Rolland, *Le théâtre du peuple* (Paris, 1913), 116.
[64]Jules Romains, *L'armée dans la ville* (Paris, 1911), x.

the actor."[65] The participation of Meyerhold's spectator would, however, be emotional, not physical. His task would be "to employ his
imagination *creatively* in order to fill in those details *suggested* by the
stage action" in the sort of stylized theatre Meyerhold wished to substitute for the "Apollonian fantasy" of naturalism.[66]

It was this sort of concern that Meyerhold brought to the Moscow
Art Theatre in 1905 when Stanislavski invited him to return to direct
the new Studio. At this point, seven years after the opening of his
theatre, Stanislavski had still produced no significant statements of
theory, but his famous productions of Chekhov and Gorki made him
the central symbol for realism in the Russian theatre and the obvious
focus for symbolist attacks. Perhaps Stanislavski's rapprochement with
Meyerhold was in part a response to these attacks, but in any case the
Moscow Art Theatre was faced at this time with a serious practical
problem. The late plays of Ibsen and the works of Maeterlinck and
other new dramatists seemed to call for an approach markedly different
from the psychological realism that had proved so successful with Chekhov. Stanislavski later recalled, in *My Life in Art*, that "realism and local
color had lived their life and no longer interested the public. The time
for the unreal on the stage had arrived." A way had to be found to
present life "not as it takes place in reality, but as we vaguely feel it in
our dreams, our visions, our moments of spiritual uplift." He was thus
led to considerations close to those of the symbolists, to an interest in
"colors, lines, musical notes and the euphony of words" which would
encourage the spectator "to create in his own imagination."[67]

Such observations suggest a convergence in the concerns of Stanislavski and Meyerhold at this time, but once again as in 1903 they found
it impossible to establish a lasting working relationship. Tensions grew
between the Studio and its parent organization, the Art Theatre, and
the political disturbances in Moscow in 1905 provided an excuse for
postponing and finally for canceling altogether the Studio's official
opening. Stanislavski continued to explore symbolist texts in his own
way, and Meyerhold departed to seek more compatible surroundings.
He seemed to find them in the new theatre established by the popular
actress Vera Komissarzhevskaya. Komissarzhevskaya, interested in the
theories and the drama of symbolism, gave up a leading position at the
Imperial Theatre to organize her own, where the "clutter of realism"
would no longer distract attention from "the soul of the actor," a theatre

[65]Meyerhold, "The Stylized Theatre," in *Meyerhold on Theatre*, 60.
[66]Ibid., 63.
[67]Constantin Stanislavski, *My Life in Art*, trans. J. J. Robbins (New York, 1956), 428,
434.

that would show *"suggestions* of things and not the things themselves."[68] To aid her in attaining this vision, she appealed to two of the leading theatre experimenters of the period, the poet Aleksandr Blok (1880–1921) as dramatist and Meyerhold as director.

Before turning to poetry, Blok had studied to become an actor, but he showed no further interest in the theatre until 1906, when his association with Komissarzhevskaya resulted in his major play, *The Fairground Booth*, and his major statement of dramatic theory, "The Dramatic Theatre of V. F. Komissarzhevskaya." The essay is a fairly typical symbolist amalgam of Wagner and Nietzsche, stating that the theatre, like poetry, arises "from the earth's primitive element, rhythm," which controls "both planets and the souls of terrestrial creatures." Drama, "the very incarnation of art," is "the highest creative manifestation of this rhythm."[69] It must answer the collective need of the people, who bear within themselves "the spirit of music" and who demand not distraction but something higher, a "reconciliation of contradictions" and a "bestowing of wings."[70]

Blok later disclaimed *The Fairground Booth* as an attempt at such a theatre, but its use of popular elements of traditional folk drama—the farce, the clown, the commedia—certainly suggests an attempt to recapture a naive theatrical consciousness. In any case, both play and concept proved enormously stimulating to Meyerhold's thought. Blok's play seemed the ideal vehicle for his exploration of the ideas he was developing from the writings of Georg Fuchs (1868–1932), the director of the Munich Art Theatre.

In *Die Schaubühne der Zukunft* (1904) and *Die Revolution des Theaters* (1909), Fuchs joined Appia in a denunciation of the "peep-show stage" of the naturalists: the theatre can never truly reproduce nature, he says, and the trend of the stage toward greater and greater realistic detail (as with the German Meininger company) only calls attention to the fact that "compared to nature, all scenes are quite untrue, impossible, and silly."[71] As a result, audiences have become increasingly disenchanted with the theatre and have lost the sense of enchantment, of festival, and ultimately of fulfillment as a people that theatre originally offered them. To regain its lost power, the theatre must renounce literalism and literature and restore the actor to a position of primacy. Realistic scenery not only distracts but pulls the actor back into the

[68]Fyodor Komissarzhevsky (Theodore Komisarjevsky), *Myself and the Theatre* (New York, 1920), 71.
[69]Aleksandr Blok, *Sobraniye Sochineniy*, 12 vols. (Leningrad, 1932–36), 12:7; quoted (in French) in Sophie Bonneau, *L'univers poétique d'Alexandre Blok* (Paris, 1946), 387.
[70]Ibid., 389.
[71]Georg Fuchs, *Revolution in the Theatre*, trans. Constance Kuhn (Ithaca, 1959), 99.

depths of the stage, thwarting his "instinctive forward urge" toward the audience.[72] To accommodate this urge, essential to the effectiveness of theatre, Fuchs suggests the use of a "relief stage" with the actor close to the spectator, free from the stifling box of scenery and defined by light, which is "the most important factor in the development of stage design."[73] The dominance of literature has restricted the creativity of the actor and unfortunately placed him under the control of the director, since "the actor needs a ringmaster if he is not to give in to the theatrical impulse, the creative urge within himself; if he is to fulfill the function that has been forced upon him as a walking illustration of a literary text."[74] Ideally, this situation should be reversed. Instead of forcing the actor to give way to the text, the author should construct a text based on "a delicate understanding of the possibilities of form which are inherent in the personalities of the performers."[75]

The influence of these ideas is clear in Meyerhold's essay "The Naturalistic Theatre and the Theatre of Mood" (written in 1906 and published in 1908), which condemns the naturalistic theatre for leaving nothing to the audience's imagination and for distracting from the actor, who should always be "the principal element in the theatre."[76] The idea of the relief stage and of actor-audience proximity also clearly influenced his productions for Komissarzhevskaya, but—not surprisingly—he saw the director as a much more positive force than Fuchs did. In 1908 he contributed an essay, "The New Theatre Foreshadowed in Literature," to a collection entitled *Theatre: A Book about the New Theatre*, which argued that "the theatre must employ every means to assist the actor to blend his soul with that of the playwright and reveal it through the soul of the director."[77] The shift is significant, since Meyerhold's theatre always reflected his own vision—often, in the opinion of his critics, at the actors' expense. Doubtless his reading of Craig, which began in 1907, encouraged him in this emphasis.

Although the *Theatre* collection was dedicated to Stanislavski, it was essentially a summary of the concerns of the major contemporary symbolists, almost all of whom contributed to it. A pronouncement by the director of the Moscow Art Theatre would have seemed very odd in this company; even had it been desired, Stanislavski would still probably have had little to say in the way of a theoretical statement. According

[72]Ibid., 69.
[73]Ibid., 85.
[74]Ibid., 115.
[75]Ibid., 121.
[76]Meyerhold, "The Naturalistic Theatre and the Theatre of Mood," in *Meyerhold on Theatre*, 32.
[77]Meyerhold, "The New Theatre Foreshadowed in Literature," in ibid., 38.

to his own report, it was only during the summer of 1906, while vacationing in Finland, that he began to reflect on the process of artistic creation by the actor and to develop some of the principles that would eventually be incorporated into his system. The first sketch of this system, never published but available to members of the Moscow Art Theatre, seems to have been drawn up about 1909, but many years would pass before Stanislavski had developed his ideas sufficiently to make them public.

Even though it was dominated by symbolist thought, *Theatre* was by no means a unified aesthetic statement, since deep divisions existed among the symbolists themselves. The vision of drama as an ecstatic communal ceremony, as advocated by Ivanov and Sologub, was championed in this collection by Sologub's essay "The Theatre of One Will," while Dionysian ecstasy was firmly rejected in the article "Theatre and Modern Drama" by the leading symbolist Andrey Bely (1800–1934). Bely's attack was particularly significant because in the years just after 1900, he had expressed ideas similar to those of Ivanov and Sologub. "The seeds of future drama and opera are found in the dithyrambs honoring Dionysus," he wrote in 1902 in the *World of Art*, and he designated as the goal of symbolism the return of drama to its origins in the mystery play.[78] The focus of this new mystery, he later suggested, should be the "Feminine incarnate . . . embodying the all-unified beginnings of mankind."[79]

Beginning about 1906, however, his writings began to reflect the tension so common in symbolist theorists between the abstract vision of drama and its physical presentation. In "The Symbolist Theatre" (1907) as well as "Theatre and Modern Drama," he viewed with equal suspicion the choric mysteries of Sologub and the experiments of Blok and Meyerhold for Komissarzhevskaya. Neither approach seemed suitable for achieving what Bely had come to consider the goal of symbolist drama— the recreation of life from within by individual vision and activity. One cannot hope to create a Dionysian chorus by putting white robes and garlands upon "an *art nouveau* lady, a stockbroker, a workingman and a member of the Privy Council" and setting them to dance around a sacrificial victim. The ancient sense of community is not so easily gained; the prayers of the celebrants will not harmonize, and the physical presence of the theatre will prevent transcendence into a higher realm. "Life remains life, theatre remains theatre."[80]

[78]Andrey Bely, "Formy iskusstva," *Mir iskusstva* 12 (1902); trans. George Kalbouss, in *Andrey Bely: A Critical Review*, ed. Gerald Janecek (Lexington, 1978), 148, 150.
[79]Ibid., 150.
[80]Bely, "Theatre and Modern Drama," trans. Laurence Senelik, in *Russian Dramatic Theory from Pushkin to the Soviets* (Austin, 1981), 158–60.

No more successful, in Bely's view, are the attempts of Blok and Meyerhold to express a higher realm through an actor's interpretation of a text. An actor seeking to tap the sources of life while imitating a character outside himself can only hideously distort the process of transfiguration. His individual psychology destroys "the rhythm of his own relationship to the symbolic bond." The modern director, who seeks to overcome the actors' individuality and succeeds only in converting them into puppets, adds his own distortion to material they have already distorted.[81] Meyerhold, as we have seen, insisted that the visions of actors and director could be successfully fused into a higher vision, but Blok was much less willing to defend his dramatic experiments on this score. He did not contribute to the *Theatre* collection, but his essay "On Drama" (1907) shows him as unwilling as Bely to defend Russia's attempts at true symbolist drama. In an argument recalling Pushkin, he explains that since traditional dramatic technique, language, pathos, and action never developed in Russia as they did in western Europe, Russian dramatists have tended to develop only a drama of vague lyricism. Modern civilization which Blok, like Bely, sees as fragmented, contradictory, ironic, and focused on the individual, has encouraged this tendency, so that the most successful modern literary form is subtle and evanescent lyric poetry, "capable of recording contemporary uncertainties and contradictions, the vagaries of drunken wits and the vaporings of idle forces."[82] In modern Russia a lyric drama closely akin to such poetry is possible, but this is far removed from, even antagonistic to, a true drama that speaks to the basic needs of all mankind.

A much more positive vision of theatre is offered by Bryusov in his contribution to *Theatre*, "Realism and Convention on the Stage," which seeks a middle ground between Stanislavski's realism and Meyerhold's symbolism. Both "realistic" and "conventional" theatre, says Bryusov, lead to unresolvable contradiction. The first, seeking ever closer imitations of reality, only calls attention to the basic unreality of the stage. The second, seeking to escape this trap, falls into another. As it stylizes or makes abstract the elements of production, it encounters the obstacle of the human body. The end result is a theatre of marionettes, or of pure abstraction. One path extinguishes theatre by merging it with life, the other by merging it with thought. Both deny the essence of theatre, which as Aristotle observed is action: "As shapes are to sculpture and line and color to painting, so action, direct action, appertains to drama

---

[81] Ibid., 167–68.
[82] Blok, "On Drama," in ibid., 107.

and the stage."[83] Thus the living actor is essential, and around him should be objects that are actual but not obtrusive, illusionistic, or unharmonious. The simple architectural background of the Greek stage, or the tapestries and draperies of the Elizabethan, should serve as a model for staging that is neither realistic nor conventional, but forms a simple background for the rightful owners of the stage—the actors.

The suggestion found in both Bely and Bryusov, that the theatre of convention (whose outstanding representative was Meyerhold) was destroying the creativity of the actor and thereby the art as a whole, was heard frequently at this time; it formed a leitmotif in a sort of counteranthology to *Theatre*, published later the same year, called *The Crisis in the Theatre*. The modern theatre, suggested the contributors to this volume, being torn between puppet show and mystery, was fast losing whatever relevance it might have for contemporary man. Such concerns were clearly reflected in Komissarzhevskaya's decision to sever her relationship with Meyerhold at the end of 1907, a decision warmly applauded by Bely and by her brother Fyodor.

Meyerhold, who continued his experiments at other theatres, showed no inclination to modify his views. In *On the Theatre*, a collection of his own critical writings that appeared in 1913, a key essay ("The Fairground Booth," 1912) defends theatricality and stylization, the puppet and the mask, and the elevation of form over content. Meyerhold recalls that Bely himself stated in his 1902 essay that "the impossibility of embracing the totality of reality justifies the schematization of the real (in particular by means of stylization)." He even agrees with Bely's later observation that the theatre must remain the theatre, the mystery the mystery. But for Meyerhold this means that the theatre should seek its most profound effects through its own means; the mime, the mask, the juggler, the puppet, the improvised action. Through these, the drama can suggest the "vast unfathomed depths" beneath visible reality. Particularly useful is the grotesque— a concept Meyerhold uses, in a way reminiscent of Hugo, to defend a dialectic of opposites, a playing of farce against tragedy and form against content so as to force the spectator, through ambivalent reactions, to a deeper vision of reality and an attempt "to solve the riddle of the inscrutable."[84]

The period's leading counterstatement to Meyerhold's defense of theatricalism was the essay "Rejecting the Theatre" (1912) by the theatre reviewer Yuli Aikhenwald (1872–1928). This is essentially an elaboration of a point raised by Bryusov in "Realism and Convention," that the conventionalized theatre, by denying the art of the actor, runs the

[83]Valery Bryusov, "Realism and Convention on the Stage," in ibid., 179.
[84]Meyerhold, "The Fairground Booth," in *Meyerhold on Theatre*, 137, 139.

risk of eventually eliminating the stage itself, since intellectual abstractions can as easily be conjured up in the mind of the intelligent reader. Aikhenwald broadens the warning to apply to all theatre, and—more like Lamb than Bryusov—suggests that in the end drama is essentially literary, and the gross materializations of the stage, whether realistic or conventional, are inferior to the imagination of the discriminating reader. Indeed, Aikhenwald refuses even to accept the actor as a creative artist: he simply recites words, written by someone else and alien to himself, for the benefit of an illiterate or semiliterate public. In direct opposition to Wagner, Aikhenwald calls drama a hybrid of other arts and thus inferior to music, dance, poetry, and literature in their pure, unalloyed forms.

A related, though less radical position was taken by Leonid Andreyev (1871–1919), the most successful experimental dramatist of the period, whose *Life of Man* was produced in 1907 by both Meyerhold and Stanislavski. Although Andreyev was not a member of any of the various Russian symbolist groups, his "Letter on the Theatre" (1913) echoes their general distrust of traditional theatre and is clearly indebted to Maeterlinck. He proposes a new theatre of "panpsyche" which will renounce the action and spectacle that has always characterized the drama, along with such themes as hunger, ambition, or love; it will turn inward to focus upon "human thought, with all its suffering, joys, and struggles." Instead of external action, it will depict "the quiet and external immobility of living experience." Symbolist theatre has so far failed to achieve this goal because, instead of turning inward, it has attempted to etherealize reality and thus achieved only grotesque stylization. The "weighty and carnal figure" of the actor has been "bent into grotesque shapes, his voice has been strained and contorted," but the result has been only falsity, and audiences have returned with relief to the recognizable if shallow world of realism.[85]

Fyodor Komissarzhevsky (1882–1954), who shared the direction of his sister's theatre with Nikolay Evreinov after Meyerhold's departure, agreed with Bryusov that the theatre could survive as an art only by accepting the centrality of the actor. On this ground he opposed Meyerhold's work for his sister, and in a 1912 essay published in *Debating the Theatre*, a collection gathered in rebuttal to Aikhenwald, he argued that Aikhenwald's indifference to staging resulted from that critic's lack of understanding of the actor's art. The middle ground between realism and convention, which Bryusov sought in scenic arrangement, Komissarzhevsky sought in acting style. Both Meyerhold and Stanislavski,

[85]Leonid Andreyev, "Andreyev on the Modern Theatre," trans. Manart Kippen, *New York Times*, Oct. 5, 1919, sec. 4, p. 3.

he felt, restricted the essential creative function of the actor by making him merely an imitator—Meyerhold of physical actions, Stanislavski of psychological states.

Indeed, it was probably about this time that Stanislavski became particularly interested in techniques for releasing the creative power of the subconscious, and the key term "emotional memory," drawn from the French psychologist Théodule Ribot, entered his work. In *The Art of the Actor and the Theory of Stanislavski* (1916), Komissarzhevsky praises Stanislavski for his work in studying the inner psychological ensemble of a character but faults him for beginning with a reasoned analysis of psychological moods. Ultimately, this denies the subconscious and turns "genuine living experience into reasoned simulation," replacing penetration of the author's text with "the worldly colorless anti-artistic experiences of the actor himself."[86] Such an approach might help the actor who was already creative, but it cannot inspire creativity. Stanislavski himself eventually came to a very similar conclusion; in the 1930s he turned away from an emphasis on psychological analysis to what he called "the method of physical actions" (see chapter 19).

Komissarzhevsky calls his own approach "synthetic." He denies Aikhenwald's contention that the blending of arts is a weakness in drama, and echoes Wagner in calling for a theatre in which all the arts unite to "convey simultaneously the same feelings and ideas to the spectator. The rhythm of the music must be in harmony with the rhythm of the words, with the rhythm of the movements of the actors, of the colors and lines of the decors and costumes, and of the changing lights."[87] It is the actor, whom Komissarzhevsky calls "the universal actor," who must accomplish this unification. He must master all the means of expression—music, poetry, dance, song, mime; he must understand "the art of composition of bodies, of lines and colors" and how the body moves "through the medium of music." He must then synthesize all these elements, subordinating them "to his conception of the part and to the single rhythm of his emotions."[88]

Komissarzhevsky's codirector, Nikolay Evreinov (1879–1953), was interested less in the actor than in the theatrical process itself—in what "theatrical" means and how material becomes "theatricalized." In 1907 he founded the Ancient Theatre, which sought to recapture the theatrical consciousness of earlier periods, stifled during the nineteenth century by the triumph of realism. In explaining the goals of this venture, he quoted the critic E. A. Znosko-Borovski (1884–1954), who

[86]Quoted in Oliver M. Saylor, *The Russian Theatre under the Revolution* (Boston, 1920), 251–52.
[87]Komissarzhevsky, *Myself*, 149.
[88]Ibid., 144–45.

urged producers to study "particularly theatrical eras" as an antidote to realism and to attempt the reproduction not only of important works of the past but of as much of the original performance conditions as possible. The theatre, said Evreinov, "is not dramatic literature" but a totality of drama, acting, staging, and audience; a proper revival of past works should attempt to revive "a whole complex of the social and intellectual life of a given epoch, where the spectacle itself occupies only a part of the scene."[89] Thus Evreinov, like William Poel in England and André Antoine in France, attempted period performances with appropriately costumed audiences in suitable performance spaces—churches, castle halls, and public squares.

The success of these productions won Evreinov his invitation to join Komissarzhevskaya in 1908. The same year he outlined his general theory of the theatre in an article called "An Apology for Theatricality." Theatricality, he asserts, is one of man's basic instincts; it existed before any aesthetic sense developed. All other arts, developed from theatre, are based upon formation, while theatre is based upon the "more primitive, easier to realize" goal of transformation.[90] The basis of theatre is not religion, dance, or any other art, but the desire to change, to be something other than oneself; if the modern stage attempts to become a temple, a pulpit, a tribunal, a school, or a mirror of life, it betrays this basis. Realism, a useless double of life, and symbolism, which subverts the direct joy of visual perception by emphasizing the internal, are both hostile to the true spirit of theatre.

This idea is taken further in *The Theatre as Such* (1912) and *The Theatre for Oneself* (1915–1917), the major chapters of which were combined for an English translation entitled *The Theatre in Life* (1927). In these books Evreinov develops the implications of his theory far beyond the traditional theatre, calling for a recognition of the theatrical in life itself. We should revive the long-suppressed theatrical instinct, stage-manage our life, recognize the joy and power of seeing this life as theatrical expression and of assuming new roles to extend the range of our experience and our interaction with our fellow beings.

In Evreinov, the experimental spirit in Russian theatre, which since the symbolist revolt had turned against participation in contemporary reality, returned to that participation from another direction. At the same time, other theorists, particularly those drawn toward Marxist and socialist concerns, continued to uphold a view of art more directly

---

[89]Nikolay Evreinov, *Histoire du théâtre russe*, trans. G. Welter (Paris, 1947), 383–84. The first edition of the Russian original, *Istoria russkogo teatra*, appeared in New York in 1955.
[90]Ibid., 375.

in line with the nineteenth-century critics who emphasized its social and political dimensions.

The first major Russian Marxist critic was Georgy Plekhanov (1857–1918), who introduced the phrase "dialectical materialism" to the arts. Among his predecessors in critical theory, Plekhanov was most interested in Hegel, Belinsky, and Taine, all of whom regarded art as interdependent with all human life and thought. Belinsky and Taine had gone further, seeing art as the product of a particular society. But even in Taine, whom Plekhanov much admired, there was a fundamental contradiction. Taine, said Plekhanov, correctly called art the product of human psychology, which changes as the environment changes, but he incorrectly credited changes of environment to the development of human thought and knowledge. In the first assertion he took a materialist view, in the second an idealist, and thus created a permanent conflict within his system. Plekhanov used Marx's insight to resolve the conflict by making the system wholly materialist. Plekhanov argued that varying human conditions are determined not by changes in human thought but "by the state of their productive forces and their relations of production."[91]

Plekhanov's most significant application of this principle to drama is in his essay "Henrik Ibsen" (1906–1908). Here he argues that Ibsen's dissatisfaction with the petty bourgeois world of nineteenth-century Norway drove him to revolt but offered him no political solution. In contemporary society the proletariat "represents the only class capable of being inspired with zeal for everything noble and progressive," but Ibsen's society possessed no such class. It was "an utterly undeveloped mass, sunk in mental torpor."[92] Thus Ibsen, like his hero Brand, was doomed to a purely negative revolution. Unable to grasp the importance of political action, he turned to individual liberation, which led him into symbolism and abstraction. This very vagueness endears Ibsen to the "thinking group" of the modern bourgeoisie, who are drawn to symbolism for the same reason: abstract visions of human betterment can substitute for the threats of social revolution. For the present, the proletariat cannot economically concern itself with art, but it can still revere Ibsen for the revulsion he felt for the status quo; his historical situation allowed him to offer something, as no more modern artist could do, to both of the "irreconcilably-opposed classes in contemporary society."[93]

---

[91]Georgy Plekhanov, "Historical Materialism and Art," trans. Eric Hartley, in *Art and Social Life* (London, 1953), 56.

[92]Plekhanov, "Ibsen, Petty Bourgeois Revolutionist," trans. Emily Kent et al., in Angel Flores, *Henrik Ibsen* (New York, 1937), 62.

[93]Ibid., 92.

Such pronouncements give much of Plekhanov's specific criticism a tone of social utility, but he condemned his predecessors Chernyshevsky and the civic critics for overstressing the utilitarian function of art. Plekhanov, like Mehring, admired Kant and was never able to reject completely the Kantian view of disinterested pleasure in art. At the conclusion of his essay "French Dramatic Literature and French Eighteenth Century Painting from the Sociological Standpoint" (1905), he attempts to reconcile "disinterested" aesthetic pleasure with social utility. The individual, he suggests, can enjoy art purely aesthetically, but social man seeks utility first, even when he thinks he is responding only to the beauty in art. If utility were not at all involved, an object would not appear beautiful.[94] Thus, for social man at least, Plekhanov seeks to reconcile moral instruction and aesthetic pleasure on terms very close to those of the critics of the eighteenth century. Later Marxist critics, who were not disturbed by a strictly social interpretation of art, condemned this approach as willfully ambiguous.

The next major Marxist theorist of literature, the Hungarian Georg Lukács (1885–1971), did not join the Communist Party until 1918, and did not take on the task of developing the critical strategies suggested by Mehring and Plekhanov until after 1930. From his pre-Marxist years came a number of significant critical writings that established the young scholar as a major critic, even though he renounced these after his political conversion. Lukács became interested in the drama as a student at the University of Budapest, where he wrote plays and helped to found a theatre organization, the Thalia, which—like the Freie Volks-bühne in Berlin—sought to bring modern drama to the working class. In 1906 Lukács went to Berlin to continue his studies and there wrote a draft of his first book, *A History of the Development of Modern Drama*, published in Hungarian in 1911. Its second chapter was published in German in 1914 as "Zur Soziologie des modernen Dramas." Another significant consideration of the drama by Lukács also appeared in 1911, the "Metaphysik der Tragödie," the last of a collection of ten essays. His other major work of literary criticism from his pre-Marxist period, *Die Theorie des Romans* (1916), contains only scattered observations on the drama.

In his autobiographical sketch, *Mein Weg zu Marx* (1933), Lukács cites the writings of sociologists Georg Simmel (1858–1918) and Max Weber (1864–1920) as " my models for a 'sociology of literature' in which the elements of Marx, though of course diluted and faded, were already

---

[94]Plekhanov, "French Dramatic Literature and French Eighteenth Century Painting from the Sociological Standpoint," trans. Eric Hartley, in *Art*, 165.

present, even if they were scarcely recognizable."[95] At that time, Lukács accepted Simmel's view that Marx in his concern with commodity fetishism was describing only a particular case of a general "tragedy of culture"—the replacement of the subjective by the objective, of a culture of persons by a culture of things. In the preface to his *Philosophie des Geldes* (1900), the work by Simmel most influential on the young Lukács, Simmel explicitly removes himself from Marx, noting that the economic changes Marx observed are themselves "the result of more profound valuations and currents of psychological or even metaphysical preconditions."[96]

Anguish over the modern condition, which elevates the mechanical creations of man over man himself, permeates the writings of both Simmel and Weber, and it is this alienation that clearly interested Lukács at the time. Simmel did, however, also address specifically the problems of artistic production in the modern era. Thus in "Der Schauspieler und die Wirklichkeit" (1912), he takes issue with two popular misconceptions of the art of acting: that it attempts to reproduce reality, and that it serves only as an illustration of a poetic text. He suggests as an axiom that "the dramatic arts as such transcend both poetry and reality."[97] The dramatic actor, like the poet, "creates within himself a complete unity with its unique laws," having its roots "in the same fundamentals as do all other art forms," even though he uses another art—the poet's—as his medium.[98] His task is not to transform the dramatic work into reality but to transform reality, the psychological integration of his previous experience, into a work of art. Thus Simmel sees acting, like other arts, as requiring a commitment to life processes rather than to the mechanization that threatens all modern culture. True acting is "an expression of the primary artistic energy of the human soul, which assimilates both the poetic art and reality into one living process, instead of being composed of these elements in a mechanical fashion."[99]

Lukács's "Zur Soziologie des modernen Dramas" (1911) is based upon the modern alienation described by Simmel. The drama manifests clearly the tensions of bourgeois culture in general, he says, and the modern dramatist shares the alienation of all modern artists, cut off from the shared body of belief that bound him to his public in the precapitalist

---

[95]Georg Lukács, *Schriften zur Ideologie und Politik* (Neuwied, 1967), 324.

[96]Georg Simmel, *The Philosophy of Money*, trans. Tom Bottomore and David Frisby (London, 1978), 56.

[97]Simmel, *The Conflict in Modern Culture and Other Essays*, trans. K. P. Etzkorn (New York, 1968), 95.

[98]Ibid., 96.

[99]Ibid., 97.

period. In theatrical art this has resulted in a sundering of drama and theatre: the drama has become didactic and biased, a "ground for the struggle of classes," a means for the bourgeoisie "to inspire, to encourage, to exhort, to attack, and to teach"; unable to create an art for the people on these terms, the drama has withdrawn to the printed page, and the theatre has turned to "mindless entertainment."

More important, Lukács continues, in neither of the two is there any longer a trace of "the festive, the religious, or even at the least some sort of religious feeling,"[100] and the loss of this metaphysical center has made all serious modern drama problematic. Without a mythology, without a sense of the heroic, it is reduced to the material of daily life, and this "is no longer dramatic; it no longer possesses the possibility of mixing the timeless poetic and the sensations of the moment in a naive synthesis."[101] Historical distancing is now substituted for myth, but it is much more conscious (in Schiller's terms, the naive has given way to the sentimental) and has much more concern for the accuracy of facts and empirical data. Historical distancing may provide a certain reduction of the sense of the trivial and accidental that threatens depictions of everyday life, but it still cannot provide an agreed-upon ethical system that can be developed in aesthetic terms, and thus cannot avoid the ideological relativity that plagues all modern drama. "When a mythology is absent . . . the basis on which everything must be justified is character,"[102] yet character itself is a shifting, unstable thing, a search for the vital center which contemporary life does not offer. Man's major struggle becomes simply a defense of his individuality against the encroaching circumstances of life and the tendency of rationalism and capitalism to seek uniformity in human personalities.

This defense, although Lukács recognizes it as lonely and even at times heroic, is itself problematic, however, because it is based upon no positive ethical structure. Man drifts toward isolation, which is inimical to the drama; toward the expression of loneliness in dialogue increasingly "fragmented, allusive, impressionistic";[103] and toward pathology, which the critic Alfred Kerr (1867–1948) characterized as "the permitted poetry of naturalism."[104] The subjectivity of the characters pervades the entire world of the play; events become tragic or comic not in essence but simply from the point of view. Lukács condemns the shifting emotional responses of the modern tragicomedy, for though

---

[100]Lukács, *Werke*, 17 vols. (Darmstadt, 1964–81), 15:57.
[101]Ibid., 115.
[102]Lukács, "The Sociology of Modern Drama" (abridged), trans. Lee Baxandall, *Tulane Drama Review* 9, 4 (Summer 1965): 168.
[103]Ibid., 163.
[104]Alfred Kerr, *Die Welt im Drama*, 192, quoted in ibid., 169.

the comedy may be deepened thereby, the "purity of style" is destroyed and the tragedy reduced "to the level of the banal and trivial, if indeed it is not distorted into grotesquery."[105] The cure must be sought not in art but in life. Until an ethical center is rediscovered, the sort of center shared by classic dramatists and their public, the problems of modern drama will remain unsolved.

Lukács's essay "Metaphysik der Tragödie" (1911) contains little of the historical or sociological concerns that characterize "Zur Soziologie des modernen Dramas," although reference to the "terrifyingly soulless" state of contemporary nature and society echoes the earlier work. At the beginning of the century, many of the leading German dramatists and dramatic theorists turned against both naturalism and symbolism to call for a return to classic principles and even to classic form and subject matter, and Lukács had become interested in their experimentation. Paul Ernst (1866–1913), Samuel Lublinski (1868–1910), and Wilhelm von Scholz (1874–1922) were the leaders in this neoclassic revival, and it was the plays and theories of Ernst, the best known of the three, that provided the inspiration for Lukács's essay.

Lukács's interest in Ernst is understandable when one realizes that this neoclassicism in fact grew from the same roots as the sociological writings of Simmel. Ernst himself had become involved with the Social Democratic Party while a student in Berlin, and he was at first drawn to naturalism as an artistic movement that seemed harmonious with his social concerns. But by the early 1890s he, like Mehring, had begun to feel that naturalism was incapable of achieving the political ends he had hoped for. In "Die neueste litterarische Richtung in Deutschland" (1891), he condemned naturalism for its ignorance of the process of development of modern society and its lack of support for socialism. At the same time, he was involved in organizing a radical element within the party to oppose its decline in revolutionary zeal and its drift toward political compromise, its attempts to seek reform not by confrontation but by forming unions and petitioning parliament. His disillusionment with the party led to his resignation from it in 1896, when he turned his attention to literature. His attempts to deal with modern social questions in the drama did not satisfy him, however, since he felt that the conventions of naturalism had made the theatre a place of resignation and hopelessness. In "Das Drama und die moderne Weltanschauung" (1899), he complained that modern drama "believes man has no free will"; the hero of classical drama, on the other hand, "though he might suffer

---

[105]Ibid., 165.

or be defeated," nevertheless "left with the spectator or reader the strongest impression of human worth and power."[106]

By 1900 Ernst had come to a conclusion similar to that of Simmel, that the forces of objectivity and alienation were too strong to succumb to political attack in the near future. The worker, on whom socialism based its hope and naturalism its characters, could not yet create a new society because his struggle for material needs gave him no time to conceive of ideals. In these bleak conditions, if the drama were to serve as a way of keeping alive a vision of man that was not yet politically realizable, the drama must return to the aristocratic hero, who could preserve this ideal until the masses were able to share it. In "Die Möglichkeit der klassische Tragödie" (1904), Ernst argues that the opposition of the hero to necessity has always been essential to great tragedy, and that modern social and economic conditions make possible a new formulation of this opposition. The development and expansion of capitalism "has created unprecedented, very close ties between all members of society," but these ties have their own rules and obligations, which take no account of the individual. Thus "for the individual they become blind fate."[107]

In 1904, the same year as this essay by Ernst, a strikingly similar view of the drama was advanced in France by André Gide (1869–1951), who also considered the contemporary world stultifying to the human spirit and the contemporary drama a pathetic reflection of man's loss of hope. Gide traced the source of the oppression not to socioeconomic causes but to the imposition upon all individuals of arbitrary values and moral systems; nevertheless, his solution was the same as that of Ernst—the exaltation of the individual in the drama as a means of keeping alive man's spirit of freedom.

In "De l'évolution du théâtre" (1904), Gide calls the period's interest in realism a reflection of illness in both art and nature. Whenever art languishes, it goes back to nature for a cure, but this is an illusion because art and nature are rivals; beauty results not from nature but from artifice and constraint. In periods when "life is full to overflowing," art willingly embraces the constraints that give it the greatest power, but when life itself becomes stifled and constrained, the roles are reversed, and both art and life suffer. Art "aspires to liberty only in periods of sickness."[108]

Such, says Gide, is the case today, when society is stifled by the weight of conventional morals. Now the stage can at best show "bankruptcies

---

[106]Paul Ernst, *Der Weg zu Form* (Berlin, 1906), 30–31.
[107]Ibid., 130.
[108]André Gide, *Oeuvres complètes*, 14 vols. (Paris, 1932–39), 4:206.

of heroism" in the manner of Ibsen, in which the only alternatives open to man are meek resignation to contemporary moral codes or hypocritical acceptance of them.[109] Since Gide, like Ernst, sees no likelihood of immediate change in this situation, he calls on the theatre to seize the initiative and to provide new models of heroism for the world. In this way, perhaps both art and society may be saved.

Lublinski's path from socialism to neoclassicism paralleled that of Ernst. His *Bilanz der Moderne* (1904), strongly Marxist in orientation, condemned both romanticism and naturalism for presenting symbols and partial perspectives and avoiding real portrayals of society. During the next few years, however, inspired in part by Ernst and Nietzsche, Lublinski sought a subjective freedom that Marx did not seem to provide. In *Der Ausgang der Moderne* (1907), he renounced the views advanced in *Die Bilanz*, dismissed the working class as "living in too difficult a struggle with material reality to take part in cultural improvement,"[110] and advanced the single hero—expressing his individuality in conflict with society—as the only source of tragedy and the highest expression of humanity. He also declared his intellectual affinity with Wilhelm von Scholz, whom he credited with laying the "aesthetic and philosophical groundwork" for modern tragedy, and with Ernst, who had solved its "literary and technical problems" and prevented it from becoming a purely formal exercise.[111]

Scholz, who seems to have been less engaged with social questions than Ernst or Lublinski, came to neoclassic concerns through a consideration of how the drama engages and works upon its audience. In *Gedanken zum Drama* (1905), he condemns drama that seeks only the transient tension of suspense, and calls for drama that engages its public through "emotional tension" resulting from "the struggle of will against will."[112] The struggle must be an inevitable one based upon necessity, not imposed upon the hero. Thus, although the hero may be opposed by external forces, Scholz would prefer a "self-generating conflict" growing out of contradictory drives within the hero himself, such as the balanced claims of self-assertion and recognition of universal moral law.[113]

Lukács's "Metaphysik der Tragödie" deals primarily with the tragedies of Ernst, but draws upon each of these neoclassic critics. Tragedy, says Lukács, expresses the tension between the empirical, corrupting world of everyday life and the crystalline vision of real life, uncom-

[109]Ibid., 216.
[110]Samuel Lublinski, *Der Ausgang der Moderne* (Berlin, 1907), 14.
[111]Ibid., 159.
[112]Wilhelm von Scholz, *Gedanken zum Drama* (Munich, 1905), 5.
[113]Ibid., 67.

promised and totally fulfilled. This higher life can be approached through transcendent forms, a key example of which is tragedy. Tragedy is a miraculous but necessarily momentary manifestation of real life in the midst of empirical life. It "ruthlessly turns life into a clear, an unambiguous equation—which it then resolves."[114] Man is too weak to bear this revelation more than momentarily, but while it is occurring, he is separated from historical reality to enter the world of essence. Tragedy takes place in that world, outside of space or time, and this is the metaphysical reason for the unities, to which the French and Lessing mistakenly attempted to apply a rationalistic explanation. The experience of tragedy is akin to the trace of the mystic, a "form-creating" experience, but the essence of the former is self-fulfillment, of the latter, self-oblivion: "the one, at the end of his road, is absorbed into the All, the other shattered against the All."[115]

The influence of Neo-Kantian, indeed of Neoplatonic, thought can be seen in Lukács's dualism and in the suggestion that the forms the soul seeks are *a priori*, static and eternal; but the dynamic of this essay is more suggestive of Kierkegaard (the subject of an earlier essay in the same collection) in his search for the absolute and for authentic existence. The essay has thus been claimed by Lucien Goldmann and others as a forerunner of modern existentialism, although that was not the course Lukács himself followed. When his study of Marx brought him back to a more specific concern with the social and historical context of literature, he looked back on "Zur Soziologie" as a much more significant indication of his later thought than the "Metaphysik."

Still other critical strategies were applied to the analysis of tragedy during this period by other German writers, those of psychological analysis by Sigmund Freud (1856–1939) and those of phenomenology by Max Scheler (1874–1928). Freud is best known to students of dramatic theory for his use of dramatic characters (most notably Oedipus) to illustrate certain psychoneurotic conditions; for his study of jokes, which indirectly bears upon the conditions of comedy; and to a lesser extent for his psychological criticism of certain scenes and characters in the drama, such as the three caskets scene in *The Merchant of Venice* or Rebecca West in Ibsen's *Rosmersholm*.

Less well known is the single essay in which Freud directly addresses the theory of drama, "Psychopathic Characters on the Stage," probably written in 1905. Taking as his basis Aristotle's remarks on purgation, he suggests that the drama provides a safe means of "opening up

---

[114]Lukács, *Soul and Form*, trans. Anna Bostock (Cambridge, Mass., 1971), 153.
[115]Ibid., 160.

sources of pleasure or enjoyment in our emotional life,"[116] analogous to the release children gain at play. There is a direct enjoyment coming from the identification with a hero, free from all political, social, or sexual concerns, but also an indirect masochistic satisfaction at the defeat of this figure, experienced without pain or risk to ourselves. "Suffering of every kind is thus the subject-matter of drama," provided that the audience is compensated for its sympathy by the psychological satisfactions of psychical stimulation. The suffering should be mental, not physical, since the latter discourages both enjoyment and psychic activity. It must arise from "an event involving conflict and it must include an effort of the will together with resistance."[117]

The first and grandest example, says Freud, was the classic tragedy's struggle against the divine. Then, as religious belief diminished, the hero was pitted instead against human society or other powerful individuals (though here the "rebellious source of enjoyment" is lost). Next came the psychological drama, where the conflict occurs in the hero's mind between different impulses, and results not in death but in renunciation of one of these impulses. Finally, the psychological drama can become psychopathological if the conflict is between a conscious impulse and a repressed one, as in *Hamlet*. The repressed impulse cannot be openly recognized, for then only neurotic spectators could derive pleasure from it. For more normal persons to sympathize with the hero, they must enter his illness with him, and this can be achieved only if the dramatist keeps the repressed impulse somewhat hidden, so that our own resistance is not aroused to diminish our pleasure in the liberation.

The phenomenology of Edmund Husserl (1859–1938), developed in the early years of the new century, inspired another interpretation of tragedy in "Zum Phänomen des Tragischen" (1915), the work of Husserl's student Max Scheler. Husserl's concern was with the process of cognition, the determination of what exists on the basis of what appears. Scheler's particular focus within this system is upon the emotive dimension of consciousness, which he believes is objectively determined by a series of values; these, as much as rational activity, condition the actions an individual pursues. The sum of these actions defines both the individual within the world and the world in the conception of the individual. Both of these perspectives are necessarily partial, since only an infinite, perfect individual could, like God, relate directly to the totality of God's world.

---

[116]Sigmund Freud, *The Standard Edition of the Complete Psychological Works*, trans. James Strachey et al., 24 vols. (London, 1953–74), 7:305.
[117]Ibid., 307.

Out of this system of partial perspectives, of conflicting values in individual conceptions of the world, arises tragedy; indeed, says Scheler, tragedy can be found "only in that realm where there are objects of value and where these work in one way or another on each other."[118] The "working on each other" is critical for Scheler, since although tragedy involves the destruction of a value, this destruction "as such is not tragic." It becomes so only when the value is forced into destruction by other competing values, and the "purest and clearest" tragedy results when "objects of equally high value appear to undermine and ruin each other."[119] Tragedy portrays the makeup of the cognitive world—its associations, its powers and beliefs, and the necessary disjunctures in these. Participants in a tragedy should have nothing to do with "tragic guilt," since the power of tragedy is lessened if all are not following their highest values and conceptions of duty. "Disaster becomes tragic only when everyone has done his duty and, in the usual sense of the word, no one has incurred 'guilt.' "[120]

On related grounds Scheler denies the traditional idea of "necessity" in tragedy. If someone has failed in his duty or even omitted certain measures available to him to avert the calamity, or if someone is tainted and doomed from the outset, tragedy is not possible. Tragic necessity lies beyond all such considerations; it appears only as a transcendent reality, both inevitable and unpredictable, from "the essence and essential relation of the inevitability and inescapability of things founded in society."[121] Only when the spectator witnesses the tragic outcome being resisted by every conceivable power of the participants can he experience the "specific tragic grief and tragic sympathy," along with the "unique peace and reconciliation of the emotions," which is the end of tragedy.[122]

An important new dimension was given to considerations of tragedy at about this time by the theories developed by a group of scholars at Cambridge, who were interested in Greek tragedy as an anthropological rather than an aesthetic phenomenon, and who viewed its relationship with ritual under the inspiration not of Nietzsche but of the highly influential anthropologist and student of early rites, Sir James Frazer (1854–1941). Drawing upon the ritual cycle of death and rebirth as seen in a sacrificed and resurrected king in Frazer's *The Golden Bough* (1890), Gilbert Murray (1866–1957) identified a ritual structure that

[118]Max Scheler, "On the Tragic," trans. Bernard Stambler, *Cross Currents* 4, 2 (Winter 1954): 180.
[119]Ibid., 181.
[120]Ibid., 187.
[121]Ibid., 186.
[122]Ibid., 188.

he believed lay beneath all Greek tragedy. This structure, described in "Excursus on the Ritual Forms Preserved in Greek Tragedy" (1912), was composed of an *agon* (representing light against dark, summer against winter), a *pathos* (representing the sacrificial death), a *messenger* (since the actual death is seldom performed on stage), a *threnos* or lamentation, and an *anagnorisis* or recognition of the slain God, followed by his *apotheosis* or epiphany.[123]

Murray's influential essay appeared in the book *Themis* by Jane Ellen Harrison (1850–1928), which provided a much more detailed study of the sacrificed and resurrected God in Greek art and legend. An earlier rival theory of tragedy's origin by William Ridgeway (1853–1956) looked to commemorations of dead heroes rather than to worship of some god or daimon; Harrison absorbs Ridgeway's view by claiming the hero figure itself as a secondary manifestation of the sacrificed god. "As hero he is a functionary; he wears the mask and absorbs the ritual of an *Eniautos-Daimon* [Harrison's term for the spirit of the changing year]."[124]

In *The Origin of Attic Comedy* (1914), F. M. Cornford (1874–1943) traced Greek comedy back to the same seasonal ritual of death and rebirth, moving in this case from agon to culminating ritual marriage. The traditional ritual echoing the life of the year-spirit, he said, gave "the abstract conception or movement of plot" to both comedy and tragedy; tragedy, depicting human destiny, kept this movement central, while comedy, more interested in individual psychology and the follies of human character, retained it largely as a matter of convenience. The fatal pride, the hubris of the tragic protagonist, was also echoed in comedy, in the fraudulent, boasting *Alazon* who was placed in opposition to the modest *Eiron*, the comic hero.[125]

All the Cambridge critics were primarily concerned with the historical and anthropological bases of comedy and tragedy; Murray specifically disclaims aesthetic criticism as a part of his observations.[126] Nevertheless, their insistence that drama—especially tragedy—had to be considered in the light of ritual made a permanent impression on modern critical thought, even after the details of their theory had been devastatingly attacked by the preeminent modern scholar of the Greek theatre, A. W. Pickard-Cambridge (1873–1952) in his book *Dithyramb, Tragedy and Comedy* (1927).

[123]Jane Ellen Harrison, *Themis* (Cambridge, 1912), 342–43.
[124]Ibid., xiv.
[125]F. M. Cornford, *The Origin of Attic Comedy* (Cambridge, 1934), 183.
[126]Harrison, *Themis*, 363.

18

The Twentieth Century, 1914–1930

JACQUES COPEAU (1879–1949), the most influential theatre director of his generation in France, often declared himself an enemy of abstract theorizing. As early as 1905, he wrote that nothing shocked him so much as the concern with any specific mode—"poetic theatre, realist theatre, psychological play, comedy of idea, comedy of manner, comedy of character"—which "*a priori* and systematically excludes from dramatic art any aspect of human truth, any ambition toward beauty."[1] In 1913, on the eve of the opening of his Vieux Colombier theatre, he announced, "We represent no school. . . . We support no formula. . . . We feel no need of a revolution. . . . We do not believe in the efficacy of aesthetic formulas which are born and die every month in little *cénacles*."[2]

Nevertheless, Copeau's "Essai de rénovation dramatique" (1913), while devoid of the avant-garde posturing so popular in artistic manifestos of the period, presents a clear and in some ways even revolutionary program. Copeau deplores the modern condition of the theatre, given over to commercialism, cheap sensationalism and exhibitionism, ignorance, indifference, and lack of discipline—debasing both itself and its public. He proposes a new theatre raised "on absolutely solid foundations" which can serve as a rallying place for actors, authors, and audience "who are possessed by the desire to restore beauty to the scenic spectacle."[3] The means Copeau suggests set him apart from both the commercial and the avant-garde theatres of his day. He follows the symbolists in placing the poet and the text in a primary role and stresses

---

[1] Jacques Copeau, "Critiques d'un autre temps," *Nouvelle revue française* 21 (Dec. 1923): 225.
[2] Ibid., 243.
[3] Ibid., 234.

that the work of the director must always remain subservient to these. Similarly, he calls for extreme simplicity in the physical setting, the famous *tréteau nu* (bare boards) which would allow the actor and author to present the text without "theatrical" intrusion.[4] The repertoire of his theatre would emphasize the great works of the past as models for the present, presented in repertoire to avoid the systematic exploitation of particular successes.

These ideals won many adherents in France and elsewhere, but every one of them—the primacy of the text, the veneration of the classics, the emphasis on the actor, the disencumbering of the stage—was sharply opposed by the first major avant-garde movement of the new century. This was futurism, which achieved its greatest impact in the years during which the Vieux Colombier was being planned and established. Futurism was launched in Paris by a manifesto of Filippo Marinetti (1876–1944) that appeared on the front page of the *Figaro* of February 20, 1909. In this violent, rhapsodic statement Marinetti called for a new art suited to the new century, dedicated to speed and to struggle, to the mob, the factory, and the machine. The racing automobile was to replace the Victory of Samothrace as the symbol of beauty, and the traditions of a numbing past were to be cast aside. War was to be idealized, not only because it represented action and struggle but because it contributed to the destruction of the past. Marinettti called upon the new artists to "destroy the museums, libraries, academies of every kind" and to "fight moralism, feminism, every opportunistic or utilitarian cowardice."[5]

During 1909 and 1910 Marinetti organized futurist evenings, called *serate*, which involved the reading of futurist poetry and manifestos to demonstrative and often hostile audiences; he also wrote a series of essays on futurism and how it might be developed in various arts. These were collected under the title *Le futurisme* (1911). His 1910 "Manifeste des auteurs dramatiques futuristes" appears here as "La volupté d'être sifflé." It advances the theatre as "among all literary forms, the one that can serve Futurism most effectively."[6] To achieve this, dramatists must spurn proven formulas and popular success, along with traditional psychology and subject matter. They should instead seek "to force the soul of the audience away from base everyday reality and to lift it into a blinding atmosphere of intellectual intoxication," a realm of "terrestrial, marine, and aerial velocities, dominated by steam and electricity."[7]

[4]Ibid., 248.
[5]Filippo Marinetti, "Manifesto of Futurism," trans. R. W. Flint, in *Marinetti: Selected Writings* (New York, 1972), 42.
[6]Marinetti, "The Pleasure of Being Booed," in ibid., 113.
[7]Ibid., 114.

The new society of the twentieth century, a society of scientific revolution and machine power, demands a new art reflecting its dynamic power. Smug, satisfied, traditionalist audiences will resist this, but authors and actors must reject the applause that rewards mediocrity and learn to enjoy "the pleasure of being booed."[8]

This rather vague program was given more focus in Marinetti's second and most famous pronouncement on futurist theatre, "Il teatro di varietà" (1913), which was soon reproduced in abridged form in the London *Daily Mail* and in Craig's *Mask*. This essay denounces contemporary theatre as vacillating stupidly between historical reconstruction and photographic reproduction, and urges the futurist dramatist to look to the variety theatre for new inspiration. There, instead of the exaltation of the inner life and "stupid analyses of feelings," may be found what Marinetti opposes to psychology: *fisicofollia* (body-madness), an exaltation of "action, heroism, life in the open air, dexterity, the authority of instinct and intuition."[9] Amazement and surprise are the effects to be sought; the audience is to be constantly taken off guard by such devices as incorrect tickets or glue in their seats. Tradition should be not merely ignored but actively destroyed, and all classic art systematically prostituted on stage.[10] Form, color, words, and physical action should be displayed and enjoyed for their own sake, not in reference to externally established values. The essay concludes with dynamic fireworks of disconnected words, phrases, and noises. The concerns of this essay could be clearly seen in the *sintesi*, brief dramatic scenes performed by the futurists which sought to capture the speed, surprise, irreverence, and immediacy Marinetti admired in the variety theatre.

In the spring of 1913 Marinetti met Meyerhold in Paris while Meyerhold was producing his first work outside of Russia, D'Annunzio's *Pisanelle*. Since Meyerhold's major essay, "The Fairground Booth," had just appeared, it is possible that he suggested to Marinetti the theatrical power of such popular forms, though Marinetti would have been little interested in the symbolist undertones of Meyerhold's approach. Nor did Meyerhold, whose theoretical writings are sprinkled with the names of contemporaries whose ideas he found stimulating, seem to have gained much from Marinetti. Indeed, looking back on this period in 1929, he remarked that Marinetti had merely reinforced the anarchy that was "an unhappy tradition of the Italian theatre."[11]

---

[8]Ibid., 115.
[9]Marinetti, "The Variety Theatre," in ibid., 120.
[10]Ibid., 121.
[11]Vsevolod Meyerhold, "The Reconstruction of the Theatre," trans. Edward Braun, in *Meyerhold on Theatre* (New York, 1969), 258.

The relationship between the Russian and the Italian avant-gardes at this period has been the subject of much controversy, since a futurist movement, with some clear points in common but even more clear differences, did appear in both countries. Certainly the first and most famous Russian futurist manifesto, "A Slap in the Face of Public Taste" (1912), bore a strong resemblance to the pronouncements of Marinetti. "Throw Pushkin, Dostoyevsky, Tolstoy, *et al.*, *et al.* overboard from the ship of modernity," it urged. The more recent symbolists, Bryusov, Andreyev, and Blok, were equally scorned by the four young authors of this document, who expressed "insurmountable hatred" for all previous language and "horror for fame and reputation," and who saw themselves, like Marinetti's actors, standing proudly amid a "sea of boos and indignation."[12]

One of the signers of this document, Vladimir Mayakovsky (1893–1930), became the leading spokesman for Russian futurist theatre. In the summer of 1913, he published "Theatre, Cinematography, Futurism," an article condemning the modern stage, and Stanislavski in particular, for leading the drama down the sterile path of realism. The triumph of cinema, he said, which can achieve realism more effectively, should free the theatre to become again a significant art.[13] Mayakovsky's first play, *Vladimir Mayakovsky*, was created this same year as an example of the new drama. Similar ideas were expressed the following year by the futurist critic Vadim Shershenevich (1893–1942) in "A Declaration about the Futurist Theatre," which appeared in the newspaper *Nov.* He attacked not only Stanislavski but also Meyerhold, for stressing eclecticism and for repressing the actor, whose movement was the true basis of theatre. The word should no longer rule, he contended, but be replaced by "intuitive improvisation."[14]

In January and February of 1914, Marinetti visited Moscow and St. Petersburg, arousing much interest in futurism but at the same time demonstrating that his outlook was quite different from that of the Russians. Marinetti found his hosts metaphysical and nationalistic, still bound to the past; they considered him anarchic and lacking in true artistic sensitivity. In St. Petersburg, Marinetti attended the studio just founded by Meyerhold to carry out experiments with pantomime, variety theatre, and the grotesque; he even worked with a class of actors dealing with the concept of the grotesque in a three-minute production of *Othello*.

Back in Italy, Marinetti championed this type of concentrated drama

[12]Vladimir Mayakovsky et al., "A Slap in the Face of Public Taste," trans. H. Segall in E. and C. Proffer, *The Ardis Anthology of Russian Futurism* (Ann Arbor, Mich., 1980), 179.
[13]Mayakovsky, "Theatre, Cinematography, Futurism," in ibid., 182.
[14]Quoted in Vladimir Markov, *Russian Futurism* (Berkeley, 1968), 147.

in an article written in collaboration with Emilio Settimelli (b. 1891) and Bruno Corra (b. 1892), "Il teatro futurista sintetico" (1915). Its subtitle, "atechnical—dynamic—simultaneous—autonomous—alogical—unreal," summarizes the goals of the new "synthetic" drama, which its creators hoped would help encourage the "much-prayed-for great war."[15] Traditional techniques such as the building of climaxes, foreshadowing, and logical connections were to be abolished. The new theatre should reshape reality rather than photograph it, challenge accepted logic, and be extremely compact, compressing "into a few minutes, in a few words and gestures innumerable situations, sensibilities, ideas, sensations, facts, and symbols."[16] It should be a "gymnasium" to train the spirit for life in the new world of speed and scientific progress.

Other Italian theorists considered how to bring futurism to physical staging. Chief among these were Enrico Prampolini (1894–1956) and Fortunato Depero (1892–1960). Prampolini's "Scenografia e coreografia futurista" (1915) condemns even such experimental designers as Appia and Craig as having only "made some limited innovations, some objective syntheses." He calls instead for an abstract stage directed toward the emotional sensations of the audience, toward feelings aroused by color and space rather than by the poet's words or the actor's gestures. Instead of painted backdrops, the stage should employ "electromechanical architecture, given powerful life by chromatic emanations from a luminous source provided by electric reflections of multicolored panes of glass, arranged and coordinated analogically with the psyche of each scenic action."[17] Depero's "Il teatro plastico" (1919) speaks in even more ecstatic terms of electrical and mechanical magic shows in which animate and inanimate forms would struggle, merge, and be transformed in a kind of cosmic machine-ballet.[18] Giacona Balla's designs for Stravinsky's *Feu d'artifice*, presented by the Ballets Russes in Rome in 1917, was the most famous manifestation of such ideas in the theatre.

The futurist movement remained a significant part of the Italian theatrical scene until about 1930, but after World War I it contributed little that was new to dramatic theory. The two major manifestos after 1915, "Il teatro della sorpresa" (1921) by Marinetti and Francesco Cangiullo and "L'atmosfera scenica futurista" (1924) by Prampolini, essentially repeated positions already established in earlier writings. Moreover,

---

[15]Marinetti et al., "The Futurist Synthetic Theatre," in *Marinetti*, 123.

[16]Ibid., 124.

[17]Enrico Prampolini, "Futurist Scenography," trans. V. N. Kirby, in Michael Kirby, *Futurist Performance* (New York, 1971), 204.

[18]Fortunato Depero, *Il teatro plastico* (Luglio, 1970), 147–48.

the success of Pirandello and others after 1920 tended to eclipse the futurists, who had never achieved—or indeed sought—major theatrical success.

While futurism was developing in Italy and Russia, parallel and occasionally overlapping experimental movements were launched elsewhere: dada in Zurich and expressionism in Germany. The ties between these movements, at least in their early years, were obvious in the program of the first dada soirée, given April 14, 1917, in Zurich. The major offering was the play *Sphinx und Strohmann* by Oscar Kokoshka (b. 1886), later claimed as one of the fathers of expressionism, and among the prefatory events was the reading of one of Marinetti's manifestos.

The dadaists, more extreme even than the futurists in their iconoclasm but without a unifying spokesman like Marinetti, left few discursive statements on their idea of theatre. Tristan Tzara's (1896–1963) note, in his *Chronique zurichoise* (1919), on this first evening's offering is one of the clearest, and the kinship with futurism is obvious: "This performance decided the role of our theatre, which will entrust the stage direction to the subtle invention of the explosive wind; the scenario in the audience; a visible direction by grotesque means: the Dadaist Theatre. Above all, masks and revolver shots, the effigy of the director. Bravo and Boom Boom."[19] In a rather more coherent note, "Le dadaisme et le théâtre" (1922), Tzara hailed the passing of realism and of the "illusionist theatre." Freed of the burden of imitating life, the theatre could "preserve its artistic autonomy, that is to say, live by its own scenic means." Actors could be freed from the "cage" of the proscenium theatre, and scenic and lighting effects be arranged in full view of the spectators, making them a part of the theatre world.[20]

The call for "artistic autonomy" in the theatre instead of imitation of life is one that echoes through much French theatre theory of this period. It is closely related to Guillaume Apollinaire's (1880–1918) concept of surrealism, defined for the first time in his program notes to the ballet *Parade* (1917) by Cocteau, Picasso, and Satie. This "*surréaliste*" work, said Apollinaire, "translated reality" into a coherent ensemble of painting, dance, mime, and plastic art—a total theatre piece. Instead of seeking to imitate reality, it suggested it "by a kind of synthesis-analysis embracing all the visible elements and something more, if possible, an integral schematization which seeks to harmonize contradictions while at times deliberately renouncing the immediate aspect

[19]Tristan Tzara, *Oeuvres complètes*, 5 vols. (Paris, 1975), 1:564.
[20]Ibid., 606.

of the object."[21] Apollinaire returned to this concept in the preface and prologue to his 1917 play, *Les mamelles de Tirésias*. In a famous passage he compares the work of the surrealist to the wheel, an invention of man to imitate walking, but one that bears no resemblance to the leg. Similarly, the stage "is no more the life it represents than the wheel is a leg," and it must create reality on its own terms. The dramatist, says the prologue, must avoid realism, and pay no heed to conventional time or space:

> His universe is his stage
> Within it he is the creating god
> Directing at his will
> Sounds gestures movements masses colors
> Not merely with the aim
> Of photography the so-called slice of life
> But to bring forth life itself in all its truth.[22]

The preface to Jean Cocteau's (1889–1963) *Les mariés de la Tour Eiffel* (1922) cites *Ubu roi* and *Les mamelles de Tirésias* as precursors, and echoes their rejection of conventional reality. Like Apollinaire, Cocteau calls for a new art combining many elements—"the fantastic, the dance, acrobatics, mime, drama, satire, music, and the spoken word."[23] In a memorable phrase, he rejects traditional verse drama as poetry in the theatre in favor of a "poetry of the theatre," achieved by all the means available to the staged performance.[24] He rejects also the realism of Antoine in favor of a deeper realism which, because we are so accustomed to the clichés of the naturalist theatre, will surprise us as bizarre, even fantastic. Anticipating the popular critical term of the mid-twentieth century, Cocteau calls such theatre "absurd" because "instead of attempting to keep this side of the absurdity of life, to lessen it, to organize and arrange it as we organize and arrange the story of an incident in which we played an unfavorable part, I accentuate it, I emphasize it, I try to paint *more truly than the truth*."[25] Clearly, the absurd of Cocteau is close to the surrealism of Apollinaire.

Between 1905 and 1913, when Paris was witnessing the birth of futurism and the first cubist paintings, one fascinated visitor was the Polish poet and painter Stanislaw Witkiewicz (1885–1939). After trav-

[21]Quoted in Daniel Oster, *Guillaume Apollinaire* (Paris, 1975), 111.

[22]Guillaume Apollinaire, *The Breasts of Tiresias*, trans. Louis Simpson, in Michael Benedikt and George Wellwarth, *Modern French Theatre* (New York, 1966), 66.

[23]Jean Cocteau, Preface to *The Wedding on the Eiffel Tower*, trans. Michael Benedikt, in ibid., 98.

[24]Ibid., 96.

[25]Ibid., 95.

eling to the South Seas with the anthropologist Malinowski and participating in the Russian Revolution, Witkiewicz returned to Poland in 1918 to embark on a remarkably innovative career. One part involved the production of plays and dramatic theory so experimental that only after the Beckett-Ionesco revolution of the 1950s (see Chapter 20) was his work widely understood and appreciated. Upon his return to Poland, Witkiewicz became associated with a group called the Formists, whose doctrines coincided significantly with the ideas on art he had been developing since his years in Paris.

The Formists spoke of different sorts of reality to which the artist could give equally legitimate form: naturalism depicted material reality; surrealism, psychological reality; futurism or expressionism, the reality of the free imagination. In the essay "On a New Type of Play" (1920), Witkiewicz calls for a theatre based not upon external reality or psychological reality, but upon pure form, as were certain experiments in painting. The basis may be either realistic or fantastic, but either should be reworked into a creative synthesis of sound, decor, movement, and dialogue "so as to create a whole whose meaning would be defined only by its purely scenic internal construction."[26] Each element—a gesture, a color, a musical note, a shaft of light—must be seen as a formal element and accepted not for itself but as a part of this whole, "just as we accept as inevitable a particular part of a composition on a canvas or a sequence of chords in a musical work."[27] (As we shall see, Eisenstein in Russia was just at this time working in much the same direction with his theatre of "montage.")

A supplementary essay, "A Few Words about the Role of the Actor in the Theatre of Pure Form" (1921), was stimulated by the appearance of Komissarzhevsky's book on the theories of Stanislavski. Witkiewicz agrees readily enough with Stanislavski's emphasis on the acting ensemble in preference to the star system, but he firmly rejects the idea of an actor's "experiencing" the inner life of the role. He should instead seek to grasp "the *formal conception* of the work (as distinct from its real-life mood) and its character apart from all real-life probabilities."[28] He must subordinate himself not merely to the acting ensemble but to the entire work, and choose tones and gestures not on the basis of imitation or of psychological truth but for their contribution to the whole—a line may be given in a psychologically realistic way or it may be given only as a pattern of sound or as the stimulus of an image. The overall form

[26]Stanislaw Witkiewicz, *The Madman and the Nun and Other Plays*, trans. Daniel C. Gerould and C. S. Durer (Seattle, 1968), 292.

[27]Ibid., 293.

[28]Witkiewicz, "A Few Words about the Role of the Actor in the Theatre of Pure Form," trans. D. C. Gerould, in *Twentieth Century Polish Drama* (Ithaca, N.Y., 1977), 154.

is the responsibility of the director, but the duty of the actor is "to keep himself firmly under control," to "forget completely about life," and to devote himself entirely to building up the total theatrical experience.[29]

German expressionism—the most significant theatre avant-garde of this period—shared with futurism, surrealism, and dada a rejection both of naturalism, with its fidelity to surface reality and interest in social questions, and symbolism, with its worship of beauty and visions of otherworldly paradises. The new movements exalted subjectivity and vitalism, and favored abstraction, distortion, and lyric excess over mimesis and formal beauty. Common enemies and some shared concerns allowed a certain amount of cross-fertilization among these contemporary movements, but significant differences nevertheless divided them. The futurists' fascination with modern machinery and the products of industrial society was by no means shared by the majority of the expressionists; on the contrary, they tended to feel that the spirit of the individual was being crushed by these developments. Futurism stressed externals—light, color, speed, physical risk—while expressionism, like the surrealists after Breton, sought to explore the mysteries of the inner life. The psychological rhapsodies of Nietzsche helped to orient the young Germans of the new century in this direction, and in the drama both Frank Wedekind and Carl Sternheim were important precursors, but probably the major single influence was the late plays of Strindberg, widely read and performed in Germany during the formative years of expressionism.

Clearly, an interest in revealing the workings of the unconscious marks even the so-called naturalistic plays of Strindberg; in the article "Des arts nouveaux" (1894), subtitled "the role of chance in artistic creation," he speaks of a painter who allows his spatula to move at random, "keeping nature's model in mind without trying to copy it." This results in "a charming mixture of the unconscious and the conscious" wherein the artist "works like capricious nature, without predetermined aim."[30]

After 1900, Strindberg undertook more radical dramatic experiments with the unconscious, as may be seen in *A Dream Play* (1902), whose brief preface calls the work an attempt "to reproduce the disconnected but apparently logical form of a dream." Conventional time and space disappear as the psyche roams freely over fragments of reality; "imagination spins and weaves new patterns made up of memories, experiences, unfettered fancies, absurdities and improvisations.

[29]Ibid., 156.
[30]August Strindberg, "The New Arts," trans. Albert Bermel, in *Inferno, Alone and Other Writings* (New York, 1968), 99.

The characters are split, double and multiply; they evaporate, crystallize, scatter and converge."[31] The only controlling element is the free-flowing consciousness of the dreamer. In the essay "Truth in Error" (1907), Strindberg's "teacher" advances a Swedenborgian idea that might be taken as a motto for much of the expressionist movement: "The world is a reflection of your interior state, and of the interior states of others."[32]

"August Strindberg is our watchword," claimed the expressionist René Schickele (1883–1940) in 1912,[33] and his opinion was seconded by Kurt Pinthus (1886–1975) in "Zur jüngsten Dichtung" (1915). Ibsen, said Pinthus, sought to reveal "the determinism of presumed truth" through a "scientific analysis of psychic relations," realizing too late (as his final play confesses) that such intellectual analysis leads to death. Strindberg, on the other hand, was the first to attempt in a "seminally explosive" way to release mankind, "an obliging Atlas, from the Alpine weight of Reality which he had been bearing."[34]

Unlike futurism or the later surrealist movement, expressionism had no single leader, no central manifesto. The term was first used in art criticism, then applied to certain young German dramatists who, after 1912, began to deal with material in highly subjective and often radically distorted ways. Alfred Döblin's (1878–1957) *Lydia und Mäxchen* (1906) and the better known *Mörder, Hoffnung der Frauen* (1907) by the painter Kokoschka were important precursors to Reinhard Sorge's (1892–1916) *Der Bettler* (1912), the first fully developed example of the new style. Its protagonist, the Poet (who, like Strindberg's dream characters, takes on another role, the Son, in the central part of the play), dreams of a "new drama" which will liberate mankind. He rejects plot in the traditional sense of the term, for true plot "cannot be expressed, not in words, for it is silent, not in the actors' gestures, for it indeed has gestures but they cannot be imitated, not in figures, for it indeed has an image but it is filled by eternal relations, by impulses and a thousand souls that cannot be reproduced."[35]

Walter Hasenclever's (1890–1940) *Der Sohn* (1914), presenting similarly abstract characters in somewhat more traditional dramatic form, was widely accepted as the major work of the new movement. In "Versuch eines zukunftigen Dramas" (1914), Pinthus criticizes even Wedekind and Sternheim for conditioning their characters by external reality,

[31]Strindberg, *Six Plays*, trans. Elizabeth Sprigge (New York, 1956), 193.
[32]Strindberg, *En Blå Bok* (Stockholm, 1962), 216.
[33]René Schickele, "August Strindberg," *Die Aktion* 2, 4 (Jan. 22, 1912): 104.
[34]Kurt Pinthus, "Zur jüngsten Dichtung," in Paul Raabe, *Expressionismus: Der Kampf um eine literarische Bewegung* (Munich, 1965), 71.
[35]Reinhard Sorge, *Der Bettler* (Berlin, 1919), 152.

while in Hasenclever's play "the perspective throughout is that of the son. Thus we must see the characters, not as was the custom up until the present in an objective manner, but as the son sees them."[36] The interest is no longer in the development of plot or character but in the expression of "a soul swollen with tragedy." Such tragedy, because it touches the hidden life of every man, is instantly recognizable, says Pinthus, though it was never explored by the realists, the neoclassicists, or the neoromantics. "No son in reality ever spoke as this son does; but in every human son's soul in such a situation all this is felt, more or less unconsciously."[37] Hasenclever himself spoke of the theatre not only as a means of expressing the inner man but as a "medium between philosophy and life" that seeks to expose "the unexpressed schism between what exists and what man needs."[38]

Another leading contributor to prewar expressionism, Paul Kornfeld (1889–1942), accompanied his first play, *Die Verführung* (1913), with an essay on expressionist acting. He condemns actors who attempt the illusion of spontaneity on stage or who visit bars to see how people act when they are drunk. On stage one should speak and act as no one has ever done in real life. "In short, let him not be ashamed of the fact that he is acting. Let him not deny the theatre or try to feign reality." Free of the crosscurrents of conflicting passions and interests in real life, the actor can portray emotions with crystal clarity. Once emotional memory and observation are banished, the actor will find that the expression of a feeling artificially stimulated is "purer, clearer, and stronger" than any feeling aroused by real stimuli.[39] Only the actor is free to externalize himself this completely.

The First World War was not greeted by the expressionists with the enthusiasm found among the futurists. The majority of the former saw the war as another manifestation of the depersonalizing social system, which was always the expressionists' adversary. By 1916, the main concern of expressionism was denunciation of the war, and a call for a new world order based on brotherhood and a belief in the fundamental goodness of man. In a 1916 preface to *Der Sohn*, Hasenclever claimed it as a political drama that portrayed "the struggle of the spirit against reality" and taught "that we are all sons, but that we are more than sons; we are brothers."[40] Ernst Toller (1893–1939), the chief exponent of this view, called *Die Wandlung* (1919), his first play, "a political pam-

---

[36]Pinthus, "Versuch eines zukunftigen Dramas," *Die Schaubühne* 10 (1914): 393.
[37]Ibid., 394.
[38]Walter Hasenclever, "Das Theater von Morgen," *Die Schaubühne* 12 (1916): 477.
[39]Paul Kornfeld, "Epilogue to the Actor," trans. Joseph Bernstein, in Walter Sokel, *An Anthology of German Expressionist Drama* (New York, 1963), 7.
[40]Quoted in "Kunst und Definition," *Neue Blätter für Kunst und Dichtung* 1 (1918): 40.

phlet" whose aim was "to renew the spiritual content of human society." The political poet and the religious poet taught the same message, said Toller, "that man feels himself answerable for himself and for every brother in human society."[41]

Georg Kaiser (1878–1945), expressionism's leading playwright, shared this vision, too. Though he scorned the trappings of realism, he shared with dramatists like Shaw a view of the theatre as an intellectual forum. The drama, he says in his essay "Der Mensch im Tunnel" (1922), trains man in one of the most difficult but essential parts of life, the ability to think. "Writing a drama means: thinking a thought through to its conclusion," he begins, citing Plato's dialogues as outstanding examples of this process.[42] The dramatist must seek always to push back the frontiers and to encourage others to join him. He must show his fellow men the purpose of being, which is "the attainment of record achievements," moving always toward a more comprehensive vision of reality.[43]

If the major authors of expressionist drama in its peak years from 1918 to 1922 shared this religious/political view of their work, a less tendentious view of drama as an exploration of inner life also had its adherents. In "Theater und anderes" (1918), Kornfeld contrasted older drama based on man's character with new drama based on the soul. In the former, man was portrayed as "the sum of attributes and abilities, ruled by a psychological causality similar to a material one." The modern drama of the soul, on the contrary, "argues that man is no mechanism, that conscious subjectivity is destructive, and that psychological causality is as unimportant as material."[44] Much the same point would be made by Adamov and Ionesco 30 years later.

Similarly, Friedrich Koffka (1888–1951), in "Über die Zeit und das Drama" (1919), rejects character as proper to epic but not to drama, since epic shows man as a phenomenon, a part of the world order, while drama shows him as a force, standing outside of or even opposed to the world. In terms suggesting the later existentialists, Koffka describes man as living contentedly in the world until "there comes a day when suddenly something unknown awakes in him, a dark, as if subterranean, power," elemental and indescribable, which launches him on a course of alienation and conflict with the world. Echoing Nietzsche, he concludes, "In the midst of the glowing Apollonian course of life

[41]Ernst Toller, *Schöpferische Konfession* (Berlin, 1920), 48.
[42]Georg Kaiser, "Man in the Tunnel," trans. Walter Sokel, in Sokel, *Anthology*, 12.
[43]Ibid., 13.
[44]Kornfeld, "Theater und anderes," *Das Junge Deutschland* 1 (1918):11–12.

and the peaceful world, Dionysus awakes. From nothing but this event Drama is born, and the great tragic writers dealt with nothing else."[45]

Hasenclever's "Über der Tragische" (1921) also locates the tragic conflict in the relationship between "the world as it exists and men who must live in it," but his description of the conflict harks back to the early romantics: "All perception is tragic; it is the reflection of human forms on the boundaries of the possible. When these bounds are surpassed, thought is surpassed; causality is neutralized; the formulas of logic no longer apply."[46] A generation later this same concept of perception as tragic and of the collapse of causality and logic would appear again in the theories and plays of Ionesco and the "absurdists."

An even closer parallel to subsequent experimentation was provided by the work of Ivan Goll (1891–1950), whose career touched upon dada and surrealism as well as expressionism. The preface to Goll's play *Die Unsterblichen* (1920) calls for an *Überdrama* as the third and final phase of drama's development. First came the Greek drama, depicting struggles between the gods and men, then ill-begotten plays dealing in a limited manner with the problems of individuals. The new superdrama will show "man's struggle with all that is thinglike and beastlike around him and within him." The basic opposition in such drama will be between the soul of man and external reality, which Goll describes in symbolist terms. All "external form" must be destroyed; the theatre must return to its "primary symbol," the mask, and to a perception like that of the child. To counteract the enormous dullness and stupidity of contemporary man, the theatre must create its own enormities, drawn from "a grotesque that does not cause laughter."[47]

The challenge of expressionism to traditional form and accepted dramatic conventions made it a phenomenon of major significance to the critic Oskar Walzel (1864–1944), who was attempting to establish an approach to poetic theory less dependent than those of his predecessors upon the analysis of ethical or ideological content. In his early writings, Walzel was attracted to the theories of Wilhelm Dilthey, insofar as Dilthey provided an alternative to Comtean positivism. Walzel found very useful Dilthey's famous three types of world view, each associated with a different type of dramatic structure, though the psychological foundations of the system worked against the more strictly formal analysis Walzel wished to develop.

The appearance of the *Kunstgeschichtliche Grundbegriffe* (1915) of the art historian Heinrich Wölfflin (1864–1945) provided Walzel with a much

---

[45]Friedrich Koffka, "Über die Zeit und das Drama," *Masken* 15, 14 (1919): 315–16.
[46]Hasenclever, "Über der Tragische," *Menschen* 4, 2 (1921): 18.
[47]Ivan Goll, "Two Superdramas," trans. Walter Sokel, in Sokel, *Anthology*, 9–11.

more compatible system. Wölfflin contrasted Renaissance and baroque art on the basis of five pairs of formal oppositions: the graphic (line) and the painterly (color), surface and depth, closed form (well-defined and self-contained) and open form, multiplicity and unity, clarity and vagueness. Walzel felt that these or similar polarities could also be used to analyze dramatic structure; he experimented with all but graphic and painterly, but the pair he found most stimulating was open and closed (also called atectonic and tectonic) form. These terms he first employed in an analysis of Shakespeare, "Über Shakespeares drama-tische Baukunst" (1916), launching an international vogue of consid-eration of the "baroque" qualities in Shakespearean structure and establishing Wölfflin's categories as standard critical tools for subsequent German literary theorists. Open and closed form remained the most popular, but the rest were also used—even line and color, which entered dramatic theory as line-based versus scene-based dramaturgy.

Walzel's major work, *Gehalt und Gestalt in Kunstwerk des Dichters* (1923), attempts to correct the traditional emphasis on content (*Gehalt*) by show-ing how that content relates to and interrelates with structure (*Gestalt*). Walzel sees the process of literary history as an alternation between opposing *Gestalten*—but not in Hegelian fashion, since their opposition is so complete that no synthesis is ever possible[48]—and the most recent reversal in *Gestalt* as having occurred just after the turn of the century, when the closed, or tectonic, form of scientific naturalism gave way to various open, or atectonic, forms, the most important of which was expressionism.

After Walzel's book appeared, the new plays being written suggested that the time for the next reversal had arrived. Few expressionist or indeed experimental works of any kind appeared in Germany after 1923. More conventional forms, and subjects reminiscent of turn-of-the-century realism, reappeared as part of a movement called the *Neue Sachlichkeit*, a term first applied in 1925 to a group of paintings exhibited in Munich, then to literature. One of the leading spokesmen for the new school, Wilhelm Michel, outlined its program in "Physiognomie der Zeit und Theater der Zeit" (1928). Instead of the "work of art," *Neue Sachlichkeit* drama would show "the 'thing' itself, life itself, the authentic object. Illusion is no longer acceptable." In terms clearly anticipating Brecht and the documentary theatre, Michel called for the stage to show "actual life and its forces without mediation, with 'incar-nation,' without placing it in a harmonious and aesthetic frame." A "problematic" era required a "direct theatre," a "theatre of real action,"

---

[48]Oskar Walzel, *Gehalt und Gestalt in Kunstwerk des Dichters* (Berlin, 1923), 116.

which would accumulate evidence and stimulate discussion of contemporary problems.[49]

Yet while experimentation in playwriting declined, there remained at least one major center for experimentation in production techniques—the Bauhaus, an influential school of design founded in Weimar in 1919, which at least in its early years carried on certain expressionist concerns. Lothar Schreyer (1886–1966), whom Walter Gropius (1883–1969) invited in 1921 to develop a theatre studio at the Bauhaus, was editor of *Der Sturm*, the leading journal for expressionist writing and graphics. The first issue of the Bauhaus's own theatre journal, the *Bauhausbühne*, which appeared in December 1922, contained manifestos by Gropius, "Der Arbeit der Bauhausbühne," and Schreyer, "Das Bühnenwerk." These agree on an ultimate metaphysical aim for theatre, which Gropius describes in Schillerian terms as "placing in physical evidence a supersensuous idea," and Schreyer in Hegelian ones as "the resolution of contradictions by law, the law which is the order that gives life to all living things." Gropius is more specific in suggesting the means to this end: the new scenic space should be based on the spirit of construction (*Bau-Geist*) and should unite movement, organic and mechanical bodies, form, light, color, verbal and musical sound; the actor should be the sort of "inspired workman" who was the Bauhaus ideal, "incarnating an immaterial idea" through his mastery of the laws of "movement and repose, optics and acoustics." Schreyer speaks much more vaguely of "mechanical means freed from mechanism, organic means freed from the organic, light and soul, the living parts of the work," and of the theatre producing life "as life produces life. The message of the interior man acting upon the interior man."[50]

When Schreyer left the Bauhaus in 1923, the theatre division came under the supervision of Oskar Schlemmer (1888–1943), much closer to Gropius than Schreyer had been in his interest in the materials and processes of construction and in the formal and mechanical possibilities of the human body. Soon after the Bauhaus moved from its first home in Weimar to Dessau, there appeared a special issue of the journal the *Bauhaus-Buch* devoted to the theatre, with an introduction by Gropius and articles by Schlemmer and two Hungarian Bauhaus designers, Farkas Molnár and László Moholy-Nagy (1895–1946).

The best-known of these articles is Moholy-Nagy's "Theater, Zirkus, Varieté," which calls for a "total theatre" of the future. It praises the dadaists and futurists for breaking with the "logical-intellectual (liter-

[49]Wilhelm Michel, "Physiognomie der Zeit und Theater der Zeit," *Masken* 22 (1928): 6–8.

[50]Walter Gropius, "Der Arbeit der Bauhausbühne," and Lothar Schreyer, "Das Bühnenwerk," *Die Bauhausbühne, Erste Mittelung* (Weimar, 1922).

ary) theatre" of the past, but faults them for retaining man as the dominant element.[51] In the theatre of the future, man must be employed "on an equal footing with the other formative media" and express not individual concerns but the activities common to all men. This will be achieved though a "great dynamic-rhythmic process" combining many contrasting formal elements, comic and tragic, trivial and monumental (as does circus or vaudeville), and all available media—color, light, sound, machinery—in a totally flexible performance space, which may be extended even to include the audience.[52]

Molnár's "U-Theater" and Gropius's Total Theater of 1926 were the most famous attempts to realize this vision. The goal of theatre architecture, Gropius wrote in 1928, is "to make the theatre instrument as impersonal, as flexible, and as transformable as possible in order to place no restraint upon the director and to allow him to express the most diverse artistic conceptions."[53]

Schlemmer was much less willing to give up man's central position in the theatre. Like Appia, he saw the tension between man the living organism and the nonliving environment on the stage as the critical opposition of the art. But man himself, Schlemmer noted, is both spiritual and mechanical. "He follows his sense of himself as well as his sense of embracing space."[54] In "Mensch and Kunstfigur" Schlemmer recalls the interest of Craig, Kleist, and Bryusov in the marionette, but argues that the puppet can never achieve the essence of drama, which is "Dionysiac in its origin, Apollonian as the visible symbol of the unity of nature and spirit." The ideal stage figure would be both formal and spiritual, both man and marionette (actually something rather close to Craig's *Über-Marionette*); Schlemmer calls it the *Kunstfigur*.[55] Like Meyerhold, Schlemmer was much influenced by Taylor's motion studies, which he saw as a means toward the most efficient and "purest" human gestures, derived from life itself and not from abstract symbolic form.

The Bolshevik rise to power in Russia in 1917 might have been expected to produce a distinct shift toward Marxism in dramatic theory, yet it was another decade before the new regime began to impose a theory of art derived from its view of dialectical and historical materialism. In the meantime, the party made do with a smattering of observations on drama drawn from such populist and engaged theorists as Belinsky, Rousseau, Wagner, and Rolland, and from the scanty com-

---

[51]László Moholy-Nagy, "Theatre, Circus, Variety," trans. A. S. Wensinger, in *The Theatre of the Bauhaus* (Middleton, Conn., 1961), 52.
[52]Ibid., 57–58.
[53]Gropius, "Vom modernen Theaterbau," *Die Scene* 18 (1928): 4.
[54]Oskar Schlemmer, "Man and Art Figure," trans. Wensinger, in *Bauhaus*, 25.
[55]Ibid., 29.

ments of Marx and Engels on *Franz von Sickingen*. Eventually these led to a theory of realism and political comment, but in 1917 the dominant theoretical approach in drama was still that of the antirealists, and this view maintained its supremacy for a number of years. The more conservative and realistic theatres, most notably the Moscow Art Theatre, inadvertently encouraged this situation by remaining for some time highly suspicious of the new order, which received far more enthusiastic support from the experimenters—Mayakovsky, Blok, and Meyerhold. Theatre historians have often suggested that the Communists accepted these avant-garde artists with reluctance, having no ready alternative; but if Lenin seemed indifferent to the avant-garde, this was certainly not the case with the first People's Commissar of Education, Anatoly Lunacharsky (1873–1933), who headed Soviet theatre policy during the early years of the Revolution.

In a 1908 essay, "Socialism in the Theatre," he attacks the traditional "bourgeois" theatre as "coarse, base and vulgar," with only occasional hints of ideas, based on the false assumption that a tired worker requires only light entertainment after his day's toil. On the contrary, says Lunacharsky, the theatre should deal with ideas—not in the refined, neurasthenic manner of the period, but in a way that will engage the common people even if it strikes "nervous young ladies and the soured cream of society" as crude. It should be a theatre of "rapid action, major passions, rare contrasts, whole characters, powerful sufferings, and lofty ecstasy," a "noisy, rapid, glittering" theatre. "Its satire will strike one's cheeks loudly; its woe will make one sob. Its joy will make one forget oneself and dance; its villainy will be terrifying."[56] Such observations show Lunacharsky exploring much the same ground as Meyerhold and even, though in less mystic terms, Ivanov, both of whom were given supervisory positions under the new regime.

Lunacharsky's 1908 essay does not call for a renunciation of the classics as part of the renewal of theatre; rather, Shakespeare and Schiller must be recaptured from the bourgeoisie "in order to link great art with the great lords of the future—the people." On these grounds he defended traditional approaches to drama against Meyerhold and others who argued that a new social order demanded a clean break with the past. Still, Lunacharsky did not discourage experimentation, and productions of classic works in this period were often so radically original as to be essentially new creations. This was indeed the stated policy of Moscow's State Exemplary Theatre, founded in 1919. Its theorist, F. A. Stepun (b. 1884) claimed in "Tragedy and the Contem-

---

[56]Anatoly Lunacharsky, "Sotsializm i teatr," *Teatr*, 1908; quoted in Nikolai Gorchakov, *The Theatre in Soviet Russia*, trans. Edgar Lehrman (New York, 1957), 108-9.

porary Life" that only the "super-art of the past" could worthily celebrate the proletarian, the "super-man of the future," though this "super-
art," the classics, had to be thoroughly reinterpreted to show its contemporary relevance. Our task, Stepun wrote of his production of *Oedipus*, "is to show not ancient Greece but contemporary Russia."[57]

Much more extreme was the approach of the Proletarian Cultural
Educational Organization, the Proletcult, led by Alexander Bogdanov,
who demanded a complete rejection of the past and the creation of a
totally new culture of the workers. The precise form that a workers'
theatre should take was, however, a subject of considerable debate.
Some theorists envisioned a kind of communal festival, looking for
inspiration to symbolists like Ivanov or to the Swiss mystic Appia, whose
last major book, *L'oeuvre d'art vivant* (1921), called for a new sort of
religious celebration without auditorium, stage, play, or spectator, an
experience of the pure sense of joy of the free body moving in space
participated in by the entire community.[58] Other theorists of mass drama,
less religious and more social or political in tone, were rather more
attractive. The writings of Rolland and through them the ideas of
Rousseau and the models of the great festivals of the French Revolution
were a major source of stimulation, reaching an apotheosis in open-air
recreations of major historical events with casts of thousands directed
by Evreinov and others.

The leading theoretical statement on theatre from the Proletcult was
Creative Theatre (1919) by Platon Kerzhentsev (1881–1940). Kerzhentsev
considered the entire existing theatre so tainted by bourgeois culture
that nothing of it could be saved; the repertory, the personnel, the
production methods must all be re-created. Authors and artists must
be found among the proletariat, "to release the creative instinct of the
masses." Even a bourgeois actor with genius was useless to the new
order, since a socialist theatre could no more be created by bourgeois
artists than could a socialist magazine by bourgeois journalists.[59] Theatre artists should no longer behave as entertainers hired to amuse
their masters, but should be considered fellow workers with their audiences. The traditional creator-spectator relationship must disappear,
and the spectator should play an active part not only in performance
but in rehearsals and in all the work of the theatre.

At this same time in Berlin, Erwin Piscator (1893–1966), in opening

[57]F. Stepun, "V poiskakh geroicheskogo teatra," *Literaturnyi sovremennik* 1 (1951): 71,
74; quoted in Gorchakov, *Theatre*, 127.
[58]Adolphe Appia, *The Work of Living Art*, trans. H. D. Albright (Coral Gables, Fla.,
1960), 54–55.
[59]Quoted in Marc Slonim, *Russian Theatre from the Empire to the Soviets* (New York,
1962), 234.

his own Proletarisches Theater, argued that theatre and drama could be made to serve the proletarian audience without a complete rejection of tradition. Much of the standard repertoire, after judicious rewriting and perhaps with explanatory prologues and epilogues, "could serve the cause of the Proletarian revolution just as universal history serves to propagate the idea of class struggle." In time actors would arise from the working class, but for the time being, established actors could be used if they would learn a new approach. All the old styles must be abandoned—the reliance upon "experience" or "expression," the rejection of conscious will. The actor must become a political being, presenting material clearly and concretely to his equals in the audience in the style of a manifesto by Lenin.[60] The new author also must learn "to put his own ideas and original touches to the back of his mind and concentrate on bringing out the ideas which are alive in the psyche of the masses," and must "cultivate trivial forms which have the merit of being clear and easily understood by all."[61] Actors, authors, directors, designers, spectators should view themselves as equal participants in a common effort directed toward a common goal.

The most famous of the Proletcult directors, Sergei Eisenstein (1898–1948), focused his attention on the theatre as an instrument of ideological self-discovery for proletarian audiences. In the essay "Montage of Attractions," written for his production of an Ostrovsky play in 1923, he states that the objective of "every utilitarian theatre" is "to guide the spectator in the desired direction." Every part of the production—color, sound, and movement as well as intellectual and psychological elements—must be considered in terms of this objective. The result will be a theatre far removed from the "illusory imitativeness" and "representationality" of the past. Instead of building up a self-contained illusion of reality, the production will be composed of an assemblage of "attractions." An attraction is "any aggressive aspect of the theatre; that is, any element of it which subjects the spectator to a sensual or emotional impact." Further, these must be "experimentally regulated and mathematically calculated to produce in him certain emotional shocks" arranged in a meaningful pattern, the "montage," to enable the spectator "to perceive the ideological side of what is being demonstrated—the ultimate ideological conclusion."[62] Like Meyerhold, Eisenstein looked to the music hall and the circus for models of this new montage.

The new proletarian theatres had a strong supporter in Meyerhold,

---

[60]Erwin Piscator, *The Political Theatre*, trans. Hugh Rorrison (New York, 1978), 45.

[61]Ibid., 46–47.

[62]Sergei Eisenstein, "Montage of Attractions," trans. D. and E. Gerould, *Drama and Theatre* 9 (Fall 1970): 10.

whom Lunacharsky placed in charge of the national Theatre Department in Moscow in 1920. In the pages of its journal, the *Theatre Herald* (*Vestnik teatra*), he championed nonprofessional Proletcult productions and scored the apolitical attitudes of Moscow's professional theatres, the "sugary, outmoded romanticism" of the State Exemplary Theatre, the "psychological Meiningenism" of the Moscow Art Theatre, the "sickly gaudiness" of Tairov's Kamerny Theatre.[63] Meyerhold himself worked with young and inexperienced actors to develop a new approach called biomechanics, which attempted to relate acting to the new machine age and the new political order. By emphasizing physical training rather than inspiration or psychological insight, Meyerhold claimed that acting could be made available to a far broader segment of the population. His essay "The Actor of the Future and Biomechanics" (1922) notes that theatre and acting have always reflected their society, and the new Russian society thus demands a new vision of theatre. Since labor is "no longer regarded as a curse but as a joyful, vital necessity," the spectacle of a man working efficiently affords positive pleasure, and this should be the actor's goal.[64] His art being that of plastic forms in space, he must study the workings, the mechanics of the body, seeking not psychological insight but physical clarity, a state of "*excitation* which communicates itself to the spectator and induces him to share in the actor's performance."[65]

The other great directors of this remarkable period—Tairov, Evreinov, Vakhtangov, Komissarzhevsky—each developed an approach to the theatre somewhere between the polarities established by Meyerhold and Stanislavski. Alexander Tairov (1885–1950), with an interest in physical training and a determined rejection of past formulas, was the closest to Meyerhold, even though during the early 1920s he aroused some of Meyerhold's sharpest criticism.

Tairov's theory is outlined in his book *Notes of a Director* (1921). He, like Komissarzhevsky, calls for a "synthetic" theatre, centered upon what he calls a "master-actor" closely akin to Komissarzhevsky's "universal actor."[66] Tairov, obviously aware of this parallel, insists (not entirely accurately) that Komissarzhevsky's synthetic theatre did not seek an organic unity of its disparate elements, a unity that Tairov himself advocates.[67] The narrow bounds of existing dramatic literature, he says,

[63]Meyerhold, "On the Contemporary Theatre" and "The Solitude of Stanislavsky," in *Meyerhold on Theatre*, 168–69, 175.
[64]Meyerhold, "Biomechanics," in ibid., 197.
[65]Ibid., 199.
[66]Alexander Tairov, *Notes of a Director*, trans. William Kuhlke (Coral Gables, Fla., 1969), 54.
[67]Ibid., 66.

cannot accommodate this ideal theatre, which must create its own works by fusing the "now separated elements of the harlequinade, tragedy, operetta, pantomime and circus, refracting them through the modern soul of the actor and the creative rhythm kindred to it."[68]

The poet would not be banished from this new theatre but would be one of a group of contributing artists, giving finished form to the actor's speeches and to sequences of action. Tairov rejects Craig's vision of the single creative genius, since no man can be a master of all the arts the theatre requires. A director is needed to guarantee unity, but not on his own terms; rather, he "concentrates in himself the creative will of the whole collective."[69] Equally rejected is the Proletcult attempt to bring the audience into the artistic process, since this will inevitably introduce chance, and "where there is an element of chance, there is no art."[70] Even when the masses are utilized as controlled and rehearsed crowds, as in certain experiments of Reinhardt and Evreinov or as visualized in the cosmic and mystical communal pageant of Alexander Scriabin's (1871–1915) unfinished *Mysterium*, they will be inferior artistically to trained professional actors. Indeed, Tairov sees the spectator only as a witness to the art, in no way essential to it. There can be rehearsals "so inspired that no subsequent performance can compare with them."[71]

In the relaxation of socialist demands that followed the implementation of Lenin's New Economic Policy in 1921, theatrical experimentation continued to flourish despite the misgivings of Proletcult critics. The dominance of socialist realism still lay in the future, though the Twelfth Party Congress in 1923 urged that Russian dramatists produce works "using the episodes of the heroic struggle led by the working class,"[72] and Lunacharsky, in an influential article in the newspaper *Izvestya* this same year, called on the Russian theatre to return to Ostrovsky and to the spirit of his drama, based on character study and realistic depictions of the concerns of everyday life.

Each theatre felt free, however, to interpret the "back to Ostrovksy" advice in its own way. Late in 1923 the conservative Maly mounted a perfectly traditional realistic version of *The Forest*, while Meyerhold responded in January 1924 with a highly stylized interpretation of the same play, reducing the characters to grotesque "social masks" and developing their movements from biomechanic exercises. "A play," he said in reference to this production, "is simply the excuse for the rev-

[68]Ibid., 99.
[69]Ibid., 101.
[70]Ibid., 137.
[71]Ibid., 141.
[72]Slonim, *Russian Theatre*, 303.

elation of its theme on the level at which the revelation may appear vital today."[73] Tairov soon followed with a production challenging realism in quite a different way; he removed all specific details from costumes and all realistic inflections from speech and gestures from acting, and he used a neutral setting consisting only of a wooden bridge and ramps. In 1926, Stanislavski in turn responded to these productions with a brilliant revival in his own style of Ostrovsky's *The Burning Heart*. During the rehearsals he observed, "Our task is to struggle for realism. We must not give the 'stylish' critics the slightest reason to think that we have even the slightest sympathy for Meyerhold's tricks."[74]

Piscator's highly controversial production of Schiller's *Die Räuber* in 1926 forced him also to deal with the question of how a socially engaged theatre should relate to the classics. Piscator aroused protest from both left and right; the conservative critic Herbert Ihering (b. 1888) accused him of "dragging the sacred classic of the nation through the mud," while the liberal Bernhard Diebold (b. 1886) said he should not present the classics at all, at least for several years, to encourage new plays by socialist authors. To attempt relevant updating of plays by Schiller or Shakespeare, Diebold contended, required such modification of content and transformation of form as "to render them aesthetically incomprehensible."[75]

The Proletcult vision of a new art by and for the workers was attacked by Lev Trotsky (1879–1940) in his book *Literature and Revolution* (1924). The party, says Trotsky, should encourage progressive tendencies in art by commentary or clarification but should not attempt to stimulate or control art. That is the work of the "historic processes of history," to which both party and proletariat only contribute.[76] Automatic condemnation of non-party artists and support of proletarian artists are equally misguided. The transitional nature of present society should be accepted and whatever seems positive and promising should be encouraged whatever its source. Trotsky voices some skepticism about contemporary theatre experimentation such as biomechanics but refrains from condemning it. He suggests that the theatre seek a new realistic revolutionary repertoire, particularly Soviet comedy, which seems particularly appropriate for the transitional society. In the future, when theatre "will emerge out of its four walls and will merge

[73]Meyerhold, "Meyerhold o svoyom *Lese*," *Novy Zritel* 7 (1924): 6; quoted in *Meyerhold on Theatre*, 190.

[74]Gorchakov, *Rezhisserskie uroki K. S. Stanislavskogo* (Moscow, 1951), 390; quoted in Gorchakov, *Theatre*, 433 n.

[75]Herbert Ihering, *Reinhardt, Jessner, Piscator oder Klassikertod?* (Berlin, 1926), and Bernhard Diebold, "Tod der Klassiker," *Frankfurter Zeitung*, July 2, 1929; quoted in Piscator, *Das politische Theater* (Berlin, 1929), 87–89.

[76]Lev Trotsky, *Theatre and Revolution*, trans. anon. (New York, 1957), 218.

with the life of the masses," biomechanics and other such experimentation may be more appropriate.[77]

Trotsky considers the revival of tragedy in the new society more difficult than comedy, since its focus is still unclear. The theme of ancient tragedy was the helplessness of man in the face of nature, expressed as fate. The Renaissance focused upon the individual and individual passion. In Shakespeare this "is carried to such a high degree of tension that it outgrows the individual, becomes super-personal, and is transformed into fate of a certain kind." As the romantics expressed it, character became destiny. The internal contradictions of bourgeois society gradually eroded the dream of individual emancipation, and awakened man to the realization that until he becomes master of his social organization, it "will hang over him as his fate." Thus modern tragedy lies in the conflict between the individual and the collective, or in the conflict between two hostile collectives in the same individual.[78] There seems more of Hegel than of utopian socialism in this, since Trotsky's tragic vision implies a continual becoming and suggests that the ideal socialist state will never be achieved. Even when the average human has risen to the heights of an Aristotle, a Goethe, or a Marx, "above this ridge new peaks will rise."[79]

The sort of tolerance manifested by Lunacharsky toward experimental theatre and by Trotsky toward nonproletarian art was seen less often as the 1920s passed. A much narrower and more politically engaged theory of the theatre was already clearly in evidence at the Fifteenth Congress of the Party in 1927; the Central Committee proved far more responsive than before to demands from leftist literary organizations that the government insist upon a more clearly socialist theatre. A resolution was passed noting that class warfare was "an important factor that must be considered in planning and accomplishing theatre policy." Governmental indifference to theatre offerings had encouraged the appearance of bourgeois ideology, manifested either by a continuation of the "decadent and socially unhealthy phenomena of the pre-Revolutionary theatre" or by the appearance of "new phenomena which directly or indirectly reflect opinions which the Proletariat finds alien and hostile."[80]

After 1927, censorship steadily tightened, and only the best-established authors and directors were able to stretch the bounds of permitted experimentation. One of the last theatrical avant-garde groups

[77]Ibid., 238–39.
[78]Ibid., 242–43.
[79]Ibid., 256.
[80]S. N. Krylov, ed., *Puti razvitiia teatra* (Moscow, 1927), 478; quoted in Gorchakov, *Theatre*, 441 n.

to appear was the Oberiu (from the initials of the Association for Real Art), launched in 1928 against the unpropitious background of Stalin's first five-year plan and the rise to power of the proletarian writers' organizations. Daniil Kharms (c. 1905–1938), the member of the group most interested in the theatre, helped to frame the *Oberiu Manifesto* (1928), which advanced a theory of leftist art quite opposed to that of the writers' societies. Instead of emphasizing realistic subject matter, Oberiu attempted an "organically new concept of life" that would "penetrate into the center of the word, of dramatic action, and of the film frame." Efforts to make art resemble life have falsified both, since art has a logic of its own and, to depict an object from life, must adjust it to fit its own laws. In the theatre, the customary logical sequence of action should be replaced by a "theatrical sequence" (like Eisenstein's "montage"). The dramatic plot should give way to the "scenic plot, which arises spontaneously from all the elements of our spectacle."[81] There should be no attempt to subordinate individual elements; they best advance the scenic plot if they remain autonomous and of equal value. Their conflicts and interrelationships are the basis of theatre. (This concept of the isolation of elements would occur later in Brecht's epic theatre, but in more congenial surroundings.)

Ever since the Revolution, Russia's avant-garde artists had attempted to defend the possibility of a formalist, nonrealistic art that would nevertheless remain concerned with life in general and the new social order in particular. Against this, the proletarian writers and critics insisted upon a realistic approach and a message clear even to the most uneducated audiences. By 1930, when Oberiu disbanded, the battle was essentially over and the triumph of the latter view of theatre complete.

The artistic experiments in European theatre during the opening years of the twentieth century raised only faint echoes in England and America, but after 1914 an important group of American directors, designers, and critics began to champion a number of ideas, derived from European experimentation, under the collective title of the "new stagecraft." Their central critical voice was the journal *Theatre Arts*, founded in 1916 by Sheldon Cheney (b. 1886). A manifesto of the magazine, "What We Stand For," appeared in the final issue of the first volume. It denounced commercialism, naturalism, and the star system, and called for a "new race of artist-directors" who would consider "well-written plays, or inspired acting or pretty settings" not as ends in themselves "but only as contributions to a larger unity, a synthesis or har-

---

[81]Daniil Kharms et al., "The Oberiu Manifesto," trans. George Gibian, in *Russia's Lost Literature of the Absurd* (Ithaca, N.Y., 1971), 194.

mony of all the lesser arts—a newer, truer art *of the theatre*."[82] Theorists like Appia, Craig, Symons, and Evreinov were represented in the magazine's pages, along with their American disciples; the latter were led by Kenneth Macgowan (1888–1963), who joined Cheney as coeditor in 1919, and Robert Edmund Jones (1887–1954), the leading designer of the new movement, who followed Cheney as editor in 1922.

In "The New Path of the Theatre" (1919), Macgowan put forward three ideas upon which he said modern stage art must be based—simplification, suggestion, and synthesis. The first rejected the cluttered stage of realism; the second emphasized the evocative—a single candlestick or Saracenic arch; the last implied "a complex and rhythmic fusion of setting, lights, actors, and play."[83] Jones's concept was rather more mystic. "Notes on the Theatre" (1924), reminiscent of Craig or Yeats, rejected all "explicitness on the stage" along with the "tyranny of the writer, the maker of words." Theatre should rather seek an ecstatic vision of "the immense, brooding, antithetical self of the world, a completion of everyday incompleteness, the unconscious awakening from the dream of life into a perception of living, spiritual reality." It should deal with indications, suggestions, evocations, embodiments "not of character but of passion," with movements "greater than those of human life."[84]

Macgowan and Jones served as codirectors of the Provincetown Players with Eugene O'Neill (1888–1953), in whose scattered theoretical comments as well as in his plays may be seen a similar strong interest in European experimentation. In a program note for Strindberg's *The Ghost Sonata* (1924) at the Provincetown Playhouse, he called Strindberg "the most modern of the moderns" and praised the expressionists for breaking through the restraints of realism to find "some form of 'supernaturalism' " which would "express in the theatre what we comprehend intuitively of that self-defeating self-obsession which is the discount we moderns have to pay for the loan of life."[85] The theatre, he said, should deal not with the relations between man and man but with those between man and God, and with the most basic human quest: to find a meaning for life and a way "to comfort the fears of death."[86] In focusing upon such questions he indeed echoed the concerns of many of the German expressionists and symbolists; like many of them he also became interested in the mask as a device for exploring spiritual states. In "A Dramatist's Notebook" (1933), he advocated the use of the mask

[82]Sheldon Cheney, "What We Stand For," *Theatre Arts* 1 (1917): 149.
[83]Kenneth Macgowan, "The New Path of the Theatre," *Theatre Arts* 3 (1919): 88.
[84]Robert E. Jones, "Notes on the Theatre," *Theatre Arts* 8 (1924): 323–25.
[85]Quoted in Oscar Cargill et al., *O'Neill and His Plays* (New York, 1961), 108.
[86]Ibid., 115.

as a "symbol of inner reality," of "those profound hidden conflicts of the mind which the probings of psychology continue to reveal to us."[87] The theatre of masks would necessarily be a "non-realistic imaginary theatre," a kind of temple "where the religion of a poetical interpretation and symbolical celebration of life" would be communicated to spiritually starved human beings.[88]

For O'Neill, tragedy was the natural consequence of the human condition: existence itself is tragic; anguish, man's penalty for his awareness. Such a view of tragedy, rarely found in the writings of the Renaissance or the seventeenth and eighteenth centuries, gained prominence in the theories of Schopenhauer, Kierkegaard, and Nietzsche. "Man, by the very fact of being man, of possessing consciousness," suggested the Spanish philosopher Miguel de Unamuno (1864–1936), "is a diseased animal." The realization that man's only existence is in consciousness and that this consciousness is the merest fleeting phenomenon gives rise to what Unamuno called "the tragic sense of life," which may be possessed by individuals or whole people, but which will inevitably confront all who think deeply about human existence.[89] Much of the twentieth-century speculation concerning tragedy takes a similar view of the close relationship between consciousness and the "tragic sense of life."

In his book *The Drama and the Stage* (1922), the American critic Ludwig Lewisohn (1882–1955) also saw tragedy as the expression of the inevitable suffering of humanity, but his focus was more utilitarian than metaphysical. The war, he hoped, had buried forever the old ideas of guilt and vengeance, based upon human interpretation of absolute moral standards. Modern tragedy must seek to "understand our failures and our sorrows"; its pity will be pity "for our common fate," its terror "a terror lest we wrong our brother or violate his will," and its reconciliation "a profound sense of the community of human suffering."[90] In order to accomplish this most fully, drama should strive always to expand its audience, allying itself with human progress and seeking to bring "the gravest and most stirring of the arts" to an ever-increasing number of people.[91]

Lewisohn's major rival, George Jean Nathan (1882–1958), completely rejected this democratic view of tragedy in *The Critic and the Drama* (1922). In his opinion, tragedy, like all great art, appeals only to the

[87]Ibid., 116–17.
[88]Ibid., 120–21.
[89]Miguel de Unamuno, *The Tragic Sense of Life*, trans. J. E. Crawford Flitch (London, 1926), 17–18.
[90]Ludwig Lewisohn, *Drama and the Stage* (New York, 1922), 23.
[91]Ibid., 15.

"reflection, sympathy, wisdom, gallant gentleness, experience" of the spiritually superior minority. To them it brings a "wistful sadness" at the spectacle of "what they might, yet alas cannot be." The critic who seeks to make such special insight relevant to the masses risks ending, like Sarcey, by considering the worth of drama only in its effect on the crowd. For the crowd, however, no higher vision is likely, at best only a "mystical and awe-struck" experience which should not "make them glad they are alive, but rather speculate why they are permitted to be alive at all."[92]

W. M. Dixon's (1866–1946) book *Tragedy* (1924) took, like Lewisohn, a democratic view of the genre but considered its effect much more uplifting. Dixon thought the "pessimistic" theories of critics like Nietzsche and Schopenhauer ingenious but misdirected. The aim of tragedy, he says, is not to document the hopelessness of the human condition but to show how "great and astonishing" is the world of which man is a part. Tragedy encourages us to expand our imagination toward infinity, toward "greater intelligences and wider purposes" than our own. This vision, reinforced by the "order and beauty" of the poet's expression, makes the experience of tragedy ultimately a joyful one.[93] Modern drama, Dixon warns, risks losing this joy "by its secularization, by its self-imposed limitation" in shifting from cosmic to social and psychological concerns.[94]

I. A. Richards (1893–1979) also discussed the effect of tragedy in his extremely influential *Principles of Literary Criticism* (1924), but his approach was distinctly more scientific in orientation. Richards was interested in applying the new insights offered by psychology to the experience of art. In terms reminiscent of Coleridge, he suggested that the effective work of art organizes and balances emotional responses, and that the most powerful art deals with the balance of opposing emotions. The catharsis of tragedy arises from just such an opposition. "Pity, the impulse to approach, and Terror, the impulse to retreat, are brought in Tragedy to a reconciliation which they find nowhere else, and with them who knows what other allied groups of equally discordant impulses."[95] The best tragedies (few in number, according to Richards) are among the highest experiences man has discovered. All psychological suppressions and sublimations are here cast aside, and in confronting impulses otherwise avoided, tragedy harmonizes and creates joy from them. It does not teach that "all's right with the world"

[92]George Jean Nathan, *The Critic and the Drama* (New York, 1922), 31–32.
[93]W. M. Dixon, *Tragedy* (New York, 1924), 225–28.
[94]Ibid., 68–71.
[95]I. A. Richards, *Principles of Literary Criticism* (London, 1934), 245.

or that somehow, somewhere, justice will triumph, but rather that "all is right here and now in the nervous system."[96]

Two further statements on tragedy, both appearing in 1927, found Richards's emphasis on the balance of psychological forces quite unacceptable. Gilbert Murray, in *The Classical Tradition in Poetry*, continued to champion the vibrations of ancient myth within the work as the primary source of tragic pleasure, reinforced by "beauty of form in the execution."[97] It is true that we are both drawn toward the tragic hero as a "savior and champion" and repulsed by "his sins and pollutions, and their awful expiation," but catharsis expresses much more than the balance of these impulses. According to ancient myth and ritual, "the sins he expiates are really ours," and in our deepest being we recognize that his atonement and sacrifice reestablishes our own harmony with the universe.[98]

F. L. Lucas (1894–1967) attempted in *Tragedy* to rid Aristotelian criticism of its modern encrustations, among them the speculations of modern psychological criticism. The attraction of tragedy, says Lucas, arises from curiosity, the fascination of life itself and the joy of emotional experience. We go to tragedies not "to get rid of emotions, but to have them more abundantly; to banquet, not to purge."[99] Thus tragedy must show us something that strikes us as both significant and true to life. Its pleasure comes not from emotional balance or a lesson learned but from the broader experience it gives us of the human condition, "the truth with which it is seen and the fineness with which it is communicated."[100]

In all these considerations of tragedy, questions of presentation rarely arise, though Lucas does devote a chapter to "Diction and Spectacle," apparently in deference to Aristotle. He deplores the modern tendency to emphasize visual elements at the expense of the text and suggests that the theatre "needs an audience, not spectators"; "those whose only sense is visual should have elsewhere to go."[101] Lucas does not go so far as Lamb in rejecting performance, but he would always insist on the ear being favored over the eye.

Despite their disagreements on the precise workings of tragedy, English and American theorists of this period still generally felt confidence in the contemporary relevance of the genre itself—a belief that its observations on moral order, on the human condition, on guilt and

---

[96]Ibid., 246.
[97]Gilbert Murray, *The Classical Tradition in Poetry* (Cambridge, 1927), 67.
[98]Ibid., 68.
[99]F. L. Lucas, *Tragedy* (London, 1957), 73.
[100]Ibid., 78.
[101]Ibid., 166.

atonement were still operative for modern man. In Germany, the attitude toward the genre, marked by the pessimistic social theorists at the turn of the century, was much more problematic. Walter Benjamin (1892–1940), in his evocative and mystic *Ursprung des deutschen Trauerspiels* (1928), developed in his own manner the suggestion of Lukács that modern alienation and the loss of a metaphysical center has removed the basis for tragic insight. A distinction must be made, says Benjamin, between the tragedy of classic Greece and the modern "Trauerspiel" (an alternate German word for tragedy; literally, "mourning play"), which he considers a development of the consciousness of the baroque period. Though critics have attempted to conflate tragedy and *Trauerspiel*, Benjamin calls them radically different genres, based on different foundations and seeking different effects. Other conflations that he specifically rejects include the attempt of the naturalist theorists to substitute natural causation for Greek tragic fate and Scheler's conflict of levels between hero and environment, which totally ignored "the unique Greek form of such conflicts."[102]

Following Lukács, Benjamin posits history as the basis of the modern *Trauerspiel* and myth as that of Greek tragedy. The Greek tragic hero was a sacrifice of a unique type, looking in two directions: back toward the ancient laws of the gods, and forward to a new community and nation. The sacrifice was at the same time an atonement in the traditional sense, an exposure of the inadequacies of the Olympian system, and the first representative action of a new consciousness, given for a people not yet aware of its importance. This last suggests the tragic theory of Hölderlin, but Hölderlin posited a preexisting order to which the hero directed the attention of humanity. Benjamin's hero is much more clearly existentialist, and Benjamin approvingly quotes Lukács: "The essence of these great moments is the pure experience of self."[103]

Particularly helpful to Benjamin in developing his concept of tragedy were the comments of the Jewish philosopher Franz Rosenzweig (1886–1929) in *Der Stern der Erlösung* (1921). Rosenzweig considers the classic hero in the first section of his book, which deals with the isolation and independence in classic antiquity of the three Kantian elements of existence—God, World, and Man: God was aloof from this world; the World contained its own Logos; and Man was isolated within the self. The Greek tragic hero was an embodiment of this isolation: "By keeping silent, he breaks down the bridges which connect him to God and the World, elevates himself above the realm of personality, which defines

---

[102]Walter Benjamin, *The Origin of German Tragic Drama*, trans. John Osborne (London, 1977), 101, 106.
[103]Georg Lukács, *Soul and Form*, trans. Anna Bostock (Cambridge, Mass., 1970), 156.

itself and sets itself apart from others through speech, into the icy solitude of the self."[104] In the second part of his book, Rosenzweig considers the "paths" that overcome the isolation of God, Man, and World: Creation, Revelation, and Redemption. In the section on Redemption, the path that unites man with his neighbor and with the world, he contrasts modern and classic tragedy. The modern hero is not isolated from the world but "is tossed to and fro" in it, "wholly receptive, wholly alive and full of undisguised fear of the open grave."[105] He is no neutral, abstract self but an individual unique personality with limited awareness, seeking to gain consciousness both of self and the world. His goals and concerns are quite opposite to those of the Greek tragic hero. Instead of taking refuge in silence and the self, he commits himself to the world in language and action, striving at last to unite himself with the absolute Other. The ultimate, never realized aim of the modern tragic hero is sainthood.[106]

For Benjamin, whose focus is not upon redemption but upon the baroque fascination with lamentation, worldly suffering, and death, Rosenzweig's saint is primarily a martyr, one persona of the baroque tragic hero, the other being the absolute sovereign who often combines the roles of tyrant and victim. He is embedded in the world, in history, in the domain of speech and action, but Benjamin stresses the process, the suffering, rather than Rosenzweig's goal, the reconciliation. Thus, in terms of man and the universe, Benjamin essentially reverses the schema of Rosenzweig. Classic tragedy depicts a "cosmic achievement," while the modern *Trauerspiel* is enacted in "an inner world of feeling" that separates human existence and mortality from any transcendental meaning.[107] In such drama the symbol, which could suggest transcendence, is replaced by the allegory, the device of mortality. "What allegories are, in the realm of thoughts, ruins are in the realm of things": they are indicative of the corruption of existence and signposts on the road to death, which is the only door to possible meaning but is inaccessible to the world of drama.[108]

The sense of living in a world in decline, so widespread in early twentieth-century Germany (Oswald Spengler's [1880–1936] *Der Untergang des Abendlands*, in 1918, falls between the early writings of Lukács and Benjamin on tragedy), appears in American theory in Joseph Wood Krutch's (1893–1970) *The Modern Temper* (1929). Its chapter entitled "The Tragic Fallacy" argues that tragedy is no longer possible, since

[104]Franz Rosenzweig, *Der Stern der Erlösung*, 2 vols. (Frankfurt, 1921), 1:103.
[105]Ibid., 2:157.
[106]Ibid., 156.
[107]Benjamin, *Origin*, 119.
[108]Ibid., 178.

man has lost the conviction that his actions are significant. In "the universe as we see it both the Glory of God and the Glory of man have departed," and with them tragedy, which conquered pain and despair by an intimation of higher order and harmony.[109] The universe can now offer instead only pathos or farce. We may still read tragedies, thanks to a sort of nostalgia, but we can no longer write them; in time, even the faint echo of consolation offered by reading them will probably disappear. This argument, as we shall see, stimulated a lively debate over the possibility of tragedy among American theorists during the following decade.

Another controversy, that dealing with the "theatricality" of theatre and the importance of performance to the dramatic script, which was carried on with such vigor between Spingarn and Matthews in the early years of the century, continued to be a focus of critical attention. During this period the debate frequently centered on the function of the actor—whether acting should be regarded essentially as a creative art or merely as a medium (as transparent as possible) for the creative work of the dramatist. Spingarn, relying upon the early writings of Croce, considered the actor merely one of the externalizations of dramatic art and thus of little aesthetic concern; his view was echoed by Nathan, who rejected any claims of acting to be an art, since even the best actor creates nothing but remains "simply an adaptable tool in the hands of the dramatist," lacking either originality or independence.[110] Lewisohn took a position closer to that of Matthews, insisting that the actor remain faithful to the author's original vision but, with that proviso, allowing him a significant share of the creation of the dramatic work. He must "grasp the poet's intention" and, with the aid of "imaginative observation" and "personal plasticity," mold himself into the being "which the poet and he have combined to fashion."[111]

Croce, in the meantime, had shifted somewhat away from the total dismissal of performance that had so influenced Spingarn. In *Ariosto, Shakespeare e Corneille* (1919), he does dismiss stage interpretations as guides to the meaning of the original text—not on the grounds that they are irrelevant externalizations, however, but because they necessarily transform the original into a new work of art. Since actors always bring to the work "their own particular manner of feeling," their performance relates to the original in the same manner as do music and paintings inspired by the plays, "which are music and painting, and not those plays."[112]

[109]Joseph Wood Krutch, *The Modern Temper* (New York, 1929), 141.
[110]Nathan, *Critic*, 91.
[111]Lewisohn, *Drama*, 42.
[112]Benedetto Croce, *Ariosto, Shakespeare and Corneille*, trans. Douglas Ainslie (New York, 1920), 330.

This idea required a greater separation between text and performance than most theorists were willing to accept, and other critical writings in Italy soon stimulated Croce himself to modify his position. The theatre historian Silvio D'Amico (1887–1955) in his book *Maschere* (1921) insisted, like Brander Matthews, that drama is always "created presupposing ideally, if not always materially, a scenic integration" and must be analyzed in those terms.[113] A brilliant young critic, Piero Gobetti (1901–1926), responded in Crocean terms, in his article "L'interpretazione" (1921), that D'Amico had confused the work of the actor with the work of the poet. He likens the actor to the critic, whose work can and should be judged on the basis of the artistic integration and expression of personal feelings; these feelings, however, are stimulated not directly by nature but by a preexisting poetic work. "The work of the poet should be judged as the work of the poet, and the work of the actor as the work of the actor."[114] Flaws in the poetic work must not be allowed to condition judgment of the actor's achievement, while the text must be considered complete in itself, and inadequacies in it must not be tolerated on the grounds that they might disappear in performance; on that basis, no dramatic work could ever be judged a failure, because the proper presentation of it might always occur sometime in the future.

Croce, in his *Conversazioni critiche* (1931), praised Gobetti's response to the "vulgar and common theory" that "a work composed for the theatre can be judged only with reference to the theatre."[115] He did not, however, approve of the parallel Gobetti drew between critic and actor, since he felt that performance cannot illuminate a text as criticism can. He preferred to view the actor as a translator, attempting—with inevitable loss—to express the text in another language, to make it accessible in some measure "to those who cannot or do not know how to read it; to make it more readily and easily apprehended in days and hours of diversion and relaxation, to underline certain parts for better understanding, etc."[116] Croce continued to espouse this "translation" theory until near the end of his life, though his final writings suggest a willingness to consider the art of the theatre as something more independent and holistic. "Diction, gesture, and scenery become one in the performance," he wrote in *Terze pagine sparse* (1948), "a single act of artistic creation in which they cannot be separated."[117]

Luigi Pirandello's (1867–1936) most extended and best-known crit-

---

[113]Quoted in Piero Gobetti, *Opere complete*, 3 vols. (Turin, 1969–74), 3:10.
[114]Ibid., 12.
[115]Croce, *Conversazioni critiche*, 5 vols. (Bari, 1924–39), 3:71.
[116]Ibid., 72.
[117]Croce, *Terze pagine sparse*, 2 vols. (Bari, 1955), 2:267.

ical essay, "L'Umorismo" (1908), was primarily a refutation of the Crocean assertion that humor, like the comic and the tragic, is essentially undefinable, that there is no such thing as humor in the abstract but only individual humorous works. Pirandello's response, analyzing humor as a juxtaposition of contraries, deals with a number of general aesthetic concerns but not with the theatre as such. Its challenge to Croce sparked a lifelong antagonism between the two men, but in critical essays that did concern the theatre, Pirandello took positions distinctly more in harmony with Croce.

The most important of these are "Teatro e letteratura" (1918) and "Teatro nuovo e teatro vecchio" (1922). The statement in the latter, that every complete work creates a world "unique in itself, and beyond comparison" which is "simply 'that which it is' in itself and for itself eternally,"[118] is quite Crocean—as is the related warning that critics who insist upon applying previous standards to new works will inevitably misunderstand them. "Teatro e letteratura," as the title suggests, considers the tension between text and performance, and here again Pirandello essentially echoes Croce. He considers the written text the completed artistic form; what is seen in the theatre is only a "scenic translation" of it: "So many actors, so many translations, more or less faithful, more or less fortunate, but like any translation, always and necessarily inferior to the original."[119] Those authors who insist that they write for the theatre and not for literature thus write "for the translation" incomplete works like the scenarii of the commedia dell'arte, and have little claim to the title of creative artist.[120]

A similar position is implied if not directly expressed by T. S. Eliot (1888–1965) in his famous passage on the "objective correlative" in *Hamlet* (1919). Taking the expression of emotion as a central function of art, Eliot suggests that the artist seeks "a set of objects, a situation, a chain of events which shall be the formula of that *particular* emotion" and which shall inevitably arouse it when read or performed. The sense of artistic "inevitability" that Eliot describes could arise from a combination of text plus performance, but clearly Eliot himself sees it embedded in the text alone. "If you examine any of Shakespeare's most successful tragedies, you will find this exact equivalence."[121] Both word and action have been determined by the poet to achieve a precise and calculated emotional response.

Lorenz Kjerbüll-Peterson (b. 1891), director of the Mannheim the-

---

[118]Luigi Pirandello, "The New Theatre and the Old," trans. Herbert Goldstone, in H. M. Block and Herman Salinger, *The Creative Vision* (New York, 1960), 127.
[119]Pirandello, "Theatre and Literature," in ibid., 111.
[120]Ibid., 112.
[121]T. S. Eliot, *Selected Prose* (New York, 1975), 48.

atre in Germany, also focused on the emotional response of the audience, but his book *Psychology of Acting* (1925) is really concerned only with how the play works in the theatre. All art, he suggests, is characterized by "aesthetic illusion" of "conscious self-deception"—Coleridge's "willing suspension of disbelief." For any work to stimulate this paradoxical response, it must contain both illusion-fostering and illusion-hindering elements, encouraging the receiver's consciousness to vacillate constantly between the two. The theatre audience presents a particular problem, since it is essentially a psychological mob; as such, it has a tendency to abandon itself to emotion and lose the balance essential to art. The theatre must employ many elements to prevent this loss—the curtain, the proscenium frame, the use of programs, and so on—but the most important device for audience control is the living actor, who must be constantly aware of and adjusting the shifting balance. Since no actor ever completely embodies a role, he challenges the spectator to complete the "mystic unity of person and character" which is one of the "principal charms of the theatre."[122]

It is the responsibility of the actor, however, to encourage this process in his particular audience, a kind of translation that Kjerbüll-Peterson sees as far more profound and demanding than merely making a text visual. The great actor will "represent the spirit of the epoch intensified";[123] he will study how to touch the particular concerns of his audience, echo their fears and hopes, and, recognizing the constant variability of a mob, "constantly observe his audience in order to react to their slightest movements at the proper time in the appropriate manner."[124] The ability to fine-tune the balance of illusion is the source of the unique power of the theatre.

The American critic most associated with the concept of theatre as translation is Stark Young (1881–1963), whose book *The Theatre* (1927) devotes a central chapter to this idea. Young totally rejects the Croce-Pirandello assertion that translations are necessarily inferior. Theatre is a re-creation in its own terms of a text, just as the text is a re-creation in its own terms of the raw material of life. The success of either re-creation depends more on the ability of the artist than on the quality of the material used. A performance may thus be either inferior or superior to its primary text, but that text must in any case acknowledge the needs of the theatre. Young's definition of a play puts him squarely in the Matthews camp: "a piece of literature about a section of life

[122]Lorenz Kjerbüll-Peterson, *Psychology of Acting*, trans. Sarah T. Barrows (Boston, 1935), 75–76.
[123]Ibid., 114.
[124]Ibid., 123.

written in such a way that it will go over the footlights, in such a way that what it has to say it can say in the theatre."[125]

Further support for this position was provided by two of the most widely read English critics and directors of the period: Ashley Dukes (1885–1959) and Harley Granville-Barker (1877–1946). In "Dramatist and Theatre" (1924), one of the many articles he contributed to *Theatre Arts*, Dukes calls for an end to the reign of the "Napoleonic dramatist" who seeks to crush actors and directors "under a dead weight of rigid conception," as do Shaw and the recent realists.[126] As a better model, he urges Shakespeare, who "created work of a plastic quality that can be handled and moulded by his fellow craftsmen," who wrote "not to dictate, but to contribute; not to impose, but to collaborate," finding his true freedom as an artist in the renunciation of total authority.[127]

Granville-Barker's *On Dramatic Method* (1931) discusses the same idea in more detail. The dramatist must view the actor not as interpreter but as collaborator, and his central problem is how best to provide for this collaboration. The few great dramatists have achieved a workable balance between two opposed concerns: "The character as it leaves the dramatist's hands has to be re-created in terms of the actor's personality; and the problem for the dramatist is how to write it so that he may prevent it—*his* character—from perishing in the process."[128] Like an iceberg, the written text is eight-tenths submerged, and the hidden depths are revealed only in the theatre. The dramatist must fashion those hidden parts, which will be revealed by acting and all the other aspects of production, in a way that will fulfill his own vision while inspiring original creative work in others. The illuminating *Prefaces to Shakespeare* (1927) explore how Shakespeare worked to achieve this double goal. Granville-Barker admits that a dramatist may envision something too great for the "imperfect medium" of the human actor to convey, but this does not lead him, like Lamb, to despair of the theatre. "Set the actor impossible tasks and he will do better by them than the possible ones; let him be himself to the utmost, he will the better be Hamlet or Lear."[129]

The position taken by Jacques Copeau and his followers in France was close to that argued by Granville-Barker. Copeau, as we have seeen, always recognized the primacy of the text but at the same time felt that the text must stimulate, even demand, theatricalization. A more extended consideration of this process than Copeau ever developed was

[125]Stark Young, *The Theatre* (New York, 1954), 48.
[126]Ashley Dukes, "Dramatist and Theatre," *Theatre Arts* 8 (1924): 687.
[127]Ibid., 685.
[128]Harley Granville-Barker, *On Dramatic Method* (New York, 1956), 29.
[129]Ibid., 36.

offered by his friend, the playwright Henri Ghéon (1875–1944), in a series of lectures given at Copeau's theatre, the Vieux Colombier, in 1923 and published as *L'art du théâtre*. Ghéon dismisses the "total theatre" concept of Wagner as a complex balance of elements difficult if not impossible to achieve; he concentrates upon the traditional drama, which recognizes the text as primary. This does not mean that the text is complete in itself; the play written only to be read is an "essentially falsifying makeshift."[130] The dramatist must create "a dream that is realizable, viable, playable, and, if I may coin a pretty poor word, 'exteriorizable.' " His words must call forth "image, gesture, movement, action, life," but not with such "implacable precision" as to leave "no room for the actor's imagination."[131] He must provide a range of possibilities among which an actor may choose, a series of pregnant hints, of stimulating fragments for the actor to make complete. There must also be an audience receptive to the author's vision, one that stands "on the same intellectual and moral ground" as author and actor. Only a truly organic society can have a true theatre.

Louis Jouvet (1887–1951), Copeau's clearest successor, echoes Copeau's distaste of theory—"abominable in itself, a system of damnation, a condemnation, a sterilization of the spirit"[132]—and insisted that a man of the theatre must work "by intuition and never by system."[133] Still, his articles and his book *Réflexions du comédien* (1938) outline his own theory of the drama, one closely in harmony with Copeau. Jouvet deplores realism, since the theatre should always appeal to the spirit and display more than the ear can hear or the eye can see in everyday life. The future theatre should "elevate the rights of the spiritual over those of the material, the word over the action, the text over the spectacle."[134] The work of the author must always be taken as the basis of performance; the author is his link with the audience and the director his servant. The director must "find the tone, the climate, the state of soul which ruled the poet at the conception" and seek to call up that "living and fluid source" in an audience the author may have known nothing about.[135]

In 1927, Jouvet, with Georges Pitoëff (1884–1939), Charles Dullin (1885–1949), and Gaston Baty (1882–1951), formed an association, the Cartel des Quatre, which dominated the French stage of the 1930s. In their theoretical statements Pitoëff and Dullin, like Jouvet, generally

---

[130]Henri Ghéon, *The Art of the Theatre*, trans. Adele M. Fiske (New York, 1961), 8.
[131]Ibid., 9.
[132]Louis Jouvet, *Témoignages sur le théâtre* (Paris, 1951), 191.
[133]Ibid., 85.
[134]Ibid., 14.
[135]Ibid., 190.

follow in the footsteps of Copeau, disclaiming any system but agreeing on the centrality of the text and on a search for a spiritual and non-naturalistic approach to staging. The most beautiful theatre in the world, says Dullin, would draw its beauty "from the constant elevation of the spirit which it seeks and not from the display of useless luxury."[136] And, says Pitoëff, "It is better to sacrifice the entire decorative side than to sacrifice the word";[137] he calls for a presentation more concerned "with deeper significance than with external appearances."[138]

Only one member of the Cartel des Quatre departed sharply from the general theoretical position established by Copeau. This was Gaston Baty, who expressed no reservations concerning theoretical speculation about theatre; in two books, *Le masque et l'encensoir* (1926) and *Rideau baissé* (1949), and in numerous articles he developed an aesthetic at variance with the Copeau tradition. He did accept the text as a crucial element but compared its role in the theatre to that of the word in life. The word's domain is immense, since it includes "all intelligence, everything a man can understand and formulate," but beyond the word lies experience inaccessible to rational analysis. If the theatre wishes to present "an integral vision of the world," it must use plastic expression, color, light, music, gesture, and so on, to evoke the world beyond the word and the text.[139]

Le masque et l'encensoir begins with an argument for the common origin of theatre and religion, both of which seek by combinations of literary and plastic elements to engage both the intellectual and spiritual parts of man; in all of his writings Baty stresses that man's spiritual side must be addressed in drama and that it is the nontextual aspects of the art which do this. Baty thus champions the Wagnerian idea of a total work of art in which "painting, sculpture, dance, literature, and music" are "united, ordered, their means harmonized and each exalted."[140] Accused of rejecting the text in favor of "theatrical" values, Baty replied in an article (1923) that the director must submit always to two laws: "obedience to the text," and "rejection of anything nonessential." Nevertheless, he must add to the text whatever it lacks. "If nothing more than a translation of literature is sought, we should content ourselves with literature."[141] In the staging, all nontextual elements should

[136]Charles Dullin, *Souvenirs* (Paris, 1946), 71–72.
[137]Georges Pitoëff, *Notre théâtre* (Paris, 1949), 37.
[138]Ibid., 15.
[139]Gaston Baty, *Rideau baissé* (Paris, 1949), 219.
[140]Ibid., 79.
[141]Baty, "Réponse à l'enquête de Xavier de Courville sur le théâtre et la mise en scène," *Revue critique des idées et des lettres*, August 25, 1923.

be given equal weight; setting and lighting should be recognized as elements as significant as acting.

Soon after his arrival in Paris, Baty organized Les Compagnons de la Chimère, a group of actors, designers, dancers, and musicians with a vision of theatre similar to his own. Early in 1922 they began to issue the *Bulletin de la Chimère*, to which Baty was a regular contributor. Soon the group was joined by authors with similar interests, headed by Jean-Jacques Bernard (1888–1972) and Denys Amiel (1884–1971), who became the leading theorists of what was called the "théâtre du silence" (theatre of silence), although Bernard preferred the term "théâtre de l'inexprimé" (theatre of the unexpressed). In the fifth number of the *Bulletin* (1922) Bernard's "Le silence au théâtre" stated that the theatre has no worse enemy than literature, which "expresses and dilutes what should only be suggested." In terms reminiscent of Maeterlinck, he called attention to the "submerged dialogue beneath the heard dialogue" and desired "the revelation of the deepest feelings" not by "the replies themselves but by the shock of the replies."[142]

In the *Bulletin*'s seventh number (1923), Amiel suggested a theatre "based almost entirely on the use of silence with words occurring at intervals like echoes ... serving as a kind of synoptic center around which the action may develop."[143] The preface to Amiel's collected works (1925) compares looking into a theatre text with looking into an aquarium, "seeing through the transparency all that silent world below, descending, moving about, now and then touching the surface." He tries to show how people "sitting peaceably, speaking calmly, using the gestures of polite society" might be torn in their hearts by "envy, jealousy, the passions of the ancestral beast."[144]

Apparently, the unexpressed world of Bernard and Amiel was not the mystic realm of Maeterlinck but something much more akin to the discoveries of psychoanalysis. Bernard in 1930 indeed called Maeterlinck a precursor of his concerns but condemned precisely Maeterlinck's lack of psychological specificity: "The allusive language, instead of enlightening the spectator concerning the emotions of the characters, seems to hide them. Or sometimes one has the impression that there is nothing behind the allusive language; that it is employed for its own sake."[145] The Freudian subconscious thus becomes a tool for giving sharper definition to the mystic realm of the symbolists.

[142]Jean-Jacques Bernard, "Le silence au théâtre," *Bulletin de la Chimère* 5 (May 1922): 67.
[143]Denys Amiel, "Silence," *Bulletin de la Chimère* 7 (Apr. 1923): 65.
[144]Amiel, *Théâtre* (Paris, 1925): i.
[145]Bernard, *Témoignages* (Paris, 1933), 27.

19

The Twentieth Century, 1930–1950

THE 1930S, A PIVOTAL DECADE IN MODERN DRAMATIC THEORY, saw the appearance of the major theoretical works of three of the most influential theorists of the century—Brecht, Artaud, and Stanislavski. Stanislavski's reputation was already well established before this period, of course, and a certain amount of critical material on his system had appeared in Russia before 1930. Yet Stanislavski himself wrote little on his life or work until near the end of his career, and the western European and American audiences who were dazzled by the Moscow Art Theatre tours in 1923 were given only tantalizing hints of the means by which Stanislavski achieved such brilliant results. A former student at the Moscow Art Theatre, Richard Boleslavsky (1879–1937), took advantage of the enthusiasm generated by the tours to launch a school of acting in the fall of 1923; in November *Theatre Arts* published the first of his six "lessons" on acting which, collected in 1933, served for many years as the basic introduction for most American actors to certain strategies of the Russian approach.

Stanislavski's *My Life in Art* was begun in America during the 1923 tour, dedicated to America, and first published in English translation. It offered some hints about the development of the famous system but little in the way of specific theory or technique. A few more hints appeared in his brief article, "Direction and Acting," written for the Encyclopaedia Britannica of 1929. Here Stanislavski emphasized the sense of truth and the importance of emotional memory (both also stressed by Boleslavsky) and mentioned such concepts as the "unbroken line" and the "super-objective" in a manner more tantalizing than illuminating.

In France in 1930, Stanislavski at last—at the urging of his American friends Norman (1868–1937) and Elizabeth Hapgood (b. 1874)—out-

376

lined four books that would summarize his lifetime of research into the art of acting and to which *My Life in Art* would serve as a kind of preface. The production of this major work proceeded slowly, and it was not until 1936 that the first volume, translated by Elizabeth Hapgood, appeared in America as *An Actor Prepares*. A somewhat larger version was published in Russia two years later.

Even without the stimulus of *An Actor Prepares*, interest in Russian theatre grew steadily in America during the early 1930s, doubtless reinforced by the general interest in Soviet culture shown by American artists as part of the heightened social consciousness that marked the Depression years. Something of the orientation of the period is suggested by the fact that the first history of the Theatre Guild, written by Walter Eaton (1878–1957) in 1929, describes the organization of that by no means leftist group entirely in Russian terms. Its board of directors is characterized as a "revolutionary theatrical soviet" challenging "the dictum that the theatre must always have a czar."[1]

The Group Theatre, founded in 1931, was an offshoot of the Theatre Guild with a distinctly more political orientation; it relied heavily on the Russian theatre experiments for inspiration. Lee Strasberg (1901–1982), in charge of actor training for the Group, had several early speeches of Stanislavski to his students translated, along with Vakhtangov's "Preparing for the Role," which became a central document for Strasberg. The actor must work, says this essay, for "scenic faith," which shows "toward the circumstances suggested in the play an attitude as serious as though they really existed." In order to achieve this attitude, the actor must draw upon himself; whatever he does must be organic to him—to his nerves, his blood, his thoughts. It is essential "to live your own temperament on the stage and not the supposed temperament of the character. You must proceed from yourself and not from a conceived image."[2] Only by going beyond believing, to actually living the role, can an actor avoid all convention and cliché.

Harold Clurman (b. 1901), one of the founders, suggested the Group's orientation in "What the Group Theatre Wants" (1931). A good play meant not one which aspired "to some literary standard of 'art' or 'beauty' " but one which presented contemporary social or moral problems in the belief "that to all of them there may be some answer."[3] Such social concern was widespread in the theatre of the 1930s, but both then and later there was confusion about precisely what theory of the theatre the Group represented. Clurman tells in his memoirs,

[1] Walter Eaton, *The Theatre Guild: The First Ten Years* (New York, 1929), 6, 8.
[2] Trans. B. E. Zakhava, in Toby Cole, *Acting: A Handbook of the Stanislavski Method* (New York, 1947), 120.
[3] *Playbill*, Mansfield Theatre, Dec. 10, 1931, 4–5.

The Fervent Years, how he and Strasberg were invited at this period to a symposium on "Revolution and the Theatre" at the John Reed Club and introduced as "middle-of-the-roaders" compared with the Right of the Theatre Guild and the Left of recently organized workers' groups.[4] Though Clurman resisted such pigeonholing, it was not an inaccurate assessment of the Group Theatre's image. Its unwillingness to embrace either the politics or the practices of such leading leftist groups as the Prolet-Bühne (developed within the German Workers Club) or the Workers' Laboratory Theatre (associated with the Workers International) naturally made it appear suspiciously conservative to those groups; at the same time, its social engagement and generally leftist orientation in theory exposed it to charges of Bolshevism from conservatives. A middle-of-the-road position was difficult to maintain in the 1930s, which—like the 1960s—tended to polarize positions. The article "A Theatre Is Born" (1931) by Hallie Flanagan (1890–1969), future director of the Federal Theatre Project, suggested the dynamic: "There are only two theatres in the country today that are clear as to aim: one is the commercial theatre which wants to make money; the other is the workers' theatre which wants to make a new social order."[5]

Theatre Arts, though favorably inclined toward the new workers' theatres, was insufficiently committed to political questions to serve as an organ for this new consciousness, and a major rival appeared in 1933: *New Theatre* evolved from *Workers' Theatre*, which had been founded in 1931 to coordinate the efforts of proletarian stages across the nation. Under both titles the journal denounced the capitalistic view of drama as a search for beauty and called it instead a weapon in man's struggle for justice. The influence of Marxist dramatic theory was clear from the first issue, which urged workers to familiarize themselves with the arts of the stage for use in supporting their struggles, and to seek behind the "dry enumerations of names, dates, and the like" in capitalist histories of the stage "the social and economic conditions that give rise to each particular form."[6] The change to a more general title marked a change from almost exclusive preoccupation with proletarian theatre to the application of socialist principles in all aspects of contemporary theatre. Among the contributing editors to the reorganized journal were Hallie Flanagan, Lee Strasberg, Mordecai Gorelik (leading designer of the Group Theatre), and dramatist John Howard Lawson.

Not surprisingly, *New Theatre* reflected, along with its political concerns, the Group Theatre's interest in Russian acting theory. In the

---

[4]Harold Clurman, *The Fervent Years* (New York, 1957), 60.
[5]Hallie Flanagan, "A Theatre Is Born," *Theatre Arts* 15 (1931):915.
[6]*Workers Theatre* 1 (April 1931); quoted in *Theatre Arts* 15 (1931): 911.

first issue appeared a group of acting notes written by Mikhail Chekhov (1865–1936) in 1922 while working at the Moscow Art Theatre's First Studio.[7] These, emphasizing the actor's internal work—concentration, imagination, scenic faith, and so on—harmonized closely with Boleslavsky and Vakhtangov.

This same year, however, Stella Adler (b. 1902) studied with Stanislavski in Paris and returned with a conflicting idea of the Russian system, one which put much less stress on personal experience and more on imagination and study of the text. Strasberg in particular resisted this new interpretation, and the long-awaited publication of *An Actor Prepares* in 1936 seemed to confirm Strasberg's position, particularly since Stanislavski's projected subsequent volumes were left incomplete at his death.

During the 1930s and 1940s, the period of Stanislavski's greatest influence in America, his system was known primarily through the partial perspective offered by *An Actor Prepares*. The emphasis of this book is on developing inner resources and on freeing the mind and body to respond to the demands of a script. Stanislavski returns to the "magic if" of *My Life in Art* as a device for stimulating imagination, supported by an actor's faith in his creation and enriched by his memories of personal emotions. He calls for a consistent guiding purpose throughout the play, the "super-objective," which has the power to "draw all of an actor's creative faculties and to absorb all the details and smaller units of a play or plot." While breaking the play into small coherent units, each with its own goal, the actor must never lose sight of this overriding aim. Coherently ordered, the smaller units will create a "through-line of action," uniting all of the actor's inner work and subordinating it to the super-objective. Stanislavski calls these three concepts—inner grasp, super-objective, and through-line of action—the most important features of the actor's creative process.[8]

The second book on his system, edited from several drafts, appeared in English as *Building a Character* in 1949. Chapters on such subjects as making the body expressive, diction, and tempo-rhythm in speech demonstrated clearly that Stanislavski had by no means ignored external technique in his interest in inner exploration. Indeed, transcriptions from his later rehearsals and the publication (1961) of some of his last notes in *Creating a Role* all suggest that by 1930 Stanislavski had evolved away from an emphasis on the inner life as the source for a role to one on study of the text and its required physical actions as a means of

[7]Trans. Mark Schmidt in Cole, *Acting*, 105–15.

[8]Constantin Stanislavski, *An Actor Prepares*, trans. E. R. Hapgood (New York, 1936), 256.

stimulating the inner life. A new line was sought, the "line of physical being," and a new strategy: actors were advised to begin "with the simplest objectives and actions" leading to the "physical life of a part," which leads to the spiritual life and actual sense of life in a play and part, which "in turn transmutes itself into the inner creative state."[9] Stanislavski's late view of feeling as a "reflex" to the stimuli of physical actions in the creative moment suggests the possible influence of Pavlov, whose theories were becoming enshrined as the basis of all Russian work in psychology; whatever the inspiration, Stanislavski does not seem to have regarded this "method of physical actions" as a rejection of his earlier system but as a further development of it. The actor's work proceeds in a circle from physical action and script analysis to creation of inner life back to external action in the role—all as part of the same process.

It was doubtless this new orientation that Stella Adler sensed in Paris in 1933, but with no further documentation of Stanislavski's thought available than *An Actor Prepares* for almost another generation, Strasberg's more psychological interpretation prevailed, becoming the basis for the American "Method," then generally accepted as a faithful reproduction of the Stanislavski approach. This orientation was clearly seen in the *Theatre Workshop*, a quarterly that appeared in 1936, replacing the foundering *New Theatre* and again including among its directors Gorelik, Strasberg, and Lawson. The first issue, a special on the art of acting, included a major essay by Vakhtangov's successor, I. M. Rapoport (1901–1970): another detailed commentary on the development of "outer and inner features," stressing "stage attitude" (the actor's belief that corresponded to Vakhtangov's "scenic faith") as "the foundation on which the role is built."[10]

Further Russian articles with similar emphases appeared in subsequent issues. *Theatre Workshop* II (1937) offered two lectures on "The Creative Process" by Stanislavski's student, the director Ilya Sudakov (1890–1969): one on inner technique, stressing concentration, truth, and sense-memory; the other on training of the voice and body. *Theatre Workshop* III (1937) featured "Principles of Directing" by Boris Zakhava (1896–1976), a graduate of Vakhtangov's Third Studio. Zakhava argued that significant theatre could not grow from "the subjective desire of a single creative personality" but only from "the united will of the collective."[11] He condemned Craig and Sologub for their denial of the creative contribution of the actor, and Aikhenwald for the mistaken

---

[9]Stanislavski, *Creating a Role*, trans. E. R. Hapgood (New York, 1961), 223.
[10]Cole, *Acting*, 67.
[11]Ibid., 185.

idea that when the playwright's work is done, the creative task is complete. Any true artist must use "given material as an expression of one's own reaction to life."[12] This is how Shakespeare used his sources and how actors and directors must use Shakespeare. Otherwise they are mere technicians and illustrators, as Aikhenwald accused them of being. Directors have no more right to dictate to actors than playwrights have to dictate to directors. The raw material of the director is not the body of the actor but the actor's own creativity, which the director must stimulate and encourage.[13]

By 1937, internal conflicts were beginning to break up the Group Theatre, and though Clurman kept the venture alive for another four years, it never again equaled its former significance. Strasberg, who withdrew in 1937, continued his own work on the Method, outlining his approach in "Acting and the Training of the Actor" in John Gassner's *Producing the Play* (1941). The art of acting gradually evolved, says Strasberg, as actors learned to speak rather than to declaim, to react to other actors, to create the illusion of a real person, and finally to relate to the entire world of the play. The great accomplishment of modern acting theory has been the rejection of "any system with detailed illustrations as to what the actor would do in any given situation" in favor of "a method, by means of which he will evolve for himself the proper results."[14] The aim of that method is to make an actor's own resources accessible to him so that he will have the proper mental, physical, and emotional equipment for every demand. Only in this way can he give total credibility to the author's lines.

The designer Mordecai Gorelik (b. 1899), who remained with the Group Theatre to the end, studied the evolution of theatrical production in his book *New Theatres for Old* (1940). His theoretical kinship to Clurman and others in the Group is evident throughout the book, which begins by defining the purpose of drama as "to influence life by theatrical means."[15] Its artists must clarify their understanding of their own lives and employ this understanding to enlighten their audiences. Gorelik's clear sympathy is for what he calls the "tribunal" theatre, a "theatre of inquiry" that adheres to the "rules of evidence," presenting impartial verdicts on its own times.[16] Its goal should be neither a detached art for art's sake nor the propagandistic manipulation of public opinion, but "a useful and practical knowledge of the world."[17]

[12]Ibid., 191.
[13]Ibid., 189.
[14]John Gassner, *Producing the Play* (New York, 1953), 141.
[15]Mordecai Gorelik, *New Theatres for Old* (New York, 1948), 5.
[16]Ibid., 466–67.
[17]Ibid., 471.

John Howard Lawson (b. 1894), the best known leftist playwright of the period, was also associated in the early 1930s with the Group, and in 1936 published his *Theory and Technique of Playwriting*, which attempted to harmonize the drama of social engagement with the Freytag-Sarcey-Archer tradition of dramatic theory. Lawson cites Brunetière, Archer, and Jones on crisis and conflict, but he finds each inadequate. He prefers Brunetière's conflict to Archer's crisis as the essence of drama, but argues that the conflict must be always a *social* one. Jones neglects to mention the conscious will as the force that generates the conflict. This will must be directed toward a specific goal, which "the social viewpoint of the audience" can accept as realistic, and must be sufficiently powerful to "bring the conflict to a point of crisis."[18] The mere *strength* of the will does not, as Brunetière suggested, determine the value of the drama—rather, it is the *quality* of the will and of the forces it opposes. In each of these adjustments, Lawson may be seen moving away from purely structural concerns to those of content, and particularly social content.

No other twentieth-century writer has influenced the theatre both as dramatist and theorist as profoundly as Bertolt Brecht (1898–1956), whose central concern was the theatre's social and political dimension. His first theoretical writings, mostly criticisms for the socialist paper *Der augsburger Volkswille* between 1919 and 1921, are fairly conventional pieces, but various entries in his notebooks from the early 1920s show him groping toward a new idea of the drama, emphasizing not similitude but the marvelous and wonderful.[19] These thoughts began to crystallize into a theory about 1926, when German theatre seemed in the eyes of many to be essentially moribund. The *Vossische Zeitung* of April 4 noted that "more and more voices are raised that the decline of the theatre is beginning or is already established. It is an old claim that tragedy is impossible in our time, but the complaint is new that the drama itself as an art form is outmoded."[20] Expressionism had clearly run its course; the true spirit of classicism seemed beyond recapturing; film, radio, and sports drew an increasingly greater share of the public.

Partially in response to this general concern and partially in seeking a suitable dramatic technique for a projected play dealing with economic concerns in America, Brecht began to develop what he called *"episches Drama."* He remarked to his secretary, Elizabeth Hauptmann, that his subject was impossible for a traditional treatment: "As soon as

---

[18]John Howard Lawson, *The Theory and Technique of Playwriting* (New York, 1936), 168.
[19]Bertolt Brecht, *Tagebücher 1920–1922* (Frankfurt, 1975), 187.
[20]Quoted in Jan Knopf, *Brecht Handbuch* (Stuttgart, 1980), 429.

one realizes that the modern world is no longer reconcilable with the drama then the drama can no longer be reconciled with the world." Among Brecht's ideas at this time for a new drama of the modern world was that the actor play "from memory (quoting gestures and attitudes)."[21]

Other statements of the same year provide further suggestions. In an interview Brecht states that his new "epic theatre" will be addressed to reason instead of empathy, since "feelings are private and limited. Against that the reason is fairly comprehensible and can be relied on."[22] An early version of the famous *"Verfremdungsprinzips"* (principle of estrangement, or alienation) occurs in the article "Ovation für Shaw" which makes the essence of Shaw's approach to characterization "his delight in dislocating our stock associations."[23] In 1926 also Brecht began studying Marx's *Das Kapital*, and found Marx extremely helpful in systematizing many of the concerns he felt—the search for a pattern and direction in human effort, an explanation and even a cure for the corruption in modern society, and in the Hegelian dialectic a stimulating tool for dramaturgical exploration. "This man Marx," he observed in *Schriften zum Theater*, "was the only spectator for my plays I'd ever come across."[24]

The first full statement of Brecht's dramatic theory appears as a set of notes to his opera *Aufsteig und Fall der Stadt Mahagonny* (1930), which contains the often reproduced table of changes of emphasis between "Dramatic Form" and "Epic Form." This table elaborates the distinction already made between the emotional response to drama and the rational response to the epic. The former encourages the spectator to become engulfed in the plot, to accept it as an unalterable linear development of experience. The latter distances the spectator, presents its action as alterable, and forces the spectator to consider other possibilities and to judge between them.[25] Another possible distinction would be between "aesthetic" and "political" theatre, since Brecht's essay insists that the new epic theatre be viewed in political terms. The heritage of both Wagner and Marx is clear in the opening section, which characterizes art as merchandise, produced not for the general good or according to the desires of the artist, but according to the "normal laws of mercantile trade." Only that art is permitted which serves the apparatus of the existing society, and anything which threat-

---

[21]Elizabeth Hauptmann, "Notizen über Brechts Arbeit 1926," *Sinn und Form* 2 (1957): 242.

[22]*Brecht on Theatre*, trans. John Willett (New York, 1964), 15.

[23]Ibid., p. 11; *Schriften zum Theater*, 3 vols. (Frankfurt, 1963–67), 1:99.

[24]*Brecht*, 24; *Schriften*, 1:181.

[25]*Brecht*, 37; *Schriften*, 3:1009–10.

ens change is suppressed.[26] But if this analysis echoes Wagner, the solution is radically different. Brecht sees Wagner's *Gesamtkunstwerk* as one of the most powerful devices in the existing system, submerging the spectators in a work of art, casting a spell over them, and stifling any disturbing element that might lead them to reflection. Brecht, on the contrary, calls for a radical separation of the elements so that each may provide commentary on the others and force the spectator to weigh alternatives and make decisions.[27]

Brecht's theatre is devised not for some future socialist society, but for the bourgeois society of the present, and its goal is educative: to expose the hidden contradictions within that society. Once text, music, and setting are free to "adopt attitudes"; once "illusion is sacrificed to free discussion"; once the spectator is "forced, as it were, to cast his vote"—then a change has been launched which is the first step toward achieving "the theatre's social function."[28] Brecht saw *Mahagonny* as functioning on two levels: the traditional level of opera as simply a pleasurable experience, and the level of instruction. To achieve the latter, he suggested in a footnote, everything must be made *"gestisch,"* gestic, since "the eye which looks for the gest in everything is the moral sense."[29] Brecht is distinctly less clear on this important term than he is on estrangement; perhaps his clearest statement occurs in "Über gestische Musik" (1932?), where he distinguishes between *Gestus* and traditional gesture. Both make external something otherwise hidden, but gesture reveals subjective personal states, while *Gestus* is always social—it makes corporeal and visible the relationships between persons. A laborer's task, for example, is a social *Gestus* because "all human activity directed toward the mastery of nature is a social undertaking, an undertaking between men."[30] Thus *Gestus* functions to keep always before the spectator the social implications of epic theatre.

Throughout the *Mahagonny* essay, Brecht expresses his concern that the new epic form may not succeed in breaking free from the expectations of traditional "culinary" theatre, may not force the spectator accustomed to passive acceptance into a more engaged role. Partly as a manifestation of this concern and partly out of a desire to explore the possibilities of a true socialist theatre for a future period when compromise forms like *Mahagonny* would no longer be necessary, Brecht at this same time began working on another type of drama, the *Lehrstück* ("teaching play"). "Die Grosse und die kleine Pädagogik" (c. 1930)

[26]*Brecht*, 34; *Schriften*, 3:1006.
[27]*Brecht*, 37; *Schriften*, 3:1010.
[28]*Brecht*, 39; *Schriften*, 3:1013.
[29]*Brecht*, 36; *Schriften*, 3:1006.
[30]*Brecht*, 104; *Schriften*, 2:753.

distinguishes between the "lesser pedagogy" of the epic theatre, which "merely democratized the theatre during the prerevolutionary period" and the "greater pedagogy," which "transforms the role of playing completely, abolishes the system of spectator and performer," and converts "all individual interests into the interests of the state."[31] In the production of *Lehrstücke*, small groups of workers would participate in mutual instruction. In the notes to *Die Horatier und die Kuratier* (1934), Brecht says that "whoever presents a teaching play must perform it as a student" and that it teaches "not by being seen but by being played. Fundamentally, no spectator is necessary for a teaching play."[32] In short, the epic drama is created for the instruction of the spectator, the teaching play for that of the performer.

The essay "Verfremdungseffekte in der chinesischen Schauspielkunst" (1936?) is Brecht's first extended discussion of the central concept of *Verfremdung*, or alienation. He cites the traditional Chinese acting style as a model for actors in epic theatre, who seek to make the audience think about their work by making it "strange." The bourgeois theatre presents events as universal, timeless, and unalterable; the epic, or "historicizing," theatre uses *Verfremdung* to render even everyday events "remarkable, particular, and demanding inquiry."[33] Thereafter, the *V-Effekt* is a standard part of Brecht's critical vocabulary. The essay "Über experimentelles Theater" (1939) advances *Verfremdung* as an alternative to the sympathetic understanding evoked by traditional pity and terror. "To alienate an event or a character is simply to take what to the event or character is obvious, known, evident and produce surprise and curiosity out of it."[34]

So influential has this concept been, and so closely has it become identified with Brecht, that it might be well to note that Brecht did not create it; rather, he put new emphasis on an idea of quite ancient lineage. Even Aristotle's *Poetics* (chapter 22) spoke of the poet's obligation to make familiar language unfamiliar by use of metaphor, ornament, and strange or rare words. Francis Bacon, whom Brecht often cited approvingly for his interest in scientific experimentation instead of unconsidered acceptance of traditional (Aristotelian) precepts, advised in his *Novum Organum* the use of "estrangement." He suggests a variety of approaches for perceiving "singularity" and inciting "wonder" to counteract the "depraved habit" of the understanding, which

---

[31]Brecht, "Die Grosse und die kleine Pädagogik," *Alternative* 78/79 (Aug. 1971): 126.
[32]Brecht, *Schriften*, 3:1022, 1024.
[33]*Brecht on Theatre*, 96–97; *Schriften*, 3:1087–91.
[34]Brecht, "On the Experimental Theatre," trans. C. R. Mueller, *Tulane Drama Review* 6, 1 (Sept. 1961):14; *Schriften*, 1:301.

is "necessarily corrupted, perverted, and distorted by daily and habitual impressions."[35]

The German romantics found this process of great interest; indeed Novalis, one of the most original of the romantic poets, defines romantic poetry as "the art of surprising in a pleasing way, of making a subject strange and yet understandable and interesting."[36] In more recent times, Viktor Shklovsky (b. 1893), leader of the Russian formalists, in his most famous article "Art as Technique" (1917) established the *priyom ostra-nenije* (technique of making strange) as a cornerstone of Russian formalist theory, arguing that poets use metaphor and imagery not, as traditional theory maintained, to express the unfamiliar but to make the familiar strange and wonderful.[37] Since Brecht was in Moscow when he witnessed the performance by the Chinese troupe of Mei Lan-fang that inspired his *Verfremdung* essay, it is possible that his coinage owes something to Shklovsky, though clearly Brecht had been developing this idea for some time. In any case the political dimension of Brecht's usage sets it apart from that of any of these possible precursors.

An interest in developing a drama relevant to the concerns of the common man and to the problems of contemporary society was widespread in the 1930s, but Brecht's radical approach to this issue was by no means readily or universally accepted even by other German theorists who shared his concerns. A very different approach was suggested by Odön von Horváth (1901–1938), whose theories and dramas emerged from relative obscurity in the late 1960s to provide an important challenge to Brecht. Horváth's major concern was with the *Volksstück*, a term he took from the traditional popular theatre of Vienna, and his central theoretical statements on this form are found in an interview with Willi Cronauer and in the "Gebrauchsanweisung" (both 1932).

Horváth emphasizes that he is "deliberately destroying the form and ethos" of the old *Volksstück* in order to create something new, a drama that will depict the concerns of the people "seen through the eyes of the people," and "call upon the instincts rather than the intellect of the people."[38] Obviously, this injects a much more psychological note than is found in Brecht's theories; indeed, Horváth's central aim is a Freudian "unmasking of the unconscious," and his fundamental motif is "the eternal combat between the conscious and the subconscious."[39] By a

---

[35]Francis Bacon, *Novum Organum* (New York, 1902), 2.32.185.
[36]Quoted (in German) in R. H. Stacy, *Russian Literary Criticism* (Syracuse, 1974), 166.
[37]"Iskusstvo, kak priyom," trans. in *Russian Formalist Criticism: Four Essays*, ed. L. T. Lemon and M. J. Reis (Lincoln, Neb., 1965), 12.
[38]Odön von Horváth, *Gesammelte Werke*, 4 vols. (Frankfurt, 1971), 4:662–63.
[39]Ibid., 659–60.

"synthesis of seriousness and irony," Horváth proposes to expose "the extremely private instinctive impulses" of his characters and thereby of his audiences. The traditional *Volksstück* denied this psychological reality, along with such other realities as those of language and of society. The "people" of Horváth's Germany are the petty bourgeois, who speak not in dialect or in the clever turns of the traditional *Volksstück* but in the "jargon of culture," built upon clichés and received ideas. Horváth's new drama seeks to expose to his public the conflict between this empty and pretentious jargon and the authentic agonies of repressed psychological impulses and an equally repressed recognition of an unjust socioeconomic system.

A much more serious challenge to Brecht's theories during the 1930s was mounted by Georg Lukács, who returned at this time to the study of literature, but now from a distinctly Marxist perspective. Drawing upon the observations of Marx and Engels, he proposed a literature of "realism," that is, of accurate presentation of the total sociohistorical situation of a given society. Its characters should be neither so unique as to have no general applicability nor so abstract as to be interchangeable, but should unite the general and the particular to form "types" illustrative of the universal laws of society. The bourgeoisie before 1848, when it was still a progressive class, could still produce "realistic" works, but in present society, said Lukács, only the proletariat has this clarity of vision.

In the Berlin proletarian journal *Die Linkskurve*, for which he wrote between 1931 and 1933, Lukács condemned most contemporary proletarian literature for not having attempted the blend of the general and particular that would produce the "typical." At one extreme, he said, the propagandistic writers created abstract models of action, such as the "decent non-Communist who suddenly converts to Communism," instead of "living people and their relations, which are in a constant state of flux."[40] At the other, creators of "reportage" or "montage" sought objectivity by presenting isolated facts or clusters of facts and equally missed the totality of a social process. Lukács's major example of this error was the work of novelist Ernst Ottwalt (1901–1936?), but he also cited the plays of Brecht: Ottwalt and Brecht had reacted to the psychological, subjective tradition of bourgeois literature by concentrating on objective fact, thereby losing "the dialectical interaction of subjectivity and formal elements."[41]

These attacks launched a major theoretical debate within Marxist criticism that was carried on throughout the 1930s and echoed for

[40]Georg Lukács, "Willi Bredels Romane," *Die Linkskurve* 3, 11 (Nov. 1931):24.
[41]Lukács, "Reportage oder Gestaltung," *Die Linkskurve* 4, 7 (July 1932):25.

decades after. Brecht did not respond immediately, but Ottwalt, who was working with Brecht as coauthor on *Kuhle Wampe* (1932), submitted to *Linkskurve* a Brechtian defense. "It is not the duty of our literature to stabilize the reader's consciousness but to alter it," he argued, accusing Lukács of advocating works unsuitable to the present transitional era, complete and harmonious works which would leave audiences "satisfied with things the way they are."[42]

Ottwalt's defense revealed an essential difference between Brecht and Lukács: Brecht saw social reality as contradictory in its essence, and rationality as skeptical and experimental (though Ottwalt's "transitional period" masks this skepticism); Lukács, more Hegelian, felt that art could unite contradictions to express an essential "totality." Lukács's response, "Aus der Not eine Tugend," provided further, if indirect, evidence: he rejected Brecht's view that the "old" theatre showed man as unchangeable, calling such a view "mechanical and false to the true sense of Marx's thesis," since Marx showed the dialectical process at work throughout history, and Lukács himself found much to value in the pre-Marxist literary tradition. He saw Brecht's stress on contradiction not as Marxist but as a disguised bourgeois expression of meaninglessness, so common in twentieth-century decadent art.[43]

Lukács's position was supported by Andor Gábor (1884–1953), another Hungarian Marxist then living in Berlin. In the same issue of *Linkskurve*, his article "Zwei Bühnenereignisse" attacked two proletarian dramas for their indebtedness to the "false and misleading" ideas of Brecht. He reproduced Brecht's comparative table from the *Mahagonny* preface and, ignoring Brecht's warning that this showed only a change of emphasis, accused him of "idealism" in creating such abstractions as a man with only feeling or with only reason. As a result, said Gábor, Brecht could not or would not present man on the stage "as he loves and lives," in the fullness of his emotional *and* rational life, but created instead "a stage of consciousness and not of being," suitable only for "bourgeois idealists."[44]

Hitler's seizure of power early in 1933 ended this phase of the debate, along with *Linkskurve* and the Communist Party itself in Germany. Lukács and Gábor escaped to Moscow, Brecht and Ottwalt to Denmark. In Russia, Lukács found support for his position in the doctrine of socialist realism just then emerging. The term appeared in the spring of 1932, and in October, Stalin solidified its usage by remarking that if an artist "truthfully depicts our life, he cannot but notice and depict

[42]Ernst Ottwalt, " 'Tatsachenroman' und Formexperiment: Eine Entgegnung an Georg Lukács," *Die Linkskurve* 4, 10 (Oct. 1932):22, 24.
[43]Lukács, "Aus der Not eine Tugend," *Die Linkskurve* 4, 12 (Dec. 1932): 18, 24.
[44]Andor Gábor, "Zwei Bühnenereignisse," *Die Linkskurve* 4, 12 (Dec. 1932):29.

in it that which leads to socialism. This exactly will be socialist art. This exactly will be socialist realism."[45] The Congress of Soviet Writers held in 1933 began to work out the implications of this doctrine. Andrei Zhdanov (1896–1948), secretary of the Central Committee and in charge of ideological affairs, stressed that socialist realism meant not only "truthfulness and historical concreteness of the artistic portrayal" but also "the ideological remoulding and education of the toiling people in the spirit of socialism." Writers should, in Stalin's words, be "engineers of human souls," and socialist literature should be tendentious and proudly so.[46] The drama, as the genre best suited to the education of the masses, was given particular attention by the Soviet Central Committee.[47]

Lukács essentially subscribed to the orthodox interpretation of socialist realism, though he was less inclined than Zhdanov to seek tendentiousness and more tolerant of authors of earlier periods who, he felt, could create significant realistic art despite their class background. He was much more closely in harmony with the Soviet literary authorities on the decadence and worthlessness of nonrealistic, or "formalistic," literary experimentation. As early as 1933 he published an article " 'Grösse und Verfall' des Expressionismus," which condemned expressionism as a decadent, regressive form, an early manifestation of the development of Fascist ideology.

This position was reaffirmed by Lukács's disciple Alfred Kurella (1895–1975) in an early issue of *Das Wort*, a Moscow-based journal purportedly serving as an international forum for anti-Fascist authors, but also providing an instrument for acquainting the rest of Europe with current Soviet literary theories. Kurella's attack on expressionism inspired a series of articles during 1937 and 1938 in *Das Wort*, collectively called the *"Expressionismusdebatte."* The key essays in this exchange appeared at its conclusion: "Diskussionen über Expressionismus" by Ernst Bloch (1885–1977) and, as a final word, Lukács's "Es geht um den Realismus." Bloch and Lukács had been closely acquainted for some 30 years and at the time of the First World War had even planned collaborating on work on aesthetics. But as early as 1918, Bloch's first major work, the mystic *Geist der Utopie*, contained a celebration of expressionist and modernist experimentation unacceptable to Lukács. The famous exchange of articles in *Das Wort* thus essentially summed up a debate between these two theorists that had been developing for almost two decades.

[45]Quoted in Herman Ermolaev, *Soviet Literary Theories, 1917–1934* (Berkeley, 1963), 145.
[46]Andrei Zhdanov, *Problems of Soviet Literature*, trans. anon. (Moscow, 1935), 21.
[47]Ermolaev, *Soviet*, 142 and notes.

Bloch's article condemned Lukács (and his spokesman Kurella) for insisting upon a black and white view of reality, in which "all forms of opposition to the ruling class which are not Communist from the outset are lumped together with the ruling class" and thus denied any critical utility. This view arises from Lukács's idea of a "closed and integrated reality"—a heritage from classical German philosophy: since he denies that the bourgeois system contains disjunctures, contradictions, fissures in its surface interrelations, he must also condemn legitimate attempts to exploit those disjunctures and to find new values within the fissures, not as healthy criticism but as decadent and empty "playing."[48]

Lukács, in response, willingly accepted the charge of assuming a totality in bourgeois culture; he quoted Marx—"the relations of production of every society form a whole"—and repeated his earlier insistence upon the reflection of objective reality in literature and the dangers of subjectivity and self-indulgent experimentation. A technique like montage may be dazzling in its diversity and may even achieve occasional striking effects with political import, but it can never give the shape to reality and to a world of interrelationships that is the essential obligation of Marxist art.[49]

Although Brecht was a coeditor of *Das Wort*, he was far away in Denmark, and his actual influence was negligible—as the general antiexperimental tone of the 1937–1938 debate makes clear. In fact, he wrote several essays in response to Lukács but decided against submitting them for publication. Walter Benjamin, who shared a part of his Danish exile, reports conversations suggesting both that Brecht wished to avoid a direct theoretical confrontation with Lukács and that he felt misgivings about challenging the political powers in Moscow which apparently supported Lukács's position. His *Arbeitsjournal* of this period leaves no doubt, however, as to Brecht's opinions: it was Lukács who was still entrapped in the bourgeois literary tradition, since he saw no difference, no conflict between his so-called "realism of the proletariat" and the realism of traditional bourgeois culture. In fact, realism "has now been as nicely corrupted as socialism by the Nazis," and Lukács himself should be styled a "murxist" whose "only significance consists in the fact that he is writing from Moscow."[50]

Two of the essays Brecht wrote in 1937 in response to Lukács, "Weite und Vielfalt der realistischen Schreibweise" and "Volkstümlichkeit und Realismus," finally appeared in 1954 and 1958, and others were included in the 1967 edition of his *Schriften zur Kunst und Literatur*. All

[48] Ernst Bloch, "Diskussionen über Expressionismus," *Das Wort* 6 (1938):110–12.
[49] Lukács, "Es geht um den Realismus," *Das Wort* 6 (1938): 135–38.
[50] Brecht, *Arbeitsjournal*, 2 vols. (Frankfurt, 1973), 1:13, 25, 39.

treat Lukács much more gently than did the *Arbeitsjournal*, but the incompatibility of his views and Brecht's is evident. Brecht credits Lukács with some "notable essays" on realism, though these "in my opinion, define it rather too narrowly." Realism should be "broad and political," free alike from "aesthetic restrictions" and "convention."[51] An artist whose works truly expose the causal network of society for the proletariat need not fear that the people will not understand, even if the approach is unfamiliar. Indeed, a true art for the people must move and develop as the people move, seeking new approaches as society itself evolves. Art that refuses to do this will lose its contact with life and become merely a sterile repetition of earlier works. "One cannot decide if a work is realist or not by finding out whether it resembles existing, reputedly realistic works which must be counted realist for their time. In each individual case the picture given of life must be compared, not with another picture, but with the actual life portrayed."[52] Thus Brecht argued that not he but Lukács, with his veneration for realists like Balzac, was drifting away from reality toward formalism.

Walter Benjamin's essays *Versuche über Brecht*, written during the 1930s and published in 1966, provide another defense of epic theory and practice. The Brechtian drama had many points in common with Benjamin's *Trauerspiel*—it was fragmented, device-baring, shock-producing—but it had a positive program for curing the desolation of society which the *Trauerspiel* merely reflected in melancholy anguish. Benjamin's defense was clearly conditioned by the arguments of Lukács. The artist, like the worker, must consider his position in the production process. If he simply unthinkingly accepts the production methods of the past (such as early nineteenth-century realism), even his most "proletarian" creations will tend to be assimilated on traditional terms, simply as entertainment—what Brecht called "culinary" theatre. Brecht was the first artist to demand a change in production apparatus, the breaking of illusion, to prevent such assimilation. Looking to film, radio, and photography but perhaps also recalling the theory of Eisenstein, Benjamin calls this technique montage. By bringing action "to a stand-still in mid-course" it "compels the spectator to take up a position towards the action, and the actor to take up a position towards his part."[53]

The expansion of Hitler's power drove Brecht from Europe to America in 1941. There he found the familiar Lukács controversy awaiting him. In 1937, Mordecai Gorelik had published in *Theatre Workshop* the

[51]Brecht, "Volkstümlichkeit und Realismus," *Sinn und Form* 4 (1958):109.
[52]Ibid., 112.
[53]Walter Benjamin, *Understanding Brecht*, trans. Anna Bostock (London, 1973), 100.

first statement in America of Brecht's theories; it was followed in the next issue by a rebuttal from John Howard Lawson, who essentially echoed Lukács and called Brecht's ideas "discredited and thoroughly un-Marxist."[54] Brecht responded to this in his "Short List of the Most Frequent, Common, and Boring Misconceptions about the Epic Theatre." Central among these were the beliefs that the theory of epic theatre was overintellectual and abstract, and that it was against emotions.

The years in America produced comparatively few further critical statements from Brecht. Upon his return to Europe in 1947, however, he drew up his major statement, the *Kleines Organon für das Theater* (1949). This brought together the various elements of epic theory—the historicizing of the present, the *Verfremdungseffekt*, the actor's distance from his role, the division of the action into individual and dialectically opposed episodes (each with its basic *Gestus*), the separation of the various arts of the drama for similar mutual estrangement—and developed them in terms of their ability to awaken man to the possibility of change in all things.[55]

The first section of Brecht's manifesto stresses, a bit surprisingly, that the proper basis of theatre is entertainment, and that pleasure is its only justification. The audience of the scientific age, however, requires a sort of entertainment that reflects the modern, scientific view of reality; on these primarily aesthetic rather than political grounds, Brecht now defends epic theatre. It brings into the field of human relationships, he says, the scientific spirit that men already employ in their dealings with nature and the world, and thus creates an entertainment relevant for and harmonious with the modern consciousness.

Brecht proposed to explore all these ideas more fully in his *Messingkauf Dialogues*, but as these were never completed, the *Kleines Organon*, a "short condensation" of the *Dialogues*, became the basic summary of Brechtian theory.

Antonin Artaud (1896–1948), whose influence on subsequent theatre has rivaled that of Brecht, also viewed the drama as an instrument of revolution, a tool for the reordering of human existence. Like Brecht, he sought to dissociate theatre as it ought to be, "the achievement of mankind's purest desires," from what it was, "a facile and false" purveyor of transitory pleasure attended "as one goes to a bordello."[56] Artaud's vision, however, was of a theatre that would change man not socially but psychologically, by setting free the dark, latent forces festering in the individual soul. Brecht and Artaud, then, came to rep-

---

[54]*Theatre Workshop*, nos. 3 and 4 (1937).

[55]Brecht, *Versuche*, 12 (Berlin, 1958), 137.

[56]Antonin Artaud, "Le théâtre de l'atelier," *Oeuvres complètes*, 17 vols. (Paris, 1956), 2:155.

resent positions almost diametrically opposed, the one associated with a theatre stimulating the spectator to reason and analysis, the other with one regarding discursive thought as a barrier to the awakening of the body's inner spirit. In Artaud we see the metaphysical concerns of the symbolist and surrealist theorists taken to their most radical extension.

Artaud's first significant theatre statement, "L'évolution du décor" (1924) takes issue with his former patrons in the Cartel des Quatre, calling for "the spirit and not the letter of the text" and denouncing the goal of "retheatricalizing the theatre." Instead, the theatre should "throw itself back into life," not in the manner of the naturalists but on a more mystical, metaphysical level. Designers and performers must seek to open the hidden life of great plays and to create a theatre where the public comes "not to observe, but to participate."[57]

These ideas were developed further in the manifestos Artaud wrote between 1926 and 1929 in support of his producing organization, the Théâtre Alfred Jarry. He promised a theatre that would show audiences "the anguishes and concerns of their real lives," where the spectator would undergo "a real operation, involving not only his mind, but his senses and his flesh." It would be a theatre of magic, addressed not to the eye or to the mind but to "the most secret recesses of the heart."[58]

André Breton, now committed to a political role for surrealism, expelled Artaud from the movement for his apostate view of revolution as "no more than a change in the internal conditions of the soul." Artaud did not deny the charge; indeed, in 1927 he characterized Breton's revolution, preoccupied with "the necessity of production" and "the conditions of workers," as a "revolution for castrates." The roots of man's problems lay far deeper than in social organization, he said; the only revolution worthy of support would have to free the internal man.[59]

Naturally, such statements led politically engaged critics to characterize Artaud as a formalist, a defender of art for art's sake, a position he also rejected in "Le Théâtre Alfred Jarry" (1929). While his goal was a theatre as free as music, poetry, and painting, a "total spectacle" of pure experience, it had "nothing to do with art or with beauty"; it was extratheatrical, a reintegration of life itself, a vision akin to hallucination of human actuality, the "actuality of sensation and concerns" in its totality.[60]

During the early 1930s Artaud created the series of essays that formed

---

[57]Artaud, "L'évolution du décor," *Oeuvres*, 1:213–16.
[58]Artaud, "Le Théâtre Alfred Jarry," *Oeuvres*, 2:13–14, 23.
[59]Artaud, "Manifeste pour un théâtre avorté," *Oeuvres*, 2:25.
[60]Artaud, "Le Théâtre Alfred Jarry," *Oeuvres*, 2:34.

his most influential work, *Le théâtre et son double* (1938). The first of these, "Sur le théâtre Balinais" (1931), recorded a major event in his life and thought: his observation of the Balinese dancers at the Paris Colonial Exposition. In one of the 1926 manifestos, Artaud had said that acting and staging "should be thought of merely as the visible signs of a secret and invisible language,"[61] but a model for such signs eluded him until he witnessed the Balinese dancers. Here at last was realized "the idea of pure theatre where everything, conception and realization alike, has value, has existence only in proportion to its degree of objectification *on the stage*." Words were eliminated; the actors themselves became "animated hieroglyphs" whose cries and gestures awakened an intuitive response in the audience untranslatable into logical and discursive language.[62]

From the beginning of his career as a poet, Artaud had been haunted by the inadequacy of words to capture inner life, a theme constantly repeated in his 1924 *Correspondence avec Jacques Rivière*. The Balinese dancers seemed to suggest a solution to this problem, a means of avoiding the pitfalls of language. Here was expressed a system of spiritual signs, "a secret psychic impulse which is Speech before words."[63] "La mise en scène et la métaphysique" (1931) and "Théâtre oriental et théâtre occidental" (c. 1935) developed this idea. The theatre must be freed from subordination to the text as the body from subordination to the mind. Language, if used, should no longer be humanistic, realistic, and psychological but religious and mystic, the language of incantation.[64]

The term "cruelty" was selected by Artaud to characterize the new theatre in 1932, after he had considered and rejected "absolute," "alchemical," and "metaphysical." He issued two manifestos for the *théâtre de la cruauté* in 1932 and 1933 and supplemented these by letters and the essays "Le théâtre alchimique" (1932), "En finir avec les chefs-d'oeuvre" (1933), and "Le théâtre et la peste" (1934). From the beginning Artaud resisted a moral or physical interpretation of cruelty. Bloodshed and martyred flesh, he observed in his first "Lettre sur la cruauté," constitute "a very minor aspect of the question." Cruelty is rather a cosmic "rigor, implacable intention and decision, irreversible and absolute determination," which holds both torturer and victim in its grasp.[65] Thus, though bloodshed is a minor part of this suffering center, it is a part. The basis is the turbulent force of the creative power

[61] Ibid., 30.
[62] Artaud, *The Theatre and Its Double*, trans. M. C. Richards (New York, 1958), 53–54.
[63] Ibid., 60.
[64] Ibid., 46.
[65] Ibid., 101.

itself, an irrational impulse whose permanent law is evil.[66] The dark creative principle exposed by the theatre suggests Schopenhauer's dark and cruel Will, or perhaps more directly Nietzsche's spirit of Dionysus; but the spectator in Artaud's theatre, entrapped in being, is not offered the mystic release Schopenhauer suggested, nor does Artaud posit an Apollonian counterforce arising in the art. The theatre's only true task is to reveal the heart of darkness in life itself.

All the trappings of modern, especially Western society—its morality, its taboos, its social institutions—were, in Artaud's view, doomed attempts to deny and repress this cosmic cruelty, and like Freudian repressions, they steadily undermined the spiritual health of Western man. The disparity between feelings and language that tortured Artaud from the beginning he now saw as a personal manifestation of a general cultural crisis, an attempt, in Nietzschian terms, to build an Apollonian society without recognition of the Dionysian. In the rhapsodic essay "Le théâtre et la peste" (1933), Artaud likens the theatre to the plague, as a releaser and revealer of this repressed spirit; it is "the bringing forth, the pushing into the open a depth of latent cruelty"; it "liberates dark powers and possibilities." The critic Franco Tonnelli perceptively calls this process "anti-purgation."[67] It seeks not to relieve the soul of certain dark passions and restore peace and equilibrium, but rather to confront the perhaps too complacent soul with dark and painful energies that admit of no reconciliation.[68]

Stimulating less controversy but equally open to misinterpretation was Artaud's concept of the "double." In a 1936 letter, Artaud explained the title of his major book thus: "If the theatre is the double of life, life is the double of the true theatre." This has nothing to do, he says, with Wilde's paradox of nature imitating art, but with the "doubles of the theatre that I have found so many years since: metaphysics, the plague, cruelty."[69] The double of the theatre is not everyday, observed reality, daily becoming more empty and meaningless; it is "archetypical and dangerous reality," which Artaud, in the essay "Le théâtre alchimique" (1932), had argued was the goal of alchemical and other occult experimentation. In traditional occult terms, Artaud traced the origin of the drama to the second phase of creation, where "matter and materialization" arose from the undivided original spirit.[70]

Artaud also uses the concept of the double in speaking of the actor's art in "Un athlétisme affectif" (1936). The actor must see his body as

---

[66]Ibid., 103.
[67]Franco Tonnelli, *L'esthétique de la cruauté* (Nizet, 1972), 19.
[68]Artaud, *Theatre*, 31.
[69]Artaud, "Lettre à Jean Paulhan," Jan. 25, 1936, *Oeuvres*, 5:272.
[70]Artaud, *Theatre*, 48, 50.

a double of a "specter," perpetual, plastic, and never achieved, "like the Ka of the Egyptian mummies." Every part of the body has a special mystic power, and every emotion an organic base. Even different methods of breathing can and should be analyzed for symbolic content. "Through the hieroglyph of a breath," Artaud concludes, "I can find once more the idea of a sacred theatre."[71] In the years after 1936, the theatre for Artaud became increasingly identified with the body. His 1947 poem "Le théâtre et la science" states that theatre "is not a scenic parade where one develops a myth virtually and symbolically, / but a crucible of fire" where "by the trampling of bones, limbs, and syllables / bodies are remade."[72] In that crucible were spent Artaud's tormented final years, during which he produced nothing to rival the essays collected in *Le théâtre et son double*.

The dominance of the text-oriented critical tradition of Copeau and Jouvet prevented the ideas of Artaud from exerting much influence in France for many years. The theoretical spirit of the early 1940s there is excellently captured in *L'essence du théâtre* (1943) by Henri Gouhier (b. 1898). Four brief "testimonials" by members of the Cartel precede the volume, reaffirming the Copeau aesthetic. "Our aim," says Pitoëff, "is only to aid the author's thought to be revealed more perfectly to the spectator." "The master of the theatre is the author," says Dullin. Jouvet expresses interest in a historical study of theatre architecture.[73] Baty, predictably, comes closest to Artaud, calling for a theatre that will not merely speak of the world but "render it sensible."[74] Still, his vision is in many ways the opposite of Artaud's. Baty would move outward from man to encompass all creation, and even God, in pantheistic harmony; Artaud would move inward, to find conflict and upheaval.

Gouhier's own theory naturally also follows Copeau. The text is "not all of the play" but is its "germ," and the staging must remain always faithful to it. Still, the theatre cannot be judged as a literary genre; it is a separate art, based on the "exteriorization of the will" and the "making present by the presences" of actors and scenery.[75] This creation of stage reality is the nearest man comes to divine creation, and is thus his spirit's most ambitious effort to overcome the weakness of the human condition.[76] There is not a hint of Artaud here, five years after the appearance of his major book, though Professor Gouhier

[71] Ibid., 134, 141.
[72] Alain Virmaux, *Antonin Artaud et le théâtre* (Paris, 1970), 264.
[73] Henri Gouhier, *L'essence du théâtre* (Paris, 1943), iv, v.
[74] Ibid., viii.
[75] Ibid., 45, 48.
[76] Ibid., 231.

would eventually come to place Artaud center stage in a 1974 study, *Antonin Artaud et l'essence du théâtre*.

Even Artaud's early champions, Jean-Louis Barrault (b. 1910) and Jean Vilar (1912–1971), though they scoffed at the subservience of the previous generation to the "author's intention," remained committed to a theatre of text (both, for example, revered Claudel) and communicated little of the dark vision at the center of Artaud's writings. Vilar, in "Le metteur en scène et l'oeuvre dramatique" (1946), cites with approval Artaud's stress on the "incantatory" nature of the text, a text which must serve as a "scenario" for the creative work of the theatre.[77] Vilar, like Pushkin and Wagner, sees great drama as possible "only in those privileged ages when some belief, be it Christian, pagan, or atheist" inspires the poet and brings him into harmony with a people who share the same belief. Since the fragmentation of society and the commercialization of art make this impossible, the artist must become involved in social concerns: "We must first construct a society, and then perhaps we can construct a worthy theatre."[78] Thus, despite Vilar's approving words for Artaud, his program was totally different; the stress on social rather than metaphysical solutions for man's problems was of course precisely the ground of Artaud's split with Breton and the surrealists.

Barrault found in Artaud an inspiration for his own theoretical concerns, which approached theatre as a total physical and psychic experience. Barrault considered Artaud one of the five essential theorists for all young theatre artists to know—the others being Aristotle, Corneille, Hugo, and Craig.[79] The essay on acting, with its cabalistic (Barrault calls them "alchemical") divisions of types of breathing, seemed particularly germane to the French actor's work on the rigorous development of physical expression, and Barrault urged a similar detailed analysis of every part of the vocal mechanism. He was much less comfortable with Artaud's rejection of language: "Speech and Gesture are not like pear and apple, dog and cat, but one and the same fruit, like a garden peach and a wild peach."[80] In fact, Barrault had little interest in radical change in the theatre; he sought to deepen and enrich the existing tradition. His rather conventional "spectrum of theatre"—with "pure gesture" at one end, "pure speech" at the other, and Shakespeare and Molière at the center—has little to do with the sort of apocalyptic vision found in Artaud.

[77]Jean Vilar, *De la tradition théâtrale* (Paris, 1955), 86.
[78]Ibid., 101.
[79]Jean-Louis Barrault, *Reflections on the Theatre*, trans. Barbara Wall (London, 1951), 50.
[80]Ibid., 53.

Jean-Paul Sartre (1905–1980) saw the drama as a portrayal of the process of commitment, dealing not with facts but with "rights," where every character "acts because he is engaged in a venture and because this venture must be carried to its conclusion, justifies it by reasons, believes he is right to undertake it."[81] This process must be relevant to the audience's own concerns but must also be distanced, to give perspective. In the theatre man sees himself "not as others see him, but as he is."[82] The essence of theatre, for Sartre as for Brecht, is a combination of objective distance and the presentation of situations relevant to the spectator's concerns. The lecture "Le style dramatique" (1944), which contains these observations, also echoes Brecht in looking to gesture as the basis of drama. Theatre language should be always directed toward action, not realism or psychological expression; it must demand gesture; and it must contribute directly to a developing pattern of commitment.

The emphasis on gesture was applauded by Barrault, one of the speakers who commented on Sartre's talk (others were Vilar, Camus, and Cocteau). Barrault suggested that dramatic style begins with "a breathing out of a breathing in," that gesture is implied in the very sound of certain consonants and vowels. Artaud's influence can be seen here, as well as in Barrault's reference to an "alchemy" of the word "not as idea but as action, as gesture," and in his suggestion that even gibberish "could make an extraordinarily dramatic language." Sartre, whose drama of choice and belief demanded discursive language, was predictably cool to these proposals.[83]

Later in the 1940s, Sartre developed the idea of a "theatre of situations" as a successor to the "theatre of character." In "Forger des mythes" (1946), he expresses the hope that in such drama the young playwrights of France are returning to tragedy "as the Greeks saw it"— in the assertion of a Hegelian right. Unlike the thesis drama or the defeatist drama of naturalism, this new theatre shows "a man who is free within the circle of his own situations, who chooses, whether he wishes to or not, for everyone else when he chooses for himself."[84] This choice, a result of man's free will, taken in the face of the "world's absurdity," involves the most fundamental questions of how man views and defines himself, and thus can assume the significance of modern myth.

In laying out this approach to tragedy for modern man, Sartre is very close to Albert Camus (1913–1960), and despite his protests, Ca-

---

[81]Jean-Paul Sartre, *Sartre on Theatre*, trans. Frank Jellinck (New York, 1976), 14.
[82]Ibid., 12.
[83]Ibid., 26.
[84]Ibid., 36.

mus was then and has often since been considered an "existentialist" dramatist, basically in agreement with Sartre. The "world's absurdity" mentioned by Sartre is most fully developed in Camus's highly influential "Le mythe de Sisyphe" (1943), and man's creation of meaning in the face of a world apparently indifferent to it is the central concern of both authors. By the late 1940s, however, a clear difference in their ideas became evident, and their public schism in the early 1950s was accompanied—in traditional French fashion—by a war of articles and pamphlets. Camus found Sartre's Marxism an embracing of a tainted partial perspective, a betrayal of individual consciousness in favor of the collective. Sartre accused Camus of an unwillingness to become engaged in the processes of history, even if that engagement involved accepting a degree of moral guilt.

The political and philosophical ramifications of this controversy were developed in the essays of the early 1950s by both authors, and the theatrical works of each supported their opposed positions. The debate is less clearly reflected in their dramatic theory, but its traces can be seen in Camus's major theoretical statement on drama, "Sur l'avenir de la tragédie" (1955). His suggested bases for modern tragedy recall Hebbel more than Hegel. Looking to the Greek and Renaissance experience, he observes that "the tragic age always seems to coincide with an evolution in which man, consciously or not, frees himself from an older form of civilization and finds that he has broken away from it without having found a new form that satisfies him."[85] Camus sees a kind of pendulum effect in history between societies based on religion and those based on man. Both the Greeks and the Renaissance authors portrayed the heroic individual in conflict with the order of the world, but in both cases, as reason and the rights of the individual triumphed, tragedy disappeared. In modern times man has turned human intellect, human science, human history into a new deity, which has now "assumed the mask of destiny." The individual, seeking freedom from this new god, is once more in the ambiguous and contradictory state that can give rise to tragic expression.[86]

The possibility and meaning of tragedy in the modern world aroused fresh interest in America and England, too, during the 1930s and 1940s, beginning with responses to Krutch's pessimistic 1929 assessment of the future of tragic vision. Kenneth Burke (b. 1897), in his *Counter-Statement* (1931), accepts the argument that any work of art reflects to some extent its own time, but he rejects the Spenglerian analysis of decay and decline that he sees reflected in Krutch. Burke grants

[85]Albert Camus, *Lyrical and Critical*, trans. Philip Thody (London, 1967), 179.
[86]Ibid., 185.

that modern society no longer shares a common ideology or moral system (the traditional bases for "objective" art such as the drama), and that modern art therefore has become more centered on the artist's "subjective" experience. Still, the "tragic spirit" has not diminished, and the concerns of tragedy—"man's intimate participation in processes beyond himself" and a committed stand in relation to these processes— are as accessible as ever. Though science replaced the traditional metaphysical system of belief, it has been replaced by a belief in the "slow, unwieldy movement of human society."[87] The tragic hero thus may in the future relate not to a divine but to a *historic* process.

Mark Harris (b. 1907), in *The Case for Tragedy* (1932), seems unaware of Burke's writings but follows a somewhat similar argument. He insists from the outset that aside from philosophic and aesthetic concerns, one must always keep in mind the sociological concerns of the drama, the values "which happened to be cherished" by the spectator's era and which are "objectified for him in the dramatic spectacle."[88] Those who, like Krutch, would deny the possibility of modern tragedy are simply attempting to apply to a new order values that are no longer accepted. Though the nexus of the modern system of value is no longer in heaven or man, science has found a new nexus in nature; and modern tragic authors, like O'Neill and Ibsen, tend to show nature as triumphant and thus lack the reconciliation typical of the humanistic or metaphysical tragedies of the past. So long as man seeks value, in whatever form, in the universe and fears challenges to that value, a tension is created that makes tragedy possible, for tragedy always "places in jeopardy" the personal or collective values of the time.[89]

Eric Bentley (b. 1916) also defends modern tragedy, created in modern terms, in *The Playwright as Thinker* (1946). As his title suggests, Bentley advocates a theatre of ideas, opposed equally to the light entertainment of the commercial stage and to the nonverbal theatricalism of Craig and the symbolists. Bentley stresses the balance of tragedy: it must be neither too optimistic, "for that would be to underestimate the problem," nor too pessimistic, "for that would be to lose faith in man." It should be "a broad and deep account of the life of the individual," in which "neither man's problems nor his ability to cope with them are belittled."[90] Similarly one should avoid the extremes of the expressionist, who tried to seize "the essence of life without the content," and the surrealist, who sought content without essence. Far more satisfactory are modern dramatists like Sartre and Brecht, who in complementary

---

[87]Kenneth Burke, *Counter-Statement* (New York, 1931), 200.
[88]Mark Harris, *The Case for Tragedy* (New York, 1932), xv.
[89]Ibid., 182.
[90]Eric Bentley, *The Playwright as Thinker* (New York, 1946), 33.

ways consider the basic dramatic tension of modern times: the tension between society and the individual.[91]

No suggestion that tragedy has become problematic or that modern tragedy must alter its concerns appears in Maxwell Anderson's (1888–1959) essay "The Essence of Tragedy" (1939). Anderson argues that human consciousness has changed little since Greek times, that the bases of comedy and tragedy have remained essentially the same throughout history, and that the theorist need seek only what all the acknowledged great works have in common, both in structure and function. In structure, Anderson looks to Aristotle, as filtered through the late nineteenth-century formal critics like Archer: "A play should lead up to and away from a central crisis, and this crisis should consist in a discovery by the leading character which has an indelible effect on his thought and emotion and completely alters his course of action."[92] This crisis is normally placed, as Freytag suggested, near the end of the center act of the play. The hero must be flawed so that after the crisis he may change for the better. Thus he contributes to the moral evolution of the species and fulfills the function of tragedy as "a religious affirmation, an age-old rite restating and reassuring man's belief in his own destiny and ultimate hope."[93]

Kenneth Burke returned to the subject of drama in *The Philosophy of Literary Form* (1941), but now as a central reference point for his evolving philosophic system. Anticipating the strategies of a number of later sociologists and anthropologists, Burke suggested that since human beings enact roles, define themselves by actions, and participate in social dynamics in life as in drama, "human relations should be analyzed with respect to the leads discovered by a study of the drama."[94] Burke takes ritual drama as his "Ur-form, 'the hub,' with all other aspects of *human* action treated as spokes radiating from this hub."[95] This does not mean that he necessarily accepts ritual drama as drama's original form, in the manner of Gilbert Murray, only that it provides him with the best available "vocabulary or set of coördinates" for studying all social phenomena. This study (to be elaborated in Burke's subsequent writings) he called Dramatism; he proposed to break down more carefully his earlier analysis—of social and poetic action as a strategy for encompassing a situation—by means of five dramatic terms: act, scene, agent, agency, purpose.[96]

[91]Ibid., 194.
[92]Maxwell Anderson, *The Essence of Tragedy* (Washington, 1935), 7.
[93]Ibid., 9.
[94]Burke, *The Philosophy of Literary Form* (New York, 1941), 310.
[95]Ibid., 103.
[96]Ibid., 106 n.

The Grammar of Motives (1945) is based upon these terms, and in discussing the "dialectic of tragedy," Burke uses them to explain "tragic rhythm." This formulation recalls Hegel: an agent undertakes an act of assertion, which calls forth "a counter-assertion in the elements that compose its context." The original agent must then "suffer" the process of understanding the counter-assertion, thereby transcending the "state that characterized him at the start."[97] One begins with an action, the *poiema* (meaning both act and poem), which arouses the opposition of *pathema* (suffering and situation), leading to *mathemata* (knowledge or learning). Burke subsequently applied this rhythm to the analysis not only of imaginative literature in general but to most human action.

Francis Fergusson (b. 1904) accepted Burke's concept of "tragic rhythm" and emphasis upon action, but feared that Burke's rational, conceptual, and linguistic basis was ultimately too reductive for useful criticism of drama. In purely formal terms, he says, Greek tragedy and a Platonic dialogue might follow the same rhythm, but at this level of abstraction, other crucial questions are largely ignored, those dealing with "the being which the artist envisages, and the histrionic, rather than rational, action whereby he imitates or represents it."[98] Oedipus's change in ideas, for example, is not dialectic; it comes not from thinking but "from suffering and direct experience—a development of the man himself."[99] In *The Idea of a Theatre* (1949), Fergusson argues that either creation or enjoyment of drama requires a "histrionic sensibility," which he compares to having an ear trained for music.[100] The primacy that Burke gave grammatically to ritual drama, Fergusson accepted literally, looking back for support to the Cambridge anthropologists, though he found Burke's tripartite rhythm (which he translated as "purpose, passion, and perception") a more useful tool than Murray's agon, pathos, messenger, threnos, anagnorisis, and theophany.

Fergusson's conversion of Burke's general strategy for the analysis of human action into a ritual pattern underlying tragedy naturally involves some narrowing and adjustment of terms. The Burke/Hegel dialectic between act (*poiema*) and situation (*pathema*) is scarcely recognizable in purpose and passion. Purpose as Fergusson defines it is rather closer to the shaping drive suggested by Stanislavski's through-line of action. As for tragic rhythm, Fergusson uses it not only for description but for evaluation. Agreeing with Krutch that modern drama has been seriously flawed by a loss of cultural wholeness, Fergusson produces as evidence plays in which the tragic rhythm is weak or trun-

[97]Burke, *The Grammar of Motives* (New York, 1945), 38.
[98]Francis Fergusson, *The Human Image in Dramatic Literature* (New York, 1957), 203.
[99]Ibid., 202.
[100]Fergusson, *The Idea of a Theatre* (Princeton, 1949), 236.

cated. Yet unlike Krutch, Fergusson sees hope for renewal. We may learn "to recognize and appreciate the fragmentary perspectives we do have," hoping that some day the total pattern will be again accessible in all its clarity.[101]

Cleanth Brooks (b. 1906), a leading champion of the textually-oriented American school of New Criticism in the 1940s, shared with Burke a dramatistic view of all poetry. In the tradition of Eliot and I. A. Richards, or—at a further remove—of Coleridge, he viewed all poetry as a synthesis of opposing forces, a poem as a pattern of resolved stresses. Tragedy, "where the tension between attraction and repulsion is most powerful," is thus properly regarded as the highest form of poetry.[102]

The New Criticism movement's basic statement on drama as a separate poetic genre was the text *Understanding Drama* (1945) by Brooks and Robert B. Heilman (b. 1906). Here, after a general introduction to the drama as a literary form, a series of plays—"arranged in a scale of ascending difficulty" from *Everyman* to *The Way of the World*—was analyzed, according to the principles of this school, in terms of characterization, structure, theme, symbol, and Brooks's central critical concerns: unity, balance, metaphor, and irony. "Dramatic" is defined in an accompanying glossary as "presented by means of characters in action and marked by the tension of conflict."[103] As a genre, Brooks and Heilman consider drama closer to poetry than to prose fiction, since these two forms share a high concentration of effect in language, and both are strictly controlled by the restrictions of the form.[104]

Una Ellis-Fermor (1894–1958), in *The Frontiers of Drama* (1945), also attempts to abstract the essentials of dramatic form, on the assumption that each art, like any organism, carries within its embryo "certain principles that determine its growth and features."[105] These she attempts to discover by seeking the related characteristics of all great plays and by investigating those plays "upon the borders" whose creators attempted to subjugate material not normally considered suitable for this art. In this manner she develops the usual features of drama: a conflict of strong passions, a clearly shaped series of related deeds coordinated by a "certain grand simplicity of idea." Conversely, certain material such as religious experience, complex ideas, or epic events cannot readily be encompassed in the limited scope of the drama. Ellis-

---

[101]Ibid., 227.

[102]Cleanth Brooks, *The Well-Wrought Urn* (New York, 1947), 230.

[103]Cleanth Brooks and Robert B. Heilman, *Understanding Drama* (New York, 1945), 500.

[104]Ibid., 26.

[105]Una Ellis-Fermor, *The Frontiers of Drama* (New York, 1945), 1.

Fermor considers tragedy in the light of another limitation, that of mood, because its achievement depends upon the maintenance of "a strict and limiting balance between two contrary readings of life and their sequent emotions at work within the poet's mind."[106] This balance is much the same as that suggested by Bentley, a recognition both of evil and pain and of some ultimate reconciliation or interpretation in terms of good. Since this balance is always accessible to the superior artist, Ellis-Fermor sees no obstacle to the creation of modern tragedy, but she warns against confusing it with the drama of social concern. The latter deals with remedial ills or shows human misery with no hope of release, either of which rejects the balance of tragedy, which shows both evil and good as inevitable.

The theory of tragedy advanced in James Feibleman's (b. 1904) *Aesthetics* (1949), though couched in more philosophic terms, is ultimately very similar. Feibleman analyzes both tragedy and comedy as explorations of the disjuncture between the actual and the possible; his arguments are often reminiscent of German romantic theory. "Essence," says Feibleman, in direct opposition to Sartre, "is a larger and more inclusive category than existence," and both comedy and tragedy hint at this larger category. Every actual thing is "fragmentary, in constant striving to complete itself," which inevitably brings it into conflict with "other fragments which are engaged in the same pursuit." In this conflict, sooner or later, all values are defeated, since nothing in the world of actuality is eternal.

Tragedy, in Feibleman's analysis, mourns the loss of these defeated values but at the same time "tacitly but emphatically" recognizes the being of another world, beyond that of actuality, where these values are preserved and whence they may at some future time return.[107] Comedy is an indirect treatment of what tragedy treats directly, and is more intellectual than emotional. "While tragedy is concerned with values *qua* values, comedy is concerned with the limitations on those values."[108] Tragedy thus preaches acceptance; comedy preaches action, since comedy implies that the limitations can be overcome and the conditions improved. Nevertheless, tragedy is the deeper form, since whatever improvements are made, all products of actuality must perish; we may hope, but not be certain, that they will someday return.

America's major serious dramatists of the 1940s, Arthur Miller (b. 1915) and Tennessee Williams (1911–1983), defended tragedy as a possible modern genre, but each proposed a rethinking of the genre

[106]Ibid., 127.
[107]James Feibleman, *Aesthetics* (New York, 1949), 67–68.
[108]Ibid., 77.

in the light of contemporary concerns. Soon after the opening of his *Death of a Salesman* in 1949, Miller contributed two related essays to the *New York Times*: "Tragedy and the Common Man" and "The Nature of Tragedy." In the second essay Miller views tragedy in terms close to those of Anderson. Any stage work must involve conflict, either external as in melodrama, or internal as in drama and tragedy. What distinguishes tragedy from the merely pathetic is that tragedy "brings us not only sadness, sympathy, identification and even fear; it also, unlike pathos, brings us knowledge or enlightenment." This knowledge, like Anderson's affirmation, shows "the right way of living in the world," through the negative example of characters like ourselves who realize, too late, that what they are is not what they might have been. The tragic hero "has missed accomplishing his joy," but shows us that this joy is possible.[109]

In the better-known first essay, Miller defends modern tragedy on somewhat different grounds, focusing not on opportunity for fulfillment but on the strength of the hero's commitment. The tragic feeling is aroused in us by a character "ready to lay down his life, if need be, to secure one thing—his sense of personal dignity." The "tragic flaw" is simply "his inherent unwillingness to remain passive in the face of what he conceives to be a challenge to his dignity, his image of his rightful status." His action against a degrading scheme of things enlightens us by pointing "the heroic finger at the enemy of man's freedom."[110] The German romantic emphasis on freedom versus necessity seems to be echoed in this view, but there is also a striking similarity to the almost contemporary statements of Sartre on the hero's defiance of the absurd world. The central theme of this essay, however, is not the definition of tragedy but the defense of the common man as tragic hero, and Miller insists that the traditional elevated hero is merely an outmoded convention. The desire to justify one's existence, to seek self-fulfillment is felt at least as strongly by the common man.

In the preface to *The Rose Tattoo* (1950), entitled "The Timeless World of a Play," Williams suggests that the distancing of the dramatic world, its existence "outside of time," is the source of both its lasting strength and its current weakness. In the theatre, freed from our haunting sense of impermanence, we can view human actions and emotions openly and clearly. Relieved of self-consciousness, we recognize and pity man asserting his dignity by deliberately choosing "certain moral values by which to live."[111] Williams does not feel that this process is as automatic

[109] Arthur Miller, *The Theatre Essays*, ed. Robert Martin (New York, 1978), 11.
[110] Ibid., 4–5.
[111] Tennessee Williams, *The Rose Tattoo* (New York, 1950), ix.

as it was in earlier times or as Miller suggests. Modern man has become so guarded in acknowledging his feelings and sensibility even to himself that the "timeless and emotional" world of the play works upon him only temporarily, if at all, and remains distinct from his life outside the theatre. Perhaps only by "a certain foolery, a certain distortion toward the grotesque" can the modern dramatist force his audience to recognize the relationship between its world of temporality and the timeless world of drama.[112]

America's third leading dramatist of the 1940s, Thornton Wilder (b. 1897), attempted to sketch in brief the essential features of theatrical art. His perceptive little essay "Some Thoughts on Playwriting" (1941) advances "four fundamental conditions of the drama" as distinct from other arts, and considers some implications of each. Under the first condition, that theatre is a collaborative art, Wilder discusses the relationship between script and interpretation, with particular attention to the actor. The actor must serve as collaborator, and the writer must create each character "in such a way that it will take advantage of the actor's gift."[113] The second condition, that theatre is addressed to a group mind, requires a broad field of interest and a clear forward movement in the action. Here Wilder places himself in the tradition of Sarcey, Archer, and Matthews. The third condition, that theatre lives by conventions, exposes the search for realistic illusion as an error, since conventions encourage the necessary "collaborative activity of the spectators' imagination" and raise the action from the specific to the general.[114] Finally, the theatre takes place in perpetual present time, representing pure existence. This deprives the dramatist of many descriptive and explanatory devices utilized by the writer of novels, but in exchange it gives him the enormous power of the living form.

The theatre's "perpetual present time" (remarked by Wilder) or "timeless world" (by Williams) was for Gertrude Stein (1874–1946) a source not of power but of distraction and irritation, since it rarely harmonized with the emotional present of the audience. Emotion, she stated in "Plays" (1934), is always in "syncopated time," always "either behind or ahead of the play."[115] Though the business of art should be "to completely express the complete actual present," the drama's devotion to crisis and climax is alien to the experience of excitement and relief in real life, its introduction and development of characters far more abrupt and arbitrary than in real time. Thus Stein called for and attempted to create a theatre that would be "timeless" or "perpetually

---

[112]Ibid., x.
[113]Augusto Centeno, ed., *The Intent of the Artist* (Princeton, 1941), 89.
[114]Ibid., 95.
[115]Gertrude Stein, *Writings and Lectures*, ed. Patricia Meyerowitz (London, 1967), 58.

present" in a more radical manner than Williams or Wilder suggested. It would reject such traditional concerns as crisis and climax, beginning, middle, and end, foreshadowing, character development, and intrigue in favor of a flow of existence—a concept reminiscent of Bergson. The spectator would not attempt to enter the emotional world of such a drama but merely observe it as he would a landscape, which is simply there. "You may have to make acquaintance with it, but it does not with you." Thus the disjuncture between the development of emotion on stage and in the audience is no longer a matter for concern: "The relation between you at any time is so exactly that that it is of no importance unless you look at it."[116]

The final group of theorists of drama from this period have only recently gained widespread attention with the application of semiotic methods to theatre analysis. The first significant attempts were carried out in the 1930s and 1940s in Czechoslovakia by some members of the group of scholars known as the Prague Linguistic Circle. Drawing upon the methodologies of Russian formalism and the structural linguistics of Ferdinand de Saussure (1857–1913), the Circle published in 1928 a set of "Theses." These laid the foundations for a semiotic study of art by distinguishing between the practical function of language, when it is primarily directed toward what is denoted in the external world, and the poetic function, "when language is directed toward the sign itself."[117]

In the key essay "Art as Semiotic Fact" (1934), Jan Mukařovský (1891–1975) insists upon the elucidation of the semiotic character of art as essential to the understanding of its function. Taking the sign as "a reality perceivable by sense perception that has a relationship with another reality which the first reality is meant to evoke," Mukařovský considers the nature of this second reality when the sign is an artistic one. In Saussure's theory, the sign is composed of a "signifier" (such as the word "red") which cultural usage has established to evoke a "signified" (here the concept of the color). Mukařovský observes that certain of the arts, especially the so-called "representational" ones, might use signifiers in this "informational" way, but that all signs in art are primarily "autonomous." Rather than being restricted to a signified with a specific "existential value," they refer to "the total content of social phenomena" of any given milieu—"philosophy, religion, politics, economics, and so on."[118] Mukařovský's brief essay "An Attempt at a Structural Analysis of a Dramatic Figure" (1931) analyzes a limited set

[116]Ibid., 75.
[117]*Thèses: Travaux du cercle linguistique de Prague* (Prague, 1929), 14.
[118]Jan Mukařovský, *Structure, Sign, and Function*, trans. John Burbank and Peter Steiner (New Haven, 1978), 84.

of "autonomous" signs, the gestural signs utilized by Chaplin in *City Lights*.

The Prague linguists who were particularly interested in the analysis of the theatre drew heavily on the first major Czech work on theatre theory, *The Aesthetics of the Art of Drama* (1931) by Otakar Zich (1879–1934). Although Zich was not in fact a member of the structuralist school, his concerns overlapped theirs in a number of important ways. He rejected the fusion of Wagner's *Gesamtkunstwerk* to consider the mutual interaction of various elements in dramatic art and came very close to the Saussurian signifier and signified in his distinction between the material or physical (audial and visual) elements and the imagery or conceptual elements of dramatic action, dramatic character, dramatic plot, and dramatic place.

The development of these ideas in semiotic terms was first undertaken by the folklorist Petr Bogatyrev (1893–1970), whose interest in popular forms allowed him to qualify some of the generalizations made by Zich on the basis of the drama of realism. In "Semiotics in the Folk Theatre" (1938) and "Forms and Functions of Folk Theatre" (1940), Bogatyrev suggests transformation as the central feature of the theatre. There all aspects of material reality, especially the actor, become something different; at the same time, the transformation must be to some degree transparent. The spectator is aware of the actor both as person and as character and thus both as a living person and as a system of visual and aural signs. Zich's realistic theatre plays down this "special artistic duplexity," while folk theatre recognizes its great artistic potential.[119]

Bogatyrev also disagrees with Zich on the uniform stylization of theatrical performances in different periods, again pointing to the mixture of styles utilized by folk theatre to enrich the potential vocabulary of signs. One aspect of theatrical transformation is the shifting of signs from one style to another. The real and the abstract may also change place: a real object, such as a ring, may stand for an abstraction, like love or wealth; an abstract object, such as a pile of cubic forms, may stand for a real object, such as a mountain, or for another abstraction, such as the ladder to success. Every new performance explores these transformational possibilities anew; it "struggles against traditional signs and strives to put new signs in their place."[120] Moreover, the unusually dense sign system in the theatre allows it to appeal to a large and diffuse audience, since the same action may be comprehended simultaneously

---

[119]Petr Bogatyrev, "Forms and Functions of Folk Theatre," trans. Bruce Kochis, in *Semiotics of Art: Prague School Contributions*, ed. Ladislav Matejka and Irwin Titunik (Cambridge, Mass., 1976), 48.

[120]Ibid., 47.

but by means of different signs "by spectators of various tastes, various aesthetic standards."[121]

Karel Brušák, in "Signs in the Chinese Theatre" (1939), stressed other aspects of signification by considering yet another theatrical tradition. Brušák considered Chinese drama insignificant from a literary point of view; "performance is paramount," and the elements of performance "carry numerous obligatory signs standing for referents that are often very complex."[122] To Brušák, the importance Bogatyrev and Zich give to individual interpretations is a bias of Western criticism, which deals with a theatre including "numerous chance shaping factors ranging from a producer's conception to an actor's diction." Chinese theatre, on the contrary, offers a "generally homogeneous" structure and a stock of several essentially fixed systems of "lexicalized signs," which can be decoded with moderate precision.[123]

Jindřich Honzl (1894–1953), director of the avant-garde Liberated Theatre in Prague, in "Dynamics of Sign in the Theatre" (1940), unites Zich's structuralist approach with Bogatyrev's emphasis on transformation. Everything that makes up reality on the stage stands for something else; thus the theatre is essentially a complex of signs, all easily transformable. A visual sign may change to an aural one; an actor may take on the function of scenery, or vice versa. It is this very changeability that has caused so much confusion in defining dramatic art or locating its essence. Honzl suggests that the essence be sought in the old idea of action, but with the realization that word, actor, costume, scenery, and music may all advance the action as "different conductors of a single current that either passes from one to another or flows through several at one time."[124] The changes in this current reflect different performances, different styles, different periods. In "The Hierarchy of Dramatic Devices" (1943), Honzl focuses on a particular kind of transformation, that of poetic reference into action not shown but imagined by the audience. This device, common in classic theatre and relatively rare in realism, Honzl considers a major source of theatrical power, since theatrical perception is based upon "an opposition between mental representation and reality" synthesized into an emotionally charged "seeing" by the spectator's act of interpretation.[125]

Jiří Veltruský, in "Man and Object in the Theatre" (1940), agrees with Honzl that the transformability of theatrical signs and the flexibility

---

[121]Ibid., 44.
[122]Karel Brušák, "Signs in the Chinese Theatre," trans. by the author, in ibid., 59.
[123]Ibid., 73.
[124]Jindřich Honzl, "Dynamics of Sign in the Theatre," trans. Susan Larson, in ibid., 91.
[125]Honzl, "The Hierarchy of Dramatic Devices," trans. Susan Larson, in ibid., 123.

of the flow of action through different sign systems are central. This flexibility, Veltruský suggests, makes the theatre particularly effective in a process akin to Shklovsky's defamiliarization. Shifting signs "can be used to link together unconventionally various aspects of reality," allowing the theatre to develop powerful social statements by showing "new ways of perceiving and understanding the world."[126] In a 1942 essay, Veltruský warns that Honzl's image of action shifting from sign to sign like a flowing current should not suggest a conflation of different sign systems: "Words cannot be fully translated into gestures, pictures, music, the meaning of a picture cannot be fully conveyed by language, music, the play of facial muscles, etc." Each type of sign refers to the same reality, but none captures that reality in its entirety. Thus the theatre should be considered a laboratory of "contrastive semiotics."[127]

Mukařovský's "On the Current State of the Theory of the Theatre" (1941) may be taken as a kind of summation of this first generation of semiotic/structural criticism of theatre. The aim of such criticism, says Mukařovský, is to demonstrate that despite all the material tangibility of its means, the theatre is essentially "an immaterial interplay of forces moving through time and space and pulling the spectator into its changeable tension, into the interplay which we call a stage production, a performance."[128] The analysis of this interplay has encouraged the study of certain basic elements of theatre—particularly the text, the dramatic space, the actor, and the audience, for each of which Mukařovský summarizes what seem to be the central critical problems. When semiotics reemerged as a major critical concern in the late 1960s, these areas of investigation laid out by Mukařovský still defined its basic orientations.

[126]Jiří Veltruský, "Man and Object in the Theatre," trans. Paul Garvin, in *A Prague School Reader on Esthetics, Literary Structure, and Style* (Washington, 1955), 106–7.
[127]Veltruský, "Notes Regarding Bogatyrev's Book on Folk Theatre," trans. Ladislav Matejka, in Matejka and Titunik, *Semiotics*, 281–82.
[128]Mukařovský, *Structure*, 203.

20

The Twentieth Century, 1950–1965

THE INTERNATIONAL IMPACT OF *En attendant Godot* (1953) by Samuel
Beckett (b. 1906) focused attention on a new style of antirealist drama
in France that would become the most successful avant-garde theatre
the century had yet produced. Grouping Beckett's work with the early
plays of Eugène Ionesco (b. 1912) and Arthur Adamov (1908–1971),
French literary and theatrical reviewers hailed a new movement. The
appearance of Camus's *Mythe de Sisyphe* in 1951 had made "the absurd"
a fashionable literary catchword, and a number of writers seized upon
it to classify the new drama—despite the protests of both the existentialist dramatists like Sartre and Camus, and recipients of the appellation like Ionesco and Adamov. In "Cerisy-la-Salle" (1953), Ionesco
called "absurd" a fashionable term which was "vague enough to mean
nothing any more and to be an easy definition of anything." He considered the world "not absurd but incredible." One can in fact make
sense of existence, discover laws, establish "reasonable" rules. Only
when one seeks the sources of existence or tries to understand it as a
whole does incomprehensibility appear.[1] In *L'homme et l'enfant* (1968),
Adamov expressed his opposition to the label even more strongly, finding it both incorrect and irritating. "Life is not absurd, only difficult,
very difficult."[2]

Nevertheless, Martin Esslin's (b. 1918) influential *Theatre of the Absurd*
(1961) again evoking Camus's book as the philosophic touchstone of
the new drama, essentially established this term for English criticism.
The French, attempting to separate the tradition of Sartre and Camus

[1]Eugene Ionesco, *Notes and Counter Notes*, trans. Donald Watson (New York, 1964),
216–17.
[2]Arthur Adamov, *L'homme et l'enfant* (Paris, 1968), 111.

from that of Beckett and Ionesco, have shown more willingness to accept Ionesco's offered alternate term, "théâtre de dérision."

Beckett, Ionesco, and the early Adamov were in fact united less by a common philosophical position than by a commonality in what they rejected: the accepted conventions of the traditional French theatre, the emphasis upon the word, the linkage of cause and effect, a bias toward realism, and the psychological development of character. The existentialist playwrights, emphasizing situation, helped to undermine the psychological approach, as did the writings of Edmond Husserl and Maurice Merleau-Ponty (1908–1961), whose turn from reflexes to the structures organizing these reflexes had already affected the French novel. Adamov made this change a sort of campaign, calling his work an Artaud-inspired protest against the "so-called psychological works" filling the stage.[3] The foreword to *La parodie* and *L'invasion* (1950), in terms strongly reminiscent of Artaud, pleads for "a living theatre, that is, a theatre where gestures, attitudes, the true life of the body have the right to free themselves from the convention of language, to pass beyond psychological conventions, in a word to pursue to the ultimate their deepest signification."[4]

Ionesco's diary for April 10, 1951, calls *La cantatrice chauve* "abstract theatre. Pure drama. Anti-thematic, anti-ideological, anti-social-realist, anti-philosophic, anti-boulevard-psychology, anti-bourgeois, the rediscovery of a new free theatre."[5] *Les chaises* he considers "an attempt to push beyond the present frontiers of drama"; it is neither psychological, social, cerebral, nor poetic.[6] In "Notes sur le théâtre" (1953), he says he wishes to strip dramatic action of "all that is particular to it: the plot, the accidental characteristics of the characters, their names, their social setting and historical background, the apparent reasons for the dramatic conflict, and all the justifications, explanations, and logic of the conflict," and to achieve an abstract conflict "without psychological motivation."[7] Thus freed from all external distractions, the theatre can concern itself with more basic material, what Ionesco in 1954 called "theatre from within": man's "most deeply repressed desires, his most essential needs, his myths, his indisputable anguish, his most secret reality and his dreams"–all normally hidden by "social crust and discursive thought."[8] For such expression, words are not the only medium available and often not the best for the dramatist. "Everything is lan-

[3]Adamov, *Théâtre*, 4 vols. (Paris, 1955), 2:9.
[4]Adamov, *Ici et maintenant* (Paris, 1968), 14.
[5]Ionesco, *Notes*, 181.
[6]Ibid., 190.
[7]Ibid., 217–18.
[8]Ibid., 223–24.

guage in the theatre," says Ionesco in a passage recalling the Prague linguists, "words, gestures, objects, action." The author is "not only allowed, but recommended to make actors of his props, to bring objects to life, to animate the scenery and give symbols form."[9]

Esslin considered Jean Genet (b. 1910), together with Beckett, Ionesco, and the early Adamov, a major absurdist playwright—a choice certainly defensible in terms of Genet's technique but less so in terms of his philosophic outlook. A general vision of the human condition with images of isolation, meaninglessness, and the breakdown of language unites the first three of these authors, but Genet's plays turn more toward a fascination with patterns of domination and submission, often with sadomasochistic overtones, couched in metaphors of elaborate ceremony and ritual. In a 1954 preface to *Les bonnes* (1947), Genet calls the celebration of the Mass the greatest drama available to modern Western man, whose theatre has lost, perhaps irrevocably, the element of the numinous. Theatre should be "a profound web of active symbols capable of speaking to the audience a language in which nothing is said but everything portended." Genet, like Artaud, feels that Eastern theatre still offers this, while in the West the actor "does not seek to become a sign charged with signs. He merely wishes to identify himself with a character."[10]

The first appearance (1954) of Brecht's Berliner Ensemble in Paris made a profound impression. In "La révolution Brechtienne," an editorial for a special issue of *Théâtre populaire* devoted to Brecht (January-February 1955), Roland Barthes (1915–1980) discusses the challenge posed by Brecht, a challenge to "our habits, our tastes, our reflexes, the very 'laws' of the theatre in which we live."[11] Brecht's theatre takes up the great progressive themes of our time—that art can and must intervene in history, dealing not with aesthetic universals but with social and political needs, explaining rather than expressing, insisting that the world can be other than it is. In "Mère Courage aveugle" (1955) Barthes suggests that Brecht, in renouncing participation, restored theatre to its original purpose as civic ritual. He revealed traditional dramaturgies as radically false, "dramaturgies of abdication," and offered instead a drama of "maieutic power," which "represents and brings to judgment," simultaneously "overwhelming and isolating."[12]

Barthes's "Les tâches de la critique Brechtienne" (1956) proposes four levels of analysis for considering this new theatre. The first is

---

[9]Ibid., 29.
[10]Jean Genet, "A Note on Theatre," trans. Bernard Frechtman, *Tulane Drama Review* 7, 3 (Spring 1963):37.
[11]Roland Barthes, *Critical Essays*, trans. Richard Howard (Evanston, Ill., 1972), 38.
[12]Ibid., 35.

sociology, the means by which various contemporary publics attempt to deal with Brecht. The second is ideology, not the "message" of the plays but the general method of explanation. The third is semiology, especially interesting in Brecht because of the distance he puts between signifier and signified in his rejection of illusion. Finally comes morality, involving for Brecht analysis of a historical situation in the light of a belief in the potential for change.

Costume as a part of the Brechtian *Gestus* inspired Barthes's "Les maladies du costume de théâtre" (1955). Brecht's production of *The Mother* shows that costume as *Gestus* is concerned neither with naturalism nor with traditional display: it is instead an argument, based on a "precise vestimentary code," and selected to communicate "ideas, information, or sentiments."[13] Such an element must not be parasitical but relate organically to other components of the production, a sign working with and relating to other signs. (The emphasis on Brecht's use of the sign was taken up again by Barthes in the 1960s when, influenced by structural linguistics, he developed further the semiotic study of art.)

The Brecht productions in Paris came at a critical moment for Adamov, who was in the process of moving toward a more socially engaged theatre. In "Théâtre, argent et politique" (1956), he renounced his early work for its indifference to political matters and cited Brecht as his new model. Historical drama has traditionally sought to create a "fallacious identification" between spectator and hero, he says, while Brecht, by creating a critical distance, allows the spectator to consider the historical process more objectively, to become aware of the continual "antagonism of classes, one of which is always oppressed by another."[14] The dominant class, for its own protection, has encouraged a drama of fatalism, but Brecht exposes this deception by showing social conditions as alterable. *Paolo Paoli* (1957) was Adamov's first major drama to utilize this new approach; in a program note of 1959 he calls it the result of his discovery that "a work of art, and especially a theatre piece, acquires reality only if placed in a defined social context," that new techniques are meaningless if not put "in the service of an ideology," which today means "in the service of Marxism-Leninism."[15]

In "Qui êtes-vous Arthur Adamov" (1960), an article written for the bulletin of Planchon's Théâtre de la Cité, Adamov suggested that the theatre must show "both the curable and incurable aspect of things." The incurable is "that of the inevitability of death. The curable aspect

---

[13]Ibid., 46–47.
[14]Adamov, *Ici*, 42.
[15]Ibid., 93.

is the social one."[16] Indeed, much of the drama in France during this period might be considered drama either of the incurable, following Beckett, or of the curable, following Brecht.

The suspicion with which Adamov in the late 1950s looked back on his earlier experimental works was shared by others, among them the English critic Kenneth Tynan (b. 1927), who in "Ionesco: Man of Destiny?" (1958) expressed his concern over the growing popularity and influence of a drama seemingly devoid of any positive humanistic values, of faith in logic or communication. A significant exchange of articles followed in the pages of the *London Observer*, providing one of the most thoughtful exchanges of the period on the question of the drama's relation to society. Ionesco, responding to Tynan, distinguished between the merely "social" and "true society," which is "revealed by our common anxieties, our desires, our secret nostalgias." Political concerns are merely pale reflections of these deeper realities; "it is the human condition that directs the social condition, not vice versa." Drama in turn should deal with these basic realities: "the pain of living, the fear of dying, our thirst for the absolute."[17]

Tynan answered that Ionesco was attempting to isolate art from life and thus from any value outside itself, an impossible and morally questionable goal. "Every human activity, even buying a packet of cigarettes, has social and political repercussions," and to deny this is an abdication of moral responsibility. "If a man tells me something I believe to be an untruth, am I forbidden to do more than congratulate him on the brilliance of his lying?" Tynan inquired.[18]

Echoes of earlier debates could be heard here: the Marxist critics against those they called formalists; the socially engaged realists of the late nineteenth century against the proponents of art for art's sake. Ionesco willingly accepted the "formalist" label in his essay "La Coeur n'est pas sur la main" (1959). The function of art, Ionesco said, is not teaching but testifying about existence through its structure or inner logic. Like Langer, he called it "a way of knowing that involves the emotions," tied to no "ideology or closed system of thought." Art's purpose is simply to be what it is; indeed, that appears to be all that one can say about the entire universe. The business of existence is to exist.[19]

A very similar view of contemporary drama was expressed by the German dramatist Wolfgang Hildesheimer (b. 1916) in his "Erlanger

---

[16]*Cité-Panorama* 9 (1960), quoted in Martin Esslin, *The Theatre of the Absurd* (New York, 1960), 73.

[17]Ionesco, *Notes*, 91.

[18]Ibid., 100.

[19]Ibid., 102.

Rede über das absurde Theater" (1960). Ionesco's theatre, suggested Hildesheimer, is neither Aristotelian nor epic; it shows a universe in which questions are asked but no answers are given or even implied. Drama is a sort of "symbolic ceremonial, in which the spectator assumes the role of man who questions, while the play represents the world that gives no reasonable response."[20] The playwright must feel this absurdity to write about it, as only a religious dramatist can write authentic religious drama; his play, like the world it reflects, simply exists, without purpose, without cause and effect. This places a new challenge before the actor, trained in the theatre of logic. He must feel and express the same alienation in his interpretation as is found in the script, an even more radical alienation than that sought by Brecht in his epic theatre.[21]

Michel de Ghelderode (1898–1962), the Flemish dramatist, was never really part of the "théâtre de dérision"; his career was nearly over when the new wave headed by Beckett and Ionesco appeared, and his grotesque lyrical dramas, mixing gothicism and realism, had little in common with theirs. Still, the new attention to experimental theatre in France worked to his benefit, and however much his plays differed from those of Ionesco, his attitude toward the relationship of drama to society was quite similar. In the most extended discussion of his theories, the Ostend Interviews of 1951, he spoke of his plays as arising "not from an intellectual emotion but from a visual emotion. Theatre begins always with the eyes."[22] Ghelderode shared the symbolist interest in marionettes; he found in them theatre in its "pure, savage, and original state," a theatre of magic, of symbolic sounds, colors, and objects. "Objects are signs, and the visionary arrangement of such signs is the function of theatre."[23] Such theatre may be rejected as irrational and visionary, but it cannot be expected to yield a discursive message. In an interview shortly before his death, Ghelderode specifically condemned engaged and thesis plays. He recognized Brecht as a theatrical genius but called him a misguided one, who denied divination in favor of materialism and refused to acknowledge that theatre is "an art of instinct and not of reason."[24]

In "More than a Play" (1950), Eric Bentley suggested that a strong religious element still characterized the French theatre, appearing both as orthodox (Ghéon and Claudel) and as magical and heretical (Artaud).

[20]Wolfgang Hildesheimer, "Erlanger Rede über das absurde Theater," *Akzente* 7 (Dec. 1960):548.
[21]Ibid., 556.
[22]Michel de Ghelderode, *Seven Plays*, trans. George Hauger (New York, 1960), 15–16.
[23]Ibid., 23.
[24]Samuel Draper, "An Interview with Michel de Ghelderode," *Tulane Drama Review* 8, 1 (Fall 1963):46–47.

The latter variety "attacks the bourgeois world order and the liberal, materialistic, secular philosophies" and champions "the reality of instincts and visions."[25] Barrault had been instrumental in bringing both aspects of religious drama to the stage, and the only serious artistic and intellectual rival of this theatre, Bentley concludes, is that of Brecht, which seeks a political rather than magical goal. Thus the contemporary French theatre, and perhaps other theatre as well, seems to be facing the choice between politics and magic, Brecht and Barrault. Both, Bentley warns, run the risk of compromising theatre art itself by seeking an extratheatrical end. In *What Is Theatre?* (1956), Bentley attempts to define the elusive art of theatre. After considering the special qualities of theatre space, the actor, and the audience, Bentley turns to the dramatist, whose goal, like that of any author, is "to search for the human essence,"[26] which theatre allows him to do in a particularly daring, public, audacious way. Brecht among contemporaries perhaps comes closest to this, but Bentley mistrusts Brecht's self-confidence in his solution. Our highest sense of humanity has been lost, and the drama should lead us in search of it with "the audacity of Dionysos and the controlling hand of Apollo."[27]

The interest in bringing theatre back into harmony with orthodox religion, which Bentley noted in France in the work of Claudel and Ghéon, appeared elsewhere in Europe at this same time, most significantly in the plays of Eliot in England and those of Ugo Betti (1892–1953) in Italy. Among Betti's last writings is his most complete statement on this subject, "Teatro e religione" (1953). He notes a growing tendency in serious theatre to deal with needs which "although variously expressed are essentially religious,"[28] needs which seek universal and absolute values. Today's dramatist must enter into the spiritual desert where many live and, starting from zero, "prove again certain things to everyone." He must show the desire in even the most cruel, selfish, and lost souls for "mercy, harmony, solidarity, immortality, trust, forgiveness, and, above all, for love" far greater than "the pale imitations offered by this world." By expressing and exploring this need, the dramatist establishes "one side of a perimeter," whose complete figure is at last revealed as God.[29]

At Betti's death a glowing tribute was paid to him as a "passionately involved" modern dramatist by the young Spanish playwright Alfonso

---

[25]Eric Bentley, *In Search of Theatre* (New York, 1953), 382.
[26]Bentley, *What is Theatre?* (New York, 1956), 264.
[27]Ibid., 270.
[28]Ugo Betti, "Religion and the Theatre," trans. Gino Rizzo and William Meriwether, *Tulane Drama Review* 5, 2 (Dec. 1960):4.
[29]Ibid., 12.

Sastre (b. 1926), who was himself seeking a way to make the theatre more deeply relevant to human needs. In "Teología del drama" (1953), Sastre essentially echoes Betti in proposing as a theme "the tragedy of a world without Christ, the tragedy of a world with its back turned on the truth."[30] Soon after this, largely under the influence of Sartre, Sastre moved away from a specifically Christian to a more generally humanistic "engaged" theatre, but he carried into his new orientation a suspicion of total commitment to any specific political program, which brought him closer in thought to Camus than to Sartre. He had warned in "El teatro revolucionario" (1952) that political engagement tends to blind one to the truths in the adversary's position. Engagement, he contended, must be based on "an objective vision of sociopolitical realities" rather than on an *a priori* commitment to any social or political position, which is "unacceptable, not only for the theatre, but for any social activity, artistic or otherwise."[31] In *Drama y sociedad* (1956), a collection of his early essays, Sastre added some new observations. He explains how a dramatist can write engaged drama without preconception, by a rather Brechtian process: without openly espousing any particular doctrine, he "attempts to stimulate prepolitical states of emotion and awareness—states which frequently encourage a purifying political action."[32]

Sastre believed that Aristotle need not be abandoned, only updated, as he first explained in "Tragedia" (1953). The plot of tragedy must include "painful events which arouse in the sufferer or at least in the spectator fundamental questions about the meaning of those events" and about "the possibility of reducing their effect by human effort." Pity and fear thus serve to stimulate the spectator "to make meaningful social decisions, ranging from individual assistance to revolution," and *katharsis* consists of two phases: "immediate or personal purification and social purification."[33] These two phases are treated as a double focus in tragedy in "Drama y sociedad," where Sastre speaks of the "permanent" and the "corruptible." He relates the first, involving metaphysical conditions, to the theory of Aristotle and to Unamuno's "tragic sense of life." The second has to do with social conditions and inspires a wish to improve them. The categories recall Adamov's "incurable" and "curable," but Sastre resisted the choice that Adamov felt must be made between the two.

"Teatro épico, teatro dramático, teatro de vanguardia" (1963) praises both Beckett and Brecht, but considers each as having a partial per-

[30]Alfonso Sastre, "Teología del drama," *Correo literario* 85 (Dec., 1953):10.
[31]Sastre, "El teatro revolucionario," *Guía* (Aug. 1952):22.
[32]Sastre, *Drama y sociedad* (Madrid, 1956), 71.
[33]Sastre, "Tragedia," *Correo literario* 70 (Apr. 15, 1953):10.

spective. By a strategy derived from Hegel, or more proximately from Lukács, Sastre proposes a *"realismo profundo"* that would fuse Becket and Brecht, showing "the tragic quality of individual human existence as well as the perspective of historical development," balancing Beckett's pessimism with Brecht's "naive optimism."[34] The opening section of Sastre's book *Anatomía del realismo* (1965) calls this strategy "a negation of Brecht's negation of the Aristotelian drama," the next necessary step after Brecht's own criticism.[35]

Antonio Buero Vallejo (b. 1916) accepts neither of the two aspects of tragedy postulated by Sastre. "A play is not a treatise or even an essay," he states in the "Palabra final" to his play *Historia de una escalera* (1950). "Its mission is to reflect life, and life is usually stronger than ideas."[36] This attitude—together with his call for the "rehabilitation" of Unamuno's tragic sense in the theatre, and his praise for existentialism's revelation of the radical character of human life "as a problem whose solution can never be fully attained"[37]—seems to place Buero clearly on the side of Adamov's "incurable." Yet Buero distances himself equally from Beckett and Brecht even though, like Sastre, he expresses admiration for both. His essays "La tragedia" (1958) and "Sobre la tragedia" (1963) return to the early romantic vision of a tragedy of hope, based on the conflict between freedom and necessity. It demonstrates "man's desire to free himself from the bonds—external or internal, social or individual—which enslave him."[38] Despair cannot exist without hope, and from these opposites the tragic dramatist creates a higher reconciliation, "something great and unchangeable which lies beyond tragedy but which can be reached only through it."[39]

The Living Theatre, probably the best known experimental group of the 1960s, became in its later years for many the prototype of the engaged theatre, but its theory and practice throughout its existence remained closer to Artaud than to Brecht, and its message more mystical than political. When Judith Malina (b. 1926) and Julian Beck (b. 1925) organized their venture in 1947, they were interested in establishing a permanent repertory that would offer moving and meaningful plays. "What we wanted to do most," said Beck in a later interview, "was to enhance the blossoming forth of poetry in the theatre, while preserving a certain realism, of course."[40] This goal remained constant

[34]Sastre, *Anatomía del realismo* (Madrid, 1965), 129.
[35]Ibid., 8.
[36]Antonio Buero Vallejo, *Historia de una escalera* (Barcelona, 1950), 155.
[37]Bernard Dulsey, "Entrevista a Buero Vallejo," *Modern Language Journal* 50, 3 (Mar. 1966):153.
[38]Buero Vallejo, "Sobre la tragedia," *Entretiens sur les lettres et les arts* 22 (1963):57.
[39]Buero Vallejo, *Hoy es Fiesta* (Madrid, 1957), 100.
[40]Pierre Biner, *The Living Theatre*, trans. anon. (New York, 1972), 20.

through a variety of experimentation during the 1950s. In a 1961 interview, Beck stated, "We believe in the theatre as a place of intense experience, half dream, half ritual, in which the spectator approaches something of a vision of self-understanding, going past the conscious to the unconscious, to an understanding of the nature of things." Poetry, or else a language "laden with symbols and far removed from our daily speech" seemed for this the proper vehicle.[41]

Under the influence of the avant-garde musician John Cage, Beck and Malina sought to open up the creative process, to encourage their actors to seek their own style and break free from the authority of the director. They were attracted for a time to Brecht but came to feel that he, like Shaw, had made a fatal error in assuming that one could not speak directly to an audience about human problems; both therefore sought to disguise their message—Shaw with wit, Brecht with theatrical diversion—allowing the audience to enjoy the distraction and ignore the essence. Artaud, whom Beck and Malina discovered in 1958, seemed to offer a better approach. They saw in Artaud the ultimate revolutionary, who recognized that the "steel world of law and order" created to protect us from barbarism also cut us off from all our deepest impulses and sensations, turning us into the heartless monsters who wage wars and oppress and exploit our fellows. If, following Artaud, we could release our trapped feelings, "we might find all this suffering intolerable, the pain too great to bear, we might put an end to it," to feel instead "the joy of everything else, of loving, of creating, of being at peace, and of being ourselves."[42]

In preparation for the Living Theatre's production of Brecht's *Mann ist Mann*, Beck discussed Brecht's acting theory with the company and established a workshop headed by Joseph Chaikin (b. 1935) to explore techniques in nonnaturalistic acting. Chaikin shared Beck's view that a better theatre and a better society should be sought, in America at least, not by stimulating an audience to Marxist class consciousness but by freeing the individual unconscious. The "sophistication of our time," says Chaikin in his notebooks, has "closed off a great deal of our total human response." Actors "must open up again, become naive again, innocent, and cultivate our deeper climates—our dread, for example."[43]

While Brecht attempted to demonstrate that society and the historical process are not unalterable, Chaikin's own company, the Open Theatre (founded in 1963), worked to present a parallel refutation of the Freudian idea of the unalterability of human nature. Its work was thus closely

---

[41]William Glover, "The Living Theatre," *Theatre Arts* 45, 12 (Dec. 1961):63.
[42]Kenneth H. Brown, *The Brig* (New York, 1965), 25.
[43]Quoted in Robert Pasolli, *A Book on the Open Theatre* (New York, 1970), 95.

allied to the theories of the existential psychoanalysts of the 1960s, such as David Cooper and R. D. Laing, who rejected Freud's positing of society as a norm to which the patient should be "adjusted"; they argued that so-called aberrant behavior might be a legitimate response to sicknesses in society itself. The Open Theatre viewed the traditional "dramatic character" as Brecht viewed the "Aristotelian action," as an illustration of determinism, and evolved a similar strategy for undermining it: whatever character realities were established at the beginning of an action were soon destroyed or transformed into others, which were in turn soon supplanted, often with little transition, so that the audience was prevented from relaxing into any fixed view of the characters—a psychological *Verfremdungseffekt*.

Viola Spolin's *Improvisation for the Theatre* (1963) provides a methodology for the Open Theatre approach. She agrees that the basis of creativity is personal freedom, a state resisted by the "authoritarianism that has changed its face over the years from that of the parent to the teacher and ultimately the whole social structure."[44] Attempting to satisfy this external judge, we lose our ability to relate personally and organically to the world, losing touch with both our selves and our art. Improvisation for Spolin is a means of overcoming this loss. Since life and theatre constantly place crises and choices before us, theatre can train us in a spontaneous, natural choice of alternatives, a constant recreation of self in response to the world, which Spolin calls transformation.[45] Thus she comes from a different direction to the same conclusion as several members of the Prague linguistic circle, that the continuing appearance of new reality is the essence of theatre. Transformation became a central concept and technique at the Open Theatre. According to Peter Feldman, Chaikin's assistant director, "the transformation, besides questioning our notion of reality in a very graphic way, also raises certain questions about the nature of identity and the finitude of character."[46] Fittingly, the last major production of the Open Theatre, in 1971, was entitled *The Mutation Show*.

Another aspect of Spolin's theory was her belief that children's play and game structure are "different in degree but not in kind from dramatic acting."[47] This concept—recalling Schiller's *Spieltraub* and Evreinov's interest in transformation and the theatricalization of life—was reinforced during the later 1960s by the work of contemporary sociologists and became a major concern in dramatic theory.

The influence of Brecht and of French experimentation began to be

---

[44]Viola Spolin, *Improvisation for the Theatre* (Chicago, 1963), 7–8.
[45]Ibid., 392, 394.
[46]Quoted in Pasolli, *Open Theatre*, 95.
[47]Spolin, *Improvisation*, 5.

felt in the theory and practice of the English theatre about 1956, the year that John Osborne's (b. 1929) *Look Back in Anger* ushered in a new era in British playwriting. Characteristically, the English dramatists of Osborne's generation were less extreme than their continental contemporaries in experimentation and less inclined to theoretical pronouncements about their work. Nevertheless, the conflict between the theatre of political engagement and that of metaphysical speculation may be traced, if in muted form, here as well.

The political side was distinctly the more evident of the two. A set of credos from the new generation called *Declaration* appeared in 1957, including statements by Tynan and Osborne. The introduction to the volume insisted that the so-called "Angry Young Men" represented no united movement but did share an indignation with contemporary society and values, and wished to change them. Tynan, in "Theatre and Living," found only three attitudes toward life open to the dramatist: the faithful mirroring of it, good or evil; the attempt to change it; or the denial of it by withdrawal into private fantasy. Tynan acknowledged sympathy only with the second: art "must go on record; it must commit itself," and the drama must be "vocal in protest."[48]

Osborne's "They Call it Cricket" stated that he wished to give his audiences "lessons in feeling. They can think afterwards."[49] This has been quoted to suggest a vagueness or lack of political concern in Osborne, but the ensuing pages, condemning in the strongest terms the arrogance and folly of contemporary British society, indicate otherwise. The dramatist, Osborne feels, should not suggest specific tactics of reform; that is the proper task for economists, sociologists, psychologists, and legislators. Drama's contribution to a new socialist society is to raise the proper questions: the meaning of human work, the value of life, the expectations, hopes, and fears. It should demonstrate the proper values but not seek "to discover the best ways of implementing them."[50]

John Arden (b. 1930) likewise insists that the theatre must address social matters in its own terms. Pure social criticism is "dangerously ephemeral" he says in "Telling a True Tale" (1960), and the theatre must counter by expressing it "within the framework of the traditional poetic truths."[51] In a letter to *Encore* in 1964, he warns against drama that gives easy or obvious answers, mere placebos to moral and social questions. The audience must be presented with an honest view of the ambiguous and contradictory situations life offers, and its instruction

[48] Tom Maschler, ed., *Declaration* (London, 1957), 111–12.
[49] Ibid., 65.
[50] Ibid., 83.
[51] John Arden, "Telling a True Tale," *Encore* 7, 3 (May-June 1960):25.

must be by indirection and implication. It shows choices and the effects of choices; the audience must consider the root causes that made each choice occur.[52]

Much more openly concerned with the social relationships of the drama, Arnold Wesker (b. 1932) issued a sort of manifesto in "Let Battle Commence" (1958). He calls for a teaching theatre, giving spectators "an insight into an aspect of life which they may not have had before."[53] New audiences should be sought among the working classes, who have traditionally considered the theatre the domain of bourgeois intellectuals and irrelevant to their own experience. Doing so will be difficult, for the dramatist must address this new public on its own terms and in its own language, while they must deal with a totally new set of values, requiring a change as significant as religious conversion. Wesker's "Art—Therapy or Experience" (1964) charged the entire British cultural and educational system with considering art a leisure activity for the upper and middle classes, instead of the answer to a "burning need" and the compelling curiosity to understand "the marvelous nature and complexity" of human lives. Education in the arts is impossible until educators realize that the work of art is "a battle field, where ideas are fought and values affirmed."[54]

The proper role and form of an engaged theatre, always a central concern of Marxist aesthetics, was a subject of considerable and sometimes heated debate in German theory, both East and West, during this period. In *Das Prinzip Hoffnung* (1954), Ernst Bloch applied his interpretation of Marxism to a wide variety of cultural phenomena, including music, painting, design, dance, architecture, film, circus, and popular fiction. In a chapter devoted to the theatre, he draws upon both Brecht and Schiller to define its purpose: "to influence the desires of the world toward real possibilities—as a paradigmatic institution."[55] Bloch insists that despite the pressures to convert both art and popular culture into escapism, mere entertainment, spiritualized abstraction, or self-contained artifact, the human spirit continues to express through these manifestations its repressed need for fulfillment. Art is "a laboratory and at the same time a festival of real possibilities," and the theatrical performance is an anticipatory appearance (*Vor-Schein*) of material that is not yet in existence but toward which human consciousness is striving.[56] Art thus prefigures, even though it cannot bring into full being, the "concrete utopia" that exists "at the horizon of every

[52]Arden, "Letter," *Encore* 11, 5 (Sept.-Oct. 1964):52.
[53]Arnold Wesker, "Let Battle Commence," *Encore* 5, 4 (Nov.-Dec. 1958):19.
[54]Wesker, "Art—Therapy or Experience," *Views* 4 (Spring 1964):47.
[55]Ernst Bloch, *Gesamtausgabe*, 15 vols. (Frankfurt, 1959), 5:492.
[56]Ibid., 249.

reality." Brecht's concept of *Verfremdung* is adjusted by Bloch to reflect this: estrangement in the theatre rises not from the spectators' becoming aware of the contradictions in present social reality, but from their catching glimpses of the "beautiful strange," the utopia of fulfillment to which their inner vision responds while still embedded in the contemporary reality where such fulfillment can not yet be achieved.[57]

Official East German literary policy from the beginning of the 1950s had been to encourage "socialist realism" and discourage "decadent" and "experimental" forms, essentially the position taken by Lukács in the expressionism debate. This policy was challenged in 1956 at a conference of directors and playwrights, however, and a "dialectical theatre," drawing more evenly upon the theories of both Brecht and Lukács, was proposed. Peter Hacks (b. 1928), the chief spokesman for this position, discussed it in two 1957 essays in *Neue Deutsche Literatur*: "Das Theater der Gegenwart" and "Das realistische Theaterstück." The official view of socialist realism held that East German society could solve all social conflicts, and that drama portraying such conflicts therefore misrepresented reality. Hacks calls for a more "dialectical" view of realism, which recognizes the inevitability of conflict in all phenomena and regards the spectator as someone "involved in change." He cites Brecht as the pioneer of this idea of theatre, developed in opposition to the bourgeois theory of Lessing.[58] Conflict and contradiction are equally important, Hacks notes, in Lukács's doctrine of the "typical." The proletarian hero should possess "the typical contradictions of his society" and be placed in "the typical contradictory situations of his period." He is not "a hero reduced by flaws; he is hero and non-hero at the same time."[59]

During the 1960s Hacks proposed another approach to socialist drama, particularly in the essays "Versuch über das Theaterstück von Morgen" (1960) and "Das Poetische" (1966). He suggested two ways of presenting socialist reality: a dramatist could depict the historical process in action, as in Hacks's "epic-sociological" dramas of the 1950s, or he could anticipate the fulfilled pattern of history, thus "poeticizing" the material, as he was now attempting in his "classical" dramas. Hacks justified this shift on the grounds that his audiences had already liberated themselves from the oppressive social conditions that were the concern of the epic-sociological drama and had embarked upon the quest for self-fulfillment within a free humanist society.[60] The new classic play is thus "in

---

[57]Ibid., 430.
[58]Peter Hacks, "Das Theater der Gegenwart," *Neue Deutsche Literatur* 5, 4 (April 1957):128.
[59]Hacks, "Das realistische Theaterstück," *Neue Deutsche Literatur* 5, 10 (Oct. 1957):104.
[60]Hacks, *Das Poetische* (Frankfurt, 1972), 29.

harmony with the perspective of the viewer." It contains conflict, which is essential to drama, but "since its social reality rests upon secure foundations, these conflicts do not become demonic, the basis of tragic phenomena."[61] Brecht's *Einfühlung* and *Verfremdung* clearly influence the terms Hacks uses to describe spectator reactions. The *Identifikationswert* (identification factor) creates an emotional sympathy with the play's hero, while the *Unwirklichkeitswert* (unreal factor) opens the spectator to the play's poetic vision of the workings of an as yet unachieved utopia.[62] This latter idea seems to owe much to Bloch's concept of the "beautiful strange." Much more than Brecht, Hacks emphasizes in Hegelian fashion the combination of the two reactions for the success of the drama of the future.

In his 1958 book, *Wider den missverstandenen Realismus*, Lukács returned to the themes of the expressionism debate but now called the enemy of "realism" not "expressionism" but "modernism." While expressionism depicts the general condition of man in a "social and historical environment," open to change and improvement, modernism depicts man as "solitary, asocial, unable to enter into relationships with other human beings" in a world without direction or goal.[63] Although his central positive example is Thomas Mann and his negative one is Franz Kafka, Lukács also returns again to Brecht, suggesting that in his later plays Brecht wisely abandoned the sterile modernist approach—parallel to "the pretentious, empty experimentalism of Ionesco"—to return to traditional "living beings grappling with the forces of their environment."[64]

Once again Lukács's intolerance of experimentalism aroused protest, and the "modernism" debate of the late 1950s stirred echoes of the expressionism debate of two decades before. Lukács's major opponent this time was Theodor Adorno (1903–1969), one of the best-known members of the Frankfurt Institute for Social Research. In "Erpresste Versöhnung," his 1958 review of Lukács's book, Adorno charges Lukács with confounding art and life by focusing upon content to the exclusion of style and form. The artist must always recognize that his creation is to some degree implicated in the total system of rationality of his own time, and if he wishes to defy that totality, he must somehow do so within the process of creation itself, not simply in the subject matter but in the way the subject matter is treated.[65]

---

[61]Ibid., 36.
[62]Ibid., 121, 126.
[63]Georg Lukács, *The Meaning of Contemporary Realism*, trans. J. and N. Mander (London, 1962), 20.
[64]Ibid., 86–87, 89.
[65]Theodor Adorno, "Erpresste Versöhnung," *Monat* 122 (Nov. 1958), 44.

In the essay "Versuch, das Endspiel zu verstehen" (1961), Adorno defends Beckett, perhaps the leading "modernist" dramatist, as perhaps the most successful creator of truly engaged theatre. Traditionally, a play has three levels of meaning: the meaning of the dialogue, the overall meaning, and the metaphysical meaning. Traditional engaged drama has found meaning at one or another of these levels, but Beckett sets them in opposition. The meaning sought at the dialogue level is denied at the overall and the metaphysical levels, so that no meaning is offered, even that of "absurdity."[66]

Adorno takes up this idea again in his famous essay "Engagement" (1962). Beckett is praised as an artist who, like Kafka, "explodes from within the art which a committed approach subjugates from without and thus only in appearance." Work like Beckett's "compels a change of attitude" instead of merely calling for it, as traditional "committed works" do.[67] Adorno's major examples of less successful "committed" authors are Brecht and Sartre. Both seek to pit a subjective good—Sartre's existentialist hero, Brecht's proletariat—against the forces of objectivity and reification, yet neither achieves within the actual construction of the plays a reflection of the subjective-objective struggle as Beckett does.[68] Sartre presents his theses with "flat objectivity"—the spontaneity he advocates encounters no resistance, and his work is assimilated into the system he seeks to reject. Brecht, by attempting to deny illusion, an inescapable part of theatre, only creates a new order of illusion, a bogus social reality that comes no closer than Sartre to encouraging real social understanding. The anonymity of postindustrial man and the helplessness of postatomic man is betrayed by dramas which, as Lukács advises, show "reality" in terms of developed characters and choices.

Much in this position recalls the earlier Lukács and more generally the tone of cultural despair so common in German intellectual circles at the turn of the century. Little wonder, then, that Adorno's theory was attacked as advocating not realistic appraisals of social reality but resignation and hopelessness. The journal *Theater Heute* in 1963 surveyed 11 contemporary playwrights on the question of how contemporary reality should be presented on the stage. In the most extended response, Rolf Hochhuth (b. 1931), whose *Der Stellvertreter* had just premiered with enormous effect, directly challenged Adorno as the principal spokesman for a view that Hochhuth called unacceptable to drama: the view that meaning is impossible in today's world, that the

---

[66]Adorno, *Noten zur Literatur*, 4 vols. (Frankfurt, 1961), 2:86-87.

[67]Adorno, "Commitment," trans. Francis McDonagh, *New Left Review* 87-88 (Sept.-Dec., 1974):86-87.

[68]Ibid., 78.

actions and choices of individuals are unimportant, and that drama which suggests otherwise is a distortion of reality. "Unpopular as this may be at the moment, one of the most essential tasks of the drama is to maintain that man is a responsible being," argues Hochhuth, adding that if Marxism insists that "the individual has disappeared in the bourgeois era, due to the industrial organization of society," then drama is no longer possible, since the individual is its basis. In a subsequent revision of this article for a Lukács *Festschrift* in 1966, Hochhuth quoted as support Schiller's "eternally valid artistic law—'only through the individual have I perceived the whole.' "[69] Like Lukács, Hochhuth has little tolerance for the abstraction or stylization of either Beckett or Brecht. He prefers the use of specific historical material treated realistically, as in his own documentary dramas, though this does not imply—as he points out in the "Historische Streiflichter" appended to *Der Stellvertreter*—a naturalistic presentation of raw data: "Reality was respected throughout, but much of its slag had to be removed." Again, Schiller is cited as the authority. The dramatist seeks "symbolic" truth and thus cannot use "a single element of reality as he finds it." His work "must be idealized in *all* its parts if he is to comprehend reality as a whole."[70]

Adorno became aware of Hochhuth's attack only when the article appeared in the Lukács *Festschrift*, and he responded in an open letter to the *Frankfurter Allgemeinen Zeitung* in February 1967. He denies the necessity of the individual in drama, insisted upon by Lukács and Hochhuth; he recalls that Hegel and Marx had said of individualism that it is "not a category of nature but historically decided, arising from labor." In the modern industrial world, continues Adorno, the individual has given way to "anonymous configurations which can no longer be understood by the person unacquainted with theory, and which in their infernal coldness can no longer be tolerated by the anxious consciousness." Dramatists are tempted falsely to personalize these objective circumstances, as Hochhuth has done, an approach to which Adorno applies the American word "phoney."[71] A more honest choice would be to create a form that reflects "the absurdity of the real" as realism cannot do. Brecht had the proper instinct, but could not escape an individualist bias, which Beckett at last managed to do.

The response of Peter Weiss (b. 1916) to the 1963 *Theater Heute* survey was much less definite than that of Hochhuth. Weiss suggests that the portrayal of the contemporary world can legitimately involve many

---

[69]Rolf Hochhuth, "Das Absurde ist die Geschichte," *Theater Heute* 4, 13 (1963):73.

[70]Hochhuth, *The Deputy*, trans. Richard and Clara Winston (New York, 1964), 287–88.

[71]Adorno, "Offener Brief an Rolf Hochhuth," *Theater Heute* 8, 7 (July 1967):1.

subjects and many approaches; the theme of "a reasonable, enlightened portrayal of benevolent events" is as valid as the countertheme of "the confusion and fluidity of all events and an autistic dream world." What is essential is that the drama be clear and comprehensible, since it must always "share, renew, or call something into question; the spectator should always learn something."[72]

In the course of the following two years, during which his *Marat/Sade* brought him an international reputation, Weiss moved to a theoretical position much closer to Hochhuth's. In a November 1964 interview, he condemns the hopelessness of Beckett, who "lives like a kind of embryo in a world too strong for him" and denies the power of art to change life. The stage should rather show the circumstances of contemporary life in such a way that spectators will react by saying, "We must change that. It can't go on that way." However, Weiss avoided a specific political commitment until late in 1965, when he announced, in "Peter Weiss' Entscheidung," his conversion to revolutionary socialism. Ideally, he said, a work of art should be free "politically and aesthetically," but in the present world of competing ideologies, and particularly in divided Germany, "every word that I write down and release for publication is political."[73] A choice then must be made as to which ideology is more likely to lead at last to the desired freedom for art, and Weiss chooses socialism.

Most of Weiss's subsequent articles have been essentially political, but in "Notizen zum dokumentarischen Theater" (1968), he considers the type of drama that might be best suited to contemporary political needs. His projected "documentary theatre" collects authentic material and presents it "adjusted in form but not in content." The goal, "to make a model of actual contradictions, a pattern open to change, out of the fragments of reality," suggests Brecht, although Weiss emphasizes the dramatist's choice of positions rather than the public's. The drama should present both sides of political disputes, but it is the duty of the dramatist to make clear which is the superior one. "Objectivity" should be shunned as a concept used by the group in power "to justify their own actions" and to protect their present advantage.[74]

Max Frisch (b. 1911), in his essay "Der Autor und das Theater" (1964), admits the inevitable political dimension of the drama, which is produced by and witnessed by persons participating in society. Nevertheless, a play should be created "out of love of theatre, nothing else," and thus be governed by the rules of art, not politics.[75] There is little

---

[72]Peter Weiss, "Dies hier ist Bühne ...," *Theater Heute* 4, 13 (1963):70.
[73]Weiss, "Peter Weiss' Entscheidung," *Theater Heute* 6, 10 (Oct. 1965): 14.
[74]Weiss, *Rapporte* 2 (Frankfurt, 1971), 98–99.
[75]Max Frisch, *Gesammelte Werke*, 12 vols. (Frankfurt, 1956), vol 5, pt. 2, p. 349.

evidence, he argues, that any of the millions of spectators who have seen Brecht's plays have in fact changed their political opinions as a result, and it is clearly in response to Brecht that Frisch calls his *Biedermann und die Brandstifter* (1958) a "Lehrstück ohne Lehre" (teaching play with nothing taught). Art, because it stresses the importance of the individual, is naturally subversive, but it cannot effectively engage in direct political action.

A central work of postwar German dramatic theory, Peter Szondi's (b.1929) *Theorie des modernen Dramas* (1956) draws—like Lukács, Benjamin, and Adorno—upon the Hegelian idea, reflected in Marx, that form and content are inseparably bound in a dialectic relationship. Therefore, he attacks the "traditional view" (the view attributed at this same time by Adorno to the later Lukács) that separates form and content, that emphasizes the latter and makes the former "historically indifferent."[76] The evolution of modern drama, in Szondi's interpretation, clearly refutes this assumption. Modern drama is a creation of the Renaissance, fully synthesized in France in the seventeenth century. Such devices as prologue, epilogue, and chorus were abandoned in favor of the dialogue as human interaction became drama's central concern. This created a closed "absolute" form, apparently self-contained, denying both author and audience. The spectator was not allowed to participate as spectator, but only as imaginary sharer in the stage action. He could choose "only total separation or total identification."[77] The distinctive features of this drama—the unities, the maintenance of illusion, the determinism arising from the avoidance of chance—all contributed to enforcing this self-contained world.

Toward the end of the nineteenth century, Szondi's analysis continues, the content of drama began to change from "events of human interactions shown in the present," and the change created a crisis within the traditional form. Dramatists like Maeterlinck explored the dramatic possibilities of non-events; others like Strindberg dealt with internal states instead of interactions; still others like Ibsen and Chekhov focused on the past or future.[78] Important works were created during this period of instability, but tension of this sort between form and content could not be maintained for long. The early twentieth century saw some dramatists attempting to save traditional form, and others attempting to evolve new forms to suit a new content. Among the attempts to save the old form were naturalism, pieces almost devoid of content like the well-made play, and the various attempts to return to

[76]Peter Szondi, *Theorie des modernen Dramas* (Frankfurt, 1956), 11.
[77]Ibid., 17.
[78]Ibid., 75.

some version of classicism, perhaps most successful in the "situational" dramas of Sartre. The experiments that began to acknowledge the new content introduced in various ways a subject-object relationship into drama, a recognition of the presence of both creater and public, breaking open the absolute form of traditional drama. The most successful of these Szondi calls "epic," a term he applies to a wide range of experimentation of which Brecht is only one example. Such works point outside themselves, present a "microcosm representing a macrocosm" which is explained and set forth by an "epic I," a creative presence that acknowledges an audience to whom this demonstration is directed.[79] Aside from Brecht, Szondi sees this process at work in expressionism, in Piscator's "political reviews," in Eisenstein's montage, in Pirandello, in the interior monologues of O'Neill, in Wilder, and in Miller's *Death of a Salesman*.

Lucien Goldmann (b. 1913) drew upon the writings of Lukács, several of which he translated into French, and upon the Marxist tradition in general for his interest in social realism and his conviction that form and content are inseparably related and both conditioned by social forces. In his view, the study of literary works thus inevitably involves a study of the social and political sources of these works. In *Le dieu caché* (1955), Goldmann posits three possible critical approaches to a text: positivistic (textual analysis), intuitive (personal feelings), and dialectic, which seeks to fit the work into larger and more complete contexts.[80] Goldmann cites Dilthey's concept of world view as a move toward this third approach, elaborated and made more accurate and scientific by Lukács. The critic using this approach should consider a work in light of "the whole complex of ideas, aspirations, and feelings which links together the members of a social group (a group which, in most cases, assumes the existence of a social class) and which opposes them to members of other social groups."[81] He then proceeds to analyze both the tragedies of Racine and the philosophy of Pascal in the light of the conflict between the coherent world view of seventeenth-century rationalism and the concept of a God of transcendent being and values.

This analysis leads in turn to a general theory of tragedy, which Goldmann elaborates more fully in *Jean Racine: Dramaturge* (1956). He defines tragedy in terms echoing Lukács's *Die Seele und die Formen*: "a spectacle under the permanent regard of God."[82] God never intervenes but nonetheless requires adherence to absolute values in a world of compromise, contingency, and circumscribed existence. All tragedy re-

[79]Ibid., 141.
[80]Lucien Goldmann, *The Hidden God*, trans. Philip Thody (New York, 1964), 8–12.
[81]Ibid., 17.
[82]Goldmann, *Jean Racine: Dramaturge* (Paris, 1956), 17.

flects this conflict. The Greek tragic hero sets himself against both the world and the human community, represented by the chorus. In Racine the authentic community has been lost, so the chorus has disappeared, and the isolated hero brings about his own destruction either by refusing to accept the flawed world or by attempting to impose upon the world his own desires.

The Marxist interest in the historical and sociopolitical dimensions of theatre pointed the way to a more general study of theatre as a sociological phenomenon, a theoretical approach which has steadily increased in importance in the second half of the twentieth century. The major strategies of such an approach were outlined in 1956 by Georges Gurvitch (1894–1965) in a remarkably prescient article, "Sociologie du théâtre," which summarized the proceedings of a 1955 conference on "Le théâtre et la société" at Royaumont. The "profound affinity of the theatre with society," Gurvitch suggests, opens possibilities of sociological investigation in both directions, the examination of "theatricality" in society or of social organization in theatre.

Anticipating the subsequent research of writers such as Goffman and Turner, Gurvitch calls attention to the theatrical element in all social ceremonies, even in "a simple reception or a gathering of friends."[83] Moreover, "each individual plays several social roles," those of class, profession, political orientation, and so on. As for the theatre itself, it is composed of a set group of performers, portraying a social action, encased in another social dynamic made up of performance and public. On these grounds Gurvitch suggests a range of possibilities for sociological research in theatre: first, the public, particularly its degrees of diversity and cohesion; second, the relationship between the play and its style, its interpretation, and its particular social setting; third, the internal organization of the acting profession, and its relationship to other professions and to society as a whole; fourth, the relationship between the content of plays and their society; fifth, the changes in the interpretation of this content and the relationship of these changes to changing social configurations; sixth, the social functions of theatre itself in different societies.[84]

Turning to a consideration of theatre as an instrument of social experimentation, Gurvitch dismisses the psychodramas of Moreno as far too controlled and goal-directed to serve as models. Anticipating the experimentation of guerilla theatres and of such directors as Boal, Pörtner, and Schechner (see Chapter 21), Gurvitch proposes "theatrical

[83]Georges Gurvitch, "Sociologie du théâtre," *Les lettres nouvelles* 34-36 (Jan.-June 1956): 197.
[84]Ibid., 202-4.

representations camouflaged in real life, without the members of the group suspecting what is happening" or representations designed "to stimulate collective actions, freeing the public from precise and structured social cadres and inciting them to participate in the play of the actors and to extend it into real life."[85]

Gurvitch's observations on the "theatricalism" of social life were explored in some detail by sociologists and anthropologists in the late 1950s—Erving Goffman in *The Presentation of Self in Everyday Life* (1959), Neal Gross et al. in *Explorations in Role Analysis* (1958), R. Caillois in *Les jeux et les hommes* (1958), and M. Leiris in *La possession et ses aspects théâtraux chez les Ethiopiens de Gondar* (1958)—but theorists of the theatre did not develop Gurvitch's proposals until later.

The sole major example during the 1960s was Jean Duvignaud (b. 1921), whose *Sociologie du théâtre* (1963) was a pioneering study in such investigation. Surveying the course of theatre in Europe, Duvignaud finds significant relationships between playwriting, staging, and the organization and assumptions of society, but he rejects the theory that drama is "a simple reflection of the collective reality."[86] Instead, Duvignaud proposes four types of theatre, each responding to a different sort of social configuration. In "traditional societies," such as that of the Middle Ages, theatre reflects the beliefs of a generally stable system, attempting to depict man in his totality. A second type, exemplified by the Renaissance and classic Greece, appears when technical, economic, and social changes have so shifted within a traditional society as to force radical changes of structure. The theatre then expresses the tension felt within society, producing heroes who embody the collective desire both "to transgress the old rules" and "to punish this attempt at freedom."[87] Fools, madmen, criminals, visionaries, and heretics people such stages. The theatre of the "Italianate stage" in Europe represents a third type, when a power elite appropriates culture and civilization to itself and attempts to define and control the human condition within a rigid dramaturgy. Major dramatists within this type tend to be subversive, seeking to suggest the hidden domains of thought and action overtly denied by the theatre in which they work. The fourth is the modern type, the product of a highly relativistic and mobile society, a theatre seeking to present the diversity of available experience. In none of the four types does the theatre, as is generally believed, provide an answer to certain needs; it reflects desires still seeking definition. It poses questions to which answers are not yet available, opening vistas on the

[85]Ibid., 208-9.
[86]Jean Duvignaud, *Sociologie du théâtre* (Paris, 1963), 550.
[87]Ibid., 180.

future rather than solidifying the present. Thus theatre is and always has been "a revolt against the established order."[88]

Duvignaud's *L'acteur* (1965) deals primarily with society's relations to the actor and secondarily with the actor's own view of his art and his social function. Since the actor serves as the embodiment of the dreams man is not yet ready to acknowledge in society, he must remain always outside that society, an outcast, yet one with a mysterious power, like the *mana* described by the anthropologists.[89] Societies with no hope for change feel no need for theatre, but Duvignaud discusses three evolving "historic" types of societies with somewhat different attitudes toward the actor. Under monarchies, the actor leads a double life, as normal court functionary and as free spirit outside the class structure. His representation of a richer, freer existence, breaking through the established social barriers, makes him both threatening and fascinating, sought after and cursed. In liberal societies he becomes a product of consumption, placed in solidified roles which nevertheless reflect the hidden fears of the present or the half-formed ideologies of the future. In contemporary society, still burdened by conflicting ideologies, political systems, nationalities, and an unsettled technology, his task is still "to reveal in the flesh the still invisible, unrecognized tendencies of the society,"[90] the *Vor-Schein* of Bloch, a vision now of authentic and total existence in a society free of classes and other restrictive barriers.

The social role of drama was also considered by the Communist theorist Louis Althusser (b. 1918) in "Notes sur un théâtre materialiste" (1962), written on the occasion of a Parisian production of a late nineteenth-century Italian *verismo* drama by Giorgio Strehler's Piccolo Teatro. Althusser perceives and praises in this Italian work the same "internal dissociation" and "unresolved alterity" that made plays like Brecht's *Mother Courage* and *Galileo* such outstanding examples of "materialist theatre."[91] Classical theories of drama, he says, have considered the audience as either psychologically identifying with characters in the drama or consciously remaining outside the drama and viewing it objectively from the perspective of a "clear consciousness of self." Though the latter has been mistakenly associated with Brechtian theatre, neither is in fact what Brechtian or materialist theatre seeks to achieve. The spectator is inevitably involved in the drama but on a more basic level than that of psychological identification. He is "the brother of the char-

[88]Ibid., 566.
[89]Duvignaud, *L'acteur* (Paris, 1965), 275.
[90]Ibid., 204-5.
[91]Louis Althusser, *For Marx*, trans. Ben Brewster (London, 1977), 142.

acters, caught in the spontaneous myths of ideology, in its illusions and privileged forms."[92]

The question then becomes what the drama is to do with this inevitable cultural and ideological identification. Traditional drama, as Althusser sees it, reaffirmed and deepened cultural myths without escaping them, while Brecht sought to "displace" self-consciousness, to break or remove the mirror at the center of the drama, to "always defer" the center of the dramatic world, and to place it outside the illusion, toward reality. The imbalance and hence the dynamic of his drama arises from the tension between the "spontaneous ideology" depicted and the real conditions of the characters' existence, invisible to them but visible to the spectator "in the mode of a perception which is not given, but has to be discerned, conquered and drawn from the shadow which initially envelops it and yet produced it." This effect depends not upon "epic" acting style, placards, austere sets, or exposed lighting—all the trappings of the Brechtian theatre—but upon the internal dynamics of the Brechtian drama itself, "at once criticizing the illusions of consciousness and unravelling its real conditions."[93]

While theatrical theorists working in the Hegelian and Marxist tradition naturally stressed the manner in which theatre is conditioned by historical, social, and economic processes, other theorists have sought to identify the universal features of the drama that are equally applicable to different periods and nations. Among the most important of these have been those modern philosophers who turned to a consideration of aesthetics, an area neglected by a good deal of twentieth-century philosophy.

The work of Ernst Cassirer (1874–1945) on symbolism opened a particularly fruitful line of research. His *Philosophie der symbolischen Formen* (1923–1929) considered the various "functions of the human spirit" such as art, cognition, myth, and religion as all concerned with "symbolic forms," each creating an "image-world" which does not merely reflect the empirically given but in fact creates it "in accordance with an independent principle." Each of these functions provides a different road "by which the spirit proceeds towards objectivization, i.e., its self-revelation."[94] Cassirer devoted little systematic attention to art as such, and that little primarily to lyric poetry. The application of the philosophy of symbolic forms to the arts was more centrally the concern of Susanne Langer (b. 1895).

Langer's first major book, *Philosophy in a New Key* (1942), follows

[92]Ibid., 148.
[93]Ibid., 146–47.
[94]Ernst Cassirer, *The Philosophy of Symbolic Forms*, trans. Ralph Manheim, 2 vols. (New Haven, 1953–57), 1:78.

Cassirer in defining man essentially as a maker of symbols. These may be broadly divided into two types: the discursive, which deal with logical processes and whose major expression is language, and the nondiscursive, which deal with emotional states and whose major expression is art. Art for Langer is not the expression of emotions; it is about them, as language is about concepts. Art's symbols work simultaneously rather than serially, and they are shifting and multiple rather than specific; but they are by no means arbitrary or impossible to study, as the modern philosophers devoted to logic and semantics have implied.

Music, the purest expression of nondiscursive symbols and the art most familiar to Langer, is the primary illustration she uses in the first book, but in *Feeling and Form* (1953) she considers each of the major arts in turn, among them the drama. Each creates a "virtual" or symbolic realm of its own for the portrayal of some aspect of feeling, and just as discursive language brings order to the intellectual life, these symbolic realms bring order to the perceptual one. They educate us in feeling. The essential product of all poetic art (including drama) is an illusion of the processes of human life, "virtual history." The drama presents virtual history in the mode of enactment, as a series of actions working toward a completed pattern, a fulfilled form. The mode of literature in general is Memory, while that of drama is Destiny.[95] Quoting a 1933 British essay, "The Nature of Dramatic Illusion" by Charles Morgan, Langer calls this mode "form in suspense." The dramatist must create this form in so clear an outline that it provides a stimulus and a "poetic core" for actors and designers, while still leaving them scope for their own contributions. Both actors and dramatists must remember that they are creating virtual, not real history; this is the confusion that has led to the traditional debates over verisimilitude and emotional identification. An actor "does not undergo and vent emotions; he conceives them, to the smallest detail, and enacts them."[96]

Langer believes that the debate over the moral function of drama is based on the same misunderstanding. Moral questions are considered in drama only as thematic material, contributing to the primary goal of the art, the creation of a "pattern of felt life."[97] They are to drama what representation of objects is to painting—useful but not indispensable. Theoretical speculation on the great dramatic forms, comedy and tragedy, has also been beclouded, she says, by an emphasis on subject matter or mood rather than on the distinct organizing "rhythm" of each. Comedy illustrates man's contest with a threatening world, and

[95]Susanne Langer, *Feeling and Form* (New York, 1953), 307.
[96]Ibid., 323.
[97]Ibid., 326.

his triumph "by wit, luck, personal power, or even humorous, or ironical or philosophical acceptance of mischance."[98] Tragedy depicts the
more sombre rhythm of growth, maturity, decline, and death; in it man
undergoes his ultimate testing, and displays his fullest potential. The
destiny of comedy is fortune; that of tragedy is fate. But both are
created forms, artistic or symbolic expressions of human destiny, not
depictions of the real world. Seeking philosophical or ethical significance in the great dramas leads inevitably to confusion, since their
ultimate aim is neither philosophical nor ethical but symbolic. The
commanding form of the work expresses neither ideas nor specific
emotions but "the whole life of feeling," the totality of our subjective
being.[99]

Mikel Dufrenne's *Phénoménologie de l'expérience esthetique*, published in
1953 (the same year as *Feeling and Form*), agrees with Langer in emphasizing feeling: "The very height of aesthetic perception is found in
the feeling which reveals the expressiveness of the work."[100] However,
while Langer stresses the symbolic, communicative aspect of this feeling, Dufrenne—a phenomenologist—stresses perception: "The aesthetic object moves me to do nothing but perceive."[101] At its deepest
and fullest level, perception involves not only reflection but feeling,
defined by Dufrenne as the "reciprocity of two depths"—that of the
expressed world in the work of art and that of the spectator. Like
Langer, Dufrenne insists that art is a reflection not of reality but of
feeling, and so the question of "realism" is not a central one: "The
affective quality of the world matters more than its geography."[102]
Indeed, Dufrenne echoes Oscar Wilde in placing this affective world
first. Perception "begins with art," and art can be applied to reality
"because reality is, in a sense, its handiwork."[103] Man and reality both
belong to something more basic—to being itself—which exists prior to
the object in which it is manifested and to the subject which perceives
the manifestation. Neither subject nor object is necessary for being, but
both are necessary for a *consciousness* of being, which is what the spectator achieves by contemplation of the art object.

Another system seeking a common ground in all manifestations of
poetic expression was that developed by Northrop Frye (b. 1912). His
central work, *Anatomy of Criticism* (1957), views literature, as do Langer

---

[98]Ibid., 331.
[99]Ibid., 366.
[100]Mikel Dufrenne, *The Phenomenology of the Aesthetic Experience*, trans. Edward S. Casey
et al. (Evanston, 1973), 49.
[101]Ibid., 86.
[102]Ibid., 179.
[103]Ibid., 543, 547.

and Cassirer, as a symbolic system. But Frye, more in the tradition of Frazer, Jung, and Fergusson, sees behind these symbols not the emotional life of man but a set of archetypes whose coherent system evokes "the total dream of man."[104] This dream, common to man in all periods, structures in symbolic form man's basic needs, drives, and attempts to relate to the natural rhythms of the universe.

No single work could embody this total mythic consciousness, and Frye seeks to show how individual works or types of works fit into the total pattern. He suggests that four basic genres, comedy, romance, tragedy, and satire, correspond to the four seasons, spring, summer, autumn, and winter. Each at its extreme merges into the next, and each is subdivided into six phases that work through progressively smaller archetypal rhythms. Tragedy, for example, moves from the heroic to the ironic, from works dealing with the birth of the hero or the sufferings of his mother, through tragedies of youth and maturity, to those of death and demonic torture.

A similar system of interlocking forms, based upon the relationship of the audience to the myth presented, is used by Frye to explore the relationships of various specifically dramatic genres. Thus traditional religious drama, which he calls the *auto*, blends gradually into the secular study of a hero, which in turn blends into tragedy. As tragedy becomes less concerned with the hero and the inevitable and more with the sources of suffering, it becomes ironic, and reaches the "dead center" of complete realism. Comedy then emerges, first dealing with the world as it is, then becoming an increasingly idealized concept, and turning at last to music, dance, spectacle, and an attempt to draw the audience into its world. As this form, a kind of masque, becomes more subjective and psychological, it becomes also disturbing—a satyr play beyond the control of reason. Here we reach the point described by Nietzsche as that of the birth of tragedy, where the demonic meets the divine and the mythic cycle is complete.

All drama, indeed all literature (for despite passing nods at music and spectacle, Frye's vision of drama is essentially literary), is thus assembled into a total system which, once generally understood, is essentially discursive. The aim of this system is to explain why the genres have developed as they have, how they interrelate, and why particular themes, concerns, characters and situations occur in particular works. Frye's intention is to explain literary phenomena, not to judge between them, as his "Polemical Introduction" makes clear: "Criticism has no

---

[104]Northrop Frye, *Anatomy of Criticism* (Princeton, 1957), 118.

business to react against things, but should show a steady advance toward undiscriminating catholicity."[105]

A much more mechanical attempt at a categorization of all possible plots was made in 1950 by Etienne Souriau (b. 1892) in *Les deux cent mille situations dramatiques*. Looking back to Gozzi's famous claim and to Polti's 1894 book, Souriau proposed analyzing dramatic plots not, like Frye, on the basis of mythic archetypes but on the possible functional arrangement of various elements. Souriau posits six "functions" which by different combinations create a "morphology" or "calculus" of all possible dramatic situations. For ease in transcription, he gives them astrological names and symbols. The Lion represents the "thematic force" of the drama, embodied in its principal character. The Sun represents the goal sought by the Lion; the Earth, whoever or whatever will profit by the achieving of this goal. Mars is a rival or opponent. The Scale is the arbitrator who awards the goal to the Lion or to Mars. The Moon serves as a helper of any of the other five. The various "functions" may be filled by more than one character, and a single character may fulfill several functions. More than one situation also will be found in most plays, requiring a rearrangement of the "horoscope" representing each one. By means of an *"ars combinatoria"*— dividing, doubling, and variously arranging these functions—Souriau claims that his system can generate in fact 210,141 dramatic situations, covering every possible arrangement found in the world's drama.[106]

Drawing upon the work of Souriau and the Russian formalist Vladimir Propp (1895–1970), who attempted a similar analysis of the morphology of the folktale, the French linguist A. J. Greimas attempted in *Sémantique structurale* (1966) to establish a system accounting for verbal meaning of all kinds. Souriau's "functions" are here converted into more linguistically oriented nominal groups (*actants*) which have six possible "roles"—subject, object, sender, receiver, opponent, and helper. Single sentences are then analyzed in terms of actants, much as Souriau analyzes single dramatic situations.[107] Both directly and indirectly (through Greimas), Souriau exerted a distinct influence on semiotic studies of theatre as these developed in the late 1970s.

Paul Ginestier's *Le théâtre contemporain dans le monde* (1961), with a preface by Souriau, attempts to develop Souriau's insights into a more general theory of theatre. A drama, like a plant, says Ginestier, may be analyzed by "transversal slices" that reveal an "architectonic cohesis," which we find profoundly satisfying. A "dramatic geometry" of these

---

[105]Ibid., 25.
[106]Etienne Souriau, *Les deux cent mille situations dramatiques* (Paris, 1950), 144.
[107]A. J. Greimas, *Sémantique structurale* (Paris, 1966), 155–56.

structures can be set up, though this will provide only a partial analysis, since it will exclude their dynamic functioning interrelationship.[108] Ginestier seeks to conquer this methodological problem by a "dialectic" (Hegelian) strategy, composed of three analytic steps. The first "scientific" analysis moves from "geometric" analysis of the structure of parallel scenes, triangular arrangements, and other balanced patterns in character relationships to general observations on character. The second step, "psychological" analysis, begins with the central character, the hero, and attempts to demonstrate how the work is organized architectonically around him. The third step, "philosophic" analysis, combines the first two to show how theatre works dialectically as "physical simplification and spiritual triumph." Three "psychic morphologies" of drama are here developed. The first is the "conquest of the personality," based on activity, showing a hero's horizontal movement toward a goal. The second is the "call of misfortune," based on emotion, which shows the downward movement of the fall of man as a victim of fate. The third is the "conquest of the absolute," based on resonance, which shows upward movement from the physical world of relative values to the spiritual world of absolutes.[109]

The German critic Emil Staiger (b. 1908), like Langer, came to poetic theory with a strong interest in music and found part of his inspiration in the philosophy of Cassirer. His *Grundbegriffe der Poetik* (1946), however, evolves a much different view of the literary arts, reflecting in large measure the intellectual heritage of Hegel and, more specifically, of Heidegger. Central to Staiger are Heidegger's three fundamental modes of *Dasein* (being-in-the-world): *Befindlichkeit*, the way being "finds" itself placed in the world, expressed through moods or emotional attitudes; *Verfallen*, the sense of "decline" being experiences in contact with the world; and *Verstehen*, the "understanding" of an existential purpose beyond this contact. These three modes of existence correspond to the three modes of time (*Ekstasen*), past, present, and future; and though all three modes are always accessible, basic existence is always dominated by one of them. Although Heidegger himself did not apply this system to analysis of literary types, Staiger, looking back to Hegel and the romantic theorists, suggests a parallel between the *Ekstasen* and the traditional trivium of epic, lyric, and dramatic.[110]

His musical interest leads Staiger to emphasize the lyric, the poetic mode of *Befindlichkeit*, but he follows Hegel in calling the dramatic the third and highest stage of poetic expression. The lyric poet looks in-

---

[108]Paul Ginestier, *Le théâtre contemporain dans le monde* (Paris, 1961), 6–7.
[109]Ibid., 158.
[110]Emil Staiger, *Grundbegriffe der Poetik* (Zurich, 1951), 237–38.

ward, the epic poet outward, the dramatic poet toward a totality that involves ultimate meanings and destinations. "Everything depends—in the real sense of the word—upon the end."[111] To what end (*worumwillen*) is the central question of the dramatic mode. On this point Staiger comes close to Langer's concept of drama as the mode of destiny. Thus he calls lyric the style of remembrance (*Erinnerung*), epic that of presentation (*Vorstellung*), and dramatic that of suspense (*Spannung*). He is less concerned than Langer or Hegel with physical presentation; more crucial is the attitude of poet and audience. Thus the dramatic may in fact predominate in works epic or lyric in form.

Staiger also explains certain conventions and practices of the drama in philosophic terms. He feels there are two basic dramatic styles, "pathetic" and "problematic." In the first, a protagonist absorbs the public into his passionate experience, creating the elevation and lack of individual humanity traditionally associated with the tragic hero.[112] The second focuses not upon articulation of understanding but upon fulfillment of destiny. Epic and lyric elements are reduced to a minimum, and audiences are stimulated to focus on the ultimate solution to a problem. The traditional unities aid in the concentration of this focus.[113] In both types of tragedy Staiger follows the traditional German romantic view of tragedy as a genre demonstrating the failure of finite humanity to impose its limited order on the infinite cosmos. Comedy, by contrast, shows humanity content to live within the boundaries of the finite.

While Staiger suggested that specific formal manifestations in literary works could be best understood as manifestations of philosophic content, specific formal analysis, especially of drama, received very little attention in his work. A series of other German theorists during the 1950s, looking back to the writings of Wölfflin and Walzel early in the century, gave more specific attention to the interaction of form and content. Arnulf Perger (b. 1883) praises Walzel's general approach in *Grundlagen der Dramaturgie* (1952) but rejects Walzel's basic categories of "open" and "closed" form as too vague for the drama. Instead, he suggests *Einortsdrama* (drama set in a single place) and *Bewegungsdrama* (drama of motion). Each has typical concerns: the *Einortsdrama*, a conflict between closely related people, be they commoners or kings; the *Bewegungsdrama*, unfolding events. The first gives a "slice of life"; the second, life "in the round." The dramatist, considering the expectations of his public and his own concerns, will choose between these basic

[111]Ibid., 106.
[112]Ibid., 154.
[113]Ibid., 167–68.

modes (each with many variations), and his choice will determine both his handling of the material and its physical presentation. Perger specifically considers the result of this choice in terms of plot structure, character development, and dramatic idea. The question of setting (*das Raumproblem*) thus becomes "the ruling concern of dramatic art."[114] Perger's concern with the *Raum* provided a focus for a significant number of later theorists and producers of theatre in Germany.

The second volume of Robert Petsch's (1875–1945) *Wesen und Formen des Dramas* was left incomplete at his death, but its contents were summarized in some detail by Fritz Martini in 1953. In the published first volume (1945), Petsch briefly discusses the "poetic-dramatic" and "mimic-theatrical" tension in the drama, then analyzes plot construction, character, speech, music, verse, and the use of time and space. His second volume considers various typologies of the drama and their implications for content and form. The first typologies he discusses emphasize content and style: the traditional "tone or mood" categories of comedy, tragedy, and drama; national, historical, or sociological types such as the commedia, Greek tragedy, baroque Catholic drama, and French neoclassicism; subject divisions such as religious, historical, or love interest; stylistic types, such as naturalistic-mimetic, realistic-classic, or fantastic-romantic. He then turns to typologies of form, with particular attention to Walzel's concepts of "open" and "closed" drama, the working out of which in fact involves content as fully as form. Associated with closed form are "an idealistic premise, spiritually developed types, symmetry of lines, reduction of the mimic-theatrical, tightness of plot, elevated language, and emphasis on inner action"—all qualities associated in Petsch's first book with the "poetic-dramatic" polarity of theatre. The open form naturally represents the opposite "mimic-theatrical" pole, involving "a broad colorful spectrum of scenes, a loose pictorial composition, conflicting motives, ideals expanded to infinity, self-contained acts and scenes, kaleidoscopic changes, unresolved and incomplete action." Unlike Walzel, Petsch posits a "mediating form" between these two, exemplified by German classicism and particularly by Schiller. Here a "ruling freedom is joined with a measured strength," and a synthesis is maintained between unity and variety, and between freedom and constraint of form.[115]

A number of articles and monographs in Germany during the 1950s sought to apply the categories of Walzel to various dramatists and periods, and Volker Klotz in 1960 attempted to draw together all as-

[114]Arnulf Perger, *Grundlagen der Dramaturgie* (Graz, 1952), 11.
[115]Fritz Martini, "Robert Petsch: Wesen und Formen des Dramas," *Deutsche Viertel-jahrsschrift für Literaturwissenschaft und Geistesgeschichte* 27 (1953): 301.

pects of this question in his general study, *Geschlossene und offene Form im Drama*. Each form is considered in terms of its assumptions concerning plot, time, place, character, structure, and language. The single dominating principle of the closed form, says Klotz, is that "the part represents the whole," while in the open form "the whole appears in parts."[116] Closed drama stresses harmony, order, completeness. Its actions are symmetrical, its tragic hero sacrificed to a clear higher value. The characters are normally aristocratic but representative of all men. Their actions and speech are elevated, abstracted from empirical reality. Open drama seeks to suggest the multiplicity, ambiguity, and lack of focus in the empirical world by presenting fragmentary sections implying more than they show. The hero confronts not a symmetrical opponent but an array of shifting contingencies, and his fall establishes no clear order or unity. Characters, speech styles, and settings are varied, suggesting the boundless variety of reality.

In his concluding section, Klotz suggests possible combinations of the two forms. Schiller, for example, began as an "open" dramatist and became more "closed," while Grabbe evolved in the opposite direction. Certain historical periods favor one type or another; the closed form is "particularly suited to aristocratic and hierarchic societies or societies with a certain stability of belief and of social classes."[117] Yet there have rarely been periods when at least some examples of the opposing style were not produced. Thus in the drama of particular periods as in the work of particular dramatists, the analyst must usually speak of tendencies rather than of exclusive dramaturgical practices.

The methodological approach represented by Staiger and Petsch was criticized by Roman Ingarden (b. 1920) in an appendix added in 1960 to his *Das literarische Kunstwerk* (1931). This essay, "Von den Funktionen der Sprache im Theaterschauspiel," argues that these theorists, in their concern with form, have scarcely touched upon the complex and crucial question of how language is used in the staged drama. Ingarden's consideration of this question follows the same phenomenological strategy pursued in the major part of his book; that is, he is concerned not at all with evaluation or the social, moral, or political implications of a work, but purely with describing the manner in which the literary world is constructed and how it creates the effects of the literary experience. The drama is dealt with briefly in two sections in the main body of Ingarden's book. In section 30, theatrical dialogue is considered as an example of "boxing" (*Einschachtelung*), like the direct quotation of a character in a novel whose statements, because they are a quotation,

---

[116]Volker Klotz, *Geschlossene und offene Form im Drama* (Munich, 1960), 227.
[117]Ibid., 237.

have another level of intentionality than those of the direct narration. The dramatic text is divided into the "main text," composed of such quotations, and the "side text" of stage directions, and so forth. In section 57, Ingarden speaks of the staged drama as a "borderline case" of a literary work. He rejects the concept of staging as a "realization" of a literary creation, because staging adds certain nonlinguistic but meaningful elements of its own and reinterprets other elements in the original.[118]

Ingarden's appendix stresses the complexity of the theatrical world, which consists of three different domains: one that is actually represented, one that is both represented and discussed, and one that is only discussed.[119] Language itself serves four major functions in this world: "representation," supplementing the concrete world offered by the staging; "expression" of the experiences and emotions of the characters; "communication" with other characters; and "influencing" the actions of others. (This emphasis on language as action anticipates the work of the Oxford philosopher John Austin and the subsequent work in speech-act theory which has, in turn, provided one of the sources for more recent semiotic theory in theatre.) Moreover, asserts Ingarden, whether a theatre is "open" or "closed" in form, it demands a special attitude toward language from the spectators—which adds additional levels to these four normal linguistic functions. The spectator must apprehend each utterance as an "act," a link in the "chain of human vicissitudes developing through the conversations" which makes up any drama. In addition to this particular level, common to all drama, particular styles and periods call for other levels of awareness. A clear example is the highly mannered speech of poetic drama, where the characters "behave as if they do not notice that these verses and declamations are often not at all appropriate to the situation."[120]

Roland Barthes's *Sur Racine* (1960) contains, like Klotz's book, both a personal interpretation and a survey of recent scholarship, but while Klotz sees a critical convergence of "open" and "closed" interpretation of drama, Barthes stresses the diversity of interpretation and defends it as essential to the health of the discipline. *Sur Racine* is actually three essays written for different occasions. The first, and most extended, analyzes the Racinian hero and his world in terms of internal (structural) relationships and psychology, attempting to do so as far as possible entirely from within the work.

The shorter second essay, "Dire Racine," condemns traditional de-

---

[118]Roman Ingarden, *The Literary Work of Art*, trans. George Grabowicz (Evanston, Ill., 1973), 322.
[119]Ibid., 379.
[120]Ibid., 391, 395.

livery in which the actor, instead of simply abandoning himself to the rhythm of the Alexandrine, attempts to "sing" the lines or to "analyze" them for the audience, losing the effect of the whole in the concern for detail. We should accept the strangeness of Racine rather than attempt to make him familiar if we wish to experience his power, says Barthes; only in this way may we today catch a glimpse of the "lost world" that tragedy represented. To perform tragedy, "it is necessary and sufficient to act as if the gods existed, as if one had seen them, as if they had spoken."[121]

Barthes's final essay, "Histoire ou littérature," considers the continuing question, first raised by nineteenth-century criticism, of the relationship between historical and literary events. Two traditional types of analysis, historical and psychological, are available for literary analysis. The first, viewing literature as an institution, inevitably leads away from the individual work into history proper, the study of the collective. The second confronts the inevitable problem of subjectivity, since no ultimate expression of the self can be attained. The critical "languages" applied to Racine—psychoanalytic, existential, tragic, and others still to be invented—can never provide a final objective analysis, since criticism, like literature itself, seeks "to institutionalize subjectivity."[122] The would-be interpreter of Racine must accept this paradox, committing himself and acknowledging his commitment to a mode of interpretation, even while realizing that all such modes are utterly subjective and historical.

Western Europe in the first part of the twentieth century had experienced very little of the sort of radical interpretive freedom represented by Meyerhold, for example. The iconoclasm of the futurists and dadaists made little impact on the text-centered approach of Copeau and his followers in France and did not affect the English-language theatre at all. By 1960, however, the widely held assumption that each play calls for a certain more or less predictable production interpretation began to be seriously challenged, primarily (as in Barthes) in the name of historical relativism.

A parallel observation appears in Michel Saint-Denis's (1897–1971) *Theatre: The Rediscovery of Style.* The reality of each country is made up of "its historical personality, which is constantly being modified." No artist can avoid reflecting his own country and his own time, and works from other periods and other countries must "be brought to life in contemporary terms."[123] This does not mean that the historical style

[121]Roland Barthes, *On Racine*, trans. Richard Howard (New York, 1964), 148.
[122]Ibid., 172.
[123]Michel Saint-Denis, *Theatre: The Rediscovery of Style* (New York, 1960), 48, 50.

of a script is to be ignored, only that one cannot and should not attempt to recreate that precise style with modern actors for a modern audience. The actor must find a way to unite his contemporary consciousness with "the form, the poetical color and rhythm" of the original, and the director must be both "submissive and creative." His goal is both difficult and challenging—to "substitute himself for the dead dramatist and recreate the play."[124] Aurélieu Weiss (1893-1962), in *Le destin des grandes oeuvres dramatiques* (1960), argues that though there is a "permanent human truth" in all great works, inevitable changes in customs and manners change the ways we view these works. They remain alive and relevant through "inevitable adaptation."[125] Elsewhere he credits the actor with contributing significantly to this process. Every successful Hamlet will be different; the actors do not reproduce the author's role but transform it into "the substance of their souls."[126]

Probably the first major director in England and America to be generally associated with this relativistic approach to interpretation was Tyrone Guthrie (1900–1971), who addressed this question in some detail in "Directing a Play," a lecture given in 1962. He dismissed as "nonsense" the general assumption that there exists an "ideal performance which completely realizes the intention of Shakespeare" or any dramatist, partly because any important creation draws significantly upon the subconscious and partly because plays in order to survive must state their general philosophy in such a way that new interpretations can make it relevant to changed historical circumstances. Thus any work of art will always be a partial perspective of that observer at that historical moment, and every performance can only be that performing group's comment on the play, their interpretation of an open-ended score, to which the audience will add yet another level of interpretation. A director has really only two alternatives: either to try to make the play "what you think Shakespeare was after, which clearly is not precisely what Shakespeare was after, but it's the impression he's made upon you"; or else to copy "some other Shakespearean production that you've admired," which is no service to Shakespeare, to the theatre, or to that other interpretation that you have re-created.[127]

The process by which meaning is created in the theatre in general is the concern of J. L. Styan's (b. 1923) *The Elements of Drama* (1963), an attempt to chart the largely unexplored middle ground between literature and performance. The first section, "The Dramatic Score,"

---

[124]Ibid., 67, 78.

[125]Aurélieu Weiss, *Le destin des grandes oeuvres dramatiques* (Paris, 1960), 158.

[126]Weiss, "The Interpretation of Dramatic Works," trans. Emerson Marks, *Journal of Aesthetics and Art Criticism* 23 (1964-1965): 317.

[127]J. Robert Wills, ed., *The Director in a Changing Theatre* (Palo Alto, 1976), 89-90.

considers the text as a collection of elements designed to produce "animation—not of actors acting and speaking, but of our imaginative impressions."[128] The second section, "Orchestration," considers how the dramatic elements are put together to build sequences of impressions and create the rhythms, the balance, and the theatrical patterns necessary to lead the audience to an understanding of the performance. The third section, "Values," explores this understanding from the audience's point of view. The spectator is led to compare the play with his own experience of life, to judge its quality and its ordering of impressions along with the quality of his own interest, and to reach at last a judgment on the value of the fulfilled intention of the performance. He also is a creative artist, whose participation requires both skill and discipline. Styan's conclusion anticipates his own future research and that of an important element of more recent theatre theory, the aesthetics of reception: the play, paradoxically, "is not on the stage but in the mind."[129]

The subject of tragedy in modern times continued during this period to engage the attention of theorists, particularly in England and America, though defenders of the traditional concept of tragedy as a mode of ordering the universe were few. Those who felt that tragedy was still a relevant genre tended to stress its darker—even its demonic—element, or else to follow Kierkegaard in approaching it by way of paradox, suggesting that the tragic spirit could be best expressed in the modern theatre in comedic terms. A striking example of the former approach appears in *Shakespeare's Tragedies* (1950) by Clifford Leech (b. 1909), who sees the tragic world as not merely devoid of meaning but actively malevolent. Leech, like Richards and Ellis-Fermor, speaks of a balance of forces in tragedy but with no similar resulting impression of goodness and order. On the contrary, evil usually predominates in the tragic world and is balanced only temporarily by the almost superhuman internal strength of the hero. Terror is balanced not by pity but by pride in the endurance with which the hero confronts a malevolent destiny. "In a planned but terrible universe we see man justifying his existence."[130]

Karl Jaspers (1883–1969), in *Von der Wahrheit* (1947), views tragedy as a possible path to something transcendent but an equally possible stimulus to man's darkest impulses. Like Unamuno, Jaspers regards the tragic vision as inseparable from consciousness: "Man seems truly awake only when he has such knowledge." Tragic guilt thus arises

---

[128]J. L. Styan, *The Elements of Drama* (Cambridge, 1963), 64.
[129]Ibid., 288.
[130]Clifford Leech, *Shakespeare's Tragedies* (London, 1950), 171.

naturally from existence and action; the tragic hero is the exceptional man who, by calling into question the established political, social, moral, or religious order, exposes both its limitations and his own. He thus reveals the transcendent, which does not triumph but "makes itself felt only through the whole situation."[131] Tragedy is not an end in itself but a process that points toward an unattainable complete truth.

This positive aspect of tragic knowledge may easily be lost, however, and the "tragic sense of life" may become an end in itself. Then a tragic philosophy, a philosophy of nihilism, may result, as Jaspers felt had happened in his own Germany under the Nazis. A turmoil of nihilistic impulses was the result, a "delight in meaningless activity, in torturing and in being tortured, in destruction for its own sake, in the raging hatred against the world and man coupled with the raging hatred against one's own despised existence."[132]

The meaninglessness or apparent malevolence of the universe, the horror of modern war, and the shadow of atomic destruction led many theorists after the Second World War to feel that the kind of exultation available through tragedy, even such dark tragedy as that proposed by Leech or Jaspers, was no longer attainable; they looked instead to dark comedy or comedy with tragic implications as a more suitable genre for the modern consciousness. The central statement of this approach is probably the speech "Theater probleme" (1954) of the playwright Friedrich Dürrenmatt (b. 1921). Dürrenmatt argues that the drama must depict the subjective world of which it is a part, and that the modern world, anonymous and bureaucratic, offers neither representative figures nor tragic heroes—only victims. Tragedy "assumes guilt, trouble, moderation, range of vision, responsibility. In the routine muddle of our century, in this last dance of the white race there are no longer any guilty people nor any responsible ones either." Nevertheless, "the tragic element" is still possible, even if pure tragedy is not. It can be generated out of comedy, which is still accessible to us, "as a terrible moment, as a chasm beginning to open." Such imagery sounds close to Ionesco, but Dürrenmatt strikes a more positive note by stressing the refusal to despair when confronted with the "senselessness, the hopelessness of this world," and the attempt to replace the consolation of the lost world-order by restoring it within the individual.[133]

Like Hugo, Dürrenmatt associates the grotesque with the idea of tragicomedy. In the essay "Anmerkung zur Komödie" (1952), which

[131]Karl Jaspers, *Tragedy Is Not Enough*, trans. H. A. T. Reiche et al. (London, 1952), 31, 52.
[132]Ibid., 101.
[133]Friedrich Dürrenmatt, *Writings on Theatre and Drama*, trans. H. M. Waidson (London, 1976), 81–82.

serves as a sort of preface to "Theaterprobleme," he suggests that the grotesque is the only proper artistic response to such horrors as world war and the atomic bomb. Again, he stresses that for all its cruelty, the grotesque is "not the art of the nihilists, but much more that of the moralists, not the art of decay, but of salt."[134]

This insistence on the positive aspect of such theatrical expression inevitably forced Dürrenmatt to deal with the question of engagement in the drama, to define his theory in relation to those concepts of writers like Sartre and Brecht. His speech "Friedrich Schiller," presented upon his receiving the Schiller Prize in 1959, provided him with an occasion to do so. Recalling Schiller's distinction between the naive and the sentimental, Dürrenmatt suggests that the naive poet accepts the world as it exists, while the sentimental or reflective poet calls it into question. The latter thus becomes a rebel, and if he is to be morally consistent, he will not stop at questioning the world but begin to urge change; that is, he will move from rebel to revolutionary. In our own time as in Schiller's, however, this logic is defective: since the revolutionary doctrine that a man "can and must change the world" is unrealizable for the individual, it can serve only as a political slogan to incite the mob.[135] The modern poet is confronted by a world both unacceptable and— through his efforts, at any rate—unchangeable. Schiller, facing this dilemma, provided another answer: to accept necessity in the external realm of nature but to assert freedom within the individual. His example should remind us that "man is only in part a political being" and that his destiny will be fulfilled not politically but in what "lies beyond politics and comes after it."[136]

During the 1950s, before the works of Beckett, Ionesco, or Dürrenmatt had made any impact in the English or American theatre, the blending of tragic and comic elements in contemporary drama received distinctly less attention there than on the continent. The tradition of the Cambridge anthropologists, fortified by the work of Carl Jung (1875–1961) and clearly evident in the theory of Fergusson, continued to exercise a much stronger influence.

Herbert Weisinger's (b. 1913) *Tragedy and the Paradox of the Fortunate Fall* (1953) suggests that there are "a few basic patterns in art" of particular power and vitality, among which is that which echoes the primeval archetype of death and rebirth, entering myth and ritual as the *felix culpa* paradox. This mythic pattern has been in turn utilized

[134]Ibid., 58.
[135]Ibid., 107-8.
[136]Ibid., 111.

as the "ideological background" of tragedy, the ultimate power of which arises from recognition of the archetype.[137]

Richard B. Sewall (b. 1908), in "The Tragic Form" (1954), finds in tragedy a depiction of the paradoxical nature of man and the universe. Tragic suffering and insight come when the hero confronts "ambiguities without and within."[138] The confrontation, suffering, and insight make up the "tragic form," and bear a close resemblance to the elements of Fergusson's "tragic rhythm."

Harold H. Watts (b. 1906), in "Myth and Drama" (1955), treats comedy and tragedy as secular versions of the two basic mythic views of existence: the cyclic view, which offers the promise of continual reestablishment of order and harmony; and the linear view, which shows a world moving relentlessly forward into the unknown, where choices are irreversible and their consequences both unforeseen and inevitable.[139] The work of Northrop Frye, especially *Anatomy of Criticism*, brings this mythically oriented theory to its fullest development.

D. D. Raphael (b. 1916), in the manner of Hegel or Schopenhauer (whom he cites, but whom he criticizes as metaphysicians who attempted to fit tragedy into their own "ready-made metaphysics"), looks at tragedy as a more general human phenomenon. His book *The Paradox of Tragedy* (1960) takes up the old question of tragic pleasure, which, he suggests, arises from our sympathy for the hero as a being like ourselves, combined with our admiration for his greatness of spirit—a view of tragedy somewhat reminiscent of Corneille. The conflict of this elevated tragedy is between two forms of the sublime: "the awe-inspiring strength of necessity and the *grandeur d'âme* which inspires admiration." Though the hero is defeated by necessity, the audience is led to feel that "the sublimity of the hero's spirit is superior to the sublimity of the power which overwhelms him."[140]

Murray Krieger (b. 1923), in *The Tragic Vision* (1960), denies the possibility of creating such a hero in the modern theatre. "Tragic vision" is accessible to the individual, who may experience Dionysian terror though direct and personal confrontation with a meaningless universe. The Apollonian balance, however, has been lost, and this vision "can no longer be made through tragedy to yield to an order and a shared religious vision."[141] Instead of being pitted against universals, the mod-

[137]Herbert Weisinger, *Tragedy and the Paradox of the Fortunate Fall* (East Lansing, Mich., 1953), 115.
[138]Richard B. Sewall, "The Tragic Form," *Essays in Criticism* 4 (1954):358.
[139]Harold H. Watts, "Myth and Drama," *Cross Currents* 5 (1955).
[140]D. D. Raphael, *The Paradox of Tragedy* (Bloomington, 1960), 27–28.
[141]Murray Krieger, *The Tragic Vision* (Chicago, 1960), 17.

ern hero confronts in the drama only parochial and limited ethical practicality.

George Steiner (b. 1929) suggests in *The Death of Tragedy* (1961) that although the modern world does offer certain major configurations of belief and symbolic form to the dramatist, none of them provides the sort of mythology needed to center the imagination and organize the inner landscape for the expression of tragedy. The classic configuration leads to a dead past, and Christianity and Marxism cannot form the basis for tragedy, because their metaphysics—the one transcendent, the other secular—are essentially optimistic. Steiner expresses admiration for the power of certain modern dramatists, notably Beckett, but agrees with Lukács that their works lack the essence of drama, "the creation of characters endowed with the miracle of independent life."[142]

The difficulty if not impossibility of writing modern tragedy is accepted by Lionel Abel (b. 1910) with little regret, since he feels that Western dramatists, from Shakespeare to the present, have been evolving a "comparably philosophic" form of drama. This possible replacement is the subject of his book *Metatheatre* (1963). Metatheatre shows life as consciously theatricalized, with characters aware of their own dramatic dimension, like Hamlet.[143] The world is treated not as external and alien but as a "projection of human consciousness." Order is not, as in tragedy, imposed from without but "continually improvised by men." There is thus no ultimate world image, but a continual unfolding of human dreams and imaginings. The goal of metatheatre is not transcendence; it is wonder at the capacity of this human imagination.[144]

In the 1960s, Dürrenmatt's assertion that in modern times the tragic vision could be attained most effectively in comedic terms began to be echoed in a variety of theoretical statements on the contemporary blending of these traditionally opposed genres. Harold Pinter (b. 1930) took a position strikingly like that of Dürrenmatt in a 1960 British radio interview, observing that "everything is funny; the greatest earnestness is funny; even tragedy is funny," and that his plays sought to "get to this recognizable reality of the absurdity of what we do and how we behave and how we speak." Pinter saw, too, the abyss of meaninglessness opening within the expression of modern comedy: "There is a kind of horror about and I think that this horror and absurdity go together."[145]

The German dramatist Tankred Dorst (b. 1925), in "Die Bühne ist der absolute Ort" (1962), agrees that the proper theatre for the modern

---

[142]George Steiner, *The Death of Tragedy* (New York, 1961), 350.
[143]Lionel Abel, *Metatheatre* (New York, 1963), 60.
[144]Ibid., 113.
[145]Interview with Hallam Tennyson, Aug. 7, 1960, in Esslin, *Absurd*, 239–39.

world is not tragedy; it consists rather of farces, grotesques, and parables created for audiences "unsure, skeptical, perhaps even a bit suspicious," who come to the theatre with questions but expect no answers from the dramatist "who has no more great material or metaphysical world plan than they do."[146] The new "postpsychological" era demands a new "negative" dramaturgy. Such devices as masks, disguises, and plays within plays can be used to call attention to the indeterminacy of the stage world, says Dorst, and thus reflect the parallel indeterminacy of values, morals, and social norms in the world of the spectator. Instead of metaphysical speculation or political engagement, the stage presents "absolute appearance and simulated postures," a play of tensions and conflicts without resolution.[147]

J. L. Styan also believes that the dramatist "who can swing between the extremes of tragedy and farce within the same framework" is today the one seen as most relevant,[148] but Styan's study of such drama, *The Dark Comedy* (1962), sees this mixture neither as uniquely modern nor as necessarily tied to the expression of loss of values and beliefs. Closer in this respect to Hugo than to Dürrenmatt, Styan suggests that in the hands of the boldest and most controlled dramatists, this mixture encompasses the greatest range of human experience and arouses the spectator to the highest degree. Styan compares the construction of such drama to walking a tightrope. When most successful, the play is taken "to the very edge of disintegration," stimulating the audience to an extreme stage of tension and alertness. Then "if the dramatic chemistry has been perfectly calculated," a synthesis and reconciliation of the parts will be achieved that is of unparalleled scope and power.[149]

It was essentially this romantic view of mixed tragedy and comedy that James Thurber (1894–1961) expressed in "The Case for Comedy" (1960), which supported the genre known as "tragicomedy" as "the true balance of life and art, the saving of the human mind as well as of the theatre"; humor and pathos, tears and laughter are, "in the highest expression of human character and achievement, inseparable."[150] The American playwright Jack Richardson (b. 1935) quotes Thurber approvingly in the preface to his *Gallows Humor* (1961). Comedy is not something "categorically separated from life's lamentation," a "harmless, vapid antidote to the numbing effects of tragedy," but an equally essential part of life; the artist who restricts himself to one pattern or the other is severely limited. True comedy has much in

---

[146]Tankred Dorst, *Grosse Schmärede an der Stadtmauer* (Cologne, 1962), 113.
[147]Ibid., 115.
[148]Styan, *The Dark Comedy* (Cambridge, 1968), 282.
[149]Ibid., 117.
[150]James Thurber, "The Case for Comedy," *Atlantic* 206 (Nov. 1960):98.

common with tragedy; Don Quixote, Falstaff, M. Jourdain suffer from what under other circumstances might be called a tragic flaw. At its best, comedy is "far more closely applicable to *Oedipus Rex* than to *Under the Yum-Yum Tree*."[151]

The Hyacinth Room (1964) by Cyrus Hoy (b. 1926) elaborates upon Feibleman's suggestion that both comedy and tragedy arise from a juxtaposition of the finite and the infinite. But instead of sharing Feibleman's focus upon events and situations, Hoy looks to the dual nature of man, his infinite spiritual aspirations, and his finite corporeal powers. The blending of comedy and tragedy occurs in irony, says Hoy, when the hero becomes conscious of this inevitable conflict and brings this consciousness to the audience. The drama then presents "in a single incongruous image the grandeur to which man aspires, and the degradation to which he is perversely driven."[152]

A somewhat similar path is followed in Karl Guthke's (b. 1933) *Modern Tragicomedy* (1966). Guthke, like Hoy, sees the blend of tragedy and comedy as a new and distinct genre, in which the two do not exist to set each other off but to create a unified if contradictory mood: we "laugh with one eye and weep with the other."[153] Guthke finds that certain repeated structural patterns characterize this genre and set it apart from such related modes as satire, melodrama, and the grotesque, but all of these involve some discrepancy between a character and his surroundings that has both comic and tragic dimensions.

Despite the growing acceptance of dark comedy or tragicomedy as the new major metaphysical mode of the drama, a few theorists during this period challenged the "death of tragedy" concept. Elder Olson's (b. 1909) *Tragedy and the Theory of Drama* (1961) covers a variety of material—action, plot, character, dialogue, emotion, and effect—"from the point of view of the working dramatist,"[154] with tragedy as a central concern. Olson finds the argument against the loss of elevated characters "trivial," and the argument that universal beliefs are no longer available unproven. He does not accept the Krutch distinction between the creation and historical appreciation of tragedy, arguing to the contrary that the fact that we are still affected by tragedy proves the genre still healthy. The lack of modern tragedies arises not from any crisis in belief but from the fact that tragedy "fell into the hands of poets who were not dramatists and thus came into disrepute."[155]

Even more positive is *The Voice of Tragedy* (1963) by Mitchell Leaska

---

[151]Jack Richardson, *Gallows Humor* (New York, 1961), 8–9.
[152]Cyrus Hoy, *The Hyacinth Room* (New York, 1964), 232.
[153]Karl Guthke, *Modern Tragicomedy* (New York, 1966), 59.
[154]Elder Olson, *Tragedy and the Theory of Drama* (New York, 1961), 2.
[155]Ibid., 256.

(b. 1934), which reverses the traditional reason for the decline of the genre, treating tragedy not as the expression of a common faith but itself that faith. "In tragedy we have the scripture of unity, and in its performance, the liturgy of a humanist religion, a religion as effective and enduring as those of old."[156] Tragedy has historically appeared, says Leaska, where a spirit of freedom and fierce individualism has encountered a spirit of humanism that attempted to adjust the demands of the individual to the needs of society. Modern America, he suggests, shares this character with antique Greece and Renaissance England, and is thus the potential cradle of another great era of tragic creation.

Eric Bentley considers both tragedy and tragicomedy, along with melodrama, comedy, and farce, in *The Life of the Drama* (1964), a book that takes a fresh look at the old Aristotelian categories of plot, character, thought, language, and spectacle (wishing to explore a little more fully the relationship between text and stage, Bentley renders the last as "enactment"). Bentley sees the irreducible minimum of tragedy as "suffering and endurance." The only transcendence *always* present is that "implied in the power to write the play." The cosmos the poet creates through plot, character, dialogue, and idea is the only one he can "guarantee" to offset tragedy's experience of chaos.[157] In modern tragicomedy the vision is darker, since the comedy serves not to lighten but to deepen the tragedy. Yet Bentley sees in the creation of the artwork itself a positive reaction: "All art is a challenge to despair," and the deeper the level of despair modern tragicomedy strikes, the deeper the hope it implies as art.[158] Once again a kind of transcendence is made available, not within the message or the action of the drama, but within the experience of the artist's triumph over chaos and hopelessness.

---

[156] Mitchell Leaska, *The Voice of Tragedy* (New York, 1963), 293.
[157] Bentley, *The Life of the Drama* (New York, 1964), 282.
[158] Ibid., 353.

21

The Twentieth Century since 1965

As we have seen, a continuing point of debate in modern theatre theory has been over whether the theatre should be viewed primarily as an engaged social phenomenon or as a politically indifferent aesthetic artifact; a significant amount of contemporary theoretical discourse can still be oriented in terms of this opposition. Until the mid-1960s, the theorists who inclined toward an autonomous view of the theatre frequently looked to Artaud as their central modern spokesman; then a major new influence appeared in the productions and theories of the Polish director Jerzy Grotowski (b. 1933), who by the end of the decade came to rival Stanislavski himself as a theorist of acting and a central figure of modern theatrical consciousness. Grotowski's international influence may be dated from the 1966 performance in Paris of *The Constant Prince*, at the invitation of Barrault, a dazzling production characterized by many French critics as the long-awaited fulfillment of "Artaudian theatre."

Even before this success, Grotowski's student Eugenio Barba (b. 1936) had begun preparing the way for Grotowski with a book published in Italy in 1964 and two articles in the *Tulane Drama Review* (1965). These appeared at a crucial time for this journal and for the American experimental theatre. During the 1960s, American theatre entered its richest period of experimentation since the time of the new stagecraft, and—as in the decade before and after 1920—one journal in particular served as a sort of clearinghouse of the new ideas, seeking out and encouraging new theoreticians and practitioners in America and spreading news of work in Europe and elsewhere. What *Theatre Arts* was to the 1920s, the *Drama Review* was to the 1960s; it was fitting that in the winter issue of 1962, as *TDR* was steadily growing in influence, Gordon Rogoff, one of the last editors of *Theatre Arts*, presented a kind of obituary of the older journal, a victim of commercialism and Broadway pressures.

TDR began in 1955 as the *Carleton Drama Review*, each issue devoted to critical articles tied to a seasonal play and lecture cycle at Carleton College (in Northfield, Minnesota). In 1957 the journal and its editor, Robert W. Corrigan, moved to Tulane University in New Orleans and changed its name. Many of its articles were now devoted to new voices in the European theatre, most of them still virtually unknown in America—to Brecht most of all, but also to Artaud; to Dürrenmatt and Frisch; to Ionesco, Genet, and Adamov; to Ghelderode and Vilar; to Betti and Sastre. In 1962, Richard Schechner followed Corrigan as editor, maintaining the same general focus of the magazine. Thus *TDR* 19 (Spring 1963) featured Genet and Ionesco; *TDR* 22 (Winter 1963) focused on Artaud; *TDR* 23 (Spring 1964) discussed The Living Theatre, which had been closed for nonpayment of taxes.

Until 1964, the clear emphasis of *TDR* was on dramatic literature; then the attention moved to contemporary production. The pivot of the change was perhaps the two-issue reassessment of the influence of Stanislavski in America (Fall-Winter 1964), which Corrigan in a ten-year retrospective (Summer 1966), rightly called one of the magazine's finest achievements. Significantly, almost prophetically, the next issue (Spring 1965) contained Barba's two articles introducing the work of Grotowski.

The Polish director, Barba reported, was attempting—in the tradition of Appia, Craig, and Meyerhold—to build a new aesthetic for the theatre, to restore something of its original ritual purity by creating a "modern secular ritual."[1] To replace lost religious elements Grotowski was seeking archetypical images and actions that force the spectator into an emotional involvement. Grotowski himself described the process as a "dialectic of derision and apotheosis," turned toward a system of "taboos, conventions, and accepted values," which during the production created a "multiface mirror" by the constant arousal and destruction of these values and taboos. Such an approach has nothing in common with "literary theatre," which faithfully restates a text and seeks to illustrate the author's ideas. In Grotowski's "autonomous" theatre, the text is one element among many, a source of archetypes but essentially raw material to be freely cut and transformed. The peripeties of the production may be unrelated to the text but achieved "through purely theatrical means."[2]

---

[1] Eugenio Barba, "Theatre Laboratory 13 Rzedow," *Tulane Drama Review* 9, 3 (Spring 1965):154.
[2] Ibid., 157-59.

Such an attitude toward the text requires a new attitude also toward the actor. The academic or literary theatre employed either the "elementary actor," essentially a neutral illustration, or the "artificial actor," the creator of a structure of vocal and physical effects. Grotowski seeks to develop a third type, a more advanced artificial actor called the "archetypical actor," who uses his technique to express images drawn from the collective unconscious. The archetypical actor must be rigorously trained physically and vocally in an antinaturalistic style with highly controlled rhythm and dynamics, forcing the body to an expressiveness that seems to transcend natural boundaries and approach the visionary actors of Artaud or the über-marionettes of Craig. The conventional stage is forsaken for smaller, more intimate forms of collective contact in which the spectator is made deeply aware of the physicality and presence of the actor and forced—against the defenses of logic, social convention, and habit—to confront the world of the archetype.[3]

A collection of Grotowski's articles, interviews, speeches, and introductions to specific productions (primarily from the years 1965 to 1968) were gathered in English translation in the book *Towards a Poor Theatre* (1968). Here Grotowski repeats his conviction that the essence of theatre lies in the relationship between actor and spectator; he calls a theatre focused on this relationship the "poor theatre," opposed to the synthetic rich theatre that betrays this essence by attempting, in vain, to unite literature, painting, sculpture, architecture, lighting, and acting in a "total theatre" experience. Such efforts produce at best only a hybrid still technologically inferior to film and television.[4]

In his discussion of actor training, Grotowski refers to renouncing nonessential and distracting elements as a "via negativa—not a collection of skills but an eradication of blocks." Like Artaud, he wants to make the actor the transparent sign of an organic impulse; he sometimes speaks in terms that might in fact have come from Artaud. "Impulse and action are concurrent: the body vanishes, burns, and the spectator sees only a series of visible impulses."[5] Grotowski separates himself on practical grounds, however, hailing Artaud as a prophet and visionary but one who never undertook, as the Polish Lab Theatre was doing, a practical investigation of a methodology for achieving this vision. Grotowski calls the annihilation of the actor's body, freeing it from resistance to any psychic impulse, a sacrifice and an atonement by which a "secular holiness" is achieved.[6] It is thus that the lost ritual

[3]Ibid., 161-62.
[4]Jerzy Grotowski, *Towards a Poor Theatre* (New York, 1968), 21.
[5]Ibid., 16.
[6]Ibid., 34.

power of theatre can be restored—not for everyone, but for those members of the public who feel a true need for psychic self-examination and are willing to use the confrontation with the performance and the self-penetration of the actor as a means of unlocking their own inner selves. Instead of the collective spiritual want of the *Volk* addressed by the Wagnerian *Gesamtkunstwerk*, Grotowski looks to the individual spiritual want of a small number of individuals, addressed by totally open actors in a necessarily intimate confrontation.

The Winter 1965 issue of *TDR*, coedited by Schechner and Michael Kirby, focused on what Kirby in an introductory statement called "The New Theatre," a theatre that corresponds to the abstract and nonobjective in painting and includes such manifestations as "happenings," events, and chance theatre. Kirby's book *Happenings*, appearing this same year, called the happening "a new form of theatre, just as collage is a new form of visual art," and defined it as "a purposefully composed form of theatre in which diverse alogical elements, including nonmatrixed performing, are organized in a compartmental structure."[7] That it is "purposefully composed" differentiates the happening from chance theatre, since the elements of a happening may be determined by chance but are arranged in an intentional manner. Their relationship is, however, alogical; they are brought together according to a private structural scheme of the artist, which is not, as in traditional theatre, transformed into an "information structure" accessible to the spectator.[8] Plot and story line, exposition and climax, cause and effect are abandoned in favor of the "compartmental structure," in which each theatrical unit stands alone, with no information passed between it and any other. Acting in a happening is "nonmatrixed," involving simple specific tasks without the matrix of time, place, and character essential to traditional theatre.

Among the influences lying behind this and related new forms of theatre, Kirby cites Kurt Schwitters, whose *Merzbühne* project in 1921 suggested assembling solid, liquid, and gaseous bodies in a sort of futurist display; the development of increased attention to the audience-presentation relationship by the dadaists and their successors, leading from their collages through environments to the happening; the theatre of pure spectacle and audience involvement suggested by Artaud; and the experimental work of dancers such as Merce Cunningham and Paul Taylor. In Kirby's view, John Cage (b. 1912), with his interest in the environment of performance and the introduction

[7]Michael Kirby, *Happenings* (New York, 1965), 11, 21.
[8]Ibid., 13.

of chance elements, as well as his general concern with extending the boundaries of art, was "the backbone of the new theatre."[9]

Cage, interviewed by Kirby and Schechner in *TDR*, resisted even the open definition of happenings proposed by Kirby because it still included intentionality. Inevitably, Cage insisted, this would lead back to the artist's attempt to impose an idea upon the public, and thus to the controlled and focused traditional theatre. The artist must aim outside himself, at an experience as open and undirected as our intellectual biases will permit. Theatre should be seen simply as "something which engages both the eye and the ear" so that one can "view everyday life itself as theatre." The only exclusion Cage suggests is the totally private experience, since theatre must always be a "public occasion."[10]

A similar emphasis on the open-endedness, indeterminacy, and ephemerality of performance may be seen in the French *théâtre panique* of the mid-1960s, the leader of which was Fernando Arrabal (b. 1932). *Panique* falls clearly in the tradition of Jarry's pataphysics (a "science of imaginary solutions" which would extend "beyond metaphysics"[11]), dada, and surrealism (Arrabal was part of the Breton circle in the early 1960s) and shares with them a combination of serious aesthetic speculation and parody of traditional theorizing. Arrabal's manifesto (or antimanifesto) "L'homme panique" (1963), called *panique* "neither a group nor an artistic movement; rather a style of life, or rather, I don't know what it is." *Panique* is best expressed in "festivals, theatrical ceremonies, play, art, and indifferent solitude" and is characterized by "confusion, humor, terror, chance, and euphoria." By a sequence of puns and pseudomathematical formulas, Arrabal "demonstrates" that "Life is Memory and Man is Chance" and that the fundamental concern of the artist should always be to unite "the mechanics of memory and the rules of chance. The more the work of the artist is governed by chance, confusion, the unexpected, the richer, the more stimulating, the more fascinating it will be."[12] Arrabal cites Strindberg's 1894 essay "The Role of Chance in Artistic Creation" as an important precursor of this *panique* idea. Another aspect is the subject of Arrabal's essay "Le théâtre comme cérémonie 'panique' "—its encompassing of the widest possible variety of elements: "tragedy and guignol, poetry and vulgarity, comedy and melodrama, love and eroticism, happenings and en-

---

[9]Kirby, "The New Theatre," *Tulane Drama Review* 10, 2 (Winter 1965): 24.
[10]Kirby and Richard Schechner, "An Interview with John Cage, " *Tulane Drama Review* 10, 2 (Winter 1965): 51.
[11]Alfred Jarry, *Oeuvres complètes* (Paris, 1972), 668-69.
[12]Fernando Arrabal et al., *Le panique* (Paris, 1973), 48, 52–53.

sembles, bad taste and aesthetic refinement, the sacred and the profane, executions and celebrations of life, the sordid and the sublime."[13]

The Mexican dramatist Alexandro Jodorowsky (b. 1930), another of the founders of *panique*, suggests that in this way the theatre can find its essence in what was hitherto considered a problem—its ephemerality. His "Vers l'éphémère panique" (1965) condemns as misguided and hopeless the tradition of attempting to make "permanent" an ephemeral art. Such an attempt has led to an emphasis on text rather than on life, on mechanical repetition (never in fact achieved) rather than on improvisation, on fixed settings and architectural spaces rather than on surroundings that can change with the life of the performance. The *panique* actor improvises and immerses himself in the perishable. He will subordinate words to gesture rather than vice versa, and his words will not bear conceptual content but arise as spontaneous expression, "the pure and simple expression of experience." He rejects both the traditional idea of losing himself in a character and that of showing the actor beneath the character. He seeks instead his own "true mode of expression," becoming not a "lying exhibitionist" but a "poet in a state of trance."[14] Artaud is not mentioned, but Jodorowsky's new actor, which he calls a "creative athlete," seems clearly influenced by Artaudian thought and, perhaps for that reason, bears a certain kinship to Grotowski as well.

Jerome Savary, who directed Arrabal's *Le labyrinthe* in 1967, continued to reflect a number of these same ideas in his own subsequent theoretical statements and productions. In *Nos fêtes* (1968) he calls for productions rejecting the text and seeking new means of physical expression and more flexible technical ways "to restore to the theatre its true dignity."[15] In a 1970 interview published in *TDR*, he recommends a theatre that is no longer tied to literary expression but is a feast, a celebration, in which everyone feels free to participate. He criticizes Grotowski and the Living Theatre for placing themselves spiritually above their audiences, thus discouraging any sense of unity or desire for participation.[16]

The American Theatre of the Ridiculous shares with the *théâtre panique* a fascination with the outrageous and the extreme and with sexual and artistic perversity. But the practitioners of the Ridiculous in its various manifestations have placed less emphasis on the philosophic implications of their work (indeed, they have championed the Ridiculous as the only "non-academic" avant-garde) than on its reflection of—

---

[13]Ibid., 98.
[14]Ibid., 85, 88.
[15]Jerome Savary, *Nos fêtes* (Paris, 1968), 161.
[16]Bettina Knapp, "Sounding the Drum," *Drama Review* 15, 1 (Fall 1970): 92.

even homage to—the antiesthetic products of mass and popular culture. The playwright Ronald Tavel (b. 1941) cites as influences *art nouveau* and pop, camp, and psychedelic art. The Ridiculous, says Tavel in "The Theatre of the Ridiculous" (1966), rejects both naturalism and absurdity, and seeks to build "word and emotive associations" from the detritus of the contemporary world. "A quotidian nothingness" is built on "a foundation of subliminal cement."[17] When this "subliminal" consciousness is set free, it creates an order "beyond the trap of words" and also beyond those limitations placed on man by the two great competitors of art, politics and religion.

Tavel's emphasis on the nonverbal and the emancipation of subliminal impulses suggests Artaud, an influence made specific in a 1968 interview with Ridiculous actor/playwright Charles Ludlam (b. 1943), who says the Ridiculous unites Artaud's "pure physical theatre" with a "verbal sound source," creating from both total theatre and life experience: "The world is our work."[18] After 1967, Ludlam, Tavel, and their colleague John Vaccaro separated, with Tavel creating his own works, Vaccaro seeking as a director to depict contemporary anxieties, and Ludlam combining as an actor-manager the images and approaches of a variety of dramatic forms past and present. In a 1975 manifesto Ludlam suggested certain axioms for a theatre of ridicule, stressing paradox and self-mockery, seeking themes that threaten "to destroy one's whole value system" treated "in a madly farcical manner without losing the seriousness of the theme."[19]

Richard Kostelanetz (b. 1940) suggested in *The New American Arts*, which appeared in 1965 (the same year as Kirby's study of happenings), that this sort of experimentation was already exhausted. He reversed this assessment, however, in *The Theatre of Mixed Means* (1968), which looked beyond happenings to a general movement that Kostelanetz then considered both significant and growing. In this new movement, drama and other related arts are no longer integrated in a traditional manner but developed independently, each "used for its own possibilities."

Happenings, in Kostelanetz's classification, are the most open form of such theatre, with a vague script allowing flexibility of space and time. *Kinetic environments* are somewhat more restrictive, with space more specifically defined and the behavior of participants or components more precisely planned. *Staged happenings* define the space still further, making a clear division between audience and performers, and en-

[17]Ronald Tavel, "The Theatre of the Ridiculous," *Tri-Quarterly* 6 (1966): 94–95.
[18]Dan Isaac, "Interview," *Drama Review* 13, 1 (Fall 1968): 116.
[19]Charles Ludlam, "Ridiculous Theatre, Scourge of Human Folly," *Drama Review* 19, 4 (Dec. 1975): 70.

couraging observation rather than participation. Finally, *staged performances* are completely planned and carried out before an observing audience. The last, of course, are close to traditional theatre except that they do not emphasize the spoken word; like all new theatre, they "thoroughly mix the media of communication and most pieces have no words at all." Nor do the performers assume characters; they remain themselves or simply neutral agents.[20] The emphasis in such theatre is on an experience, not an idea; upon spatial rather than linear perception; and upon the process of creation rather than a final product. Such work obviously cannot be judged according to such conventional concerns as plot, character, and theme; a new critical vocabulary must be evolved, based upon the artist's use of time, space, and materials. The new critic must ask "how well a particular piece articulates and enhances the situation—time, space, and elements—it chooses for itself."[21]

Tadeusz Kantor (b. 1915), Poland's best-known director after Grotowski, developed during the 1960s a unique approach that builds actions upon chance and the techniques of the happening, then joins them to dramatic texts for performance. His "autonomous theatre" or "zero theatre" manifesto of 1963 rejects the assumption that a performance should "translate a dramatic text into stage ideas, interpret or bring it up-to-date" or even that it should remain in a "logical, analogical, parallel or reverse relation" with the script. Instead, performance should confront the text in an "atmosphere of shock and scandal" to break open "the suppressed sphere of imagination of the audience."[22] Kantor's "Manifesto 70" (1970) seems even closer to describing the happening, calling for a work with "no form, no esthetic qualities, no perfection ... which conveys nothing and relects nothing ... which defies interpretation, which points nowhere, has no purpose or place, a work which is life itself—transient, ephemeral, unbridled, which simply is." Yet Kantor emphasizes the space between such a work and its audience in a manner quite opposed to the happening. By its very existence, "this work places the neighboring reality in an unreal, one might say artistic, situation."[23]

After 1970, Kantor increasingly emphasized the separation, the closed and alien nature of the artwork from the audience's point of view. In the manifesto "The Theatre of Death" (1975), he calls this sense of the alien the basis of art, taking Craig's marionette, the romantic interest

---

[20]Richard Kostelanetz, *The Theatre of Mixed Means* (New York, 1968), 4, 7.

[21]Ibid., 281.

[22]Quoted in "A Work of Art Is Closed," interview with Tadeusz Kantor, *The Theatre in Poland* 247 (1979): 9.

[23]Quoted in August Grodzicki, "Tadeusz Kantor and his 'Cricot-2' Theatre," *The Theatre in Poland* 228 (1977): 11.

in the double, and the image of death as echoes of this insight. The concept of life "can be vindicated in art only through the *absence of life in its conventional sense*," including "the whole orthodoxy of linguistics and conceptualism." The primeval power of the actor grew from the audience's realization of his radical otherness, as a figure "deceptively similar" yet "infinitely *distant*, shockingly *foreign*, as if *dead*." Kantor's theatre seeks to recover the "primeval force" of the shocking confrontation of the familiar and the alien, the living and the dead.[24]

The experiments of the German dramatist Peter Handke (b. 1942) may be related to manifestations like the happening in a different way. Far from denying the written text, Handke foregrounds it. He follows the philosopher Ludwig Wittgenstein (1889–1951) in his fascination with language as the basis of reality, so much so that his major plays have been sometimes characterized as illustrations of Wittgenstein's ideas. In terms of theatre experimentation, however, Handke's rejection of illusion and empathy, and his emphasis on the experience of immediate reality, bring him close to theorists like Cage. The experiential awareness sought by others in images, Handke seeks in words. His first four plays—called *Sprechstücke*, doubtless in implied contrast to Brecht's *Lehrstücke*—are designed "not to revolutionize, but to make aware"; not to teach, but "to point to the world by way of words."[25] The most famous of these "speaking-plays," *Publikumsbeschimpfung* (1966), subjects its spectators to harangues, insults, and philosophic speculation. Traditional illusion and empathy are totally rejected. Instead, says Handke in a 1972 note to the play, the work attempts to make the audience "conscious that they are there, that they exist."[26]

The approach is totally opposed to the outwardly directed, politically engaged Brechtian theatre, as Handke made clear in two 1968 articles in *Theatre Heute*, "Horváth ist besser" and "Strassentheater und Theatertheater." In the first, he labels Brecht's work "trivial," presenting clear problems with simple solutions that have no relation to the complexity of real life as Handke has experienced it "in my own consciousness."[27] The second accuses Brecht of confusing the nature of theatre with that of political action. A politically engaged theatre cannot remain in the theatre but must confront real life—in the streets, the factories, the schools—with disruptive actions that reveal the falsity and idyllicism of that life. When theatre remains in the theatre, it is in the domain of play and self-discovery but not of social change. Its function there

[24]Tadeusz Kantor, "The Theatre of Death," trans. Vog T. and Margaret Stelmasynski, in *Twentieth Century Polish Theatre*, ed. Bohdan Drozdowski (London, 1979), 98, 103.
[25]Peter Handke, *Publikumsbeschimpfung* (Frankfurt, 1966), 95.
[26]Handke, *Stücke* (Frankfurt, 1972), 203.
[27]Handke, "Strassentheater und Theatertheater," *Theater Heute* 9, 4 (Apr. 1968): 27.

must be to develop "the inner, hidden rooms of play in the spectator" and, through the encouragement of greater sensitivity and self-awareness, to aid the spectator's "coming into the world."[28] Similarly in a 1969 interview Handke distinguished his new theatre from that of the past by saying that it sought to make the audience "aware of the theatre world, not of the world outside the theatre." Theatrical objects have a special mode of existence. A table's "theatrical function" is to show "what a table on stage can be good for—including a wide range of practical, symbolic, and scenic functions."[29] Drama seeks to prove nothing, Handke adds, in a note to *Der Ritt über den Bodensee* (1970); actors, objects, and language are presented as a "free play of powers."[30]

Richard Foreman (b. 1937), founder in 1968 of the Ontological-Hysteric Theatre, issued three free-form "Ontological-Hysteric Manifestos" (1972, 1974, 1975) that show a strong affinity for the theory of Handke, stressing the phenomenological fact of the theatre experience (and indeed in their form and structure the phenomenological act of writing manifestos). Foreman considers all traditional theatre, including even such recent experimentation as that of Brook, Grotowski, and Chaikin, to be based on the same premise—that a spectator is to be "trapped" into some sort of emotional commitment.[31] Foreman, citing Ludwig Wittgenstein and Gertrude Stein as precursors, proposes instead a theatre calling attention to moment-by-moment existence and to the "intersecting process" that is the "perpetual constituting and reconstituting of the self." This new theatre "leaves a *tracing in matter* of this intersecting" and promotes "a courageous 'tuning' of the old self to new awareness."[32] The goal is not to place some imagined idea or emotion before an audience but on the contrary to lead the audience to question its assumptions and in this disintegration reveal the "elusive now" that no artist can imagine or fix. The artwork should encourage the spectator to see what is there, and to see himself seeing; it should "ground us in what-it-is-to-be-living."[33] Using a metaphor from physics, Foreman suggests that the work of art should produce a spark of antimatter, matter being "the on-going ideas which are the world, which are the dead husks of far earlier creative moments." Like that spark, the work is immediately annihilated, adding its dead husk to the world, but it provides an instant of vision into immanent reality, and the immediate succession of such instants should be the goal of art.[34]

[28] Artur Joseph, *Theater unter vier Augen* (Cologne, 1969), 7.
[29] Ibid., 34.
[30] Handke, *Stücke* 2 (Frankfurt, 1973), 57.
[31] Richard Foreman, *Plays and Manifestos*, ed. Kate Davy (New York, 1976), 70.
[32] Ibid., 74.
[33] Ibid., 145.
[34] Ibid., 189.

Foreman's work is often linked with that of two other leading American avant-garde directors of the 1970s, Robert Wilson and Lee Breuer. Although Wilson and Breuer, both strongly oriented toward the visual, have produced little extended theoretical observation, Bonnie Marranca, who presents works by each in her *The Theatre of Images* (1977), believes that Foreman's emphasis on sense impression, upon developing the audience's consciousness of "being there" in the theatre, upon expanding "the audience's capacity to perceive" informs the work of all three. Marranca sees such experimentation as the culmination of approaches developed out of happenings and the theatre of mixed means described by Kostelanetz. The aim of this new theatre is to create "a new stage language, a visual grammar 'written' in sophisticated perceptual codes."[35]

The influential English director Peter Brook (b. 1925), in his book *The Empty Space* (1968), discusses a range of contemporary approaches to the art of theatre. Like Guthrie and Barthes, Brook stresses that a director must deal with a play according to the demands of his own time and his own audience. A play cannot "speak for itself"; one must "conjure its sound from it."[36] Directors who avoid this challenge, as Guthrie warned, simply copy previous interpretations. Much modern production, especially of the classics, falls into this trap of old formulae, old methods, old effects, which Brook designates collectively as the "deadly" theatre. The two major modern challenges to the deadly theatre are what Brook calls the "holy theatre" and the "rough theatre." The first, exemplified by Artaud and Grotowski, is visionary, seeking to make the invisible visible; the second, exemplified by Brecht, brings renewal to theatre by returning to the popular sources of real life.

Beyond the holy theatre and the rough theatre, Brook suggests a more all-encompassing form, the "immediate theatre," which can unite spectator and performance in a communal celebration of experience, briefly achieving a totality that may leave a permanent image in the minds of its participants. Clearly, Brook considers Weiss's *Marat/Sade*, which he directed in 1964 (one of the decade's most famous productions), as a play headed in this direction. In the preface to the English version of the play, Brook lauds Weiss for the density of his drama. A good play, says Brook, sends out a rich texture of messages, "often several at one time, often crowding, jostling, overlapping one another," stirring the intelligence, the emotions, and the memory; a poor play has a much thinner texture, leaving gaps where inattention creeps in.[37]

[35]Bonnie Marranca, *The Theatre of Images* (New York, 1977), xv.
[36]Peter Brook, *The Empty Space* (New York, 1968), 38.
[37]Ibid., v.

Weiss combined Brechtian, Artaudian, absurdist, intellectual, and emotional impressions to create an extremely dense dramatic structure. (And though he does not say so, Brook's own vivid theatrical imagination considerably increased this density.)

After *Marat/Sade*, as we have seen, Weiss moved away from this sort of dramatic blend to the more openly political documentary theatre. The influence of Artaud and of Ionesco and Beckett could still be found in the German drama of the late 1960s and the 1970s, but the majority of the new dramatists saw their work in more distinctly political terms. This was true even when, after 1970, the documentary theatre declined in popularity and Brecht became a less central figure for theorists. Handke's attack on the "idyllic vision" of Brecht and his stated preference for the realism of Horváth in the late 1960s was echoed by several of the leading dramatists of the new generation, who combined a socially engaged view of the theatre with a technique strongly reminiscent of naturalism.

The best known of this group is Franz Xaver Kroetz (b. 1946), whose two 1971 articles, "Liegt der Dummheit auf der Hand?" and "Horváth von heute für heute," echoed Handke's choice of Horváth over Brecht, focusing on language as the key to Brecht's distance from reality. Brecht's figures are not, like Horváth's, trapped in a linguistic world created by their rulers. They are "fluent," with a "fund of language" of their own which opens to them "the way to a positive utopia, to revolution."[38] Horváth on the contrary depicted a loss of speech, resulting from a loss of meaning when "language is no longer able to summon up the recollection of what was originally meant."[39] While Horváth's *Volk* was the petty bourgeoisie, Kroetz depicts the proletariat, whose loss of language is a striking example of the degradation of the people in capitalist culture.

By the mid-1970s, however, Kroetz began to look more favorably upon Brecht as a model for transcending the "fixed boundaries" of Horváth-style "descriptive realism." The "utopianism" Kroetz earlier found questionable in Brecht seemed to him, as he admitted in a 1975 interview, a significant part of engaged theatre: "In the best sense art can suggest a believable, possible better reality; at its best the criticism of society is the vision of a better society."[40] The article "Zu Bertolt Brechts 20. Todestag" (1977) goes further still, calling "inadequate" a dramatist who, like Horváth, merely sympathizes with the victims of the social system, who attempts only "to present what one observes,"

[38]Franz Xaver Kroetz, "Liegt der Dummheit auf der Hand?" *Süddeutsche Zeitung* 20/21 (Nov. 1971): 4.
[39]Kroetz, "Horváth von heute für heute," *Theater Heute* 12, 12 (Dec. 1971): 13.
[40]Quoted in Ursula Schregel, *Neue deutsche Stücke im Spielplan* (Berlin, 1980), 79.

leaving the means of changing conditions in society for the spectator "to work out on his own." Rather, the dramatist should follow Brecht, using a dialectic world view and the techniques of socialist realism to create a fable with characters capable of change, which can "show the light of dawn in the darkest night."[41]

Politically oriented drama and theatrical theory were relatively uncommon in America, after the wave of interest in the 1930s and 1940s, until the late 1960s, when involvement with such questions strikingly reappeared. The revived interest was fueled at first by the arms race and the Cold War, then by an increasing awareness of tension over the military involvement in Vietnam, then by a growing concern with other unresolved social tensions, particularly economic and racial. Herbert Blau's (b. 1926) *The Impossible Theatre: A Manifesto* (1965) stands at the brink of this new surge of attention to engaged theatre in America. Blau condemns contemporary American theatre—whether on Broadway, in the universities, or in regional houses—as essentially a "stronghold of non-ideas."[42] It evades or minimizes the dangers and conflicts of its period, thus failing to fulfill its true role as the "Public Art of Crisis."[43] Theatre should pit its imagination, courage, and joy against the outrages humanity commits upon itself, looking beyond the immediate divisions and popular causes to the often less immediate goals of universal humanity and brotherhood. It should be a forum for the suppressed or ignored civic and civil side of man.[44] The same aspect of the theatre that constantly tempts it to compromise is also the source of its greatest potential power: that it is the most public of all the arts, the art which must function "at the dead center of community."[45]

The general humanist commitment preached in *The Impossible Theatre* was soon overshadowed by calls for the theatre to undertake social tasks of a much more immediate and specific nature. Theatre began to be considered as a forum for political statement, even as a weapon. The Summer 1966 issue of *TDR* may be taken as symptomatic of this shifting interest. A brief play by Robert Head, *Kill Viet Cong*, provided striking evidence that the growing uneasiness with American involvement in Vietnam might prove an important stimulus to politically engaged theatre. The political role of the theatre was a recurring and hotly debated theme in the abridged report of a *TDR* theatre conference, and Saul Gottlieb in "The Living Theatre in Exile" noted that the Becks based scene 4 of *Mysteries and Smaller Pieces* on such slogans as "Stop the War

[41]Heinz Arnold and Theo Buck, *Positionen des Dramas* (Munich, 1977), 251.
[42]Herbert Blau, *The Impossible Theatre: A Manifesto* (New York, 1965), 7.
[43]Ibid., 16.
[44]Ibid., 102.
[45]Ibid., 309.

in Vietnam. Ban the Bomb. Freedom Now. Change the World. Do It Now. Make It Work. Feed the Poor. Amnesty."[46]

One piece was entirely concerned with drama as political action: "Guerilla Theatre" by R. C. Davis, director of the San Francisco Mime Troupe, repeated, in stronger and more colorful language, Brecht's assertion that the only way for art not to be political is for it to support the ruling powers. Since the ruling powers in America are "debilitating, repressive, and nonaesthetic," said Davis, theatre is challenged on both social and artistic grounds to "teach, direct toward change, and be itself an example of change." Davis gives a set of directives and suggestions for theatre operating within society in a manner analogous to guerilla warfare—aligning itself with the populace, struggling always for a more just new order, but choosing the fighting ground carefully and never engaging the enemy head on. Naturalistic symbolism or "happenings for the chic" must be rejected in favor of forms of "effective protest or social confrontation."[47] Brecht is of course more directly useful than Artaud, but both reflect European historical concerns; the American theatre must ultimately find its own way. In a Mime Troupe program of the late 1960s, for example, the company's members spoke of themselves as the American equivalent of the Red Army "Art and Propaganda" teams, moving out among the populace in the parks and streets while the avant-garde theatres remained in their cellars.[48]

The 1965 *Huelga* (strike) of Filipino and Chicano migrant farm workers in California inspired the foundation of a number of politically oriented Chicano theatres, the most famous of which was El Teatro Campesino. Its director and chief playwright, Luis Valdez, came from the San Francisco Mime Troupe and brought with him some of the philosophy of that company. In a 1967 interview he predicted that America was entering an increasingly political period, a period of growing social problems, and that the future American theatre would have to be "a theatre of political change."[49] Like Davis, Valdez championed a specific kind of realism, not naturalistic but symbolic and emblematic in striking theatrical terms. The "dramatic situation, the thing you're trying to portray on the stage, must be very close to the reality that is *on* the stage." Thus when a figure representing the ranch owner is shown standing on the backs of two workers this is "not imitation" but rather "a theatrical reality that will hold up on the flatbed of a truck."[50]

[46]Saul Gottlieb, "The Living Theatre in Exile," *Tulane Drama Review* 10, 4 (Summer 1966): 141.

[47]R. C. Davis, "Guerilla Theatre," *Tulane Drama Review* 10, 4 (Summer 1966): 132.

[48]Quoted in Arthur Sainer, *The Radical Theatre Notebook* (New York, 1975), 29.

[49]Beth Bagby, "El Teatro Campesino," *Tulane Drama Review* 11, 4 (Summer 1967): 79.

[50]Ibid., 77–78.

Thus the guerilla theatre moves toward the political equivalent of Grotowski's poor theatre—theatre stripped to the essential emblematic presence of the actor before the audience.

Raymond Williams (b. 1921) suggests in *Modern Tragedy* (1966) that social disorder, war, and revolution are the contemporary subjects which express man's eternal concern with order and disorder. Every age expresses this concern in its own way, and Williams dismisses as narrow and historically biased the theory that the modern era cannot create tragedy because its view of order and disorder is no longer defined in religious or institutional terms. Our own beliefs and fears are not those of previous ages, but they are as commonly held and as accessible for tragic treatment. The modern concern with social disorder and violence is tragic in its origins, since it moves and involves all humanity, and tragic in its action, which pits men not against gods or institutions, but against other men. The insight that the only adequate action against disorder, the revolutionary act, produces other disorder, new alienation, is a tragic insight though not a negative one. It places us beyond either a simple resignation to disorder or a utopian belief that a single act of "heroic liberation" can solve the problem. It does not confirm disorder but makes us aware of it and aware of the necessity of continuing struggle—the necessity of a process of becoming, which is the only possible alternative to fixity and to the confirmation of disorder in its most radical form.[51]

Richard Schechner explored his own reactions to the new political and social orientation of the theatre of the mid-1960s in "The Politics of Ecstasy," an essay contributed to an anthology significantly entitled *Revolution* (1968). He returned, perhaps unconsciously, to the position of Wagner in *Die Kunst und die Revolution*: Art in its original and proper form is communal, socially constructive, and transcendent or ecstatic; but it has become individualistic and commercialized, practiced by artists who—like workers—sell their talent "by the piece or by the hour."[52] Since we cannot simply re-create the traditional theatre of societies unlike our own, we must seek ritual roots accessible to all cultures; and these roots, since they express the essential sense of community, must be discovered by the dedicated efforts of groups. To work in this direction, Schechner organized his own Performance Group in New York.

The new theatre Schechner describes in "Politics of Ecstasy" bears a striking resemblance to the Living Theatre, which achieved an almost mythic status during its years of European exile. In 1968–1969, it returned for a tour of America, arousing controversy and critical debate

---

[51]Raymond Williams, *Modern Tragedy* (Stanford, 1966), 83, 203.
[52]Richard Schechner, *Public Domain* (New York, 1968), 218.

everywhere it appeared. The company's challenges to existing order—social, theatrical, and sexual—made it anathema to conservative elements, but even some of its most avid supporters were disturbed or shocked to find that a group so associated in popular mythology with political protest should be so out of harmony with the assumptions and strategies of political theatre as it had developed in America during the years of the Becks' exile in Europe. For all its opposition to political oppression, the Living Theatre remained more oriented toward Artaud than toward Brecht. In a final interview in San Francisco, Julian Beck stressed again the theatre's desire to free the individual to feel and to create. The brain, he said, has become separated from the body and from feeling, and language has been corrupted and perverted. The theatre should attempt "some kind of communication of feeling and idea that push toward some other area that is beneath words or beyond words," not to destroy language but to "deepen it and amplify it and to make the communication real rather than a series of lies."[53] In January 1970, the Living Theatre issued its final declaration. Having become institutionalized in its current form, it was dividing into separate cells to continue, like guerilla bands, to struggle outside the existing order for a new art and a new society.

If the politically oriented concept of theatre that was developing in America in the late 1960s could not easily accommodate the mystic, spiritual, and psychological elements in the Living Theatre, certainly the work and theory of Grotowski—oriented entirely in that direction—presented far greater difficulties. American participants at a training course in Denmark in the summer of 1969 condemned the Polish director for his apparent indifference to social questions. In a subsequent French interview, Grotowski responded to the criticism. Man's primary duty is not of a social order, he said; his duty is "to respond to the challenge of life and to answer it in the manner of nature." Action is indeed required—not social/political action, however, but action of self-understanding, leading to the unity of body and soul.[54] Eugenio Barba echoed these ideas in an interview that same fall. The theatre cannot save society, he said, but it can play a significant role when, as in classic Greece, it becomes "an integral part of a firmly cemented social structure." Modern theatre should explore "behavior patterns"; these are neither social, political, nor religious but "biological reactions that spring up in extreme situations" and that the theatre elicits, channels, and disciplines.[55]

[53]Quoted in Renfreu Neff, *The Living Theatre: USA* (New York, 1970), 235.
[54]Grotowski, "External Order/Internal Intimacy," trans. George Reavez, *Drama Review* 14, 1 (Fall 1969): 172, 174.
[55]Eugenio Barba, "A Sectarian Theatre," *Drama Review* 14, 1 (Fall 1969): 57.

Particular attention to theatre as a form of social and political action developed at this time among American black writers, headed by LeRoi Jones (b. 1934), who in the late 1960s took the Muslim name Amiri Baraka. Baraka was a key figure in the shift, which began to occur about 1965 in many parts of the American black community, from civil rights protest to a more militant emphasis on black ethnicity, black culture, and black political power. Baraka, already a well-known young playwright, expresses the new orientation in "The Revolutionary Theatre" (1966). All theatre, he states, has a political/social message, though the dominant classes that control the establishment theatre always deny this. Broadway is "a theatre of reaction whose ethics, like its aesthetics, reflect the spiritual values of this unholy society." The new Revolutionary Theatre, a Theatre of Victims, must be anti-Western, exposing the real horror and oppression in this world which is hidden by traditional theatre. It will be hated and feared by the white establishment because its purpose will be "to destroy them and whatever they believe is real."[56]

The Summer 1968 issue of *TDR* was devoted to Black theatre, and to avoid the possibility of filtering ideas through the consciousness of the "white media," the editorial board turned the responsibility for the issue over to Ed Bullins (b. 1935), the most significant black playwright to appear after Baraka, relinquishing even the editorial veto they had retained over the invited editors of other special issues. In the lead article, "The Black Arts Movement," Larry Neal called Black Art the "aesthetic and spiritual sister of the Black Power concept," requiring a separate symbolism, mythology, criticism, and iconography "from the traditional western cultural aesthetic."[57] Like many Marxist critics, Neal considered the existing cultural system so corrupted by the ruling class that it was beyond reform by even the most radical means; it could only be destroyed and replaced. The new Black artists, he said, must therefore break completely with traditional white values and look to the Third World, the world of the oppressed, for inspiration in developing an art that celebrates community rather than the individual.

In the 1970s there was a rapid decline of the revolutionary impetus in the Black movement; Baraka attributed it in large part to the willingness of many to avoid the challenge and to be assimilated instead into the established socioeconomic mainstream. By 1974, he had become convinced that America's racial problem could be solved only by a change in the entire class structure. His introduction to *The Motion of History* (1978) quotes with approval Mao Tse-tung's demand for the unity of politics and art. Baraka looks back on his own theory and

---

[56]Amiri Baraka, *Selected Plays and Prose* (New York, 1979), 131.
[57]Larry Neal, "The Black Arts Movement," *Drama Review* 12, 4 (Summer 1968): 29.

practice of theatre as evolving from petty bourgeois radicalism through nationalism to grasp at last the Marxist-Leninist science of revolution. Evidence that his later works threaten the system more fundamentally is provided by the fact that it proved easier to get plays "screaming 'Hate Whitey' " published than those calling for "the building of a revolutionary communist party in America."[58]

In France, the influence of Artaud spread steadily after 1960 and was, of course, strikingly reinforced by the Grotowski productions in 1966. Brecht, whose influence had been much greater before 1960, seemed about to be eclipsed, and with him the idea of a politically engaged theatre. The director Roger Planchon (b. 1931), one of Brecht's strongest supporters, warned his contemporaries against the irrationality and the fundamentally reactionary tendencies in Artaud—who, he said, was an excellent poet but a writer quite lacking in the "logical structure one finds in Brecht."[59] Planchon credited Grotowski with achieving very striking effects, but only within a narrow and largely irrelevant type of theatre. "In abandoning the text, the dialogue," Grotowski's actors "have discovered unknown lands. But the day they leave these unknown lands, they will also abandon the discoveries they have achieved."[60]

The apparent drift of the progressive elements in the French theatre toward this alogical and ahistorical approach proved weaker than Planchon feared. The student and worker uprisings of 1968 stimulated fresh consideration of the relationship between theatre and the social order, especially in Paris, where the Living Theatre's participation in the student occupation of the national theatre, the Odéon, made it a somewhat reluctant symbol of the defiance of the old order. Vilar's Avignon festival that summer was challenged as a bastion of traditional ideas in an open letter from young theatre radicals in Paris. Their "Treize questions aux organisateurs et aux participants du festival d'Avignon" constituted a manifesto condemning as "repressive and authoritarian" any idea of culture as "a domain reserved for paying specialists." It called for a theatre of "collective creation" with no schism between artistic activities and "political, social, and everyday events," a theatre of "political and psychological liberation," of "direct rather than represented action," which would place the spectator no longer in "an alienated and underdeveloped situation."[61]

Such concerns closely reflected those of the Living Theatre, invited to participate in the Avignon festival. The Becks, too, were seeking a

---

[58]Baraka, *The Motion of History* (New York, 1978), 16.
[59]Roger Planchon, "Planchon on Brecht," *Drama Survey* 6, 3 (Spring 1968): 334.
[60]*Cité-Panorama*, no. 10, 1969; cited in Emile Copfermann, *Roger Planchon* (Lausanne, 1969), 269.
[61]Copfermann, *La mise en crise théâtrale* (Paris, 1972), p. 105.

theatre tying art and life more closely together, collectively created by a community that would "function truly like an anarchist society"—a society of artists working in cooperation and without authority as a model for the world outside.[62] This convergence of interest, plus the notoriety arising from their action at the Odéon, made it impossible for Beck and Malina to serve as mediators between the young critics and the festival, as they at first attempted to do. After they were forbidden to give free performances, they openly joined the revolutionary side, and departed from Avignon issuing a statement that they could not serve "both the people and the state" so long as the latter wanted the knowledge and power of art to be confined "to those who can pay for it."[63]

Arrabal also participated in the student uprisings in Paris, and this experience, coupled with his arrest the previous year in Spain on charges of obscenity, encouraged him to take a distinctly more political stance in his subsequent writings, even while maintaining his concern with man's "secret desires and inner impulses." In a 1972 interview, he calls his most recent experiments *théâtre de guerilla* instead of *théâtre panique* though there is still an echo of Artaud in this dangerous and revelatory theatre, "baroque, excessive, and savage." There is a new attitude toward the audience, too. While the *théâtre panique* assaulted them in the extremity of its images and unexpectedness of its juxtapositions, the *théâtre de guerilla* seeks a different kind of shock, a physical involvement in the actual experience of political repression. "I want them to feel surprised, terrified, taken off guard—as if they had just suddenly been plucked off the street and put into a prison."[64]

Armand Gatti (b. 1924) is probably the dramatist most closely associated with the politically oriented, antiinstitutionalist theatre of post-1968 France. As early as 1959, however, his first produced play, *Le crapaud-buffle*, showed him already interested in theatre as a political instrument. "The theatre is for me a means of combat," he said in an interview that year. "Later, when there is no longer anything to combat, the theatre may become at last what it ought to be—a universal festival."[65] By 1965, Gatti had evolved a theory of "time-possibility" which he opposed to the "time-duration" of traditional bourgeois theatre, an opposition suggestive of Brecht's epic versus Aristotelian drama. Embedded in the very grammar of traditional theatre and the society

---

[62]Pierre Biner, *The Living Theatre*, trans. anon. (New York, 1972), 163.

[63]Copfermann, *Mise en crise*, 106.

[64]Mel Gussow, "Arrabal—A Storm over the Wounded," *New York Times*, May 10, 1972, 40.

[65]Jacqueline Autrusseau, "Le mythe de la grandeur au petit T. N. P.," *Les lettres françaises*, Oct. 15, 1959, 9.

it reflects, he said, is a fixed and fallacious system of past, present, and future, whereas the mind moves easily and freely among the three. By emphasizing possibility rather than duration, the theatre can show an action from many perspectives and without a sense of closure, encouraging its audience to see the world as open to change.[66]

During the latter 1960s, Gatti became increasingly concerned with the specific audience to which modern theatre should be addressed. In "Notes au spectateur idéal," a 1967 interview, he argued that the function of today's theatre should be to allow "the most disinherited classes to gain an understanding of themselves and their potential."[67] Feeling that this could be best achieved by allowing members of these classes to participate with actor and author in the creation of the drama, Gatti, sometimes with a small band of actors and sometimes alone, began working with culturally deprived groups to create dramatic statements reflecting their concerns—somewhat in the manner of American guerilla theatre troupes like the San Francisco Mime or the Campesino. From these experiments came "a completely new aesthetic, a new style, a new kind of theatre," which Gatti calls "mini-pièces."[68] They are created, he explained in a 1969 interview, out of "a complete lack of means" and without an author, "since they always depend primarily on the performers and their context." The goal is not simple participation in the spectacle but "reflection on the problems that are posed," reflection that may lead to the resolution of these problems, "doubtless not that same evening but one day, later, in contact with reality."[69]

In a 1980 speech Gatti places the foundations of his theatre "in the eternal association which can exist between history and Utopia." Since both traditional theatre space and the language of the prevailing system of social reality block any attempt to deal honestly with either history or Utopia, theatre must be taken "out of the theatre." New locations must be found for performance and a new language must be developed suitable to these new locations—the factory or the street—and to the people who inhabit them.[70] Gatti, like Kroetz, sees the victims of political, social, and economic repression as deprived even of a language in which to understand their social reality; aiding them to find their language is the mission of theatre.

The French director most prominently associated with the conver-

[66]Jean-Louis Pays, "Entretien avec Armand Gatti," *Les lettres françaises*, Aug. 19, 1965, 1.

[67]Jean Michaud-Mailland, "Notes au spectateur idéal," *Les lettres françaises*, June 15, 1967, 22.

[68]Helmut Bauer, "Das Theater und die Revolution," *Die Zeit*, July 22, 1969, 10.

[69]Armand Gatti, "Entretien," *Travail théâtrale* 3 (Apr.-June 1971): 10.

[70]Gatti, "Armand Gatti on Time, Place, and the Theatrical Event" trans. Nancy Oakes, *Modern Drama* 25, 1 (Mar. 1982): 70–71.

gence of theatre and political action in the late 1960s is probably André Benedetto of the Nouvelle Compagnie d'Avignon. His "Manifeste" of April 1966 echoes Brecht in seeing the contemporary theatre as an instrument "to put consciousness to sleep" and to show the world as unalterable. Traditional culture and the classics, in their support of the prevailing ideology, "make up the most formidable enterprise of alienation, degradation, and reconciliation of irreconcilables ever conceived by any society up to the present."[71] Within a system so universal and so coercive, reform is impossible, and meaningful theatre must become subversive and revolutionary. Its method, says Benedetto in a 1971 interview, cannot be direct political action; rather it must seek to "harmonize divergent elements in the revolutionary process" by focusing on "the common enemy, the dominant ideology." Like Gatti, he renounces traditional theatre spaces, language, and characterization, but works with a fairly stable company of actors. Their approach, like that of Chaikin in the Open Theatre, is polyvalent and transformational, each actor seeking not to create a character but to "reveal himself to his utmost possible limit."[72]

The popular audience, Benedetto says in "Le petit héros populaire" (1975), finds this approach quite congenial. It is a more critical audience than the traditional one, for which Brecht's epic theatre was more suitable. The new popular audiences create their own *Verfremdung*; they do not project themselves onto the characters but observe and judge, demanding to know "why things go the way they are shown, why actions are thus and not otherwise."[73]

Ariane Mnouchkine (b. 1939), director of the Théâtre de Soleil in Paris, agrees with Gatti and Benedetto on the revolutionary essence of theatre. Hegel's idea of tragedy, she observes in a 1975 discussion, is flawed in suggesting that the enemy, external or internal, is invincible. The theatre should demonstrate that "the enemy can be conquered, that the world can be changed."[74] Her view of the relationship between theatre and audience differs, however, from that of either Benedetto or Gatti. She does not accept the former's already critically aware audience but argues that a popular public which does not yet exist must be created. On the other hand, she rejects Gatti's view of the theatre as a tool to be put into the hands of the dispossessed so that they may thereby express their concerns. The theatre, she says in a 1971 interview, should seek to establish a rapport with the public, but theatre

---

[71]André Benedetto, "Manifeste," *Travail théâtrale* 5 (Oct.-Dec. 1971): 28.
[72]Benedetto, "Entretien," *Travail théâtrale* 5 (Oct.-Dec. 1971): 8.
[73]Benedetto, "Le petit héros populaire," *Travail théâtrale* 21 (Oct.-Dec. 1975):46.
[74]*Esprit*, June 1975; quoted in Raymonde Temkine, *Mettre en scène au présent I* (Lausanne, 1977), 128 n.

should be created by a performance ensemble, whose work is modified by the public only in the sense that public comments after each production should influence the creation of the next.[75] This is part of the raw material used by the actors, working collectively to reflect the concerns of their own time in "the most elementary, the most direct possible form."[76]

Probably no contemporary theorist has exlored the political implications of the performance-audience relationship in so searching and original a manner as the Latin American director Augusto Boal. Like Brecht, he rejects "Aristotelian" drama as an instrument of the established class structure, but he is far more detailed and explicit than Brecht as to just how Aristotelian drama functions in that capacity. His major work, *Teatro do oprimido* (1974), views the origins of theatre in a manner reminiscent of Wagner and Appia, as a celebration of an entire people, later taken over by the aristocracy, who divided the art and turned it to their own ends. Boal sees these ends as essentially propagandistic and coercive, and the divisions as conscious and politically motivated. Aristotle constructed "the first, extremely powerful poetic-political system for intimidation of the spectator, for elimination of the 'bad' or illegal tendencies of the audience."[77] The two divisions imposed on the earliest theatre support this system: the first, dividing actors and public, converts the latter into spectators, unable to influence the course of the action; the second divides the protagonists, representing the aristocrats, from the chorus, representing the people. The spectators are encouraged to feel empathy with the tragic hero, to recognize in his *hamartia* their own antisocial urges, and through the fall of the hero and his recognition of error, they are led to reject those urges. This is the basic function of catharsis, the purging of antisocial elements.[78]

The bourgeois theatre, Boal continues, retained the exceptional individuals of classic theatre to use in its struggle against feudalism, but when a new opponent, the proletariat, appeared, the individual was steadily reduced. Hegel and Hugo diminished him by pitting him against eternal and immutable values, and realism made him a product of his environment.[79] Finally, in the theatre of Ionesco, even communication was removed, and man became completely dehumanized and abstract. In opposition to this, a new theatre, radically different in both style and content, must arise from the proletariat.

[75]Ariane Mnouchkine, "Entretien," *Travail théâtrale* 2 (Apr.-June 1971): 11.
[76]Mnouchkine, *1789* (Paris, 1971), 84.
[77]Augusto Boal, *The Theatre of the Oppressed*, trans. Charles A. and Marie-Odilia McBride (New York, 1979), xiv.
[78]Ibid., 46.
[79]Ibid., 75.

Boal sees Brecht as pointing the way by proposing a poetics totally opposed to the "idealist poetics" of Aristotle and Hegel. In idealist poetics, social thought conditions social being; dramatic action is created by the spirit. In Brecht's Marxist poetics, social being determines social thought; dramatic action arises from social relations. Boal thus rejects the Hegelian individual orientation of, for example, Hochhuth, who would say, "Kennedy invaded Girón Beach," in favor of the Brechtian statement, "Economic forces led Kennedy to invade Girón Beach."[80] Brecht begins where the bourgeois theatre ends, with abstraction, with characters not free to act; but he encourages his audience to see this condition as alterable by rejecting catharsis, which leads to tranquility and acceptance. Building upon Brecht's system and his own vision of the original function of theatre, Boal seeks to break down the walls between actors and spectators. In the "theatre of the oppressed," the spectator no longer delegates power to the actor but "himself assumes the protagonistic role, changes the dramatic action, tries out solutions, discusses plans for change." The theatre becomes a "rehearsal for revolution."[81]

The latter part of Boal's book explores a variety of experiments in the direction of such a theatre, some of them very close to the techniques of Gatti. The experiment most fully developed at Boal's Arena Theatre of São Paolo is the "Joker" system, which attempts to demonstrate the freedom of the individual "within the strict outlines of social analyses." The system mixes reality and fantasy, empathy and distance, details and abstraction; it tries to present simultaneously a performance and its analysis. The key is the "Joker," a figure who stands between play and audience, commenting, guiding, creating, and breaking the illusion. He functions in a way opposite to that of the protagonist, urging the audience to view the play critically rather than seeking to draw them emotionally into it.[82]

The leading politically engaged dramatist of Italy, Dario Fo (b. 1926), in 1968 joined an association of Communist cultural organizations devoted to bringing the arts to the disadvantaged working class. However, Fo's inclusion of the Italian Communist Party among his targets for satirical attack led to the formation of his own independent theatrical collective, La Commune, in 1970. Fo shares with Hochhuth and Weiss an interest in documentary theatre, but his painstaking research is then converted into highly theatrical expression through the use of traditional devices drawn from the popular theatre—farce, slapstick, and

[80]Ibid., 92–93.
[81]Ibid., 122.
[82]Ibid., 182-86.

commedia routines. His essay "Teatro di situazione uguale teatro popolare" (1971) explains Fo's approach. He insists upon a theatre of
"precise documentation" but one which is not "cold and didactic." The
documentary theatre will not become significant until it is fully realized
by theatrical means, seizing the public in such a way that "the didactic
information is acquired not as a lesson but as a spectacle." Fo hastens
to add that this should be achieved "with a minimum of technical
means."[83]

In a 1974 interview, Fo explained that his theatre had to be created
outside the conventions and the physical spaces of the traditional, bourgeois theatre, which like the ostrich "digests everything." Its language,
its problems, its physical surroundings are all alien to the worker, who
still does, however, respond to the traditions and appeal of the popular
theatre (the point made by Davis of the San Francisco Mime Troupe).
Thus Fo's goal—"to advance certain democratic appeals, to form public
opinion, to stimulate, to create moments of dialectical conflict"—had to
be approached first "on the level of style, of expressive means," by
research into popular theatre and into the role of gesture as the inseparable accompaniment of theatrical discourse.[84]

In England, Edward Bond (b. 1934) brought to the drama a political
commitment similar to that of these continental figures, and though
his theoretical observations do not echo their preoccupation with reaching or developing a proletarian audience, he does stress the obligation
of modern drama to create an "image and consciousness" for the working class, which has hitherto been systematically excluded from culture
and thereby from the development of its human image.[85] The job of
the writer, says Bond in "The Writer's Theatre" (1971), is "to analyze
and explain our society."[86] Though philistines charge art with being
arbitrary, random, or fantastic, in fact it is society itself, based upon
injustice and expediency, that is arbitrary, and any legitimate art challenges society with necessary truths. Such truths, says Bond in his preface to *Bingo* (1974), "express the justice and order that are necessary
to sanity but are usually destroyed by society."[87] The program notes to
We Came to the River (1976) stress the importance of art to all suffering
humanity. Theatre's major responsibility is to express "the conviction
that we can have a rational relationship with the world and with each

[83]Dario Fo, "Teatro di situazione uguale teatro popolare," *Sipario* 300 (May 1971): 43.
[84]"Intervista con Dario Fo," in Lanfranco Binni, *Attento te. . . !* (Verona, 1975), 388–89.
[85]*Edward Bond: A Companion to the Plays*, ed. M. Hay and P. Roberts (London, 1978), 70.
[86]Ibid., 45.
[87]Edward Bond, *Bingo and The Sea* (New York, 1975), xi.

other" and to bring its audience "to recognize a common, shared humanity, which is shattered by the class structure of society." Bond, like Bloch, sees the best opportunity for such theatrical expression in the fissures of society; "the critical parts of society where the old and irrational break down" are where re-creation and the rational potential of humanity must be shown as operative.[88]

In a 1978 interview, Howard Brenton (b. 1943) characterized his plays as "written unreservedly in the cause of socialism." The greatest drama has always been involved in proving "in two hours of scenes, events, jokes, and entertainment, that an unpopular idea is actually a good idea." The true test of a drama is not originality but the ability to articulate "common concerns, hopes or fears" and to provide "an answer or the ghost of the possibility of an answer" to these concerns. Unless a play enters the "arena of public action" by enlightening its public and suggesting what they should do next, it is a failure and worthless.[89]

Other socially oriented but less specifically political theories of theatre provided an important segment of critical writing after 1965. In "Approaches to Theory/Criticism" (1966), Richard Schechner calls for a reexamination of the theories of the Cambridge anthropologists. Their work, though brilliant and insightful, was limited and is "no longer suited to our perceptions of theatre."[90] A broader anthropological view of the interrelationship of all of man's public performance activities is needed—one that considers play, games, sports, theatre, and ritual. Schechner cites a number of writers in the social sciences whose work suggests new approaches to theatre analysis. J. Huizinga's study of play in *Homo Ludens* discusses features common to games, sports, and theatre. Mathematical (Martin Shubik) or transactional (Eric Berne) game analysis procedures might be applied to theatre structure. Erving Goffman's *The Presentation of Self in Everyday Life* (1959) discusses the ubiquity of "performance" in human activity. The thesis of theorists like Goffman and Berne, that the psyche is not fixed but constantly playing new roles according to situations, provides sociological support for an interest in transformational acting.

The Summer 1967 issue of *TDR* pursued this idea: an article by Arthur Wagner reported on the use of Eric Berne's transactional analysis as a directorial approach to a production of *Benito Cereno*, and there was an interview with Berne himself. Berne suggested that an actor's

[88]*Edward Bond*, 70.

[89]Malcolm Hay and Philip Roberts, "Howard Brenton: Introduction and Interview," *Performing Arts Journal* 3, 3 (Winter 1979): 137, 140.

[90]Richard Schechner, "Approaches to Theory/Criticism," *Tulane Drama Review* 10, 4 (Summer 1966): 26.

work should be considered "not as playing a character but as dealing with a series of specific interpersonal transactions." At the same time, there is a hidden drive, not truly autonomous, that justifies the denouement, so that a good play works simultaneously on an open and a hidden level.[91]

The overlapping of theatre and life is further explored in Schechner's "6 Axioms for Environmental Theatre" (1968). Schechner proposes a "continuum of theatrical events" ranging from public occasions and demonstrations, through happenings and environmental theatre, to traditional theatre. Each overlaps others and weaves together social transactions, creating what Goffman has characterized as a network of expectations and obligations.[92] Viewing theatre as a set of transactions allows us to expand our theoretical approaches beyond the traditional studies of literature, acting, and directing. We may consider the primary transactions among performers, among audience members, or between these two groups—as well as the secondary ones among production elements, between these and performers or audience, or between total production and space. In addition to this "transactional" view, Schechner proposes five other concerns of "environmental theatre," most of them dealing with space. "Environmental" space will probably not be traditional but totally transformed, or even "found." The same space is shared by audience and performance, and the focus is variable and flexible. All production elements speak for themselves, and none is necessarily subordinated to the rest. This includes the text, which has no necessary primacy and in fact may disappear altogether.

Many of these concerns, as we have seen, also emerge in the politically oriented theory of this period. The general openness of this approach, and the freedom of production elements to speak for themselves, strongly suggests Brecht; the rejection of traditional space and predetermined text, plus the moving of the performers into the real world and space of the spectator, suggests Gatti and Benedetto. No specifically political note is present in Schechner's theory, however. His orientation is toward Grotowski and such experiments as the happenings, more to opening up theatre and theory to a fuller relationship with the complexities of the modern consciousness. His support of audience participation is less akin to that of Gatti than to that, for example, of Ann Halprin, organizer of the San Francisco Dance Workshop, who argues in "Mutual Creation" (1968) that because the modern world contains too much for one mind to master, the theatre should no longer depend

[91]Eric Berne, "Notes on Games and Theatre," *Tulane Drama Review* 11, 4 (Summer 1967): 90.
[92]Schechner, "6 Axioms for Environmental Theatre," *Drama Review* 12, 3 (Spring 1968): 43.

upon one mind to determine "everything for everybody." Simply allowing things to happen with everyone participating is not only "more enjoyable and more unpredictable" but also demonstrates "what is possible and not just what you think *should* be."[93]

The German theorist Claus Bremer (b. 1924), in a series of essays collected as *Thema Theater* (1969), also advocates a modern theatre of indeterminacy, though less on the basis of the overwhelming complexity of the modern world than on that of the loss of absolutes. In an essay on the *Mitspiel* (an audience participation form being developed at this time by Paul Pörtner), Bremer states that the contemporary theatre must "pursue the consequences of the lack of an absolute, and must present each individual point of view as equally valid." The hierarchy of author, actor, spectator must disappear; each must assume functions of the other. Recalling Perger's emphasis on physical surroundings (the *Raumproblem*), and a 1965 conference at Bregenz on "Theatralische Raumgestaltung" that focused upon the aesthetic and social implications of theatre space in various periods,[94] Bremer raises the question of the proper space for modern drama. "A theatre that holds nothing as absolute, I told myself, can establish no fixed boundary between auditorium and stage." The particular advantage of theatre over film, radio, and television is precisely this, that it can open itself to its audience, and admit all perspectives. Its new public should be less like that of film or television and more like that of "sports, jazz, and the tavern."[95]

Joachim Hintze's *Das Raumproblem im modernen deutschen Drama und Theater* (1969) devotes relatively little attention to the interpretation of audience and performance space, but explores the implications of a series of twentieth-century views of theatre space. The most attention is given to naturalism and expressionism, but the final chapter considers three types of contemporary room experimentation. The *Gerichtsraum* is used for courtroom dramas, such as Peter Weiss's *Die Ermittlung* (1965), which confront the audience as a sort of unacknowledged jury, with evidence drawn from historical events. The *Modellraum*, particularly associated with the theatre of Brecht, involves elements from real life abstracted for the stage "in order to serve a didactic purpose and influence the relations between stage and auditorium."[96] A more general category is what Hintze calls the "theatrically autonomous room," which

[93] Ann Halprin, "Mutual Creation," *Drama Review* 13, 1 (Fall 1968): 174.
[94] Papers from this conference were reproduced in *Maske und Kothurn* 13, nos. 3 and 4 (1965).
[95] Claus Bremer, *Thema Theater* (Frankfurt, 1969), 14, 16.
[96] Joachim Hintze, *Das Raumproblem im modernen deutschen Drama und Theater* (Marburg, 1969), 207.

may or may not include the spectator but in any case recognizes the theatre as a world of its own, not as an illusory slice of life.

As the concept of the "theatrically autonomous room" has gained importance in contemporary German theatre theory and practice, so has the work of Wilfried Minks, the designer and theorist most associated with this approach. The products utilized to construct the "Minks-Bühne" are drawn from modern technology, and the design created from them does not weld them into a unified and unique "work of art" but places them in an alterable and altering system of technologically reproducible units. Minks seeks a design that is neither realistic nor abstract but "matter-of-fact, just as a natural landscape is," one created for the theatre world, living and developing a relationship with actors and audience, and contributing "not only optically, but sensually" to a total theatre experience.[97]

Paul Pörtner (b. 1925), Germany's leading experimenter in the early 1970s in enlarging the creative role of the spectator, explains his theories in *Spontanes Theater* (1972). The first part of the book discusses the artists and theorists Pörtner considers his predecessors; the second traces his own career. Pörtner divides modern theatre into two general types, "total" and "autonomous," which he equates with Grotowski's "rich" and "poor" theatre. The total theatre creates distance between itself and its spectators, while the autonomous seeks to establish contact.[98] The first major theorist of the autonomous theatre and of the interpenetration of theatre and life was Evreinov. Pörtner's "spontaneous" theatre has been most influenced in theory by Evreinov, Artaud, and Jakob Moreno, whose work with psychodrama revealed a great deal about the process of eliciting theatrical creation from spectators. Among more recent parallel experiments, Pörtner lists Piscator, the Living Theatre, Arrabal, and Gatti. Pörtner himself moved from improvisational theatre (which built upon suggestions from the audience) through variable theatre (in which the audience selected one of several alternative developments) to the *Mitspiel*, where the author provides a beginning situation, then allows the spectators not only to select one of several lines of development but actually participate in the evolving action.

Pörtner sees the *Mitspiel* as political theatre, not in its content but in the more fundamental matter of its structure and workings. The traditional theatre, he notes, whether controlled by dramatist, director, or actors, has always been authoritarian, forcing content or experience

[97]Wilfried Minks, "Bühnenräume solten die Selbstverständlichkeit von Landsschaften haben," *Theater Heute* 11, 9 (Sept. 1970): 38.
[98]Paul Pörtner, *Spontanes Theater* (Cologne, 1972), 93.

upon the audience. In the *Mitspiel*, "the public shall not have something said to them from above, from the stage or platform, but shall say something themselves, determine for themselves what shall be played and how." The goal is "to bring into being communication among all the participants."[99]

Ulrich Pfaendler's *Drama und Mitspiel* (1975) relates Pörtner's experiments to the traditional forms of open and closed drama. Closed drama poses, develops, and concludes a defined problem during the performance, with a solution provided by the author. The audience participates only through identification with the hero or other characters. In the open drama, a problem from real life is presented and developed by analogy, stimulating a process within the spectator, who is then responsible for a solution outside the theatre. In the *Mitspiel*, a real problem is reconstructed in the theatre, developed and solved by experimentation involving the active participation of the audience.[100] The emotional identification of the closed form and the rational analysis of the open are here fused into something close to a life situation. The *Mitspiel* approaches real life more closely than either open or closed drama. Time and place of performance become identical with reality, and even in the controlled opening section of the work, the actors must remain close to reality so that the audience participants can subsequently relate to them. Speech must be natural, even banal, as opposed to the "formal, information-filled" dialogue of traditional theatre. Actors should be cast as closely as possible to the roles they play, not only in age and appearance but—even more important—in beliefs and sociopolitical orientation, so that they may move freely into improvisational work with the public as they explore the problems posed. In this way the *Mitspiel* can become the theatrical "embodiment of the democratic process."[101]

A sociological approach to theatrical theory closely akin to Schechner's suggestions in the late 1960s was explored by Elizabeth Burns in *Theatricality* (1972) (though Burns is apparently unaware of the *TDR* essays on this subject, which she calls "wholly the concern of French scholars" such as Gurvitch and Duvignaud). The book deals with "the phenomenon of theatricality as it is manifested in theatre and social life."[102] After general remarks on the theatre as a metaphor, the "Theatrum Mundi," Burns outlines the traditional theory of the origin of classic and medieval theatre from religious ritual, and discusses the new set of "language conventions" required for theatre to develop as a

[99]Ibid., 82.
[100]Ulrich Pfaendler, *Drama und Mitspiel* (Basel, 1975), 203, 204.
[101]Ibid., 207, 208.
[102]Elizabeth Burns, *Theatricality* (London, 1972), 6.

separate entity—conventions that establish the assumed world of the theatre and persuade the audience to accept this world as rhetorically valid. Burns then turns to the playing of roles in social life and to the actor's relationship to this process—as "presenter" of a mode of behavior; as "interpreter," adding dimensions of his own to a text; and as "constructor of alternative existences" outside the established world of social roles. Theatre both borrows material from life—adjusted to its own conventions—and gives back models for the theatrical aspects of social behavior. Ritualization and patterning permeate all our activities, and the theatre idealizes this process, presenting it "legitimated and stylized," uninterrupted by accident or other interference. The constant "feed in and feed-back" of theatricality between stage and audience is the essence of drama.[103]

Uri Rapp draws upon Duvignaud and upon recent sociological and anthropological research in his *Handeln und Zuschauen* (1973), which considers theatre both as a social situation and as the embodiment of social interrelations. Taking "action and observation" as the keys to the drama, Rapp discusses the parallel development of these social phenomena, inside and outside the theatre, through role playing, arrangement of situation, presentation, observation of self and others, and so on. The unity of social man is in fact "an open-ended aggregate of played, playable, fantastical, and anticipated roles," and human society "created the theatre as a model, a copy in which society's own signification could be symbolized."[104]

A special issue of *TDR* (September 1973), guest-edited by Richard Schechner, stressed the application of social science's strategies to the study of theatre. Schechner called for more work on "performance theory," involving the study of sports, ritual, play, and other daily life "performance" in humans, as well as play and ritualized behavior in animals; analyze nonverbal communication; consider the implications of psychotherapy for theatre; investigate the ritualized forms of ancient and alien cultures; and seek unified theories of performance related to theories of behavior.[105] Schechner's lead article distinguished between drama, or the original text; script, that which can be transmitted from this text into a new situation; theatre, the specific event enacted by performers; and performance, the entire constellation of human activity surrounding this event. Traditional illusionistic theatre at-

---

[103]Ibid., 231–32.
[104]Uri Rapp, *Handeln und Zuschauen* (Darmstadt, 1973), 168.
[105]Schechner, "Performance and the Social Sciences," *Drama Review* 17, 3 (Sept. 1973): 3.

tempted to weld these together, while modern experiments often call attention to the "seams" or disjunctures between them.[106]

Schechner's continuing interest in performance theory led to the publication later in the decade of two collections of essays: *Ritual, Play and Performance* (1976) and *Essays on Performance Theory 1970–1976* (1977). The first, coedited by Schechner, included texts from ethnologists Konrad Lorenz and Jane van Lawick-Goodall, sociologist Erving Goffman, anthropologist Victor Turner, and communication scientist Ray Birdwhistell—as well as his own "From Ritual to Theatre and Back" (1974), which suggested that Western theatre's great periods occurred when ritual and theatre were most nearly in balance. Schechner views both as performance, but theatre emphasizes entertainment, audience separation, and the present world, while ritual emphasizes efficacy, audience participation, and an absent Other.[107] The second collection, of Schechner's own essays, overlaps to some extent both the earlier anthology and the special issue of *TDR*. The essay "Towards a Poetics of Performance" (1975) gives particular attention to Goffman and Turner, who use the concepts and terminology of the theatre to discuss certain social manifestations, Goffman considering role playing and the theatrical "framing" of situations, Turner a dramaturgical pattern in the development and resolution of social crises. The four steps of Turner's "social dramas"—a breach of regular norm-governed social relations, the crisis caused by this breach, redressive action, and reintegration of the disturbed group or recognition of irreparable schism—are applicable, Schechner believes, to the basic pattern of traditional drama as well, drama itself being an expression of the necessary ceremonial adjustments that a society must make in order to survive.[108]

Turner himself, in his book *From Ritual to Theatre* (1982), considers some of the implications of his anthropological studies. He does not agree with Schechner that traditional drama tends to echo the four-stage patterns of "social drama"; rather, it exaggerates the third phase, the ritualized action of redress. He sees the poetic development of this phase as akin to Dilthey's fifth movement of *Erlebnis*, in which experience is expressed to other members of a culture for their observation and reflection. Art and ritual, Turner suggests, are generated in areas of "liminality," where normally fixed conditions are open to flux and change, and man may undertake periodic reorganization of his view of himself and his world. In comparatively holistic tribal and agrarian

---

[106]Schechner, "Drama, Script, Theatre, and Performance," *Drama Review* 17, 3 (Sept. 1973): 9.
[107]Schechner, "From Ritual to Theatre and Back," *Educational Theatre Journal* 26, 4 (Dec. 1974): 467.
[108]Schechner, *Essays on Performance Theory* (New York, 1977), 60–61.

societies, liminal phenomena often appear as rather predictable cultural manifestations such as rites of passage. Even total inversions of the normative social process can be thus integrated into that process. The more fragmentary modern industrial societies typically produce "liminoid" phenomena, conceived not as integrated antistructure but as play, a leisure activity outside the normative process, allowing experimentation with varied structure.[109]

Some liminal tendencies remain in the modern theatre, as in the work of Grotowski, but Turner views such modern "rites of initiation" as basically totalitarian, removing one set of status roles only to firmly implant another. Complex modern societies are unlikely to find much consensus on any social questions, and the theatre can perhaps best serve them through an open-ended liminoid playfulness, providing a multitude of possible models and interpretive meanings for the typical events of the epoch.

In the 1980s some theorists have warned against too close an identification of theatre processes with sociological (Goffman) or with anthropological (Turner) phenomena. Clifford Geertz's essay "Blurred Genres: The Figuration of Social Thought" (1980) judges Turner's "ritual approach" most valuable in showing how drama in the form of social action confirms known form, and also how it aids in the transformation of its society. Its disadvantage is that it submerges individual details and specific contents in the charting of general rhythms, making "vividly disparate matters look drably homogeneous."[110] As a counterweight, Geertz suggests the theorists of symbolic action, such as Burke, Frye, and Langer, who focus upon the rhetoric of drama: not how an action is shaped, but what it says. A synthesis fusing the Burkean pattern (each part of society as enactment of an order) and the Turner pattern (social ceremonies as a force to hold polity together or to change it) would provide a richer model for anthropological study and perhaps for theatre theory as well.

The extension of theatrical metaphor into the analysis of life situations outside the theatre is the central concern of the book *Role Playing and Identity* (1982) by Bruce Wilshire (b. 1932). Using a phenomenological approach derived from Husserl, Merleau-Ponty, and Heidegger, Wilshire first considers the manner in which theatre mimics life. He advances as the "essential theatrical theme" a process of "standing in" and "authorization." The actor "stands in" for a recognizable example of the human family and we "authorize" him to do so. At the same time, he authorizes us as "potential mimics, since we stand in with the

[109]Victor Turner, *From Ritual to Theatre* (New York, 1982), 52.
[110]Clifford Geertz, "Blurred Genres," *American Scholar* 37 (Spring 1968), 173.

character through him."[111] Traditional concepts of imitation and empathy are too narrow to suggest this process, which teaches us something about the conditions of our own self-identity through a "perceptually induced mimetic phenomenon of participation."[112] The enactments of theatre share the same universal conditions of life posited by Heidegger: language, being with others, projection of personality, and mood.[113]

The second part of Wilshire's book evolves a theory of the identity of the self, arguing that an exclusively mentalistic or memory-based theory is inadequate, that a comprehensible self requires "a body which is able to 'express' itself, to deploy and display itself in a theatre-like way in space and time."[114] One of the most basic drives and motivations for action is the effort to define a self, to seek the particular significance of the individual body. But the Apollonian quest is attended by a fear of isolation from others: hence the corresponding Dionysian urge to lose the individual identity in the crowd. Only the artist and the person committed to the development of the artlike in his life can synthesize these opposed joys and fears. Theatre experiments constantly with the "mimetic fusion with others, disruptions from them, and attendant transformation of personality" that mark "the course of selves through time."[115]

In the final section of the book, Wilshire discusses the limits of the theatrical metaphor in life, the inability of art to encompass the "indissoluble residuum of uncanniness and particularity in the factuality of human existence"[116] and the inescapable ethical responsibility for roles and actions which in real life are a condition of identity. The self-observing and self-responsible "observer" of roles, the being that attempts to weave together the episodes and experiments of life into a conscious structure of self, is a phenomenon of real life, not of acting; and the indifference of Goffman's approach to this fact "blurs fundamental distinctions between off and onstage."[117]

One of the most important directions that American theatre theorists took after 1970 was toward a consideration of the theatre as a performed art, though without rejecting a critical interest in the written text (significantly, some began to speak of the text not as a play but a "playscript"). Although as a group these theorists exhibit little direct

---

[111]Bruce Wilshire, *Role Playing and Identity* (Bloomington, 1982), 6–7.
[112]Ibid., 26.
[113]Ibid., 109.
[114]Ibid., 139.
[115]Ibid., 228, 232.
[116]Ibid., 245.
[117]Ibid., 280.

influence from continental structuralism, some designate their theory as structuralist, and all are concerned with works of theatre as functioning systems and with the relationships between their various constituent parts. J. L. Styan's already discussed *Elements of Drama* (1963) may be taken as the first significant modern manifestation of this approach, though Granville-Barker's emphasis on the dynamics of performance, the concern of Freytag, Sarcey, and Archer with dramatic structure, and Kenneth Burke's interest in the shifting, mutually illuminating, and conditioning elements of the dramatic situation might be listed as earlier strategies reflected in the work of these post-1970 theorists.

The title of Jackson Barry's (b.1926) *Dramatic Structure: The Shaping of Experience* (1970) reveals his commitment to this kind of analysis. Barry dissociates himself at once, however, from such earlier theorists of dramatic structure as Freytag, whose systems he considers essentially spatial and static—unsuited for the theatre, where temporality is the essential quality. Theatre "shapes the materials of experiences" into patterns giving "an image of man's interaction in time."[118] (This temporal patterning, as we shall see, is a central concern of the American "structural" critics.) Drama begins, Barry suggests, with a certain "Basic Pattern of Events," reflecting the assumptions made by an audience about the way life itself is structured. The Greeks found the pattern of a successful man struck down a significant reflection of human experience; the Elizabethans tended to view life as a progressive historical process; the nineteenth century exhibited a strong belief in determinism; and the twentieth century has inclined toward random and unstructured patterns.

From such basic patterns, the dramatist derives the intermediate pattern of the specific play, which is in turn subdivided into actions and beats. All dramatic structure reflects a tension between two basic patterns of time: the improvisational, or Heraclitean, which sees time as a specious present moving constantly "step by step into an unknown future," and the retrospective, which sees a completed portion of time with a definite shape.[119] There is an echo of Burke's dramatic pentiad in Barry's suggestion that an action becomes dramatic when it is performed with a sense of purpose under the influence of time, place, and situation.

Bernard Beckerman (b. 1921) attempts to establish in *Dynamics of Drama* (1970) a modern method of analyzing and discussing this art. Theatre, he suggests, "occurs when one or more human beings isolated

---

[118]Jackson Barry, *Dramatic Structure: The Shaping of Experience* (Berkeley, 1970), 56.
[119]Ibid., 70.

in time and/or space present themselves to another or others."[120] His parallel definition of drama adds "in imagined acts" after "present themselves."[121] Since theatre is a temporal art, this presentation must occur in the form of activity; Beckerman proposes a "vertical" analysis of such activity, using as elements "not plot and character but units of time," which Beckerman calls "segments." All theatrical action is essentially composed of varying types of segments that increase in tension to a crux, then relax. The dramatic segment adds to this pattern levels of symbolic meaning, stimulating a critical response in the imagination of the audience. Each segment requires a precipitating context to point the direction of its action, a "project" that focuses the energies of each performer, a buildup to the crux, and a subsequent relaxation; these elements are constantly varied to maintain interest. A basic variation is between active and reactive segments, the first, traditionally favored by dramatic theorists, based on resistance and confrontation, the second on a sustained emotional release that is generally more oriented toward the experience than the goal.[122] Further variations may be introduced by changes in intensity, by different types of crux, and by variations in the external activity that contains the internal action.

Audiences, Beckerman continues, are not usually specifically aware of the patterns of action, yet they may experience them isomorphically as a kind of psychic echo. Their detailed empathetic response will be determined by associated factors, the "ground," and the pure "experience" itself will be further conditioned by an inescapable element of meaning. Meaning appears in four aspects: descriptive or literal; participational (always central in theatre); referential, looking to external experience; and conceptual or imaginative. Only the full course of the action will establish these meanings, since they, like character, are built up out of the sequence of segments, whose arrangement and interplay are determined by the dramatist on the basis of such concerns as causation, repetition, and emphasis.

A Structural Approach to the Analysis of Drama (1971) by Paul M. Levitt (b. 1935) takes the rather more mechanical French scene, instead of Beckerman's segment, as the basic building block of the drama. Levitt defines structure as "the place, relation, and function of scenes in episodes and in the whole play."[123] The analysis of this structure suggests the traditional modes of theorists of the well-made play: the implications of an early or late point of attack, the linkage of scenes, the

---

[120]Bernard Beckerman, *Dynamics of Drama* (New York, 1970), 10.
[121]Ibid., 20.
[122]Ibid., 80, 86.
[123]Paul M. Levitt, *A Structuralist Approach to the Analysis of Drama* (The Hague, 1971), 66.

importance of entrances and exits, the variation of scenes through such techniques as recurrence and reversal.

Bert States (b. 1929), in *Irony and Drama: A Poetics* (1971), is somewhat closer in approach to the continental structuralists, focusing upon certain recurring functions and relationships in the drama, but States's acknowledged major theoretical source is Kenneth Burke, whose *Grammar of Motives* provides the central concept of this study, which is that the essence of drama lies in a basic pattern of irony and dialectic, concentrating on the moment of peripety. Drama does not simply imitate action but imitates it in a habitual way, reflecting the manner in which dialectical man, in the face of the variety of nature, endows the events of nature "with a certain radical, and therefore comforting form."[124] In this form acts do not merely produce further acts but tend to produce counteracts. Drama concentrates on the moment of ironic reversal from A to non-A, seeking the "mastered moment" that joins opposites in a dialectical synthesis and convinces the spectator that "all that can be said on the subject has been said."[125] States discusses a spectrum of dramatic form from the most highly synthesized example of the ironic-dialectic, which is traditional tragedy, through dramas of conflict between necessary and accidental and dramas emphasizing either the ironic as in Chekhov or the dialectic as in Ibsen, to the epic of Brecht (in which the descriptive begins to merge with the dramatic), and finally to the purely lyric-descriptive, the drama's opposite pole. Such a spectrum provides "a model of strategies by which the playwright (or poet) may express experience."[126]

Roger Gross (b. 1931), in *Understanding Playscripts* (1974), distinguishes between the drama (an artistic genre and a species of literature), the play (a kind of occurrence), and the playscript (a symbolic notation on which a certain kind of play is based).[127] He then considers the process of interpretation (by both artists and audience) in the theatre. Artists who interpret the script, the director in particular, must understand the process of signification and the "influence of all of the sign-field," and they must become expert in the knowledge of the internal and external relationships (matrices) that create the apprehensible structure of the work.[128] This knowledge then must be turned toward the public and its comprehension of the work. The interpretive artists seek to reduce the ambiguity of each sign by attributing to it a meaning "which integrates that sign with all other signs in the work in one

---

[124]Bert States, *Irony and Drama: A Poetic* (Ithaca, N.Y., 1971), 14.
[125]Ibid., 141.
[126]Ibid., 228.
[127]Roger Gross, *Understanding Playscripts* (Bowling Green, Ohio, 1974), 4.
[128]Ibid., 43.

meaning-structure."[129] This is an open-ended process, since under-standing is always tentative and provisional, but the goal is a perfor-mance with the greatest possible degree of apprehensible relevance, continuity, coherence, and congruity. In his emphasis on the sign and theatrical communication, Gross has a close affinity to such Europeans as Kowsan and Ruffini, who at this same time were developing a modern semiotics of the theatre.

J. L. Styan's *Drama, Stage, and Audience* (1975) shares this affinity, focusing even more directly upon communication through the arrange-ment of both verbal structures and such nonverbal elements as cos-tumes, properties, and light. Dramatic perception "involves a capacity beyond literary, a sensitivity to the kind of amalgam of the arts natural to the theatre."[130] Genre and style are "ways of seeing"; they are dif-ferent aesthetic abstractions from the norm of everyday life, which must be recognized by the audience not only for the proper emotional response but indeed for any real communication of meaning to take place. Theatre theorists must therefore consider the historical condi-tions of performance: the attitudes of audiences in different periods to the physical configuration of the stage, to improvisation and the actors' belief, to such matters as asides and prologues. This is not to suggest that drama is merely a reflection of already established ideas; it is rather a collective act of creation, the harnessing of "the ingredients of human imagination for community experience." Theatre always en-courage its community to stretch the mind and extend the perception.

Michael Kirby issued in 1975 a "Manifesto of Structuralism" that attempted to distinguish "structuralist theatre" from other types of theatre, all of which have structure but do not make it dominant. Kirby specifically denies any relationship between his usage and that of such figures as Freud, Jung, and Levi-Strauss. He wishes instead to designate a kind of theatre that seeks its concepts and emotions "according to certain structural principles."[131] These principles are elaborated in Kir-by's essay "Structural Analysis/Structural Theory" (1976), which faults traditional theatre analysis for emphasizing content and neglecting form, as manifested in such matters as visual continuity, momentum, and shape. In both theory and practice, semantic elements have tended to "take over" the theatrical work. Structuralist theatre attempts to counter this tendency by reflecting "the pure workings of the mind," since it is this, "rather than the informational context, that is significant."[132]

Richard Hornby (b. 1938) also warns the reader, at the beginning of

---

[129]Ibid., 121.
[130]J. L. Styan, *Drama, Stage, and Audience* (London, 1975), 56.
[131]Kirby, "Manifesto of Structuralism," *Drama Review* 19, 4 (Dec. 1975): 82–83.
[132]Kirby, "Structural Analysis/Structural Theory," *Drama Review* 20, 4 (Dec. 1976): 68.

Script into Performance: A Structuralist View of Play Production (1978), that his concept of structure and structuralism "is different both from traditional notions of dramatic structure and from the concepts of many contemporary structuralists."[133] Hornby views the playscript as an intrinsic pattern of complex relationships to be revealed by performance. The structuralist method, therefore, "1. reveals something hidden, 2. is intrinsic, 3. incorporates complexity and ambiguity, 4. suspends judgment, and 5. is wholistic."[134] The four most influential contemporary theorists—Stanislavski, Brecht, Artaud, and Schechner—all are in some sense structuralists, but all have mistakenly or inadvertently done great damage to the theatre by downgrading the significance of the playwright. All but Brecht share a bias against literature, and Brecht's American followers have interpreted him as having such a bias. As a counter to this, Hornby urges a return to Aristotle's emphasis on plot, defined as the arrangement of incidents, and suggests that theorists turn to the dynamics of this arrangement in light of such concepts as choice, sequence, progression, duration, rhythm, and tempo. Form for Hornby is the articulation of content, which of course places his "structuralism" in almost direct opposition to that of Kirby, remote as both are from European critical usage of the term.

Two books appearing in 1975 depart from structurally oriented analysis to focus upon theatre as a quasi-magical space, created primarily by the shamanistic figure of the actor. David Cole (b. 1939) leans more heavily on a religious-ritualistic view in *The Theatrical Event: A "Mythos," A Vocabulary, A Perspective*; he sees theatre's function, like that of ritual, as the re-creation of the "*illud tempus*," a mythical time of origins which can be made "present again at any moment by the performance of a ritual."[135] Cole likens the actor's research for his role, the seeking in the script and in the inner life another life that comes to "possess" him, to the trance-journeys and possession of the traditional shaman. Actor and shaman alike create a being both fascinating and frightening, making the familiar mystically strange. Stage space, scenery, visual configurations, and lighting—like the actor's body—exist in a double world, both as themselves and as part of the *illud tempus*, both as reality and as ideogram. This manifestation of mythic presence, the bringing into being of an Image, is the only true concern of the theatre. All other concerns, which Cole terms as a group "political," are ultimately extraneous, and any attempt to force theatre to serve these rather than

---

[133]Richard Hornby, *Script into Performance* (Austin, Tex., 1978), x.
[134]Ibid., 24.
[135]David Cole, *The Theatrical Event: A "Mythos," a Vocabulary, a Perspective* (Middletown, Conn., 1975), 7.

its own concerns will be resisted and subverted by the workings of the theatre itself.[136]

Michael Goldman's (b. 1936) *The Actor's Freedom* (1975) speaks of acting in strikingly similar terms, as terrific, uncanny, simultaneously exciting and terrible, dangerous and attractive; it calls the confrontation between actor and audience that arouses these ambivalent feelings the essence of drama.[137] Goldman's interpretation of this confrontation is more psychic and less anthropological than Cole's, but both stress the theatre's response to the self's longing for clarification, its desire "to possess the present and to possess itself in the present, in a way that ordinary space, time, and selfhood do not allow."[138] Drama has been preoccupied with the central fears and freedoms of every age, attempting to come to terms with a volatile and menacing world. In the face of that world, the actor becomes a representative of freedom, of "all that freedom threatens and is threatened by."[139] The ultimate goal is self-identification, for the theatre seems particularly designed to provide examples of that clarity of self which human consciousness is capable of imagining, and which the self in the world longs for but cannot achieve.

This view of the function of acting closely parallels that expressed by Joseph Chaikin in *The Presence of the Actor* (1972): acting is a demonstration of self, but self clarified by imagination. "Because we live on a level drastically reduced from what we can imagine, acting promises to represent a dynamic expression of the intense life."[140]

The most recent major theoretical approach to the theatre, semiology or semiotics, developed out of structuralism; indeed, Jonathan Culler argues, in *Structuralist Poetics* (1975), that they are different aspects of the same study. The former considers social and cultural phenomena not simply as material objects or events but as "objects or events with meaning, and hence signs"; the latter considers the same phenomena as without essence but "defined by a network of relations, both internal and external." It is possible to focus on one or the other of these, but study of either presupposes the insights of the other.[141]

The work of the Prague linguists in the 1930s laid the foundations for a semiotics of the theatre, but their investigations were not pursued further for several decades. When the semiological method began to be applied to art after World War II, it was first employed in the study

---

[136]Ibid., 156.
[137]Michael Goldman, *The Actor's Freedom* (New York, 1975), 7.
[138]Ibid., 161.
[139]Ibid., 110.
[140]Joseph Chaikin, *The Presence of the Actor* (New York, 1972), 2.
[141]Jonathan Culler, *Structuralist Poetics* (Ithaca, N.Y., 1975), 4.

of literature, then gradually in painting, music, and the cinema, where a considerable body of semiotic theory was built up before the theatre became, once again, a significant object of such study.

The complexity of the theatre, combined with its ephemerality, presents formidable methodological problems. As early as 1943 Eric Buyssens, in *Les langages et le discours*, called the presentation of opera "the richest combination of semical facts." He did not, however, attempt an analysis, which in his opinion should deal not only with words, music, gesture, dance, costumes, scenery, and lighting, but audience reactions, social relationships, and even the personnel of the theatre, the ushers, the firemen, the police. An accurate semiotic study of such a phenomenon would have to consider the communication that takes place for a few hours within "an entire world."[142]

It was not until the late 1960s that semioticians began to consider the theatre seriously. A brief but sharply focused statement of such concerns was given by Roland Barthes in "Littérature et signification" (1963), in response to a question from *Tel Quel*, the leading journal of the French New Criticism at this time, asking how he would relate his interest in semiology to the theatre in general and to Brecht in particular. Barthes called theatre "a kind of cybernetic machine" which, as soon as the curtain rises, sends out a variety of simultaneous messages (from setting, costume, and lighting as well as the positions, words, and gestures of the actors), some of which remain (the setting), while others constantly change (words and gestures). This "informational polyphony, " this "density of signs," is a fundamental characteristic of theatre and makes it one of the greatest challenges to semiotic analysis.[143]

Brecht's theories, said Barthes, anticipated and support a semiotic approach to theatre by his emphasis on the intellectual rather than the emotional, and by his realization that the theatrical sign is part of an alterable system of signification. Brecht does not, however, seek a theatre of political signification. He does not wish "to transmit a positive message (this is not a theatre of the signified) but to show that the world is an object to be deciphered (this is a theatre of the signifier)." At the point when Brecht's signifiers are about to solidify into a positive signified, he holds them in suspense, a suspense parallel to his own historical moment, when his political vision is not yet achieved. This is a dramatic strategy far more audacious, difficult, and necessary than the suspension of sense that the avant-garde seeks by "pure subversion of

---

[142]Eric Buyssens, *Les langages et le discours* (Brussels, 1943), 56.
[143]Roland Barthes, *Critical Essays*, trans. Richard Howard (Evanston, Ill., 1972), 261–62.

ordinary language and of theatrical conformism."[144]

A specific and highly influential preliminary codification of theatrical sign systems was attempted by Tadeusz Kowsan (b. 1922) in "The Sign in the Theatre" (1968). Kowsan suggests 13 systems of auditive, visual, spatial, and temporal theatrical signs: these are word, tone, mime, gesture, movement, makeup, hairstyle, costume, accessory, decor, lighting, music, and sound effects.[145] He recalls from the Prague linguists the importance of interchangeability of signs between different systems and of signs with several meanings in theatre. In Saussurian terms, several signs may have the same signified, one sign may have several signifieds, or several signs may work together to produce a single signified. The idea of connotation, Kowsan suggests, may help analyze some cases but is inefficient in the more complicated ones. An important methodological step is the determination of a means of segmenting the spectacle for analysis, and he tentatively suggests "a slice containing all the signs emitted simultaneously, a slice the duration of which is equal to the sign that lasts least."[146]

Steen Jansen's "Equisse d'une théorie de la forme dramatique" (1968) also claims to approach drama as a "semiologic fact" but is rather more oriented toward structuralism. He views the "dramatic form" from two perspectives: as the "dramatic text," the basis of all "realizations" of the work, and the "dramatic work," the ensemble of the means that unite the elements of the text into a coherent whole.[147] The emphasis of the text is upon situation; that of the work is upon structure. The analysis of dramatic text can be pursued as Ingarden suggested, on the level of dialogue or the level of scenic indication. The dramatic work is also subject to double analysis, through the linkage of elements (following the linear development of the action) or through the ensemble of elements (looking backward from the completion).

Another structural-semiotic approach to theatre was developed in Romania by the mathematician Solomon Marcus (b. 1925), who began in the early 1960s to apply mathematical analysis to linguistic structures. In 1966, at the University of Bucharest, Marcus presented a course on mathematical and semiotic strategies in the study of theatre, the contents of which were summarized in the concluding chapter of his book *Poetica matematică* (1970). Unlike Kowsan or Jansen, Marcus is concerned only with the analysis of the written text, as were the predecessors he cites as dramatic theorists of mathematical orientation: Polti

[144]Ibid., 263–64.
[145]Tadeusz Kowsan, "The Sign in the Theatre," *Diogenes* 61 (Spring 1968): 73.
[146]Ibid., pp. 78-79.
[147]Steen Jansen, "Equisse d'une théorie de la forme dramatique," *Langages* 12 (Dec. 1968):73–74.

and Souriau, who attempted to codify the presumed limited number of dramatic situations mentioned by Gozzi; Ginestier, with his geometical typology of the early 1960s; and Felix von Cube, who attempted to apply information theory to dramatic analysis in the essay "Das Drama als Forschungsobjekt der Kybernetik" (*Mathematik und Dichtung*, 1965).

The difficulty with all these earlier approaches, according to Marcus, was that they began with basic data already "very complex, very rich in intuitive and semantic aspects, thus very dependent on our subjectivity."[148] By contrast, Marcus begins with what he considers "the most primitive and objective data contained in a theatrical play," the inventory of characters and the segmentation into scenes. Drawing upon Saussure's emphasis on binary oppositions in linguistic study, and Ginestier's analogy of the function of a character in a play to that of a word in a text, Marcus bases his analysis upon a table or matrix with columns equal to the characters and rows equal to scenes, presence or absence being indicated by 1 or 0.

Mihai Dinu (b. 1942), a student in Marcus's 1966 course, has published a number of articles developing the implications of this mathematical strategy. "Structures linguistiques probabilistes issues de l'étude du théâtre" (1968) argues that Markovian analysis can reveal "the sentiments of sympathy and antipathy of the characters" and trace "with extreme precision the phases of a conflict" even when its content is unknown and the dialogue itself is ignored.[149] Probability theory and information theory provide potential tools for studying Markovian configurations. For example, the less probable a specific configuration of characters is, the greater the quantity of information its realization will provide.[150] In "L'interdépendance syntagmatique des scènes dans une pièce de théâtre" (1972) and "Continuité et changement dans la stratégie des personnages dramatiques" (1973), Dinu directs this analysis toward how scenes are linked in terms of character relationships, and how classic dramatists evolve changing configurations and stress the importance of particular characters and relationships.[151]

Certain adjustments to this method and a warning about its limits appear in "On Marcus' Methods for the Analysis of the Strategy of a Play" (1974) by Barron Brainerd (b. 1928) and Victoria Neufeldt

---

[148]Solomon Marcus, "Editorial Note," *Poetics* 6, 3/4 (Dec. 1977): 203.

[149]Mihai Dinu, "Structures linguistiques probabilistes issues de l'étude du théâtre," *Cahiers de linguistique théoretique et appliqué* 5 (1968): 45.

[150]Ibid., 39.

[151]Dinu, "L'interdépendance syntagmatique des scènes dans une pièce de théâtre," in ibid., 9 (1972): 55–70, and "Continuité et changement dans la stratégie des personnages dramatiques," in ibid., 10 (1973): 5–26.

(b. 1939). They find such analysis "a useful tool for bringing out nuances of plot structure," but caution that it should not be "relied upon by itself to yield an explication of play structure unaided by other critical considerations," among them the thematic features of the play.[152]

The Brainerd-Neufeldt essay appears in a special issue of *Poetics*, edited by Marcus, on "Poetics and Mathematics." In 1977, Marcus edited another special issue, entirely on theatrical theory, entitled "The Formal Study of Drama." Articles on mathematical analysis of theatre by nine Romanian mathematicians and aestheticians consider the syntactic, semantic, and pragmatic aspects of drama through strategies derived from system theory, cybernetics, and the computer sciences, as well as from the mathematical fields of graph theory, combinatorics, logic, code theory, probability, game theory, and formal languages. In his introduction, Marcus suggests that the typology of catastrophe theory, as proposed by René Thom, is a promising new tool for the analysis of situations in the drama that involve "gradual evolutions having discontinuous, abrupt effects."[153] Marcus's own updated comments on his system, "The semiotics of theatre, a mathematical-linguistic approach," promised for a 1979 issue of *Poetics*, had not yet appeared by 1982.

The first general text on semiology to devote a section to theatre was Georges Mounin's *Introduction à la sémiologie* (1970), but Mounin's major concern is in fact to warn against an *a priori* view of theatre as a language with "theatrical signifiers and signifieds, Brechtian 'syntax,' scenographic 'codes,' and so on."[154] The communication model falsifies the nature of theatre, since communication—in the normal linguistic sense of the word— between the public and any part of the theatre (actors, author, setting) does not exist. Except in a very limited manner, the audience is quite unable, for example, to respond to the emitter of messages. A much closer model would be that of a "very complex type of stimulus response" (a model that some theorists will resist not because it is inaccurate but because using it is less "culturally elevated" than regarding the theatre in linguistic terms).[155] The proper goal of a semiology of theatre should be to seek the means by which theatre selects and organizes its various stimuli in order to lead the spectators to that process of interpretation known as the aesthetic experience.

As Mounin predicted, however, most semiologists of theatre continued to follow the linguistic model and to reject his denial of theatrical "communication." Franco Ruffini, for example, in "Semiotica del tea-

---

[152]Barron Brainerd and Victoria Neufeldt, "On Marcus' Methods for the Analysis of the Strategy of a Play," *Poetics* 10 (1974): 73.
[153]Marcus, "Editorial Note," *Poetics* 6, 3/4 (Dec. 1977): 207.
[154]Georges Mounin, *Introduction à la sémiologie* (Paris, 1970), 87.
[155]Ibid., 92–93.

tro: ricognizione degli studi" (1974), admits that the codes of sender and receiver differ in theatre, but insists that communication requires only that they know each other's codes, not that "the two codes coincide nor that they translate each other's messages exactly, nor that the two-way communication occur along the same channel."[156]

The first book-length consideration of semiotics and theatre was Tadeusz Kowsan's *Littérature et spectacle dans leurs rapports esthétiques, thématiques et sémiologiques* (first published in 1970, revised and augmented in 1975). The first part of Kowsan's study deals with the characteristics and varieties of "spectacle," which he defines as "a work of art necessarily communicated in both space and time."[157] He subdivides spectacle into eight groups depending on the presence or absence of plot, man, and language; they range from traditional drama as a type with all three elements to fireworks or water displays as types with none of the three. Dramatic literature overlaps the field of spectacle when it is presented, but exists purely in the field of temporal arts when it is only read.

What unites literature and spectacle is the fable or plot, and Kowsan's second section considers the use of fables in dramatic literature. Throughout the history of drama, Kowsan finds a preference for "known subjects, great myths, other literary works or historical facts," a fact that he credits to the theatre's function as an art less concerned with creating new fables than with treating material in a new manner, in the virtual mode of space and time.[158] The final section of the book considers various sign systems through which this virtual mode is achieved—essentially an elaboration of the 13 systems already advanced by Kowsan in his 1968 article.

In 1972, André Helbo founded in Brussels a review, *Degrés*, for the interdisciplinary study of semiotics; in 1974, he began a series, "Creusets," to address specific concerns in this field of research. The second volume in the "Creusets" series, *Sémiologie de la représentation* (1975), presented eight essays on theatre semiotics, designed, Helbo states, not to resolve or restate traditional problems, but "to stir up some fecund disturbance."[159] Half of these articles focus upon text, half on performance. Among the former, essays by Helbo and by the Italian semiotician Umberto Eco (b. 1932) warn against too literal an application of the language communication model to theatre research. Helbo, in "Le code théâtrale," stresses the importance of "code" over "message" in the theatre, since the spectator is rarely offered a single message but

---

[156]Franco Ruffini, "Semiotica del teatro: ricognizione degli studi," *Biblioteca teatrale* 9 (1974): 40.
[157]Tadeusz Kowsan, *Littérature et spectacle* (Warsaw, 1975), 25.
[158]Ibid., 157, 159.
[159]André Helbo, ed., *Sémiologie de la représentation* (Brussels, 1975), 10.

is rather called upon to recognize the workings of and to play with a variety of interpretive possibilities in a complex system of codes.[160]

Eco, using Charles Peirce's illustration of the drunken man, discusses the complexity and variability of the theatrical sign, depending on the theatrical context with its many possible connotations and on the varied strategies that spectators bring to the decoding of this phenomenon. For aid in the reading of the "signals" emitted by such a figure, Eco—like Schechner—looks to recent research in kinesics, proxemics, and paralinguistics.

Among the essays on performance are the already cited article by Marcus and a study by Pavel Campeanu, which anticipates the increased interest of semioticians in theatre audiences after 1980. Campeanu distinguishes between theatre and more open forms like sports on the grounds that theatre "has always an obligatory program for the protagonists which the spectators are called upon to discover."[161] This does not, however, imply a simple communication model in which the audience receives some specific knowledge. Theatre is concerned ultimately not with "informational density but with emotional density," and it operates always both on the level of signs (which have a generally circumscribed relation to everyday experience) and on that of symbols (which open themselves to creative elaboration outside these boundaries).[162]

Marco de Marinis summarized the available research on theatre semiotics in a 1975 article, "Problemi e aspetti di un approccio semiotico al teatro," concluding that the application of informational and cybernetic methodologies to theatre had not yet produced the anticipated results. This failure, De Marinis suggests, is due to a methodological emphasis on the written text and a tendency to regard "the concrete dimensions of the spectacle" as "marginal or irrelevant." Any effective semiotic approach to theatre must, despite the difficulties, consider theatre as "a complex set of interrelations of heterogeneous models, reducible only with difficulty (or not reducible at all) to a homogeneous higher model."[163] De Marinis quotes approvingly the observation of Julia Kristeva (in her 1968 article "Le geste, pratique ou communication?") that "the linguistic methodology developed from systems of verbal communication is only *one possible* approach, not exhaustive and

---

[160]Ibid., 18.
[161]Ibid., 99.
[162]Ibid., 105–106.
[163]Marco de Marinis, "Problemi e aspetti di un approccio semiotico al teatro," *Lingua e stile* 10, 2 (1975): 355.

not even essential, to the *general text*, which encompasses in addition to the voice different types of *productions* such as *gesture, writing, economy*."[164]

Patrice Pavis's *Problèmes de sémiologie théâtrale* (1976) seeks to establish the theoretical bases for a semiology of theatre suggested but not extensively developed by Kowsan and others. Pavis begins with the nature and function of the theatrical sign: its four primary relations are semantic, referential, syntactic, and pragmatic; its three fundamental functions (derived from the philosopher Peirce) are icon, index, and symbol. Pavis calls theatre "the privileged domain of the icon," since actors, setting, properties, costumes, and language are all literal or mimetic representatives of real things. Index, which points to something else, is of lesser but still considerable importance, since it attracts and focuses the receiver's attention—a major concern in theatre.[165] Symbols are "free figures" operating on several levels, as icon and index, as message and code. Pavis sees the process of theatrical understanding as basically circular. The spectator receiving the complex messages of the stage begins to construct provisionary codes, allowing the various icons to be assigned stable signifieds. The signs thus constructed can change to signifiers of still other signs on the level of codes by the linkage of connotations. This process is in turn to some extent controlled by other primarily indexical signs, which point back to the message, completing a message/code cycle that is in continual operation.[166]

Pavis's second section considers the "three dimensions" of the theatrical sign—semantic, syntactic, and pragmatic. The comic strip is used as a semantic example to demonstrate the differing functions of visual and linguistic signifiers, index here being associated with "showing" and icon with "naming." Syntactics involves the laws by which signs relate to and combine with other signs to create the narrative code of theatre. Pragmatics moves outside the structure of the message to involve the connotative decoding of the text, its meaning for the receiver. Pavis next considers the "actantial" systems of Souriau and others, proposing a much simpler model of four functions—a force, a counterforce (*opposant*), an arbitrator who decides the outcome, and an *adjuvant* that may aid or oppose either force.[167]

In his final section, Pavis first considers the question of segmentation of the dramatic text; he suggests that units be considered on the basis of related "connotations and groups of connotation," each portion "making comprehensible the connotations involved in that part of the

---

[164]Julia Kristeva, "Le geste, pratique ou communication?" *Langages* 10 (1968): 63.
[165]Patrice Pavis, *Problèmes de sémiologie théâtrale* (Montreal, 1976), 15–16.
[166]Ibid., 22.
[167]Ibid., 96.

message."[168] He then considers varieties of theatre, according to differing emphases on denotation (specific referents) or connotation (ambiguity); icon or index; the semantic, pragmatic, or syntactic dimension. The theatre of psychological realism, for example, emphasizes denotation, icon, and the semantic. Oriental theatre tends to rely on internal codes rather than imitating those of everyday life. Racine draws his intrigue directly from an actantial model, while Shakespeare surrounds this model with a proliferation of diverse signs.[169] Even the most "realistic" theatre, however, does not imitate reality but signifies it "by presenting it as a codifiable system."[170]

It is not always clear whether Pavis is speaking of text, performance, or a combination of the two as he explores the "theatrical sign." Anne Ubersfeld, in *Lire le théâtre* (1977), frankly restricts herself to the semiotic examination of the dramatic text, though always in view of its relationship to performance. More than any other literary text, she says, the dramatic text is *troué*, marked with "holes," which in performance are filled by another text, that of the staging, the *mise en scène*.[171] Both "texts" are composed of "an ensemble of signs making up the message in a process of communication."[172] Ubersfeld rejects Mounin's idea of communication as too restrictive, looking instead to the variety of communicative functions distinguished by the linguist Jakobson: emotive, connotative, referential, phatic, metalinguistic, and poetic. Ubersfeld begins her textual analysis with a study of actants, related to the work of Pavis and Souriau but drawing more directly upon the semiotician Greimas. Here a "giver" wants the "subject," aided by a "helper" or resisted by an "opponent," to desire an "object" for the sake of a "receiver"—a scheme that Ubersfeld applies in terms of dialectic couples and balanced triangles to a wide variety of plays.

In treating character, Ubersfeld rejects the traditional idealist and psychological approaches; she sees character rather as a focal point for a variety of concerns, a place of mediation between text and performance, director and author. Syntactically, it fulfills a position in the actantial structure; poetically, it refers by connotation to a wide semantic field. It is both subject and object of the play's discourse, a semiotic ensemble with distinctive traits and a role with various codes. Space and time in theatre also serve multiple purposes, and the reader of the text must seek those syntactic structures that imply the spatial and temporal realization of the performance. Space always exists both as

[168]Ibid., 108.
[169]Ibid., 132.
[170]Ibid., 127–28.
[171]Anne Ubersfeld, *Lire le théâtre* (Paris, 1977), 24.
[172]Ibid., 40.

"an icon of such-and-such a social or sociocultural space and as an ensemble of signs aesthetically constructed like an abstract painting."[173] Time works on the levels of real time, the time of the action, and theatrical time, which mediates between the other two in different ways according to the dramatic mode. Dramatic discourse is treated in the final chapter as a rapport among four "voices"—the author, the character sender, the character receiver, and the audience. The written text serves a double purpose, as an "ensemble of phonic signs emitted by the actors," and as a command not only for its own enunciation but, through its structures or indices, for the nonspoken audiovisual signs implied by its enunciation.[174]

Ubersfeld's is the most thorough and ambitious attempt to date to study the dramatic text semiotically as a basis for performance, but De Marinis challenged her approach in 1978 with the assertion that a true semiotics of theatre "must move away from a consideration of the (written) text as spectacle to one of the spectacle as (semiotic) text."[175] In two major articles jointly titled "Lo spettacolo come testo" (1978–1979), in successive issues of the Italian semiotics journal *Versus*, De Marinis developed such a consideration. (The first part concluded a special issue on "Teatro e semiotica," edited by De Marinis, which contained discussion of the aims, methods, and problems of theatre semiotics; its relationship to other theatre studies; the text/performance relationship; the problems of notation and ephemerality; and the specificity of theatre codes. Among the leading theatre semioticians who contributed articles were Kowsan, Helbo, Jansen, Ruffini, and Pavis—whose comments appeared in English at the conclusion of his *Languages of the Stage* in 1982.)

The most obvious feature of the spectacle, says De Marinis, is its absence. A performance once completed is unrecapturable, and this ephemerality has naturally discouraged research, because of both the difficulty of original analysis and the impossibility of scientific "confirmation" by subsequent scholars. Nevertheless one cannot build a semiotics of performance from the "virtual *mise en scène*" of the written text, which has its own semiotics; the features of the "spectacle text (TS)" itself must be sought, composed of the "unity of verbal and nonverbal theatrical manifestations which make the spectacle a complete signifying process."[176] The spectacle text is multicoded, multidimensional, and pluralistic in material. A variety of manifestations may mark its "beginning" or "end," among them the arrival and departure

[173]Ibid., 164.
[174]Ibid., 256.
[175]De Marinis, "Lo spettacolo come testo 1," *Versus* 21 (Sept.-Dec. 1978): 67.
[176]Ibid., 68.

of the public, the curtain, the curtain call, the appearance and disappearance of actors. Its coherence may be internal or may be attributed by the analytic receiver. Each spectacle creates a new textual system based on many codes, specific and variable, evolved within theatre or taken from elsewhere and given new theatrical meanings, constantly shifting and evolving new interrelationships. The spectator is encouraged to attempt plural readings, some of which will be pertinent and some not, as he works inductively toward the understanding of codes and deductively from codes provisionally recognized. The circle is not closed, however, for the connotative process of interpretation will always move the spectator far beyond simple decoding.

De Marinis dismisses the semiotic search for general "minimal units," as well as for "general theatrical codes." Each production evolves its own segmentation in terms of its individual codes and subcodes, and meaning is created "within the spectacle, not by means of any external systems."[177] De Marinis takes from Eco the idea of ostentation as the fundamental sign-producing process in the theatre. (The concept of ostentation is introduced briefly in Eco's article "Semiotics of Theatrical Performance" (1977), an English reworking and elaboration of his 1975 essay for Helbo. Ostended signs are not "actively produced," says Eco, but "picked up among the existing physical bodies" and "presented as signifying devices."[178] Since, as Honzl observed, everything on stage is a sign, the mere placing of an object on stage is a process of ostentation.)

Stage performance, De Marinis continues, always involves communication on at least two levels, infrascenic (between characters) and extrascenic (between stage and audience). Even those performances that emphasize physical stimulus and deemphasize text and narrative—such as those of Chaikin, Grotowski, Schechner, and the Living Theatre—in fact program their stimuli and thus semanticize and encode them. De Marinis finds that the analysis of the audience's role in the spectacle, both the pure and simple decoding of the performance signs and the vastly more complex process of interpretation, has been the most neglected area of theatre semiotics and needs much greater attention.[179]

Michael Kirby, who also contributed to the 1978 special issue of *Versus*, seems in general to echo the position taken by De Marinis. The semiotics of theatre "must learn to deal with actual performance," leaving the analysis of scripts to the semiotics of literature. Meaning in performance is "self-sufficient and does not depend on or exist in

---

[177]Ibid., 70–71.
[178]Umberto Eco, "Semiotics of Theatrical Performance," *Drama Review* 30, 1 (1977): 110.
[179]De Marinis, "Lo spettacolo come testo 2," *Versus* 22 (Jan.-Apr. 1979): 23, 28.

relation to a script." Kirby concludes, however, with an assertion that moves the discussion in a quite different direction: just as codes may be created in the theatre, they may also be consciously "destroyed, made unspecific"; or a performance may be created beyond the scope of semiotics "that has no meaning, that uses no codes."[180]

Kirby saw his own idea of "structuralist theatre" as leading to this sort of "nonsemiotic performance," which he described more fully in a 1982 article by that name in a special theory and performance issue of *Modern Drama*. Arguing that a communication model lies behind all semiotic analysis, Kirby considers his "structuralist" performance inaccessible to that approach. Such a performance is not about meanings or information but about relationships among them; they are raw material, like sounds and images. Chance and other nonintentional elements are employed to "deconstruct" codes and meaning. The audience experience is "primarily sensory, dealing with relationships on the perceptual continuum of vision and hearing." The audience does not "decode" but engages at most in the more open-ended process of "interpretation."[181] (This thinking brings Kirby close to the French critics who, in the early 1980s, began to view performance in deconstructionist terms.)

Two books appearing at the end of the 1970s attempted an overview of theatrical research, with a strong emphasis on the recently developed field of semiotics. First came *L'univers du théâtre* (1978) by Gilles Girard, Réal Ouellet, and Claude Rigault, then *The Semiotics of Theatre and Drama* (1980) by Keir Elam.

The contemporary interest in performance is reflected in *L'univers*, which defines theatre first as a "*social place* where something transpires for people voluntarily assembled," and only secondarily and "by reduction" as a "dramatic text read by an individual."[182] The first half of the book, on representation, is organized along traditional semiotic lines, drawing heavily on Kowsan's organization. A section on acting considers actor training and the sociology of the actor, as well as the implications for character and role of such recent semiotic approaches as those of Jansen and Marcus. The latter half of the book deals more with text, considering the fable in terms of actantial models, partition of the script, traditional genres, and more open contemporary forms—which reflect "the multitude of possible combinations to be drawn from the constituent elements of dramatic communication already evoked,"

---

[180]Kirby, "Intervento," ibid., 38.
[181]Kirby, "Nonsemiotic Performance," *Modern Drama* 21 (March 1982): 110.
[182]Gilles Girard et al., *L'univers du théâtre* (Paris, 1978), 10.

and which may be regarded as "a vast metalanguage seeking to decode the dramatic phenomenon."[183]

Elam's book focuses more directly (though not exclusively) on semiotics. It opens with a distinction between drama, the written text which may be approached linguistically by various theories of discourse and narration, and theatre, which has to do "with the production and communication of meaning in the performance itself."[184] Though Elam deals with both, his survey naturally reflects the bias of antecedent research and is thus heavily weighted toward text-oriented analysis. After a brief survey of the development of theatre semiotics beginning with the work of the Prague school, he considers both drama and theatre in the light of communication and codes. His discussion of these concepts is much more wide-ranging than that in *L'univers*, extending into such nontheatrical but potentially useful communication research as kinesics and proxemics. Following Eco, he gives particular attention to ostentation and to the importance of "deixis"—gesture and language that establishes the actor's relationships to the stage space and to others.[185]

The chapters on dramatic logic and dramatic discourse, constituting more than half the book, focus essentially on drama rather than theatre; they consider the status of the fictional world, actantial models, and the referential and performance qualities of dramatic language. The last is clearly a central concern for Elam, as his strong interest in deixis and speech-act theory demonstrates. Drawing upon Alessandro Serpieri's "Ipotesi teorica di segmentazione del testo teatrale" (1978), Elam argues that "all stylistic and semiotic functions in the drama" derive from "the deictic orientation of the utterance toward its context." This leads him to propose shifts in deictic orientation as the long-sought "markers" of basic units of segmentation for semiotic analysis of drama.[186]

From speech-act theory, and particularly from the work of John Austin, Elam takes the concepts of "illocutionary" and "perlocutionary" speech acts. The first is the act performed *in* saying something, such as promising, questioning or asserting; the second is the act performed *by means of* saying something, such as persuading or moving to action. Elam characterizes dramatic discourse as "a network of complementary and conflicting illocutions and perlocutions." Just as deixis orients us within the dramatic world, speech acts orient us within the dynamics of that world. Elam cites Richard Ohmann's observation in "Literature as Act" (1973) that "movement of the characters and changes in their

---

[183]Ibid., 184.
[184]Keir Elam, *The Semiotics of Theatre and Drama* (London, 1980), 2.
[185]Ibid., 72.
[186]Ibid., 141, 145.

relations to one another within the social world of the play appear most clearly in their illocutionary acts."[187] But Elam himself goes further, seeing dramatic dialogue as primarily a mode of praxis "which sets in opposition the different personal, social, and ethical forces of the dramatic world."[188]

The December 1980 special issue of *Etudes littéraires*, "Théâtre et théâtralité: essais d'études sémiotiques," echoes many of the themes stressed by Elam. The issue's purpose, according to special editor Jeannette Savona, was "to elucidate the notion of theatricality" and to attempt an understanding of the specificity of theatrical discourse."[189] Savona herself and Ross Chambers contributed articles exploring Austin's "illocutionary" discourse in the theatre, while Ivo Osolsobě considered "ostentation," and André Helbo went back once again to refute Mounin, the favorite straw man of theatre semiotics. Among the theoretical articles in this special issue, only Régis Durand's "La voix et le dispositif théâtral" struck a distinctly different note, by introducing concepts and attitudes drawn less from the tradition of structuralism and semiotics than from deconstruction, a critique of that tradition that had previously been little applied to theatre theory.

Deconstruction, whose first major practitioner was Jacques Derrida, has sought to avoid the tendency of structuralism and semiotics to settle upon stable, self-authenticating, definitive meanings or systems of meaning. Derrida specifically challenges the Saussurian assumption of language as a signifying system, a system of primary reality lying behind the individual manifestations of speech or behind the "derived speech" of writing. Derrida takes the "primary reality" to be itself—like writing—already derived, already conditioned by prior structures of which it bears only the traces. In Derrida's own work, this analsyis is applied to theatrical concerns most penetratingly in two essays on Antonin Artaud in *L'écriture et la différence* (1967): "La parole soufflée" and "Le théâtre de la cruauté et la clôture de la représentation."

In opposition to those theatre theorists who have taken Artaud as the prophet who will free theatre for its fullest development, Derrida sees Artaud's vision as paradoxical; its achievement would mean not the fulfillment but the erasure of theatre. Derrida analyzes Artaud as one of the metaphysical theorists who seek a fundamental unity, a metaphysical plenitude which stands behind written texts and of which they are but pale, derived reflections. The theatre of cruelty is an attempt to capture "pure presence," the "unity prior to dissociation" without

[187]Richard Ohmann, "Literature as Act," in Seymour Chatman, ed., *Approaches to Poetics* (New York, 1973), 83.
[188]Elam, *Semiotics*, 159.
[189]Jeannette Savona, "Présentation," *Etudes littéraires* 13, 3 (Dec. 1980): 383.

the interior difference that characterizes writing.[190] The paradox of this quest, a paradox recognized by Artaud himself, is that such an authentic presence must exist outside of time and consciousness. Once realized, it is already involved in repetition, already carrying within itself the fatal "double," and yet only in this way can it be manifested as "theatre." Artaud's theory thus circles always around this central paradox, that theatre from its moment of concept has been the repetition of the unrepeatable, an endless and impossible attempt to recapture a lost and endlessly deferred presence.[191]

More specific attention has been given to the theatre by a French theorist with similar orientation, Jean-François Lyotard, who provided the major inspiration for Durand's article. Lyotard expressed certain misgivings about the modern semiotic approach to theatre almost from its initiation. He was a participant—along with Umberto Eco, Erwin Goffman, and other theorists from Italy and Japan—in one of the first discussions of the subject, held during the annual International Festival of Theatre in Venice in 1972. There the work of Japanese actors performing at the festival was submitted to semiotic analysis, to the bemusement and occasionally the irritation of the artists themselves, who tended to view this process as both alien and sterile. Lyotard on that occasion denounced his fellow Westerners for perpetuating the Occidental view of the Japanese as lifeless "objects" for intellectual analysis. The living art of Japan was being subjected, in his opinion, to "semiotic imperialism."[192]

The following year in "La dent, la paume," Lyotard questioned the general validity of a theatre theory based on semiotics—not on cultural but on philosophical grounds, much in the manner of Derrida. The theory of theatrical signs, says Lyotard, is based on absence (*nihilisme*), since the signs, as Peirce argued, replace something not present. Theatricality plays with "hiding and showing." However, modern consciousness cannot accept any longer the primacy of this hidden "other"; "there is nothing to replace, no established position is legitimate or all are, and consequently the sense is itself only a substitute for a displacement." On these grounds Lyotard proposes a "theatre of energies" rather than of signs, built upon "libidinal displacements" instead of upon "representative substitutions."[193]

Durand responds that the theatre can be productively viewed from both perspectives, as a place of tension between displacement and substitution, as a machine not of cybernetics but of "impulses," which,

---

[190]Jacques Derrida, *Writing and Difference*, trans. Alan Bass (Chicago, 1978), 174.
[191]Ibid., 249–50.
[192]Quoted in Ricard Salvat, *El teatro de los años 70* (Barcelona, 1974), 261.
[193]Jean-François Lyotard, *Les dispositifs pulsionnels* (Paris, 1973), 95–96.

from its discontinuities (between stage and audience or between different elements of the "text"), seizes "energies and intensities, and maintains and transforms them, producing certain effects."[194] The alternative to a theatre "smothered by conversation" is not necessarily a theatre of gestures and cries, as Artaud thought, but rather a "theatre of impulses and intensities the movements and variations of which are experienced." The critical concern in the achievement of this is that the necessities of representation not force a "condensation and a flattening" of the rich field of energies, a reduction of the drama's "plurality of voices."[195]

Around 1980, a new orientation toward semiotic study of the theatre appeared to be developing. The structural and linguistic approach of the majority of studies up to that time, best summarized in Elam, were increasingly challenged by other approaches, directed toward performance, the performance/text synthesis within the theatre, or the dynamics of audience reception. A study that looks in this direction, though not from a semiotic point of view, is Gerald Hinkle's *Art as Event* (1979), a short book arguing that critical understanding of the performing arts has been hampered by the application to them of strategies evolved in arts such as literature, where performance is not essential. The performance aspect of arts like theatre relates them more directly to our perception of life as an "event-full" process, as described by Whitehead. Theatre should thus preferably be viewed as "1) more an event than an object in perception, 2) more an enactment than an episode in experience, and 3) more the point-of-departure for participation than for reflection."[196] The theatrical "event" is a Whiteheadian nexus made up of six combined "loci"—the text, the director, the cast, the crew, the audience, and the actuality created by the actors' dual consciousness of self and of character.

This shift to the pragmatic (interpretive) aspect of the sign is articulated in semiotic terms in Achim Eschbach's *Pragmasemiotik und Theater* (1979), which sees "action" (*Handlung*) as the basis for theatre semiotics, but insists that essential to the understanding of action is the process of reception. Eschbach ascribes the relative neglect of this process by previous theatre semiotics to the influence of Saussure, whose signifier-signified model ignores the necessary third element in signification: the interpretant—which is given attention by Peirce. Indeed, reception is build directly into Peirce's famous definition of a sign as "something which stands to somebody for something in some respect or capacity,"

[194]Régis Durand, "La voix et le dispositif théâtral," *Etudes littéraires* 13, 3 (Dec. 1980): 389.

[195]Ibid., 395.

[196]Gerald Hinkle, *Art as Event* (Washington, 1979), 40.

the interpretant being "the equivalent sign created in the mind of that person."[197] For Eschbach, the interpretant, involving the sociohistorical dynamic by which Peirce's "somebody" understands his "something," opens theatre to infinite signification—parallel to Peirce's infinite semiosis—since "the realization of verbal and nonverbal signifying acts refers always to the shifting universe of action in which author, actors, and spectators are implicated."[198] Theatre is particularly open to this process because the written text is semiotically unfulfilled, and the elements added in staging will inevitably relate to the historically determined intepretant. Using Weiss's *Gesang vom lusitanischen Popanz* as his central example, Eschbach argues that the work is so written as to "achieve its full, multimedia effect only on the stage," the performance itself becoming the completed "text."[199] He then analyzes the play in terms of Kowsan's 13 signifying systems (although Eschbach mistakenly attributes them to a Swiss theorist, P. Schweiger).

The already mentioned article by Ross Chambers in the 1980 *Etudes littéraires*, "La masque et le miroir," looks in this same direction as a result of Chambers's dissatisfaction with the illocutionary approach to theatre discourse, which he finds limited and imprecise. As an act of "enunciation," theatre must be approached by a "relational theory" that "takes into account the relationship between the stage and the auditorium." Like Eschbach, Chambers notes that a work of art is soon freed from its "author" and addressed to constantly changing receivers in varied contexts. Its understood "performative" is therefore something like "I invite you to interpret me," the "you" being "a perfectly indeterminate to-whom-it-may-concern."[200]

The relatively minor attention given to the audience's contribution by the first generation of modern theatre semioticians is demonstrated by the fact that Elam's book devotes only 9 of 210 pages to this subject, but more recent work suggests that this may develop into one of the major areas of theoretical investigation of the 1980s. An important part of the foundation for such study is the *Rezeptionsaesthetik* developed in Germany during the 1970s, particularly by Hans Robert Jauss and Wolfgang Iser. Rainer Warning, whose *Rezeptionsaesthetik* (1975) was the first major analysis of this approach, traces it back to the Prague school, recalling that Mukařovský had insisted upon a certain "indeterminacy in the specific referentiality of the work of art," since the

[197]Charles Peirce, *Collected Papers*, 8 vols. (Cambridge, Mass., 1931–58), 2:135, para. 228.
[198]Achim Eschbach, *Pragmasemiotik und Theater* (Tübingen, 1979), 146.
[199]Ibid., 150.
[200]Ross Chambers, "Le masque et le miroir," *Etudes littéraires* 13, 3 (Dec. 1980): 402–3.

individual perceiving it "by no means responds with only a common reaction but with all of the momentum of his position in the world and in reality."[201] Jauss's *Literaturgeschichte als Provokation* (1970) deals only with literary texts and readers, but its assumptions and methodology have proved highly useful for theorists of reception as well. Particularly important is Jauss's insistence upon the open-endedness of the text, its concretization the product of a constantly varying dialectic between the work's "horizon of expectations" and the varying "horizon of expectations" of the reader.[202]

The changing orientation of theatre semiotics can easily be seen in two collections of essays that appeared in 1981, *La relation théâtrale*, edited by Régis Durand, and a special issue of *Poetics Today* entitled "Drama, Theater, Performance: A Semiotic Perspective." The title of Durand's collection recalls Chambers's "relational" approach, and indeed Durand describes the focus of the collection as "not so much on the different elements (text, author, director, actor, auditorium, decor, audience, etc.) as on the complex system of relations that unites and transforms them."[203] Each of the seven articles in this collection focuses in some way upon the audience-text relationship. Monique Dubar considers the effect of Jarry's *Ubu roi* upon a group of hypothetical readers, while Claude Gauvin and Victor Bourgy examine devices of audience manipulation and orientation in medieval and Renaissance English drama and in Shakespeare. The remaining four articles deal more abstractly with reception theory. One is a translation of Richard Schechner's "Toward a Poetic of Performance." Anne Ubersfeld explores the Freudian concept of repression in its possible relation to the complex patterns of belief, illusion, and contradiction in the theatre experience. Patrice Pavis, in "Pour une ésthetique de la réception théâtrale," suggests a variety of strategies for the analysis of the audience contribution to a performance experience: reception (drawing in part on Jauss's ideas of horizons of expectation), reading, hermeneutics, and perspective; he uses Marivaux's *Jeu de l'amour et du hasard* to illustrate several of these approaches. André Helbo's "Le discours théâtral" explores in a preliminary way the dynamic that Helbo proposes as basic to the creation of the theatrical object: the dialectic between discourse and theatre, between the "theatricality inherent in the signifying prac-

---

[201] Jan Mukařovský, *Kapital aus der Äesthetik* (Frankfurt, 1976), 97, quoted in Rainer Warning, *Rezeptionsaesthetik* (Munich, 1975), 14.
[202] Hans Robert Jauss, *Aesthetische Erfahrung und literarische Hermeneutik* (Munich, 1977), 18.
[203] Régis Durand, ed., *La relation théâtrale* (Lille, 1980), 7.

tice of language" (in particular, its spatialization) and the "act of theatrical discourse where the stage creates language."[204]

The 1981 special issue of *Poetics Today* provides a somewhat more balanced selection of contemporary theatre semiotics, with three articles on the written text (one repeating in part the Serpieri article admired by Elam), two on the relationship between text and performance, three on performance itself (one dealing with the mobility of theatre signs, two with the body and gesture), and three on the audience/stage relationship, the central concern of the Durand collection. Of the last three, the most original is Frank Coppieters's "Performance and Perception." Coppieters notes that the little research done in England and America on theatre audiences has relied almost exclusively on "mass methods and statistical analysis," a social science approach that he rejects on the grounds that "the study of *people* and their everyday social world requires methods which are different, and especially more refined, than those narrowly or blindly borrowed from the scientific study of things." For an alternate strategy, Coppieters looks to ethnomethodology, especially the ethnogenic approach of Rom Harré and his associates at Oxford; he urges detailed studies of individual audience members as "typical members of social collectives" and of particular occasions as "typical kinds of social events."[205]

Patrice Pavis's *Languages of the Stage* (1982)—a collection of English translations of various essays written between 1978 and 1982—reflects, as Pavis himself observes, a change in perspective since his earlier *Problèmes de sémiologie théâtrale*, a change not only in his own work but in the field of theatre semiotics as a whole. A global approach to the subject now seems, if not impossible, "at least extremely problematical"; theorists are turning instead to the consideration of "specific objects, a *mise en scène*, a decor, an acting style—using methods inspired by semiology."[206] This book comprises several such "attempts" (*essais*), among them two articles on the language of the body (one on Brecht's *Gestus* and the other on mime as discourse), three that discuss the present state of theatre semiology and its relation to other theatre research, two specific examples of semiotic analysis, and four on performance and text reception. Among the last group is an English version of the audience reception essay that appeared in Durand and "Towards a Semiology of the Mise en Scène?" a discussion that considers the creation of a performance text from a dramatic text as a process of "stage writing," in which a director, as both reader and writer, "develops a

---

[204]Ibid., 104.
[205]Frank Coppieters, "Performance and Perception," *Poetics Today* 2, 3 (Spring 1981): 35, 36.
[206]Pavis, *Languages of the Stage* (New York, 1982), 9.

metatext which generates the stage enunciation," which is in turn presented for the pragmatic reception of the public, the final member of the semiological "theatrical team."[207]

Anne Ubersfeld's preface to her *L'école du spectateur* (1982) agrees with Pavis that it is "perhaps already too late" to attempt a synthesis of the "various semiologies and semiotics" of theatre. Nevertheless, her book does offer at least a tentative "summary but synthetic view of representation," designed to aid the spectator in "sharpening his eyes and ears, stimulating his reflection and increasing his pleasure" in the theatre.[208] *L'école du spectateur*, subtitled *Lire le théâtre 2*, may best be understood as the companion volume to Ubersfeld's earlier work. In *Lire le théâtre* she described the dramatic text as incomplete (*troué*) and considered the dynamic implications of that incompleteness. Now she considers what occurs in completing the text, in filling the holes. Individual chapters deal with the specific nature of the sign in representation, the semiotic functions of space and time in the theatre, the theatrical object, the work of the actor (including the creation of character and the structure of his verbal and gestural discourse), the way in which the director creates the theatre universe, and how this relates to text, actors, and audience.

The two final chapters discuss the spectator, who is not only "the object of the verbal and scenic discourse, the receiver in the process of communication, the king of the feast," but also "the subject of a doing, the craftsman of a praxis which is continually developed only with the praxis of the stage."[209] Ubersfeld identifies the various ways in which the spectator performs this activity—generally with reference to instructions given by the text, the performance, or the performance situation—and the various sources of audience pleasure. There is the pleasure of discovery, of analyzing the signs of performance, of invention (when the spectator must find his own meanings for the theatrical signs), of identification with another being, of experiencing temporarily the impossible or the forbidden; finally, there is the total pleasure suggested by the Indian *rasa*, "the union of all affective elements, plus the distancing that gives peace."[210] Ubersfeld closes, however, not on this harmonious note but on a suspended one of limits and "desire as lack." Ultimately, the spectator must experience the "absence" of theatre, the lack of total fulfillment of total presence, both physical and intellectual. To accept the role of spectator, one must accept this condition of unfulfilled desire.

[207]Ibid., 135 (trans. Susan Melrose).
[208]Ubersfeld, *L'école du spectateur* (Paris, 1982), 7.
[209]Ibid., 303.
[210]Ibid., 342.

In the early 1980s, semiotics seems well established as the dominant new approach to theatrical theory, though only a handful of major writings have yet appeared in English. Poststructuralism, which has mounted so stimulating a challenge to semiotics and structuralism in recent nontheatrical literary theory, has as yet inspired little theatre-oriented work; the growing interest in semiotics, however, would naturally suggest that theory paralleling Derrida's challenge to Saussurian assumptions in general literary theory will inevitably follow.

Indeed, scattered examples have already appeared, among them the articles by Lyotard and Durand already discussed and, more recently, two essays by Chantal Pontbriand and Josette Féral in the March 1982 special theory issue of *Modern Drama* and a variety of articles by Herbert Blau appearing between 1979 and 1983. Pontbriand's "The eye finds no fixed point on which to rest . . . " and Féral's "Performance and Theatricality: The Subject Demystified" clearly are developed from a common intellectual background, though Féral makes more direct use of French poststructuralism. Both insist upon an understanding of the difference between theatre and performance, citing Richard Foreman's work as a central example of the latter and quoting the American theorist of minimalist art, Michael Fried: "The success, even the survival of the arts has come increasingly to depend on their ability to defeat theatre."[211] The strategy of these two theorists suggests that poststructuralist theatrical theory on this continent may well combine insights drawn on the one hand from French theorists like Derrida, Lyotard, and Lacan, and on the other from the American tradition of happenings, chance art, and the "theatre of images" of Foreman and Wilson.

Féral sees "theatricality" as composed of two different parts: the theatrical part inscribes the subject in the symbolic, in "theatrical codes"; the performance part undoes these codes and "competencies," allowing the subject's "flows of desire to speak."[212] The first builds structures which the second deconstructs. Here we reach the "limits of theatre" mentioned by Ubersfeld, whose vocabulary at this point, like Féral's, borrows from the French neo-Freudian critic, Jacques Lacan. According to Lacan, both the conscious and the unconscious are linguistically structured, with the eternally unfulfilled subject engaged always in a dialectic and search for ("desire" for) a primal Other. On these grounds, Ubersfeld's closing description of theatre as perpetually unfilled desire and Féral's "flows of desire" meet. Féral's approach is more openly deconstructionist, however, since it specifically views performance as de-

[211]Gregory Battcock, ed., *Minimal Art* (New York, 1968), 139.
[212]Josette Féral, "Performance and Theatricality," *Modern Drama* 25, 1 (Mar. 1982): 178.

systemitizing theatre. This theatre, the object of Fried's attack, is always narrative, always representational, and always involved with signification and the codification of meanings. Performance works without narrativity, with "pieces of body" and "pieces of meaning."[213] Pontbriand calls it "a process, an inchoative breaking-up."[214]

In performance, says Féral, the actor neither "plays" nor "represents" himself but is a source of "production and displacement." He becomes "the point of passage for energy flows—gestural, vocal, libidinal, etc.— that traverse him without ever standing still in a fixed meaning or representation," and he "plays at putting those flows to work and seizing networks." Theatricality is the bonding of this dynamic of performance with theatre in "endless play" and in "continuous displacements of the position of desire."[215]

The recent writings of Herbert Blau—the six essays collected in *Blooded Thought* (1982) and the subsequent "Universals of Performance; or, Amortizing Play" (1983) and "Ideology and Performance" (1983)— provide the most extensive development of these strategies yet attempted by an American theorist. The concern with drama as a socially relevant ensemble art reflected in Blau's earlier *The Impossible Theatre* is replaced in these essays by a concern with the basic process of theatre and of performance and its relation to the consciousness of the individual actor and spectator. In a sense Blau begins where Féral ends. He too sees performance as a realm of displacement, libidinal flow, and desire. But he cannot accept the suggestion of Féral (and earlier of Artaud) that "performance" might offer the opportunity for experience uncontaminated by the signification and codification of "theatre." "There is nothing more illusory in performance than the illusion of the unmediated," insists Blau. "It is a very powerful illusion in the theatre, but it *is* theatre, and it is *theatre*, the truth of illusion, which haunts *all* performance, whether or not it occurs in the theatre."[216]

The pursuit of unmediated experience by Artaud and others (giving rise to the illusion that "performance," by rejecting "theatre," could achieve this) has been a failure, forcing upon us the realization that there is something in the nature of *both* theatre and performance which "implies no *first time*, no origin, but only recurrence and reproduction."[217] In common with Freud, and more immediately with Derrida

---

[213]Ibid., 179.
[214]Chantal Pontbriand, "The eye finds no fixed point on which to rest . . . ," *Modern Drama* 25, 1 (Mar. 1982): 157.
[215]Féral, "Performance," 174, 177.
[216]Herbert Blau, "Universals of Performance; or, Amortizing Play," *Sub-stance* 37-38 (1983): 143.
[217]Ibid., 148.

and Lacan, Blau sees this inevitable repetition as a product of an irreducible dualism, of our knowledge of death at the origin of life; it is "death which rejects pure presence and dooms us to repetition." Life can defend itself against death "only through an economy of death, through deferment, repetition, reserve."[218] The contact of life and death, a primal violence not directly apprehensible by the psyche, haunts all repetition (and all performance) with the remainder, the trace within repetition of something not repetition. "There is something in the nature of theatre," says Blau, "which from the very beginning of theatre has always resisted being theatre."[219] This something, a resistance, a "rub," encourages the never-to-be-realized dream of a realized original experience instead of the re-presentation of performance.

Thus performance, like consciousness itself, begins with a sense of division, and Blau views with suspicion the suggestions of theorists like Turner that in performance some transcultural communitas may be achieved. "Performance is a testament to what separates," and if anything in it can cross cultures, it is the universal sense of a primordial breach, suggested by the performer who, "in a primordial substitution or displacement, is born on the site of the Other."[220] Again, the influence of Lacan and Derrida is clear, but this approach also strikingly echoes German romanticism, in which the idea of a primordial individuation also appeared, giving rise to reflexivity and consciousness, but at the price of an eternal sense of loss and an ambivalent desire for a return to that original state of Buddhist nirvana, as sought by Schopenhauer, or Dionysian ecstasy as described by Nietzsche.

But consciousness and reflexivity, like Schiller's related concept of the sentimental, once gained, is not easily discarded, as the romantics well knew, and attempts to do so simply add new layers to the reflexive process—in more modern terms, they add new substitutions, new displacements. "Every radical advance in the theatre has come from another illusion first subverting and then impacting the one before,"[221] and the recognition of the inevitability of this process is the essential first stage in dealing with it. Blau sees a certain relation between his own work and that of Richard Foreman in that both are explorations of "perception reflecting upon itself,"[222] but Blau in both theory and practice is concerned not simply with the articulation of this process but with the illumination of its originating point, that "privileged in-

---

[218]Ibid., 150.

[219]Ibid., 143.

[220]Ibid., 157.

[221]Blau, "Look What Thy Memory Cannot Contain" (1981), in *Blooded Thought* (New York, 1982), 93.

[222]Blau, "Ideology and Performance," *Theatre Journal* 35, 4 (Dec. 1983): 449.

stant" when performance *begins*, when by the workings of consciousness whatever was there before performance "precipitates" into performance.[223]

Within performance is what Blau sometimes refers to as a ghost, a memory of what preceded performance, of what performance makes present (or in another Blau term, "amortizes"), but which was not present before. Performance gives "visible body to what is not-there, not only the disappearance of origin but what never disappeared because it was never constituted."[224] Blau's question, "Theatre makes present, but makes *what* present?" is thus the central question of performance, but admits no possible answer, since memory, and thought itself, cannot penetrate beyond the barrier of precipitation. What theory can do at most, and what Blau attempts, is to push as close to this barrier as possible, trying to capture the dynamics of that creative instant when what is not becomes what is, born into reality with a memory of what it was before.

The complex and always evolving play of incompleteness, substitution, repetition, and deferring that this generation of critics has brought into theatre theory promises to open this theory to the same range of new perspectives already opened by recent critical work in other genres. In coming years the dialectic Féral suggests between theatre (viewed in semiotic terms) and performance (as a radical deconstructive challenge to those terms) and the kind of exploration being done by Blau into the dynamic by which performance comes into existence suggest rich new fields for theoretical speculation which theatre and performance theory have at this time barely begun to cultivate.

[223]Blau, "Universals," 155.
[224]Blau, "Look What," 84.

Index

Abel, Lionel, 450
Absurd, the, 344-345, 350, 398-399, 405, 411-413, 416, 426-427, 465
Acting, 24, 26, 29, 33, 39, 59-60, 65-66, 68, 99, 105, 138-140, 143, 150, 152-153, 159-162, 170-171, 190-194, 217-218, 224-225, 227, 230, 232-237, 239, 250-251, 264-265, 276-277, 279-281, 288, 290-296, 303-305, 311, 318-325, 329, 341, 345-346, 348, 352-353, 355-359, 361, 368-386, 394-397, 406, 408-410, 417, 421, 431, 433, 435, 444-446, 456, 459, 462, 473, 475-476, 483, 485-486, 492-494, 499, 502-503, 510-511, 513-515
Adamov, Arthur, 349, 411-415, 418-419, 455
Addison, Joseph, 127-128, 130, 135-136
Adler, Stella, 379-380
Admiration, 72, 83, 89, 100, 107, 109, 117, 159, 164, 168, 449
Adorno, Theodor, 425-427, 429
Aikhenwald, Yuli, 323-325, 380-381
Althusser, Louis, 433-434
Amalarius of Metz, 36
Amiel, Denys, 375
Ancients and moderns, 43, 54, 56, 60, 110, 114, 122-123, 171, 181
Anderson, Maxwell, 401, 405
Andreyev, Leonid, 324, 341
Antitheatrical writings, 28-30, 60, 70, 79-81, 110, 112, 121, 123-125, 151-152, 156, 254
Antoine, André, 279-280, 326, 344
Apollinaire, Guillaume, 343-344
Appia, Adolphe, 293-296, 304, 319, 342, 353, 355, 362, 455, 475

Appropriateness. *See* Decorum
Archer, William, 235, 308-310, 382, 401, 405, 487
Arden, John, 422
Ariosto, Orazio, 51
Aristarchus, 21
Aristophanes, 15-16, 25, 185, 196, 204, 242
Aristophanes of Byzantium, 21-22
Aristotle, 15-27, 31-34, 37-55, 71-73, 77-78, 81-82, 85, 87-89, 94, 96-99, 101-103, 107-111, 117-118, 120, 123-124, 126-128, 138, 156, 163, 167-169, 171, 174-175, 185, 190, 193, 201, 236, 257-258, 265, 311-312, 334, 365, 385, 397, 401, 418-419, 421, 453, 472, 475-476, 491
Aristoxenus of Tarentium, 21
Arnold, Matthew, 231-232, 236
Arrabal, Fernando, 458-459, 472, 481
Artaud, Antonin, 376, 392-397, 413, 416, 419-420, 454-457, 459-460, 464-465, 467, 471-472, 481, 491, 505-507, 513
Ascham, Roger, 78
Audience, 38, 40-42, 44, 46, 48-55, 59, 61-62, 73, 85-86, 93, 98, 116, 120, 125, 136, 151-153, 165, 167, 178, 182, 192, 199, 211, 213, 216, 221-225, 243, 245, 247, 268, 279-284, 289, 291-292, 311-321, 326, 333, 336, 339-340, 343, 354, 363-365, 371, 384-385, 387, 393, 408-411, 420, 423-425, 428-429, 431, 433, 440, 446, 451, 456, 460-461, 463-465, 472-484, 488-490, 496-499, 502-503, 507-511
Auger, Louis, 204

Library of Congress Cataloging in Publication Data

Carlson, Marvin, 1935-
   Theories of the theatre.

   Includes index.
   1. Theater—History. 2. Dramatic criticism—History. I. Title
PN2039.C26   1984   792'.01   84-7658
ISBN 0-8014-1678-7 (alk. paper)